"The extracts that follow are intended essentially to convey the scope and quality of Augustine's doctrine. Theoretically, the best way to achieve this double aim would be to choose the most comprehensive passage or passages in Augustine's works on any particular important topic and then add, frequently in snippets merely, additional or modifying matter from other works. This, however, would be to treat the doctrine as if it had little or no connection with Augustine's life—whereas, of course, it notoriously has. It would be to treat his teaching as static, whereas it is dynamic and even (as I have tried to suggest) poetical, visionary, salvationist. It is not dead matter to be carved up in sample pieces. Moreover, Augustine's life and experience, book or letter, sermon or prayer, are as interesting as, and in influence perhaps even more significant than, the teaching itself, which in any case is so often a reflection of his experience. . . .

"Accordingly, I have opted for extracting not in passages, but as far as possible in Books. . . .

"To make guidance to the treatment of the topic fairly complete, however, I have added before each extract brief introductory notes, brief recent bibliography and brief references to the relevant important matter in other works of Augustine.

"Finally, I give at the end of the *Reader* a Bibliographical Guide containing full references for names or works cited in my Introductions, as well as a short Index of the main topics covered so that one can quickly discover what Augustine has here to say on them and where to go for more."

—from the Introduction

AN
AUGUSTINE READER

Edited, with an Introduction,
by John J. O'Meara

IMAGE BOOKS

A Division of Doubleday & Company, Inc.

Garden City, New York

Image Books edition: 1973
Image Books edition published September 1973

Book I from NINE SERMONS OF ST. AUGUSTINE, translated
by Edmund Hill. Copyright © 1958 by Longmans, Green & Co.,
Ltd. Used by permission of The Macmillan Company and Longmans, Green & Co., Ltd.

ISBN: 0-385-06585-X
Library of Congress Catalog Card Number 73–80800
Copyright © 1973 by John J. O'Meara
All Rights Reserved
Printed in the United States of America

CONTENTS

Biographical Guide   7

Introduction   11

A.D.
386–387 *Soliloquies,* Book 1   34
394–418 *Letters* (Correspondence with St. Jerome)   65
397–400 *Confessions,* Books 7, 8 (Manichaeism and
         Neoplatonism) and 11 (Creation and
         Time)   127
401   *On Baptism,* Book 1 (against the Donatists)   204
407   *Sermon on Psalm 22*   235
399–419 *On the Trinity,* Books 2 and 8   252
413–427 *City of God,* Books 5 and 22   314
418   *The Grace of Christ and Original Sin,*
         Book 2 (against the Pelagians)   443
396–426 *Christian Instruction,* Book 4   491

Bibliographical Guide   545

Index of Topics   555

BIOGRAPHICAL GUIDE*

A.D.

354   Born at Tagaste, in Numidia.

361   At school in Tagaste. Seriously ill.

367   Away at school in Madauros.

369–370   Studies interrupted. Idle at home. Death of father, Patricius.

370   In Carthage for higher studies. Liaison with a concubine.

372–373   Birth of their son Adeodatus. Reading of Cicero's *Hortensius*. Joins Manichaeans.

374   Teaching rhetoric at Tagaste.

375   Death of a friend.

376   Teaching rhetoric at Carthage.

380–381   His first (not extant) work: *De pulchro et apto* (*On the Beautiful and Fitting*)

382–383   Doubtful on Manichaeism.

383   Leaves for Rome. Seriously ill.

384   Nominated to a high rhetoric post in Milan by Symmachus, an important pagan. Influence of St. Ambrose. His mother, Monica, joins him.

386   Reading of Platonist books.
Conversion.
First (extant) works.

387   Baptism at Milan. Death of Monica.

388   Return to Africa, Carthage and Tagaste.

* The chronological order of Augustine's works is given in the Bibliographical Guide on pp. 545.

390	Death of Adeodatus.
391	Ordained at Hippo.
396	Becomes bishop of Hippo.
411	Condemnation of Donatists at Carthage.
412	Condemnation of Coelestius, the Pelagian, in Africa.
418	Pope Zosimus condemns Pelagius and Coelestius.
426	Nominates his successor, Eraclius.
430	Vandals attack Numidia. Death of Augustine.

AN
AUGUSTINE READER

INTRODUCTION

Augustine of Hippo was lucky in his time. At the beginning of the fourth century A.D., the century in which he was born in a small town in North Africa, the Christian Church, though spreading its influence everywhere, was still subject to a pagan power. By the end of that century the church had for all practical purposes taken over the Roman Empire—and he was a bishop already famous.

There is a well-known and useful line from an epistle of the Latin poet Horace—*Graecia capta ferum victorem cepit* (*Epistles* 2.1.156) ("Greece, the captive, captured her wild conqueror"). Rome's legions kept marching along the straight and ever penetrating Roman roads; her laws ran everywhere; her prosperity was enjoyed by all. But Greek art, philosophy, letters, education and even religion occupied, somewhat unhappily, the mind of Rome. In this sense Arnold Toynbee's characterization of Rome as a late Hellenic rally is evidently true.

When in turn the Christian Church took over the Roman Empire, it too was in danger of being captured by Hellenism. How could it have been otherwise? By now only a minority of Christians were Jews with a Jewish understanding of the Old and New Testaments. The majority were citizens of the far-flung Roman Empire, thinking with the minds of Cicero and Vergil.

Just when the church became the Establishment in the West and had urgent need to politicize its revelation—to make it appear rational—Augustine was at hand to serve. This is what I mean when I say that he was lucky in his time. He set the mold in which Western Christendom was laid: he set it firmly and he set it fully. No one before or since had ever had such an opportunity in this regard. He, moreover, had the desire and confidence to seize that chance.

This is one of the reasons why Augustine must be of interest to us. The thought patterns, determining action for fifteen hundred years, were set (not initiated, let it be noted) by him. We nowadays would ask: what were his qualifications for so (in retrospect) momentous a task? His range of knowledge, his experience, his character cannot but be of great interest to us. As it happens, he had an unusual personality and we have his own delineation of it in an extraordinary book—his *Confessions*. This knowledge, experience and character will engage our attention for much of the rest of this Introduction, and they will be illustrated in the more personal excerpts in the *Reader*. But we must also examine a little the philosophy, so to speak, which he brought forth from a merging of Hellenistic thought and religion (not excluding demonology) on the one hand and Hebraic revelation on the other—this will be seen in most of the extracts that follow.

LIFE

Aurelius Augustinus was born in Tagaste in Numidia—now Souk-Ahras in Algeria, about sixty miles south of Bône—on November 13, A.D. 354. His parents, Patricius and Monica, although having connections with Berber stock, were Roman in outlook and Latin was the vernacular of the growing boy. There were at least two other children in the family. Patricius was a modest landowner and town councilor, but was not wealthy. He died in 370, when Augustine was sixteen years of age. Monica was a pious, patient, and insistent woman, whose ambition it was to win both her husband and Augustine to Catholicism. She succeeded and died at Ostia in the year of Augustine's baptism, A.D. 387. It is often suggested that Monica had undue influence on Augustine.

After local schooling to the age of ten Augustine went some fifteen miles south to Madauros for high school education. This was mainly in the Latin authors Terence, Sallust, Cicero and Vergil. He was taught a little Greek and hated it. At Carthage he subsequently took up the career of rhetorician —in effect a kind of university professor—in which he was to win distinctions in Africa and such success subsequently in Rome and Milan (then the emperor's court) that he could reasonably entertain the expectation of becoming governor of a province. One should bear very much in mind that his formation and career were almost exclusively in Latin rhetoric, that is in literature and public speaking.

Away from home in the year of his father's death, the sixteen-year-old boy would seem to have succumbed somewhat to the flesh. A little later he took a mistress who gave him a son whom he called Adeodatus—"given by God." He was faithful to her and she to him for fifteen years—until he planned a regular marriage with another. Then she was sent away, with sorrow in both their hearts. It would seem that her social condition did not allow her to expect or him to offer marriage. He clearly loved her, as he also loved their brilliant son, who, alas, died young. Augustine does not conceal that his own and his mother's worldly ambitions and the social mores of the time made their separation inevitable. He nevertheless tells the story against himself, and this is the plainest evidence that he was deeply attached to her and did not, in the circumstances, treat her—as it is sometimes suggested—brutally. It is simply not fair to apply to him the outlook of our times.

At any rate, the testimony of others, his success in studies, his fidelity to one woman and, perhaps above all, his growing preoccupation with religious and intellectual ideals tend very much to give the lie to his own strictures on these teen-age years in his *Confessions*, written nearly two decades later.

In his nineteenth year Augustine felt a strong call, stimulated by reading Cicero's *Hortensius* (now lost), to give himself to higher things and contemn mere worldly ambition. The curious result of this was his embracing of Manichaeism which promised to teach him all things through reason—unlike Catholicism, which demanded also faith.

Augustine had imbibed Catholicism, as he says, with his mother's milk. He had not been baptized, however, for the baptismal wiping out of sin was thought better postponed until at least wild oats were safely sown. Manichaeism was dualistic, positing the existence of two principles, good and evil. While it incorporated many non-Christian elements in its revelation and was actively hostile to Christianity in many ways, and notably to Christianity's acceptance of the Old Testament, it was, in North Africa, nevertheless so "Christian" in other ways, and particularly in its enthusiasm for St. Paul's Epistles, that it was said that one could pass from Manichaeism to Christianity or vice versa without any great noticeable change—indeed, Augustine the bishop was accused of being a crypto-Manichaean all along. Nevertheless Monica was so displeased with her son's joining the Manichaeans that she turned him out of her house. Moreover, Augustine's own rigorous controversy with the Manichaeans later indicates that for him too at that stage there was a great divide.

Augustine remained a Manichaean for nearly all his impressionable and formative twenties, excusing his sins as caused by evil and aspiring to the good. He gradually realized that the Manichaeans did not, any more than the Catholics, base their system on reason alone—nor were their lives always exemplary. Still, he tried to spread their gospel while declining to join the higher echelons of the sect. In the end he became so disillusioned with their bizarre beliefs and their exaggerated criticism of the Old Testament that he resumed, at about the age of thirty, the religion of his earlier life. In the meantime, his mother had long before allowed him back. His defiance of her, however, in this—and indeed other—important matters, should not go unnoted.

That Augustine should have subscribed to material dualism in his twenties made his conversion to belief in an immaterial God and his understanding of the problem of evil in the world extremely difficult. What is more, it cannot but have left its mark deeply on him, tainting for him any life of the senses with the suggestion of sin.

By now, about 384, he had abandoned Carthage, his unruly pupils and his mother for Rome (where he found that the pupils did not pay!) and the patronage of Symmachus, a leader of the surviving pagans of the day. He was recommended to a high post, Master of Rhetoric, at the Court in

Milan. There the tempo of his life increased: he made important public speeches, he canvassed powerful friends, he kept up the arduous grind of teaching. He put away his mistress and planned for marriage with a girl who had a suitable dowry—but was too young. His search for truth was impatient and despairing. He resolved to join the followers of the New Academy, who professed that one could not know anything and therefore one must assent to nothing. His health was deteriorating. He was so profoundly unhappy that he envied a drunken beggar his intoxication.

But gradually things began to improve. His mother had followed him to Milan, and this led him to attend upon Ambrose, the bishop. Listening for the rhetoric of his sermons, he began to realize that Ambrose was supplying him with the solution to many Manichaean and personal arguments against the Bible. Ambrose insisted with St. Paul: "The letter kills, but the spirit gives life" (2 Cor. 3:6). Scripture was to be understood not literally but allegorically. Even more, he found either in Ambrose's sermons or in the discourse of intellectual friends in Milan an immaterial philosophy that at one stroke enabled him to conceive of a spiritual God and have some explanation of the problem of evil as simply a privation or defect of being and (most wonderful of all) seemed to fit with Catholic teaching, especially on Providence and the Trinity. That philosophy was Neoplatonism and its recent interpreters in Rome were Plotinus (A.D. 205–270) and his disciple Porphyry (A.D. 232–305). The excitement of that momentous discovery burned in him as a bright flame for many a long year. He returned again and again to the mystical impulse to ascend the scale of being from creatures to the One that Plotinus had given him. Never again could any worldly thing have real value for him. Augustine's attitude was henceforth absolutist: there was no truth, no justice or any other virtue unless it took account first of God. This made an already zealous Augustine zealous beyond measure.

Augustine now felt that intellectually he must become formally a Catholic—but he was held back by the flesh. Part of the problem was undoubtedly created by the differing dualisms of both Manichaeism and Neoplatonism. For a Platonist, the body was the tomb of the soul and had to be shunned. How could one aspire to union with the Father while continuing to have truck with the senses? Augustine understood Catholicism to demand the same, at least from him. But he found that his will was sleepy and sluggish, while habit was awake and strong. It took the stories of the conversions of Antony (the father of monasticism) and of the African rhetor Victorinus and other conversions to bring him to a crisis wherein he found himself bidden by the mysterious voice of an unseen child to open the Scriptures and read what his eye first fell on. It was: "Put on the Lord Jesus Christ, and make not provision for the flesh, to fulfill its lusts" (Rom. 13:14). On the spot his will was adamant. He was converted. Henceforth Augustine was the apostle of grace, unaccountable and irresistible. In 387 he was baptized by Ambrose.

In the following year Augustine returned to Africa with the intention of living in a Christian community and writing a series of Christian literary and philosophical works. Though he became, unwillingly, a priest in 391 and a bishop in 396, engaged till his death in 430 in resounding and extended controversies with successively Manichaeans, Donatists and Pelagians, interpreted the Scriptures daily, attended to heavy administrative (some civil) duties, had a vast correspondence (he wrote to many of the notables of his day) and wrote the seminal theological books for Western Christendom, in one way the great adventure of his life was already over. Few authors have so clearly depended on their own experiences to generate their theories as did Augustine: his life, but above all, his early life, profoundly influenced his teaching.

WORKS

Augustine's works run to over a hundred in number, exclusive of some eight hundred *Sermons* and over two hundred *Letters*—some of them the equivalent of books. The *Sermons*, of course, are mainly exegetical—interpretation of the Scriptures—but they have many a human and sometimes controversial touch. The *Letters* are testimony to his influence throughout the known world: his opinions and advice were sought by emperors and ministers, popes and saints. They

mark his changing interests and are invaluable for understanding the development of his ideas. His works are mainly
concerned with his controversies with the Manichaeans, Donatists and Pelagians. But the first and third of these controversies are also encountered in the *Confessions* (thirteen
books) and the *City of God* (twenty-two books) respectively.
The Manichaeans we have mentioned very briefly already.
The Donatist schism arose in A.D. 312, when those who had
remained constant in a recent persecution refused to have
dealings with those who had acquiesced. It is sometimes
thought (but this has been questioned more recently) that
it was African and rural in outlook as opposed to the
official Roman and urbanized church represented by Augustine. In every town the schism was only too apparent—bishop
against bishop, church against church. What was involved,
therefore, was essentially doctrine on the church itself. Augustine tried every manner of persuasion, in the end resorting
reluctantly to physical coercion by the powers of the state
to bring this controversy to a close.

The Pelagian controversy was more serious. Here virtuous
and intelligent men—Pelagius, Coelestius and Julian of
Eclanum—defended their view of the self-sufficiency of human
nature (without the aid of grace) partly from the earlier
writing of Augustine himself. Moreover the great questions
of free will and predestination were inevitably involved: here
Augustine tended to harden his formulas beyond what the
church would later accept—all in defense of his preoccupation with grace.

Apart from these pastoral and administrative writings, the
more important of his more formal works are the *Dialogues
of Cassiciacum,* the *Confessions,* the *Trinity* and the *City of
God.*

The *Dialogues* (386–87), written after his conversion in a
semi-catechetical semi-Platonic manner, discuss knowledge,
happiness and order in a manner so philosophical as to have
given rise to the idea, now firmly rejected, that Augustine
was really converted, not to Catholicism, but to Neoplatonism
in A.D. 386. In fact, they are, for all their philosophy, pre-
dominantly based on Christ as the Truth and the Way. Of the
three dialogues mentioned, that on Order is the most pro-

found (indeed, it is somewhat obscure) and has a number of anticipations (as has the *Trinity*) of the more mystical speculation of later Western writers subject to Greek theological influence—such as Eriugena, for example. Augustine composed at the same time as these *Dialogues* his *Soliloquies*, which are prayerful, intimate and more personal.

The *Confessions* (397–400) is a great and unique work, rhetorical and emotional, poetic and subtle. It is fatally easy to misunderstand it—to begin with, the confession is not of sin only, but of faith and praise to God. In nine books Augustine outlines in a rhetorical moralistic and selective way his life, guided as it was by providence and saved by grace, from birth to his conversion at the age of thirty-two: much is taken up with his reactions to Manichaeism and Neoplatonism. The tenth book covers more factually the period between his conversion and the time of writing as a bishop some twelve years later. The last three books are a commentary on the first chapter of Genesis. The *Confessions* gives rise to great problems in connection with its structure and historicity. But few can read it without being moved and in some way exalted by its obsessive ascent from the dragging body to the soaring mind.

The *Trinity* (399–419) in fifteen books employs all the resources of exegesis to win from the Scriptures in its earlier part and from Reason in its later part some understanding of this great Christian mystery. Here particularly Augustine exploits analogies with the powers of the human soul to discover in them—mind, knowledge, love; memory, intelligence, will—some faint shadow of Father, Word and Spirit. In this difficult book later writers on creation and mysticism found much help and inspiration.

Finally we come to the *City of God* (413–427), begun after the sack of Rome by Alaric in 410 but in one way or another in prospect for long before. The first ten of its twenty-two books attack in turn the Roman official view that *temporal* prosperity is dependent upon worship of the many false gods (Books 1–5) and the Greek philosophical view that happiness in the afterlife is dependent upon this worship (Books 6–10). It is to be stressed that this part of the *City of God* is against polytheism, not against Roman virtue or

Greek philosophy, both of which are commended and considered to be providentially arranged aids to the spread and understanding of the Christian revelation. The final twelve books of the work fall into three equal groups dealing with the scriptural account of the origin of man (Books 11–14), his history (Books 15–18) and final destiny (Books 19–22). The title of the *City of God* is taken from Psalm 87:3 and refers not to a political city, but to the society of the saved (both men and angels) here and hereafter. This society is not identical with the church. The work is equally about the City of Earth (or the Devil), that is, the society of those who will be, indeed are, damned. The work is theological and might be said to give a theology of history—not a philosophy of it. It has little, moreover, to say on politics. It heralds the coming of the Christian era and explicitly proclaims its Hebraic, Roman and Greek sources. It is a great Christian prose epic—not without its baffling *longueurs*.

DOCTRINE

Augustine was not a systematic theologian, though there is much system in his theology. His theological speculation is, however, extensive and has had a dominating influence in the West. He is, therefore, essentially a theologian. He is even less—much less—a systematic philosopher, though he was excited by philosophy in his youth and at the time of his conversion was greatly impressed by it. Nevertheless, although he always retained something of the philosophic manner, related (when convenient) his doctrine to reason and continued to profess admiration (with certain explicit reservations) for Plato, Plotinus and Porphyry, his stance from the time of his conversion is determined by his acceptance of the Christian doctrines of the Incarnation and Resurrection of the body. In effect, he at least dispensed with the Platonists and in practice often contradicted them. It is, however, anachronistic to distinguish strictly between philosophy and theology in his period. We must, therefore, present his doctrine without such strict distinction.

He has little new or important to give in the theory of knowledge except the seeming anticipation of Descartes' *cogito, ergo sum* (for Augustine, *dubito, ergo sum*), his Neo-platonic emphasis on purification as prerequisite to knowledge and especially his theory of illumination. This theory is part and parcel of his doctrine on grace. Intellectual ideas (as distinct from ideas arising from sense perception) cannot arise in the mind unless they are illuminated by another (God) as by their sun: God is the only and inner teacher of the soul.

The relation of faith to reason is, of course, a basic problem in Augustine. At the time of his conversion he professed to regard them as two independent ways to—in a sense, revelations of—God which mutually assisted one another. They could be independent (for a very few, however, in the case of reason only). Later he modified his notions on their independence. Since faith depended on verifying the credibility of the testimony one believed in, faith depended upon reason. Reason, on the other hand, operated on its own. It was incapable itself, however, of reaching the truths that revelation proposed for its understanding and was, in *time,* preceded by faith: to understand anything, you must first accept it. "I believe that I may understand."

Christian revelation is verified by reason in four ways: the miracles of Christ, the fulfillment of prophecies, the multitude of believers, the holiness and heroism of Christianity. The sources of faith are the Scriptures, tradition and over all the teaching power of the church.

God exists as the necessarily posited source of all being, all truth and all good. God, however, is ineffable. God's most obvious attribute, to Augustine, is simplicity. Augustine's formulation of his doctrine on the Trinity was a remarkable advance in the West and has endured. Here three points made clear by him are important: the concept of the nature of the Trinity as being before the persons; the attribution of all operations of the Trinity outside itself to the Trinity as one; and the explanation of the procession of the persons in terms of human psychology.

Creatures were made *ex nihilo* distinct from God, and by his will and all at once. While God may intervene at any time, "new" creatures are but developments of "seeds" (*rationes seminales*) existing from the one creation. Angels too were created by God, among them the demons, who dwelt in the atmosphere, could sense our thoughts and were skilled and keen to mislead us.

Man's *soul* is immaterial, and man is an unmixed composite of body and soul. Body is a good. Adam's soul was a separate creation. Other human souls would seem to have been generated if the transmission of original sin was to be explained.

In many ways, the center of Augustine's theology and view of history is the *Incarnation*. Belief in the Incarnation was the final challenge at his conversion, the parting of the ways from the Neoplatonists and the unerring and sustaining universal way of salvation. History looked forward and backward to that event, incredible to the proud but believed by the whole world. Christ's predecessors—the sibyl of Cumae, for example—were saved by Christ whose City of God existed from the beginning. Christ, equal to the Father, is God and is man with a real body and a real soul. In Christ the union is of two natures in one single person.

God's sovereignty over the human will, according to Augustine, is absolute. *Grace,* unmerited, precedes all good actions, including faith. Here Augustine's theories of illumination and grace are at one. Nevertheless, man's *will is free.* God's foreknowledge reconciles both elements in the problem. Adam was punished for his (original) sin by the deprivation of privileges, and his descendants, because of their moral union with him, share his guilt. There is reason to believe that Augustine taught that sensual pleasure in intercourse is the necessary condition for the transmission of original sin to Adam's descendants. Damnation of some kind is the punishment for original sin *alone* (as in the case of unbaptized infants). Predestination to salvation is absolutely gratuitous, but God, nevertheless, wills to give *all* men the power to save and the freedom to damn themselves.

Augustine was insistent that "outside the *Church* there is no salvation." But God, Augustine insisted, nevertheless did employ his grace independently of the church. In the last analysis, Christ, who established the church, alone is our teacher. The church's holiness will not be perfect until heaven; here on earth she sanctifies through the sacraments. Her authority is supreme: "I for my part," Augustine pro-

claims, "would not believe in the Gospel, if the authority of
the Catholic Church did not bid me to do so" (*Contra
epistulam quam vocant Fundamenti*, 5.6).

Augustine taught that our end in life is happiness, that is,
the enjoyment of God, the Supreme End. He as Truth il-
lumines our minds, and we are moved to love him and our
fellow men. Evil is not evil nor good good because God
forbids one and commends the other: rather is it that he
forbids evil because it is evil and commends good because it
is good. Charity, or *love*, is behind every precept. In the
afterlife the good will be resurrected and enjoy Heaven, the
evil punished in Hell: Purgatory will exist until the Last
Judgment.

INFLUENCE

Augustine shares from time to time with Vergil the title
of "Father of the West"—but Augustine's must surely be the
greater claim. He was, of course, himself profoundly affected
by Vergil. In the pages of Vergil's *Aeneid* he had learned of
Love and Mission—of Dido and Aeneas. The struggle in the
heart of Vergil was the struggle in the heart of Augustine:
love appeared to be the only and all-conquering value. It was
also self-indulgent and destructive. Duty must transcend it—
obedience to God and the service of his purpose with man-
kind. Augustine shows all the passion of Dido and all the
temptations to weakness of Aeneas. But he follows Aeneas,
and consciously. *Mens immota manet, lacrimae volvuntur
inanes* (*Aeneid* 4.449) ("His mind stays unmoved, tears roll
down unavailing"). This was an intellectual struggle for
Vergil. It was "real" for the character Aeneas. It was real
also for Augustine.

It is, I think, true to say that the young Augustine is more
attractive than the old, that the *Confessions* is his most interesting book and that much of the tension in it disappears
on his conversion. Like Aeneas' desertion of Dido and vision
of Destiny, Augustine's abandonment of the flesh and vision
of a Neoplatonic-Christian Father marked the end of "human
nature's daily food" and heralded a long campaign, with its
endless battles and controversies, to found a holy empire: it

is a higher, nobler pursuit—but it may have less human appeal.

To the extent that Augustine followed Vergil and Aeneas in deserting love to found a Rome, he fell back on the Roman Stoic organization for virtue and public service. Gone for the most part was the beckoning attraction of the flesh; gone too for the most part, Platonic mysticism. They never wholly went. From time to time in the later Augustine (as in the "later" books of the *Aeneid*) emerge—*veteris vestigia flammae* (*Aeneid* 2.23), "the scars," as C. Day Lewis renders it, "of the old flame."

At any rate, Augustine's contribution to the *tempora Christiana*, the Christian era, was paramount and enduring. Fulgentius of Ruspe, Isidore of Seville, Caesarius of Arles, Prosper of Aquitaine, Pope Gregory the Great in Italy all proclaim their debt to him. Charlemagne conceived his planned Renaissance not with reference to Augustus, but to Augustine. In the early Middle Ages Augustine's teaching on predestination was the source of much theological controversy in which Gottschalk and Johannes Scottus Eriugena played important and rather unhappy roles. In the wider field of theology Augustine continued to dominate—"after the Apostles the master of the Churches"[1]—until the thirteenth century and the advent of Aquinas. The *City of God* especially was credited with the prescription of the mutual rights of State and Church—with perhaps little real justification.

In the world of asceticism the influence of the *Regula Sancti Augustini* (attributed to Augustine and certainly inspired by his influence) grew apace. The foundation of the Canons Regular, Premonstratensians and Dominicans ensured the persistence of Augustine's ascetical ideals; while the abbey of the Canons of St. Victor, founded at Paris in 1108 and made famous by its sons, Hugh, Richard and Adam, spread the influence of his spirit of humanism and mysticism.

In some ways Aquinas tended to supplant Augustine in the world of Christian philosophy and theology, if only because he had available to him in a rediscovered Aristotelian-

---

[1] D. C. Lambot, *Oeuvres théologiques et grammaticales de Godescalc d'Orbais, Spicilegium sacrum Lovaniense*, t. 20, 1945, p. 327.

ism a system that was more adaptable as a rational under-
pinning for developed Christian revelation than was the
dominant Platonism of the era of Augustine. Moreover,
Aquinas was much more systematic and acceptable to the
Scholastic mode. In fact, of course, Aquinas, a Dominican
disciple of Augustine, transmitted the received inheritance
of Christian teaching in the West—and this, as Aquinas makes
clear on many an occasion, is mainly Augustinian. It is to
be remembered, too, that, whatever his sympathy for Platonism had been in the beginning, Augustine had repudiated its basic tenets that conflicted with the Christian doctrine
on the Incarnation and Resurrection. But the Franciscans,
through Bonaventure and Duns Scotus, and the Order of the
Hermits of St. Augustine, through Giles of Rome (d. 1316)
and Gregory of Rimini (d. 1356), kept the distinctive Augustinian approach alive.

The Reformation marked, in a sense, the return of Augustine to the center of the stage—especially in its revival of the
controversy on predestination. The reformers tended to take
the more extreme views of Augustine's interpretation of St.
Paul's teaching on the consequences of original sin, concupiscence, the powerlessness of man, salvation by grace and
justification by faith. It should not be forgotten that Luther
was an Augustinian monk whose religious name was Augustine and that he declared not that he had read Augustine but
that he had swallowed him whole! In due course, the revival
of interest in Augustine and the advent of printing led to the
important editions of Augustine's works by Amerbach (Basel,
1508), Erasmus (Basel, 1527–29) and Johann van der
Meulen (Antwerp, 1576–77). These editions mark the beginning of a renaissance in Augustinian studies which still
endures.

The seventeenth century, especially in France, was the
Augustinian century *par excellence*. Cardinal de Bérulle and
his spiritual sons St. Vincent de Paul, Condren, Olier of St.
Sulpice and St. John Eudes spread the influence of Augus-
tine's spiritual ideals. Unfortunately, the old Augustinian-
Pelagian controversy broke out once again on the posthu-
mous publication (Louvain, 1640) of Jansenius' *Augustinus*.
The controversy had been gathering force from the time of

Baius (1513–89) and the dispute of the Jesuit Molina (1536–1600) with the Dominicans. Now it broke forth with great virulence. The Jansenism of Port-Royal (a name intended, it is said, to remind one of Augustine's see of Hippo Regius), of St. Cyran and the Great Arnauld had an immense influence that continued, one might say, until today.

Side by side with these more theological and religious developments, the apparent correspondence of the basic epistemological positions of Augustine and Descartes gave a strong impulse towards the revival of interest in Augustinian philosophical approaches (as seen, for example, in Malebranche). In this way Augustine has been introduced, so to speak, to the modern age. But indeed, one might go further: certain, more mystical, aspects of the work of Teilhard de Chardin suggest that the spirit of Augustine is alive and working powerfully. And some now blame him for the alleged puritanism of traditional Christian attitudes to sex, but we shall say something on this almost immediately.

PERSONALITY

In the end, one wants to find out, if one can, the most important thing about Augustine—his personality, the kind of man he was. There is no doubt that, for all his luck or circumstances, his impact on the world has been very great. Some would say that it was for good, some for evil. He was a sign to be contradicted. In short, both he and his teaching are complicated, arousing love and hate, or at least like and dislike, in almost everyone who knows them. A totally rounded, consistent picture of Augustine would be suspect.

Some authors see the elements of tension and inconsistency in his birthplace and his birth: Africa made him intense and extreme; his mother gave him goodness and sensibility, especially religious sensibility; his father made him unscrupulous and a bully. All of these elements were in him in one way or another at one time or another in his life. But the assignment of the source or nice calculation of measure can never be more than plausible.

He had other obvious qualities too—a love of ideas and on the whole an even greater and more sustained love of action.

He was loyal, persistent, aggressive. He was also disloyal (and
to his mother!), indecisive, without confidence. He was me-
thodical and clear in purpose over all: in detail he could be
sidetracked and become irrelevant. Were all these inconsistent
qualities simply inherited, as some would think, from Monica
and Patricius? We can never know.

We can, however, point to evidence of influences more
discernible, even if not more fundamental. Augustine was
singularly responsive to his environment and experiences.
Apart from what may have come to him with his blood and
in his home, there were other factors in his life that shaped
his outlook and temperament.

The first of these was his intellectual—and religious—formation. This was made up of Latin schooling (as pupil and
teacher), Manichaean "reason," Neoplatonic intellectual aspirations and the Bible. All of these marked him deeply and,
one is tempted to say (bathetic as it may seem), equally.

Augustine was trained in a narrow Latin literature with a
dominating, professionally rhetorical slant. This gave or developed in him his finally most obviously realized qualities:
eclecticism in ideas and a somewhat detached, indeed, on occasion irresponsibly loyal, absoluteness in moral choice. It
also gave him a technique: the technique of persuasion and
orderly exposition. But there is more: it gave him the Roman
love to serve and rule—which he describes with such sympathy
in the fifth book of the *City of God*. God was substituted for
Jupiter, Juno and Minerva.

Still, he had the nagging need to get to the bottom of things
—to follow the Cicero of the *Hortensius* rather than the Cicero
of the *Academica*. Why was there evil in the world? Why do
we yield to our baser instincts? Whence do we come? Whither
do we go? The Manichaeans, while reverencing Christ and
St. Paul, promised a satisfying rational answer. But Augustine was disappointed. Nevertheless there remained with him
forever, from this almost ten-year encounter, so overwhelming a conviction that he was utterly powerless before the
principle of evil, that the idea of grace, unmerited, became
virtually a necessity for him; and pessimism deeply marked
his emotional outlook as can be seen from the twenty-second
book of the *City of God* included in this *Reader*.

Yet his experience of Neoplatonism, of the doctrine of Plotinus and Porphyry, had the opposite effect: from them he got his countervailing optimism—that all created nature is good and that evil is no more than the absence or privation of that good. It also enabled him to conceive of a spiritual Being who illumined our minds and arranged all things in his Providence for good. The three Neoplatonic hypostases, moreover, seemed to correspond to the Christian Trinity. Porphyry seemed even to suggest that his Supreme Being was the God of the Hebrews, that grace was given to men and that some Mediator (but Porphyry denied that it was Christ, because of his birth of a virgin and death on a cross), some Universal Way, brought man back to God. Above all, the reading of Plotinus seems to have stimulated a mystical, visionary flair in Augustine which remained with him till the end. For him the Plotinian return to the Father is inextricably bound up with the New Testament's return of the Prodigal. This spiritual discovery ultimately made possible for him the embracing of the Scriptures and Catholicism and sustained him in a kind of mystical suspense throughout his life. It would be a mistake, however, to think that Augustine made a profound study or had a profound understanding of Neoplatonism: the lightheartedness with which he stressed the apparent correspondences between certain Neoplatonic and Christian doctrines suggests that he was more interested in discerning and using such possible correspondences than in penetrating them. His great forte was vision. This vision gave a strongly "salvationist" character to his thought and action and is the mainspring of his later life. It is to be noted that it involved some departure from an historical attitude. Here we see in Augustine the Aeneas of the later books of the *Aeneid:* the ever-willing warrior committed to a goal and the endless battles that come between.

Finally, the Bible became for him literally the oracle of God, peremptory and final. It was his daily food which he shared with his flock. A very large part of his life as bishop lay in expounding the Scriptures: we have a sample of his method in the second book on the *Trinity* given later on. All other sources of information wilted away before Augustine's consuming passion for God's word.

So much for his intellectual formation. He was formed, too, by the experiences of his life, of which the greatest, the vantage point from which he viewed his own life and the life of every man, was his conversion. This event was marked by such evident intervention of Providence in so many quite improbable ways, that Augustine was ready to see God's finger everywhere. Out of apparent evil had come so much good for him that he felt open to construe any event in a providential light. This gave him a distinctly unscientific attitude to many problems. It also reinforced a detachment from the historical truth of things which is discomfiting. It is to some degree part and parcel of his and his contemporaries' vivid and real belief in demons, dreams and miracles; but it is also an *unquestioning* acceptance in advance of God's providence, which could always intervene to interrupt the established order of things. This at once allowed him to adopt positions that were either too extreme or improbable and seem on occasion to us a little irresponsible—notably in relation to grace. But he did this in much simpler things. He advanced, for example, without grounds the theory that the Academic philosophers were not skeptics but crypto-Platonists and then added: "This theory I have sometimes thought probable. If it is false, I do not mind" (*Against the Academics* 3.20.43). But there are many other instances. In some ways Augustine indulged in some make-believe.

Not so, however, in dealing with the Manichaeans, Donatists and Pelagians. Here he showed a compensatingly excessive grasp of the practical measures that would ensure success. Whatever his initial hesitations and reluctance, he finally used the civil force to bring Donatism to an end in Africa. Likewise with the Manichaeans—a recent comment on Augustine's method of controversy with one of them, Felix, is that it was *fort choquante*. Similarly did this hound of heaven, this *procureur général* of the church, pursue the Pelagians. He even insisted too much with Jerome, as the correspondence here reproduced will show. At best, it is an unattractive trait; at worst it is righteous (perhaps too righteous) bullying. In fact, it was the product of excessive zeal for the very best of ends.

Perhaps the quality most associated with Augustine in the

popular mind is sensuality, sublimated in later life in the single-minded love of God: "I came to Carthage where all around me roared the sizzle of shameful loves. I was not in love yet, but I was in love with the desire to love, and because of a deep want in myself I hated myself for not wanting enough. I looked around for something to love, in love with loving. I hated a life without trouble and entanglements. To love and to be loved was very sweet to me, especially if I could enjoy the body of my lover. And so I polluted the river of friendship with the dirt of concupiscence and clouded its brightness with the hell of my lust. I threw myself into love in which I wanted to be trapped. I was loved and secretly succeeded in binding myself with pleasure" (*Confessions* 3.1.1). Thus wrote the new bishop of his sixteenth or seventeenth year. As an older man he distinguished the city of God from the city of this world on the basis of the love of God and the love of self: "And so two loves have made two cities—namely the earthly, love of self even to contempt of God; but the heavenly love of God even to contempt of self" (*City of God* 14.28). One of the best-known maxims of Augustine is the apparently very permissive one: *Dilige et quod vis fac* (*Tract. in Joh. Ep.* P.L. 35.2033)— "Love and do what you will"—which, however, really means "Love God, and do what you will *then* want to do."

The need to love is, undoubtedly, an important quality in Augustine. But it is an exaggeration to claim that the church's traditional attitude and teaching on sex and marriage is mainly traceable to Augustine's reaction from youthful sexual excesses to sublimated love of God.

A strong and professionally competent statement of the case against Augustine appeared in 1963 in an article by L. Janssens in the *Ephemerides Theologicae Lovanienses* (39.4, pp. 787–826) which asserted that Augustine introduced a dualism into married life: his pessimistic attitude to sexual pleasure demanded that he should find justification for its use—this was found both in the need for procreation (*bonum prolis*) and precaution against a partner's adultery (*bonum fidei*). On the other hand, true conjugal love was a *purely spiritual thing* (*bonum sacramenti*), in regard to which sexual relations could have no positive signification whatever.

In fact, carnal desire was for him an evil (*malum*) and a disease (*morbus*) and could only be an obstacle to the flowering of conjugal love. The more desire is repressed, the stronger is the *caritas coniugalis*. Hence Augustine, according to Janssens, wishes that all Christian couples could practice complete continence so as to be united not in the flesh but in *caritas*.

Janssens is careful to point out some of the sources of these ideas: Stoics, Neo-Pythagoreans, Essenes and Gnostics. He is also careful to state that although Augustine was the principal agent in the transmission of these ideas into Christian theology, he was not the only Church Father responsible. There were also Justin Martyr, for example, Athenagoras, Clement of Alexandria, Origen, Ambrose and Jerome. All of these were determined that the Christian view of marriage would be no whit less ascetical than the Stoic or Neo-Pythagorean or what you will. He notes too that of the three great controversies that dominated Augustine's life—with the Donatists, the Manichaeans and the Pelagians—the two latter provided him with a field only too favorable for the development of such pessimistic ideas.

It must be admitted, then, that Augustine did not *reduce* the age-old Western—perhaps simply human—inhibitions on the vital appetite of sex. His former Manichaean beliefs, his Neoplatonic conversion and education in the classics, his personal turning away from the life of the senses to the life of the spirit and, perhaps above all, his stance on the Pelagian controversy, where his need to stress the insufficiency of nature led him to associate original sin directly with the sexual pleasure—all made it too easy for him to endorse and transmit in full the attitudes of many predecessors. It is to these attitudes rather than to personal reaction to his earlier life *alone* that his role in the transmission of puritan sexual ideas is to be referred.

Augustine did have a loving nature and attracted faithful and loyal friends. He was emotional and responsive. But it is hard to escape the conclusion that his love from the beginning, however it manifested itself, was a consuming love of God: "Our heart will not rest, until it rests in you" (*Confessions* 1.1.1). Here his love joins his mother's, with whom at

Ostia before her death in A.D. 387, he shared the highest mystical experience (so far as we know) of his life. Here is the real key to Augustine. This love is the passion of his life. It explains his embarrassing absoluteness. It is an affair, primarily, of the heart and less of the intelligence.

> Too late I have loved you, beauty old and new! Too late I have loved you. Yet you were within me, while I was outside! There I was searching for you—without any beauty in myself I poured myself out upon the beautiful things you made! You were with me, but I was not with you. Those things kept me far away from you, which if they did not exist in you, would not exist at all. You called me, you shouted to me, you shattered my deafness! You flashed and shone upon and drove away my blindness! You exuded perfume and I drew in breath and smell for you! I taste and have hunger and thirst. You touched me and I burned for your peace. (*Confessions* 10.27.38).

Augustine has said it himself: *Exarsi in pacem tuam*—he was "on fire for God's peace." Fire can be difficult to control.

An aspect of Augustine's passion was its obsessiveness. The enormous extent of his works conceals much circling around what is in the long run a narrow range of ideas. The intensity of his passion and vision sustained him by itself. One might expect that readers, having neither the vision nor the passion, might find in Augustine mere repetitiveness. And yet it is not quite so. For Augustine had an extraordinary power of both memory and assimilation. The ever-recurring themes have ever-new settings and ever-new treatments. Augustine was undoubtedly an artist, call him poet or musician as you will. Artists have an obsessive quality, a tendency to essay the same thing over and over again in, ultimately, so clearly the same way that we can recognize a piece of Bach —or Gershwin—a painting by Gainsborough—or Kandinsky —almost in an instant. And yet there is always some development, some difference. Augustine might be said to be another Vergil—or another Aeneas (Vergil's *alter ego*); but he had to find expression for his epic intuition in some way that was appropriately contemporary and his own. If his *Confessions* is his *Odyssey,* his *City of God* is his *Iliad*—and they were both necessarily theological and in prose. Van der Meer in his *Augustine the Bishop* (London and New York, 1961) has called him simply "the greatest poet of Christian Antiquity, without ever having written any poetry worth mentioning." It is a paradox that Augustine himself would particularly appreciate.

THE EXTRACTS

The extracts that follow are intended essentially to convey the scope and quality of Augustine's doctrine. Theoretically, the best way to achieve this double aim would be to choose the most comprehensive passage or passages in Augustine's works on any particular important topic and then add, frequently in snippets merely, additional or modifying matter from other works. This, however, would be to treat the doctrine as if it had little or no connection with Augustine's life—whereas, of course, it notoriously has. It would be to treat his teaching as static, whereas it is dynamic and even (as I have tried to suggest) poetical, visionary, salvationist. It is not dead matter to be carved up in sample pieces. Moreover, Augustine's life and experience, book or letter, sermon or prayer, are as interesting as and in influence perhaps even more significant than, the teaching itself, which in any case is so often a reflection of his experience.

For these reasons I believe that Augustine's works must be excerpted, so to speak, in whole Books. He is usually a slow and indeed for us rather tedious and frequently enigmatic writer. Dipping into him is not enough. While the structure of any particular work of his is clear, the relevance, drift and even meaning of any particular passage is often not so clear. One is amazed to discover on rereading a passage in Augustine after a lapse of time that one had not only failed to see the real meaning on first prolonged acquaintance, but even failed to notice its obscurity. Alas, the experience can be repeated later with the same passage! While there is some chance of being sure of his real meaning if one takes him in a large context, there is serious danger of either not understanding or of misunderstanding him if one consults him in isolated passages, however long.

Accordingly, I have opted for extracting not in passages, but as far as possible in Books. Among these Books are ones relating to the dominant experience of his life—his conversion—which, as I have tried to say, is important in later influence and in any case determines to some extent Augustine's own teaching. But these books (*Confessions* 7 and 8) also give fairly fully his ideas on Manichaeism and Neoplatonism and much else besides. Usually I have also tried to pick *structurally* important books, so that in reading them one can get a taste of the quality of the whole work. Thus for the *Trinity* I have chosen one book each to represent the exegetical approach to the mystery of the Trinity in the first part (Books 1–7) and the merely "rational" approach in the second (Books 8–15). (Incidentally, this allows me to give a sample of his biblical exegesis whether in book or homily.) Again, from the *City of God* I have chosen the last of the books dealing with Roman polytheism and civil life (Book 5) and the last book of all (Book 22) dealing with man's end as seen in Christian revelation. (Lack of space, its unfamiliar character and the danger of some duplication with *Confessions* 7 restrained me from giving Book 10, the last of those dealing with Greek polytheism and philosophy.) Here again, there has, incidentally, been included some treatment of important themes such as politics (there is much less of this in Augustine and the *City of God* than is commonly thought) and predestination.

To make guidance to the treatment of the topic fairly complete, however, I have added before each extract brief introductory notes, brief recent bibliography and brief references to the relevant important matter in other works of Augustine.

Finally, I give at the end of the *Reader* a Bibliographical Guide containing full references for names or works cited in my Introductions, as well as a short Index of the main topics covered so that one can quickly discover what Augustine has here to say on them and where to go for more.

Soliloquies
(A.D. 386–387)
Book 1

The *Soliloquies* (two books) were written at the same time as the *Dialogues* (*Contra Academicos, De beata vita* and *De ordine*), which were composed at Cassiciacum, in the country not very far from Milan. There Augustine and his mother, some friends and pupils were passing together the autumn and winter months between Augustine's conversion in 386 and baptism in 387. During the day he discussed the problems of the *Dialogues* mainly with his students. At night he spoke to God more intimately in the *Soliloquies*–which open with an elaborate and rather intellectual prayer. Nevertheless, the *Soliloquies* also treat of some of the ideas that occupied the mind of Augustine as he planned to devote himself to a life of philosophy within Christianity–a life that he saw being led by certain Christian-Platonist friends of his in Milan. The *Soliloquies* are ostensibly a dialogue (and so a sample of his use of dialogue) between Augustine and Reason, mainly on the relations of faith and reason, on which he had not yet fully developed his views. Here already, however, we find one of his most important statements on "illumination" (1. 12–15), which, with the connected theme of grace, is at the heart of Augustine's doctrine. Here (2.1.1) too we meet his anticipation of Descartes' maxim: "I think, therefore I am" (see *Bibliothèque Augustinienne*, Paris, 1959, vol. 35, pp. 486 f.). The influence of Neoplatonism, strong in the other dialogues of the time, is seen here in the explanation of evil, in the sharp separation of sensible and intellectual perception and in the necessity for purification before one can know or ascend to God in elevation of mind. The translation given here is by R. E. Cleveland (London, 1910) (with some minor adaptations).

SPECIAL TOPICS

1. *The Neoplatonism of Augustine at his conversion in* A.D. *386*

For a long time it was thought by some scholars—such as Harnack and Boissier—that Augustine was converted not to Catholicism but to a Neoplatonism with a tincture of Catholicism. The idea was based on an alleged conflict between the *Dialogues of Cassiciacum* (which were taken to be dominantly Neoplatonic, contemporary and historical) and the *Confessions,* which is dominantly Catholic, was written fourteen years after the conversion and is in part at least fictional. While there is some evidence that might be used for any or all of the propositions here implied, no serious scholar now supports the view referred to—especially since P. Courcelle's *Recherches sur les Confessions de s. Augustin* (Paris, 1950), which demonstrated that Ambrose and others in Milan synthesized Neoplatonism and Christianity. There was some illusion in this synthesis, as Augustine was to discover. But his conversion to Catholicism was sincere and primary, even though he entertained ideas—such as the need to reject the sensible and the independence of reason—that later he was to abandon. On the other hand, in accepting Christ both as Truth and Incarnate he was at variance with Neoplatonism. See J. O'Meara, *Against the Academics,* Ancient Christian Writers, vol. 12 (London, 1952), pp. 19–23; *The Young Augustine* (New York, 1965), pp. 131 ff.; "Augustine and Neo-platonism," *Recherches Augustiniennes,* vol. 1 (Paris, 1958), pp. 91–111.

2. *Reason and Faith*

At the time of writing the *Soliloquies,* Augustine had such confidence in Platonist reasoning that he held that a few men could achieve by reason alone the knowledge attainable directly by Revelation—though even they could, and should, profit from Revelation. This optimistic view reflected his impression of Neoplatonism and his belief that as reason and Revelation came from the same source—God—ultimately they could not conflict and profited from the same illumination. Revelation helped to raise questions that reason, otherwise, would never think of. Even at this early stage he proclaimed that belief led to understanding: *credo ut intellegam*. Moreover, he declared that if Neoplatonic reason were to conflict with Christ's authority, he would follow Christ (*Contra Academicos* 3.43). Indeed, the ultimate argument he uses against the skeptical Academics is that in Christ man possesses Truth. See J. O'Meara, "St. Augustine's View of Authority and Reason in A.D. 386," *The Irish Theological Quarterly*, Oct. 1951, pp. 338–46; Portalié, pp. 114–19. Other Augustine texts on faith: *De utilitate credendi*; *Epistulae* 120, 147; *Enchiridion*.

3. Illumination

The Augustinian doctrine of illumination is of a piece with his connected doctrine on grace—central and difficult. Augustine started from Plato's doctrine of the intelligible world, but did not separate the ideas from God. The question arises, therefore, how, if we cannot see God (on which he insists), we can perceive the ideas. Augustine asserts that we do. As to *how* we see them, he tells us (as here in the *Soliloquies*) that we see them in the divine light. Various efforts have been made to explain this metaphor—some involve pantheism; some seem to contradict some at least of his other, admittedly not transparent, statements; and still others fall short of what he seems to say. Portalié (pp. 112 f.) "explains" illumination as "a mysterious influence of God which does not consist in the objective manifestation of God to us, but in the effective production of a kind of image in our soul of those truths which determine our knowledge." See also Gilson, pp. 77–96. Other Augustine texts on illumination: *De Magistro* 40; *De Trinitate* 12.15.

SOLILOQUIES

BOOK I

1

1. For many days I had been debating within myself many and diverse things, seeking constantly, and with anxiety, to find out my real self, my best good, and the evil to be avoided, when suddenly one—I know not, but eagerly strive to know, whether it were myself or another, within me or without—said to me:

Reason. Now consider: suppose you had discovered something concerning that which you are so constantly and anxiously seeking to know; to what would you entrust it, in order that you might give your attention to things following?

Augustine. To memory, of course.

R. Is the memory an adequate custodian of all things which the mind discovers?

A. Hardly; in fact it cannot be.

R. Such things must, then, be written down. But how will you do this, when your health does not admit of the labor of writing them? They cannot be dictated, for they demand absolute solitude.

A. What you say is true, and so I do not see how I am to proceed without embarrassment.

R. Pray for health and help in accomplishing your desires, and write this prayer down also, that by these first fruits you may become more courageous. Then summarize briefly the conclusions at which you have arrived. Do not make any

effort to attract a crowd of readers; a few of your own towns-
men will suffice.

A. I will do as you advise.

2. O God, founder of the universe, help me, that, first of
all, I may pray aright: and next, that I may act as one worthy
to be heard by you: and, finally, set me free. God, through
whom all things are, which of themselves could have no
being; God, who does not permit that to perish, whose tendency it is to destroy itself! God, who has created out of nothing
this world, which the eyes of all perceive to be most beautiful! God, who does not cause evil, but does cause that it
shall not become the worst! God, who reveals to those few
fleeing for refuge to that which truly is, that evil is nothing!
God, through whom the universe, even with its perverse part,
is perfect! God, to whom dissonance is nothing, since in the
end the worst resolves into harmony with the better! God,
whom every creature capable of loving, loves, whether consciously or unconsciously!

God, in whom all things are, yet whom the shame of no
creature in the universe disgraces, nor his malice harms, nor
his error misleads! God, who does not permit any save the
pure to know the true! God, father of truth, father of wisdom,
father of the true and perfect life, father of blessedness,
father of the good and the beautiful, father of intelligible
light, father of our awakening and enlightening, father of
that pledge which warns us to return to you!

3. You do I invoke, God, truth, in whom and by whom
and through whom are all things true which are true: God,
wisdom, in whom and by whom and through whom are all
wise who are wise: God, true and perfect life, in whom and
by whom and through whom those live who do truly and
perfectly live: God, blessedness, in whom and by whom and
through whom are all blessed who are blessed: God, the good
and the beautiful, in whom and by whom and through whom
are all things good and beautiful, which are good and beautiful: God, intelligible light, in whom and by whom all shine
intelligibly, who do intelligibly shine: God, whose kingdom
is that whole realm unknown to sense: God, from whose
kingdom law for even these lower realms is derived: God,
from whom to turn is to fall; to whom to turn is to rise; in

whom to abide is to stand: God, from whom to go out is to waste away; to whom to return is to revive; in whom to dwell is to live: God, whom no one, unless deceived, loses: whom no one, unless admonished, seeks: whom no one, unless purified, finds: God, whom to abandon is to perish; whom to long for is to love; whom to see is to possess: God, to whom faith excites, hope uplifts, love joins: God, through whom we overcome the enemy, you do I supplicate!

God, whose gift it is that we do not utterly perish: God, by whom we are warned to watch: God, through whom we discriminate good things from evil things: God, through whom we flee from evil and follow after good: God, through whom we yield not to adversity: God, through whom we both serve well and rule well: God, through whom we discern that certain things we had deemed essential to ourselves are truly foreign to us, while those we had deemed foreign to us are essential: God, through whom we are not held fast by the baits and seductions of the wicked: God, through whom the decrease of our possessions does not diminish us: God, through whom our better part is not subject to our worse: God, through whom death is swallowed up in victory! God, who turns us about in the way: God, who strips us of that which is not, and clothes us with that which is: God, who makes us worthy of being heard: God, who defends us: God, who leads us into all truth: God, who speaks all good things to us: God, who does not deprive us of sanity nor permit another to do so: God, who recalls us to the path: God, who leads us to the door: God, who causes that it is open to those who knock: God, who gives us the bread of life: God, through whom we thirst for that water, which having drunk, we shall never thirst again: God, who convinces the world of sin, of righteousness, and of judgment: God, through whom the unbelief of others does not move us: God, through whom we reprobate the error of those who deem that souls have no deserving in your sight: God, through whom we are not in bondage to weak and beggarly elements: God, who purifies and prepares us for divine rewards, propitious, come to me!

4. In whatever I say come to my help, O you one God, one true eternal substance, where is no discord, no confusion, no change, no want, no death: where is all harmony, all illu-

mination, all steadfastness, all abundance, all life: where nothing is lacking and nothing redundant; where begetter and begotten are one: God, whom all things serve which do serve and whom every good soul obeys! God, by whose laws the poles rotate, the stars pursue their courses, the sun leads on the day, the moon tempers the night, and the whole order of the universe—through days by the alternations of light and darkness; through months by the waxing and waning of moons; through years by the successions of spring, summer, autumn and winter; through cycles by the completing of the sun's course; through vast eons of time by the return of the stars to their first risings—preserves by these unvarying repetitions of periods, so far as sensible matter may, the marvellous immutability of things; God, by whose laws forever standing, the unstable motion of mutable things is not allowed to fall into confusion and is, throughout the circling ages, recalled by curb and bit to the semblance of stability: by whose laws the will of the soul is free, and rewards to the good, and penalties to the wicked, are everywhere distributed by unchangeable necessity: God, by whom all good flows toward us, all evil is driven from us: God, above whom, outside whom, without whom, is nothing: God, beneath whom, in whom, with whom, is everything: who has made man after your own image and likeness, which he who knows himself discovers: hear, hear, hear me! My God, my master, my king, my father, my cause, my hope, my wealth, my honor, my home, my country, my salvation, my light, my life! Hear, hear, hear me, in that way of yours, known best to few!

5. At last I love you alone, you alone follow, you alone seek, you alone am I ready to serve: for you alone, by right, are ruler; under your rule do I wish to be. Command, I pray, and order what you will, but heal and open my ears that I may hear your commands, heal and open my eyes that I may see your nod; cast all unsoundness from me that I may recognize you! Tell me whither to direct my gaze that I may look upon you, and I hope that I shall do all things which you command!

Receive, I pray, master and most merciful father, me, your

fugitive! I have suffered already enough punishment, long enough been in bondage to your enemies whom you have under your feet, long enough been the sport of delusions.

Receive me, your household servant, fleeing from them, for even these received me, though alien to them, fleeing from you! I feel that I ought to return to you: let your door open to me knocking: teach me how to come to you! I have nothing other than the will: I know nothing other than that the fleeting and the falling should be spurned, the fixed and eternal sought after. This do I, father, for this is all I know: but how to make my way to you I know not. Do you suggest it, make it plain, equip me for the journey!

If they who take refuge in you find you by faith, give me faith! if by virtue, give me virtue! if by knowledge, give me knowledge! Increase my faith, increase my hope, increase my charity, O goodness of yours, unique and admirable!

6. After you am I groping, and by whatever things you may be felt after, even these do I seek from you! For if you desert a man, he perishes: but you desert him not, for you are the sum of good, and no man, seeking you aright, has failed to find you; and every one seeks you aright whom you cause to so seek you. Cause me, O father, to seek you; let me not stray from the path, and to me, seeking you, let nothing befall in place of yourself! If I desire nothing beside yourself, let me, I implore, find you now; but if there is in me the desire for something beside yourself, do you yourself purify me, and make me fit to look upon you!

For the rest, whatever concerns the welfare of this mortal body of mine, so long as I do not know how it may serve either myself or those I love, to you, father, wisest and best, do I commit it, and I pray that you will admonish me concerning it as shall be needful. But this I do implore your most excellent mercy, that you convert me in my inmost self to you, and, as I incline toward you, let nothing oppose; and command that so long as I endure and care for this same body, I may be pure and magnanimous and just and prudent, a perfect lover and learner of your wisdom, a fit inhabitant of a dwelling place in your most blessed kingdom!

Amen and Amen!

2

7. A. Behold, I have prayed to God.

R. What, then, do you desire to know?

A. Those things for which I have prayed.

R. Sum them up, briefly.

A. I desire to know God and the soul.

R. And nothing more?

A. Nothing whatever.

R. Begin then to seek. But first make clear to me how God may be so demonstrated to you that you can say: "It is enough."

A. I do not know how he can be so demonstrated to me that I can say, "It is enough"; for I believe that I know nothing in the way that I wish to know God.

R. What, then, are we to do? For do you not consider that it must first be known what it is to know God sufficiently, so that, when you have attained to that much knowledge, you need seek no further?

A. I do indeed think so, but by what plan it shall become possible to do this, I do not perceive. For what have I ever known which is like God so that I could say: "as I know this, so do I desire to know God!"

R. Having known nothing like God, from what source do you know that you have not yet known him?

A. Because, should I have known anything like God, I would, without doubt, love it; but, as it is, I love only God and the soul, and know neither the one nor the other.

R. Do you not, then, love your friends?

A. How, loving the soul, should I not love them?

R. Is it in this way, then, that you love gnats and bugs?

A. I said that I love, not animals, but the soul.

R. Either, then, your friends are not men or you love them not; for every man is an animal, and you say you do not love animals.

A. They are men and I love them, not in that they are animals, but in that they are men: that is, from the fact that they possess rational souls, which I love even in thieves. For it is permitted me to love reason in anything whatever, although I may justly hate him who makes a bad use of it. So much the more, then, do I love my friends, by as much as they make a good use of that rational soul, or as much, indeed, as they desire to do so.

3

8. R. I accept this, but yet if some one should say to you, I will cause you to know God as well as you know Alypius,[1] would you not thank him and say: "That is enough"?

A. I would indeed thank him, but I would not say: "That is enough."

R. And why, may I ask?

A. Because I do not know God even as I know Alypius, and I do not know Alypius well enough.

R. See to it, then, that you are not arrogant in desiring to know God well enough—you who do not even know Alypius well enough!

A. That does not follow. For, in comparison with the stars, what is more trifling a matter than my dinner? Yet, while I do not know what I shall have to-morrow for dinner, and am wholly ignorant of that, I do not deem it arrogant to affirm that I do know in what sign the moon will rise.

R. Will you, then, be satisfied to know God after the fashion in which you know in what sign the moon will rise to-morrow?

A. No, that is not enough, for it is by my senses that this is known. Also I know not whether God, or some occult natural cause, might not suddenly change the ordinary course of the moon, and if this should happen, all that I had taken for granted would become false.

R. And do you believe this could happen?

A. I do not. But I seek what I may know, not what I may believe. For it may, indeed, be truly said that we believe all that we know, but not that we know everything that we believe.

R. Do you, then, in your present undertaking, reject all testimony of the senses?

[1] His friend and fellow bishop.

A. I do altogether.

R. How about your intimate friend, whom you have said you know only partially; do you know him by sense or by intellect?

A. The knowledge which I have of him by sense—if indeed anything is truly known by sense—is worthless and is enough: that part by which he is truly my friend is the mind itself, and I wish to pursue that by the intellect.

R. And can he not otherwise be known?

A. In no other way.

R. Do you venture, then, to declare that your friend, and he, too, your most intimate friend, is unknown to you?

A. And why should I not venture? For I consider that a most just law of friendship which prescribes that one shall love his friend, not less, and not more, than himself. Therefore, since I do not know myself, what reproach can it be to me that I declare him to be unknown to me, especially since, as I believe, he does not really know himself?

R. If, then, those things which you desire to know are such as are pursued by the intellect, when I said that, since you did not even know Alypius, you were arrogant in desiring to know God, you should not have cited your dinner and the moon as illustrations, since these, as you have said, pertain to sense.

4

9. But how does that concern us? Now answer me: if those things which Plato and Plotinus[2] said concerning God are true, is it enough for you to know God as they knew him?

A. It does not necessarily follow that, even if those things which they said are true, they knew them to be so. For many persons discourse most fluently of things of which they are ignorant, as I, just now in prayer, have desired to know many things, which, although I have mentioned them, I would not desire to know if I already knew them. But am I, therefore, the less able to mention them? For I have given utterance, not to things which my intellect comprehends, but

2 Platonic philosopher (A.D. 205–270).

which, gathered here and there, and committed to the memory, I have reinforced by all the faith of which I am capable. But to know is another thing.

R. Tell me now, I beg: do you, at least, know what, in the science of geometry, a line is?

A. That I certainly do know.

R. And do you not, in this admission, stand in awe of the Academicians?[3]

A. Not at all. For it is the wise whom they forbid to err, and I am not wise. At this point, therefore, I do not fear to admit the knowledge of such things as I know. When, as I desire, I shall have attained to wisdom I will do as she shall exhort.

R. I do not object: but I was going to ask if you know the ball which is called a sphere in the same way as you know a line?

A. I do.

R. And do you know one as well as the other, or one more or less than the other?

A. I know both equally, for in nothing am I deceived in either.

R. And have you perceived these by the senses or by the intellect?

A. In this matter my experience with the senses has been as with a ship: for when they had carried me where I was going, and I had dismissed them, and was as if placed on dry land, and had begun to turn these matters over in thought, I was, for a long time, unsteady of foot. Therefore it seems to me that one could sooner swim on dry land than perceive geometrical truths by the senses, although in learning the rudiments they are of some use.

R. You do not, then, hesitate to call your acquaintance, such as it is, with these things knowledge?

A. No, if the Stoics, who ascribe knowledge only to the wise, permit. I certainly do not deny that I have such perception of these things as they concede even to the unwise. But I do not indeed very much fear the Stoics. I hold these things concerning which you have been asking in positive knowl-

---

[3] Philosophers who maintained that nothing can be known.

edge. Go on, then, that I may see your purpose in these questions.

R. Do not be in haste; we have time enough. Be very cautious what you accept, lest you concede something rashly. I am studying to make you happy in the certainty of things in which you will fear no downfall, while you, as if this were an easy matter, demand that I make haste.

A. May God cause it to be as you say! Question now as you will, and if I repeat this offense rebuke me more severely.

10. R. Very well. Is it clear to you that it is impossible to divide a line lengthways?

A. It is clear.

R. How about crossways?

A. That, of course, can be done to infinity.

R. And is it not equally evident that, of all the circles that, in a sphere, pass by a part more or less far from the center, there are not two which can be equal to one another?

A. It is.

R. And do the line and the sphere seem one and the same thing to you, or do they differ somewhat?

A. Who would not see that they differ greatly?

R. Since, then, you have an equal knowledge of each notwithstanding that, as you say, they differ greatly, it follows that although objects of knowledge differ, yet the knowledge by which one is known is identical with the knowledge by which the other is known.

A. Who has denied that?

R. You, yourself, a little time ago. For, when I asked you how you desired to know God, so that you might say: "It is enough"; you replied that you were unable to say, for the reason that among the things you know there is nothing like God. How, then! The line and the sphere,—are they alike?

A. Who could say that?

R. But I had not asked what you knew like God, but what you know in the same way as you desire to know God. For, though the line and the sphere are in no way similar, yet your knowing of the one is identical with your knowing of the other. Therefore tell me: would it be enough for you to know God, as you know the sphere of geometry, that is, to doubt nothing concerning God as you doubt nothing concerning it?

5

11. A. I answer you, that, however vehemently you urge and argue, I do not, nevertheless, dare to say that I desire to know God as I know these things. For not only do these things, that is, the sphere and God, differ, but the knowing of the one cannot be the same as the knowing of the other. In the first place, the line and the sphere do not differ so much that one science may not treat of each, while no geometry has professed to treat of God. And, in the second place, were my knowledge of these things of the same sort as is the knowledge which I desire to have of God, I should rejoice that I know them as much as I expect to rejoice in the cognition of God. But now I more than despise these things in comparison with him; and it seems to me, that, should I attain to the cognition of him, and see him in the way he can be seen, these things would perish from my memory altogether. Indeed, even now, it is an effort to recall these to mind, because of my absorbing desire for him.

R. Be it so, then, that the knowledge of God would rejoice you very much more than the knowledge of these inferior things: yet this fact does not result from the unlikeness of their apprehension. Or is it by one kind of seeing you gaze upon the earth and by another upon the tranquil sky, since the sight of the latter charms you so much more than that of the former? And, the eyes being trustworthy, if you were asked whether you were as sure that you had looked upon the earth as upon the sky, you would reply that you were, although not so delighting in the aspect of the earth as in the beauty and splendor of the sky.

A. This illustration, I confess, moves me, and I am constrained to agree, that, as much in kind as the earth differs from the heavens, so much do the demonstrations of the sciences, though certain and exact, differ from the intelligible majesty of God.

6

12. R. It is well that you are thus moved. For reason, who speaks to you, promises that God himself shall be even so demonstrated to your mind as is the sun to your eyes. For the eyes of the mind are the senses of the soul. Now the truths of science are made visible to the mind, as the light of the sun makes visible to the eyes the earth and terrestrial objects. But it is God himself who shines. And I, reason, am such to the mind as is sight to the eyes: for to have eyes that you may look is one thing, and to so look that you may see is another. And so it is that the task of the soul is threefold, that it possess eyes fit for use, that it look, that it see. Now the eyes of the soul are fit when she is pure from every fleshly taint, that is, when all desire of mortal things is purged and far away, which task faith alone is, at the outset, equal to. For this cannot be made manifest to a soul marred and diseased by lust, since unless sound she cannot see, nor will she apply herself to the labor of making herself sound if she does not believe, that, when so, she will be able to see. And, furthermore, though one may have this faith and believe that the matter is as has been stated, and that his ability to see can come about only in this way, yet if he despair of recovery, will he not give himself up, and despise and disobey the orders of his physician?

A. That is perfectly true, especially since one who is ill of necessity feels these orders to be severe.

R. Hope, then, must be added to faith.

A. I believe so.

R. And how if the soul have this faith, and also hope that she can be healed, and yet does not love nor desire the promised light, but is constrained from long habit, which has made them pleasant, to deem it her duty to abide content with her shadows, will she not none the less reject her physician?

A. She will forthwith.

R. Therefore a third, charity, is needed!

A. Nothing is so absolutely necessary.

R. Without, then, these three, no soul is sound enough to see, that is, to perceive her God?

13. When, then, you shall have sound eyes, what remains?

A. That the soul look.

R. The gaze of the soul is reason; but since it does not follow that every one who looks, sees, that right and perfect looking, which is followed by seeing, is called virtue, for virtue is rectified and perfected reason. But that very act of looking, even though the eyes be sound, cannot turn them toward the light unless three things persist: faith—by which the soul believes that, that toward which the gaze has been directed, is such that to gaze upon it will cause blessedness: hope—by which, the eyes being rightly fixed, the soul expects this vision to follow: and love—which is the soul's longing to see and to enjoy it. Such looking is followed by the vision of God himself, who is the goal of the soul's gaze, not because it could not continue to look, but because there is nothing beyond this on which it can fix its gaze. This is truly perfected reason—virtue—attaining its proper end, on which the happy life follows. And this intellectual vision is that which is in the soul a conjunction of the seer and the seen: as seeing with the eyes results from the conjunction of the sense of sight and the sensible object, either of which being lacking, nothing can be seen.

7

14. When now it has come about that the soul sees, that is, intellectually apprehends God, let us see whether these three things are still necessary to her. How shall faith be necessary when the soul has now sight? Or hope, since it has the thing hoped for? Charity alone is nothing diminished, but rather, indeed, very greatly augmented. For when the soul shall have seen this true and unique beauty she will love it the more, and unless with mighty love she fix upon it her gaze, nor turn it thence to anything whatever, she cannot abide in this most blessed vision. But even while the soul is in the body, although it may behold most fully, that is, may apprehend God, nevertheless since the senses of the body serve in their own proper office, though they may cause doubt,

they cannot cause delusion, and that which opposes them and believes rather that which is contrary to them to be true, may, so far, be called faith. Again, since God being apprehended, the soul may in this lower life attain blessedness, yet because she must still suffer much molestation by the flesh, she must hope that after death all these troubles will cease to exist. Neither, therefore, may hope desert the soul in this life; but when, after this life, the soul shall have found herself complete in God, love, by which she is held there, abides; for she cannot be said still to have faith that these things are true, since she is solicited by no intrusion of the false; nor that anything remains to be hoped for, since she now possesses all securely. Three things, then, concern the soul: that she be sound, that she look, that she see. Another three, faith, hope and charity, are all needful for health of soul, and reason's gaze; while for the vision itself, all, indeed while in the body; but, after this life, charity alone.

8

15. Be attentive now, while, so far as is at present necessary, I disclose to you by similitude of sensible objects some truth concerning even God himself. God, undoubtedly, is intelligible even as are these obvious intelligibilities of science; with, however, a wide difference. For the earth is visible and light is visible, but the earth cannot be seen unless made visible by light. So is it with those things treated of by the sciences, which he who apprehends concedes to be most true, and yet it is not credible that they can be apprehended, unless made manifest by some illumination, by some other sun, as it were their own. Thus, as of the sensible sun, we may predicate three things: namely, that it is, that it shines, that it makes objects visible; even so may we predicate three things of that most mysterious God whom you long to know: viz., that he is, that he is apprehended, that he causes other things to be apprehended. These two things, i.e. yourself and God, I dare to teach you. Now tell me how you receive these things: as probabilities or as truths?

A. As probabilities, obviously, and I am stimulated, I admit, to hope for something more. For, excepting those two statements concerning the line and the sphere, nothing has been said by you which I should venture so far as to declare absolute knowledge.

R. That is not to be wondered at, for, so far, nothing has been so demonstrated as to compel your perception.

9

16. But why do we loiter? The journey should be pursued. Now let us see whether we are in a sound condition, *for that is the first step.*

A. It is for you to find, if, either in myself or in yourself, anything can be detected. I will reply to your question so far as I am conscious of anything.

R. Do you love anything beside the knowledge of God and of yourself?

A. As I now feel, I can answer, "nothing:" but it is safer to say "I do not know." For it has frequently been my experience, when I did not believe it possible to be moved by anything else, yet, something coming into my mind would disturb me far beyond what I had believed possible. And again, although something passing through my mind as a mere suggestion would not much disturb me, yet the very fact of its coming did disturb me more than I had supposed: but it now seems to me that I can be disturbed by only three things, namely: the fear of losing those I love, the fear of pain, and the fear of death.

R. You love, then, life in the companionship of those dearest to you, your own good health, and your life itself in the flesh; for, were it not so, you would not fear their loss?

A. I confess it is so.

R. The sole fact, then, that your friends are not all with you, and that your health is not wholly sound, occasions you some distress of mind, for that, I see, must follow.

A. You see rightly; I cannot deny it.

R. How if you should suddenly feel and become certain that you were sound of body, and should see all those whom you love enjoying together with yourself ease and plenty; would you be almost transported with joy?

A. Almost, indeed. Nay! If this, of all other things, might, as you say, suddenly fall to my lot, how could I contain my-self, or how conceal my excess of joy?

R. You are, therefore, even now, agitated by all diseases and perturbations of the mind. What impudence is it, then, that such eyes should wish to look upon that sun!

A. You come to your conclusions as if I did not feel pre-cisely how far my health has improved, or what plague has retreated and what still holds its ground. Suppose I grant you this!

10

17. R. Are you not aware that the eyes of the body, even though sound, being frequently hurt and turned away by the light of this sensible sun, flee for refuge to shade? So you are thinking over your improvement, not of that which you desire to see! nor yet of this discussion, how you consider us to have advanced:—Do you not desire riches?

A. They are not, now, my first object. I am now three and thirty years of age, and I have ceased to desire riches for almost fourteen years, nor, if they happened to be offered to me, would I have any other interest in them, save such as a freeman requires for his maintenance and use. A single book of Cicero's[4] immediately and easily persuaded me that riches should not be craved, but if they fell to our lot should be wisely and carefully administered.

R. What about honors?

A. These, I confess, I have but recently ceased to wish for.

R. And how about a wife? Would not one beautiful, modest, docile and cultivated, or at least, one who could be easily taught by yourself, bringing, also,—since you despise opulence,—a marriage portion sufficient to prevent her being a tax upon your leisure, especially if you might confidently hope that no annoyance could come to you because of her, would not such a wife greatly delight you?

A. No matter how you portray her or load her with de-sirable things, I have decided that nothing is so much to be shunned as intercourse, for I feel that nothing so much casts

---

[4] *Hortensius;* cf. *Confessions* 3.4.7.

down the mind of man from its citadel as do the blandishments of women, and that physical contact without which a wife cannot be possessed. Therefore if it pertain to the office of a wise man (and I am not yet sure that it does) to give himself the care of a family, whoever sustains the marriage relation for the sake of this alone is, I may indeed concede, to be admired, but not, therefore, to be imitated; for the attempt has in it more of peril than the event can have of satisfaction. Enough, however, that for the sake of my freedom of mind, I have, and as I believe, rightly and usefully, decided neither to desire, nor seek, nor take a wife.

R. I do not now ask what you have resolved upon, but whether at the present time you have actually overcome desire itself, or whether you still struggle against it? For this concerns the soundness of your eyes.

A. I now neither seek nor desire anything whatever of this sort. It is with horror and loathing that I even remember it. What more can you ask? And this good increases in me every day. For, as much as the hope of seeing that superior beauty, for which I am so consumed by vehement desire, increases, so much does all desire and delight converge to that direction.

R. And now about the enjoyment of food: how much does that concern you?

A. As to those things which I have cut off from my diet, they do not disturb me; those still allowed I enjoy when before me, yet so that even they could be entirely withdrawn without causing me any annoyance. When they are not immediately present, the appetite for them does not dare to intrude itself, as an impediment to my thoughts. But ask me no more concerning food or drink or baths, or any other pleasure of the flesh. I desire to have them only in proportion to the benefit they can confer upon my health.

11

18. R. You have made great progress. Nevertheless some things remain which greatly hinder the seeing of that light. But I now attempt something which it seems to me easy to find out; for either nothing remains to be overcome, or, of all these things which we believe to have been eradicated, the

root infection still remains;—in which case we have made no
progress whatever. Now I ask you whether, if you were persuaded that not otherwise than by an ample competence
equal to the supply of all your mutual necessities, would it
be possible for you to pursue the study of wisdom in company
with your many very dear friends, would you not choose
and desire riches?

A. I admit that I would.

R. And how, if it should be shown that, your authority
being increased by public honors, you could persuade many
to be wise, and that your intimate friends themselves could
not curb their worldly desires and turn wholly to seeking
after God, unless they themselves should become persons of
consequence; and that this, except by your own importance
and dignity, could not be accomplished, would not these material things be greatly to be desired and urgently to be sought
after?

A. It is as you say.

R. Now concerning a wife: I will not argue, for perhaps
there can exist no such necessity that she should be taken. If,
however, by means of her ample patrimony, it were possible that all those whom you desire to have live with you
in one place, could be comfortably supported, herself also
cordially agreeing to this arrangement, and if, especially, by
reason of nobility of birth, she were of sufficient influence
to bring within easy reach of you those honors which you
have just now admitted to be necessary,—I do not know
whether it would be proper for you to despise these things.

A. How should I dare to hope for such things?

19. R. You speak as if I were asking what you hope for.
I am not now asking what, among things denied, would displease you: but what, being offered, would please you. A
dead plague is one thing, a sleeping one another. And here
this saying of certain learned men is pertinent: all fools are
mad, as all dunghills stink, yet one does not always realize
this fact, but only when they are stirred up.[5] It is of the
greatest importance to us whether carnal desire is stupefied
by despair of satisfaction, or expelled by health of mind.

[5] Cf. Cicero, *Tusc. Disp.* 4.24.54.

A. Although I cannot make any answer to this, yet you will never persuade me that, in the inclination of mind which I now feel to be mine, I am to believe I have made no progress.

R. I believe that this seems so to you because, although it is possible that you should wish for such things, it would, nevertheless, not be for their own sake, but for some other reason, that they would appear desirable to you.

A. This is what I have been wishing to say: for as to riches, when, formerly, I desired them, it was because I wished to be rich; and honors, the desire for which I have admitted did, until recently, dominate me, I was wont to wish for because of I know not what glamour about them which fascinated me. And when I sought a wife, I sought her for nothing else than for the sake of getting pleasure without loss of reputation. There was then in me a desire for these things in themselves, but I now absolutely spurn them all. Yet, if these things which I do long for can be reached only through those, I seek them, not that they may be fondly treasured but submissively tolerated.

R. Excellent! For I do not consider that those things which are asked for solely on account of something else can be said to be desired at all.

12

20. R. But now I ask you why you desire that those men whom you love should live with you, or should live at all?

A. In order that we may together inquire into God and our own souls. For thus, he who first found out something could, without labor, easily impart it to the others.

R. But how if they do not care to inquire into these things?

A. I will persuade them so that they will care to.

R. But suppose you are not able to do this, either because they have already themselves made these discoveries, or deem them to be things which cannot be discovered; or because they are preoccupied with the cares and desires of other things.

A. I will still keep hold of them and they of me, as if we were able.

R. But suppose their presence is really an impediment to you in your researches. Would not that embarrass you; and if they cannot be otherwise, would you not prefer to be alone rather than so situated?

A. I confess that I would.

R. You do not then crave either that they live or live with you, save for the purpose of finding wisdom?

A. Such is the case.

R. And how if your own life were proved to be an impediment to the attainment of wisdom—would you wish it to continue?

A. I would flee from it forthwith.

R. And suppose that you were shown that whether in or out of the body you could equally well attain to wisdom, would you care whether here or in another life you should enjoy that which you delight in?

A. If I might rest assured that nothing worse were in store for me hereafter, and no backward step from that to which I have already advanced, I would not care.

R. You fear then to die, lest you shall be involved in some worse evil by which the knowledge of God shall be taken away from you?

A. Such as I have conceived it, not only do I fear lest it shall be taken away from me, but also lest the entrance upon those things, at sight of which I stand marvelling, shall be closed to me; although what I now grasp will, I trust, remain with me.

R. You desire then that life shall remain to you, not on its own account but on account of wisdom?

A. So it is.

21. R. Fear of pain remains, which probably moves you by its own intrinsic power.

A. Even that I do not very greatly fear on any other account than because it hinders me in my researches. Not long since, although I was tormented with a very severe toothache, so that I was unable to do any continuous thinking, except on subjects with which I was already familiar, and was altogether prevented from undertaking any researches in which concentration of mind was necessary, yet, even then, it seemed to me that should that illumination disclose itself to my mind, I should either lose all consciousness of the pain, or would certainly support it as if it were nothing. Up to this time I have had no more serious pain to bear, but since frequently realizing how much more intolerable pain might fall to my lot, I am constrained to agree with Cornelius Celsus,[6] when he says that the greatest good is wisdom, and the greatest evil physical pain. Nor does the argument for this saying seem to me absurd. For, he says, since we are compounded of two parts, namely, of mind and body, the superior part is the mind and the inferior the body: and the greatest good is the best of the better part, and the greatest evil the worst of the worst part, and wisdom is the best thing in the soul and pain the worst in the body. Therefore he concludes, as I think not at all falsely, that the greatest good is to be wise, the greatest evil to suffer pain.

R. Later on we will see about that. For perhaps wisdom herself, toward whom we are urging our way, will persuade us otherwise. If, however, this is shown to be true, we will, doubtless, entertain the same opinion as to the greatest good and the greatest evil.

13

22. Now let us inquire what kind of a lover you are of that wisdom, whom, with most chaste regard and embrace and with no interposing veil, but as if nude, in a way she does not permit save to very few of her most favored suitors, you desire to grasp and to gaze upon. For surely were you consumed with desire for some most beautiful woman, it would be but just that she should not yield herself to you, if she had discovered that another beside herself were loved by you. Nor will this most chaste beauty of wisdom disclose herself to you, except you are consumed by desire for her alone.

A. Why then am I, unhappy I, so long kept waiting in suspense and excruciating agony? Surely I have proved that I love no other, for that which is not loved for itself is not

[6] Lived under the Emperor Tiberius (A.D. 14–37) and wrote an encyclopedia of which the medical part is extant.

loved at all. But wisdom I love for herself alone, and other
things—life, leisure, friends—which I wish to have in addition,
I fear to be without, on her account only. How boundless
must be the love I bear to that beauty, when not only do I
not envy other lovers, but even seek many more who may
with me long for her; with me gaze, marvelling, upon her;
with me lay hold upon, with me enjoy her; so much the more
shall they be my friends, as she shall be loved by us in
common!

23. R. It is altogether fitting that such should the lovers of
wisdom be. She, union with whom is pure and without con-
tamination, seeks such. But she is not won in one way alone.
It is according to his soundness and strength that each one
comes to know this unique and most veritable good. There
is an intellectual illumination of an ineffable and mysterious
sort. Ordinary light may, so far as it can, teach us something
concerning that higher light. There are eyes so vigorous and
sound as, though scarcely open, to turn full upon the sun
without shrinking. To such, light is, in a way, health itself,
nor do they need a physician, save only perhaps for advice.
To such it is enough to believe, to hope, to love. But there
are others whose eyes are hurt by that very effulgence
which they so vehemently long to look upon, and often turning from it go with delight back to their shadows. Such as
these may be truly said to be sound, but no attempt to show
them that which they are not able to look upon is without
danger. They need first to be exercised by a salutary encour-
agement of desire, and an equally wise postponement of its
satisfaction.

They should, first, be shown some things which are not
in themselves luminous, but can be seen only by reflected
light, such as a garment or a wall, or anything of that sort.
After that, something else, which, though not itself luminous, yet glows with more beauty by reflection than does the
former, as gold or silver or something similar; but not so
brightly as to hurt the eye. Next, they should look upon some
moderate terrestrial fire, then upon the stars, then the moon,
then the glow of dawn, and the growing splendor of sunrise.
And whoever accustoms himself to these things, whether in
unbroken order, or with some omissions, will come to look

upon the sun itself without shrinking and with great delight. The most excellent teachers use some such method as this with those eagerly desirous of wisdom, who already see, but whose sight is not acute. For it is the office of good discipline to attain wisdom by a certain order of approach, and without that order it is scarcely credible that the approach can be happy. But we have, I think, written enough for today. Health must be considered.

14

24. Another day having arrived:—

A. Give now if you can, I beg, I implore, this order. Proceed; do what you will, by any means, in any way. Command things however difficult, however arduous, and, nevertheless, if they are within my power, I shall certainly, through them, attain to that which I desire.

R. One thing alone can I teach you; nothing else do I know: the things of sense must be abandoned, and the greatest caution must be used, so long as we carry about this body, lest some adhesive impediment of sense should clog our wings, whose task, when whole and perfect, it is to bear us upward away from these shadows to that higher light, which it befits not to disclose itself to those shut up in this cave, unless they shall have been such, that, when they escape, their prison being either rent asunder or decayed away, they shall be able to mount up to their native atmospheres. And so, when you shall have become such, that nothing whatever of earth can charm you, in that very moment, in that very instant of time, believe me, you shall look upon that which you desire.

A. When, then, shall that be, I pray you? For I do not think it possible to arrive at that complete contempt of these inferior things, until I shall have first beheld that in comparison with which they become vile.

25. R. This is as if the eyes of the body should say: "When I shall have seen the sun, I will no longer love darkness." For, though it seems right that this should be the order by which to proceed, it is, in fact, a long way from it. For the eye loves darkness for the very reason that it is not sound, and yet, unless sound, it cannot gaze upon the sun. The mind is

often deceived in this, and boasting and thinking itself sound, as if it had occasion, it complains that it does not see. But that beauty knows when it should disclose itself; for she, herself, assumes the office of physician, and knows better who may be fit to look upon her than do they themselves who are made fit.

Thus we, having emerged so far, seem to ourselves to see; but how deep we have been sunk or to what point we have risen, we are not permitted to either feel or think; and so, because we have not a worse disease, we conclude that we have none. Do you not observe how, only yesterday, we announced, as if secure, that we were no longer hindered by any fleshly plague, and that we loved wisdom alone, and sought for and desired other things on her account only? How worthless, how foul, how execrable, how horrible, seemed to you a woman's embrace, as we were inquiring between ourselves concerning the desire for a wife! And yet, that very night, being wakeful, when we again discussed the same matter, how far other you felt than you would have supposed, when thrilled with these imagined blandishments and that amorous softness!—far less, indeed, than its wont, but yet, far otherwise than you had been asserting. May that most confidential physician of yours therefore demonstrate to you both what, by his care, you have escaped, and what yet remains to be cured!

26. A. Silence, I beseech you, silence! Why do you so torment me; why probe so deep? Now I weep beyond endurance! Henceforth I promise nothing, I presume nothing, lest you ask again concerning these things. You say truly that he whom I ardently desire to see will, himself, know when I am restored to health. Let him do what pleases him; let him disclose himself when it pleases him! I now commit myself wholly to his care and clemency. For I believe, for all time, he will not cease to uplift to himself those so inclined. I will pronounce nothing concerning my soundness until I shall have looked upon that beauty.

R. May you indeed do nothing other. But now restrain yourself from tears and gird up your mind. You have wept overmuch, and the pain in your chest is seriously affected by it.

A. Would you set a bound to my tears when I can see no bound to my misery? Or do you bid me consider the health of my body when my real self may be consumed with infection? Nay, I implore you, if you are of any avail for me, that you endeavor to lead me onward by some less tedious route, that, by some proximity of that light, which, if I have advanced somewhat, I am now able to bear, it will shame my eyes to return to those shadows I have left; if, indeed, those things can be said to be abandoned which can still venture to cajole my blindness.

15

27. R. Let us, if you please, conclude this first volume that we may set out upon a second by some propitious way; for this inclination of yours must not cease for want of suitable exercise.

A. I refuse absolutely to consent that this little book shall be concluded until you shall have opened to me some little glimmer concerning the nearness of that light on which I am intent.

R. Your divine healer consents to grant you this much: for I know not what effulgence touches me and invites me to lead you thither. Be, therefore, intently receptive.

A. Lead on; seize and hurry me whither you will.

R. Do you affirm truly that you will to know God and the soul?

A. Such is my whole concern.

R. And nothing more?

A. Absolutely nothing.

R. What! Do you not desire to comprehend truth?

A. As if I could truly have acquaintance with these except through that!

R. That, then, must first be known, in order that these may be.

A. I agree to that.

R. Let us, then, first see whether, since truth and true are two words, it appears to you that they stand for two things or only for one?

A. For two things, it seems to me. Thus, chastity is one

thing, the chaste another: and so of many others. I believe, therefore, truth is one thing, and that which is said to be true another thing.

R. And which of them do you consider the more excellent?

A. Truth, in my judgment: for as chastity is not the offspring of the chaste, but the chaste of chastity, so, if anything be true it is true by reason of truth.

28. R. When a chaste person dies do you consider that chastity dies also?

A. Not at all.

R. When, therefore, that which is true perishes, truth does not perish.

A. But how does anything true perish? I do not see.

R. I am surprised that you ask that question, for do we not see constantly a thousand things perish before our eyes? Or do you, perhaps, consider this tree to be a tree, but not a true tree? Or not capable of perishing? For, although you do not believe in the senses, and may reply that you are not sure whether the tree exists or not, you will, nevertheless, not, I think, deny that, if it be a tree, it is a true tree; for this judgment is a matter not of sense, but of intelligence; for if it be a false tree it is not a tree, but if it be a tree it is of necessity a true tree.

A. I concede this.

R. And how of this also; do you not concede a tree to be of that class of things which are born and die?

A. I cannot deny it.

R. It is, then, concluded that a true thing may perish?

A. I do not deny it.

R. And, further, does it not appear that, though true things die, truth does not die: just as, though the chaste person dies, chastity does not die?

A. I now concede this also, and eagerly await the outcome of your efforts.

R. Pay attention, then.

A. I am all attention.

29. R. Does this proposition:—*whatever is, is, of necessity, somewhere,* seem true to you?

A. Nothing so wins my consent.

R. And do you admit that truth is?

A. I do.

R. We must, then, of necessity inquire where she may be. She is not in some portion of space, unless you, perhaps, think that something else beside a body can occupy space, or that truth is a body.

A. I think neither of these things.

R. Where, then, do you believe her to be? For we have agreed that what is, cannot be nowhere.

A. If I knew where she were, I would not be likely to continue my researches.

R. Are you, then, at least, able to conceive where she may be?

A. If you suggest it, I may be able.

R. She certainly is not in mortal things. For whatever is cannot survive in anything, if the thing in which it is does not survive. Also, it was, a little time ago, conceded that truth remains, though true things pass away. Therefore truth is not in mortal things. But truth is, and is not nowhere. Therefore there are things immortal. But nothing is true in which truth is not, and it therefore follows that nothing is, unless it be immortal: and every false tree is not a tree, and false wood is not wood, and false silver is not silver, and anything whatever which is false, is not. But everything which is not true, is false: therefore nothing can be rightly said to be except the immortal.

Now review this line of reasoning carefully, lest it should appear that some of your concessions ought not to have been made. If, however, it is valid, we have accomplished almost our entire undertaking, as will perhaps be better seen in a following book.

A. I am grateful and give you thanks; and in the silence I will diligently and cautiously review these things with myself, and with you, provided no shadows reappear, causing me pleasure, as I so vehemently dread.

R. Have constant faith in God, and commit your whole self to his care so far as you can! Refuse to be or to will as of your own power, and openly confess yourself to be a servant of this most merciful and gracious God; for so he will not forbear to uplift you to himself, and will permit nothing save what is for your good to happen, even though you know it not!

A. I hear, I believe, and I obey, so far as I have the power, and—unless you require something else of me—with all my soul I pray that I may have more and more power!

R. And meanwhile, all is well. You will do hereafter whatever he himself, having been seen, will instruct you.

Letters
(A.D. 394–418)
Correspondence with St. Jerome

Of Augustine's correspondence, which extended to all parts and all kinds of people, over two hundred letters are extant. Some of them are really books in which weighty questions are treated of exhaustively: indeed, to some extent a letter on a serious topic was a form of publication, and an author usually was aware that his letters might—in some cases probably would—have wide circulation. The *Letters* of Augustine, therefore, are, not surprisingly, seldom intimate or very informal. The most famous part of Augustine's correspondence was that with St. Jerome, the greatest part of which is given here. It started in 394, when Augustine was still a priest, and continued almost to Jerome's death in 419 or so. The letters exchanged between these two reveal much of their characters. They start badly and get worse. But in the end there is a sincere profession of mutual affection and admiration. The translation given here is by J. G. Cunningham, *Letters of St. Augustine*, 2 vols. (Edinburgh, 1872–75).

RECOMMENDED READING

F. van der Meer, *Augustine the Bishop*, London and New York, 1961, pp. 247–55.

M. E. Keenan, *The Life and Times of St. Augustine as Revealed in His Letters*, Washington, D.C., 1935.

W. J. Sparrow-Simpson, *The Letters of St. Augustine*, London, 1919.

W. H. Semple, "Some Letters of St. Augustine," *Bulletin of the John Rylands Library*, 33 (1950), pp. 111–30.

LETTERS

LETTER 28

(A.D. 394 OR 395)

TO JEROME, HIS MOST BELOVED LORD, AND BROTHER AND
FELLOW-PRIEST, WORTHY OF BEING HONOURED AND
EMBRACED WITH THE SINCEREST AFFECTIONATE DEVOTION,
AUGUSTINE SENDS GREETING.

CHAP. 1. 1. Never was the face of any one more familiar to
another, than the peaceful, happy, and truly noble diligence
of your studies in the Lord has become to me. For although
I long greatly to be acquainted with you, I feel that already
my knowledge of you is deficient in respect of nothing but a
very small part of you,—namely, your personal appearance;
and even as to this, I cannot deny that since my most blessed
brother Alypius (now invested with the office of bishop, of
which he was then truly worthy) has seen you, and has on his
return been seen by me, it has been almost completely im-
printed on my mind by his report of you; indeed, I may say
that before his return, when he saw you there, I was seeing
you myself with his eyes. For any one who knows us may say
of him and me, that in body only, and not in mind, we are
two, so great is the union of heart, so firm the intimate friendship subsisting between us; though in merit we are not alike,
for his is far above mine. Seeing, therefore, that you love me,
both of old through the communion of spirit by which we are
knit to each other, and more recently through what you know
of me from the mouth of my friend, I feel that it is not presumptuous in me (as it would be in one wholly unknown to

you) to recommend to your brotherly esteem the brother Profuturus, in whom we trust that the happy omen of his name (Good-speed) may be fulfilled through our efforts furthered after this by your aid; although, perhaps, it may be presumptuous on this ground, that he is so great a man, that it would be much more fitting that I should be commended to you by him, than he by me. I ought perhaps to write no more, if I were willing to content myself with the style of a formal letter of introduction; but my mind overflows into conference with you, concerning the studies with which we are occupied in Christ Jesus our Lord, who is pleased to furnish us largely through your love with many benefits, and some helps by the way, in the path which he has pointed out to his followers.

CHAP. 2. 2. We therefore, and with us all that are devoted to study in the African churches, beseech you not to refuse to devote care and labour to the translation of the books of those who have written in the Greek language most able commentaries on our Scriptures. You may thus put us also in possession of these men, and especially of that one whose name you seem to have singular pleasure in sounding forth in your writings.[1] But I beseech you not to devote your labour to the work of translating into Latin the sacred canonical books, unless you follow the method in which you have translated Job, viz. with the addition of notes, to let it be seen plainly what differences there are between this version of yours and that of the Septuagint,[2] whose authority is worthy of highest esteem. For my own part, I cannot sufficiently express my wonder that anything should at this date be found in the Hebrew manuscripts which escaped so many translators perfectly acquainted with the language. I say nothing of the Septuagint, regarding whose harmony in mind and spirit, surpassing that which is found in even one man, I dare not in any way pronounce a decided opinion, except that in my judgment, beyond question, very high authority must in this work of translation be conceded to them. I am more per-

[1] Origen.
[2] The revered translation of the Old Testament into Greek completed by "seventy" men in "seventy" days at the bidding of Ptolemy Philadelphus (287–247 B.C.).

plexed by those translators who, though enjoying the advantage of labouring after the Septuagint had completed their
work, and although well acquainted, as it is reported, with
the force of Hebrew words and phrases, and with Hebrew
syntax, have not only failed to agree among themselves, but
have left many things which, even after so long a time, still
remain to be discovered and brought to light. Now these
things were either obscure or plain: if they were obscure, it is
believed that you are as likely to have been mistaken as the
others; if they were plain, it is not believed that they (the
Septuagint) could possibly have been mistaken. Having stated
the grounds of my perplexity, I appeal to your kindness to
give me an answer regarding this matter.

CHAP. 3. 3. I have been reading also some writings, ascribed
to you, on the Epistles of the apostle Paul. In reading your
exposition of the Epistle to the Galatians, that passage came
to my hand in which the apostle Peter is called back from a
course of dangerous dissimulation. To find there the defence
of falsehood undertaken, whether by you, a man of such
weight, or by any author (if it is the writing of another),
causes me, I must confess, great sorrow, until at least those
things which decide my opinion in the matter are refuted, if
indeed they admit of refutation. For it seems to me that most
disastrous consequences must follow upon our believing that
anything false is found in the sacred books: that is to say, that
the men by whom the scripture has been given to us, and
committed to writing, did put down in these books anything
false. It is one question whether it may be at any time the
duty of a good man to deceive; but it is another question
whether it can have been the duty of a writer of Holy Scripture to deceive: indeed, it is not another question—it is no
question at all. For if you once admit into such a high sanctu-
ary of authority one false statement as made in the way of
duty, there will not be left a single sentence of those books
which, if appearing to any one difficult in practice or hard to
believe, may not by the same fatal rule be explained away, as
a statement in which, intentionally, and under a sense of
duty, the author declared what was not true.

4. For if the apostle Paul did not speak the truth when,
finding fault with the apostle Peter, he said: "If you, being

a Jew, live after the manner of Gentiles, and not as do the Jews, why do you compel the Gentiles to live as do the Jews?" —if, indeed, Peter seemed to him to be doing what was right, and if, notwithstanding, he, in order to soothe troublesome opponents, both said and wrote that Peter did what was wrong;[3]—if we say thus, what then shall be our answer when perverse men such as he himself prophetically described arise, forbidding marriage,[4] if they defend themselves by saying that, in all which the same apostle wrote in confirmation of the lawfulness of marriage,[5] he was, on account of men who, through love for their wives, might become troublesome opponents, declaring what was false,—saying these things, not because he believed them, but because their opposition might thus be averted? It is unnecessary to quote many parallel examples. For even things which pertain to the praises of God might be represented as piously intended falsehoods, written in order that love for him might be enkindled in men who were slow of heart; and thus nowhere in the sacred books shall the authority of pure truth stand sure. Do we not observe the great care with which the same apostle commends the truth to us, when he says: "And if Christ be not risen, then is our preaching vain, and your faith is also vain: and we are found false witnesses of God; because we have testified of God that he raised up Christ; whom he raised not up, if it be that the dead rise not."[6] If any one said to him, "Why are you so shocked by this falsehood, when the thing which you have said, even if it were false, tends very greatly to the glory of God?" would he not, abhorring the madness of such a man, with every word and sign which could express his feelings, open clearly the secret depths of his own heart, protesting that to speak well of a falsehood uttered on behalf of God, was a crime not less, perhaps even greater, than to speak ill of the truth concerning him? We must therefore be careful to secure, in relation to our knowledge of the divine Scriptures, the guidance only of such a man as is imbued with a high reverence for the sacred books, and a profound

---

[3] Gal. 2: 11–14.
[4] 1 Tim. 4: 3.
[5] 1 Cor. 7: 10–16.
[6] 1 Cor. 15: 14 f.

persuasion of their truth, preventing him from flattering himself in any part of them with the hypothesis of a statement being made not because it was true, but because it was expedient, and making him rather pass by what he does not understand, than set up his own feelings above that truth. For, truly, when he pronounces anything to be untrue, he demands that he be believed in preference, and endeavours to shake our confidence in the authority of the divine Scriptures.

5. For my part, I would devote all the strength which the Lord grants me, to show that every one of those texts which are quoted in defence of the expediency of falsehood ought to be otherwise understood, in order that everywhere the sure truth of these passages themselves may be consistently maintained. For as statements adduced in evidence must not be false, neither ought they to favour falsehood. This, however, I leave to your own judgment. For if you apply more thorough attention to the passage, perhaps you will see it much more readily than I have done. To this more careful study that piety will move you, by which you discern that the authority of the divine Scriptures becomes unsettled (so that every one may believe what he wishes, and reject what he does not wish) if this be once admitted, that the men by whom these things have been delivered unto us, could in their writings state some things which were not true, from considerations of duty; unless, maybe, you purpose to furnish us with certain rules by which we may know when a falsehood might or might not become a duty. If this can be done, I beg you to set forth these rules with reasonings which may be neither equivocal nor precarious; and I beseech you by our Lord, in whom truth was incarnate, not to consider me burdensome or presumptuous in making this request. For a mistake of mine which is in the interest of truth cannot deserve great blame, if indeed it deserves blame at all, when it is possible for you to use truth in the interest of falsehood without doing wrong.

CHAP. 4. 6. Of many other things I would wish to discourse with your most ingenuous heart, and to take counsel with you concerning Christian studies; but this desire could not be satisfied within the limits of any letter. I may do this more fully by means of the brother bearing this letter, whom I rejoice in sending to share and profit by your sweet and useful conversation. Nevertheless, although I do not reckon myself superior in any respect to him, even he may take less from you than I would desire; and he will excuse my saying so, for I confess myself to have more room for receiving from you than he has. I see his mind to be already more fully stored, in which unquestionably he excels me. Therefore, when he returns, as I trust he may happily do by God's blessing, and when I become a sharer in all with which his heart has been richly furnished by you, there will still be a consciousness of void unsatisfied in me, and a longing for personal fellowship with you. Hence of the two I shall be the poorer, and he the richer, then as now. This brother carries with him some of my writings, which if you condescend to read, I implore you to review them with candid and brotherly strictness. For the words of scripture, "The righteous shall correct me in compassion, and reprove me; but the oil of the sinner shall not anoint my head,"[7] I understand to mean that he is the truer friend who by his censure heals me, than the one who by flattery anoints my head. I find the greatest difficulty in exercising a right judgment when I read over what I have written, being either too cautious or too rash. For I sometimes see my own faults, but I prefer to hear them reproved by those who are better able to judge than I am; lest after I have, perhaps justly, charged myself with error, I begin again to flatter myself, and think that my censure has arisen from an undue mistrust of my own judgment.[8]

[7] Ps. 141: 5.
[8] Even in 403 (see Letter 71, further on) Augustine wondered if Jerome had received this letter. Jerome lets him know all in Letter 72 (A.D. 404).

LETTER 39

(A.D. 397)

TO MY LORD AUGUSTINE, A FATHER TRULY HOLY AND MOST
BLESSED, JEROME SENDS GREETING IN CHRIST.

CHAP. 1. 1. Last year I sent by the hand of our brother, the
sub-deacon Asterius, a letter conveying to your Excellency a
salutation due to you, and readily rendered by me; and I think
that my letter was delivered to you. I now write again, by
my holy brother the deacon Præsidius, begging you in the
first place not to forget me, and in the second place to receive
the bearer of this letter, whom I commend to you with the
request that you recognise him as one very near and dear to
me, and that you encourage and help him in whatever way
his circumstances may demand; not that he is in need of anything (for Christ has amply endowed him), but that he is most
eagerly desiring the friendship of good men, and thinks that
in securing this he obtains the most valuable blessing. His design in travelling to the west you may learn from his own lips.

CHAP. 2. 2. As for us, established here in our monastery,
we feel the shock of waves on every side, and are burdened
with the cares of our lot as pilgrims. But we believe in him
who hath said, "Be of good cheer, I have overcome the
world,"[1] and are confident that by his grace and guidance we
shall prevail against our adversary the devil.

I beseech you to give my respectful salutation to the holy
and venerable brother, our father Alypius. The brethren who,
with me, devote themselves to serve the Lord in this
monastery, salute you warmly. May Christ our Almighty God
guard you from harm, and keep you mindful of me, my lord
and father truly holy and venerable.

[1] John 16: 33.

LETTER 40

(A.D. 397)

TO MY LORD MUCH BELOVED, AND BROTHER WORTHY OF BEING
HONOURED AND EMBRACED WITH THE MOST SINCERE DEVO-
TION OF CHARITY, MY FELLOW-PRIEST JEROME, AUGUS-
TINE SENDS GREETING.

CHAP. 1. 1. I thank you that, instead of a mere formal salutation, you wrote me a letter, though it was much shorter than
I would desire to have from you; since nothing that comes
from you is tedious, however much time it may demand.
Therefore, although I am beset with great anxieties about the
affairs of others, and that, too, in regard to secular matters, I
would find it difficult to pardon the brevity of your letter,
were it not that I consider that it was written in reply to a yet
shorter letter of my own. Address yourself, therefore, I entreat you, to that exchange of letters by which we may have
fellowship, and may not permit the distance which separates
us to keep us wholly apart from each other; though we are in
the Lord bound together by the unity of the Spirit, even
when our pens rest and we are silent. The books in which
you have laboured to bring treasures from the Lord's store-
house give me almost a complete knowledge of you. For if I
may not say, "I know you," because I have not seen your
face, it may with equal truth be said that you do not know
yourself, for you cannot see your own face. If, however, it
is this alone which constitutes your acquaintance with yourself, that you know your own mind, we also have no small
knowledge of it through your writings, in studying which we
bless God that to yourself, to us, to all who read your
works, he has given you as you are.

CHAP. 2. 2. It is not long since, among other things, a certain book of yours came into my hands, the name of which
I do not yet know, for the manuscript itself had not the title

written, as is customary, on the first page. The brother with whom it was found said that its title is *Epitaphium,*—a name which we might believe you to have approved, if we found in the work a notice of the lives or writings of those only who are deceased. Since, however, mention is there made of the works of some who were, at the time when it was written, or are even now, alive, we wonder why you either gave this title to it, or permitted others to believe that you had done so. The book itself has our complete approval as a useful work.

CHAP. 3. 3. In your exposition of the Epistle of Paul to the Galatians I have found one thing which causes me much concern. For if it be the case that statements untrue in themselves, but made, as it were, out of a sense of duty in the interest of religion, have been admitted into the Holy Scriptures, what authority will be left to them? If this be conceded, what sentence can be produced from these Scriptures, by the weight of which the wicked obstinacy of error can be broken down? For as soon as you have produced it, if it be disliked by him who contends with you, he will reply that, in the passage alleged, the writer was uttering a falsehood under the pressure of some honourable sense of duty. And where will any one find this way of escape impossible, if it be possible for men to say and believe that, after introducing his narrative with these words, "The things which I write unto you, behold, before God, I lie not,"[1] the apostle lied when he said of Peter and Barnabas, "I saw that they walked not uprightly, according to the truth of the gospel"?[2] For if they did walk uprightly, Paul wrote what was false; and if he wrote what was false *here,* when did he say what was true? Shall he be supposed to say what is true when his teaching corresponds with the predilection of his reader, and shall everything which runs counter to the impressions of the reader be reckoned a falsehood uttered by him under a sense of duty? It will be impossible to prevent men from finding reasons for thinking that he not only might have uttered a falsehood, but was bound to do so, if we admit this canon of interpretation. There is no need for many words in pursuing this argument, especially in

[1] Gal. 1: 20.
[2] Gal. 2: 14.

writing to you, for whose wisdom and prudence enough has already been said. I would by no means be so arrogant as to attempt to enrich by my small coppers your mind, which by the divine gift is golden; and none is more able than yourself to revise and correct that work to which I have referred.

CHAP. 4. 4. You do not require me to teach you in what sense the apostle says, "To the Jews I became as a Jew, that I might gain the Jews,"[3] and other such things in the same passage, which are to be ascribed to the compassion of pitying love, not the artifices of intentional deceit. For he that ministers to the sick becomes as if he were sick himself; not, indeed, falsely pretending to be under the fever, but considering, with the mind of one truly sympathizing, what he would wish done for himself if he were in the sick man's place. Paul was indeed a Jew; and when he had become a Christian, he had not abandoned those Jewish sacraments which that people had received in the right way, and for a certain appointed time. Therefore, even although he was an apostle of Christ, he took part in observing these; but with this view, that he might show that they were in no wise hurtful to those who, even after they had believed in Christ, desired to retain the ceremonies which by the law they had learned from their fathers; provided only that they did not build on these their hope of salvation, since the salvation which was foreshadowed in these has now been brought in by the Lord Jesus. For the same reason, he judged that these ceremonies should by no means be made binding on the Gentile converts, because, by imposing a heavy and superfluous burden, they might turn aside from the faith those who were unaccustomed to them.

5. The thing, therefore, which he rebuked in Peter was not his observing the customs handed down from his fathers —which Peter, if he wished, might do without being chargeable with deceit or inconsistency, for, though now superfluous, these customs were not hurtful to one who had been accustomed to them—but his compelling the Gentiles to observe Jewish ceremonies,[4] which he could not do otherwise than by so acting in regard to them as if their observance

[3] 1 Cor. 9: 20.
[4] Gal. 2: 14.

was, even after the Lord's coming, still necessary to salvation, against which truth protested through the apostolic office of Paul. Nor was the apostle Peter ignorant of this, but he did it through fear of those who were of the circumcision. Manifestly, therefore, Peter was truly corrected, and Paul has given a true narrative of the event, unless, by the admission of a falsehood here, the authority of the Holy Scriptures given for the faith of all coming generations is to be made wholly uncertain and wavering. For it is neither possible nor suitable to state within the compass of a letter how great and how unutterably evil must be the consequences of such a concession. It might, however, be shown seasonably, and with less hazard, if we were conversing together.

6. Paul had forsaken everything peculiar to the Jews that was evil, especially this: "That, being ignorant of God's righteousness, and going about to establish their own righteousness, they had not submitted themselves unto the righteousness of God."[5] In this, moreover, he differed from them: that after the passion and resurrection of Christ, in whom had been given and made manifest the mystery of grace, according to the order of Melchizedek, they still considered it binding on them to celebrate, not out of mere reverence for old customs, but as necessary to salvation, the sacraments of the old economy, which were indeed at one time necessary, otherwise it had been unprofitable and vain for the Maccabees to suffer martyrdom, as they did, for their adherence to them.[6] Lastly, in this also Paul differed from the Jews: that they persecuted the Christian preachers of grace as enemies of the law. These and all similar errors and sins he declares that he "counted but loss and dung that he might win Christ;"[7] but he does not, in so saying, disparage the ceremonies of the Jewish law, if only they were observed after the custom of their fathers, in the way in which he himself observed them, without regarding them as necessary to salvation, and not in the way in which the Jews affirmed that they must be observed, nor in the exercise of deceptive dissimulation such as he had rebuked in Peter. For if Paul observed

5 Rom. 10: 3.
6 2 Macc. 7: 1.
7 Phil. 3: 8.

these sacraments in order, by pretending to be a Jew, to gain the Jews, why did he not also take part with the Gentiles in heathen sacrifices, when to them that were without law he became as without law, that he might gain them also? The explanation is found in this, that he took part in the Jewish sacrifices, as being himself by birth a Jew; and that when he said all this which I have quoted, he meant, not that he pretended to be what he was not, but that he felt with true compassion that he must bring such help to them as would be needful for himself if he were involved in their error. Herein he exercised not the subtlety of a deceiver, but the sympathy of a compassionate deliverer. In the same passage the apostle has stated the principle more generally: "To the weak I became weak, that I might gain the weak; I am made all things to all men, that I might by all means save some,"[8]—the latter clause of which guides us to understand the former as meaning that he showed himself one who pitied the weakness of another as much as if it had been his own. For when he said, "Who is weak, and I am not weak?"[9] he did not wish it to be supposed that he pretended to suffer the infirmity of another, but rather that he showed it by sympathy.

7. Wherefore I beseech you, apply to the correction and emendation of that book a frank and truly Christian severity, and chant what the Greeks call a "palinode."[10] For incomparably more lovely than the Grecian Helen is Christian truth. In her defence, our martyrs have fought against Sodom with more courage than the heroes of Greece displayed against Troy for Helen's sake. I do not say this in order that you may recover the faculty of spiritual sight,—far be it from me to say that you have lost it!—but that, having eyes both clear and quick in discernment, you may turn them towards that from which, in unaccountable dissimulation, you have turned them away, refusing to see the calamitous consequences which would follow on our once admitting that a writer of the divine

[8] 1 Cor. 9: 22.
[9] 2 Cor. 11: 29.
[10] Stesichorus (first half of the sixth century B.C.), having lost his sight as a judgment for writing an attack on Helen, was miraculously healed when he wrote a poem in retractation.

books could in any part of his work honourably and piously
utter a falsehood.

CHAP. 5. 8. I had written some time ago a letter to you
on this subject,[11] which was not delivered to you, because the
bearer to whom it was entrusted did not finish his journey to
you. From it I may quote a thought which occurred to me
while I was dictating it, and which I ought not to omit in this
letter, in order that, if your opinion is still different from mine,
and is better, you may readily forgive the anxiety which has
moved me to write. It is this: If your opinion is different, and
is according to truth (for only in that case can it be better
than mine), you will grant that "a mistake of mine, which
is in the interest of truth, cannot deserve great blame, if indeed
it deserves blame at all, when it is possible for you to use truth
in the interest of falsehood without doing wrong."

9. As to the reply which you were pleased to give me concerning Origen, I did not need to be told that we should, not
only in ecclesiastical writers, but in all others, approve and
commend what we find right and true, but reject and condemn
what we find false and mischievous. What I craved from your
wisdom and learning (and I still crave it), was that you should
acquaint us definitely with the points in which that remarkable
man is proved to have departed from the belief of the truth.
Moreover, in that book in which you have mentioned all the
ecclesiastical writers whom you could remember, and their
works, it would, I think, be a more convenient arrangement
if, after naming those whom you know to be heretics (since
you have chosen not to pass them without notice), you would
add in what respect their doctrine is to be avoided. Some of
these heretics also you have omitted, and I would like to know
on what grounds. If, however, it has been from a desire not
to enlarge that volume unduly that you refrained from adding
to a notice of heretics, the statement of the things in which
the Catholic Church has authoritatively condemned them, I
beg you not to grudge bestowing on this subject, to which with
humility and brotherly love I direct your attention, a portion
of that literary labour by which already, by the grace of the
Lord our God, you have in no small measure stimulated and

11 Letter 28, given here.

assisted the saints in the study of the Latin tongue, and publish in one small book (if your other occupations permit you) a digest of the perverse dogmas of all the heretics who up to this time have, through arrogance, or ignorance, or self-will, attempted to subvert the simplicity of the Christian faith; a work most necessary for the information of those who are prevented, either by lack of leisure or by their not knowing the Greek language, from reading and understanding so many things. I would urge my request at greater length, were it not that this is commonly a sign of misgivings as to the benevolence of the party from whom a favour is sought. Meanwhile I cordially recommend to your goodwill in Christ our brother Paulus, to whose high standing in these regions I bear before God willing testimony.

LETTER 67

(A.D. 402)

TO MY LORD MOST BELOVED AND LONGED FOR, MY HONOURED BROTHER IN CHRIST, AND FELLOW-PRIEST, JEROME, AUGUSTINE SENDS GREETING IN THE LORD.

CHAP. 1. 1. I have heard that my letter has come to your hand. I have not yet received a reply, but I do not on this account question your affection; doubtless something has hitherto prevented you. Therefore I know and avow that my prayer should be, that God would put it in your power to forward your reply, for he has already given you power to prepare it, seeing that you can do so with the utmost ease if you feel disposed.

CHAP. 2. 2. I have hesitated whether to give credence or not to a certain report which has reached me; but I felt that I ought not to hesitate as to writing a few lines to you regarding the matter. To be brief, I have heard that some brethren have told your Charity that I have written a book against you and have sent it to Rome. Be assured that this is false: I call

God to witness that I have not done this. But if perhaps there be some things in some of my writings in which I am found to have been of a different opinion from you, I think you ought to know, or if it cannot be certainly known, at least to believe, that such things have been written not with a view of contradicting you, but only of stating my own views. In saying this, however, let me assure you that not only am I most ready to hear in a brotherly spirit the objections which you may entertain to anything in my writings which has displeased you, but I entreat, indeed implore you, to acquaint me with them; and thus I shall be made glad either by the correction of my mistake, or at least by the expression of your goodwill.

3. Oh that it were in my power, by our living near each other, if not under the same roof, to enjoy frequent and sweet conference with you in the Lord! Since, however, this is not granted, I beg you to take pains that this one way in which we can be together in the Lord be kept up; indeed, more improved and perfected. Do not refuse to write me in return, however seldom.

Greet with my respects our holy brother Paulinianus, and all the brethren who with you, and because of you, rejoice in the Lord. May you, remembering us, be heard by the Lord in regard to all your holy desires, my lord most beloved and longed for, my honoured brother in Christ.

LETTER 68

(A.D. 402)

TO AUGUSTINE, MY LORD, TRULY HOLY AND MOST BLESSED FATHER, JEROME SENDS GREETING IN CHRIST.

1. WHEN my kinsman, our holy son Asterius, subdeacon, was just on the point of beginning his journey, the letter of your grace arrived, in which you clear yourself of the charge of having sent to Rome a book written against your humble servant. I had not heard that charge; but by our brother Sysin-

nius, deacon, copies of a letter addressed by some one apparently to me have come hither. In the said letter I am exhorted to sing the palinode, confessing mistake in regard to a paragraph of the apostle's writing, and to imitate Stesichorus, who, vacillating between disparagement and praises of Helen, recovered, by praising her, the eyesight which he had forfeited by speaking against her. Although the style and the method of argument appeared to be yours, I must frankly confess to your excellency that I did not think it right to assume without examination the authenticity of a letter of which I had only seen copies, lest perhaps, if offended by my reply, you should with justice complain that it was my duty first to have made sure that you were the author, and only after that was ascertained, to address you in reply. Another reason for my delay was the protracted illness of the pious and venerable Paula. For, while occupied long in attending upon her in severe illness, I had almost forgotten your letter, or more correctly, the letter written in your name, remembering the verse, "Like music in the day of mourning is an unseasonable discourse."[1] Therefore, if it is your letter, write me frankly that it is so, or send me a more accurate copy, in order that without any passionate rancour we may devote ourselves to discuss scriptural truth; and I may either correct my own mistake, or show that another has without good reason found fault with me.

2. Far be it from me to presume to attack anything which your grace has written. For it is enough for me to prove my own views without controverting what others hold. But it is well known to one of your wisdom, that every one is satisfied with his own opinion, and that it is puerile self-sufficiency to seek, as young men have of old been accustomed to do, to gain glory to one's own name by assailing men who have become renowned. I am not so foolish as to think myself insulted by the fact that you give an explanation different from mine; since you, on the other hand, are not wronged by my views being contrary to those which you maintain. But that is the kind of reproof by which friends may truly benefit each other, when each, not seeing his own bag of faults, observes, as

[1] Sir. 22: 6.

Persius has it, the wallet borne by the other.[2] Let me say further, love one who loves you, and do not because you are
young challenge a veteran in the field of scripture. I have had
my time, and have run my course to the utmost of my strength.
It is but fair that I should rest, while you in your turn run
and accomplish great distances; at the same time (with your
leave, and without intending any disrespect), lest it should
seem that to quote from the poets is a thing which you alone
can do, let me remind you of the encounter between Dares
and Entellus,[3] and of the proverb, "The tired ox treads with
a firmer step." With sorrow I have dictated these words.
Would that I could receive your embrace, and that by converse
we might aid each other in learning!

3. With his usual effrontery, Calphurnius, surnamed Lana-
rius,[4] has sent me his execrable writings, which I understand
that he has been at pains to disseminate in Africa also. To
these I have replied in part, and shortly; and I have sent you
a copy of my treatise, intending by the first opportunity to
send you a larger work, when I have leisure to prepare it. In
this treatise I have been careful not to offend Christian feeling in any, but only to confute the lies and hallucinations arising from his ignorance and madness.

Remember me, holy and venerable father. See how sincerely
I love you, in that I am unwilling, even when challenged, to
reply, and refuse to believe you to be the author of that which
in another I would sharply rebuke. Our brother Communis
sends his respectful salutation.

[2] *Sat.* 4. 29.
[3] Vergil, *Aen.* 5. 369 ff.
[4] Rufinus of Aquileia (c. 345–410), once a friend—but now no
longer—of Jerome.

LETTER 71

(A.D. 403)

TO MY VENERABLE LORD JEROME, MY ESTEEMED AND HOLY
BROTHER AND FELLOW-PRIEST, AUGUSTINE SENDS GREETING
IN THE LORD.

CHAP. 1. 1. Never since I began to write to you, and to long
for your writing in return, have I met with a better opportunity for our exchanging communications than now, when my
letter is to be carried to you by a most faithful servant and
minister of God, who is also a very dear friend of mine,
namely, our son Cyprian, deacon. Through him I expect to
receive a letter from you with all the certainty which is in
a matter of this kind possible. For the son whom I have
named will not be found wanting in respect of zeal in asking,
or persuasive influence in obtaining a reply from you; nor will
he fail in diligently keeping, promptly bearing, and faithfully
delivering the same. I only pray that if I be in any way worthy
of this, the Lord may give his help and favour to your heart
and to my desire, so that no higher will may hinder that which
your brotherly goodwill inclines you to do.

2. As I have sent you two letters already to which I have
received no reply, I have resolved to send you at this time
copies of both of them, for I suppose that they never reached
you. If they did reach you, and your replies have failed, as
may be the case, to reach me, send me a second time the same
as you sent before, if you have copies of them preserved: if
you have not, dictate again what I may read, and do not refuse
to send to these former letters the answer for which I have
been waiting so long. My first letter to you, which I had prepared while I was a priest, was to be delivered to you by a
brother of ours, Profuturus, who afterwards became my colleague in the episcopate, and has since then departed from
this life; but he could not then bear it to you in person, be-

cause at the very time when he intended to begin his journey, he was prevented by his ordination to the weighty office of bishop, and shortly afterwards he died. This letter I have resolved also to send at this time, that you may know how long I have cherished a burning desire for conversation with you, and with what reluctance I submit to the remote separation which prevents my mind from having access to yours through our bodily senses, my brother, most amiable and honoured among the members of the Lord.

CHAP. 2. 3. In this letter I have further to say, that I have since heard that you have translated Job out of the original Hebrew, although in your own translation of the same prophet from the Greek tongue we had already a version of that book. In that earlier version you marked with asterisks the words found in the Hebrew but wanting in the Greek, and with obelisks the words found in the Greek but wanting in the Hebrew; and this was done with such astonishing exactness, that in some places we have every word distinguished by a separate asterisk, as a sign that these words are in the Hebrew, but not in the Greek. Now, however, in this more recent version from the Hebrew, there is not the same scrupulous fidelity as to the words; and it perplexes any thoughtful reader to understand either what was the reason for marking the asterisks in the former version with so much care that they indicate the absence from the Greek version of even the smallest grammatical particles which have not been rendered from the Hebrew, or what is the reason for so much less care having been taken in this recent version from the Hebrew to secure that these same particles be found in their own places. I would have put down here an extract or two in illustration of this criticism; but at present I have not access to the manuscript of the translation from the Hebrew. Since, however, your quick discernment anticipates and goes beyond not only what I have said, but also what I meant to say, you already understand, I think, enough to be able, by giving the reason for the plan which you have adopted, to explain what perplexes me.

4. For my part, I would much rather that you would furnish us with a translation of the Greek version of the canonical Scriptures known as the work of the Seventy translators. For if your translation begins to be more generally read in

many churches, it will be a grievous thing that, in the reading of scripture, differences must arise between the Latin Churches and the Greek Churches, especially seeing that the discrepancy is easily condemned in a Latin version by the production of the original in Greek, which is a language very widely known; whereas, if any one has been disturbed by the occurrence of something to which he was not accustomed in the translation taken from the Hebrew, and alleges that the new translation is wrong, it will be found difficult, if not impossible, to get at the Hebrew documents by which the version to which exception is taken may be defended. And when they are obtained, who will submit to have so many Latin and Greek authorities pronounced to be in the wrong? Besides all this, Jews, if consulted as to the meaning of the Hebrew text, may give a different opinion from yours: in which case it will seem as if your presence were indispensable, as being the only one who could refute their view; and it would be a miracle if one could be found capable of acting as arbiter between you and them.

Chap. 3. 5. A certain bishop, one of our brethren, having introduced in the church over which he presides the reading of your version, came upon a word in the book of the prophet Jonah, of which you have given a very different rendering from that which had been of old familiar to the senses and memory of all the worshippers, and had been chanted for so many generations in the church.[1] Thereupon arose such a tumult in the congregation, especially among the Greeks, correcting what had been read, and denouncing the translation as false, that the bishop was compelled to ask the testimony of the Jewish residents (it was in the town of Oea). These, whether from ignorance or from spite, answered that the words in the Hebrew manuscript were correctly rendered in the Greek version, and in the Latin one taken from it. What further need I say? The man was compelled to correct your version in that passage as if it had been falsely translated, as he desired not to be left without a congregation,—a calamity which he narrowly escaped. From this case we also are led to think that you may be occasionally mistaken. You will also

[1] Jon. 4: 6.

observe how great must have been the difficulty if this had occurred in those writings which cannot be explained by comparing the testimony of languages now in use.

CHAP. 4. 6. At the same time, we are in no small measure thankful to God for the work in which you have translated the Gospels from the original Greek, because in almost every passage we have found nothing to object to, when we compared it with the Greek Scriptures. By this work, any disputant who supports an old false translation is either convinced or confuted with the utmost ease by the production and collation of manuscripts. And if, as indeed very rarely happens, something be found to which exception may be taken, who would be so unreasonable as not to excuse it readily in a work so useful that it cannot be too highly praised? I wish you would have the kindness to open up to me what you think to be the reason of the frequent discrepancies between the text supported by the Hebrew codices and the Greek Septuagint version. For the latter has no mean authority, seeing that it has obtained so wide circulation, and was the one which the apostles used, as is not only proved by looking to the text itself, but has also been, as I remember, affirmed by yourself. You would therefore confer upon us a much greater boon if you gave an exact Latin translation of the Greek Septuagint version: for the variations found in the different codices of the Latin text are intolerably numerous; and it is so justly open to suspicion as possibly different from what is to be found in the Greek, that one has no confidence in either quoting it or proving anything by its help.

I thought that this letter was to be a short one, but it has somehow been as pleasant to me to go on with it as if I were talking with you. I conclude with entreating you by the Lord kindly to send me a full reply, and thus give me, so far as is in your power, the pleasure of your presence.

LETTER 72
(A.D. 404)

TO AUGUSTINE, MY LORD TRULY HOLY, AND MOST BLESSED
FATHER, JEROME SENDS GREETING IN THE LORD.

CHAP. 1. 1. You are sending me letter upon letter, and often
urging me to answer a certain letter of yours, a copy of which,
without your signature, had reached me through our brother
Sysinnius, deacon, as I have already written, which letter you
tell me that you entrusted first to our brother Profuturus, and
afterwards to some one else; but that Profuturus was prevented from finishing his intended journey, and having been
ordained a bishop, was removed by sudden death; and the
second messenger, whose name you do not give, was afraid
of the perils of the sea, and gave up the voyage which he had
intended. These things being so, I am at a loss to express my
surprise that the same letter is reported to be in the possession
of most of the Christians in Rome, and throughout Italy, and
has come to every one but myself, to whom alone it was ostensibly sent. I wonder at this all the more, because the brother
Sysinnius aforesaid tells me that he found it among the rest
of your published works, not in Africa, not in your possession,
but in an island of the Adriatic some five years ago.

2. True friendship can harbour no suspicion; a friend must
speak to his friend as freely as to his second self. Some of
my acquaintances, vessels of Christ, of whom there is a very
large number in Jerusalem and in the holy places, suggested
to me that this had not been done by you in a guileless spirit,
but through desire for praise and celebrity, and *éclat* in the
eyes of the people, intending to become famous at my expense;
that many might know that you challenged me, and I feared
to meet you; that you had written as a man of learning, and
I had by silence confessed my ignorance, and had at last found
one who knew how to stop my garrulous tongue. I, however,

let me say it frankly, refused at first to answer your excellency, because I did not believe that the letter, or as I may call it (using a proverbial expression), the honeyed sword, was sent from you. Moreover, I was cautious lest I should seem to answer uncourteously a bishop of my own communion, and to censure anything in the letter of one who censured me, especially as I judged some of its statements to be tainted with heresy. Lastly, I was afraid lest you should have reason to remonstrate with me, saying, "What! had you seen the letter to be mine,—had you discovered in the signature attached to it the autograph of a hand well known to you, when you so carelessly wounded the feelings of your friend, and reproached me with that which the malice of another had conceived?"

CHAP. 2. 3. Therefore, as I have already written, either send me the identical letter in question subscribed with your own hand, or desist from annoying an old man, who seeks retirement in his monastic cell. If you wish to exercise or display your learning, choose as your antagonists, young, eloquent, and illustrious men, of whom it is said that many are found in Rome, who may be neither unable nor afraid to meet you, and to enter the lists with a bishop in debates concerning the Sacred Scriptures. As for me, a soldier once, but a retired veteran now, it becomes me rather to applaud the victories won by you and others, than with my worn-out body to take part in the conflict; beware lest, if you persist in demanding a reply, I call to mind the history of the way in which Quintus Maximus by his patience defeated Hannibal, who was, in the pride of youth, confident of success.[1]

> The rest I have forgot; for cares and time
> Change all things, and untune my soul to rhyme.
> I could have once sung down a summer's sun:
> But now the chime of poetry is done:
> My voice grows hoarse.[2]

Or rather, to quote an instance from scripture: Barzillai of Gilead, when he declined in favour of his youthful son the kindnesses of King David and all the charms of his court,

[1] Livy 22.
[2] Vergil, *Ecl.* 9. 51 ff. (Dryden).

taught us that old age ought neither to desire these things, nor to accept them when offered.

4. As to your calling God to witness that you had not written a book against me, and of course had not sent to Rome what you had never written, adding that, if maybe some things were found in your works in which a different opinion from mine was advanced, no wrong had thereby been done to me, because you had, without any intention of offending me, written only what you believed to be right; I beg you to hear me with patience. You never wrote a book against me: how then has there been brought to me a copy, written by another hand, of a treatise containing a rebuke administered to me by you? How comes Italy to possess a treatise of yours which you did not write? How can you reasonably ask me to reply to that which you solemnly assure me was never written by you? Nor am I so foolish as to think that I am insulted by you, if in anything your opinion differs from mine. But if, challenging me as it were to single combat, you take exception to my views, and demand a reason for what I have written, and insist upon my correcting what you judge to be an error, and call upon me to recant it in a humble palinode, and speak of your curing me of blindness; in this I maintain that friendship is wounded, and the laws of brotherly union are set at nought. Let not the world see us quarrelling like children, and giving material for angry contention between those who may become our respective supporters or adversaries. I write what I have now written, because I desire to cherish towards you pure and Christian love, and not to hide in my heart anything which does not agree with the utterance of my lips. For it does not become me, who have spent my life from youth until now, sharing the arduous labours of pious brethren in an obscure monastery, to presume to write anything against a bishop of my own communion, especially against one whom I had begun to love before I knew him, who also sought my friendship before I sought his, and whom I rejoiced to see rising as a successor to myself in the careful study of the Scriptures. Therefore either disown that book, if you are not its author, and give over urging me to reply to that which you never wrote; or if the book is yours, admit it frankly; so that if I write anything in self-defence, the responsibility may lie

on you who gave, not on me who am forced to accept, the challenge.

CHAP. 3. 5. You say also, that if there be anything in your writings which has displeased me, and which I would wish to correct, you are ready to receive my criticism as a brother; and you not only assure me that you would rejoice in such proof of my goodwill toward you, but you earnestly ask me to do this. I tell you again, without reserve, what I feel: you are challenging an old man, disturbing the peace of one who asks only to be allowed to be silent, and you seem to desire to display your learning. It is not for one of my years to give the impression of enviously disparaging one whom I ought rather to encourage by approbation. And if the ingenuity of perverse men finds something which they may plausibly censure in the writings even of evangelists and prophets, are you amazed if, in your books, especially in your exposition of passages in scripture which are exceedingly difficult of interpretation, some things be found which are not perfectly correct? This I say, however, not because I can at this time pronounce anything in your works to merit censure. For, in the first place, I have never read them with attention; and in the second place, we have not beside us a supply of copies of what you have written, excepting the books of Soliloquies and Commentaries on some of the Psalms; which, if I were disposed to criticise them, I could prove to be at variance, I shall not say with my own opinion, for I am nobody, but with the interpretations of the older Greek commentators.

Farewell, my very dear friend, my son in years, my father in ecclesiastical dignity; and to this I most particularly request your attention, that henceforth you make sure that I be the first to receive whatever you may write to me.

LETTER 73

(A.D. 404)

TO JEROME, MY VENERABLE AND MOST ESTEEMED BROTHER
AND FELLOW-PRIEST, AUGUSTINE SENDS GREETING IN THE
LORD.

CHAP. 1. 1. Although I suppose that, before this reaches you,
you have received through our son the deacon Cyprian, a servant of God, the letter which I sent by him, from which you
would be apprised with certainty that I wrote the letter of
which you mentioned that a copy had been brought to you;
in consequence of which I suppose that I have begun already,
like the rash Dares, to be beaten and belaboured by the missiles and the merciless fists of a second Entellus[1] in the reply
which you have written; nevertheless I answer in the meantime
the letter which you have deigned to send me by our holy
son Asterius, in which I have found many proofs of your most
kind goodwill to me, and at the same time some signs of your
having in some measure felt aggrieved by me. In reading it,
therefore, I was no sooner soothed by one sentence than I was
buffeted in another; my wonder being especially called forth
by this, that after alleging, as your reason for not rashly accepting as authentic the letter from me of which you had a
copy, the fact that, offended by your reply, I might justly
remonstrate with you, because you ought first to have ascertained that it was mine before answering it, you go on to command me to acknowledge the letter frankly if it is mine, or
send a more reliable copy of it, in order that we may, without
any bitterness of feeling, address ourselves to the discussion
of scriptural doctrine. For how can we engage in such discussion without bitterness of feeling, if you have made up your
mind to offend me? or, if your mind is not made up to this,
what reason could I have had, when you did not offend me,

[1] See Jerome's Letter 68.2.

for justly complaining as having been offended by you, that
you ought first to have made sure that the letter was mine,
and only then to have replied, that is to say, only then to have
offended me? For if there had been nothing to offend me in
your reply, I could have had no just ground of complaint. Accordingly, when you write such a reply to that letter as must
offend me, what hope is left of our engaging without any bitterness in the discussion of scriptural doctrine? Far be it from
me to take offence if you are willing and able to prove, by
incontrovertible argument, that you have apprehended more
correctly than I have the meaning of that passage in Paul's
Epistle [to the Galatians], or of any other text in Holy Scripture: nay, more, far be it from me to count it anything else
than gain to myself, and cause of thankfulness to you, if in
anything I am either informed by your teaching or set right
by your correction.

2. But, my very dear brother, you could not think that I
could be offended by your reply, had you not thought that
you were offended by what I had written. For I could never
have entertained concerning you the idea that you had not felt
yourself offended by me if you so framed your reply as to
offend me in return. If, on the other hand, I have been supposed by you to be capable of such preposterous folly as to
take offence when you had not written in such a way as to
give me occasion, you have in this already wronged me, that
you have entertained such an opinion of me. But surely you
who are so cautious, that although you recognised my style
in the letter of which you had a copy, you refused to believe
its authenticity, would not without consideration believe me
to be so different from what your experience has proved
me to be. For if you had good reason for seeing that I might
justly complain had you hastily concluded that a letter not
written by me was mine, how much more reasonably may I
complain if you form, without consideration, such an estimate
of myself as is contradicted by your own experience! You
would not therefore go so far astray in your judgment as to
believe, when you had written nothing by which I could be
offended, that I would nevertheless be so foolish as to be capable of being offended by such a reply.

CHAP. 2. 3. There can therefore be no doubt that you were

prepared to reply in such a way as would offend me, if you had only indisputable evidence that the letter was mine. Accordingly, since I do not believe that you would think it right to offend me unless you had just cause, it remains for me to confess, as I now do, my fault as having been the first to offend by writing that letter which I cannot deny to be mine. Why should I strive to swim against the current, and not rather ask pardon? I therefore entreat you by the mercy of Christ to forgive me wherein I have injured you, and not to render evil for evil by injuring me in return. For it will be an injury to me if you pass over in silence anything which you find wrong in either word or action of mine. If, indeed, you rebuke in me that which merits no rebuke, you do wrong to yourself, not to me; for far be it from one of your life and holy vows to rebuke merely from a desire to give offence, using the tongue of malice to condemn in me that which by the truth-revealing light of reason you know to deserve no blame. Therefore either rebuke kindly him whom, though he is free from fault, you think to merit rebuke; or with a father's kindness soothe him whom you cannot bring to agree with you. For it is possible that your opinion may be at variance with the truth, while notwithstanding your actions are in harmony with Christian charity: for I also shall most thankfully receive your rebuke as a most friendly action, even though the thing censured be capable of defence, and therefore ought not to have been censured; or else I shall acknowledge both your kindness and my fault, and shall be found, so far as the Lord enables me, grateful for the one, and corrected in regarded to the other.

4. Why, then, shall I fear your words, hard, perhaps, like the boxing-gloves of Entellus, but certainly fitted to do me good? The blows of Entellus were intended not to heal, but to harm, and therefore his antagonist was conquered, not cured. But I, if I receive your correction calmly as a necessary medicine, shall not be pained by it. If, however, through weakness, either common to human nature or peculiar to myself, I cannot help feeling some pain from rebuke, even when I am justly reproved, it is far better to have a tumour in one's head cured, though the lance cause pain, than to escape the pain by letting the disease go on. This was clearly seen by

him who said that, for the most part, our enemies who expose
our faults are more useful than friends who are afraid to reprove us. For the former, in their angry recriminations, sometimes charge us with what we indeed require to correct; but
the latter, through fear of destroying the sweetness of friendship, show less boldness on behalf of right than they ought.
Since, therefore, you are, to quote your own comparison, an
ox worn out, perhaps, as to your bodily strength by reason
of years, but unimpaired in mental vigour, and toiling still as-
siduously and with profit in the Lord's threshing-floor; here
am I, and in whatever I have spoken amiss, tread firmly on
me: the weight of your venerable age should not be grievous
to me, if the chaff of my fault be so bruised under foot as
to be separated from me.

5. Let me further say, that it is with the utmost affectionate
yearning that I read or recollect the words at the end of your
letter, "Would that I could receive your embrace, and that by
converse we might aid each other in learning." For my part,
I say,—would that we were even dwelling in parts of the earth
less widely separated; so that if we could not meet for converse, we might at least have a more frequent exchange of
letters. For as it is, so great is the distance by which we are
prevented from any kind of access to each other through the
eye and ear, that I remember writing to your holiness regarding these words in the Epistle to the Galatians when I was
young; and behold I am now advanced in age, and have not
yet received a reply, and a copy of my letter has reached you
by some strange accident earlier than the letter itself, about
the transmission of which I took no small pains. For the man
to whom I entrusted it neither delivered it to you nor returned
it to me. So great in my esteem is the value of those of your
writings which we have been able to procure, that I should
prefer to all other studies the privilege, if it were attainable
by me, of sitting by your side and learning from you. Since
I cannot do this myself, I propose to send to you one of my
sons in the Lord, that he may for my benefit be instructed
by you, in the event of my receiving from you a favourable
reply in regard to the matter. For I have not now, and I can
never hope to have, such knowledge of the Divine Scriptures
as I see you possess. Whatever abilities I may have for such

study, I devote entirely to the instruction of the people whom God has entrusted to me; and I am wholly precluded by my ecclesiastical occupations from having leisure for any further prosecution of my studies than is necessary for my duty in public teaching.

CHAP. 3. 6. I am not acquainted with the writings speaking injuriously of you, which you tell me have come into Africa. I have, however, received the reply to these which you have been pleased to send. After reading it, let me say frankly, I have been exceedingly grieved that the mischief of such painful discord has arisen between persons once so loving and intimate, and formerly united by the bond of a friendship which was well known in almost all the Churches. In that treatise of yours, any one may see how you are keeping yourself under restraint, and holding back the stinging keenness of your indignation, lest you should render railing for railing. If, however, even in reading this reply of yours, I fainted with grief and shuddered with fear, what would be the effect produced in me by the things which he has written against you, if they should come into my possession! "Woe unto the world because of scandals!"[2] Behold the complete fulfilment of that which he who is truth foretold: "Because iniquity shall abound, the love of many shall wax cold."[3] For what trusting hearts can now pour themselves forth with any assurance of their confidence being reciprocated? Into whose breast may confiding love now throw itself without reserve? In short, where is the friend who may not be feared as possibly a future enemy, if the breach that we deplore could arise between Jerome and Rufinus? Oh, sad and pitiable is our portion! Who can rely upon the affection of his friends because of what he knows them to be now, when he has no foreknowledge of what they shall afterwards become? But why should I reckon it cause for sorrow, that one man is thus ignorant of what another may become, when no man knows even what he himself is afterwards to be? The utmost that he knows, and that he knows but imperfectly, is his present condition; of what he shall hereafter become he has no knowledge.

[2] Matt. 18: 7.
[3] Matt. 19: 12.

7. Do the holy and blessed angels possess not only this knowledge of their actual character, but also a foreknowledge of what they shall afterwards become? If they do, I cannot see how it was possible for Satan ever to have been happy, even while he was still a good angel, knowing, as in this case he must have known, his future transgression and eternal punishment. I would wish to hear what you think as to this question, if indeed it be one which it would be profitable for us to be able to answer. But mark here what I suffer from the lands and seas which keep us, so far as the body is concerned, distant from each other. If I were myself the letter which you are now reading, you might have told me already what I have just asked; but now, when will you write me a reply? when will you get it sent away? when will it come here? when shall I receive it? And yet, would that I were sure it would come at last, though meanwhile I must summon all the patience which I can command to endure the unwelcome but unavoidable delay! Therefore I come back to those most delightful words of your letter, filled with your holy longing, and I in turn appropriate them as my own: "Would that I might receive your embrace, and that by converse we might aid each other in learning,"—if indeed there be any sense in which I could possibly impart instruction to you.

8. When by these words, now mine not less than yours, I am gladdened and refreshed, and when I am comforted not a little by the fact that in both of us a desire for mutual fellowship exists, though meanwhile unsatisfied, it is not long before I am pierced through by darts of keenest sorrow when I consider Rufinus and you, to whom God had granted in fullest measure and for a length of time that which both of us have longed for, so that in most close and endearing fellowship you feasted together on the honey of the Holy Scriptures, and think how between you the blight of such exceeding bitterness has found its way, constraining us to ask when, where, and in whom the same calamity may not be reasonably feared; seeing that it has befallen you at the very time when, unencumbered, having cast away secular burdens, you were following the Lord and were living together in that very land which was trodden by the feet of our Lord, when he said, "Peace I leave with

you, my peace I give unto you;"[4] being, moreover, men of
mature age, whose life was devoted to the study of the word
of God. Truly "man's life on earth is a period of trial."[5] If
I could anywhere meet you both together—which, alas, I cannot hope to do—so strong are my agitation, grief, and fear,
that I think I would cast myself at your feet, and there weeping till I could weep no more, would, with all the eloquence
of love, appeal first to each of you for his own sake, then
to both for each other's sake, and for the sake of those, especially the weak, "for whom Christ died,"[6] whose salvation is
in peril, as they look on you who occupy a place so conspicuous on the stage of time; imploring you not to write and scatter abroad these hard words against each other, which, if at
any time you who are now at variance were reconciled, you
could not destroy, and which you could not then venture to
read lest strife should be kindled anew.

9. But I say to your charity, that nothing has made me tremble more than your estrangement from Rufinus, when I read
in your letter some of the indications of your being displeased
with me. I refer not so much to what you say of Entellus and
of the wearied ox, in which you appear to me to use genial
pleasantry rather than angry threat, but to that which you have
evidently written in earnest, of which I have already spoken
perhaps more than was fitting, but not more than my fears
compelled me to do,—namely, the words, "lest perhaps, being
offended, you should have reason to remonstrate with me."
If it be possible for us to examine and discuss anything by
which our hearts may be nourished, without any bitterness of
discord, I entreat you let us address ourselves to this. But if
it is not possible for either of us to point out what he may
judge to demand correction in the other's writings, without being suspected of envy and regarded as wounding friendship,
let us, having regard to our spiritual life and health, leave such
conference alone. Let us content ourselves with smaller attain-
ments in that knowledge which puffs up, if we can thereby
preserve unharmed that charity which edifies.[7] I feel that I

4 John 14: 27.
5 Job 7: 1.
6 1 Cor. 8: 11.
7 1 Cor. 8: 1.

come far short of that perfection of which it is written, "If
any man offend not in word, the same is a perfect man;"[8]
but through God's mercy I truly believe myself able to ask
your forgiveness for that in which I have offended you: and
this you ought to make plain to me, that through my hearing
you, you may gain your brother.[9] Nor should you make it
a reason for leaving me in error, that the distance between
us on the earth's surface makes it impossible for us to meet
face to face. As concerns the subjects into which we inquire,
if I know, or believe, or think that I have got hold of the
truth in a matter in which your opinion is different from mine,
I shall by all means endeavour, as the Lord may enable me,
to maintain my view without injuring you. And as to any offence which I may give to you, so soon as I perceive your
displeasure, I shall unreservedly beg your forgiveness.

10. I think, moreover, that your reason for being displeased
with me can only be, that I have either said what I ought not,
or have not expressed myself in the manner in which I ought:
for I do not wonder that we are less thoroughly known to
each other than we are to our most close and intimate friends.
Upon the love of such friends I readily cast myself without
reservation, especially when chafed and wearied by the scandals of this world; and in their love I rest without any disturbing care: for I perceive that God is there, on whom I confidingly cast myself, and in whom I confidingly rest. Nor in this
confidence am I disturbed by any fear of that uncertainty as
to the morrow which must be present when we lean upon human weakness, and which I have in a former paragraph be-
wailed. For when I perceive that a man is burning with Christian love, and feel that thereby he has been made a faithful
friend to me, whatever plans or thoughts of mine I entrust
to him I regard as entrusted not to the man, but to him in
whom his character makes it evident that he dwells: for "God
is love, and he that dwells in love dwells in God, and God
in him;"[10] and if he cease to dwell in love, his forsaking it
cannot but cause as much pain as his abiding in it caused joy.
Nevertheless, in such a case, when one who was an intimate

[8] Jas. 3: 2.
[9] Matt. 18: 15.
[10] 1 John 4: 16.

friend has become an enemy, it is better that he should search out what ingenuity may help him to fabricate to our prejudice, than that he should find what anger may provoke him to reveal. This every one most easily secures, not by concealing what he does, but by doing nothing which he would wish to conceal. And this the mercy of God grants to good and pious men: they go out and in among their friends in liberty and without fear, whatever these friends may afterwards become: the sins which may have been committed by others within their knowledge they do not reveal, and they themselves avoid doing what they would fear to see revealed. For when any false charge is fabricated by a slanderer, either it is disbelieved, or, if it is believed, our reputation alone is injured, our spiritual wellbeing is not affected. But when any sinful action is committed, that action becomes a secret enemy, even though it be not revealed by the thoughtless or malicious talk of one acquainted with our secrets. Therefore any person of discernment may see in your own example how, by the comfort of a good conscience, you bear what would otherwise be insupportable—the incredible enmity of one who was formerly your most intimate and beloved friend; and how even what he utters against you, even what may to your disadvantage be believed by some, you turn to good account as the armour of righteousness on the left hand, which is not less useful than armour on the right hand[11] in our warfare with the devil. But truly I would rather see him less bitter in his accusations, than see you thus more fully armed by them. This is a great and a lamentable wonder, that you should have passed from such amity to such enmity: it would be a joyful and a much greater event, should you come back from such enmity to the friendship of former days.

[11] 2 Cor. 6: 7.

LETTER 75

(A.D. 404)

Jerome's answer to Letters 28, 40 and 71.

TO AUGUSTINE, MY LORD TRULY HOLY, AND MOST BLESSED
FATHER, JEROME SENDS GREETING IN CHRIST.

CHAP. 1. 1. I have received by Cyprian, deacon, three letters,
or rather three little books, at the same time, from your excellency, containing what you call sundry questions, but what
I feel to be animadversions on opinions which I have published, to answer which, if I were disposed to do it, would require a pretty large volume. Nevertheless I shall attempt to
reply without exceeding the limits of a moderately long letter,
and without causing delay to our brother, now in haste to depart, who only three days before the time fixed for his journey
asked earnestly for a letter to take with him, in consequence
of which I am compelled to pour out these sentences, such
as they are, almost without premeditation, answering you in
a rambling effusion, prepared not in the leisure of deliberate
composition, but in the hurry of extemporaneous dictation,
which usually produces a discourse that is more the offspring
of chance than the parent of instruction; just as unexpected
attacks throw into confusion even the bravest soldiers, and
they are compelled to take to flight before they can gird on
their armour.

2. But our armour is Christ; it is that which the apostle
Paul prescribes when, writing to the Ephesians, he says, "Take
the whole armour of God, that you may be able to withstand
in the evil day;" and again, "Stand, therefore, having your
loins girt about with truth, and having on the breastplate of
righteousness; and your feet shod with the preparation of the
gospel of peace; above all, taking the shield of faith, wherewith you shall be able to quench all the fiery darts of the

wicked: and take the helmet of salvation, and the sword of the
Spirit, which is the word of God."[1] Armed with these weapons, King David went forth in his day to battle; and taking
from the torrent's bed five smooth rounded stones, he proved
that, even amidst all the eddying currents of the world, his
feelings were free both from roughness and from defilement;
drinking of the brook by the way, and therefore lifted up in
spirit, he cut off the head of Goliath, using the proud enemy's
own sword as the fittest instrument of death,[2] smiting the profane boaster on the forehead and wounding him in the same
place in which Uzziah was smitten with leprosy when he presumed to usurp the priestly office;[3] the same also in which
shines the glory that makes the saints rejoice in the Lord, saying, "The light of your countenance is sealed upon us, O
Lord."[4] Let us therefore also say, "My heart is fixed, O God,
my heart is fixed: I will sing and give praise: awake up, my
glory; awake, psaltery and harp; I myself will awake early;"[5]
that in us may be fulfilled that word, "Open thy mouth wide,
and I will fill it;"[6] and, "The Lord shall give the word with
great power to them that publish it."[7] I am well assured that
your prayer as well as mine is, that in our contendings the victory may remain with the truth. For you seek Christ's glory,
not your own: if you are victorious, I also gain a victory if I
discover my error. On the other hand, if I win the day, the
gain is yours; for "the children ought not to lay up for the
parents, but the parents for the children."[8] We read, moreover, in Chronicles, that the children of Israel went to battle
with their minds set upon peace,[9] seeking even amid swords
and bloodshed and the prostrate slain a victory not for themselves, but for peace. Let me therefore, if it be the will of
Christ, give an answer to all that you have written, and attempt in a short dissertation to solve your numerous questions.

[1] Eph. 6: 13–17.
[2] 1 Sam. 17: 40–51.
[3] 2 Chron. 16: 19.
[4] Ps. 4: 7.
[5] Ps. 57: 7 f.
[6] Ps. 81: 10.
[7] Ps. 68: 11.
[8] 2 Cor. 12: 14.
[9] 1 Chron. 12: 17 f.

I pass by the conciliatory phrases in your courteous salutation: I say nothing of the compliments by which you attempt
to take the edge off your censure: let me come at once to the
matters in debate.

CHAP. 2. 3. You say that you received from some brother
a book of mine, in which I have given a list of ecclesiastical
writers, both Greek and Latin, but which had no title; and
that when you asked the brother aforesaid (I quote your own
statement) why the title-page had no inscription, or what was
the name by which the book was known, he answered that
it was called "Epitaphium," i.e. "Obituary Notices:" upon
which you display your reasoning powers, by remarking that
the name epitaphium would have been properly given to the
book if the reader had found in it an account of the lives and
writings of deceased authors, but that since mention is made
of the works of many who were living when the book was
written, and are at this day still living, you wonder why I
should have given the book a title so inappropriate. I think
that it must be obvious to your own common sense, that you
might have discovered the title of that book from its contents,
without any other help. For you have read both Greek and
Latin biographies of eminent men, and you know that they
do not give to works of this kind the title Epitaphium, but
simply "Illustrious Men," e.g. "Illustrious Generals," or "philosophers, orators, historians, poets," etc., as the case may be.
An epitaphium is a work written concerning the dead; such
as I remember having composed long ago after the decease
of the priest Nepotianus, of blessed memory. The book,
therefore, of which you speak ought to be entitled, "Concerning Illustrious Men," or properly, "Concerning Ecclesiastical
Writers," although it is said that by many who were not quali-
fied to make any correction of the title, it has been called
"Concerning Authors."

CHAP. 3. 4. You ask, in the second place, my reason for
saying, in my commentary on the Epistle to the Galatians, that
Paul could not have rebuked Peter for that which he himself
had done,[10] and could not have censured in another the dissimulation of which he was himself confessedly guilty; and

[10] Gal. 2: 14.

you affirm that that rebuke of the apostle was not a manœuvre of pious policy, but real; and you say that I ought not to teach falsehood, but that all things in scripture are to be received literally as they stand.

To this I answer, in the first place, that your wisdom ought to have suggested the remembrance of the short preface to my commentaries, saying of my own person, "What then? Am I so foolish and bold as to promise that which he could not accomplish? By no means; but I have rather, as it seems to me, with more reserve and hesitation, because feeling the deficiency of my strength, followed the commentaries of Origen in this matter. For that illustrious man wrote five volumes on the Epistle of Paul to the Galatians, and has occupied the tenth volume of his *Stromata* with a short treatise upon his explanation of the epistle. He also composed several treatises and fragmentary pieces upon it, which, if they even had stood alone, would have sufficed. I pass over my revered instructor Didymus (blind, it is true, but quick-sighted in the discernment of spiritual things), and the bishop of Laodicea, who has recently left the church, and the early heretic Alexander, as well as Eusebius of Emesa and Theodorus of Heraclea, who have also left some brief disquisitions upon this subject. From these works if I were to extract even a few passages, a work which could not be altogether despised would be produced. Let me therefore frankly say that I have read all these; and storing up in my mind very many things which they contain, I have dictated to my amanuensis sometimes what was borrowed from other writers, sometimes what was my own, without distinctly remembering the method, or the words, or the opinions which belonged to each. I look now to the Lord in his mercy to grant that my want of skill and experience may not cause the things which others have well spoken to be lost, or to fail of finding among foreign readers the acceptance with which they have met in the language in which they were first written. If, therefore, anything in my explanation has seemed to you to demand correction, it would have been seemly for one of your learning to inquire first whether what I had written was found in the Greek writers to whom I have referred; and if they had not advanced the opinion which you censured, you could then with propriety condemn me for what I gave as my own view, especially seeing that I have in the preface openly acknowledged that I had followed the commentaries of Origen, and had dictated sometimes the view of others, sometimes my own, and have written at the end of the chapter with which you find fault: "If any one be dissatisfied with the interpretation here given, by which it is shown that neither did Peter sin, nor did Paul rebuke presumptuously a greater than himself, he is bound to show how Paul could consistently blame in another what he himself did." By which I have made it manifest that I did not adopt finally and irrevocably that which I had read in these Greek authors, but had propounded what I had read, leaving to the reader's own judgment whether it should be rejected or approved.

5. You, however, in order to avoid doing what I had asked, have devised a new argument against the view proposed; maintaining that the Gentiles who had believed in Christ were free from the burden of the ceremonial law, but that the Jewish converts were under the law, and that Paul, as the teacher of the Gentiles, rightly rebuked those who kept the law; whereas Peter, who was the chief of the "circumcision,"[11] was justly rebuked for commanding the Gentile converts to do that which the converts from among the Jews were alone under obligation to observe. If this is your opinion, or rather since it is your opinion, that all from among the Jews who believe are debtors to do the whole law, you ought, as being a bishop of great fame in the whole world, to publish your doctrine, and labour to persuade all other bishops to agree with you. As for me in my humble cell, along with the monks my fellow-sinners, I do not presume to dogmatize in regard to things of great moment; I only confess frankly that I read the writings of the Fathers, and, complying with universal usage, put down in my commentaries a variety of explanations, that each may adopt from the number given the one which pleases him. This method, I think, you have found in your reading, and have approved in connection with both secular literature and the Divine Scriptures.

6. Moreover, as to this explanation which Origen first advanced, and which all the other commentators after him have

---

[11] Gal. 2: 8.

adopted, they bring forward, chiefly for the purpose of answering, the blasphemies of Porphyry, who accuses Paul of presumption because he dared to reprove Peter and rebuke him to his face, and by reasoning convict him of having done wrong; that is to say, of being in the very fault which he himself, who blamed another for transgressing, had committed. What shall I say also of John, who has long governed the church of Constantinople, and holding pontifical rank,[12] who has composed a very large book upon this paragraph, and has followed the opinion of Origen and of the old expositors? If, therefore, you censure me as in the wrong, suffer me, I pray you, to be mistaken in company with such men; and when you perceive that I have so many companions in my error, you will require to produce at least one partisan in defence of your truth. So much on the interpretation of one paragraph of the Epistle to the Galatians.

7. Lest, however, I should seem to rest my answer to your reasoning wholly on the number of witnesses who are on my side, and to use the names of illustrious men as a means of escaping from the truth, not daring to meet you in argument, I shall briefly bring forward some examples from the Scriptures.

In the Acts of the Apostles, a voice was heard by Peter, saying to him, "Rise, Peter, slay and eat," when all manner of four-footed beasts, and creeping things, and birds of the air, were presented before him; by which saying it is proved that no man is by nature ceremonially unclean, but that all men are equally welcome to the gospel of Christ. To which Peter answered, "Not so, Lord; for I have never eaten anything that is common or unclean." And the voice spoke to him again the second time, "What God has cleansed, that do not call common." Therefore he went to Cæsarea, and having entered the house of Cornelius, "he opened his mouth and said, 'Of a truth I perceive that God is no respecter of persons, but in every nation he that fears him and works righteousness is accepted with him.'" Thereafter "the Holy Ghost fell on all them who heard the word; and they of the circumcision who believed were astonished, as many as

12 St. John Chrysostom.

came with Peter, because that on the Gentiles also was poured out the gift of the Holy Ghost. Then answered Peter, 'Can any man forbid water, that these should not be baptized, who have received the Holy Ghost as well as we?' And he commanded them to be baptized in the name of the Lord."[13] "And the apostles and brethren that were in Judea heard that the Gentiles had also received the word of God. And when Peter was come up to Jerusalem, they that were of the circumcision contended with him, saying, 'You went in to men uncircumcised, and did eat with them.'" To whom he gave a full explanation of the reasons of his conduct, and concluded with these words: "Since then as God gave them the like gift as he did to us who believed on the Lord Jesus Christ, what was I, that I could withstand God? When they heard these things, they held their peace, and glorified God, saying, 'Then has God also to the Gentiles granted repentance to life.'"[14] Again, when, long after this, Paul and Barnabas had come to Antioch, and "having gathered the church together, rehearsed all that God had done with them, and how he had opened the door of faith to the Gentiles, certain men who came down from Judea taught the brethren, and said, 'Except you be circumcised after the manner of Moses, you cannot be saved.' When therefore Paul and Barnabas had no small dissension and disputation with them, they determined that Paul and Barnabas, and certain other of them, should go up to Jerusalem to the apostles and elders about this question. And when they were come to Jerusalem, there rose up certain of the sect of the Pharisees who believed, saying that it was needful to circumcise them, and to command them to keep the law of Moses." And when there had been much disputing, Peter rose up, with his accustomed readiness, "and said, 'Men and brethren, you know how that a good while ago God made choice among us, that the Gentiles by my mouth should hear the word of the gospel, and believe. And God, who knows the hearts, bare them witness, giving them the Holy Ghost, even as he did to us; and put no difference between us and them, purifying their hearts by faith. Now therefore

13 Acts 10: 13–48.
14 Acts 11: 1–18.

why tempt God, to put a yoke upon the neck of the disciples, which neither our fathers nor we were able to bear? But we believe that, through the grace of the Lord Jesus Christ, we shall be saved, even as they.' Then all the multitude kept silence;" and to his opinion the apostle James, and all the elders together, gave consent.[15]

8. These quotations should not be tedious to the reader, but useful both to him and to me, as proving that, even before the apostle Paul, Peter had come to know that the law was not to be in force after the gospel was given; more, that Peter was the prime mover in issuing the decree by which this was affirmed. Moreover, Peter was of so great authority, that Paul has recorded in his epistle: "Then, after three years, I went up to Jerusalem to see Peter, and abode with him fifteen days."[16] In the following context, again, he adds: "Then, fourteen years after, I went up again to Jerusalem with Barnabas, and took Titus with me also. And I went up by revelation, and communicated to them that gospel which I preach among the Gentiles;" proving that he had not had confidence in his preaching of the gospel if he had not been confirmed by the consent of Peter and those who were with him. The next words are, "but privately to them that were of reputation, lest by any means I should run, or had run, in vain." Why did he this privately rather than in public? Lest offence should be given to the faith of those who from among the Jews had believed, since they thought that the law was still in force, and that they ought to join observance of the law with faith in the Lord as their saviour. Therefore also, when at that time Peter had come to Antioch (although the Acts of the Apostles do not mention this, but we must believe Paul's statement), Paul affirms that he "withstood him to the face, because he was to be blamed. For, before certain men came from James, he did eat with the Gentiles: but when they were come, he withdrew, and separated himself, fearing them which were of the circumcision. And the other Jews dissembled likewise with him; insomuch that Barnabas also was carried away with their dissimulation. But when I saw," he

[15] Acts 14: 27 and 15: 1–12.
[16] Gal. 1: 18.

says, "that they walked not uprightly, according to the truth
of the gospel, I said unto Peter before them all, 'If you, being
a Jew, live after the manner of Gentiles, and not as do the
Jews, why do you compel the Gentiles to live as do the
Jews?' "[17] No one can doubt, therefore, that the apostle Peter
was himself the author of that rule with deviation from which
he is charged. The cause of that deviation, moreover, is seen
to be fear of the Jews. For the scripture says, that "at first
he did eat with the Gentiles, but that when certain men had
come from James he withdrew, and separated himself, fearing
them which were of the circumcision." Now he feared the
Jews, to whom he had been appointed apostle, lest by occasion of the Gentiles they should go back from the faith in
Christ; imitating the good shepherd in his concern lest he
should lose the flock committed to him.

9. As I have shown, therefore, that Peter was thoroughly
aware of the abrogation of the law of Moses, but was compelled by fear to pretend to observe it, let us now see whether
Paul, who accuses another, ever did anything of the same
kind himself. We read in the same book: "Paul passed
through Syria and Cilicia, confirming the churches. Then he
came to Derbe and Lystra: and, behold, a certain disciple
was there, named Timotheus, the son of a certain woman
who was a Jewess, and believed; but his father was a Greek:
who was well reported of by the brethren that were at Lystra
and Iconium. Him Paul wanted to go forth with him; and
he took and circumcised him, because of the Jews who were
in those quarters: for they all knew that his father was a
Greek."[18] O blessed apostle Paul, who had rebuked Peter
for dissimulation, because he withdrew himself from the Gentiles through fear of the Jews who came from James, why
are you, notwithstanding your own doctrine, compelled to
circumcise Timothy, the son of a Gentile, more, a Gentile
himself (for he was not a Jew, not having been circumcised)?
You will answer, "Because of the Jews who are in these
quarters?" If, then, you forgive yourself the circumcision of
a disciple coming from the Gentiles, forgive Peter also, who

[17] Gal. 2: 1, 2, 14.
[18] Acts 15: 41 and 16: 1–3.

has precedence above thee, his doing some things of the same kind through fear of the believing Jews. Again, it is written: "Paul after this tarried there yet a good while, and then took his leave of the brethren, and sailed thence into Syria, and with him Priscilla and Aquila; having shorn his head in Cenchrea, for he had a vow."[19] Be it granted that he was compelled through fear of the Jews in the other case to do what he was unwilling to do; why did he let his hair grow in accordance with a vow of his own making, and afterwards, when in Cenchrea, shave his head according to the law, as the Nazarites, who had given themselves by vow to God, were accustomed to do, according to the law of Moses?

10. But these things are small when compared with what follows. The sacred historian Luke further relates: "And when we were come to Jerusalem, the brethren received us gladly;" and the day following, James, and all the elders who were with him, having expressed their approbation of his gospel, said to Paul: "You see, brother, how many thousands of Jews there are who believe; and they are all zealous of the law: and they are informed of you, that you teach all the Jews who are among the Gentiles to forsake Moses, saying that they ought not to circumcise their children, neither to walk after the customs. What is it therefore? The multitude must come together: for they will hear that you are come. Do therefore this that we say to you: We have four men who have a vow on them; them take, and purify yourself with them, and pay their expenses, that they may shave their heads: and all may know that those things, of which they were informed concerning you, are nothing; but that you yourself also walk orderly, and keep the law. Then Paul took the men, and the next day purifying himself with them, entered into the temple, to signify the accomplishment of the days of purification, until an offering should be offered for every one of them."[20] O Paul, here again let me question you: why did you shave your head, why did you walk barefoot according to Jewish ceremonial law, why did you offer sacrifices, why were victims slain for you according to the

19 Acts 18: 18.
20 Acts 21: 17–26.

law? You will answer, doubtless, "To avoid giving offence
to those of the Jews who had believed." To gain the Jews,
you did pretend to be a Jew; and James and all the other
elders taught you this dissimulation. But you did not succeed
in escaping, after all. For when you were on the point of
being killed in a tumult which had arisen, you were rescued
by the chief captain of the band, and sent by him to Cæsarea,
guarded by a careful escort of soldiers, lest the Jews should
kill you as a dissembler, and a destroyer of the law; and from
Cæsarea coming to Rome, you did, in your own hired house,
preach Christ to both Jews and Gentiles, and your testimony
was sealed under Nero's sword.[21]

11. We have learned, therefore, that through fear of the
Jews both Peter and Paul alike pretended that they observed
the precepts of the law. How could Paul have the assurance
and effrontery to reprove in another what he had done himself? I at least, or, I should rather say, others before me,
have given such explanation of the matter as they deemed
best, not defending the use of falsehood in the interest of
religion, as you charge them with doing, but teaching the
honourable exercise of a wise discretion; seeking both to show
the wisdom of the apostles, and to restrain the shameless
blasphemies of Porphyry, who says that Peter and Paul quarrelled with each other in childish rivalry, and affirms that
Paul had been inflamed with envy on account of the excel-
lences of Peter, and had written boastfully of things which
he either had not done, or, if he did them, had done with
inexcusable presumption, reproving in another that which he
himself had done. They, in answering him, gave the best
interpretation of the passage which they could find; what interpretation have you to propound? Surely you must intend
to say something better than they have said, since you have
rejected the opinion of the ancient commentators.

CHAP. 4. 12. You say in your letter:[22] "You do not require me to teach you in what sense the apostle says, 'To
the Jews I became as a Jew, that I might gain the Jews;'[23]
and other such things in the same passage, which are to be

21 Acts 23: 23 and 28: 14, 30.
22 Letter 40.4.
23 1 Cor. 9: 20.

ascribed to the compassion of pitying love, not to the artifices of intentional deceit. For he that ministers to the sick becomes as if he were sick himself, not indeed falsely pretending to be under the fever, but considering with the mind of one truly sympathizing what he would wish done for himself if he were in the sick man's place. Paul was indeed a Jew; and when he had become a Christian, he had not abandoned those Jewish sacraments which that people had received in the right way, and for a certain appointed time. Therefore, even when he was an apostle of Christ, he took part in observing these, but with this view, that he might show that they were in no wise hurtful to those who, even after they had believed in Christ, desired to retain the ceremonies which by the law they had learned from their fathers; provided only that they did not build on these their hope of salvation, since the salvation which was foreshadowed in these has now been brought in by the Lord Jesus." The sum of your whole argument, which you have expanded into a most prolix dissertation, is this, that Peter did not err in supposing that the law was binding on those who from among the Jews had believed, but departed from the right course in this, that he compelled the Gentile converts to conform to Jewish observances. Now, if he compelled them, it was not by use of authority as a teacher, but by the example of his own practice. And Paul, according to your view, did not protest against what Peter had done personally, but asked why Peter would compel those who were from among the Gentiles to conform to Jewish observances.

13. The matter in debate, therefore, or I should rather say your opinion regarding it, is summed up in this: that since the preaching of the gospel of Christ, the believing Jews do well in observing the precepts of the law, i.e. in offering sacrifices as Paul did, in circumcising their children, as Paul did in the case of Timothy, and keeping the Jewish Sabbath, as all the Jews have been accustomed to do. If this be true, we fall into the heresy of Cerinthus and Ebion, who, though believing in Christ, were anathematized by the fathers for this one error, that they mixed up the ceremonies of the law with the gospel of Christ, and professed their faith in that which was new, without letting go what was old. Why do I speak

of the Ebionites, who make pretensions to the name of Christian? In our own day there exists a sect among the Jews throughout all the synagogues of the East, which is called the sect of the Minei, and is even now condemned by the Pharisees. The adherents to this sect are known commonly as Nazarenes; they believe in Christ the Son of God, born of the Virgin Mary; and they say that he who suffered under Pontius Pilate and rose again, is the same as the one in whom we believe. But while they desire to be both Jews and Christians, they are neither the one nor the other. I therefore beseech you, who think that you are called upon to heal my slight wound, which is no more, so to speak, than a prick or scratch from a needle, to devote your skill in the healing art to this grievous wound, which has been opened by a spear driven home with the impetus of a javelin. For there is surely no proportion between the culpability of him who exhibits the various opinions held by the fathers in a commentary on scripture, and the guilt of him who reintroduces within the church a most pestilential heresy. If, however, there is for us no alternative but to receive the Jews into the church, along with the usages prescribed by their law; if, in short, it shall be declared lawful for them to continue in the churches of Christ what they have been accustomed to practise in the synagogues of Satan, I will tell you my opinion of the matter: they will not become Christians, but they will make us Jews.

14. For what Christian will submit to hear what is said in your letter? "Paul was indeed a Jew; and when he had become a Christian, he had not abandoned those Jewish sacraments which that people had received in the right way, and for a certain appointed time. Therefore, even when he was an apostle of Christ, he took part in observing these; but with this view, that he might show that they were in no wise hurtful to those who, even after they had believed in Christ, desired to retain the ceremonies which by the law they had learned from their fathers." Now I implore you to hear patiently my complaint. Paul, even when he was an apostle of Christ, observed Jewish ceremonies; and you affirm that they are in no wise hurtful to those who wish to retain them as they had received them from their fathers by the law. I, on the contrary, shall maintain, and, though the world were

to protest against my view, I may boldly declare that the Jewish ceremonies are to Christians both hurtful and fatal; and that whoever observes them, whether he be Jew or Gentile originally, is cast into the pit of perdition. "For Christ is the end of the law for righteousness to every one that believes,"[24] that is, to both Jew and Gentile; for if the Jew be excepted, he is not the end of the law for righteousness to every one that believes. Moreover, we read in the Gospel, "The law and the prophets were until John the Baptist."[25] Also, in another place: "Therefore the Jews sought the more to kill him, because he had not only broken the sabbath, but said also that God was his Father, making himself equal with God."[26] Again: "Of his fulness we have all received, and grace for grace; for the law was given by Moses, but grace and truth came by Jesus Christ."[27] Instead of the grace of the law which has passed away, we have received the grace of the gospel which is abiding; and instead of the shadows and types of the old dispensation, the truth has come by Jesus Christ. Jeremiah also prophesied thus in God's name: "Behold, the days come, says the Lord, that I will make a new covenant with the house of Israel, and with the house of Judah; not according to the covenant which I made with their fathers, in the day that I took them by the hand, to bring them out of the land of Egypt."[28] Observe what the prophet says, not to Gentiles, who had not been partakers in any former covenant, but to the Jewish nation. He who has given them the law by Moses, promises in place of it the new covenant of the gospel, that they might no longer live in the oldness of the letter, but in the newness of the spirit. Paul himself, moreover, in connection with whom the discussion of this question has arisen, delivers such sentiments as these frequently, of which I subjoin only a few, as I desire to be brief: "Behold, I Paul say to you, that if you be circumcised, Christ shall profit you nothing." Again: "Christ is become of no effect to you, whoever of you are justified by the law; you

24 Rom. 10: 4.
25 Matt. 11: 13 and Luke 16: 16.
26 John 5: 18.
27 John 1: 16 f.
28 Jer. 31: 31 f.

are fallen from grace." Again: "If you be led of the Spirit,
you are not under the law."[29] From which it is evident that
he has not the Holy Spirit who submits to the law, not, as
our fathers affirmed the apostles to have done, feignedly,
under the promptings of a wise discretion, but, as you suppose to have been the case, sincerely. As to the quality of these
legal precepts, let us learn from God's own teaching: "I gave
them," he says, "statutes that were not good, and judgments
whereby they should not live."[30] I say these things, not that
I may, like Mani and Marcion, destroy the law, which I know
on the testimony of the apostle to be both holy and spiritual;
but because when "faith came," and the fulness of times,
"God sent forth his Son, made of a woman, made under the
law, to redeem them that were under the law, that we might
receive the adoption of sons,"[31] and might live no longer
under the law as our schoolmaster, but under the heir, who
has now attained to full age, and is Lord.

15. It is further said in your letter: "The thing, therefore,
which he rebuked in Peter was not his observing the customs
handed down from his fathers, which Peter, if he wished,
might do without being chargeable with deceit or inconsistency."[32] Again I say: since you are a bishop, a teacher in
the churches of Christ, if you would prove what you assert,
receive any Jew who, after having become a Christian, cir-
cumcises any son that may be born to him, observes the
Jewish Sabbath, abstains from meats which God has created
to be used with thanksgiving, and on the evening of the four-
teenth day of the first month slays a paschal lamb; and when
you have done this, or rather, have refused to do it (for I
know that you are a Christian, and will not be guilty of a
profane action), you will be constrained, whether willingly
or unwillingly, to renounce your opinion; and then you will
know that it is a more difficult work to reject the opinion of
others than to establish your own. Moreover, lest perhaps
we should not believe your statement, or, I should rather say,
understand it (for it is often the case that a discourse unduly

29 Gal. 5: 2, 4, 18.
30 Ezek. 20: 25.
31 Gal. 4: 4.
32 Letter 40.5.

extended is not intelligible, and is less censured by the un-skilled in discussion because its weakness is not so easily per-ceived), you inculcate your opinion by reiterating the state-ment in these words: "Paul had forsaken everything peculiar to the Jews that was evil, especially this, that 'being ignorant of God's righteousness, and going about to establish their own righteousness, they had not submitted themselves to the right-eousness of God.'[33] In this, moreover, he differed from them, that after the passion and resurrection of Christ, in whom had been given and made manifest the mystery of grace, accord-ing to the order of Melchizedek, they still considered it bind-ing on them to celebrate, not out of mere reverence for old customs, but as necessary to salvation, the sacraments of the old dispensation; which were indeed at one time necessary, else had it been unprofitable and vain for the Maccabees to suffer martyrdom as they did for their adherence to them.[34] Lastly, in this also Paul differed from the Jews, that they persecuted the Christian preachers of grace as enemies of the law. These, and all similar errors and sins, he declares that he counted but loss and dung, that he might win Christ."[35]

16. We have learned from you what evil things peculiar to the Jews Paul had abandoned; let us now learn from your teaching what good things which were Jewish he retained. You will reply: "The ceremonial observances in which they continue to follow the practice of their fathers, in the way in which these were complied with by Paul himself, without believing them to be at all necessary to salvation." I do not fully understand what you mean by the words, "without be-lieving them to be at all necessary to salvation." For if they do not contribute to salvation, why are they observed? And if they must be observed, they by all means contribute to salvation; especially seeing that, because of observing them, some have been made martyrs: for they would not be ob-served unless they contributed to salvation. For they are not things indifferent—neither good nor bad, as philosophers say. Self-control is good, self-indulgence is bad: between these, and indifferent, as having no moral quality, are such things

[33] Rom. 10: 3.
[34] 2 Macc. 7: 1.
[35] Phil. 3: 8. Letter 40.6.

as walking, blowing one's nose, expectorating phlegm, etc. Such an action is neither good nor bad; for whether you do it or leave it undone, it does not affect your standing as righteous or unrighteous. But the observance of legal ceremonies is not a thing indifferent; it is either good or bad. You say it is good. I affirm it to be bad, and bad not only when done by Gentile converts, but also when done by Jews who have believed. In this passage you fall, if I am not mistaken, into one error while avoiding another. For while you guard yourself against the blasphemies of Porphyry, you become entangled in the snares of Ebion; pronouncing that the law is binding on those who from among the Jews have believed. Perceiving, again, that what you have said is a dangerous doctrine, you attempt to qualify it by words which are only superfluous: viz., "The law must be observed not from any belief, such as prompted the Jews to keep it, that this is necessary to salvation, and not in any misleading dissimulation such as Paul reproved in Peter."

17. Peter therefore pretended to keep the law; but this censor of Peter boldly observed the things prescribed by the law. The next words of your letter are these: "For if Paul observed these sacraments in order, by pretending to be a Jew, to gain the Jews, why did he not also take part with the Gentiles in heathen sacrifices, when to them that were without law he became as without law, that he might gain them also? The explanation is found in this, that he took part in the Jewish rites as being himself a Jew; and that when he said all this which I have quoted, he meant not that he pretended to be what he was not, but that he felt with true compassion that he must bring such help to them as would be needful for himself if he were involved in their error.[36] Herein he exercised not the subtlety of a deceiver, but the sympathy of a compassionate deliverer." A triumphant vindication of Paul! You prove that he did not pretend to share the error of the Jews, but was actually involved in it; and that he refused to imitate Peter in a course of deception, dissembling through fear of the Jews what he really was, but without reserve freely avowed himself to be a Jew. Oh,

[36] Letter 40. 6.

unheard-of compassion of the apostle! In seeking to make the Jews Christians, he himself became a Jew! For he could not have persuaded the luxurious to become temperate if he had not himself become luxurious like them; and could not have brought help, in his compassion, as you say, to the wretched, otherwise than by experiencing in his own person their wretchedness! Truly wretched, and worthy of most compassionate lamentation, are those who, carried away by vehemence of disputation, and by love for the law which has been abolished, have made Christ's apostle to be a Jew. Nor is there, after all, a great difference between my opinion and yours: for I say that both Peter and Paul, through fear of the believing Jews, practised, or rather pretended to practise, the precepts of the Jewish law; whereas you maintain that they did this out of pity, "not with the subtlety of a deceiver, but with the sympathy of a compassionate deliverer." But by both this is equally admitted, that (whether from fear or from pity) they pretended to be what they were not. As to your argument against our view, that he ought to have become to the Gentiles a Gentile, if to the Jews he became a Jew, this favours our opinion rather than yours: for as he did not actually become a Jew, so he did not actually become a heathen; and as he did not actually become a heathen, so he did not actually become a Jew. His conformity to the Gentiles consisted in this, that he received as Christians the uncircumcised who believed in Christ, and left them free to use without scruple meats which the Jewish law prohibited; but not, as you suppose, in taking part in their worship of idols. For "in Christ Jesus, neither circumcision avails anything, nor uncircumcision, but the keeping of the commandments of God."[37]

18. I ask you, therefore, and with all urgency press the request, that you forgive me this humble attempt at a discussion of the matter; and wherein I have transgressed, lay the blame upon yourself who compelled me to write in reply, and who made me out to be as blind as Stesichorus. And do not bring the reproach of teaching the practice of lying upon me who am a follower of Christ, who said, "I am the way, the

[37] Gal. 5: 6 and 6: 15.

truth, and the life."[38] It is impossible for me, who am a
worshipper of the truth, to bow under the yoke of falsehood.
Moreover, refrain from stirring up against me the unlearned
crowd who esteem you as their bishop, and regard with the
respect due to the priestly office the orations which you deliver
in the church, but who esteem lightly an old decrepit man
like me, courting the retirement of a monastery far from the
busy haunts of men; and seek others who may be more fitly
instructed or corrected by you. For the sound of your voice
can scarcely reach me, who am so far separated from you by
sea and land. And if you happen to write me a letter, Italy
and Rome are sure to be acquainted with its contents long
before it is brought to me, to whom alone it ought to be sent.

CHAP. 5. 19. In another letter you ask why a former translation which I made of some of the canonical books was carefully marked with asterisks and obelisks, whereas I afterwards
published a translation without these. You must pardon my
saying that you seem to me not to understand the matter:
for the former translation is from the Septuagint; and wherever obelisks are placed, they are designed to indicate that the
Seventy have said more than is found in the Hebrew. But
the asterisks indicate what has been added by Origen from the
version of Theodotion. In that version I was translating from
the Greek: but in the later version, translating from the Hebrew itself, I have expressed what I understood it to mean,
being careful to preserve rather the exact sense than the
order of the words. I am surprised that you do not read the
books of the Seventy translators in the genuine form in which
they were originally given to the world, but as they have been
corrected, or rather corrupted, by Origen, with his obelisks
and asterisks; and that you refuse to follow the translation,
however feeble, which has been given by a Christian man,
especially seeing that Origen borrowed the things which he
has added from the edition of a man who, after the passion
of Christ, was a Jew and a blasphemer. Do you wish to be a
true admirer and partisan of the Seventy translators? Then
do not read what you find under the asterisks; rather erase
them from the volumes, that you may approve yourself indeed

[38] John 14: 6.

a follower of the ancients. If, however, you do this, you will be compelled to find fault with all the libraries of the churches; for you will scarcely find more than one manuscript here and there which has not these interpolations.

CHAP. 6. 20. A few words now as to your remark that I ought not to have given a translation, after this had been already done by the ancients; and the novel syllogism which you use: "The passages of which the Seventy have given an interpretation were either obscure or plain. If they were obscure, it is believed that you are as likely to have been mistaken as the others; if they were plain, it is not believed that the Seventy could possibly have been mistaken."[39]

All the commentators who have been our predecessors in the Lord in the work of expounding the Scriptures, have expounded either what was obscure or what was plain. If some passages were obscure, how could you, after them, presume to discuss that which they were not able to explain? If the passages were plain, it was a waste of time for you to have undertaken to treat of that which could not possibly have escaped them. This syllogism applies with peculiar force to the book of Psalms, in the interpretation of which Greek commentators have written many volumes: viz. first, Origen; second, Eusebius of Cæsarea; third, Theodorus of Heraclea; fourth, Asterius of Scythopolis; fifth, Apollinaris of Laodicea; and, sixth, Didymus of Alexandria. There are said to be minor works on selections from the Psalms, but I speak at present of the whole book. Moreover, among Latin writers the Bishops Hilary of Poitiers, and Eusebius of Vercelli, have translated Origen and Eusebius of Cæsarea, the former of whom has in some things been followed by our own Ambrose. Now, I put it to your wisdom to answer why you, after all the labours of so many and so competent interpreters, differ from them in your exposition of some passages? If the Psalms are obscure, it must be believed that you are as likely to be mistaken as others; if they are plain, it is incredible that these others could have fallen into mistake. In either case, your exposition has been, by your own showing, an unnecessary labour; and on the same principle, no one would ever venture

[39] Letter 28.2.

to speak on any subject after others have pronounced their opinion, and no one would be at liberty to write anything regarding that which another has once handled, however important the matter might be.

It is, however, more in keeping with your enlightened judgment, to grant to all others the liberty which you tolerate in yourself; for in my attempt to translate into Latin, for the benefit of those who speak the same language with myself, the corrected Greek version of the Scriptures, I have laboured not to supersede what has been long esteemed, but only to bring prominently forward those things which have been either omitted or tampered with by the Jews, in order that Latin readers might know what is found in the original Hebrew. If any one is averse to reading it, none compels him against his will. Let him drink with satisfaction the old wine, and despise my new wine, i.e. the sentences which I have published in explanation of former writers, with the design of making more obvious by my remarks what in them seemed to me to be obscure.

As to the principles which ought to be followed in the interpretation of the Sacred Scriptures, they are stated in the book which I have written,[40] and in all the introductions to the divine books which I have in my edition prefixed to each; and to these I think it sufficient to refer the prudent reader. And since you approve of my labours in revising the translation of the New Testament, as you say,—giving me at the same time this as your reason, that very many are acquainted with the Greek language, and are therefore competent judges of my work,—it would have been but fair to have given me credit for the same fidelity in the Old Testament; for I have not followed my own imagination, but have rendered the divine words as I found them understood by those who speak the Hebrew language. If you have any doubt of this in any passage, ask the Jews what is the meaning of the original.

21. Perhaps you will say, "What if the Jews decline to answer, or choose to impose upon us?" Is it conceivable that the whole multitude of Jews will agree together to be silent if asked about my translation, and that none shall be found

[40] *De optimo genere interpretandi.*

that has any knowledge of the Hebrew language? Or will they all imitate those Jews whom you mention as having, in some little town, conspired to injure my reputation? For in your letter you put together the following story:—"A certain bishop, one of our brethren, having introduced in the church over which he presides the reading of your version, came upon a word in the book of the prophet Jonah, of which you have given a very different rendering from that which had been of old familiar to the senses and memory of all the worshippers, and had been chanted for so many generations in the church. Thereupon arose such a tumult in the congregation, especially among the Greeks, correcting what had been read, and denouncing the translation as false, that the bishop was compelled to ask the testimony of the Jewish residents (it was in the town of Oea). These, whether from ignorance or from spite, answered that the words in the Hebrew manuscript were correctly rendered in the Greek version, and in the Latin one taken from it. What further need I say? The man was compelled to correct your version in that passage as if it had been falsely translated, as he desired not to be left without a congregation,—a calamity which he narrowly escaped. From this case we also are led to think that you may be occasionally mistaken."[41]

CHAP. 7. 22. You tell me that I have given a wrong translation of some word in Jonah, and that a worthy bishop narrowly escaped losing his charge through the clamorous tumult of his people, which was caused by the different rendering of this one word. At the same time, you withhold from me what the word was which I have mistranslated; thus taking away the possibility of my saying anything in my own vindication, lest my reply should be fatal to your objection. Perhaps it is the old dispute about the gourd which has been revived, after being forgotten for many long years since the illustrious man, who in that day combined in his own person the ancestral honours of the Cornelii and of Asinius Pollio,[42] brought against me the charge of giving in my translation the word "ivy" instead of "gourd." I have already given a suf-

[41] Letter 71.5.
[42] The critic here referred to was one Canthelius.

ficient answer to this in my commentary on Jonah. At present, I deem it enough to say that in that passage, where the Septuagint has "gourd," and Aquila and the others have rendered the word "ivy," the Hebrew manuscript has "ciceion," which is in the Syriac tongue, as now spoken, "ciceia." It is a kind of shrub having large leaves like a vine, and when planted it quickly springs up to the size of a small tree, standing upright by its own stem, without requiring any support of canes or poles, as both gourds and ivy do. If, therefore, in translating word for word, I had put the word "ciceia," no one would know what it meant; if I had used the word "gourd," I would have said what is not found in the Hebrew. I therefore put down "ivy," that I might not differ from all other translators. But if your Jews said, either through malice or ignorance, as you yourself suggest, that the word is in the Hebrew text which is found in the Greek and Latin versions, it is evident that they were either unacquainted with Hebrew, or have been pleased to say what was not true, in order to make sport of the gourd-planters.

In closing this letter, I beseech you to have some consideration for a soldier who is now old and has long retired from active service, and not to force him to take the field and again expose his life to the chances of war. Do you, who are young, and who have been appointed to the conspicuous seat of pontifical dignity, give yourself to teaching the people, and enrich Rome with new stores from fertile Africa. I am contented to make but little noise in an obscure corner of a monastery, with one to hear me or read to me.

LETTER 81

(A.D. 405)

TO AUGUSTINE, MY LORD TRULY HOLY, AND MOST BLESSED
FATHER, JEROME SENDS GREETING IN THE LORD.

HAVING anxiously inquired of our holy brother Firmus regarding your state, I was glad to hear that you are well. I
expected him to bring, or, I should rather say, I insisted upon
his giving me, a letter from you; upon which he told me that
he had set out from Africa without communicating to you his
intention. I therefore send to you my respectful salutations
through this brother, who clings to you with a singular
warmth of affection; and at the same time, in regard to my
last letter, I beg you to forgive the modesty which made it
impossible for me to refuse you, when you had so long required me to write you in reply. That letter, moreover, was
not an answer from me to you, but a confronting of my
arguments with yours. And if it was a fault in me to send a
reply (I beseech you hear me patiently), the fault of him who
insisted upon it was still greater. But let us be done with such
quarrelling; let there be sincere brotherliness between us; and
henceforth let us exchange letters, not of controversy, but
of mutual charity. The holy brethren who with me serve the
Lord send you cordial salutations. Salute from us the holy
brethren who with you bear Christ's easy yoke; especially I
beseech you to convey my respectful salutation to the holy
father Alypius, worthy of all esteem. May Christ, our almighty God, preserve you safe, and not unmindful of me, my
lord truly holy, and most blessed father. If you have read
my commentary on Jonah, I think you will not recur to the
ridiculous gourd-debate. If, moreover, the friend who first
assaulted me with his sword has been driven back by my pen,
I rely upon your good feeling and equity to lay blame on the
one who brought, and not on the one who repelled, the

accusation. Let us, if you please, exercise ourselves in the
field of scripture without wounding each other.

LETTER 172

(A.D. 416)

TO AUGUSTINE, MY TRULY PIOUS LORD AND FATHER, WORTHY OF
MY UTMOST AFFECTION AND VENERATION, JEROME SENDS
GREETING IN CHRIST.

1. THAT honourable man, my brother, and your excellency's
son, the priest Orosius, I have, both on his own account and
in obedience to your request, made welcome. But a most trying time has come upon us, in which I have found it better for
me to hold my peace than to speak, so that our studies have
ceased, lest what Appius calls "the eloquence of dogs" should
be provoked into exercise.[1] For this reason I have not been
able at the present time to give to those two books dedicated
to my name—books of profound erudition, and brilliant with
every charm of splendid eloquence—the answer which I
would otherwise have given; not that I think anything said
in them demands correction, but because I am mindful of the
words of the blessed apostle in regard to the variety of men's
judgments, "Let every man be fully persuaded in his own
mind."[2] Certainly, whatever can be said on the topics there
discussed, and whatever can be drawn by commanding genius
from the fountain of sacred scripture regarding them, has
been in these letters stated in your positions, and illustrated
by your arguments. But I beg your reverence to allow me
for a little to praise your genius. For in any discussion between us, the object aimed at by both of us is advancement
in learning. But our rivals, and especially heretics, if they see
different opinions maintained by us, will assail us with the
calumny that our differences are due to mutual jealousy. For

[1] Cf. Lactantius 6.18.
[2] Rom. 14: 5.

my part, however, I am resolved to love you, to look up to you, to reverence and admire you, and to defend your opinions as my own. I have also in a dialogue, which I recently published, made allusion to your blessedness in suitable terms. Be it ours, therefore, rather to rid the church of that most pernicious heresy which always feigns repentance, in order that it may have liberty to teach in our churches, and may not be expelled and extinguished, as it would be if it disclosed its real character in the light of day.

2. Your pious and venerable daughters, Eustochium and Paula, continue to walk worthy of their own birth and of your counsels, and they send special salutations to your blessedness: in which they are joined by the whole brotherhood of those who with us labour to serve the Lord our Saviour. As for the holy priest Firmus, we sent him last year to go on business of Eustochium and Paula, first to Ravenna, and afterwards to Africa and Sicily, and we suppose that he is now detained somewhere in Africa. I beseech you to present my respectful salutations to the saints who are associated with you. I have also sent to your care a letter from me to the holy priest Firmus; if it reaches you, I beg you to take the trouble of forwarding it to him. May Christ the Lord keep you in safety, and mindful of me, my truly pious lord and most blessed father.

(*As a postscript.*) We suffer in this province from a grievous scarcity of clerks acquainted with the Latin language; this is the reason why we are not able to comply with your instructions, especially in regard to that version of the Septuagint which is furnished with distinctive asterisks and obelisks;[3] for we have lost, through some one's dishonesty, most of the results of our earlier labour.

[3] Cf. Letter 71.3 f.

LETTER 195

(A.D. 418)

TO HIS HOLY LORD AND MOST BLESSED FATHER, AUGUSTINE,
JEROME SENDS GREETING.

AT all times I have esteemed your blessedness with becoming
reverence and honour, and have loved the Lord and Saviour
dwelling in you. But now we add, if possible, something to
that which has already reached a climax, and we heap up
what was already full, so that we do not suffer a single hour
to pass without the mention of your name, because you have,
with the ardour of unshaken faith, stood your ground against
opposing storms, and preferred, so far as this was in your
power, to be delivered from Sodom, though you should come
forth alone, rather than linger behind with those who are
doomed to perish. Your wisdom apprehends what I mean
to say. Go on and prosper! You are renowned throughout
the whole world; Catholics revere and look up to you as the
restorer of the ancient faith, and—which is a token of yet
more illustrious glory—all heretics abhor you. They persecute
me also with equal hatred, seeking by imprecation to take
away the life which they cannot reach with the sword. May
the mercy of Christ the Lord preserve you in safety and
mindful of me, my venerable lord and most blessed father.

**Confessions
(A.D. 397–400)
Books 7, 8 and 11**

The *Confessions* (thirteen books) was, it would appear, published in two stages: the first stage (Books 1–9) was begun early in 397 and had at least a restricted "publication" among Augustine's familiars; the second (Books 11–13) was finished between the second half of 398 and 400 or even perhaps 401. The first nine books are mainly autobiographical; the last three are mainly an exegesis of the first chapter of Genesis. The tenth book, commenting on Augustine's life at the time of writing in 397 or so, is an uneasy link between the first nine books and the last three. The *Confessions* is primarily a bishop's profession of faith in and praise of God and a confession of his sins. It is therefore distinctly less autobiographical than the title suggests to modern ears. Autobiographical details (which are relatively few) are selected in relation to the moral purposes of faith, praise and repentance. They are, moreover, set forth according to rhetorical and literary patterns that invite some questioning on their *total* historicity (but few scholars would deny that the events recounted are basically historical). The theme of the work, from which Augustine's readers were expected to profit, is that God's providence leads us through many apparent wanderings and misfortunes to salvation in Christ. Here we give three books: the important Books 7 and 8 from the first stage, dealing with Manichaeism and Neoplatonism, his intellectual and moral conversion and final submission to Christ; and Book 11 which contains a famous and subtle meditation on creation, "time" and foreknowledge. The best edition of the Latin text of the *Confessions* is that in the BA, vols. 13 and

14 (Paris, 1962), which gives the text of M. Skutella with
splendid introduction and notes by A. Solignac. The translation given here is by J. G. Pilkington, Edinburgh, 1876. There
is a good translation in Image Books.

SPECIAL TOPICS

1. *Augustine's early life and his intellectual* (Book 7) *and
moral* (Book 8) *conversion*
See J. O'Meara, *The Young Augustine* (New York, 1965),
pp. 131–90.

2. *Manichaeism* (Books 7, 8.9.21 f., 11.10.12 f.; cf. Books
3.6.10 f., 4, 5, 6.4.5 f.)
In the books of the *Confessions* given here, Augustine treats
of the central and most important aspects of his controversy
with the Manichaeans. The Manichaean system was founded
by Mani who was born about A.D. 216 in Babylonia. He was
lame, ascetic and had a hatred for the body. It was revealed
to him that he was the Paraclete and after many travels to
spread his religion was eventually crucified in 277. The religion that he founded was Gnostic: it taught salvation through
knowledge revealed in certain books of revelation. It drew
upon Christianity, and especially St. Paul, for some of its
doctrine; but while professing to complete Christianity—and
it had close relations with Christianity—it was severely critical
of the Christian defense of the Old Testament. Above all, it
was much pre-occupied with evil, which it explained by positing a Principle of Evil opposed to God, the Principle of Good
—both in effect material. Man's life was governed by the conjunction of planets and stars at his birth. Since the demons
manipulated the planets, one had to have recourse to religion
and astrology to outwit them. Augustine uses Neoplatonism
to refute the basic Manichaean tenets that God is material
and that evil derives from a Principle of Evil independent of
God. He also encounters the claims of astrology, on which
Manichaeism much relied, and the Manichaean attacks on
the Old Testament version of creation. See J. O'Meara, *The
Young Augustine*, pp. 61–91; P. Brown, *Augustine of Hippo*
(London, 1967), pp. 46–60, and *Religion and Society in the
Age of Saint Augustine* (London, 1972), pp. 94–118; H. C.
Puech, *Le Manichéisme* (Paris, 1949). A list of other Au-
gustine texts dealing with Manichaeism will be found in Al-
taner, pp. 507 f., Portalié, pp. 47–50 and Battenhouse, p.

158. Among these are *De Genesi contra Manichaeos; De moribus Manichaeorum; De utilitate credendi; De duabus animabus; Contra epistulam quam vocant Fundamenti;* and *De natura boni contra Manichaeos.*

3. *Neoplatonism* (Book 7)

Here and in the tenth book of the *City of God* Augustine tells how the revivers of Platonism—Plotinus (A.D. 205–270) and Porphyry (232–305), as it would seem—helped him decisively to grasp the notion of an immaterial God and to understand that evil was not something positive, but rather a defect in goodness: an essential feature in Augustine's teaching is that *everything* created is good. Christian-Platonists, of whom there was a group (which included St. Ambrose) in Milan when he was converted there, had long seen some correspondence between the Father, Word and Holy Spirit and the Plotinian One (also Father), Logos (or Word) and Soul. Augustine, as he tells us, was impressed by this as also by the Neoplatonic doctrine on Providence. On the other hand, he parted company from them—especially Porphyry—in their refusal to accept the Incarnation and resurrection of the flesh. See J. O'Meara, *The Young Augustine*, pp. 131–55; R. J. O'Connell, *St. Augustine's Confessions* (Cambridge, Mass., 1969), pp. 75–104.

4. *Creation and Time* (Book 11)

Both the Manichaeans and Porphyry raised the difficulty of how God, who must be changeless, could initiate creation. Augustine countered this difficulty by exploring the notion of time: all "time"—including the "time" of creation—is *present* to God. Furthermore, his "fore"-knowledge of what we will do, therefore, affects neither our will nor our destiny. Predestination, according to Augustine, is absolutely gratuitous on the one hand. On the other, "God in His creative decree has explicitly excluded every set of events in which grace would take away man's liberty and every situation in which man would not have the means to resist sin" (Portalié, p. 217). On creation and time, see Gilson, pp. 189–96, and J. F. Callahan, *Augustine and the Greek Philosophers* (Villanova, Pa., 1967), pp. 74–93; on foreknowledge and predestination, see Portalié, pp. 213–23.

5. *Ascent of the soul* (Book 7.10.16, 17.23, 20.26)

The descriptions given in Book 7 of Augustine's ascents of the soul are called "les vaines tentatives d'extases Plotiniennes" by P. Courcelle, *Recherches sur les Confessions de saint Augustin* (Paris, 1950, new ed. 1968), pp. 157–67. P. Henry, *La Vision d'Ostie* (Paris, 1938), dealing with the ninth book of the *Confessions,* concludes that Augustine was a mystic. A. Mandouze, *Saint Augustin* (Paris, 1968), pp. 678–714, examines the question in detail. For something in English, see J. O'Meara, *The Young Augustine,* pp. 139 ff., 147 f., 202 f., and C. Butler, *Western Mysticism* (London, 1927).

CONFESSIONS

BOOK 7

CHAP. 1—*He did not think of God as in the form of a human body, but as a corporeal substance diffused through space.*

1. Dead now was that evil and abominable youth of mine, and I was passing into early manhood: as I increased in years, the fouler I became in vanity, who could not conceive of any substance but such as I saw with my own eyes. I thought not of you, O God, under the form of a human body. Since the time I began to hear something of wisdom, I always avoided this; and I rejoiced to have found the same in the faith of our spiritual mother, your Catholic Church. But what else to imagine you I knew not. And I, a man, and such a man, sought to conceive of you, the sovereign and only true God; and I did in my inmost heart believe that you were incorruptible, and inviolable, and unchangeable; because, not knowing whence or how, yet most plainly did I see and feel sure that that which may be corrupted must be worse than that which cannot, and what cannot be violated without hesitation I preferred before that which can, and deemed that which suffers no change to be better than that which is changeable. Violently did my heart cry out against all my phantasms, and with this one blow I endeavoured to beat away from the eye of my mind all that unclean crowd which fluttered around it. And lo, being scarce put off, they, in the twinkling of an eye, pressed in multitudes around me, dashed against my face, and beclouded it; so that, though

I thought not of you under the form of a human body, yet I was constrained to image you to be something corporeal in space, either infused into the world, or infinitely diffused beyond it,—even that incorruptible, inviolable, and unchangeable, which I preferred to the corruptible, and violable, and changeable; since whatsoever I conceived, deprived of this space, appeared as nothing to me, altogether nothing, not even a void, as if a body were removed from its place and the place should remain empty of any body at all, whether earthy, terrestrial, watery, aerial, or celestial, but should remain a void place—a spacious nothing, as it were.

2. I therefore being thus gross-hearted, nor clear even to myself, whatever was not stretched over certain spaces, nor diffused, nor crowded together, nor swelled out, or which did not or could not receive some of these dimensions, I judged to be altogether nothing. For over such forms as my eyes range did my heart then range; nor did I see that this same observation, by which I formed those same images, was not of this kind, and yet it could not have formed them had not itself been something great. In like manner I conceived of you, life of my life, as vast through infinite spaces, on every side penetrating the whole mass of the world, and beyond it, all ways, through immeasurable and boundless spaces; so that the earth should have you, the heaven have you, all things have you, and they bounded in you, but you nowhere. For as the body of this air which is above the earth does not prevent the light of the sun from passing through it, penetrating it, not by bursting or by cutting, but by filling it entirely, so I imagined the body, not of heaven, air, and sea only, but of the earth also, to be open to you, and in all its greatest parts as well as smallest penetrable to receive your presence, by a secret inspiration, both inwardly and outwardly governing all things which you have created. So I conjectured, because I was unable to think of anything else; for it was untrue. For in this way would a greater part of the earth contain a greater portion of you, and the less a lesser; and all things should be so full of you, as that the body of an elephant should contain more of you than that of a sparrow by how much larger it is, and occupies more room; and so you would make the portions of yourself

present to the several portions of the world, in pieces, great
to the great, little to the little. But you are not such a one;
nor had you as yet enlightened my darkness.

CHAP. 2—*The disputation of Nebridius against the Manichæans,
on the question "whether God be corruptible or incorruptible."*

3. It was sufficient for me, O Lord, to oppose to those
deceived deceivers and dumb praters (dumb, since your word
did not sound forth from them) that which a long while ago,
while we were at Carthage, Nebridius used to propound, at
which all we who heard it were disturbed: "What could
that reputed nation of darkness, which the Manichæans are
in the habit of setting up as a mass opposed to you, have
done to you had you objected to fight with it? For had it
been answered, 'It would have done you some injury,' then
you would be subject to violence and corruption; but if the
reply were: 'It could do you no injury,' then no cause was
assigned for your fighting with it; and so fighting as that a
certain portion and member of you, or offspring of your
very substance, should be blended with adverse powers and
natures not of your creation, and be by them corrupted and
made worse to such an extent as to be turned from happiness
into misery, and need help by which it might be delivered and
purged; and that this offspring of your substance was the
soul, to which, being enslaved, contaminated, and corrupted,
your word, free, pure, and entire, might bring succour; but
yet also the word itself being corruptible, because it was from
one and the same substance. So that should they affirm you,
whatever you are, that is, your substance by which you are,
to be incorruptible, then were all these assertions false and
execrable; but if corruptible, then that were false, and at the
first utterance to be abhorred." This argument, then, was
enough against those who wholly merited to be vomited forth
from the surfeited stomach, since they had no means of escape without horrible sacrilege, both of heart and tongue,
thinking and speaking such things of you.

CHAP. 3—*That the cause of evil is the free judgment of the will.*

4. But I also, as yet, although I said and was firmly persuaded, that you our Lord, the true God, who made not only

our souls but our bodies, and not our souls and bodies alone, but all creatures and all things, were uncontaminable and inconvertible, and in no part mutable; yet I understood not readily and clearly what was the cause of evil. And yet, whatever it was, I perceived that it must be so sought out as not to constrain me by it to believe that the immutable God was mutable, lest I myself should become the thing that I was seeking out. I sought, therefore, for it free from care, certain of the untruthfulness of what these asserted, whom I shunned with my whole heart; for I perceived that through seeking after the origin of evil, they were filled with malice, in that they liked better to think that your substance did suffer evil than that their own did commit it.

5. And I directed my attention to discern what I now heard, that free will was the cause of our doing evil, and your righteous judgment of our suffering it. But I was unable clearly to discern it. So, then, trying to draw the eye of my mind from that pit, I was plunged again therein, and trying often, was as often plunged back again. But this raised me towards your light, that I knew as well that I had a will as that I had life: when, therefore, I was willing or unwilling to do anything, I was most certain that it was none but myself that was willing and unwilling; and immediately I perceived that there was the cause of my sin. But what I did against my will I saw that I suffered rather than did, and that I judged not to be my fault, but my punishment; whereby, believing you to be most just, I quickly confessed myself to be not unjustly punished. But again I said: "Who made me? Was it not my God, who is not only good, but goodness itself? Whence came I then to will to do evil, and to be unwilling to do good, that there might be cause for my just punishment? Who was it that put this in me, and implanted in me the root of bitterness, seeing I was altogether made by my most sweet God? If the devil were the author, whence is that devil? And if he also, by his own perverse will, of a good angel became a devil, whence also was the evil will in him whereby he became a devil, seeing that the angel was made altogether good by that most good creator?" By these reflections I was again cast down and stifled; yet not plunged into that hell of

error (where no man confesses to you),[1] to think that you suffer evil, rather than that man does it.

CHAP. 4—*That God is not corruptible, who, if he were, would not be God at all.*

6. For I was so struggling to find out the rest, as having already found that what was incorruptible must be better than the corruptible; and you, therefore, whatever you were, I acknowledged to be incorruptible. For there never yet was, nor will be, a soul able to conceive of anything better than you, who are the highest and best good. But whereas most truly and certainly that which is incorruptible is to be preferred to the corruptible (like as I myself did now prefer it), then, if you were not incorruptible, I could in my thoughts have reached to something better than my God. Where, then, I saw that the incorruptible was to be preferred to the corruptible, there ought I to seek you, and there observe "whence evil itself was," that is, whence comes the corruption by which your substance can by no means be profaned. For corruption, truly, in no way injures our God,—by no will, by no necessity, by no unforeseen chance,—because he is God, and what he wills is good, and himself is that good; but to be corrupted is not good. Nor are you compelled to do anything against your will in that your will is not greater than your power. But greater should it be if you yourself were greater than yourself; for the will and power of God is God himself. And what can be unforeseen by you, who knows all things? Nor is there any sort of nature but you know it. And what more should we say "why that substance which God is should not be corruptible," seeing that if it were so it could not be God?

CHAP. 5—*Questions concerning the origin of evil in regard to God, who, since he is the chief good, cannot be the cause of evil.*

7. And I sought "whence is evil?" And sought in an evil way; nor did I see the evil in my very search. And I set in order before the view of my spirit the whole creation, and whatever we can discern in it, such as earth, sea, air, stars, trees, living creatures; and whatever in it we do not see, as the

[1] Ps. 6: 5.

firmament of heaven, all the angels, too, and all the spiritual
inhabitants thereof. But these very beings, as though they
were bodies, my fancy disposed in such and such places, and
I made one huge mass of all your creatures, distinguished
according to the kinds of bodies,—some of them being real
bodies, some what I myself had feigned for spirits. And this
mass I made huge,—not as it was, which I could not know,
but as large as I thought proper, yet every way finite. But
you, O Lord, I imagined on every part environing and penetrating it, though every way infinite; as if there were a sea
everywhere, and on every side through immensity nothing
but an infinite sea; and it contained within itself some sponge,
huge, though finite, so that the sponge would in all its parts
be filled from the immeasurable sea. So I conceived your
creation to be itself finite, and filled by you, the infinite. And
I said, behold God, and behold what God has created; and
God is good, most mightily and incomparably better than all
these; but yet he, who is good, has created them good, and
behold how he encircles and fills them. Where, then, is evil,
and whence, and how crept it in hither? What is its root, and
what its seed? Or has it no being at all? Why, then, do we
fear and shun that which has no being? Or if we fear it need-
lessly, then surely is that fear evil whereby the heart is un-
necessarily pricked and tormented,—and so much a greater
evil, as we have naught to fear, and yet do fear. Therefore
either that is evil which we fear, or the act of fearing is in
itself evil. Whence, therefore, is it, seeing that God, who is
good, has made all these things good? He, indeed, the greatest
and chiefest good, has created these lesser goods; but both
creator and created are all good. Whence is evil? Or was there
some evil matter of which he made and formed and ordered
it, but left something in it which he did not convert into good?
But why was this? Was he powerless to change the whole
lump, so that no evil should remain in it, seeing that he is
omnipotent? Lastly, why would he make anything at all of it,
and not rather by the same omnipotence cause it not to be
at all? Or could it indeed exist contrary to his will? Or if it
were from eternity, why did he permit it so to be for infinite
spaces of times in the past, and was pleased so long after to
make something out of it? Or if he wished now all of a sudden

to do something, this rather should the omnipotent have ac-complished, that this evil matter should not be at all, and that he only should be the whole, true, chief, and infinite good. Or if it were not good that he, who was good, should not also be the framer and creator of what was good, then that matter which was evil being removed, and brought to noth-ing, he might form good matter, from which he might create all things. For he would not be omnipotent if he were not able to create something good without being assisted by that matter which had not been created by himself. Such like things I revolved in my miserable breast, overwhelmed with most gnawing cares lest I should die before I discovered the truth; yet was the faith of your Christ, our Lord and saviour, as held in the Catholic Church, fixed firmly in my heart, un-formed, indeed, as yet upon many points, and diverging from doctrinal rules, but yet my mind did not utterly leave it, but every day rather drank in more and more of it.

CHAP. 6—*He refutes the divinations of the astrologers, deduced from the constellations.*

8. Now also had I repudiated the lying divinations and im-pious absurdities of the astrologers. Let your mercies, out of the depth of my soul, confess unto you[2] for this also, O my God. For you, you altogether,—for who else is it that calls us back from the death of all errors, but that life which does not know how to die, and the wisdom which, requiring no light, enlightens the minds that do, whereby the universe is governed, even to the fluttering leaves of trees?—you pro-vided also for my obstinacy with which I struggled with Vindicianus, an acute old man, and Nebridius, a young one of remarkable talent; the former vehemently declaring, and the latter frequently, though with a certain measure of doubt, saying, "That no art existed by which to foresee future things, but that men's surmises had oftentimes the help of luck, and that of many things which they fore-told some came to pass unawares to the predicters, who chanced on it by speaking often." You, therefore, did pro-vide a friend for me, who was no negligent consulter of the astrologers, and yet not thoroughly skilled in those arts, but,

[2] Ps. 108: 8.

as I said, a curious consulter with them; and yet knowing
something, which he said he had heard from his father, which,
how far it would tend to overthrow the estimation of that art,
he did not know. This man, then, by name Firminius, having
received a liberal education, and being well versed in rhetoric, consulted me, as one very dear to him, as to what I
thought on some affairs of his, where his worldly hopes had
risen, viewed with regard to his so-called constellations; and
I, who had now begun to lean in this particular towards
Nebridius' opinion, did not indeed decline to speculate about
the matter, and to tell him what came into my irresolute mind,
but still added that I was now almost persuaded that these
were but empty and ridiculous follies. At this he told me that
his father had been very curious in such books, and that he
had a friend who was as interested in them as he was himself, who, with combined study and consultation, fanned the
flame of their affection for these toys, to the extent that they
would observe the moment when the very dumb animals
which bred in their houses brought forth, and then observed
the position of the heavens with regard to them, so as to
gather fresh proofs of this so-called art. He said, moreover,
that his father had told him, that at the time his mother was
about to give birth to him (Firminius), a female servant of
that friend of his father's was also pregnant, which could not
be hidden from her master, who took care with most diligent
exactness to know of the birth of his very dogs. And so it came
to pass that (the one for his wife, and the other for his servant,
with the most careful observation, calculating the days and
hours, and the smaller divisions of the hours) both were delivered at the same moment, so that both were compelled to
allow the very selfsame constellations, even to the minutest
point, the one for his son, the other for his young slave. For
so soon as the women began to be in travail, they each gave
notice to the other of what was fallen out in their respective
houses, and had messengers ready to despatch to one another
as soon as they had information of the actual birth, of which
they had easily provided, each in his own province, to give
instant news. Thus, then, he said, the messengers of the respective parties met one another in such equal distances from
either house, that neither of them could discern any difference

either in the position of the stars or other most minute points. And yet Firminius, born in a high estate in his parents' house, ran his course through the prosperous paths of this world, was increased in wealth, and elevated to honours; whereas that slave—the yoke of his condition being unrelaxed—continued to serve his masters, as Firminius, who knew him, informed me.

9. On hearing and believing these things, related by so reliable a person, all my resistance melted away; and first I endeavoured to reclaim Firminius himself from that curiosity, by telling him, that upon inspecting his constellations, I ought, if I were to foretell truly, to have seen in them parents eminent among their neighbours, a noble family in its own city, good birth, becoming education, and liberal learning. But if that servant had consulted me upon the same constellations, since they were his also, I ought again to tell him, likewise truly, to see in them the meanness of his origin, the abjectness of his condition, and everything else altogether removed from and at variance with the former. Therefore, then, looking upon the same constellations, I should, if I spoke the truth, speak diverse things, or if I spoke the same, speak falsely; thence assuredly it was to be gathered, that whatever, upon consideration of the constellations, was foretold truly, was not by art, but by chance; and whatever falsely, was not from the unskilfulness of the art, but the error of chance.

10. An opening being thus made, I ruminated within myself on such things, that no one of those dotards (who followed such occupations, and whom I longed to assail, and with derision to confute) might urge against me that Firminius had informed me falsely, or his father him: I turned my thoughts to those that are born twins, who generally come out of the womb so near one to another, that the small distance of time between them however much influence they may contend that it has in the nature of things—cannot be noted by human observation, or be expressed in those figures which the astrologer is to examine that he may pronounce the truth. Nor can they be true; for, looking into the same figures, he must have foretold the same of Esau and Jacob, whereas the same did not happen to them. He must therefore speak falsely; or if truly, then, looking into the same

figures, he must not speak the same things. Not then by art, but by chance, would he speak truly. For you, O Lord, most righteous ruler of the universe, the inquirers and inquired of knowing it not, work by a hidden inspiration that the consulter should hear what, according to the hidden deservings of souls, he ought to hear, out of the depth of your righteous judgment, to whom let man not say, "What is this?" or "Why that?" Let him not say so, for he is man.

CHAP. 7—*He is severely exercised as to the origin of evil.*

11. And now, O my helper, you had freed me from those fetters; and I inquired, "Whence is evil?" and found no result. But you did not allow me to be carried away from the faith by any fluctuations of thought, whereby I believed you both to exist, and your substance to be unchangeable, and that you had a care of and would judge men; and that in Christ, your Son, our Lord, and the Holy Scriptures, which the authority of your Catholic Church pressed upon me, you had planned the way of man's salvation to that life which is to come after this death. These things being safe and immoveably settled in my mind, I eagerly inquired, "Whence is evil?" What torments did my travailing heart then endure! What sighs, O my God! Yet even there were your ears open, and I did not know; and when in stillness I sought earnestly, those silent contritions of my soul were strong cries unto your mercy. No man knows, but only you, what I endured. For what was that which was poured through my tongue into the ears of my most familiar friends? Did the whole tumult of my soul, for which neither time nor speech was sufficient, reach them? Yet the whole went into your ears, all of which I bellowed out from the sighings of my heart; and my desire was before you, and the light of my eyes was not with me;[3] for that was within, I without. Nor was that in place, but my attention was directed to things contained in place; but there I found no resting-place, nor did they receive me in such a way as that I could say, "It is sufficient, it is well;" nor did they let me turn back, where it might be well enough with me. For to these things was I superior, but inferior to you;

[3] Ps. 37: 9–11.

and you are my true joy when I am subjected to you, and you had subjected to me what you created beneath me. And this was the true temperature and middle region of my safety, to continue in your image, and by serving you to have dominion over the body. But when I lifted myself proudly against you, and "ran against the Lord, even on his neck, with the thick bosses" of my buckler,[4] even these inferior things were placed above me, and pressed upon me, and nowhere was there alleviation or breathing space. They encountered my sight on every side in crowds and troops, and in thought the images of bodies obtruded themselves as I was returning to you, as if they would say unto me, "Whither do you go, unworthy and base one?" And these things had sprung forth out of my wound; for thou humble the proud like one that is wounded,[5] and through my own swelling was I separated from you; my too much swollen face closed up mine eyes.

CHAP. 8—*By God's assistance he by degrees arrives at the truth.*

12. "But you, O Lord, shall endure for ever,"[6] yet not for ever are you angry with us, because you commiserate our dust and ashes; and it was pleasing in your sight to reform my deformity, and by inward stings did you disturb me, that I should be dissatisfied until you were made sure to my inward sight. And by the secret hand of your remedy my swelling was lessened, and the disordered and darkened eyesight of my mind, by the sharp anointings of healthful sorrows, was from day to day made whole.

CHAP. 9—*He compares the doctrine of the Platonists concerning the Logos with the much more excellent doctrine of Christianity.*

13. And you, willing first to show me how you "resist the proud, but give grace to the humble,"[7] and by how great an act of mercy you had pointed out to men the path of humility, in that your "Word was made flesh" and dwelt among men,—you procured for me, by the instrumentality of one inflated with most monstrous pride, certain books of the Pla-

4 Job 15: 26.
5 Ps. 89: 11.
6 Ps. 102: 12.
7 Jas. 4: 6, and 1 Pet. 5: 5.

tonists, translated from Greek into Latin.[8] And therein I read,
not indeed in the same words, but to the selfsame effect, en-
forced by many and various reasons, that, "In the beginning
was the Word, and the Word was with God, and the Word
was God. The same was in the beginning with God. All things
were made by him; and without him was not made any thing
that was made." That which was made by him is "life; and
the life was the light of men. And the light shines in darkness;
and the darkness does not comprehend it."[9] And that the soul
of man, though it "bears witness to the light,"[10] yet itself "is
not that light; but the Word of God, being God, is that true
light that enlightens every man that comes into the world."[11]
And that "He was in the world, and the world was made
by him, and the world knew him not."[12] But that "He came
to his own, and his own received him not.[13] But as many as
received him, to them gave he power to become the sons of
God, to them that believe in his name."[14] This I did not read
there.

14. In like manner, I read there that God the Word was
born not of flesh, nor of blood, nor of the will of man, nor of
the will of the flesh, but of God. But that "the Word was
made flesh, and dwelt among us,"[15] I did not read there. For
I discovered in those books that it was in many and various
ways said, that the Son was in the form of the Father, and
"thought it not robbery to be equal with God," because naturally he was the same substance. But that he emptied himself, "and took upon him the form of a servant, and was made
in the likeness of men: and being found in fashion as a man,
he humbled himself, and became obedient to death, even the
death of the cross. Therefore God also has highly exalted

[8] Plotinus (A.D. 205–270) and Porphyry (232–305), who revived at Rome the philosophy of Plato (429–347 B.C.) of Athens.
Cf. J. O'Meara, *The Young Augustine* (New York, 1965), pp. 131–
55; P. Brown, *Augustine of Hippo* (London, 1967), pp. 88–100.
   [9] John 1: 1–5.
   [10] Ibid. 1: 7 f.
   [11] Ibid. 1: 9.
   [12] Ibid. 1: 10.
   [13] Ibid. 1: 11.
   [14] Ibid. 1: 12.
   [15] Ibid. 1: 14.

him" from the dead, "and given him a name above every
name; that at the name of Jesus every knee should bow, of
things in heaven, and things in earth, and things under the
earth; and that every tongue should confess that Jesus Christ
is Lord, to the glory of God the Father;"[16] those books have
not. For that before all times, and above all times, your only-
begotten Son remains unchangeably co-eternal with you; and
that of "his fulness" souls receive,[17] that they may be
blessed; and that by participation of the wisdom remaining
in them they are renewed, that they may be wise, is there.
But that "in due time Christ died for the ungodly,"[18] and
that you did not spare your only Son, but delivered him up
for us all,[19] is not there. "Because you have hidden these
things from the wise and prudent, and revealed them to
babes;"[20] that they "that labour and are heavy laden" might
"come" unto him and he might refresh them,[21] because he
is "meek and lowly in heart."[22] "The meek will he guide
in judgment; and the meek will he teach his way;"[23] looking
upon our humility and our distress, and forgiving all our
sins.[24] But such as are puffed up with the elation of would-be
sublimer learning, do not hear him saying, "Learn of me; for
I am meek and lowly in heart: and you shall find rest to your
souls."[25] "Because that, when they knew God, they glorified him not as God, neither were thankful; but became vain
in their imaginations, and their foolish heart was darkened.
Professing themselves to be wise, they became fools."[26]

15. And therefore also did I read there, that they had
changed the glory of your incorruptible nature into idols
and divers forms,—"into an image made like to corruptible
man, and to birds, and four-footed beasts, and creeping

[16] Phil. 2: 6–11.
[17] John 1: 16.
[18] Rom. 5: 6.
[19] Rom. 8: 32.
[20] Matt. 11: 25.
[21] Ibid. 11: 28.
[22] Ibid. 11: 29.
[23] Ps. 25: 9.
[24] Ibid. 25: 18.
[25] Matt. 11: 29.
[26] Rom. 1: 21 f.

things,"[27] namely, into that Egyptian food for which Esau lost his birthright;[28] for that your first-born people worshipped the head of a four-footed beast instead of you, turning back in heart towards Egypt, and prostrating your image—their own soul—before the image "of an ox that eats grass."[29] These things I found there; but I fed not on them. For it pleased you, O Lord, to take away the reproach of diminution from Jacob, that the elder should serve the younger;[30] and you have called the Gentiles into your inheritance. And I had come to you from among the Gentiles, and I strained after that gold which you willed your people to take from Egypt, seeing that wherever it was it was yours. And to the Athenians you said by your apostle, that in you "we live, and move, and have our being;" as one of their own has said.[31] And verily these books came from thence. But I set not my mind on the idols of Egypt, whom they ministered to with your gold,[32] "who changed the truth of God into a lie, and worshipped and served the creature more than the Creator."[33]

CHAP. 10—*Divine things are the more clearly manifested to him who withdraws into the recesses of his heart.*

16. And being thence warned to return to myself, I entered[34] into my inward self, you leading me on; and I was able to do it, for you were become my helper. And I entered, and with the eye of my soul (such as it was) saw above the same eye of my soul, above my mind, the unchangeable light. Not this common light, which all flesh may look upon, nor, as it were, a greater one of the same kind, as though the brightness of this should be much more resplendent, and with

[27] Rom. 1: 23.
[28] Gen. 25: 33 f.
[29] Ps. 106: 20; Ex. 32: 1–6.
[30] Rom. 9: 12.
[31] Acts 17: 28. Cf. Plotinus, *Enn.* 6.9.9.7–11 and Aratus, *Phaenomena* 5. The author is Stoic, possibly Cleanthes.
[32] Hos. 2: 8.
[33] Rom. 1: 25.
[34] Here, and in chs. 17.23 and 20.26, Augustine recounts experiences expressed in Plotinian terms; cf. J. O'Meara, *The Young Augustine,* pp. 138–42.

its greatness fill up all things. Not like this was that light, but different, very different from all these. Nor was it above my mind as oil is above water, nor as heaven above earth; but above it was, because it made me, and I below it, because I was made by it. He who knows the truth knows that light; and he that knows it knows eternity. Love knows it. O eternal truth, and true love, and loved eternity! You are my God; to you do I sigh both night and day. When I first knew you, you lifted me up, that I might see there was that which I might see, and that yet it was not I that did see. And you beat back the infirmity of my sight, pouring forth upon me most strongly your beams of light, and I trembled with love and fear; and I found myself to be far off from you, in the region of dissimilarity, as if I heard this voice of yours from on high: "I am the food of strong men; grow, and you shall feed upon me; nor shall you convert me, like the food of your flesh, into you, but you shall be converted into me." And I learned that you for iniquity correct man, and you make my soul to perish like a spider's web.[35] And I said, "Is truth, therefore, nothing because it is neither diffused through space, finite, nor infinite?" And you cried to me from afar, "Truly, 'I AM WHO I AM.'"[36] And I heard this, as things are heard in the heart, nor was there room for doubt; and I should more readily doubt that I live than that truth is not, which is "clearly seen, being understood by the things that are made."[37]

CHAP. 11—*That creatures are mutable and God alone immutable.*

17. And I viewed the other things below you, and perceived that they neither altogether are, nor altogether are not. They are, indeed, because they are from you; but are not, because they are not what you are. For that truly is which remains immutably. It is good, then, for me to cleave unto God,[38] for if I remain not in him, neither shall I in myself; but he, remaining in himself, renews all things.[39] And you

[35] Ps. 39: 16.
[36] Ex. 3: 14.
[37] Rom. 1: 20.
[38] Ps. 73: 28.
[39] Wis. 7: 27.

are the Lord my God, since you stand not in need of my goodness.[40]

CHAP. 12—*Whatever things the good God has created are very good.*

18. And it was made clear to me that those things are good which yet are corrupted, which, could not be corrupted, if they were supremely good, or unless they were good; because if supremely good, they were incorruptible, and if not good at all, there were nothing in them to be corrupted. For corruption harms, but, unless it could diminish goodness, it could not harm. Either, then, corruption does not harm, which cannot be; or, what is most certain, all which is corrupted is deprived of good. But if they be deprived of all good, they will cease to be. For if they be, and cannot be at all corrupted, they will become better, because they shall remain incorruptibly. And what more monstrous than to assert that those things which have lost all their goodness are made better? Therefore, if they shall be deprived of all good, they shall no longer be. So long, therefore, as they are, they are good; therefore whatsoever is, is good. That evil, then, which I sought whence it was, is not any substance; for if it were a substance, it would be good. For either it would be an incorruptible substance, and so a chief good, or a corruptible substance, which unless it were good it could not be corrupted. I perceived, therefore, and it was made clear to me, that you did make all things good, nor is there any substance at all that was not made by you; and because all that you made are not equal, therefore all things are; because individually they are good, and altogether very good, because our God made all things very good.[41]

CHAP. 13—*It is right to praise the creator for the good things which are made in heaven and earth.*

19. And to you there is nothing at all evil, and not only to you, but to your whole creation; because there is nothing outside which can break in, and mar that order which you appointed it. But in its parts, some things, because they do not harmonize with others, are considered evil; whereas those

[40] Ps. 16: 2.
[41] Gen. 1: 31, and Sir. 39: 21.

very things harmonize with others, and are good, and in themselves are good. And all these things which do not harmonize together harmonize with the inferior part which we call earth, having its own cloudy and windy sky proper to it. Far be it from me, then, to say, "These things should not be." For should I see nothing but these, I should indeed desire better; but yet, if only for these, ought I to praise you; for that you are to be praised is shown from the "earth, dragons, and all deeps; fire, and hail; snow, and vapours; stormy winds fulfilling your word; mountains, and all hills; fruitful trees, and all cedars; beasts, and all cattle; creeping things, and flying fowl; kings of the earth, and all people; princes, and all judges of the earth; both young men and maidens; old men and children," praise your name. But when, "from the heavens," these praise you, praise you, our God, "in the heights," all your "angels," all your "hosts," "sun and moon," all you stars and light, "the heavens of heavens," and the "waters that are above the heavens," praise your name.[42] I did not now desire better things, because I was thinking of all; and with a better judgment I reflected that the things above were better than those below, but that all were better than those above alone.

CHAP. 14—*Being displeased with some part of God's creation, he conceives of two original substances.*

20. There is no wholeness in them whom any part of your creation displeases; no more than there was in me, when many things which you made displeased me. And, because my soul dared not be displeased at my God, it would not suffer anything to be yours which displeased it. Hence it had gone into the opinion of two substances, and resisted not, but talked foolishly. And, returning thence, it had made to itself a god, through infinite measures of all space; and imagined it to be you, and placed it in its heart, and again had become the temple of its own idol, which was to you an abomination. But after you had calmed my head, unconscious, and closed my eyes lest they should "behold vanity,"[43] I ceased from myself a little, and my madness was lulled to sleep; and I

[42] Ps. 148: 1–12.
[43] Ps. 119: 37.

awoke in you, and saw you to be infinite, though in another way; and this sight was not derived from the flesh.

CHAP. 15—*Whatever is, owes its being to God.*

21. And I looked back on other things, and I perceived that it was to you they owed their being, and that they were all bounded in you; but in another way, not as being in space, but because you hold all things in your hand in truth: and all things are true so far as they have a being; nor is there any falsehood, unless that which is not is thought to be. And I saw that all things harmonized, not with their places only, but with their seasons also. And that you, who alone are eternal, did not begin to work after innumerable spaces of times; for all spaces of times, both those which have passed and which shall pass, neither go nor come, save through you, working and abiding.

CHAP. 16—*Evil arises not from a substance, but from the perversion of the will.*

22. And I discerned and found it no marvel, that bread which is distasteful to an unhealthy palate is pleasant to a healthy one; and that the light, which is painful to sore eyes, is delightful to sound ones. And your righteousness displeases the wicked; much more do the viper and little worm, which you created good, fitting in with inferior parts of your creation; with which the wicked themselves also fit in, the more in proportion as they are unlike you, but with the superior creatures, in proportion as they become like to you. And I inquired what iniquity was, and ascertained it not to be a substance, but a perversion of the will, bent aside from you, O God, the supreme substance, towards these lower things, and casting out its inner goods,[44] and swelling outwardly.

CHAP. 17—*Above his changeable mind, he discovers the unchangeable author of truth.*

23. And I marvelled that I now loved you, and no phantasm instead of you. And yet I did not merit to enjoy my God, but was transported to you by your beauty, and presently torn away from you by my own weight, sinking with grief

[44] Sir. 10: 9.

into these inferior things. This weight was carnal custom. Yet
there was a remembrance of you with me; nor did I any way
doubt that there was one to whom I might cleave, but that I
was not yet one who could cleave unto you; for the body
which is corrupted presses down the soul, and the earthly
dwelling weighs down the mind which thinks upon many
things.[45] And most certain I was that your "invisible things
from the creation of the world are clearly seen, being understood by the things that are made, even your eternal power
and Godhead."[46] For, inquiring whence it was that I admired
the beauty of bodies whether celestial or terrestrial, and what
supported me in judging correctly on things mutable, and pronouncing, "This should be thus, this not,"—inquiring, then,
whence I so judged, seeing I did so judge, I had found the
unchangeable and true eternity of truth, above my changeable mind. And thus, by degrees, I passed from bodies to the
soul, which makes use of the senses of the body to perceive;
and thence to its inward faculty, to which the bodily senses
represent outward things, and up to which reach the capa-
bilities of beasts; and thence, again, I passed on to the reasoning faculty, unto which whatever is received from the
senses of the body is referred to be judged, which also, finding itself to be variable in me, raised itself up to its own intelligence, and from habit drew away my thoughts, withdrawing
itself from the crowds of contradictory phantasms; that so it
might find out that light by which it was besprinkled, when,
without all doubting, it cried out, "that the unchangeable was
to be preferred before the changeable;" whence also it knew
that unchangeable, which, unless it had in some way known,
it could have had no sure ground for preferring it to the
changeable. And thus, with the flash of a trembling glance, it
arrived at that which is. And then I saw your invisible things
understood by the things that are made.[47] But I was not able
to fix my gaze on it; and my infirmity being beaten back, I
was thrown again on my accustomed habits, carrying along
with me nothing but a loving memory of it, and an appetite

[45] Wis. 9: 15.
[46] Rom. 1: 20.
[47] Ibid.

for what I had, as it were, smelled the odour of, but was not
yet able to eat.

CHAP. 18—*Jesus Christ, the mediator, is the only way of safety.*

24. And I sought a way of acquiring strength sufficient to
enjoy you; but I found it not until I embraced that "Mediator between God and man, the man Christ Jesus,"[48] "who is
over all, God blessed for ever,"[49] calling unto me, and saying, "I am the way, the truth, and the life,"[50] and mingling
that food which I was unable to receive with our flesh. For
"The Word was made flesh,"[51] that your wisdom, by which
you created all things, might provide milk for our infancy.
For I did not grasp my Lord Jesus,—I, though humbled,
grasped not the humble one; nor did I know what lesson that
infirmity of his would teach us. For your Word, the eternal
truth, pre-eminent above the higher parts of your creation,
raises up those that are subject unto itself; but in this lower
world built for itself a humble habitation of our clay, whereby
he intended to abase from themselves such as would be subjected and bring them over unto himself, allaying their swelling, and fostering their love; to the end that they might go on
no further in self-confidence, but rather should become weak,
seeing before their feet the divinity weak by taking our "coats
of skins;"[52] and wearied, might cast themselves down upon
it, and it rising, might lift them up.

CHAP. 19—*He does not yet fully understand the saying of John,
that "the Word was made flesh."*

25. But I thought differently, thinking only of my Lord
Christ as of a man of excellent wisdom, to whom no man
could be equalled; especially because, being wonderfully born
of a virgin, he seemed, through the divine care for us, to have
attained so great authority of leadership,—for an example of
contemning temporal things for the obtaining of immortality.
But what mystery there was in, "The Word was made flesh,"

[48] 1 Tim. 2: 5.
[49] Rom. 9: 5.
[50] John 14: 6.
[51] John 1: 14.
[52] Gen. 3: 21.

I could not even imagine. Only I had learned out of what is delivered to us in writing of him, that he did eat, drink, sleep, walk, rejoice in spirit, was sad, and discoursed; that flesh alone did not cleave to your Word, but with the human soul and body. All know thus who know the unchangeableness of your Word, which I now knew as well as I could, nor did I at all have any doubt about it. For, now to move the limbs of the body at will, now not; now to be stirred by some affection, now not; now by signs to enunciate wise sayings, now to keep silence, are properties of a soul and mind subject to change. And should these things be falsely written of him, all the rest would risk the imputation, nor would there remain in those books any saving faith for the human race. Since, then, they were written truthfully, I acknowledged a perfect man to be in Christ—not the body of a man only, nor with the body a sensitive soul without a rational, but a true man; whom, not only as being a form of truth, but for a certain great excellency of human nature and a more perfect participation of wisdom, I decided was to be preferred before others. But Alypius imagined the Catholics to believe that God was so clothed with flesh, that, besides God and flesh, there was no soul in Christ, and did not think that a human mind was ascribed to him. And, because he was thoroughly persuaded that the actions which were recorded of him could not be performed except by a vital and rational creature, he moved the more slowly towards the Christian faith. But, learning afterwards that this was the error of the Apollinarian heretics, he rejoiced in the Catholic faith, and was conformed to it. But somewhat later it was, I confess, that I learned how in the sentence, "The Word was made flesh," the Catholic truth can be distinguished from the falsehood of Photinus. For the disapproval of heretics makes the tenets of your church and sound doctrine to stand out boldly. For there must be also heresies, that the approved may be made manifest among the weak.[53]

CHAP. 20—*He rejoices that he proceeded from Plato to the Holy Scriptures, and not the reverse.*

26. But having then read those books of the Platonists, and

[53] 1 Cor. 11: 19.

being admonished by them to search for incorporeal truth, I
saw your invisible things, understood by those things that are
made;[54] and though repulsed, I perceived what that was,
which through the darkness of my mind I was not allowed
to contemplate,—assured that you were, and were infinite,
and yet not diffused in space finite or infinite; and that you
truly are, who are the same always, varying neither in part
nor motion; and that all other things are from you, on this
most sure ground alone, that they are. Of these things was I
indeed assured, yet too weak to enjoy you. I chattered as one
well skilled; but had I not sought your way in Christ our
saviour, I would have proved not skilful, but ready to perish.
For now, filled with my punishment, I had begun to desire to
seem wise; yet I did not mourn, but rather was puffed up with
knowledge.[55] For where was that charity building upon the
"foundation" of humility, "which is Jesus Christ"?[56] Or,
when would these books teach it to me? Upon these, therefore, I believe, it was your pleasure that I should fall before
I studied your Scriptures, that it might be impressed on my
memory how I was affected by them; and that afterwards
when I was subdued by your books, and when my wounds
were touched by your healing fingers, I might discern and
distinguish what a difference there is between presumption
and confession,—between those who saw whither they were to
go, yet saw not the way, and the way which leads not only
to behold but to inhabit the blessed country. For had I first
been moulded in your Holy Scriptures, and had you, in the
familiar use of them, grown sweet to me, and had I afterwards fallen upon those volumes, they might perhaps have
withdrawn me from the solid ground of piety; or, had I
stood firm in that wholesome disposition which I had thence
imbibed, I might have thought that it could have been attained by the study of those books alone.

Chap. 21—*What he found in the sacred books which are not to be
found in Plato.*

27. Most eagerly, then, did I seize that venerable writing

[54] Rom. 1: 20.
[55] 1 Cor. 8: 1.
[56] Ibid. 3: 11.

of your Spirit, but more especially the apostle Paul; and those difficulties vanished away, in which he at one time appeared to me to contradict himself, and the text of his discourse not to agree with the testimonies of the law and the prophets. And the face of that pure speech appeared to me one and the same; and I learned to "rejoice with trembling."[57] So I commenced, and found that whatever truth I had there read was declared here with the recommendation of your grace; that he who sees may not so glory as if he had not received[58] not only that which he sees, but also that he can see (for what has he which he has not received?); and that he may not only be admonished to see you, who are ever the same, but also may be healed, to hold you; and that he who from afar off is not able to see, may still walk on the way by which he may reach, behold, and possess you. For though a man "delight in the law of God after the inward man,"[59] what shall he do with that other law in his members which wars against the law of his mind, and brings him into captivity to the law of sin, which is in his members?[60] For you are righteous, O Lord, but we have sinned and committed iniquity, and have done wickedly,[61] and your hand is grown heavy upon us, and we are justly delivered over to that ancient sinner, the governor of death; for he induced our will to be like his will, whereby he remained not in your truth. What shall "wretched man" do? "Who shall deliver him from the body of this death," but your grace only, "through Jesus Christ our Lord,"[62] whom you have begotten co-eternal, and created[63] in the beginning of your ways, in whom the prince of this world found nothing worthy of death,[64] yet killed him, and the handwriting which was contrary to us was blotted out?[65] This those writings do not contain. Those pages do not contain the expression of this piety,—the tears of con-

[57] Ps. 2: 11.
[58] 1 Cor. 4: 7.
[59] Rom. 7: 22.
[60] Ibid. 7: 23.
[61] Dan. 3: 27 ff.
[62] Rom. 7: 24 f.
[63] Prov. 8: 22.
[64] John 18: 38.
[65] Col. 2: 14.

fession, your sacrifice, a troubled spirit, "a broken and a con-
trite heart,"[66] the salvation of the people, the espoused city,[67]
the earnest of the Holy Ghost,[68] the cup of our redemption.[69] No man sings there, shall not my soul be subject
unto God? For of him comes my salvation, for he is my God
and my salvation, my defender, I shall not be further
moved.[70] No one there hears him calling, "Come to me all
you that labour." They scorn to learn of him, because he is
meek and lowly of heart;[71] for "you have hid those things
from the wise and prudent, and revealed them to babes."[72]
For it is one thing, from the mountain's wooded summit to
see the land of peace,[73] and not to find the way thither,—
in vain to attempt impassable ways, opposed and waylaid by
fugitives and deserters, under their captain the "lion"[74] and
the "dragon;"[75] and another to keep to the way that leads
thither, guarded by the host of the heavenly general, where
they who have deserted the heavenly army, which they shun
as torture cannot plunder. These things did in a wonderful
manner sink into my bowels, when I read that "least of your
apostles,"[76] and had reflected upon your works, and feared
greatly.

BOOK 8

CHAP. 1—*He, now given to divine things, and yet entangled by the
lusts of love, consults Simplicianus in reference to the renewing
of his mind.*

1. O my God, let me with gratitude remember and confess
to you your mercies bestowed upon me. Let my bones be

[66] Ps. 51: 17.
[67] Rev. 21: 2.
[68] 2 Cor. 5: 5.
[69] Ps. 116: 13.
[70] Ps. 62: 1 f.
[71] Matt. 11: 28 f.
[72] Matt. 11: 25.
[73] Deut. 32: 49.
[74] 1 Pet. 5: 8.
[75] Rev. 12: 3.
[76] 1 Cor. 15: 9.

steeped in your love, and let them say, Who is like to you, O Lord?[1] "You have loosed my bonds, I will offer to you the sacrifice of thanksgiving."[2] And how you loosed them I will declare; and all who worship you when they hear these things shall say: "Blessed be the Lord in heaven and earth, great and wonderful is his name." Your words had stuck fast into my breast, and I was hedged round about by you on every side.[3] Of your eternal life I was now certain, although I had seen it "through a glass darkly."[4] Yet I no longer doubted that there was an incorruptible substance, from which was derived all other substance; nor did I now desire to be more certain of you, but more steadfast in you. As for my temporal life, all things were uncertain, and my heart had to be purged from the old leaven.[5] The "way,"[6] the Saviour himself, was pleasant to me, but as yet I disliked to pass through its straightness. And you put into my mind, and it seemed good in my eyes, to go to Simplicianus,[7] who appeared to me a faithful servant of yours, and your grace shone in him. I had also heard that from his very youth he had lived most devoted to you. Now he had grown in years, and by reason of so great age, passed in such zealous following of your ways, he appeared to me likely to have gained much experience; and so in truth he had. Out of which experience I desired him to tell me (setting before him my griefs) which would be the most fitting way for one afflicted as I was to walk in your way.

2. For the church I saw to be full, and one went this way, and another that. But it was displeasing to me that I led a secular life; now that my passions had ceased to excite me as of old with hopes of honour and wealth, a very grievous burden it was to undergo so great a servitude. For, compared with your sweetness, and the beauty of your house, which I loved,[8] those things delighted me no longer. But still very

[1] Ps. 35: 10.
[2] Ps. 116: 16 f.
[3] Job 1: 10.
[4] 1 Cor. 13: 12.
[5] 1 Cor. 5: 7.
[6] John 14: 6.
[7] Spiritual father and later successor to St. Ambrose in Milan.
[8] Ps. 26: 8.

tenaciously was I held by the love of women; nor did the
apostle forbid me to marry, although he exhorted me to something better, especially wishing that all men were as he himself was.[9] But I, being weak, made choice of the more agreeable place, and because of this alone was tossed up and down
in all other matters, faint and languishing with withering
cares, because in other matters I was compelled, though unwilling, to agree to a married life, to which I was given up
and enthralled. I had heard from the mouth of truth that
"there are eunuchs, which have made themselves eunuchs
for the kingdom of heaven's sake;" but, says he, "he that
is able to receive it, let him receive it."[10] Vain, assuredly,
are all men in whom the knowledge of God is not, and who
could not, out of the good things which are seen, find out
him who is good.[11] But I was no longer in that vanity; I had
surmounted it, and by the united testimony of your whole
creation had found you, our creator, and your Word, God
with you, and together with you and the Holy Ghost one
God, by whom you created all things. There is yet another
kind of impious men, who "when they knew God, they glorified him not as God, neither were thankful."[12] Into this also
had I fallen; but your right hand held me up,[13] and bore
me away, and you placed me where I might recover. For
you said to man, "Behold, the fear of the Lord, that is wisdom;"[14] and desire not to seem wise,[15] because, "Professing
themselves to be wise, they became fools."[16] But I had now
found the goodly pearl, which, selling all that I had,[17] I ought
to have bought; and I hesitated.

CHAP. 2—*The pious old man rejoices that he read Plato and the
Scriptures, and tells him of the rhetorician Victorinus having
been converted to the faith through the reading of the sacred
books.*

9 1 Cor. 7: 7.
10 Matt. 19: 12.
11 Wis. 13: 1.
12 Rom. 1: 21.
13 Ps. 18: 35.
14 Job 28: 28.
15 Prov. 3: 7.
16 Rom. 1: 22.
17 Matt. 13: 46.

3. To Simplicianus then I went,—the father of Ambrose (at that time a bishop) in receiving your grace, and whom he truly loved as a father. To him I narrated the windings of my error. But when I mentioned to him that I had read certain books of the Platonists, which Victorinus, sometime professor of rhetoric at Rome (who died a Christian, as I had been told), had translated into Latin, he congratulated me that I had not fallen upon the writings of other philosophers, which were full of fallacies and deceit, "after the rudiments of the world,"[18] whereas they, in many ways, led to the belief in God and his word. Then, to exhort me to the humility of Christ, hidden from the wise, and revealed to little ones,[19] he spoke of Victorinus himself,[20] whom, whilst he was at Rome, he had known very intimately; and of him he related that about which I will not be silent. For it contains great praise of your grace, which ought to be confessed to you, how that most learned old man, highly skilled in all the liberal sciences, who had read, criticised, and explained so many works of the philosophers; the teacher of so many noble senators; who also, as a mark of his excellent discharge of his duties, had (which men of this world esteem a great honour) both merited and obtained a statue in the Roman Forum, he,—even to that age a worshipper of idols, and a participator in the sacrilegious rites to which almost all the nobility of Rome were wedded, and had inspired the people with the love of

The dog Anubis, and a medley crew
Of monster gods [who] 'gainst Neptune stand in arms,
'Gainst Venus and Minerva, steel-clad Mars,[21]

whom Rome once conquered, now worshipped, all which old Victorinus had with thundering eloquence defended so many years,—he now blushed not to be the child of your Christ, and an infant at your fountain, submitting his neck to the yoke

18 Col. 2: 8.
19 Matt. 11: 25.
20 An African who formerly taught rhetoric at Rome.
21 Vergil, *Aen.* 8.736–8.

of humility, and subduing his forehead to the reproach of the cross.

4. O Lord, Lord, who has bowed the heavens and come down, touched the mountains and they did smoke,[22] by what means did you convey yourself into that bosom? He used to read, as Simplicianus said, the Holy Scripture, most studiously sought after and searched into all the Christian writings, and said to Simplicianus,—not openly, but secretly, and as a friend, —"Know thou that I am a Christian." To which he replied, "I will not believe it, nor will I rank you among the Christians unless I see you in the church of Christ." Thereupon he replied derisively, "Is it then the walls that make Christians?" And this he often said, that he already was a Christian; and Simplicianus making the same answer, the conceit of the "walls" was by the other as often renewed. For he was fearful of offending his friends, proud demon-worshippers, from the height of whose Babylonian dignity, as from cedars of Lebanon which had not yet been broken by the Lord,[23] he thought a storm of enmity would descend upon him. But after, from reading and inquiry, he had derived strength, and feared lest he should be denied by Christ before the holy angels if he now was afraid to confess him before men,[24] and appeared to himself guilty of a great fault in being ashamed of the sacraments of the humility of your word, and not being ashamed of the sacrilegious rites of those proud demons, whose pride he had imitated and their rites adopted, he became bold-faced against vanity, and shame-faced toward the truth, and suddenly and unexpectedly said to Simplicianus,— as he himself informed me,—"Let us go to the church; I wish to be made a Christian." But he, not containing himself for joy, accompanied him. And having been admitted to the first sacraments of instruction, he not long after gave in his name, that he might be regenerated by baptism,—Rome marvelling, and the church rejoicing. The proud saw, and were enraged; they gnashed with their teeth, and melted away![25] But the

[22] Ps. 144: 5.
[23] Ps. 29: 5.
[24] Luke 9: 26.
[25] Ps. 112: 10.

Lord God was the hope of your servant, and he regarded not vanities and lying madness.[26]

5. Finally, when the hour arrived for him to make profession of his faith (which at Rome they who are about to approach your grace are wont to deliver from an elevated place, in view of the faithful people, in a set form of words learned by heart), the priests, he said, offered Victorinus to make his profession more privately, as the custom was to do to those who were likely, through bashfulness, to be afraid; but he chose rather to profess his salvation in the presence of the holy assembly. For it was not salvation that he taught in rhetoric, and yet he had publicly professed that. How much less, therefore, ought he, when pronouncing your word, to dread your meek flock, who, in the delivery of his own words, had not feared the mad multitudes! So, then, when he ascended to make his profession, all, as they recognised him, whispered his name one to the other, with a voice of congratulation. And who was there amongst them that did not know him? And there ran a low murmur through the mouths of all the rejoicing multitude, "Victorinus! Victorinus!" Sudden was the burst of exultation at the sight of him; and suddenly were they hushed, that they might hear him. He pronounced the true faith with an excellent boldness, and all desired to take him to their very heart—by their love and joy they took him thither; such were the hands with which they took him.

CHAP. 3—*That God and the angels rejoice more on the return of one sinner than of many just persons.*

6. Good God, what passed in man to make him rejoice more at the salvation of a soul despaired of, and delivered from greater danger, than if there had always been hope of him, or the danger had been less? For so you also, O merciful Father, do "joy over one sinner that repents, more than over ninety and nine just persons that need no repentance." And with much joyfulness do we hear, whenever we hear, how the lost sheep is brought home again on the shepherd's shoulders, while the angels rejoice, and the drachma is re-

[26] Ps. 31: 6, 14, 18.

stored to your treasury, the neighbours rejoicing with the woman who found it;[27] and the joy of the solemn service of your house constrains to tears, when in your house it is read of your younger son that he "was dead, and is alive again, and was lost, and is found."[28] For you rejoice both in us and in your angels, holy through holy charity. For you are ever the same; for all things which abide neither the same nor for ever, you always know after the same manner.

7. What, then, passes in the soul when it more delights at finding or having restored to it the thing it loves than if it had always possessed them? Other things bear witness to this; and all things are full of witnesses, crying out, "So it is." The victorious commander triumphs; yet he would not have conquered had he not fought, and the greater the peril of the battle, the more the rejoicing of the triumph. The storm tosses the voyagers, threatens shipwreck, and every one gets pale at the approach of death; but sky and sea grow calm, and they rejoice much, as they feared much. A loved one is sick, and his pulse indicates danger; all who desire his safety are at once sick at heart: he recovers, though not able as yet to walk with his former strength, and there is such joy as was not before when he walked sound and strong. The very pleasures of human life—not those only which rush upon us unexpectedly, and against our wills, but those that are voluntary and designed—do men obtain by difficulties. There is no pleasure at all in eating and drinking unless the pains of hunger and thirst go before. And drunkards eat certain salt meats with the view of creating a troublesome heat, which the drink allaying causes pleasure. It is also the custom that the affianced bride should not immediately be given up, that the husband may not less esteem her whom, as betrothed, he did not long for.

8. This law obtains in base and accursed joy; in that joy also which is permitted and lawful; in the sincerity of honest friendship; and in him who was dead, and lived again, had been lost, and was found.[29] The greater joy is everywhere preceded by the greater pain. What means this, O Lord my

[27] Luke 15: 4–10.
[28] Ibid. 15: 32.
[29] Ibid.

God, when you are an everlasting joy to your own self, and some things around you are ever rejoicing in you? What means this, that this portion of things thus ebbs and flows, alternately offended and reconciled? Is this the fashion of them, and is this all you have allotted to them, whereas from the highest heaven to the lowest earth, from the beginning of the world to its end, from the angel to the worm, from the first movement unto the last, you put each in its right place, and appointed each its proper seasons, everything good after its kind? Woe is me! How high are you in the highest, and how deep in the deepest! You withdraw nowhere, and scarcely do we *return* to you.

CHAP. 4—*He shows by the example of Victorinus that there is more joy in the conversion of nobles.*

9. Haste, Lord, and act; stir us up, and call us back; inflame us, and draw us to you; stir us up, and grow sweet to us; let us now love you, let us "run after you."[30] Do not many men, out of a deeper hell of blindness than that of Victorinus, return to you, and approach, and are enlightened, receiving that light, which they that receive, receive power from you to become your sons?[31] But if they are less known among the people, even they that know them joy less for them. For when many rejoice together, the joy of each one is the fuller, in that they are incited and inflamed by one another. Again, because those that are known to many influence many towards salvation, and take the lead with many to follow them. And, therefore, they also who preceded them much rejoice in regard to them, because they do not rejoice in them alone. May it be averted that in your tabernacle the persons of the rich should be accepted before the poor, or the noble before the ignoble; since rather "you have chosen the weak things of the world to confound the things which are mighty; and base things of the world, and things which are despised, have you chosen, and things which are not, to bring to naught things that are."[32] And yet, even that "least of the

[30] Cant. 1: 4.
[31] John 1: 12.
[32] 1 Cor. 1: 27 f.

apostles,"[33] by whose tongue you sound out these words,
when Sergius Paulus the proconsul[34]—his pride overcome by
the apostle's warfare—was made to pass under the easy
yoke[35] of your Christ, and became a provincial of the great
king,—he also, instead of Saul, his former name, desired to be
called Paul, in testimony of so great a victory. For the enemy
is more overcome in one of whom he has more hold, and by
whom he has hold of more. But he has more hold of the
proud by reason of their nobility; and by them of more,
by reason of their authority. By how much the more welcome, then, was the heart of Victorinus esteemed, which the
devil had held as an unassailable retreat, and the tongue of
Victorinus, with which mighty and cutting weapon he had
slain many; so much the more abundantly should your sons
rejoice, seeing that our king has bound the strong man,[36]
and they saw his vessels taken from him and cleansed,[37] and
made meet for your honour, and become serviceable for the
Lord to every good work.[38]

CHAP. 5—*Of the causes which alienate us from God.*

10. But when that man of yours, Simplicianus, related
this to me about Victorinus, I burned to imitate him; and
it was for this end he had related it. But when he had added
this also, that in the time of the Emperor Julian,[39] there was
a law made by which Christians were forbidden to teach
grammar and oratory, and he, in obedience to this law, chose
rather to abandon the wordy school than your word, by
which you make eloquent the tongues of the dumb,[40]—he
appeared to me not more brave than happy, in having thus
discovered an opportunity of waiting on you only, which
thing I was sighing for, thus bound, not with the irons of
another, but my own iron will. The enemy was master of my

[33] 1 Cor. 15: 9.
[34] Acts 13: 12.
[35] Matt. 11: 30.
[36] Matt. 12: 29.
[37] Luke 11: 22, 25.
[38] 2 Tim. 2: 21.
[39] Emperor of Rome, 361–363.
[40] Wis. 10: 21.

will, and thence had made a chain for me and bound me. Because of a perverse will was lust made; and lust indulged in became custom; and custom not resisted became necessity. By which links, as it were, joined together (whence I term it a "chain"), did a hard bondage hold me enthralled. But that new will which had begun to develop in me, freely to worship you, and to wish to enjoy you, O God, the only sure enjoyment, was not able as yet to overcome my former wilfulness, made strong by long indulgence. Thus did my two wills, one old and the other new, one carnal, the other spiritual, contend within me; and by their discord they unstrung my soul.

11. Thus I came to understand, from my own experience, what I had read, how "the flesh lusts against the Spirit, and the Spirit against the flesh."[41] I truly lusted both ways; yet more in that which I approved in myself, than in that which I disapproved in myself. For in this last it was now rather not "I,"[42] because in much I rather suffered against my will than did it willingly. And yet it was through me that custom became more combative against me, because I had come willingly whither I willed not. And who, then, can with any justice speak against it, when just punishment follows the sinner? Nor had I now any longer my usual excuse, that as yet I hesitated to be above the world and serve you, because my perception of the truth was uncertain; for now it was certain. But I, still bound to the earth, refused to be your soldier; and was as much afraid of being freed from all embarrassments, as we ought to fear to be embarrassed.

12. Thus with the baggage of the world was I sweetly burdened, as when in slumber; and the thoughts wherein I meditated upon you were like to the efforts of those desiring to awake, who, still overpowered with a heavy drowsiness, are again steeped therein. And as no one desires to sleep always, and, in the sober judgment of all, waking is better, yet does a man generally defer to shake off drowsiness, when there is a heavy lethargy in all his limbs, and, though displeased, yet, even after it is time to rise, with pleasure yields

41 Gal. 5: 17.
42 Rom. 7: 20.

to it, so was I assured that it were much better for me to give up myself to your charity, than to yield myself to my own cupidity; but the former course pleased and vanquished me, the latter indulged me and fettered me. Nor had I anything to answer you calling to me, "Awake, you that sleep, and arise from the dead, and Christ shall give you light."[43] And to you showing me on every side, that what you said was true, I, convicted by the truth, had nothing at all to reply, but the drawling and drowsy words: "Presently, lo, presently;" "Leave me a little while." But "presently, presently," had no present; and my "leave me a little while" went on for a long while. In vain did I "delight in your law after the inner man," when "another law in my members warred against the law of my mind, and brought me into captivity to the law of sin which is in my members." For the law of sin is the violence of custom, whereby the mind is drawn and held, even against its will; deserving to be so held in that it so willingly falls into it. "O wretched man that I am! who shall deliver me from the body of this death" but your grace only, through Jesus Christ our Lord?[44]

CHAP. 6—*Pontitianus' account of Antony, the founder of Mona-chism, and of some who imitated him.*

13. And how, then, you did deliver me out of the bonds of carnal desire, by which I was most firmly fettered, and out of the drudgery of worldly business, will I now declare and confess to your name, "O Lord, my strength and my re-deemer."[45] Amid increasing anxiety, I was transacting my usual affairs, and daily sighing to you. I resorted as fre-quently to your church as the business, under the burden of which I groaned, left me free to do. Alypius was with me, being after the third sitting disengaged from his legal occupation, and awaiting further opportunity of selling his counsel, as I was wont to sell the power of speaking, if it can be supplied by teaching. But Nebridius had, on account of our friendship, consented to teach under Verecundus, a citi-zen and a grammarian of Milan, and a very intimate friend

43 Eph. 5: 14.
44 Rom. 7: 22–24.
45 Ps. 19: 14.

of us all; who vehemently desired, and by the right of friendship demanded from our company, the faithful aid he greatly stood in need of. Nebridius, then, was not drawn to this by any desire of gain (for he could have made much more of his learning had he been so inclined), but, as a most sweet and kindly friend, he would not be wanting in an office of friendliness, and turn down our request. But in this he acted very discreetly, taking care not to become known to those personages whom the world esteems great; thus avoiding distraction of mind, which he desired to have free and at leisure as many hours as possible, to search, or read, or hear something concerning wisdom.

14. Upon a certain day, then, Nebridius being away (why, I do not remember), there came to the house to see Alypius and me, Pontitianus, a countryman of ours, in so far as he was an African, who held high office in the emperor's court. What he wanted with us I know not, but we sat down to talk together, and it happened that upon a table before us, used for games, he noticed a book; he took it up, opened it, and, contrary to his expectation, found it to be the apostle Paul,— for he imagined it to be one of those books which I was wearing myself out in teaching. At this he looked up at me smilingly, and expressed his delight and wonder that he had so unexpectedly found this book, and this only, before my eyes. For he was both a Christian and baptized, and often prostrated himself before you our God in the church, in constant and daily prayers. When, then, I had told him that I bestowed much pains upon these writings, a conversation ensued on his speaking of Antony,[46] the Egyptian monk, whose name was in high repute among your servants, though up to that time not familiar to us. When he came to know this, he lingered on that topic, imparting to us a knowledge of this man so eminent, and marvelling at our ignorance. But we were amazed, hearing your wonderful works most fully manifested in times so recent, and almost in our own, done in the true faith and the Catholic Church. We all wondered— we, that they were so great, and he, that we had never heard of them.

[46] St. Antony, father of monasticism, a famous biography of whom was written by Athanasius.

15. From this his conversation turned to the companies in the monasteries, and their manners so pleasing unto you, and of the fruitful deserts of the wilderness, of which we knew nothing. And there was a monastery at Milan full of good brethren, without the walls of the city, under the fostering care of Ambrose, and we were ignorant of it. He went on with his account, and we listened intently and in silence. He then related to us how on a certain afternoon, at Trier, when the emperor was taken up with seeing the Circensian games, he and three others, his comrades, went out for a walk in the gardens close to the city walls, and there, as they chanced to walk two and two, one strolled away with him, while the other two went by themselves; and these, in their rambling, came upon a certain cottage inhabited by some of your servants, "poor in spirit," of whom "is the kingdom of heaven,"[47] where they found a book in which was written the life of Antony. This one of them began to read, marvel at, and be inflamed by it; and in the reading, to meditate on embracing such a life, and giving up his worldly employments to serve you. And these were of the society called Agents for Public Affairs. Then, suddenly being overwhelmed with a holy love and a sober sense of shame, in anger with himself, he cast his eyes upon his friend, exclaiming, "Tell me, I entreat you, what end we are striving for by all these labours of ours. What is our aim? What is our motive in doing service? Can our hopes in court rise higher than to be ministers of the emperor? And in such a position, what is there not brittle, and fraught with danger, and by how many dangers do we arrive at greater danger? And when do we arrive thither? But if I desire to become a friend of God, behold, I am even now made it." Thus he spoke, and in the pangs of the travail of the new life, he turned his eyes again upon the page and continued reading, and was inwardly changed where you saw, and his mind was divested of the world, as soon became evident; for as he read, and the surging of his heart rolled along, he raged awhile, discerned and resolved on a better course, and now, having become yours, he said to his friend, "Now have I broken loose from those hopes

[47] Matt. 5: 3.

of ours, and am determined to serve God; and this, from this hour, in this place, I enter upon. If you are reluctant to imitate me, hinder me not." The other replied that he would stay with him, to share in so great a reward and so great a service. Thus both of them, being now yours, were building a tower at the necessary cost,[48]—of forsaking all that they had and following you. Then Pontitianus, and he that had walked with him through other parts of the garden, came in search of them to the same place, and having found them, reminded them to return as the day had declined. But they, making known to him their resolution and purpose, and how such a resolve had sprung up and become confirmed in them, asked them not to molest them, if they refused to join themselves to them. But the others, not at all changed from their former selves, did nevertheless (as he said) bewail themselves, and piously congratulated them, recommending themselves to their prayers; and with their hearts inclining towards earthly things, returned to the palace. But the other two, setting their affections upon heavenly things, remained in the cottage. And both of them had affianced brides, who, when they heard of this, dedicated also their virginity unto God.

CHAP. 7—*He deplores his wretchedness, that having been born thirty-two years, he had not yet found out the truth.*

16. Such was the story of Pontitianus. But you, O Lord, while he was speaking, did turn me towards myself, taking me from behind my back, where I had placed myself while unwilling to exercise self-scrutiny; and you did set me face to face with myself, that I might behold how foul I was, and how crooked and sordid, bespotted and ulcerous. And I beheld and loathed myself; and whither to fly from myself I did not discover. And if I sought to turn my gaze away from myself, he continued his narrative, and you again opposed me to myself, and thrust me before my own eyes, that I might discover my iniquity, and hate it.[49] I had known it, but acted as though I knew it not,—winked at it, and forgot it.

17. But now, the more ardently I loved those whose healthful affections I heard tell of, that they had given up them-

48 Luke 14: 26–35.
49 Ps. 36: 2.

selves wholly to you to be cured, the more did I abhor myself when compared with them. For many of my years (perhaps twelve) had passed away since my nineteenth, when, on the reading of Cicero's *Hortensius,* I was roused to a desire for wisdom; and still I was delaying to reject mere worldly happiness, and to devote myself to search out that of which not the finding alone, but the mere search, ought to have been preferred before the treasures and kingdoms of this world, though already found, and before the pleasures of the body, though encompassing me at my will. But I, miserable young man, supremely miserable even in the very outset of my youth, had entreated chastity of you, and said, "Grant me chastity and continence, but not yet." For I was afraid lest you should hear me soon, and soon deliver me from the disease of concupiscence, which I desired to have satisfied rather than extinguished. And I had wandered through perverse ways in a sacrilegious superstition; not indeed assured of it, but preferring that to the others, which I did not seek religiously, but opposed maliciously.

18. And I had thought that I delayed from day to day to reject worldly hopes and follow you only, because there did not appear anything certain where to direct my course. And now the day had arrived in which I was to be laid bare to myself, and my conscience was to chide me. "Where are you, O my tongue? You said, truly, that for an uncertain truth you were not willing to cast off the baggage of vanity. Behold, now it is certain, and yet that burden still oppresses you; whereas they who neither have so worn themselves out with searching after it, nor yet have spent ten years and more in thinking on it, have had their shoulders unburdened, and gotten wings to fly away." Thus was I inwardly consumed and mightily confounded with a horrible shame, while Pontitianus was relating these things. And he, having finished his story, and the business he came for, went his way. And to myself, what did I not say within myself? With what scourges of rebuke did I not lash my soul to make it follow me, struggling to go after you! Yet it drew back; it refused, and exercised not itself. All its arguments were exhausted and confuted. There remained a silent trembling; and it

feared, as it would death, to be restrained from the flow of that custom whereby it was wasting away even to death.

CHAP. 8—*The conversation with Alypius being ended, he retires to the garden, where his friend follows him.*

19. In the midst, then, of this great strife of my inner dwelling, which I had strongly raised up against my soul in the chamber of my heart,[50] troubled both in mind and countenance, I made for Alypius, and exclaimed: "What is wrong with us? What is this? What did you hear? The unlearned start up and 'take' heaven,[51] and we, with our learning, but wanting heart, see where we wallow in flesh and blood! Because others have preceded us, are we ashamed to follow, and not rather ashamed at not following?" Some such words I gave utterance to, and in my excitement flung myself from him, while he gazed upon me in silent astonishment. For I spoke not in my wonted tone, and my brow, cheeks, eyes, colour, tone of voice, all expressed my emotion more than the words. There was a little garden belonging to our lodging, of which we had the use, as of the whole house; for the master, our landlord, did not live there. Thither had the tempest within my breast hurried me, where no one might impede the fiery struggle in which I was engaged with myself, until it came to the issue that you knew, though I did not. But I was mad that I might be whole, and dying that I might have life, knowing what evil thing I was, but not knowing what good thing I was shortly to become. Into the garden, then, I retired, Alypius following my steps. For his presence was no bar to my solitude; or how could he desert me so troubled? We sat down at as great a distance from the house as we could. I was disquieted in spirit, being most impatient with myself that I entered not into your will and covenant, O my God, which all my bones cried out to me to enter, extolling it to the skies. And we enter not therein by ships, or chariots, or feet, no, nor by going so far as I had come from the house to that place where we were sitting. For not to go only, but to enter there, was naught else but to will to go, but to will it resolutely and thoroughly; not to stagger and

[50] Is. 26: 20, and Matt. 6: 6.
[51] Matt. 11: 12.

sway about this way and that, a changeable and half-wounded will, wrestling, with one part falling as another rose.

20. Finally, in the very fever of my irresolution, I made many of those motions with my body which men sometimes desire to do, but cannot, if either they have not the limbs, or if their limbs be bound with fetters, weakened by disease, or hindered in any other way. Thus, if I tore my hair, struck my forehead, or if, entwining my fingers, I clasped my knee, this I did because I willed it. But I might have willed and not done it, if the power of motion in my limbs had not responded. So many things, then, I did, when to have the will was not to have the power, and I did not do that which both with an unequalled desire I longed more to do, and which shortly when I should will I should have the power to do; because shortly when I should will, I should will thoroughly. For in such things the power was one with the will, and to will was to do, and yet it was not done; and more readily did the body obey the slightest wish of the soul in the moving its limbs at the order of the mind, than the soul obeyed itself to accomplish in the will alone this its great will.

CHAP. 9—*That the mind commands the mind, but it does not will entirely.*

21. Whence is this monstrous thing? And why is it? Let your mercy shine on me, that I may inquire, if it may be that the hiding-places of man's punishment, and the darkest contritions of the sons of Adam, may perhaps answer me. Whence is this monstrous thing? and why is it? The mind commands the body, and it obeys forthwith; the mind commands itself, and is resisted. The mind commands the hand to be moved, and such readiness is there that the command is scarce to be distinguished from the obedience. Yet the mind is mind, and the hand is body. The mind commands the mind to will, and yet, though it be itself, it does not obey. Whence this monstrous thing? and why is it? I repeat, it commands itself to will, and would not give the command unless it willed; yet what it commands is not done. But it wills not entirely; therefore it commands not entirely. For so far forth it commands, as it wills; and so far forth is the thing commanded not done, as it does not will. For the will com-

mands that there be a will;—not another, but itself. But it
does not command entirely, therefore that is not done which
it commands. For if it were entire, it would not even command it to be, because it would already be. It is, therefore,
no monstrous thing partly to will, partly to be unwilling, but
an infirmity of the mind, that it does not wholly rise, sustained by truth, pressed down by custom. And so there are
two wills, because one of them is not entire; and the one is
supplied with what the other needs.

CHAP. 10—*He refutes the opinion of the Manichæans as to two
kinds of minds,—one good and the other evil.*

22. Let them perish from your presence,[52] O God, as "vain
talkers and deceivers"[53] of the soul do perish, who, observing
that there were two wills in deliberating, affirm that there
are two kinds of minds in us,—one good, the other evil. They
themselves truly are evil when they hold these evil opinions;
and they shall become good when they hold the truth, and
shall consent to the truth, that your apostle may say unto
them, "You were sometimes darkness, but now you are light
in the Lord."[54] But they, desiring to be light, not "in the
Lord," but in themselves, conceiving the nature of the soul
to be the same as that which God is, are made more gross
darkness; for through a shocking arrogancy they went farther
from you, "the true light, which enlightens every man that
comes into the world."[55] Take heed what you say, and blush
for shame; draw near to him and be "lightened," and your
faces shall not be "ashamed."[56] I, when I was deliberating
upon serving the Lord my God now, as I had long purposed,
—I it was who willed, I who was unwilling. It was I, even I
myself. I neither willed entirely, nor was entirely unwilling.
Therefore was I at war with myself, and destroyed by myself.
And this destruction overtook me against my will, and yet
showed not the presence of another mind, but the punishment of my own. "Now, then, it is no more I that do it, but

[52] Ps. 68: 2.
[53] Titus 1: 10.
[54] Eph. 5: 8.
[55] John 1: 9.
[56] Ps. 34: 5.

sin that dwells in me,"[57]—the punishment of a more uncon-
fined sin, in that I was a son of Adam.

23. For if there be as many contrary natures as there are
conflicting wills, there will not now be two natures only, but
many. If any one deliberate whether he should go to their
conventicle, or to the theatre, those men[58] at once cry out,
"Behold, here are two natures,—one good, drawing this way,
another bad, drawing back that way; for whence else is this
indecision between conflicting wills?" But I reply that both
are bad—that which draws to them, and that which draws
back to the theatre. But they believe that will not to be other
than good which draws to them. Supposing, then, one of us
should deliberate, and through the conflict of his two wills
should waver whether he should go to the theatre or to our
church, would not these also waver what to answer? For
either they must confess, which they are not willing to do,
that the will which leads to our church is good, as well as
that of those who have received and are held by the mysteries
of theirs, or they must imagine that there are two evil natures
and two evil minds in one man, at war one with the other;
and that will not be true what they say, namely that there is
one good and another bad; or they must be converted to the
truth, and no longer deny that where any one deliberates,
there is one soul fluctuating between conflicting wills.

24. Let them no more say, then, when they perceive two
wills to be antagonistic to each other in the same man, that
the contest is between two opposing minds, of two opposing
substances, from two opposing principles, the one good and
the other bad. For you, O true God, disprove, check, and
convince them; just as when both wills are bad, one deliberates whether he should kill a man by poison, or by the sword;
whether he should take possession of this or that estate of
another's, when he cannot do both; whether he should pur-
chase pleasure by prodigality, or retain his money by covet-
ousness; whether he should go to the circus or the theatre, if
both are open on the same day; or, thirdly, whether he should
rob another man's house, if he have the opportunity; or,

[57] Rom. 7: 17.
[58] The Manichæans.

fourthly, whether he should commit adultery, if at the same time he have the means of doing so,—all these things concurring in the same point of time, and all being equally longed for, although impossible to be enacted at one time. For they rend the mind amid four, or even (among the vast variety of things men desire) more antagonistic wills, nor do they yet affirm that there are so many different substances. Thus also is it in wills which are good. For I ask them, is it a good thing to have delight in reading the apostle, or good to have delight in a sober psalm, or good to discourse on the gospel? To each of these they will answer, "It is good." What, then, if all equally delight us, and all at the same time? Do not different wills distract the mind, when a man is deliberating which he should rather choose? Yet are they all good, and are at variance until one is fixed upon, whither the whole united will may be borne, which before was divided into many. Thus, also, when eternity delights us above, and the pleasure of temporal good holds us down below, it is the same soul which wills not that or this with an entire will, and is therefore torn asunder with grievous perplexities, while out of truth it prefers that, but out of custom cannot do without this.

CHAP. 11—*In what manner the Spirit struggled with the flesh, that it might be freed from the bondage of vanity.*

25. Thus I was sick and tormented, accusing myself far more severely than was usual, tossing and turning me in my chain till that was utterly broken, whereby I now was but slightly, but still was held. And you, O Lord, pressed upon me in my inward parts by a severe mercy, redoubling the lashes of fear and shame, lest I should again give way, and that same slender remaining tie not being broken off, it should recover strength, and enchain me the faster. For I said mentally, "Lo, let it be done now, let it be done now." And as I spoke, I all but came to a resolve. I all but did it, yet I did it not. Yet I did not fall back to my old condition, but took up my position hard by, and drew breath. And I tried again, and wanted but very little of reaching it, and somewhat less, and then all but touched and grasped it; and yet came not at it, nor touched, nor grasped it, hesitating to die to death, and to live to life; and the worse, to which I had been ac-

customed, prevailed more with me than the better, which I had not tried. And the very moment in which I was to become another man, the nearer it approached me, the greater horror did it strike into me; but it did not strike me back, nor turn me aside, but kept me in suspense.

26. The very toys of toys, and vanities of vanities, my old mistresses, still enthralled me; they shook my fleshly garment, and whispered softly, "Do you part from us? And from that moment shall we no more be with you for ever? And from that moment shall not this or that be lawful for you for ever?" And what did they suggest to me in the words "this or that?" What is it that they suggested, O my God? Let your mercy avert it from the soul of your servant. What impurities did they suggest! What shame! And now I far less than half heard them, not openly showing themselves and contradicting me, but muttering, as it were, behind my back, and furtively plucking me as I was departing, to make me look back upon them. Yet they did delay me, so that I hesitated to burst and shake myself free from them, and to leap over whither I was called,—an unruly habit saying to me, "Do you think you can live without them?"

27. But now it said this very faintly; for on that side towards which I had set my face, and whither I trembled to go, did the chaste dignity of Continence appear unto me, cheerful, but not dissolutely gay, honestly alluring me to come and doubt nothing, and extending her holy hands, full of a multiplicity of good examples, to receive and embrace me. There were there so many young men and maidens, a multitude of youth and every age, grave widows and ancient virgins, and Continence herself in all, not barren, but a fruitful mother of children of joys, by you, O Lord, her husband. And she smiled on me with an encouraging mockery, as if to say, "Can you not do what these youths and maidens can? Or can one or other do it of themselves, and not rather in the Lord their God? The Lord their God gave me to them. Why do you stand in your own strength, and so do not stand? Cast yourself upon him; fear not, he will not withdraw so that you would fall; cast yourself upon him without fear, he will receive you, and heal you." And I blushed beyond measure, for I still heard the muttering of those toys, and hung in

suspense. And she again seemed to say, "Shut up your ears against those unclean members of yours upon the earth, that they may be mortified.[59] They tell you of delights, but not as does the law of the Lord your God."[60] This controversy in my heart was nothing but self against self. But Alypius, sitting close by my side, awaited in silence the result of my unwonted emotion.

CHAP. 12—*Having prayed to God, he pours forth a shower of tears, and, admonished by a voice, he opens the book and reads the words in Rom. 13: 13; by which, being changed in his whole soul, he discloses the divine favour to his friend and his mother.*

28. But when a profound reflection had, from the secret depths of my soul, drawn together and heaped up all my misery before the sight of my heart, there arose a mighty storm, accompanied by as mighty a shower of tears. Which, that I might pour forth fully, with its natural expressions, I stole away from Alypius; for it suggested itself to me that solitude was fitter for the business of weeping. So I retired to such a distance that even his presence could not be oppressive to me. Thus was it with me at that time, and he perceived it; for something, I believe, I had spoken, wherein the sound of my voice appeared choked with weeping, and in that state had I risen up. He then remained where we had been sitting, most completely astonished. I flung myself down, how, I know not, under a certain fig-tree, giving free course to my tears, and the streams of my eyes gushed out, an acceptable sacrifice unto you.[61] And, not indeed in these words, yet to this effect, spoke I much to you,—"But you, O Lord, how long?"[62] "How long, Lord? Wilt you be angry for ever? Oh, remember not against us former iniquities;"[63] for I felt that I was enthralled by them. I sent up these sorrowful cries,—"How long, how long? To-morrow, and to-morrow? Why not now? Why is there not this hour an end to my uncleanness?"

29. I was saying these things and weeping in the most bitter contrition of my heart, when, lo, I heard the voice as of

[59] Col. 3: 5.
[60] Ps. 119: 85.
[61] 1 Pet. 2: 5.
[62] Ps. 6: 3.
[63] Ps. 79: 5, 8.

a boy or girl, I know not which, coming from a neighbouring house, chanting, and oft repeating, "Take up and read; take up and read."[64] Immediately my countenance was changed, and I began most earnestly to consider whether it was usual for children in any kind of game to sing such words; nor could I remember ever to have heard the like. So, restraining the torrent of my tears, I rose up, interpreting it no other way than as a command to me from heaven to open the book, and to read the first chapter I should light upon. For I had heard of Antony, that, accidentally coming in while the gospel was being read, he received the admonition as if what was read were addressed to him, "Go and sell that you have, and give to the poor, and you shall have treasure in heaven; and come and follow me."[65] And by such oracle was he forthwith converted unto you. So quickly I returned to the place where Alypius was sitting; for there I had put down the volume of the apostle, when I rose thence. I seized it, opened it, and in silence read that paragraph on which my eyes first fell,—"Not in rioting and drunkenness, not in chambering and wantonness, not in strife and envying; but put on the Lord Jesus Christ, and make not provision for the flesh, to fulfil its lusts."[66] No further would I read, nor did I need; for instantly, as the sentence ended,—by a light, as it were, of serenity infused into my heart,—all the gloom of doubt vanished away.

30. Closing the book, then, and putting either my finger between, or some other mark, I now with a tranquil countenance made it known to Alypius. And he thus disclosed to me what was done in him, which I knew not. He asked to look at what I had read. I showed him; and he looked even further than I had read, and I knew not what followed. This it was, "Him that is weak in the faith, receive;"[67] which he applied to himself, and told to me. By this admonition he was strengthened; and by a good resolution and purpose, very

[64] Some scholars regard this episode as fictitious, others as real, others still as a blend of the fact and fiction; cf. J. O'Meara, op. cit., pp. 178 ff.

[65] Matt. 19: 21.

[66] Rom. 13: 13 f.

[67] Rom. 14: 1.

much in accord with his character (wherein, for the better, he was always far different from me), without any restless delay he joined me. Thence we go in to my mother. We make it known to her,—she rejoices. We relate how it came to pass,—she leaps for joy, and triumphs, and blesses you, who are "able to do exceeding abundantly above all that we ask or think;"[68] for she perceived you to have given her more for me than she used to ask by her pitiful and most doleful groanings. For you did so convert me to yourself, that I sought neither a wife, nor any other of this world's hopes,—standing in that rule of faith[69] in which you, so many years before, had showed me to her in a vision. And you turned her grief into a gladness,[70] much more plentiful than she had desired, and much dearer and chaster than she used to crave, by having grandchildren of my body.

BOOK 11

CHAP. 1—*By confession he desires to stimulate his own love and that of his readers towards God.*

1. O Lord, since eternity is yours, are you ignorant of the things which I say unto you? Or do you see at the time that which comes to pass in time? Why, therefore, do I place before you so many accounts of things? Not surely that you might know them through me, but that I may awaken my own love and that of my readers towards you, that we may all say, "Great is the Lord, and greatly to be praised."[1] I have already said, and shall say, for the love of your love I do this. For we also pray, and yet truth says, "Your Father knows what things you have need of before you ask him."[2] Therefore we make known to you our love, in confessing to you our own miseries and your mercies upon us, that you may free us altogether, since you have begun, that we may

[68] Eph. 3: 20.
[69] Cf. *Conf.* 3.11.19.
[70] Ps. 30: 11.
[1] Ps. 96: 4.
[2] Matt. 6: 8.

cease to be wretched in ourselves, and that we may be blessed in you; since you have called us, that we may be poor in spirit, and meek, and mourners, and hungering and thirsty after righteousness, and merciful, and pure in heart, and peacemakers.[3] Behold, I have told to you many things, which I could and which I would, for you first willed that I should confess to you, the Lord my God, for you are good, since your "mercy endures for ever."[4]

CHAP. 2—*He begs of God that through the Holy Scriptures he may be led to truth.*

2. But when shall I suffice with the tongue of my pen to express all your exhortations, and all your terrors, and comforts, and guidances, whereby you have led me to preach your Word and to dispense your sacrament unto your people? And if I suffice to utter these things in order, time as it drops is dear to me. Long time have I burned to meditate in your law, and in it to confess to you my knowledge and ignorance, the beginning of your enlightening, and the remains of my darkness, until infirmity be swallowed up by strength. And I would not wish that to anything else those hours should flow away, which I find free from the necessities of refreshing my body, and the care of my mind, and of the service which we owe to men, and which, though we owe not, even yet we pay.

3. O Lord my God, hear my prayer, and let your mercy look on my longing, since it burns not for myself alone, but because it desires to benefit brotherly charity; and you see into my heart, that so it is. I would sacrifice to you the service of my thought and tongue; and do you give what I may offer to you. For "I am poor and needy,"[5] you rich unto all that call upon you,[6] who free from care cares for us. Circumcise from all rashness and from all lying my inward and outward lips.[7] Let your Scriptures be my chaste delights. Neither let me be deceived in them, nor deceive

[3] Matt. 5: 3–9.
[4] Ps. 118: 1.
[5] Ps. 86: 1.
[6] Rom. 10: 12.
[7] Ex. 6: 12.

by them. Lord, hear and pity, O Lord my God, light of the
blind, and strength of the weak; even also light of those
that see, and strength of the strong, listen unto my soul, and
hear it crying "out of the depths."[8] For unless your ears be
present in the depths also, whither shall we go? whither shall
we cry? "The day is yours, and the night also is yours."[9]
At your nod the moments flee by. Grant from them space
for our meditations among the hidden things of your law,
nor close it against us who knock. For not in vain have you
willed that the obscure secret of so many pages should be
written. Nor is it that those forests have not their harts,[10]
betaking themselves therein, and ranging, and walking, and
feeding, lying down, and ruminating. Perfect me, O Lord, and
reveal them unto me. Behold, your voice is my joy, your
voice surpasses the abundance of pleasures. Give that which
I love, for I do love; and this you have given. Abandon not
your own gifts, nor despise your grass that is thirsty. Let me
confess to you whatever I shall have found in your books,
and let me hear the voice of praise, and let me drink you in,
and reflect on the wonderful things of your law;[11] even from
the beginning, where you made the heaven and the earth,
to the everlasting kingdom of your holy city that is with you.

4. Lord, have mercy on me and hear my desire. For I
think that it is not of the earth, nor of gold and silver, and
precious stones, nor gorgeous apparel, nor honours and
powers, nor the pleasures of the flesh, nor necessaries for the
body, and this life of our pilgrimage; all these are added to
those that seek your kingdom and your righteousness.[12]
Behold, O Lord my God, where is my desire. The unrighteous
have told me of delights, but not such as your law, O Lord.[13]
Behold where is my desire. Behold, Father, look and see, and
approve; and let it be pleasing in the sight of your mercy, that
I may find grace before you, that the secret things of your
Word may be opened to me when I knock. I beseech, by our

8 Ps. 130: 1.
9 Ps. 74: 16.
10 Ps. 29: 9.
11 Ps. 26: 7.
12 Matt. 6: 33.
13 Ps. 119: 85.

Lord Jesus Christ, your Son, "the man of your right hand,
the Son of man, whom you made strong for yourself,"[14]
as your mediator and ours, through whom you have sought
us, although not seeking you, but did seek us that we might
seek you,—your Word through whom you have made all
things,[15] and among them me also,—your only-begotten,
through whom you have called to adoption the believing
people, and me also. I beseech you through him, who sits
at your right hand, and "makes intercession for us,"[16] "in
whom are hid all treasures of wisdom and knowledge."[17]
Him do I seek in your books. Of him did Moses write;[18]
this says himself; this says the truth.

CHAP. 3—*He begins from the creation of the world—not understanding the Hebrew text.*

5. Let me hear and understand how in the beginning you
made the heaven and the earth.[19] Moses wrote this; he wrote
and departed,—passed hence from you to you. Nor now is
he before me; for if he were I would hold him, and ask him,
and would adjure him by you that he would open to me
these things, and I would lend the ears of my body to the
sounds bursting forth from his mouth. And should he speak
in the Hebrew tongue, in vain would it beat on my senses,
nor would anything touch my mind; but if in Latin, I should
know what he said. But whence should I know whether he
said what was true? But if I knew this even, should I know
it from him? Truly within me, within in the chamber of my
thought, truth, neither Hebrew, nor Greek, nor Latin, nor
barbarian, without the organs of voice and tongue, without
the sound of syllables, would say, "He speaks the truth," and
I, forthwith assured of it, confidently would say unto that
man of yours, "You speak the truth." As, then, I cannot
inquire of him, I beseech you,—you, O truth, full of whom
he spoke truth,—you, my God, I beseech, forgive my sins;

14 Ps. 80: 17.
15 John 1: 3.
16 Rom. 8: 34.
17 Col. 2: 3.
18 John 5: 4–6.
19 Gen. 1: 1.

and do you, who did give to that your servant to speak these things, grant to me also to understand them.

CHAP. 4—*Heaven and earth cry out that they have been created by God.*

6. Behold, the heaven and earth are; they proclaim that they were made, for they are changed and varied. Whereas whatever has not been made, and yet has being, has nothing in it which there was not before; this is what it is to be changed and varied. They also proclaim that they made not themselves; "therefore we are, because we have been made; we were not therefore before we were, so that we could have made ourselves." And the voice of those that speak is in itself an evidence. You, therefore, Lord, did make these things; you who are beautiful, for they are beautiful; you who are good, for they are good; you who are, for they are. Nor even so are they beautiful, nor good, nor are they, as you their creator are; compared with whom they are neither beautiful, nor good, nor are at all. These things we know, thanks be to you. And our knowledge, compared with your knowledge, is ignorance.

CHAP. 5—*God created the world not from any certain matter, but in his own word.*

7. But how did you make the heaven and the earth, and what was the instrument of your mighty work? For it was not as a human worker fashioning body from body, according to the fancy of his mind, in some way able to assign a form which it perceives in itself by its inner eye. And whence should he be able to do this, had you not made that mind? And he assigns to it already existing, and as it were having a being, a form, as clay, or stone, or wood, or gold, or such like. And whence should these things be, had you not appointed them? You did make for the workman his body,—you the mind commanding the limbs,—you the matter from which he makes anything,—you the capacity whereby he may apprehend his art, and see within what he may do without,—you the sense of his body, by which, as by an interpreter, he may from mind to matter convey that which he does, and report to his mind what may have been done, that it within may

consult the truth, presiding over itself, whether it is done well. All these things praise you, the creator of all. But how do you make them? How, O God, did you make heaven and earth? Truly, neither in the heaven nor in the earth did you make heaven and earth; nor in the air, nor in the waters, since these also belong to the heaven and the earth; nor in the whole world did you make the whole world; because there was no place wherein it could be made before it was made, that it might be; nor did you hold anything in your hand wherewith to make heaven and earth. For whence could you have what you had not made, from which to make anything? For what is, save because you are? Therefore you did speak and they were made,[20] and in your Word you made these things.[21]

CHAP. 6—*He did not, however, create it by a sounding and passing word.*

8. But how did you speak? Was it in that manner in which the voice came from the cloud, saying, "This is my beloved Son"?[22] For that voice was uttered and passed away, began and ended. The syllables sounded and passed by, the second after the first, the third after the second, and thence in order, until the last after the rest, and silence after the last. Hence it is clear and plain that the motion of a creature expressed it, itself temporal, obeying your eternal will. And these your words formed at the time, the outer ear conveyed to the intelligent mind, whose inner ear lay attentive to your eternal Word. But it compared these words sounding in time with your eternal Word in silence, and said, "It is different, very different. These words are far beneath me, nor are they, since they flee and pass away; but the Word of my Lord remains above me for ever." If, then, in sounding and fleeting words you said that heaven and earth should be made, and did thus make heaven and earth, there was already a corporeal creature before heaven and earth by whose temporal motions that voice might take its course in time. But there was nothing corporeal before heaven and earth; or if there were,

20 Ps. 33: 9.
21 Ibid. 33: 6.
22 Matt. 17: 5.

certainly you without a transitory voice created that whence you would make the passing voice, by which to say that the heaven and the earth should be made. For whatever that were of which such a voice was made, unless it were made by you, it could not be at all. By what word of yours was it decreed that a body might be made, whereby these words might be made?

CHAP. 7—*By his co-eternal Word he speaks, and all things are done.*

9. You call us, therefore, to understand the Word, God with you, God,[23] which is spoken eternally, and by it are all things spoken eternally. For what was spoken was not finished, and another spoken until all were spoken; but all things at once and for ever. For otherwise have we time and change, and not a true eternity, nor a true immortality. This I know, O my God, and give thanks. I know, I confess to you, O Lord, and whoever is not unthankful to certain truth, knows and blesses you with me. We know, O Lord, we know; since in proportion as anything is not what it was, and is what it was not, in that proportion does it die and arise. Not anything, therefore, of your Word gives place and comes into place again, because it is truly immortal and eternal. And, therefore, to the Word co-eternal with you, you at once and for ever say all that you say; and whatever you say shall be made, is made; nor do you make otherwise than by speaking; yet all things are not made both together and everlasting which you make by speaking.

CHAP. 8—*That Word itself is the beginning of all things, in the which we are instructed as to evangelical truth.*

10. Why is this, I beseech you, O Lord my God? I see it, however; but how I shall express it, I know not, unless that everything which begins to be and ceases to be, then begins and ceases when in your eternal reason it is known that it ought to begin or cease where nothing begins or ceases. The same is your Word, which is also "the beginning," because also it speaks to us.[24] Thus, in the gospel he speaks through the flesh; and this sounded outwardly in the ears

[23] John 1: 1.
[24] John 8: 25.

of men, that it might be believed and sought inwardly, and
that it might be found in the eternal truth, where the good
and only master teaches all his disciples. There, O Lord, I
hear your voice, the voice of one speaking to me, since he
speaks to us who teaches us. But he that teaches us not, although he speaks, speaks not to us. Moreover, who teaches
us, unless it be the immutable truth? For even when we are
admonished through a changeable creature, we are led to
the truth immutable? There we learn truly while we stand and
hear him, and rejoice greatly "because of the bridegroom's
voice,"[25] restoring us to that whence we are. And, therefore, he is the beginning, because unless it remained, there
would not, when we strayed, be whither to return. But when
we return from error, it is by knowing that we return. But
that we may know, he teaches us, because he is the beginning
and speaks to us.

CHAP. 9—*Wisdom and the beginning.*

11. In this beginning, O God, you have made heaven and
earth,—in your Word, in your Son, in your power, in your
wisdom, in your truth, wondrously speaking and wondrously
making. Who shall comprehend? who shall relate it? What
is that which shines through me, and strikes my heart without injury, and I both shudder and burn? I shudder inasmuch
as I am unlike it; and I burn inasmuch as I am like it. It is
wisdom itself that shines through me, clearing my cloudiness,
which again overwhelms me, fainting from it, in the darkness
and amount of my punishment. For my strength is brought
down in need,[26] so that I cannot endure my blessings, until
you, O Lord, who have been gracious to all my iniquities,
heal also all my infirmities; because you shall also redeem
my life from corruption, and crown me with your loving-
kindness and mercy, and shall satisfy my desire with good
things, because my youth shall be renewed like the eagle's.[27]
For by hope we are saved; and through patience we await
your promises.[28] Let him that is able hear you discoursing

25 John 3: 29.
26 Ps. 31: 10.
27 Ps. 103: 3–5.
28 Rom. 8: 24 f.

within. I will with confidence cry out from your oracle, How wonderful are your works, O Lord, in wisdom you have made them all.[29] And this wisdom is the beginning, and in that beginning you have made heaven and earth.

CHAP. 10—*The rashness of those who inquire what God did before he created heaven and earth.*

12. Lo, are they not full of their ancient way, who say to us, "What was God doing before he made heaven and earth? For if," say they, "he were unoccupied, and did nothing, why does he not for ever also, and from henceforth, cease from working, as in times past he did? For if any new motion has arisen in God, and a new will, to form a creature which he had never before formed, however can that be a true eternity where there arises a will which was not before? For the will of God is not a creature, but before the creature; because nothing could be created unless the will of the creator were before it. The will of God, therefore, pertains to his very substance. But if anything has arisen in the substance of God which was not before, that substance is not truly called eternal. But if it was the eternal will of God that the creature should be, why was not the creature also from eternity?"

CHAP. 11—*They who ask this have not as yet known the eternity of God, which is exempt from the relation of time.*

13. Those who say these things do not as yet understand you, O you wisdom of God, you light of souls; not as yet do they understand how these things be made which are made by and in you. They even endeavour to comprehend things eternal; but as yet their heart flies about in the past and future motions of things, and is still wavering. Who shall hold it and fix it, that it may rest a little, and by degrees catch the glory of that ever-standing eternity, and compare it with the times which never stand, and see that it is incomparable; and that a long time cannot become long, save from the many motions that pass by, which cannot at the same instant be prolonged; but that in the eternal nothing passes away, but that the whole is present; but no time is wholly present;

[29] Ps. 104: 24.

and let him see that all time past is forced on by the future, and that all the future follows from the past, and that all, both past and future, is created and issues from that which is always present? Who will hold the heart of man, that it may stand still, and see how the still-standing eternity, itself neither future nor past, utters the times future and past? Can my hand accomplish this, or the hand of my mouth by persuasion bring about a thing so great?

CHAP. 12—*What God did before the creation of the world.*

14. Behold, I answer to him who asks, "What was God doing before he made heaven and earth?" I answer not, as a certain person is reported to have done facetiously (avoiding the pressure of the question), "He was preparing hell," says he, "for those who pry into mysteries." It is one thing to perceive, another to laugh,—these things I answer not. For more willingly would I have answered, "I know not what I know not," than that I should make him a laughing-stock who asks deep things, and gain praise as one who answers false things. But I say that you, our God, are the creator of every creature; and if by the term "heaven and earth" every creature is understood, I boldly say, "That before God made heaven and earth, he made not anything. For if he did, what did he make unless the creature?" And would that I knew whatever I desire to know to my advantage, as I know that no creature was made before any creature was made.

CHAP. 13—*Before the times created by God, times were not.*

15. But if the roving thought of any one should wander through the images of bygone time, and wonder that you, the God almighty, and all-creating, and all-sustaining, the architect of heaven and earth, did for innumerable ages refrain from so great a work before you would make it, let him awake and consider that he wonders at false things. For whence could innumerable ages pass by which you did not make, since you are the author and creator of all ages? Or what times should those be which were not made by you? Or how should they pass by if they had not been? Since, therefore, you are the creator of all times, if any time was

before you made heaven and earth, why is it said that you did refrain from working? For that very time you made, nor could times pass by before you made times. But if before heaven and earth there was no time, why is it asked, What did you then? For there was no "then" when time was not.

16. Nor do you by time precede time; else you would not precede all times. But in the excellency of an ever-present eternity, you precede all times past, and survive all future times, because they are future, and when they have come they will be past; but "you are the same, and your years shall have no end."[30] Your years neither go nor come; but ours both go and come, that all may come. All your years stand at once, since they do stand; nor were they when departing excluded by coming years, because they do not pass away; but all these of ours shall be when all shall cease to be. Your years are one day, and your day is not daily, but to-day; because your to-day yields not with to-morrow, for neither does it follow yesterday. Your to-day is eternity; therefore did you beget the co-eternal, to whom you said, "This day have I begotten you."[31] You have made all time; and before all times you are, nor in any time was there not time.

CHAP. 14—*Neither time past nor future, but the present only, really is.*

17. At no time, therefore, had you not made anything, because you had made time itself. And no times are co-eternal with you, because you remain for ever; but should these continue, they would not be times. For what is time? Who can easily and briefly explain it? Who even in thought can comprehend it, even to the pronouncing of a word concerning it? But what in speaking do we refer to more familiarly and knowingly than time? And certainly we understand when we speak of it; we understand also when we hear it spoken of by another. What, then, is time? If no one ask of me, I know; if I wish to explain to him who asks, I know not. Yet I say with confidence, that I know that if nothing passed away, there would not be past time; and if nothing were coming, there would not be future time; and if nothing

[30] Ps. 102: 27.
[31] Ps. 2: 7, and Heb. 5: 5.

were, there would not be present time. Those two times, therefore, past and future, how are they, when even the past now
is not, and the future is not as yet? But should the present
be always present, and should it not pass into time past, time
truly it could not be, but eternity. If, then, time present—if it
be time—only comes into existence because it passes into time
past, how do we say that even this is, whose cause of being
is that it shall not be—namely, so that we cannot truly say
that time is, unless because it tends not to be?

CHAP. 15—*There is only a moment of present time.*

18. And yet we say that "time is long and time is short;"
nor do we speak of this save of time past and future. A long
time past, for example, we call a hundred years ago; in like
manner a long time to come, a hundred years hence. But a
short time past we call, say, ten days ago; and a short time
to come, ten days hence. But in what sense is that long or
short which is not? For the past is not now, and the future
is not yet. Therefore let us not say, "It is long;" but let us
say of the past, "It has been long," and of the future, "It will
be long." O my Lord, my light, shall not even here your truth
deride man? For that past time which was long, was it long
when it was already past, or when it was as yet present? For
then it might be long when there was that which could be
long, but when past it no longer was; wherefore that could
not be long which was not at all. Let us not, therefore, say,
"Time past has been long;" for we shall not find what may
have been long, seeing that since it was past it is not; but let
us say "that present time was long, because when it was
present it was long." For it had not as yet passed away so
as not to be, and therefore there was that which could be
long. But after it passed, that ceased also to be long which
ceased to be.

19. Let us therefore see, O human soul, whether present
time can be long; for to you is it given to perceive and to
measure periods of time. What will you reply to me? Is a
hundred years when present a long time? See, first, whether
a hundred years can be present. For if the first year of these
is current, that is present, but the other ninety and nine are
future, and therefore they are not as yet. But if the second

year is current, one is already past, the other present, the
rest future. And thus, if we fix on any middle year of this
hundred as present, those before it are past, those after it
are future; therefore a hundred years cannot be present.
See at least whether that year itself which is current can be
present. For if its first month be current, the rest are future;
if the second, the first has already passed, and the remainder
are not yet. Therefore neither is the year which is current
as a whole present; and if it is not present as a whole, then
the year is not present. For twelve months make the year,
of which each individual month which is current is itself
present, but the rest are either past or future. Although
neither is that month which is current present, but one day
only: if the first, the rest being to come, if the last, the rest
being past; if any of the middle, then between past and future.

20. Behold, the present time, which alone we found could
be called long, is abridged to the space scarcely of one day.
But let us discuss even that, for there is not one day present
as a whole. For it is made up of four-and-twenty hours of
night and day, of which the first has the rest future, the last
has them past, but any one of the intervening has those before it past, those after it future. And that one hour passes
away in fleeting particles. Whatever of it has flown away is
past, whatever remains is future. If any portion of time be
conceived which cannot now be divided into even the minutest particles of moments, this only is that which may be called
present; which, however, flies so rapidly from future to past,
that it cannot be extended by any delay. For if it be extended,
it is divided into the past and future; but the present has no
space. Where, therefore, is the time which we may call long?
Is it future? Indeed we do not say, "It is long," because it is
not yet, so as to be long; but we say, "It will be long." When,
then, will it be? For if even then, since as yet it is future, it
will not be long, because what may be long is not as yet; but
it shall be long, when from the future, which as yet is not,
it shall already have begun to be, and will have become present, so that there could be that which may be long; then does
the present time cry out in the words above that it cannot be
long.

CHAP. 16—*Time can be perceived or measured only while it is passing.*

21. And yet, O Lord, we perceive intervals of times, and we compare them with themselves, and we say some are longer, others shorter. We even measure by how much shorter or longer this time may be than that; and we answer, "That this is double or treble, while that is but once, or only as much as that." But we measure times passing when we measure them by perceiving them; but past times, which now are not, or future times, which as yet are not, who can measure them? Unless, perchance, any one will dare to say, that that can be measured which is not. When, therefore, time is passing, it can be perceived and measured; but when it has passed, it cannot, since it is not.

CHAP. 17—*Nevertheless there is time past and future.*

22. I ask, Father, I do not affirm. O my God, rule and guide me. "Who is there who can say to me that there are not three times (as we learned when boys, and as we have taught boys), the past, present, and future, but only present, because these two are not? Or are they also; but when from future it becomes present, does it come forth from some secret place, and when from the present it becomes past, does it retire into anything secret? For where have they, who have foretold future things, seen these things, if as yet they are not? For that which is not cannot be seen. And they who relate things past could not relate them as true, did they not perceive them in their mind. Which things, if they were not, they could in no wise be discerned. There are therefore things both future and past.

CHAP. 18—*Past and future times cannot be thought of but as present.*

23. Suffer me, O Lord, to seek further; O my hope, let not my purpose be confounded. For if there are times past and future, I desire to know where they are. But if as yet I do not succeed, I still know, wherever they are, that they are not there as future or past, but as present. For if there also they be future, they are not as yet there; if even there they be past, they are no longer there. Wherever, therefore, they are, whatever they are, they are only so as present. Although past

things are related as true, they are drawn out from the memory,—not the things themselves, which have passed, but the words conceived from the images of the things which they have formed in the mind as footprints in their passage through the senses. My childhood, indeed, which no longer is, is in time past, which now is not; but when I call to mind its image, and speak of it, I behold it in the present, because it is as yet in my memory. Whether there be a like cause of foretelling future things, that of things which as yet are not the images may be perceived as already existing, I confess, my God, I know not. This certainly I know, that we generally think before on our future actions, and that this premeditation is present; but that the action whereon we premeditate is not yet, because it is future; which when we shall have entered upon, and have begun to do that which we were premeditating, then shall that action be, because then it is not future, but present.

24. In whatever manner, therefore, this secret preconception of future things may be, nothing can be seen, save what is. But what now is is not future, but present. When, therefore, they say that things future are seen, it is not themselves, which as yet are not (that is, which are future); but their causes or their signs perhaps are seen, which already are. Therefore, to those already beholding them, they are not future, but present, from which future things conceived in the mind are foretold. Which conceptions again now are, and they who foretell those things behold these conceptions present before them. Let now so multitudinous a variety of things afford me some example. I behold daybreak; I foretell that the sun is about to rise. That which I behold is present; what I foretell is future,—not that the sun is future, which already is; but his rising, which is not yet. Yet even its rising I could not predict unless I had an image of it in my mind, as now I have while I speak. But that dawn which I see in the sky is not the rising of the sun, although it may go before it, nor that imagination in my mind; which two are seen as present, that the other which is future may be foretold. Future things, therefore, are not as yet; and if they are not as yet, they are not. And if they are not, they cannot be seen at all; but they

can be foretold from things present which now are, and are seen.

CHAP. 19—*We are ignorant how God teaches future things.*

25. You, therefore, ruler of your creatures, what is the method by which you teach souls those things which are future? For you have taught your prophets. What is that way by which you, to whom nothing is future, teach future things; or rather of future things teach present? For what is not, of a certainty cannot be taught. Too far is this way from my view; it is too mighty for me, I cannot attain unto it;[32] but by you I shall be enabled, when you shall have granted it, sweet light of my hidden eyes.

CHAP. 20—*How time may properly be designated.*

26. But what now is manifest and clear is, that neither are there future nor past things. Nor is it fitly said, "There are three times, past, present, and future;" but maybe it might be fitly said, "There are three times; a present of things past, a present of things present, and a present of things future." For these three do somehow exist in the soul, and otherwise I see them not: present of things past, memory; present of things present, sight; present of things future, expectation. If of these things we are permitted to speak, I see three times, and I grant there are three. It may also be said, "There are three times, past, present, and future," as usage falsely has it. See, I trouble not, nor contradict, nor reprove; provided always that which is said may be understood, that neither the future, nor that which is past, now is. For there are but few things which we speak properly, many things improperly; but what we may wish to say is understood.

CHAP. 21—*How time may be measured.*

27. I have just now said, then, that we measure times as they pass, that we may be able to say that this time is twice as much as that one, or that this is only as much as that, and so of any other of the parts of time which we are able to tell by measuring. Therefore, as I said, we measure times as they

[32] Ps. 139: 6.

pass. And if any one should ask me, "Whence do you know?" I can answer, "I know, because we measure; nor can we measure things that are not; and things past and future are not." But how do we measure present time, since it does not have space? It is measured while it passes; but when it shall have passed, it is not measured; for there will not be anything that can be measured. But whence, in what way, and whither it passes while it is being measured? Whence, but from the future? Which way, save through the present? Whither, but into the past? From that, therefore, which as yet is not, through that which has no space, into that which now is not. But what do we measure, unless time in some space? For we say not single, and double, and triple, and equal, or in any other way in which we speak of time, unless with respect to the spaces of times. In what space, then, do we measure passing time? Is it in the future, whence it passes over? But what we yet measure not, is not. Or is it in the present, by which it passes? But no space, we do not measure. Or in the past, whither it passes? But that which is not now, we measure not.

CHAP. 22—*He prays God that he would explain this most entangled enigma.*

28. My soul yearns to know this most entangled enigma. Do not shut up, O Lord my God, good Father,—through Christ I beseech you,—do not shut up these things, both usual and hidden, from my desire, that it may be hindered from penetrating them; but let them dawn through your enlightening mercy, O Lord. Of whom shall I inquire concerning these things? And to whom shall I with more advantage confess my ignorance than to you, to whom these my studies, so vehemently kindled towards your Scriptures, are not troublesome? Give that which I love; for I do love, and this you have given me. Give, Father, who truly know how to give good gifts to your children.[33] Give, since I have undertaken to know, and trouble is before me until you open it.[34] Through Christ, I beseech you, in his name, holy of holies, let no man

[33] Matt. 7: 11.
[34] Ps. 73: 16.

interrupt me. For I believed, and therefore do I speak.[35] This
is my hope; for this do I live, that I may contemplate the delights of the Lord.[36] Behold, you have made my days old,[37]
and they pass away, and in what manner I know not. And we
speak as to time and time, times and times,—"How long is the
time since he said this?" "How long the time since he did
this?" and, "How long the time since I saw that?" and, "This
syllable has double the time of that single short syllable."
These words we speak, and these we hear; and we are understood, and we understand. They are most manifest and most
usual, and the same things again lie hid too deeply, and the
discovery of them is new.

CHAP. 23—*That time is a certain extension.*

29. I have heard from a learned man that the motions of
the sun, moon, and stars constituted time, and I did not assent.
For why should not rather the motions of all bodies be time?
What if the lights of heaven should cease, and a potter's
wheel run round, would there be no time by which we might
measure those revolutions, and say either that it turned with
equal pauses, or, if it were moved at one time more slowly,
at another more quickly, that some revolutions were longer,
others less so? Or while we were saying this, should we not
also be speaking in time? Or should there in our words be
some syllables long, others short, but because those sounded
in a longer time, these in a shorter? God grant to men to see
in a small thing ideas common to things great and small. Both
the stars and luminaries of heaven are "for signs and for
seasons, and for days and years."[38] No doubt they are; but
neither should I say that the circuit of that wooden wheel was
a day, nor yet should he say that therefore there was no time.

30. I desire to know the power and nature of time, by
which we measure the motions of bodies, and say (for example) that this motion is twice as long as that. For, I ask,
since "day" declares not the stay only of the sun upon the
earth, according to which day is one thing, night another, but

35 Ps. 116: 10.
36 Ps. 27: 4.
37 Ps. 39: 5.
38 Gen. 1: 14.

also its entire circuit from east even to east,—according to
which we say, "So many days have passed" (the nights being
included when we say "so many days," and their spaces not
counted apart),—since, then, the day is finished by the motion
of the sun, and by his circuit from east to east, I ask, whether
the motion itself is the day, or the period in which that motion is completed, or both? For if the first be the day, then
would there be a day although the sun should finish that
course in so small a space of time as an hour. If the second,
then that would not be a day if from one sunrise to another
there were but so short a period as an hour, but the sun must
go round four-and-twenty times to complete a day. If both,
neither could that be called a day if the sun should run his
entire round in the space of an hour; nor that, if, while the
sun stood still, so much time should pass as the sun is accustomed to accomplish his whole course in from morning to
morning. I shall not therefore now ask, what that is which
is called day, but what time is, by which we, measuring the
circuit of the sun, should say that it was accomplished in half
the usual space of time, if it had been completed in so small
a space as twelve hours; and comparing both times, we
should call that single, this double time, although the sun
should run his course from east to east sometimes in that single, sometimes in that double time. Let no man then tell me
that the motions of the heavenly bodies are times, because,
when at the prayer of one the sun stood still in order that he
might achieve his victorious battle, the sun stood still, but
time went on. For in such space of time as was sufficient was
that battle fought and ended.[39] I see that time, then, is a certain extension. But do I see it, or do I seem to see it? You, O
light and truth, will show me.

CHAP. 24—*That time is not a motion of a body which we measure
by time.*

31. Do you command that I should assent, if any one
should say that time is "the motion of a body?" You do not
command me. For I hear that no body is moved but in time.
This you say; but that the very motion of a body is time, I hear

[39] Josh. 10: 12–14.

not; you do not say it. For when a body is moved, I by time measure how long it may be moving from the time in which it began to be moved till it left off. And if I saw not whence it began, and it continued to be moved, so that I see not when it leaves off, I cannot measure unless, perhaps, from the time I began until I cease to see. But if I look long, I proclaim only that the time is long, but not how long it may be; because when we say, "How long," we speak by comparison, as, "This is as long as that," or, "This is double as long as that," or any other thing of the kind. But if we were able to note down the distances of places whence and whither comes the body which is moved, or its parts, if it moved as in a wheel, we can say in how much time the motion of the body or its part, from this place to that, was performed. Since, then, the motion of a body is one thing, that by which we measure how long it is another, who cannot see which of these is rather to be called time? For, although a body be sometimes moved, sometimes stand still, we measure not its motion only, but also its standing still, by time; and we say, "It stood still as much as it moved;" or, "It stood still twice or thrice as long as it moved;" or any other way which our measuring has either determined or estimated, "more or less," as we are accustomed to say. Time, therefore, is not the motion of a body.

CHAP. 25—*He calls on God to enlighten his mind.*

32. And I confess unto you, O Lord, that I am as yet ignorant as to what time is, and again I confess to you, O Lord, that I know that I speak these things in time, and that I have already long spoken of time, and that very "long" is not long save by the stay of time. How, then, do I know this, when I do not know what time is? Or is it, perhaps, that I do not know how I may express what I know? Alas for me, that I do not at least know the extent of my own ignorance! Behold, O my God, before you I lie not. As I speak, so is my heart. You shall light my candle; you, O Lord my God, will enlighten my darkness.[40]

CHAP. 26—*We measure longer events by shorter in time.*

33. Does not my soul pour out to you truly in confession

[40] Ps. 18: 28.

that I do measure times? But do I thus measure, O my God,
and know not what I measure? I measure the motion of a
body by time; and the time itself do I not measure? But, in
truth, could I measure the motion of a body, how long it is,
and how long it is in coming from this place to that, unless I
should measure the time in which it is moved? How, therefore, do I measure this very time itself? Or do we by a shorter
time measure a longer, as by the space of a cubit the space
of a crossbeam? For thus, indeed, we seem by the space of a
short syllable to measure the space of a long syllable, and to
say that this is double. Thus we measure the spaces of stanzas
by the spaces of the verses, and the spaces of the verses by
the spaces of the feet, and the spaces of the feet by the spaces
of the syllables, and the spaces of long by the spaces of short
syllables; not measuring by pages (for in that manner we
measure spaces, not times), but when in uttering the words
they pass by, and we say, "It is a long stanza, because it is
made up of so many verses; long verses, because they consist
of so many feet; long feet, because they are prolonged by so
many syllables; a long syllable, because double a short one."
But neither thus is any certain measure of time obtained; since
it is possible that a shorter verse, if it be pronounced more
fully, may take up more time than a longer one, if pronounced
more hurriedly. Thus for a stanza, thus for a foot, thus for
a syllable. Therefore it appeared to me that time is nothing
else than protraction; but of what I know not. It is wonderful
to me, if it be not of the mind itself. For what do I measure,
I beseech you, O my God, even when I say either indefinitely,
"This time is longer than that;" or even definitely, "This is
double that"? That I measure time, I know. But I measure
not the future, for it is not yet; nor do I measure the present,
because it is extended by no space; nor do I measure the past,
because it no longer is. What, therefore, do I measure? Is it
times passing, not past? For thus had I said.

CHAP. 27—*Times are measured in proportion as they pass by.*

34. Persevere, O my mind, and give earnest heed. God is
our helper; he made us, and not we ourselves.[41] Give heed,

41 Ps. 100: 3.

where truth dawns. Lo, suppose the voice of a body begins to
sound, and does sound, and sounds on, and lo! it ceases,—it
is now silence, and that voice is past and is no longer a voice.
It was future before it sounded, and could not be measured,
because as yet it was not; and now it cannot, because it no
longer is. Then, therefore, while it was sounding, it might,
because there was then that which might be measured. But
even then it did not stand still, for it was going and passing
away. Could it, then, on that account be measured the more?
For, while passing, it was being extended into some space of
time, in which it might be measured, since the present has
no space. If, therefore, then it might be measured, lo! suppose another voice has begun to sound, and still sounds, in a
continued tenor without any interruption, we can measure it
while it is sounding; for when it shall have ceased to sound, it
will be already past, and there will not be that which can be
measured. Let us measure it truly, and let us say how much it
is. But as yet it sounds, nor can it be measured, save from
that instant in which it began to sound, even to the end in
which it left off. For the interval itself we measure from some
beginning to some end. On which account, a voice which is
not yet ended cannot be measured, so that it may be said
how long or how short it may be; nor can it be said to be
equal to another, or single or double in respect of it, or the
like. But when it is ended, it no longer is. In what manner,
therefore, may it be measured? And yet we measure times;
still not those which as yet are not, nor those which no longer
are, nor those which are protracted by some delay, nor those
which have no limits. We, therefore, measure neither future
times, nor past, nor present, nor those passing by; and yet we
do measure times.

35. *Deus Creator omnium;* this verse of eight syllables al-
ternates between short and long syllables. The four short,
then, the first, third, fifth, and seventh, are single in respect
of the four long, the second, fourth, sixth, and eighth. Each
of these has a double time to every one of those. I pronounce them, report on them, and thus it is, as is perceived
by common sense. By common sense, then, I measure a long
by a short syllable, and I find that it has twice as much. But
when one sounds after another, if the former be short, the

latter long, how shall I hold the short one, and how measuring shall I apply it to the long, so that I may find out that this has twice as much, when indeed the long does not begin to sound unless the short leaves off sounding? That very long one I measure not as present, since I do not measure it save when ended. But its ending is its passing away. What, then, is it that I can measure? Where is the short syllable by which I measure? Where is the long one which I measure? Both have sounded, have flown, have passed away, and are no longer; and still I measure, and I confidently answer (so far as is trusted to a practised sense), that as to space of time this syllable is single, that double. Nor could I do this, unless because they have passed, and are ended. Therefore I do not measure themselves, which now are not, but something in my memory, which remains fixed.

36. In you, o my mind, I measure times. Do not overwhelm me with your clamour. That is, do not overwhelm yourself with the multitude of your impressions. In you, I say, I measure times; the impression which things as they pass by make on you, and which, when they have passed by, remains, that I measure as time present, not those things which have passed by, that the impression should be made. This I measure when I measure times. Either, then, these are times, or I do not measure times. What when we measure silence, and say that this silence has lasted as long as that voice lasts? Do we not extend our thought to the measure of a voice, as if it sounded, so that we may be able to declare something concerning the intervals of silence in a given space of time? For when both the voice and tongue are still, we go over in thought poems and verses, and any discourse, or dimensions of motions; and declare concerning the spaces of times, how much this may be in respect of that, not otherwise than if uttering them we should pronounce them. Should any one wish to utter a lengthened sound, and had with forethought determined how long it should be, that man has in silence truly gone through a space of time, and, committing it to memory, he begins to utter that speech, which sounds until it be extended to the end proposed; truly it has sounded, and will sound. For what of it is already finished has truly sounded, but what remains will sound; and thus does it pass

on, until the present intention carry over the future into the
past; the past increasing by the diminution of the future, until, by the consumption of the future, all be past.

CHAP. 28—*Time in the human mind, which expects, considers, and
remembers.*

37. But how is that future diminished or consumed which
as yet is not? Or how does the past, which is no longer, increase, unless in the mind, which enacts this, there are three
things done? For it both expects, and considers, and remembers, that that which it expects, through that which it considers, may pass into that which it remembers. Who, therefore, denies that future things as yet are not? But yet there
is already in the mind the expectation of things future. And
who denies that past things are now no longer? But, however,
there is still in the mind the memory of things past. And who
denies that time present wants space, because it passes away
in a moment? But yet our consideration endures, through
which that which may be present may proceed to become
absent. Future time, which is not, is not therefore long; but a
"long future" is "a long expectation of the future." Nor is
time past, which is now no longer, long; but a long past is "a
long memory of the past."

38. I am about to repeat a psalm that I know. Before I begin, my attention is extended to the whole; but when I have
begun, as much of it as becomes past by my saying it is extended in my memory; and the life of this action of mine is
divided between my memory, on account of what I have repeated, and my expectation, on account of what I am about
to repeat; yet my consideration is present with me, through
which that which was future may be carried over so that it
may become past. Which the more it is done and repeated,
by so much (expectation being shortened) the memory is enlarged, until the whole expectation be exhausted, when that
whole action being ended shall have passed into memory. And
what takes place in the entire psalm, takes place also in each
individual part of it, and in each individual syllable: this holds
in the longer action, of which that psalm is perhaps a portion;
the same holds in the whole life of man, of which all the

actions of man are parts; the same holds in the whole age of the sons of men, of which all the lives of men are parts.

CHAP. 29—*That human life is a distraction, but that through the mercy of God he was intent on the prize of his heavenly calling.*

39. But "because your loving-kindness is better than life,"[42] behold, my life is but a distraction, and your right hand upheld me[43] in my Lord, the Son of man, the mediator between you,[44] the one, and us the many,—in many distractions amid many things,—that through him I may apprehend in whom I have been apprehended, and may be re-collected from my old days, following the one, forgetting the things that are past; and not distracted, but drawn on, not to those things which shall be and shall pass away, but to those things which are before,[45] not distractedly, but intently, I follow on for the prize of my heavenly calling,[46] where I may hear the voice of your praise, and contemplate your delights,[47] neither coming nor passing away. But now are my years spent in mourning.[48] And you, O Lord, are my comfort, my Father everlasting. But I have been divided amid times, the order of which I know not; and my thoughts, even the inmost bowels of my soul, are mangled with tumultuous varieties, until I flow together to you, purged and molten in the fire of your love.[49]

CHAP. 30—*Again he refutes the empty question, "What did God before the creation of the world?"*

40. And I will be immoveable, and fixed in you, in my mould, your truth; nor will I endure the questions of men, who by a penal disease thirst for more than they can hold, and say, "What did God make before he made heaven and earth?" Or, "How came it into his mind to make anything,

---

[42] Ps. 63: 3.
[43] Ps. 63: 8.
[44] 1 Tim. 2: 5.
[45] Phil. 3: 13.
[46] Phil. 3: 14.
[47] Ps. 26: 7.
[48] Ps. 27: 4.
[49] Ps. 31: 10.

when he never before made anything?" Grant to them, O
Lord, to think well what they say, and to see that where there
is no time, they cannot say "never." What, therefore, he is
said "never to have made," what else is it but to say, that in
no time was it made? Let them therefore see that there could be
no time without a created being, and let them cease to speak
that vanity. Let them also be extended unto those things which
are before,[50] and understand that you, the eternal creator
of all times, are before all times, and that no times are co-
eternal with you, nor any creature, even if there be any creature beyond all times.

CHAP. 31—*How the knowledge of God differs from that of man.*

41. O Lord my God, what is that secret place of your
mystery, and how far thence have the consequences of my
transgressions cast me? Heal my eyes, that I may enjoy your
light. Surely, if there be a mind, so greatly abounding in
knowledge and foreknowledge, to which all things past and
future are so known as one psalm is well known to me, that
mind is exceedingly wonderful, and very astonishing; because
whatever is so past, and whatever is to come of after ages, is
no more concealed from him than was it hidden from me
when singing that psalm, what and how much of it had been
sung from the beginning, what and how much remained to
the end. But far be it that you, the creator of the universe,
the creator of souls and bodies,—far be it that you should
know in this way all things future and past. Far, far more
wonderfully, and far more mysteriously, you know them.
For it is not as the feelings of one singing known things, or
hearing a known song, are—through expectation of future
words, and in remembrance of those that are past—varied,
and his senses divided, that anything happens to you, unchangeably eternal, that is, the truly eternal creator of minds.
As, then, you in the beginning knew the heaven and the earth
without any change of your knowledge, so in the beginning
you made heaven and earth without any difference in your
action. Let him who understands confess to you; and let him

[50] Phil. 3: 13.

who does not understand, confess to you. Oh, how exalted
are you, and yet the humble in heart are your dwelling-place;
for you raise up those that are bowed down,[51] and they
whose exaltation you are do not fall.

[51] Ps. 146: 8.

On Baptism
(A.D. 401)
Book 1

On Baptism, comprising seven books, has been called "probably [Augustine's] most significant work in the whole course
of the [Donatist] controversy" and the "most systematic"
(Battenhouse, pp. 180 and 197). The Donatist schism arose
when, in 312, Caecilianus was made a bishop, although he
was said to have compromised in the Diocletian persecution.
Donatus and his followers, professing to have clean con-
sciences, thereupon separated from the "Catholics." The
schism therefore, local to Africa, made much of the
personal worthiness of the ministers of the sacraments and,
above all, insisted on rebaptism for Catholics joining it. The
administration of the sacrament of baptism was, in practice,
the center of the controversy: hence Augustine's work. It is
well to remember that the Donatists were as numerous as the
Catholics and were not necessarily confined to the rural population. Some of their vagabond supporters, the *circumcel-
liones,* were given to violence. Although Augustine displays
in his writings against the Donatists a tolerance that is not
sufficiently remarked, he eventually accepted the interested
offer of the Roman power to end the schism, apparently with
success. His appeal (*Epistula* 185 *ad Bonifacium* 7.24) to St.
Luke's Gospel (14:22 f.: "compel them to come in") for
this policy of coercion needs very careful understanding indeed—such as is given by P. Brown, *Religion and Society in
the Age of Saint Augustine* (London, 1972), pp. 260–78.
The translation given here is by J. B. King (Edinburgh,
1872).

RECOMMENDED READING

W. H. C. Frend, *The Donatist Church,* Oxford, 1952.
P. Brown, *Augustine of Hippo,* London, 1967, pp. 212–43.

Other works—apart from the Sermon that follows here—referring to the controversy are listed in Altaner, p. 508, Portalié, pp. 50–54, and Battenhouse, pp. 180 f. Among these are *Contra epistolam Parmeniani; Contra litteras Petiliani; Contra Cresconium grammaticum; Contra Gaudentium Donatistarum episcopum;* and *Psalmus contra partem Donati.*

SPECIAL TOPICS

1. *Donatist controversy*
2. *The Church and the Sacraments*

Augustine in this book discusses particularly the seat of authority in the church. The Donatists appealed to St. Cyprian and the Council of Carthage (A.D. 256) in justification of their practice of rebaptism. Augustine, however, appealed to a later and General Council (which must be *either* Arles in 314 *or* Nicaea in 325), which reaffirmed the earlier tradition in this matter. Moreover, Augustine submits, this practice is more in accordance with scripture and logical argument. He invokes the earlier, potent African imagery of the church as Mother (e.g., 1.10.13 ff.) and the dove (1.11.15) and then proceeds to examine in particular the "notes" of unity and catholicity of the true church on the one hand and holiness on the other. His insistence on the irrelevance of the personal worthiness of the minister of the sacrament is, of course, of extreme importance in relation to all the sacraments. For Augustine's teaching on the church and the sacraments, see Portalié, pp. 230–69, and S. Grabowski, *The Church* (St. Louis, 1957).

ON BAPTISM, AGAINST THE DONATISTS

BOOK 1

Chap. 1.—1. In the treatise which we wrote against the published epistle of Parmenianus to Tichonius, we promised that at some future time we would treat the question of baptism more thoroughly;[1] and indeed, even if we had not made this promise, we are not unmindful that this is a debt fairly due from us to the prayers of our brethren. Therefore in this treatise we have undertaken, with the help of God, not only to refute the objections which the Donatists have been accustomed to urge against us in this matter, but also to advance what God may enable us to say in respect of the authority of the blessed martyr Cyprian, which they endeavour to use as a prop, to prevent their perversity from falling before the attacks of truth. And this we propose to do, in order that all whose judgment is not blinded by party spirit may understand that, so far from Cyprian's authority being in their favour, it tends directly to their refutation and discomfiture.

2. In the treatise above mentioned, it has already been said that the grace of baptism can be conferred outside the Catholic communion, just as it can be also there retained. But no one of the Donatists themselves denies that even apostates retain the grace of baptism; for when they return within the pale of the church, and are converted through repentance, it is never given to them a second time, and so it is ruled that it never could have been lost. So those, too, who in the sacri-

[1] *Contra Epist. Parmen.* 2. 14.

lege of schism depart from the communion of the church, certainly retain the grace of baptism, which they received before their departure, seeing that, in case of their return, it is not again conferred on them; therefore it is proved, that what they had received while within the unity of the church, they could not have lost in their separation. But if it can be retained outside, why may it not also be given there? If you say, "It is not rightly given without the pale;" we answer, "As it is not rightly retained, and yet is in some sense retained, so it is not indeed rightly given, but yet it is given." But as, by reconciliation to unity, that begins to be profitably possessed which was possessed to no profit in exclusion from unity, so, by the same reconciliation, that begins to be profitable which without it was given to no profit. Yet it cannot be allowed that it should be said that that was not given which was given, nor that any one should reproach a man with not having given this, while confessing that he had given what he had himself received. For the sacrament of baptism is what the person possesses who is baptized; and the sacrament of conferring baptism is what he possesses who is ordained. And as the baptized person, if he depart from the unity of the church, does not thereby lose the sacrament of baptism, so also he who is ordained, if he depart from the unity of the church, does not lose the sacrament of conferring baptism. For neither sacrament may be wronged. If a sacrament necessarily becomes void in the case of the wicked, both must become void; if it remain valid with the wicked, this must be so with both. If, therefore, the baptism is acknowledged which he could not lose who severed himself from the unity of the church, that baptism must also be acknowledged which was administered by one who by his secession had not lost the sacrament of conferring baptism. For as those who return to the church, if they had been baptized before their secession, are not rebaptized, so those who return, having been ordained before their secession, are certainly not ordained again; but either they again exercise their former ministry, if the interests of the church require it, or if they do not exercise it, at any rate they retain the sacrament of their ordination; and hence it is, that when hands are laid on them, to mark their reconciliation, they are not ranked with the laity. For Felicianus, when he separated him-

self from them with Maximianus, was not held by the Donatists themselves to have lost either the sacrament of baptism
or the sacrament of conferring baptism. For now he is a recognised member of their own body, in company with those very
men whom he baptized while he was separated from them in
the schism of Maximianus. And so others could receive from
them, while they still had not joined our society, what they
themselves had not lost by severance from our society. And
hence it is clear that they are guilty of impiety who endeavour
to rebaptize those who are in Catholic unity; and we act rightly
who do not dare to repudiate God's sacraments, even when
administered in schism. For in all points in which they think
with us, they also are in communion with us, and only are
severed from us in those points in which they dissent from
us. For contact and disunion are not to be measured by different laws in the case of material or spiritual affinities. For
as union of bodies arises from continuity of position, so in
the agreement of wills there is a kind of contact between souls.
If, therefore, a man who has severed himself from unity wishes
to do anything different from that which had been impressed
on him while in the state of unity, in this point he does sever
himself, and is no longer a part of the united whole; but wherever he desires to conduct himself as is customary in the state
of unity, in which he himself learned and received the lessons
which he seeks to follow, in these points he remains a member, and is united to the corporate whole.

CHAP. 2.—3. And so the Donatists in some matters are with
us; in some matters have gone out from us. Accordingly, those
things wherein they agree with us we forbid them not to do;
but in those things in which they differ from us, we earnestly
endeavour that they should come and receive them from us,
or return and recover them, as the case may be. We do not
therefore say to them, "Abstain from giving baptism," but
"Abstain from giving it in schism." Nor do we say to those
whom we see them on the point of baptizing, "Do not receive
the baptism," but "Do not receive it in schism." For if any
one were compelled by urgent necessity, being unable to find
a Catholic from whom to receive baptism, and so, while preserving Catholic peace in his heart, should receive from one

without the pale of Catholic unity the sacrament which he was
intending to receive within its pale, this man, should he forthwith depart this life, we deem to be none other than a Catholic. But if he should be delivered from the death of the body,
on his restoring himself in bodily presence to that Catholic
congregation from which in heart he had never departed, so
far from blaming his conduct, we should praise it with the
greatest truth and confidence; because he trusted that God was
present to his heart, while he was striving to preserve unity,
and was unwilling to depart this life without the sacrament
of holy baptism, which he knew to be of God, and not of
men, wherever he might find it. But if any one who has it
in his power to receive baptism within the Catholic Church
prefers, from some perversity of mind, to be baptized in
schism, even if he afterwards intends to come to the Catholic
Church, because he is assured that there that sacrament will
profit him, which can indeed be received but cannot profit elsewhere, beyond all question he is perverse, and guilty of sin,
and that the more flagrant in proportion as it was committed
wilfully. For that he entertains no doubt that the sacrament
is rightly received in the church, is proved by his conviction
that it is there that he must look for profit even from what
he has received elsewhere.

CHAP. 3.—4. There are two propositions, moreover, which
we affirm,—that baptism exists in the Catholic Church, and that
in it alone can it be rightly received,—both of which the
Donatists deny. Likewise there are two other propositions
which we affirm,—that baptism exists among the Donatists, but
that with them it is not rightly received,—of which two they
strenuously confirm the former, that baptism exists with them;
but they are unwilling to allow the latter, that in their church
it cannot be rightly received. Of these four propositions, three
are peculiar to us; in one we both agree. For that baptism
exists in the Catholic Church, that it is rightly received there,
and that it is not rightly received among the Donatists, are
assertions made only by ourselves; but that baptism exists also
among the Donatists, is asserted by them and allowed by us.
If any one, therefore, is desirous of being baptized, and is already convinced that he ought to choose our church as a me-

dium for Christian salvation, and that the baptism of Christ
is only profitable in it, even when it has been received elsewhere, but yet wishes to be baptized in the schism of Donatus,
because not they only, nor we only, but both parties alike say
that baptism exists with them, let him pause and look to the
other three points. For if he has made up his mind to follow
us in the points which they deny, though he prefers what both
of us acknowledge to what only we assert, it is enough for
our purpose that he prefers what they do not affirm and we
alone assert, to what they alone assert. That baptism exists in
the Catholic Church, we assert and they deny. That it is rightly
received in the Catholic Church, we assert and they deny. That
it is not rightly received in the schism of Donatus, we assert
and they deny. As, therefore, he is the more ready to believe
what we alone assert should be believed, so let him be the
more ready to do what we alone declare should be done. But
let him believe more firmly, if he be so disposed, what both
parties assert should be believed, than what we alone maintain.
For he is inclined to believe more firmly that the baptism of
Christ exists in the schism of Donatus, because that is acknowledged by both of us, than that it exists in the Catholic Church,
an assertion made alone by the Catholics. But again, he is
more ready to believe that the baptism of Christ exists also
with us, as we alone assert, than that it does not exist with us,
as they alone assert. For he has already determined and is
fully convinced, that where we differ, our authority is to be
preferred to theirs. So that he is more ready to believe what
we alone assert, that baptism is rightly received with us, than
that it is not rightly so received, since that rests only on their
assertion. And, by the same rule, he is more ready to believe
what we alone assert, that it is not rightly received with them,
than as they alone assert, that it is rightly so received. He finds,
therefore, that his confidence in being baptized among the
Donatists is somewhat profitless, seeing that, though we both
acknowledge that baptism exists with them, yet we do not both
declare that it ought to be received from them. But he has
made up his mind to cling rather to us in matters where we
disagree. Let him therefore feel confidence in receiving baptism in our communion, where he is assured that it both exists
and is rightly received; and let him not receive it in a com-

munion, where those whose opinion he has determined to follow acknowledge indeed that it exists, but say that it cannot rightly be received. Nay, even if he should hold it to be a doubtful question, whether or no it is impossible for that to be rightly received among the Donatists which he is assured can rightly be received in the Catholic Church, he would commit a grievous sin, in matters concerning the salvation of his soul, in the mere fact of preferring uncertainty to certainty. At any rate, he must be quite sure that a man can be rightly baptized in the Catholic Church, from the mere fact that he has determined to come over to it, even if he be baptized elsewhere. But let him at least acknowledge it to be matter of uncertainty whether a man be not improperly baptized among the Donatists, when he finds this asserted by those whose opinion he is convinced should be preferred to theirs; and, preferring certainty to uncertainty, let him be baptized here, where he has good grounds for being assured that it is rightly done, in the fact that when he thought of doing it elsewhere, he had still determined that he ought afterwards to come over to this side.

CHAP. 4.—5. Further, if any one fails to understand how it can be that we assert that the sacrament is not rightly conferred among the Donatists, while we confess that it exists among them, let him observe that we also deny that it exists rightly among them, just as they deny that it exists rightly among those who quit their communion. Let him also consider the analogy of the military mark, which, though it can both be retained, as by deserters, and also be received by those who are not in the army, yet ought not to be either received or retained outside its ranks; and, at the same time, it is not changed or renewed when a man is enlisted or brought back to his service. However, we must distinguish between the case of those who unwittingly join the ranks of these heretics, under the impression that they are entering the true church of Christ, and those who know that there is no other Catholic Church save that which, according to the promise, is spread abroad throughout the whole world, and extends even to the utmost limits of the earth; which, rising amid tares, and seeking rest in the future from the weariness of offences, says in the Book of Psalms, "From the end of the earth I cried to you, while my heart was in weariness: you exalted me on a rock."[2] But the rock was Christ, in whom the apostle says that we are now raised up, and set together in heavenly places, though not yet actually, but only in hope.[3] And so the psalm goes on to say, "You were my guide, because you have become my hope, a tower of strength from the face of the enemy." By means of his promises, which are like spears and javelins stored up in a strongly fortified place, the enemy is not only guarded against, but overthrown, as he clothes his wolves in sheep's clothing,[4] that they may say, "Lo, here is Christ, or there;"[5] and that they may separate many from the Catholic city which is built upon a hill, and bring them down to the isolation of their own snares, so as utterly to destroy them. And these men, knowing this, choose to receive the baptism of Christ outside of the limits of the communion of the unity of Christ's body, though they intend afterwards, with the sacrament which they have received elsewhere, to pass into that very communion. For they propose to receive Christ's baptism in antagonism to the church of Christ, well knowing that it is so even on the very day on which they receive it. And if this is a sin, who is the man that will say, grant that for a single day I may commit sin? For if he proposes to pass over to the Catholic Church, I would ask why. What other answer can he give, but that it is ill to belong to the party of Donatus, and not to the unity of the Catholic Church? Just so many days, then, as you commit this ill, of so many days' sin are you going to be guilty. And it may be said that there is greater sin in more days' commission of it, and less in fewer; but in no wise can it be said that no sin is committed at all. But what is the need of allowing this accursed wrong for a single day, or a single hour? For the man who wishes this licence to be granted him, might as well ask of the church, or of God himself, that for a single day he should be permitted to apostatize. For there is no reason why he should fear to be an apostate for a day,

2 Ps. 61: 2 f.
3 Eph. 2: 6.
4 Matt. 7: 15.
5 Matt. 24: 23.

if he does not shrink from being for that time a schismatic
or a heretic.

CHAP. 5.—6. I prefer, he says, to receive Christ's baptism
where both parties agree that it exists. But those whom you
intend to join say that it cannot be received there rightly;
and those who say that it can be received there rightly are
the party whom you mean to quit. What they say, therefore, whom you yourself consider of inferior authority, in
opposition to what those say whom you yourself prefer, is, if
not false, at any rate, to use a milder term, at least uncertain. I entreat you, therefore, to prefer what is true to what
is false, or what is certain to what is uncertain. For it is not
only those whom you are going to join, but you yourself who
are going to join them, that confess that what you want can be
rightly received in that body which you mean to join when
you have received it elsewhere. For if you had any doubts
whether it could be rightly received there, you would also
have doubts whether you ought to make the change. If, therefore, it is doubtful whether it be not sin to receive baptism
from the party of Donatus, who can doubt but that it is certain sin not to prefer receiving it where it is certain that it
is not sin? And those who are baptized there through ignorance, thinking that it is the true church of Christ, are guilty
of less sin in comparison than these, though even they are
wounded by the impiety of schism; nor do they escape a grievous hurt, because others suffer even more. For when it is
said to certain men, "It shall be more tolerable for the land
of Sodom in the day of judgment than for you,"[6] it is not
meant that the men of Sodom shall escape torment, but only
that the others shall be even more grievously tormented.

7. And yet this point had once, perhaps, been involved in
obscurity and doubt. But that which is a source of health to
those who give heed and receive correction, is but an aggra-
vation of the sin of those who, when they are no longer
suffered to be ignorant, persist in their madness to their own
destruction. For the condemnation of the party of Maximianus, and their restoration after they had been condemned,

[6] Matt. 11: 24.

together with those whom they had sacrilegiously, to use the
language of their own Council, baptized in schism, settles
the whole question in dispute, and removes all controversy.
There is no point at issue between ourselves and those Donatists who hold communion with Primianus, which could give
rise to any doubt that the baptism of Christ may not only be
retained, but even conferred by those who are severed from
the church. For as they themselves are obliged to confess that
those whom Felicianus baptized in schism received true baptism, inasmuch as they now acknowledge them as members
of their own body with no other baptism than that which they
received in schism, so we say that that is Christ's baptism,
even without the pale of Catholic communion, which they
confer who are cut off from that communion, inasmuch as
they had not lost it when they were cut off. And what they
themselves think that they conferred on those persons whom
Felicianus baptized in schism, when they admitted them to
reconciliation with themselves, viz., not that they should receive that which they did not as yet possess, but that what
they had received to no advantage in schism, and were already
in possession of, should be of profit to them, this God really
confers and bestows through the Catholic communion on
those who come from any heresy or schism in which they received the baptism of Christ; viz. not that they should begin to
receive the sacrament of baptism as not possessing it before,
but that what they already possessed should now begin to
profit them.

CHAP. 6.—8. Between us, then, and what we may call the
genuine Donatists, whose bishop is Primianus at Carthage,
there is now no controversy on this point. For God willed
that it should be ended by means of the followers of Maximianus, that they should be compelled by the precedent of his
case to acknowledge what they would not allow at the persuasion of Christian charity. But this brings us to consider
next, whether those men do not seem to have something to
say for themselves, who refuse communion with the party of
Primianus, contending that in their body there remains greater
sincerity of Donatism, just in proportion to the paucity of
their numbers. And even if these were only the party of

Maximianus, we should not be justified in despising their salvation. How much more, then, are we bound to consider it, when we find that this same party of Donatus is split up into many most minute fractions, all which small sections of the body blame the one much larger portion which has Primianus for its head, because they receive the baptism of the followers of Maximianus; while each endeavours to maintain that it is the sole receptacle of true baptism, which exists nowhere else, neither in the whole of the world where the Catholic Church extends itself, nor in that larger main body of the Donatists, nor even in the other minute sections, but only in itself. Whereas, if all these fragments would listen not to the voice of man, but to the most unmistakeable manifestation of the truth, and would be willing to curb the fiery temper of their own perversity, they would return from their own barrenness, not indeed to the main body of Donatus, a mere fragment of which they are a smaller fragment, but to the never-failing fruitfulness of the root of the Catholic Church. For all of them who are not against us are for us; but when they gather not with us, they scatter abroad.

CHAP. 7.—9. For, in the next place, that I may not seem to rest on mere human arguments,—since there is so much obscurity in this question, that in earlier ages of the church, before the schism of Donatus, it has caused men of great weight, and even bishops whose hearts were full of charity, so to dispute and doubt among themselves, saving always the peace of the church, that the several statutes of their Councils in their different districts long varied from each other, till at length the most wholesome opinion was established, to the removal of all doubts, by a general Council of the whole world:—I therefore bring forward from the gospel clear proofs, by which I propose, with God's help, to prove how rightly and truly in the sight of God it has been determined, that in the case of every schismatic and heretic, the wound which caused his separation should be cured by the medicine of the church; but that what remained sound in him should rather be recognised with approbation, than wounded by condemnation. It is indeed true that the Lord says in the gospel, "He that is not with me is against me; and he that does not

gather with me scatters abroad."[7] Yet when the disciples
had brought word to him that they had seen one casting out
devils in his name, and had forbidden him, because he did
not follow them, he said, "Forbid him not: for he that is
not against us is for us. For there is no man who shall do a
miracle in my name, that can lightly speak evil of me."[8]
If, indeed, there were nothing in this man requiring correction, then any one would be safe, who, setting himself outside
the communion of the church, severing himself from all
Christian brotherhood, should gather in Christ's name; and
so there would be no truth in this, "He that is not with me is
against me; and he that does not gather with me scatters
abroad." But if he required correction in the point where
the disciples in their ignorance were anxious to check him,
why did our Lord, by saying, "Forbid him not," prevent this
check from being given? And how can that be true which he
then says, "He that is not against you is for you?" For
in this point he was not against, but for them, when he was
working miracles of healing in Christ's name. That both,
therefore, should be true, as both are true,—both the declara-
tion, that "He that is not with me is against me, and he that
does not gather with me scatters abroad;" and also the injunction, "Forbid him not; for he that is not against you is for
you,"—what must we understand, except that the man was
to be confirmed in his veneration for that mighty name, in
respect of which he was not against the church, but for it;
and yet he was to be blamed for separating himself from
the church, whereby his gathering became a scattering; and
if it should have so happened that he sought union with the
church, he should not have received what he already possessed, but be made to set right the points wherein he had
gone astray?

CHAP. 8.—10. Nor indeed were the prayers of the Gentile
Cornelius unheard, nor did his alms lack acceptance; nay,
he was found worthy that an angel should be sent to him, and
that he should behold the messenger, through whom he might

[7] Matt. 12: 30.
[8] Mark 9: 38 f.; Luke 9: 50.

assuredly have learned everything that was necessary, without requiring that any man should come to him. But since all the good that he had in his prayers and alms could not benefit him unless he were incorporated in the church by the bond of Christian brotherhood and peace, he was ordered to send to Peter, and through him got to know Christ; and, being also baptized by his orders, he was joined by the tie of communion to the fellowship of Christians, to which before he was bound only by the likeness of good works.[9] And indeed it would have been most fatal to despise what he did not yet possess, vaunting himself in what he had. So too those who, by separating themselves from the society of their fellows, to the overthrow of charity, thus break the bond of unity, if they observe none of the things which they have received in that society, are separated in everything; and so any one whom they have joined to their society, if he afterwards wishes to come over to the church, ought to receive everything which he has not already received. But if they observe some of the same things, in respect of these they have not severed themselves; and so far they are still a part of the framework of the church, while in all other respects they are cut off from it. Accordingly, any one whom they have associated with themselves is united to the church in all those points in which they are not separated from it. And therefore, if he wish to come over to the church, he is made sound in those points in which he was unsound and went astray; but where he was sound in union with the church, he is not cured, but recognised,—lest in desiring to cure what is sound we should rather inflict a wound. Therefore those whom they baptize they heal from the wound of idolatry or unbelief; but they injure them more seriously with the wound of schism. For idolaters among the people of the Lord were smitten with the sword;[10] but schismatics were swallowed up by the earth opening her mouth.[11] And the apostle says, "Though I have all faith, so that I could remove mountains, and have not charity, I am nothing."[12]

[9] Acts 10.
[10] Ex. 32.
[11] Num. 16.
[12] 1 Cor. 13: 2.

11. If any one is brought to the surgeon, afflicted with a grievous wound in some vital part of the body, and the surgeon says that unless it is cured it must cause death, the friends who brought him do not, I presume, act so foolishly as to count over to the surgeon all his sound limbs, and, drawing his attention to them, make answer to him, "Can it be that all these sound limbs are of no avail to save his life, and that one wounded limb is enough to cause his death?" They certainly do not say this, but they entrust him to the surgeon to be cured. Nor, again, because they so entrust him, do they ask the surgeon to cure the limbs that are sound as well; but they desire him to apply drugs with all care to the one part from which death is threatening the other sound parts too, with the certainty that it must come, unless the wound be healed. What will it then profit a man that he has sound faith, or perhaps only soundness in the sacrament of faith, when the soundness of his charity is done away with by the fatal wound of schism, so that by the overthrow of it the other points, which were in themselves sound, are brought into the infection of death? To prevent which, the mercy of God, through the unity of his holy church, does not cease striving that they may come and be healed by the medicine of reconciliation, through the bond of peace. And let them not think that they are sound because we admit that they have something sound in them; nor let them think, on the other hand, that what is sound must be healed, because we show that in some parts there is a wound. So that in the soundness of the sacrament, because they are not against us, they are for us; but in the wound of schism, because they gather not with Christ, they scatter abroad. Let them not be exalted by what they have. Why do they pass the eyes of pride over those parts only which are sound? Let them condescend also to look humbly on their wound, and give heed not only to what they have, but also to what is wanting in them.

CHAP. 9.—12. Let them see how many things, and what important things, are of no avail, if a certain single thing be wanting, and let them see what that one thing is. And herein let them hear not my words, but those of the apostle:

"Though I speak with the tongues of men and of angels, and have not charity, I am become as sounding brass, or a tinkling cymbal. And though I have the gift of prophecy, and understand all mysteries, and all knowledge; and though I have all faith, so that I could remove mountains, and have not charity, I am nothing."[13] What does it profit them, therefore, if they have both the voice of angels in the sacred mysteries, and the gift of prophecy, as had Caiaphas[14] and Saul,[15] that so they may be found prophesying, of whom Holy Scripture testifies that they were worthy of condemnation? If they not only know, but even possess the sacraments, as Simon Magus did;[16] if they have faith, as the devils confessed Christ (for we must not suppose that they did not believe when they said, "What have we to do with you? I know you who you are, the holy one of God"[17]); if they distribute of themselves their own substance to the poor, as many do, not only in the Catholic Church, but in the different heretical bodies; if, under the pressure of any persecution, they give their bodies with us to be burned for the faith which they like us confess: yet because they do all these things apart from the church, not "forbearing one another in love," nor "endeavouring to keep the unity of the spirit in the bond of peace,"[18] insomuch as they have not charity, they cannot attain to eternal salvation, even with all those good things which profit them not.

CHAP. 10.—13. But they think within themselves that they show very great subtlety in asking whether the baptism of Christ in the party of Donatus makes men sons or not; so that, if we allow that it does make them sons, they may assert that theirs is the church, the mother which could give birth to sons in the baptism of Christ; and since the church must be one, they may allege that ours is no church. But if we say that it does not make them sons, "Why then," say they,

[13] 1 Cor. 13: 1 f.
[14] John 11: 51.
[15] 1 Sam. 18: 10.
[16] Acts 8: 13.
[17] Mark 1: 24.
[18] Eph. 4: 2 f.

"do you not cause those who pass from us to you to be born again in baptism, after they have been baptized with us, if they are not thereby born as yet?"

14. Just as though their party gained the power of generation in virtue of what constitutes its division, and not from what causes its union with the church. For it is severed from the bond of peace and charity, but it is joined in one baptism. And so there is one church which alone is called Catholic; and whenever it has anything of its own in these communions of different bodies which are separate from itself, it is most certainly in virtue of this which is its own in each of them that it, not they, has the power of generation. For neither is it their separation that generates, but what they have retained of the essence of the church; and if they were to go on to abandon this, they would lose the power of generation. The generation, then, in each case proceeds from the church, whose sacraments are retained, from which any such birth can alone in any case proceed,—although not all who receive its birth belong to its unity, which shall save those who persevere even to the end. Nor is it those only that do not belong to it who are openly guilty of the manifest sacrilege of schism, but also those who, being outwardly joined to its unity, are yet separated by a life of sin. For the church had herself given birth to Simon Magus through the sacrament of baptism; and yet it was declared to him that he had no part in the inheritance of Christ.[19] Did he lack anything in respect of baptism, of the gospel, of the sacraments? But in that he wanted charity, he was born in vain; and perhaps it had been well for him that he had never been born at all. Was anything wanting to their birth to whom the apostle says, "I have fed you with milk, and not with meat, even as babes in Christ?" Yet he recalls them from the sacrilege of schism, into which they were rushing, because they were carnal: "I have fed you," he says, "with milk, and not with meat: for hitherto you were not able to bear it, nor are you yet able. For you are yet carnal: for whereas there is among you envying, and strife, and divisions, are you not carnal, and walk as men? For while one says, I am of Paul; and another,

19 Acts 8: 13, 21.

I am of Apollo; are you not carnal?"[20] For of these he says above: "Now I beseech you, brethren, by the name of our Lord Jesus Christ, that you all speak the same thing, and that there be no divisions among you; but that you be perfectly joined together in the same mind, and in the same judgment. For it has been declared to me of you, my brethren, by them that are of the house of Chlöe, that there are contentions among you. Now this I say, that every one of you says, I am of Paul, and I of Apollo, and I of Cephas, and I of Christ. Is Christ divided? was Paul crucified for you? or were you baptized in the name of Paul?"[21] These, therefore, if they continued in the same perverse obstinacy, were doubtless indeed born, but yet would not belong by the bond of peace and unity to the very church in respect of which they were born. Therefore she herself bears them in her own womb, and in the womb of her handmaids, by virtue of the same sacraments, as though by virtue of the seed of her husband. For it is not without meaning that the apostle says that all these things were done by way of figure.[22] But those who are too proud, and are not joined to their lawful mother, are like Ishmael, of whom it is said, "Cast out this bond-woman and her son: for the son of the bond-woman shall not be heir with my son, even with Isaac."[23] But those who peacefully love the lawful wife of their father, whose sons they are by lawful descent, are like the sons of Jacob, born indeed of handmaids, but yet receiving the same inheritance.[24] But those who are born within the family, of the womb of the mother herself, and then neglect what they have received, are like Isaac's son Esau, who was rejected, God himself bearing witness to it, and saying, "I loved Jacob, and I hated Esau;"[25] and that though they were twin-brethren, the offspring of the same womb.

CHAP. 11.—15. They ask also, "Whether sins are remitted in

[20] 1 Cor. 3: 1–4.
[21] 1 Cor. 1: 10–13.
[22] 1 Cor. 10: 11.
[23] Gen. 21: 10.
[24] Gen. 30: 3.
[25] Mal. 1: 2 f.; Gen. 25: 24.

baptism in the party of Donatus:" so that, if we say that they are remitted, they may answer, then the Holy Spirit is there; for when by the breathing of our Lord the Holy Spirit was given to the disciples, he then went on to say, "Baptize all nations in the name of the Father, and of the Son, and of the Holy Ghost."[26] "Whose sins you remit, they are remitted to them; and whose sins you retain, they are retained."[27] And if it is so, they say, then our communion is the church of Christ; for the Holy Spirit does not work the remission of sins except in the church. And if our communion is the church of Christ, then your communion is not the church of Christ. For that is one, wherever it is, of which it is said, "My dove is but one; she is the only one of her mother:"[28] nor can there be just so many churches as there are schisms. But if we should say that sins are not there remitted, then, say they, there is no true baptism there; and therefore ought you to baptize those whom you receive from us. And since you do not do this, you confess that you are not in the church of Christ.

16. To these we reply, following the Scriptures, by asking them to answer themselves what they ask of us. For I beg them to tell us whether there is any remission of sins where there is not charity; for sins are the darkness of the soul. For we find St. John saying, "He that hates his brother is in darkness."[29] But none would create schisms, if they were not blinded by hatred of their brethren. If, therefore, we say that sins are not remitted there, how is he regenerate who is baptized among them? And what is regeneration in baptism, except the being renovated from the corruption of the old man? And how can he be so renovated whose past sins are not remitted? But if he be not regenerate, neither does he put on Christ; from which it seems to follow that he ought to be baptized again. For the apostle says, "For as many of you as have been baptized into Christ have put on Christ;"[30] and if he has not so put on Christ, neither should

[26] Matt. 28: 19.
[27] John 20: 23.
[28] Song 6: 9.
[29] 1 John 2: 11.
[30] Gal. 3: 27.

he be considered to have been baptized in Christ. Further, since we say that he has been baptized in Christ, we confess that he has put on Christ; and if we confess this, we confess that he is regenerate. And if this be so, how does St. John say, "He that hates his brother remains still in darkness," if remission of his sins has already taken place? Can it be that schism does not involve hatred of one's brethren? Who will maintain this, when both the origin of, and perseverance in schism consists in nothing else save hatred of the brethren?

17. They think that they solve this question when they say: "There is then no remission of sins in schism, and therefore no creation of the new man by regeneration, and accordingly neither is there the baptism of Christ." But since we confess that the baptism of Christ exists in schism, we propose this question to them for solution: was Simon Magus endued with the true baptism of Christ? They will answer, yes; being compelled to do so by the authority of Holy Scripture. I ask them whether they confess that he received remission of his sins. They will certainly acknowledge it. So I ask why Peter said to him that he had no part in the lot of the saints. Because, they say, he sinned afterwards, wishing to buy with money the gift of God, which he believed the apostles were able to sell.

CHAP. 12.—18. What if he approached baptism itself in deceit? were his sins remitted, or were they not? Let them choose which they will. Whichever they choose will answer our purpose. If they say they were remitted, how then shall "the Holy Spirit of discipline flee deceit,"[31] if in him who was full of deceit he worked remission of sins? If they say they were not remitted, I ask whether, if he should afterwards confess his sin with contrition of heart and true sorrow, it would be judged that he ought to be baptized again. And if it is mere madness to assert this, then let them confess that a man can be baptized with the true baptism of Christ, and that yet his heart, persisting in malice or sacrilege, may not allow remission of sins to be given; and so let them understand that men may be baptized in communions severed from

[31] Wis. 1: 5.

the church, in which Christ's baptism is given and received
in the said celebration of the sacrament, but that it will only
then be of avail for the remission of sins, when the recipient,
being reconciled to the unity of the church, is purged from
the sacrilege of deceit, by which his sins were retained, and
their remission prevented. For, as in the case of him who
had approached the sacrament in deceit there is no second
baptism, but he is purged by faithful discipline and truthful
confession, which he could not be without baptism, so that
what was given before becomes then powerful to work his
salvation, when the former deceit is done away by the truthful confession; so also in the case of the man who, while
an enemy to the peace and love of Christ, received in any
heresy or schism the baptism of Christ, which the schismatics
in question had not lost from among them, though by his
sacrilege his sins were not remitted, yet, when he corrects
his error, and comes over to the communion and unity of the
church, he ought not to be again baptized: because by his
very reconciliation to the peace of the church he receives this
benefit, that the sacrament now begins in unity to be of avail
for the remission of his sins, which could not so avail him as
received in schism.

19. But if they should say that in the man who has approached the sacrament in deceit, his sins are indeed removed
by the holy power of so great a sacrament at the moment
when he received it, but return immediately in consequence
of his deceit: so that the Holy Spirit has both been present
with him at his baptism for the removal of his sins, and has
also fled before his perseverance in deceit so that they should
return: so that both declarations prove true,—both, "As many
of you as have been baptized into Christ have put on Christ;"
and also, "The holy spirit of discipline will flee deceit;"—that
is to say, that both the holiness of baptism clothes him with
Christ, and the sinfulness of deceit strips him of Christ; like
the case of a man who passes from darkness through light
into darkness again, his eyes being always directed towards
darkness, though the light cannot but penetrate them as he
passes;—if they should say this, let them understand that this
is also the case with those who are baptized without the pale
of the church, but yet with the baptism of the church, which

is holy in itself, wherever it may be; and which therefore belongs not to those who separate themselves, but to the body from which they are separated; while yet it avails even among them so far, that they pass through its light back to their own darkness, their sins, which in that moment had been dispelled by the holiness of baptism, returning immediately upon them, as though it were the darkness returning which the light had dispelled while they were passing through it.

20. For that sins which have been remitted do return upon a man, is most clearly taught by our Lord, in the case of the servant whom he found owing him ten thousand talents, and to whom he yet forgave all at his entreaty. But when he refused to have pity on his fellow-servant who owed him a hundred pence, the Lord commanded him to pay what he had forgiven him. The time, then, at which pardon is received through baptism is as it were the time for rendering accounts, so that all the debts which are found to be due may be remitted. Yet it was not afterwards that the servant lent his fellow-servant the money, which he had so pitilessly exacted when the other was unable to pay it; but his fellow-servant already owed him the debt, when he himself, on rendering his accounts to his master, was excused a debt of so vast an amount. He had not first excused his fellow-servant, and so come to receive forgiveness from his Lord. This is proved by the words of the fellow-servant: "Have patience with me, and I will pay you all." Otherwise he would have said, "You forgave me it before; why do you again demand it?" This is made more clear by the words of the Lord himself. For he says, "But the same servant went out, and found one of his fellow-servants who was owing him a hundred pence."[32] He does not say, "To whom he had already forgiven a debt of a hundred pence." Since then he says, "was owing him," it is clear that he had not forgiven him the debt. And indeed it would have been better, and more in accordance with the position of a man who was going to render an account of so great a debt, and expected forbearance from his lord, that he should first have forgiven his fellow-servant what was due to him, and so have come to render the account

[32] Matt. 18: 23–35.

when there was such need for imploring the compassion of his lord. Yet the fact that he had not yet forgiven his fellow-servant, did not prevent his lord from forgiving him all his debts on the occasion of receiving his accounts. But what advantage was it to him, since they all immediately returned with redoubled force upon his head, in consequence of his persistent want of charity? So the grace of baptism is not prevented from giving remission of all sins, even if he to whom they are forgiven continues to cherish hatred towards his brother in his heart. For the guilt of yesterday is remitted, and all that was before it, even the guilt of the very hour and moment previous to baptism, and during baptism itself. But then he immediately begins again to be responsible, not only for the days, hours, moments which ensue, but also for the past,—the guilt of all the sins which were remitted returning on him, as happens only too frequently in the church.

CHAP. 13.—21. For it often happens that a man has an enemy whom he hates most unjustly; although we are commanded to love even our unjust enemies, and to pray for them. But in some sudden danger of death he begins to be uneasy, and desires baptism, which he receives in such haste, that the emergency scarcely admits of the necessary formal examination of a few words, much less of a long conversation, so that this hatred should be driven from his heart, even supposing it to be known to the minister who baptizes him. Certainly cases of this sort are still found to occur not only with us, but also with them. What shall we say then? Are this man's sins forgiven or not? Let them choose just which alternative they prefer. For if they are forgiven, they immediately return: this is the teaching of the gospel, the authoritative announcement of truth. Whether, therefore, they are forgiven or not, medicine is necessary afterwards; and yet if the man lives, and learns that his fault stands in need of correction, and corrects it, he is not baptized anew, either with them or with us. So in the points in which schismatics and heretics neither entertain different opinions nor observe different practice from ourselves, we do not correct them when they join us, but rather commend what we find in them. For where they do not differ from us, they are not separated

from us. But because these things do them no good so long
as they are schismatics or heretics, on account of other points
in which they differ from us, not to mention the most grievous
sin that is involved in separation itself, therefore, whether
their sins remain in them, or return again immediately after
remission, in either case we exhort them to come to the soundness of peace and Christian charity, not only that they may
obtain something which they had not before, but also that
what they had may begin to be of use to them.

CHAP. 14.—22. It is to no purpose, then, that they say
to us, "If you acknowledge our baptism, what do we lack that
should make you suppose that we ought to think seriously
of joining your communion?" For we reply, We do not acknowledge any baptism of yours; for it is not the baptism
of schismatics or heretics, but of God and of the church,
wherever it may be found, and whithersoever it may be
transferred. But it is in no sense yours, except because you
entertain false opinions, and do sacrilegious acts, and have
impiously separated yourselves from the church. For if
everything else in your practice and opinions were true, and
still you were to persist in this same separation, contrary to
the bond of brotherly peace, contrary to the union of all the
brethren, who have been manifest, according to the promise,
in all the world; the particulars of whose history, and the
secrets of whose hearts, you never could have known or considered in every case, so as to have a right to condemn them;
who, moreover, cannot be liable to condemnation for submitting themselves to the judges of the church rather than to
one of the parties to the dispute,—in this one thing, at least,
in such a case, you are deficient, in which he is deficient who
lacks charity. Why should we go over our argument again?
Look and see yourselves in the apostle, how much there is
that you lack. For what does it matter to him who lacks
charity, whether he be carried away outside the church at
once by some blast of temptation, or remain within the Lord's
harvest, so as to be separated only at the final winnowing?
And yet even such, if they have once been born in baptism,
need not be born again.

CHAP. 15.—23. For it is the church that gives birth to all, either within her pale, of her own womb; or beyond it, of the seed of her bridegroom,—either of herself, or of her handmaid. But Esau, even though born of the lawful wife, was separated from the people of God because he quarrelled with his brother. And Asher, born indeed by the authority of a wife, but yet of a handmaid, was admitted to the land of promise on account of his brotherly good-will. Therefore also it was not the being born of a handmaid, but his quarrelling with his brother, that stood in the way of Ishmael, to cause his separation from the people of God; and he received no benefit from the power of the wife, whose son he rather was, inasmuch as it was in virtue of her conjugal rights that he was both conceived in and born of the womb of the handmaid. Just as with the Donatists it is by the right of the church, which exists in baptism, that whoever is born receives his birth; but if they agree with their brethren, through the unity of peace they come to the land of promise, not to be again cast out from the bosom of their true mother, but to be acknowledged in the seed of their father; but if they persevere in discord, they will belong to the line of Ishmael. For Ishmael was first, and then Isaac; and Esau was the elder, Jacob the younger. Not that heresy gives birth before the church, or that the church herself gives birth first to those who are carnal or animal, and afterwards to those who are spiritual; but because, in the actual lot of our mortality, in which we are born of the seed of Adam, "that was not first which is spiritual, but that which is natural, and afterward that which is spiritual."[33] But from mere animal sensation, because "the natural man receives not the things of the Spirit of God,"[34] arise all dissensions and schisms. And the apostle says[35] that all who persevere in this animal sensation belong to the old covenant, that is, to the desire of earthly promises, which are indeed the type of the spiritual; but "the natural man receives not the things of the Spirit of God."

24. At whatever time, therefore, men have begun to be of

[33] 1 Cor. 15: 46.
[34] 1 Cor. 2: 14.
[35] Gal. 4.

such a nature in this life, that, although they have partaken of such divine sacraments as were appointed for the dispensation under which they lived, they yet savour of carnal things, and hope for and desire carnal things from God, whether in this life or afterwards, they are yet carnal. But the church, which is the people of God, is an ancient institution even in the pilgrimage of this life, having a carnal interest in some men, a spiritual interest in others. To the carnal belongs the old covenant, to the spiritual the new. But in the first days both were hidden, from Adam even to Moses. But by Moses the old covenant was made manifest, and in it was hidden the new covenant, because after a secret fashion it was typified. But so soon as the Lord came in the flesh, the new covenant was revealed; yet, though the sacraments of the old covenant passed away, the dispositions peculiar to it did not pass away. For they still exist in those whom the apostle declares to be already born indeed by the sacrament of the new covenant, but yet incapable, as being natural, of receiving the things of the Spirit of God. For, as in the sacraments of the old covenant some persons were already spiritual, belonging secretly to the new covenant, which was then concealed, so now also in the sacrament of the new covenant, which has been by this time revealed, many live who are natural. And if they will not advance to receive the things of the Spirit of God, to which the discourse of the apostle urges them, they will still belong to the old covenant. But if they advance, even before they receive them, yet by their very advance and approach they belong to the new covenant; and if, before becoming spiritual, they are snatched away from this life, yet through the protection of the holiness of the sacrament they are reckoned in the land of the living, where the Lord is our hope and our portion. Nor can I find any truer interpretation of the scripture, "Your eyes did see my substance, yet being imperfect;"[36] considering what follows, "And in your book shall all be written."

CHAP. 16.—25. But the same mother who brought forth Abel, and Enoch, and Noah, and Abraham, brought forth also

[36] Ps. 139: 16.

Moses and the prophets who succeeded him till the coming of
our Lord; and the mother who gave birth to them gave
birth also to our apostles and martyrs, and all good Christians.
For all these that have appeared have been born indeed at
different times, but are included in the society of our people;
and it is as citizens of the same state that they have experienced the labours of this pilgrimage, and some of them are
experiencing them, and others will experience them even to
the end. Again, the mother who brought forth Cain, and
Ham, and Ishmael, and Esau, brought forth also Dathan and
others like him in the same people; and she who gave birth
to them gave birth also to Judas the false apostle, and Simon
Magus, and all the other false Christians who up to this
time have persisted obstinately in their carnal affections,
whether they have been mingled in the unity of the church,
or separated from it in open schism. But when men of this
kind have the gospel preached to them, and receive the sacraments at the hand of those who are spiritual, it is as though
Rebecca gave birth to them of her own womb, as she did to
Esau; but when they are produced in the midst of the people
of God through the instrumentality of those who preach the
gospel not sincerely, Sarah is indeed the mother, but through
Hagar. So when good spiritual disciples are produced by the
preaching or baptism of those who are carnal, Leah, indeed,
or Rachel, gives birth to them in her right as wife, but from
the womb of a handmaid. But when good and faithful disciples are born of those who are spiritual in the gospel, and
either attain to the development of spiritual age, or do not
cease to strive in that direction, or are only deterred from
doing so by want of power, these are born like Isaac from
the womb of Sarah, or Jacob from the womb of Rebecca, in
the new life of the new covenant.

CHAP. 17.—26. Therefore, whether they seem to abide
within, or are openly outside, whatsoever is flesh is flesh, and
what is chaff is chaff, whether they persevere in remaining in
their barrenness on the threshing-floor, or, when temptation
befalls them, are carried out as it were by the blast of some
wind. And even that man is always severed from the unity
of the church which is without spot or wrinkle, who asso-

ciates with the congregation of the saints in carnal obstinacy.
Yet we ought to despair of no man, whether he is one who
shows himself to be of this nature within the pale of the
church, or whether he more openly opposes it from without.
But the spiritual, or those who are steadily advancing with
pious exertion towards this end, do not stray without the
pale; since even when, by some perversity or necessity among
men, they seem to be driven forth, they are more approved
than if they had remained within, since they are in no degree roused to contend against the church, but remain rooted
in the strongest foundation of Christian charity on the solid
rock of unity. For here belongs what is said in the sacrifice
of Abraham: "But the birds divided he not."[37]

CHAP. 18.—27. On the question of baptism, then, I think
that I have argued at sufficient length; and since this is a most
manifest schism which is called by the name of the Donatists,
it only remains that on the subject of baptism we should believe with pious faith what the universal church maintains,
apart from the sacrilege of schism. And yet, if within the
church different men still held different opinions on the point,
without meanwhile violating peace, then till some one clear
and simple decree should have been passed by a universal
Council, it would have been right for the charity which seeks
for unity to throw a veil over the error of human infirmity,
as it is written, "For charity shall cover a multitude of sins."[38]
For, seeing that its absence causes the presence of all other
things to be of no avail, we may well suppose that in its presence there is found pardon for the absence of some missing
things.

28. There are great proofs of this existing on the part of
the blessed martyr Cyprian, in his letters,—to come at last to
him of whose authority they carnally flatter themselves they
are possessed, while by his love they are spiritually overthrown. For at that time, before the consent of the whole
church had declared authoritatively, by the decree of a general Council, what practice should be followed in this mat-

[37] Gen. 15: 10.
[38] 1 Pet. 4: 8.

ter, it seemed to him, in common with about eighty of his
fellow-bishops of the African churches, that every man who
had been baptized outside the communion of the Catholic
Church should, on joining the church, be baptized anew.
And I take it, that the reason why the Lord did not reveal the
error in this to a man of such eminence, was, that his pious
humility and charity in guarding the peace and health of the
church might be made manifest, and might be noticed, so as
to serve as an example of healing power, so to speak, not
only to Christians of that age, but also to those who should
come after. For when a bishop of so important a church,
himself a man of so great merit and virtue, endowed with
such excellence of heart and power of eloquence, entertained
an opinion about baptism different from that which was to be
confirmed by a more diligent searching into the truth; though
many of his colleagues held what was not yet made manifest
by authority, but was sanctioned by the past custom of the
church, and afterwards embraced by the whole Catholic
world; yet under these circumstances he did not sever himself, by refusal of communion, from the others who thought
differently, and indeed never ceased to urge on the others that
they should "forbear one another in love, endeavouring to
keep the unity of the Spirit in the bond of peace."[39] For so,
while the framework of the body remained whole, if any infirmity occurred in certain of its members, it might rather
regain its health from their general soundness, than be deprived of the chance of any healing care by their death in
severance from the body. And if he had severed himself,
how many were there to follow! what a name was he likely
to make for himself among men! how much more widely
would the name of Cyprianist have spread than that of
Donatist! But he was not a son of perdition, one of those
of whom it is said, "You cast them down into destruction;"[40]
but he was the son of the peace of the church, who in the
clear illumination of his mind failed to see one thing, only
that through him another thing might be more excellently
seen. "And yet," says the apostle, "I show you a more excel-

[39] Eph. 4: 2 f.
[40] Ps. 73: 18.

lent way: though I speak with the tongues of men and of angels, and have not charity, I am become as sounding brass, or a tinkling cymbal."[41] He had therefore imperfect insight into the hidden mystery of the sacrament. But if he had known the mysteries of all sacraments, without having charity, it would have been nothing. But as he, with imperfect insight into the mystery, was careful to preserve charity with all courage and humility and faith, he deserved to come to the crown of martyrdom; so that, if any cloud had crept over the clearness of his intellect from his infirmity as man, it might be dispelled by the glorious brightness of his blood. For it was not in vain that our Lord Jesus Christ, when he declared himself to be the vine, and his disciples, as it were, the branches in the vine, gave command that those that bore no fruit should be cut off, and removed from the vine as useless branches.[42] But what is really fruit, save that new offspring, of which he further says, "A new commandment I give unto you, that you love one another?"[43] This is that very charity, without which the rest profits nothing. The apostle also says: "But the fruit of the Spirit is love, joy, peace, long-suffering, gentleness, goodness, faith, meekness, temperance;"[44] each of which begins with charity, and with the rest of the combination forms one unity in a kind of wondrous cluster. Nor is it again in vain that our Lord added, "And every branch that bears fruit, my Father purges it, that it may bring forth more fruit,"[45] but because those who are strong in the fruit of charity may yet have something which requires purging, which the husbandman will not leave untended. While, then, that holy man entertained on the subject of baptism an opinion at variance with the true view, which was afterwards thoroughly examined and confirmed after most diligent consideration, his error was compensated by his remaining in catholic unity, and by the abundance of his charity; and finally it was cleared away by the pruning-hook of martyrdom.

41 1 Cor. 12: 31; 13: 1.
42 John 15: 1 f.
43 John 13: 34.
44 Gal. 5: 22 f.
45 John 15: 2.

CHAP. 19.—29. But that I may not seem to be uttering these praises of the blessed martyr (which, indeed, are not his, but rather those of him by whose grace he showed himself what he was), in order to escape the burden of proof, let us now bring forward from his letters the testimony by which the mouths of the Donatists may most of all be stopped. For they advance his authority before the unlearned, to show that in a manner they do well when they baptize afresh the faithful who come to them. Too wretched are they—and, unless they correct themselves, even by themselves are they utterly condemned—who choose in the example set them by so great a man to imitate just that fault, which did not injure him only because he walked with constant steps even to the end in that from which they have strayed who "have not known the ways of peace." It is true that Christ's baptism is holy; and although it may exist among heretics or schismatics, yet it does not belong to the heresy or schism; and therefore even those who come from thence to the Catholic Church herself ought not to be baptized afresh. Yet to err on this point is one thing; it is another thing that those who are straying from the peace of the church, and have fallen headlong into the pit of schism, should go on to decide that any who join them ought to be baptized again. For the former is a speck on the brightness of a holy soul which abundance of charity would fain have covered; the latter is a stain in their lower foulness which the hatred of peace in their countenance ostentatiously brings to light. But the subject for our further consideration, relating to the authority of the blessed Cyprian, we will commence from a fresh beginning.

Sermon on Psalm 22
(Good Friday, A.D. 407)

Augustine preached incessantly in a weak voice from a *cathedra,* or chair, in the apse. His audience, mostly simple people, reacted spontaneously as he spoke—applauding, sighing, remonstrating and joining with him (to his satisfaction) in completing his favorite quotations from scripture. His sermons were mainly improvisations on a text just recited, though occasionally they might be more careful—for the consecration of a bishop or on the anniversary of a saint. The sermons were, therefore, in the main unprepared but were in general recorded formally—and sometimes informally by those who wished to use them for themselves. There are about eight hundred of his sermons extant, of which over a hundred *Expositions on the Book of the Psalms,* one hundred and twenty-four *Homilies on St. John* and a collection of over five hundred *Sermons* form the greater part. They are dated from his early days as a bishop up to 415–417, and though they naturally constitute an important section of his work, they are the least systematic. Moreover, their matter is more conveniently represented in his formal works. Van der Meer summarizes their essential character as containing Augustine's "profoundest spiritual knowledge and experience adapted to the pattern of everyday practical life." While he proclaims, therefore, the truth as found in the Bible (with indulgent exploitation of the many resources of allegory and classical learning), he appeals to his simple audience by the use of many linguistic barbarisms and—most compelling argument—confident appeals to miracles. In these ways his sermons conform in practice to the theory of preaching he sets out in the second part of the *De doctrina Christiana.* They exemplify also, dramatically, his living awareness of directing Providence: when the lector recited a long psalm instead of a short one that Augustine had expected, Augustine, remarking that he preferred "to conform to the error of the lector and the will of God rather than to follow" (*Enarrationes in Psalmos* 138.1) his own, expounded the longer psalm. The sermon given here is his exposition on Psalm 22, delivered probably in 407 (cf. A.-M. La Bonnardière, *Recherches de chronologie augustinienne*, Paris, 1965, pp. 54 ff.). It is a true sermon to his congregation, not least in its preoccupation with the Donatists. The translation given here is that by E. Hill in *Nine Sermons of Saint Augustine on the Psalms* (London, 1958), pp. 46–60.

RECOMMENDED READING

F. van der Meer, *Augustine the Bishop*, London and New York, 1961, pp. 412–52.
A. Mandouze, *Saint Augustin*, Paris, 1968, pp. 591–663.

SERMON ON PSALM 22
(delivered on a Good Friday)

We must not pass over in silence what God has thought fit to talk about in the Holy Scriptures. Now we know of course that our Lord's passion has happened once and for all. Christ died once, the just for the unjust;[1] as St. Paul says, "Christ rising from the dead dies now no more, and death shall no longer lord it over him."[2] All the same, in case we forget what has happened once and for all, we remind ourselves of it by keeping Good Friday[3] every year. Certainly Christ doesn't die again every time Good Friday comes round; and yet this yearly reminder almost seems to conjure up before our eyes what happened such a long time ago, and we are as deeply moved as if we were actually looking at our Lord hanging on the cross here and now, but looking at him in loving faith, of course, not in mockery. He was indeed mocked as he hung on the cross, but we worship him now as he sits enthroned in heaven.

Or are there perhaps even now people who mock Christ, people worse than the Jews, who at least jeered as they thought at a dying man, not at a reigning king? If only there were just one or two such scoffers, if only they could even be

[1] 1 Pet. 3: 18.
[2] Rom. 6: 9.
[3] Augustine actually says "by keeping Easter (the Pasch) every year." Easter for him and his audience did not just mean Easter Sunday, the day of the resurrection, but the whole mystery, celebrated from Thursday to Sunday, of last supper, death and resurrection.

counted! But all the chaff on his threshing-floor scoffs at him,
and the good grain grieves to see their Lord still mocked, still
set at nought. This is what I want to grieve over together
with you; because this is the proper time for mourning and
sorrow, for crying and grieving, confessing and pleading,
when we are keeping our Lord's passion. And which of us
could ever shed enough tears to match such a great sorrow?
As we have just heard the prophet saying, "Who will give
water to my head, and a fountain of tears to my eyes?"[4] Even
if our eyes were waterfalls, it would not be enough. To see
Christ brazenly, openly mocked, and by those who cannot
even make the excuse "I didn't understand!" As he sits there in
glory at his Father's right hand, in possession of the whole
world, these Donatists have the face to say to him "Here you
are, this is your kingdom for you," and in place of the whole
world they offer him just Africa!

And what about the gospel we have just heard, brothers?
Who is the woman who came into the house with the box of
ointment,[5] what does she stand for? For the church surely,
and the ointment is that good odour which St. Paul speaks of,
"We are the good odour of Christ in every place."[6] In every
place we, the faithful, are the good odour of Christ. That is
what St. Paul says. Oh no, say our neighbours here; only in
Africa is there a good odour. The rest of the world stinks.

Let us see then what our Lord himself has to say about it.
When Judas grumbled at the waste of the ointment, because
he wanted to sell the good odour of Christ, our Lord answered
"Leave the woman alone. She has done me a good turn. And
wherever this gospel is preached in the whole world, what
this woman has done shall also be spoken of."[7] Is there anything to add to that, is there anything we can take away from
it? Or did our Lord lie, or was he deceived, perhaps? They can
take their choice; either truth lied or truth was deceived.
Wherever, he says, this gospel is preached; and where will it
be? you ask—he tells you; in the whole world.

And now let us have a look at this psalm. It's a sad tale it

[4] Jer. 9: 1.
[5] John 12: 3.
[6] 2 Cor. 2: 14.
[7] Matt. 26: 10, 13.

tells, and all the sadder when it is told to those who are too
deaf to hear it. It's astonishing, brothers, to think that the
Donatists too have this psalm to-day. Well I ask you, what
do they make of it? Christ in his mercy knows; but I honestly
begin to think, for all the good it does them, they must be
stone-deaf and never hear a word. It tells of Christ's passion
and what it has achieved for the whole world, almost as if it
were another gospel; and yet it was written heaven knows
how many hundreds of years before our Lord was born. But
time is too short for us to spend as long on it as we would
like, to satisfy our sorrow; and so we must run through it
shortly as time allows.

The first verse is the very words our Lord cried out on the
cross, "Eli, Eli, lama sabachthani?" "O God, my God, why
have you forsaken me?" What can he have meant by that?
God could not possibly have forsaken him, since he himself is
God, God the Son of God, God the Word of God. In the
beginning was the Word, and the Word was with God, and
the Word was God. And the Word was made flesh, and the
Word of God made flesh hung upon the cross, and cried out
"My God, my God, why have you forsaken me?" How could
he say it, unless he were including us in himself, because we
were there in him, because the body of Christ is the church,
and we, the church, the body of Christ, were being crucified
there? Perhaps he also said it to give us a clue, as though to
say "This psalm was written about me." "Far from my salvation are the words of my crimes." *His* crimes? He who did no
sin, neither was guile found in his mouth?[8] How can he talk
about his crimes, except by way of praying for our crimes, and
treating our sins as if they were his sins, in order to make his
justice our justice?

"My God I shall cry to you by day and you will not hear,
and at night; and it shall not be for my unwisdom." Still speaking for you and for me and the other man, taking the part
of his own body the church; just as he did in the garden, when
he said "Father, if it is possible, let this cup pass from me."[9]
He cannot have meant that he was afraid to die. The soldier

[8] 1 Pet. 2: 22.
[9] Matt. 26: 39.

can scarcely be braver than his commander. St. Paul longed
to be dissolved and be with Christ,[10] he was eager to die; and
are we to say that Christ his captain was afraid to die? No,
but he took our infirmities upon himself, and prayed in the
garden on our behalf, because we the members of his body are
still afraid to die. So here in this verse, "Day and night have
I called, and you will not hear," he is speaking on our behalf.
Many people call on God in their distress and are not heard;
but it is for their own good, it is not for their unwisdom; that
is to say, it *is* for their wisdom, to make them sadder and wiser
men, to teach them the lesson St. Paul learned the hard way.
"My grace is sufficient for you," he was told, "because strength
is made perfect in weakness."[11] We have to learn that God is
a doctor, and our troubles are a nasty but necessary operation,
not a punishment leading to damnation. When you are in the
doctor's hands, you yell at the touch of his knife and his
cauterizing iron, and beg him to stop. But the doctor doesn't
listen; he takes no notice of your pleas, because he is taking
every care of your health.

"But you dwell in the holy place, O praise of Israel," you
dwell in the hearts which you have sanctified, teaching them
the value of distress, and of not being heard when they pray
to be delivered. God doesn't listen to some, and it is for their
own good; he listens to others, to their undoing. He listened
to Satan when he wanted to tempt Job,[12] he listened to the
legion of devils when they wanted to enter the herd of swine.[13]
Their prayers were answered, St. Paul's was not. Why? Why
am I saying all this? Just remember always, in weal and in
woe, through thick and thin, to say "God be thanked." There
is a big crowd here to-day, people have come who don't usually come to church; and I tell you all alike, remember to
thank God for everything, your troubles included, because it
is in trouble that the Christian proves his worth, if he doesn't
desert his God; because at the time that is best for him the
Christian is left by God to himself—left in the furnace and

[10] Phil. 1: 23.
[11] 2 Cor. 12: 9.
[12] Job 1: 11.
[13] Matt. 8: 31.

the fire is lit. There is a great parable, a great sacrament, to be learned from the goldsmith's furnace. You have the gold and the straw, and the fire in its narrow grate. And one and the same fire does two different things; it burns the straw to ashes, but the gold it refines and cleans from all its dross. Those whom God dwells in, as in his holy place, are certainly much improved by their troubles, like fine pure gold. God knows what he is doing. After all, he made us and he knows how to mend us. In all sickness and sorrow then, in all the troubles which the devil is allowed to vex you with, keep your hearts fixed on God, who never really deserts you. Even if he seems to turn a deaf ear to your tears, he will always match your prayers with his mercy. It's a good builder who put the house up, and if it has got a little dilapidated, he knows how to repair it.

And just see what he goes on to say next. "In you did our fathers hope; they hoped and you did rescue them"—the people of Israel from the land of Egypt, the three holy children from the fiery furnace, Daniel from the lion's den, Susanna from her false accusers, he rescued them all when they cried to him. Did he then fail his own Son, did he ignore him hanging on the cross? Why should he alone not be rescued?

"I am a worm and no man." But man too is a worm, so why does he say that he is no man? Because he is God. Why does he demean himself even further then, and call himself a worm? Perhaps because a worm is born from flesh without the union of male and female, just as Christ was born of the Virgin Mary. He is a worm because he is mortal, born in the flesh, but not begotten by a man on a woman; and he is no man, because he is the Word, and in the beginning was the Word, and the Word was with God, and the Word was God.

"The reproach of men and the outcast of the people." Now we come to the story of his sufferings. Let us see *what* he suffered first, and then see *why*. What was the use of it all? Our fathers hoped, and they were delivered from Egypt. Thousands have called on God and been delivered, and in this life too, without having to wait for the next. Even Job himself, whom the devil was allowed to afflict until his flesh was rotten with maggots, even Job recovered health in this life, and was

given riches twice as great as he had lost.[14] But not so our
Lord. He was scourged and there was none to help, he was
spat on and there was none to help, knocked about and
crowned with thorns and there was none to help, nailed to
the cross and no one to rescue him. He cried out "My God,
my God, why have you forsaken me?" and still no one came to
his help. Why, my brothers, why, why, why? What was to be
gained by such sufferings? Well, he endured it as the price he
had to pay. What the price was for, we shall see further on.
First, as I was saying, we shall see what he suffered, and then
we shall see why. We shall see what bitter enemies of Christ
people must be who let him pay the price and refuse him
what he bought with it. This psalm then is going to tell us
what he suffered and why. Keep those two things in mind,
what and why. As for what he suffered, it won't need much
explanation, the psalm's own words are clear enough. Listen
carefully then, Christians, to what Christ suffered, "the reproach of men and the outcast of the people."

"All they that saw me were sneering at me, they spoke with
their lips and wagged their heads; he hoped in the Lord, let
him rescue him; let him save him since he wants him." They
could speak like that because he had become man, and they
spoke as if he were only a man. "For it is you who have
drawn me out of the womb." The eternal Word of God drawn
out of the womb? Yes, because the Word was made flesh and
dwelt among us. "My God are you from my mother's breasts."
Before all ages you are my Father, but not my God; my God
only from my mother's breasts. "On you have I been cast
from the womb," to be my only hope now that I have become
a man and weak, now that the Word is made flesh. "From
my mother's womb you are my God"; before that only my
Father.

"Do not depart from me, for trouble is very near, for there
is none to help." See how forsaken he is, God-forsaken; and
woe to us if he forsakes us, for there is none to help. "Many
calves have surrounded me, fat bulls have besieged me"—the
people and the chief priests. "They have opened their mouths

[14] Job 42: 10.

at me, like a lion ravening and roaring." Listen to their roar in the gospel, "Crucify him, crucify him."[15]

"I am poured out like water, and all my bones are scattered." By his bones he means the strong parts of his body—the backbone of the church, strong in faith. He scattered his own bones when he said "Behold I am sending you like sheep among wolves."[16] And he is poured out like water, which you pour out either to wash off dirt, or to water the garden. When Christ is poured out like water, he washes the dirt off us and waters the thirst in us. "My heart has become like melting wax in my belly." His belly means the weak parts of his body, the shaky members of his church; there are no hard bones in the belly. And his heart is his wisdom, locked up and frozen in the Scriptures. No one understood the Scriptures until the Lord was crucified, and then they melted like wax in his belly, so that even the weak could understand them. That is why the veil of the temple was rent in two, because what had been covered up, namely the wisdom of Christ, was now unveiled and open for all to see. "My strength has dried up like a tile." Magnificently said: My name is made stronger by affliction, that's what he means. Just as bricks or tiles are soft before they are fired, hard and strong afterwards, so the Lord's name was despised before he suffered, but has been honoured ever since. "And my tongue has stuck to my jaws." His tongue, that's his preachers, have acquired the wisdom they preach by inside information, right from within the mind of Christ.

"And you have brought me down into the dust of death. For many dogs have surrounded me, the council of the evil-minded—a gang of schemers—have surrounded me"; just as you see it in the gospel. "They have dug my hands and my feet," making the wounds which doubting Thomas handled, exclaiming "My Lord and my God." "Because you have seen me, Thomas, you have believed. Blessed are they who do not see, and who believe."[17] They have dug my hands and my feet. "They have counted all my bones"; by stretching him

15 John 19: 6.
16 Luke 10: 3.
17 John 20: 28.

out on the cross. There could be no apter words for that
wrenching of his body on the cross than these, they have
numbered all my bones. "They indeed have examined and inspected me." They examined him, and didn't understand; they
inspected him, and didn't see. They had eyes for the flesh, but
no mind for the Word that was made flesh. "They divided
my garments among them." His garments are his sacraments.
Listen carefully now, brothers. His garments, his sacraments,
can be divided up by heresies, but there was one garment
which no one divided up; "and over my garment they cast
lots." "His coat, says St. John, was woven from the top,"[18]
from above therefore, from heaven, from the Father, from the
Holy Ghost. What is this coat which nobody can divide up?
Charity. What is it again? Unity. They cast lots for it, nobody
cut it up. Heretics have divided the sacraments among them,
charity they have not divided. And because they haven't been
able to divide it, or part it among them, they have departed
from it. But charity remains whole and undivided. It falls to
some by lot; whoever has it is safe, no one can budge him
from the unity of the Catholic Church. And if anyone begins
to have it outside the church, then he is brought in, like the
sprig of olive which the dove brought back to the ark.[19]

"But you O Lord, do not put your aid far off"—nor did he;
on the third day he rose again. "Look to my defence. Rescue
my soul from the sword," that is from death; "and my only one
from the hand of the dog." My soul and my only one, my head
and my body, myself and my church. Deliver my church
from the power of the dog. Who are the dogs? Those who
bark without knowing what for. You do nothing to annoy
them, and they bark. What has the postman done to the dog?
Yet it barks at him. Those who yap blindly, without any idea
what at or what for, they are the dogs. "Save me from the
lion's mouth." You know who the lion is; the devil going about
roaring and seeking whom he may devour.[20] "And my lowli-
ness from the horns of the unicorns," my humble life from
the proud.

18 John 19: 23.
19 Gen. 8: 11.
20 1 Pet. 5: 8.

So much for what he suffered; now for the reason why. You must be ready to ask yourselves, brothers, if a man who has no part in the stake for which Christ suffered, whatever it may be, if such a man has any right to call himself a Christian. What is this stake then, for which all his bones were counted, and his garments divided, and his coat made the stake in a game of dice? Tell us, Christ Son of God, what was the use of your passion, which you would never have endured if it had not been your will?—I will tell you the use of it, he answers; it's no secret, I put it plainly enough, but men are too deaf to hear. "I will tell your name to my brothers"—privately, perhaps, to a few special brothers?—"In the midst of the church I will sing to you." This is happening now. But let us look and see what this church is for whose sake he suffered.

"You who fear the Lord, praise him." Wherever God is feared and praised, there is the church of Christ. Do you suppose it means nothing, people throughout the world nowadays saying Amen and Alleluia? Aren't they fearing and praising God by using these words? Not according to Donatus. Your words don't mean a thing, he says, there is no fear of God in the rest of the world at all.—But just a little is left in Africa, is it? Didn't Christ then say anything to stop the mouths of these false Amen-and-Alleluia-sayers, anything to root out their tongues? Let's have a look, perhaps we shall find it. Of course *they* tell us, "In the midst of the church means our church." Well, "you who fear the Lord praise him"; let's see if they really do praise him in the midst of their church. Poor praise of Christ, isn't it, to say "All the rest of the world is lost, the devil has captured it from him, and he only has Africa left"? But let the psalm have its say, and make the thing crystal clear, with nothing that they can explain away. "All the seed of Jacob magnify him." "We are the seed of Jacob," I suppose they say. Well, we shall see. "Let all the seed of Israel fear him"—"That's us," they say.—"Yes, yes, that's you." "For he has not slighted nor despised the prayer of the poor." Which poor? Certainly not those who trust in themselves, and preen themselves on being just. Still, let them call themselves poor if they want to. "Nor did he turn his face away from me, and when I cried to him he heard me out." Why did he hear

me out? Because "with you is my praise." He looked to God
for his praise, teaching us not to put our trust in men. Let
them wriggle still, though, if they want to. We are getting hot
now, the fire is beginning to burn, for there is none who can
hide from his heat.[21] Still, let them say "We too look to him
for our praise, and don't trust in ourselves."

"In a great church I shall confess to you." Now I think we
are getting to the quick. Is a little corner of Africa really a
great church, do you suppose? A great church means the
whole world. Listen to them answering Christ back.—"What
do you mean by saying 'I will confess to you in a great
church?' What great church? You only hang on in a little
piece of Africa, you have lost the rest of the world. You may
have shed your blood for the whole world, but you have been
the victim of a brutal aggression from the devil." We know
what the answer is to that. But let us suppose we didn't know
it, wouldn't we expect our Lord to say, "Hush, I have still got
something to say which will settle the matter once and for all"?
Let's wait and see then what he is going to say. Though I
must confess, I was quite ready for my part to give judgment
and declare the matter closed, when Christ said "In a great
church," and you say "Only in a remote corner." But I suppose they will have the nerve to say, "Ours is a great church;
what do you think of Bagai and Thamugadi?"[22] All right, if he
doesn't say something to silence you for good, call Numidia a
great church if you want to.

But let's carry on. "I shall pay my vows in the presence of
them that fear him." His vows are the sacrifice he offered to
God. The faithful know what that sacrifice is,[23] what the
vows are which he pays in the presence of them that fear him.
"The poor shall eat and shall be filled." Lucky poor who eat
and are filled. The rich aren't filled because they aren't
hungry. The poor eat, Peter the fisherman, James and John
fishermen both, the publican Matthew; all poor, all ate and
were filled, because they suffered in accordance with what
they ate. The supper Christ set before them was his passion.

---

[21] Ps. 18: 7 f.
[22] Two Donatist strongholds.
[23] An oblique reference to the Eucharist.

You take your fill of it by copying it. The poor shall eat and be filled, they shall suffer and follow in the footsteps of Christ. But who are the poor? "Those who seek him shall praise the Lord." The rich are the ones who praise themselves, the poor praise the Lord. They seek the Lord because *he* is their riches. The rich look for something to fill their pockets with, the poor for something to fill their hearts. Listen where you should look for the riches of the truly poor; they are not stored in barns or banks, but "their hearts shall live for ever and ever."

Well now, where have we got to? We have seen what the Lord suffered, and we are inquiring why, and he was in the middle of telling us. "I will tell your name to my brothers, in the midst of the church I will praise you." "This church," they say, "at Thamugadi." "Let all the seed of Israel fear him." "We are the seed of Israel." "For he has not slighted nor despised the prayer of the poor." "That's us," they say. "Nor has he turned his face away from me," Christ the Lord, that is, from himself, from his church which is his own body. "With you is my praise." You want to praise yourselves. "But," they answer, "of course we praise him too." "I shall pay my vows to the Lord in the presence of them that fear him"; the sacrifice of peace, the sacrifice of charity, the sacrifice of his body which the faithful know about—but we can't talk about that now. "The poor shall eat and be filled." Let them suffer, and they shall be filled. The Lord died, and the poor must die. Why? Tell me the use of it. "All the ends of the earth shall remember and be converted to the Lord."

There you are brothers; that's it; why look to me to answer the Donatists? There is the psalm for you, we have it read to-day, they have it read to-day. We should write it up on placards and banners, and go out in procession with it, chanting "See, Christ has suffered, see, the merchant offers his price, see the price he paid, his own blood shed." He carried the price in his purse; he was pierced with a lance, and the purse was spilt, and the price of the whole earth was shed. What more have you heretics got to say? Isn't it the price of the whole world? Is Africa alone redeemed? Here it is in black and white, "All the ends of the earth shall remember and be converted to the Lord." If he had just said "the ends of the earth," you could have answered, "Here they are, in

Morocco." But it's *all* the ends of the earth"; he said *"all,"* my dear schismatic. How are you going to wriggle out of that? You have no way out left, but the way in is always open.

Now please don't go talking about it as though what *I* say matters. Look at the psalm, read the psalm. Christ has redeemed us with his blood; there is our price for you. You ask me, "What has he bought with it?" How do you expect me to find that out? Someone answers me, "How can you find out, you ass? Why, you are carrying the account book, look at that, that will give you the answer. Look, there it is; 'All the ends of the earth shall remember and be converted to the Lord.'" But the heretics have forgotten, for all that they hear it every year on this day. Do you think they put their ears away when their reader says "All the ends of the earth shall remember and be converted to the Lord"? Oh well, it's only one verse of course, and your thoughts have wandered, you were whispering to your neighbour at that moment. But he says it again; "and all the countries of the nations shall adore in his sight." You are still not paying attention, so he hammers away with yet another; "For the kingdom is the Lord's, and he shall lord it over the nations." Three verses of it, brothers, and they have sung them there to-day—or perhaps they have censored them. Quite honestly, my friends, I get so worked up, so frantic about their astonishing hardness of heart and hearing, that I sometimes wonder whether they have these verses in their books at all. There they are all trotting off to church, all intent on hearing the psalm, all listening eagerly. Well grant that they aren't paying attention; is it only one verse? "All the ends of the earth shall remember and be converted to the Lord." But you have only just woken up, you are still rubbing your eyes. "And all the countries of the nations shall adore in his sight." Shake it off now; you are still half asleep. Listen; "For the kingdom is the Lord's, and he shall lord it over the nations."

Well I don't know; they can squabble with the Scriptures if they want to, not with me. And what about your claim that you saved the Scriptures during the persecution, and didn't hand them over to be burned? You saved them only to burn yourselves. Open them, read them. If you saved them from the flames, why tear them to pieces with the tongue? You are

the real betrayers of the Scriptures, because you do not stick
to God's will and testament when it's read. I'm not interested
in who hid the Scriptures and who betrayed them, or whose
cellar they were salvaged from. They are our Father's will.
We are brothers, what are we quarrelling about? Our Father
didn't die without leaving a will. He made his will and died
and rose again. The time to argue about a will is before it has
been proved. Once it is proved argument ceases. Every one
keeps his mouth shut, the judge listens carefully, the barristers
keep mum, the ushers call for silence, everyone in court is on
tenter-hooks while the dead man's words are read, the words
of a lifeless corpse in the grave. But Christ is risen and lives for
ever in heaven. Surely you are not going to wrangle over what
is written in his will? Listen to this, almost in the first verse
of this very psalter: "You are my son, this day have I begotten you. Ask of me, and I will give you the nations for your
inheritance, and the ends of the earth for your possession."[24]
And then in this psalm, "The kingdom is the Lord's, and he
shall lord it over the nations"; his kingdom, not yours. Acknowledge the Lord then, acknowledge his possession of the
ends of the earth.

The trouble with you people is that you want to possess
something as your own private property, you aren't interested
in our all sharing in the common property of Christ. Power
on earth, not sovereignty with him in heaven, that is what you
want.—Often, you know, brothers, I have been to see these
people and said, "Let's try to examine our differences and
really get to the truth of the matter." And they answer, "You
have got your flock, I have got mine. If you leave mine alone,
I shall leave yours alone." Well, God bless my soul, isn't that
splendid? My sheep and his sheep. Didn't Christ buy any?
Surely they are neither mine nor yours, but his who put his
brand on them. If Christ is with you, then take mine, because
they aren't mine. If Christ is here, then bring yours over to
us, because they aren't yours. Are we going to let them kiss
our hands and show us great respect as if we owned them,
and let them perish, estranged from the family of Christ? "Oh,
but I don't claim to own them," he says.—We shall see about

[24] Ps. 2: 7 f.

that. I work for the name of Christ, you work for the name
of Donatus. If it's Christ you care for, Christ is everywhere.
"Lo, here is Christ,"[25] say you; He is throughout the world,
say I. That is the church I have to show, that is what Christ
has bought, what he shed his blood for, the whole world from
the rising of the sun to its setting.[26] How can you claim to
gather with Christ,[27] when you break up Christian unity, and
are only interested in staking your own private claims?

Certainly, brothers, they use the name of Christ, and call
themselves Christians. But that only means they have filched
his title-deeds to protect their own property. I believe it's quite
common for a man who is afraid some big neighbour may
come and turn him out of his house, to pretend that it belongs
to some other big man, and he makes out false title-deeds to
show it. He wants to keep the house as his own property, but
to secure it by the influential name of another. That is how
these people misuse the name of Christ. May the Lord forgive
them for it; he is good, and may he claim his own where he
finds his title-deeds, his own brand, his own mark of baptism.
May he say, "They would not have used my mark unless the
sheep were mine. Whatever I find signed with my name must
be mine." The mark, the title-deeds need not be changed, only
the actual occupier needs to be changed, so that Christ may
really enter into possession. The mark remains the same. These
Donatists really have the baptism of Christ, and when they
come over to us we recognize the mark and title-deeds of our
king, and we don't want to change them, we don't have them
baptized again. Oh poor, mean little cottage, let him whose
title-deeds you show enter into possession. The title-deeds are
Christ's, don't let yourself be occupied by Donatus.

What a lot I have been talking about, brothers! Still at least
don't forget what has been read to-day. I beg you, by this holy
day itself, by the mysteries it stands for, don't let it fade out
of your minds. "All the ends of the earth shall remember and
be converted to the Lord. All the countries of the nations shall

[25] Matt. 24: 23.
[26] Ps. 113: 3.
[27] Matt. 12: 30.

adore in his sight. The kingdom is the Lord's, and he shall lord it over the nations." Don't listen to people who pooh-pooh such a clearly proven title to possession. Whatever is said against it is said by man. But this is what God says.

On the Trinity
(A.D. 399–419)
Books 2 and 8

On the Trinity (fifteen books) was begun in summer of 399 and finished for the most part in the following six years. Because of the difficulty of the subject matter and for other reasons, Augustine had not yet completed it by 416. At this time some friends of his released the unfinished manuscript. Then Augustine, about the middle of 419, gave it its final and definitive form. The work, however, reflects Augustine's doctrinal interests as seen in his *Confessions* 13 (dating from 398) where he attempts to expound the mystery of the Trinity from the analogy of the intimate life of the human soul. It would seem that he was stimulated to this original and enduring idea by Genesis 1:26—"Let us make man in our image, after our likeness." The *Trinity* falls into two parts: the first (1–4) elucidates the scriptural teaching on the unity and equality of the Persons, their manifestations and functions; the second discusses rationally (5–7) the technical terms involved (predicaments, relation, *Trinitas, triplex*, predicables) and the analogy of the Trinity with the human soul (8–15) —*mens, notitia, amor, memoria, intellectus, voluntas*. In this treatise, which had an immense influence on the Middle Ages, Scholasticism is said to have been born. The extracts given here are taken from each of the two parts: Book 2, a good example of Augustine's scriptural exegesis, and Book 8 of his subtle rhetoric-affected speculation. The translation given here is that of A. W. Haddan, revised by W. G. T. Shedd (Edinburgh, 1873). The best edition, with introduction and notes, is that in the BA, vols. 15 and 16, Paris, 1955.

RECOMMENDED READING

M. Schmaus, *Die psychologische Trinitätslehre des hl. Augustinus*, Münster, 1927.

E. Gilson, pp. 210–24.
R. W. Battenhouse, pp. 235–56.
E. Portalié, pp. 129–35.
M. T. Clark, *Augustinian Personalism*, Villanova, Pa., 1970, pp. 13 ff.

Other Trinitarian texts in Augustine are listed in BA, vol. 15, p. 557, and vol. 33 (*La Cité de Dieu* 1–5), Paris, 1959, p. 828.

SPECIAL TOPICS

1. *Christology* (Book 2)

The co-equality of the Persons of the Trinity is central to the whole book—particularly in relation to the Son. Whereas, according to some of its interpreters the *Confessions* (Book 7.19.25) shows Augustine at the time of his conversion as not believing in the divinity of Christ (see BA, vol. 13, pp. 693 ff.) and therefore equality with the Father, in the *Trinity* (including Book 2) the divinity and equality with the Father are fully insisted upon. The Arians had maintained that there had been no theophany (appearance) of the Father in the Old Testament: the Son had this—inferior—role. Augustine in Book 2 counters this by showing that the Father did appear to men as described in the Old Testament. For more on Augustine's Christology see Portalié, pp. 152–72.

2. *The Trinity and psychological analogies in man* (Book 8)

In Book 8.10.14 Augustine declares that in carnal love there are three things: "he that loves, and that which is loved, and love." On ascending to the mind the same three are found. He goes on: "it remains to ascend also from hence, and to seek those things which are above, as far as is given to man . . . let it suffice to have said this much, that we may weave, as it were, the hinge of some starting point, whence to weave the rest of our discourse." The extent to which, characteristically, love is a starting point for his effort to understand the Trinity is explicitly stated in 8.7.10: "no other thing, then, is chiefly to be regarded in this enquiry, which we make concerning the Trinity and concerning knowing God, except what is true love, indeed, rather what is love." At an earlier stage in Book 8 (5.8) Augustine indicates that he will use similitude to understand the Trinity. In point of fact, from the very beginning of Book 8 he has been employing the similitude of our *understanding* of truth (ch. 1 ff.), our *knowledge* of good (ch. 3 ff.) and our *love* of the righteous (ch.

6 ff.). From this fundamental book, then, are developed the various triads discussed in the later books: *mens; notitia; amor* (9.2.2 ff.); *memoria; intellectus; voluntas* (10.11.17 ff.)/*amor* (14.8.11 ff.). Augustine's profound understanding of the human mind enabled him to exploit these similitudes with great subtlety. It should be remembered, however, that Augustine in his *Confessions* (13.11.12) also, written probably in the second half of A.D. 398 (see BA, vol. 15, *La Trinité*, p. 558), had already explored this similitude and had, moreover, behind him a long tradition of similar Neoplatonic similitudes (see O. du Roy, *L'Intelligence de la foi en la Trinité selon saint Augustin*, Paris, 1966). See Portalié, pp. 133–35; Battenhouse, pp. 248–55.

ON THE TRINITY

BOOK 2

PREFACE

When men seek to know God, and bend their minds according to the capacity of human weakness to the understanding of the Trinity; learning, as they must, by experience, the wearisome difficulties of the task, whether from the sight itself of the mind striving to gaze upon light unapproachable, or, indeed, from the manifold and various modes of speech employed in the sacred writings (wherein, as it seems to me, the mind is nothing else but roughly exercised, in order that it may find sweetness when glorified by the grace of Christ);— such men, I say, when they have dispelled every ambiguity, and arrived at something certain, ought of all others most easily to make allowance for those who err in the investigation of so deep a secret. But there are two things most hard to bear with, in the case of those who are in error: hasty assumption before the truth is made plain; and, when it has been made plain, defence of the falsehood thus hastily assumed. From which two faults, inimical as they are to the finding out of the truth, and to the handling of the divine and sacred books, should God, as I pray and hope, defend and protect me with the shield of his good will,[1] and with the grace of his mercy, I will not be slow to search out the substance of God, whether through his scripture or through the creature. For both of these are set forth for our contemplation to this end, that he

[1] Ps. 5: 12.

may himself be sought, and himself be loved, who inspired
the one, and created the other. Nor shall I be afraid of giving
my opinion, in which I shall more desire to be examined by
the upright, than fear to be carped at by the perverse. For
charity, most excellent and unassuming, gratefully accepts the
dovelike eye; but for the dog's tooth nothing remains, save
either to shun it by the most cautious humility, or to blunt
it by the most solid truth; and far rather would I be censured
by any one whatsoever, than be praised by either the erring
or the flatterer. For the lover of truth need fear no one's censure. For he that censures, must needs be either enemy or
friend. And if an enemy reviles, he must be borne with: but
a friend, if he errs, must be taught; if he teaches, listened to.
But if one who errs praises you, he confirms your error; if
one who flatters, he seduces you into error. "Let the righteous," therefore, "smite me, it shall be a kindness; and let him
reprove me; but the oil of the sinner shall not anoint my
head."[2]

CHAP. 1—*There is a double rule for understanding the scriptural
modes of speech concerning the Son of God. These modes of
speech are of a threefold kind.*

2. Therefore, although we hold most firmly, concerning our
Lord Jesus Christ, what may be called the canonical rule, as
it is both disseminated through the Scriptures, and has been
demonstrated by learned and catholic interpreters of the same
Scriptures, namely, that the Son of God is both understood
to be equal to the Father according to the form of God in
which he is, and less than the Father according to the form
of a servant which he took;[3] in which form he was found
to be not only less than the Father, but also less than the Holy
Spirit; and not only so, but less even than himself,—not than
himself who was, but than himself who is; because, by taking
the form of a servant, he did not lose the form of God, as
the testimonies of the Scriptures taught us, to which we have
referred in the former book: yet there are some things in the
sacred text so put as to leave it ambiguous to which rule they
are rather to be referred; whether to that by which we under-

[2] Ps. 141: 5.
[3] Phil. 2: 6 f.

stand the Son as less, in that he has taken upon him the creature, or to that by which we understand that the Son is not indeed less than, but equal to the Father, but yet that he is from him, God of God, light of light. For we call the Son God of God; but the Father, God only; not of God. Therefore it is plain that the Son has another of whom he is, and to whom he is Son; but that the Father has not a Son of whom he is, but only to whom he is Father. For every son is what he is, of his father, and is son to his father; but no father is what he is, of his son, but is father to his son.

3. Some things, then, are so put in the Scriptures concerning the Father and the Son, as to intimate the unity and equality of their substance; as, for instance, "I and the Father are one;"[4] and, "Who, being in the form of God, thought it not robbery to be equal with God;"[5] and whatever other texts there are of the kind. And some, again, are so put that they show the Son as less on account of the form of a servant, that is, of his having taken upon him the creature of a changeable and human substance; as, for instance, that which says, "For my Father is greater than I;"[6] and, "The Father judges no man, but has committed all judgment to the Son." For a little after he goes on to say, "And has given him authority to execute judgment also, because he is the Son of man." And further, some are so put, as to show him at that time neither as less nor as equal, but only to intimate that he is of the Father; as, for instance, that which says, "For as the Father has life in himself, so has he given to the Son to have life in himself;" and that other: "The Son can do nothing of himself, but what he sees the Father do."[7] For if we shall take this to be therefore so said, because the Son is less in the form taken from the creature, it will follow that the Father must have walked on the water, or opened the eyes with clay and spittle of some other one born blind, and have done the other things which the Son appearing in the flesh did among men, before the Son did them;[8] in order that he might be able to

[4] John 10: 30.
[5] Phil. 2: 6.
[6] John 14: 28.
[7] John 5: 22, 27, 26, 19.
[8] Matt. 14: 26, and John 9: 6 f.

do those things, who said that the Son was not able to do anything of himself, except what he has seen the Father do. Yet who, even though he were mad, would think this? It remains, therefore, that these texts are so expressed, because the life of the Son is unchangeable as that of the Father is, and yet he is of the Father; and the working of the Father and of the Son is indivisible, and yet so to work is given to the Son from him, of whom he himself is, that is, from the Father; and the Son so sees the Father, that he is the Son in the very seeing him. For to be of the Father, that is, to be born of the Father, is to him nothing else than to see the Father; and to see him working, is nothing else than to work with him: but therefore not from himself, because he is not from himself. And, therefore, those things which "He sees the Father do, these also the Son does likewise," because he is of the Father. For he neither does other things in like manner, as a painter paints other pictures, in the same way as he sees others to have been painted by another man; nor the same things in a different manner, as the body expresses the same letters, which the mind has thought; but "whatsoever things," he says, "the Father does, these same things also the Son does likewise."[9] He has said both "these same things," and "likewise;" and hence the working of both the Father and the Son is indivisible and equal, but it is from the Father to the Son. Therefore the Son cannot do anything of himself, except what he sees the Father do. From this rule, then, whereby the Scriptures so speak as to mean, not to set forth one as less than another, but only to show which is of which, some have drawn this meaning, as if the Son were said to be less. And some among ourselves who are more unlearned and least instructed in these things, endeavouring to take these texts according to the form of a servant, and so misinterpreting them, are troubled. And to prevent this, the rule in question is to be observed, whereby the Son is not less, but it is simply intimated that he is of the Father, in which words not his inequality but his birth is declared.

[9] John 5: 19.

CHAP. 2—*That some ways of speaking concerning the Son are to be understood according to either rule.*

4. There are, then, some things in the sacred books, as I began by saying, so put, that it is doubtful to which they are to be referred: whether to that rule whereby the Son is less on account of his having taken the creature; or whether to that whereby it is intimated that although equal, yet he is of the Father. And in my opinion, if this is in such way doubtful, that which it really is can neither be explained nor discerned, then such passages may without danger be understood according to either rule, as that, for instance, "My doctrine is not mine, but his that sent me."[10] For this may both be taken according to the form of a servant, as we have already treated it in the former book; or according to the form of God, in which he is in such way equal to the Father, that he is yet of the Father. For according to the form of God, as the Son is not one and his life another, but the life itself is the Son; so the Son is not one and his doctrine another, but the doctrine itself is the Son. And hence, as the text, "He hath given life to the Son," is no otherwise to be understood than, he has begotten the Son, who is life; so also when it is said, he has given doctrine to the Son, it may be rightly understood to mean, he has begotten the Son, who is doctrine; so that, when it is said, "My doctrine is not mine, but his who sent me," it is so to be understood as if it were, I am not from myself, but from him who sent me.

CHAP. 3—*Some things concerning the Holy Spirit are to be understood according to the one rule only.*

5. For even of the Holy Spirit, of whom it is not said, "He emptied himself, and took upon him the form of a servant;" yet the Lord himself says, "However, when he the Spirit of truth is come, he will guide you into all truth. For he shall not speak of himself, but whatsoever he shall hear, that shall he speak; and he will show you things to come. He shall glorify me; for he shall receive of mine, and shall show it to you." And except he had immediately gone on to say after this, "All things that the Father has are mine; therefore said I, that

[10] John 7: 16.

he shall take of mine, and shall show it to you;"[11] it might, perhaps, have been believed that the Holy Spirit was so born of Christ, as Christ is of the Father. Since he had said of himself, "My doctrine is not mine, but his that sent me;" but of the Holy Spirit, "For he shall not speak of himself, but whatsoever he shall hear, that shall he speak;" and, "For he shall receive of mine, and shall show it to you." But because he has rendered the reason why he said, "He shall receive of mine" (for he says, "All things that the Father has are mine; therefore said I, that he shall take of mine"); it remains that the Holy Spirit be understood to have of that which is the Father's, as the Son also has. And how can this be, unless according to that which we have said above, "But when the Comforter is come, whom I will send to you from the Father, even the Spirit of truth, which proceeds from the Father, he shall testify of me"?[12] He is said, therefore, not to speak of himself, in that he proceeds from the Father; and as it does not follow that the Son is less because he said, "The Son can do nothing of himself, but what he sees the Father do" (for he has not said this according to the form of a servant, but according to the form of God, as we have already shown, and these words do not set him forth as less than, but as of the Father), so it is not brought to pass that the Holy Spirit is less, because it is said of him, "For he shall not speak of himself, but whatsoever he shall hear, that shall he speak;" for the words belong to him as proceeding from the Father. But whereas both the Son is of the Father, and the Holy Spirit proceeds from the Father, why both are not called sons, and both not said to be begotten, but the former is called the one only-begotten Son, and the latter, viz. the Holy Spirit, neither son nor begotten, because if begotten, then certainly a son, we will discuss in another place, if God shall grant, and so far as he shall grant.[13]

CHAP. 4—*The glorification of the Son by the Father does not prove inequality.*

6. But here also let them wake up if they can, who have

[11] John 16: 13–15.
[12] John 15: 26.
[13] Cf. Bk. 15.25.

thought this, too, to be a testimony on their side, to show that the Father is greater than the Son, because the Son has said, "Father, glorify me." Why, the Holy Spirit also glorifies him. Is the Spirit, too, greater than he? Moreover, if on that account the Holy Spirit glorifies the Son, because he shall receive of that which is the Son's, and shall therefore receive of that which is the Son's because all things that the Father has are the Son's also; it is evident that when the Holy Spirit glorifies the Son, the Father glorifies the Son. Therefore it may be perceived that all things that the Father has are not only of the Son, but also of the Holy Spirit, because the Holy Spirit is able to glorify the Son, whom the Father glorifies. But if he who glorifies is greater than he whom he glorifies, let them allow that those are equal who mutually glorify each other. But it is written, also, that the Son glorifies the Father; for he says, "I have glorified you on the earth."[14] Truly let them beware lest the Holy Spirit be thought greater than both, because he glorifies the Son whom the Father glorifies, while it is not written that he himself is glorified either by the Father or by the Son.

CHAP. 5—*The Son and Holy Spirit are not therefore less because sent. The Son is sent also by himself. Of the sending of the Holy Spirit.*

7. But being proved wrong so far, men betake themselves to saying, that he who sends is greater than he who is sent: therefore the Father is greater than the Son, because the Son continually speaks of himself as being sent by the Father; and the Father is also greater than the Holy Spirit, because Jesus has said of the Spirit, "Whom the Father will send in my name;"[15] and the Holy Spirit is less than both, because both the Father sends him, as we have said, and the Son, when he says, "But if I depart, I will send him to you." I first ask, then, in this inquiry, whence and whither the Son was sent. "I," he says, "came forth from the Father, and am come into the world."[16] Therefore, to be sent, is to come forth from the Father, and to come into the world. What, then, is that

[14] John 17: 1, 4.
[15] John 14: 26.
[16] John 16: 7, 28.

which the same evangelist says concerning him, "He was in the world, and the world was made by him, and the world knew him not;" and then he adds, "He came unto his own"?[17] Certainly he was sent thither, whither he came; but if he was sent into the world, because he came forth from the Father, then he both came into the world and was in the world. He was sent therefore thither, where he already was. For consider that, too, which is written in the prophet, that God said, "Do not I fill heaven and earth?"[18] If this is said of the Son (for some will have it understood that the Son himself spoke either by the prophets or in the prophets), whither was he sent except to the place where he already was? For he who says, "I fill heaven and earth," was everywhere. But if it is said of the Father, where could he be without his own word and without his own wisdom, which "reaches from one end to another mightily, and sweetly orders all things"?[19] But he cannot be anywhere without his own Spirit. Therefore, if God is everywhere, his Spirit also is everywhere. Therefore, the Holy Spirit, too, was sent thither, where he already was. For he, too, who finds no place to which he might go from the presence of God, and who says, "If I ascend up into heaven, you are there; if I shall go down into hell, behold, you are there;" wishing it to be understood that God is present everywhere, named in the previous verse his Spirit; for he says, "Whither shall I go from your Spirit? or whither shall I flee from your presence?"[20]

8. For this reason, then, if both the Son and the Holy Spirit are sent thither where they were, we must inquire, how that sending, whether of the Son or of the Holy Spirit, is to be understood; for of the Father alone, we nowhere read that he is sent. Now, of the Son, the apostle writes thus: "But when the fulness of the time was come, God sent forth his Son, made of a woman, made under the law, to redeem them that were under the law."[21] "He sent," he says, "his Son, made of a

---

17 John 1: 10 f.
18 Jer. 23: 24.
19 Wis. 8: 1.
20 Ps. 139: 8, 7.
21 Gal. 4: 4 f.

woman." And by this term, woman,[22] what Catholic does not know that he did not wish to signify the privation of virginity; but, according to a Hebraism, the difference of sex? When, therefore, he says, "God sent his Son, made of a woman," he sufficiently shows that the Son was "sent" in this very way, in that he was "made of a woman." Therefore, in that he was born of God, he was in the world; but in that he was born of Mary, he was sent and came into the world. Moreover, he could not be sent by the Father without the Holy Spirit, not only because the Father, when he sent him, that is, when he made him of a woman, is certainly understood not to have so made him without his own Spirit; but also because it is most plainly and expressly said in the Gospel in answer to the Virgin Mary, when she asked of the angel, "How shall this be?" "The Holy Ghost shall come upon thee, and the power of the highest shall overshadow thee."[23] And Matthew says, "She was found with child of the Holy Ghost."[24] Although, too, in the prophet Isaiah, Christ himself is understood to say of his own future advent, "And now the Lord God and his Spirit has sent me."[25]

9. Perhaps some one may wish to drive us to say, that the Son is sent also by himself, because the conception and childbirth of Mary is the working of the Trinity, by whose act of creating all things are created. And how, he will go on to say, has the Father sent him, if he sent himself? To whom I answer first, by asking him to tell me, if he can, in what manner the Father has sanctified him, if he has sanctified himself? For the same Lord says both; "Say you of him," he says, "whom the Father has sanctified and sent into the world, you blaspheme, because I said, I am the Son of God;"[26] while in another place he says, "And for their sake I sanctify myself."[27] I ask, also, in what manner the Father delivered him, if he delivered himself? For the apostle Paul says both: "Who," he says, "spared not his own Son, but delivered him up for us

22 *Mulier.*
23 Luke 1: 34 f.
24 Matt. 1: 18.
25 Is. 48: 16.
26 John 10: 36.
27 John 17: 19.

all;"[28] while elsewhere he says of the Saviour himself, "Who loved me, and delivered himself for me."[29] He will reply, I suppose, if he has a right sense in these things, because the will of the Father and the Son is one, and their working indivisible. In like manner, then, let him understand the incarnation and nativity of the virgin, wherein the Son is understood as sent, to have been done by one and the same operation of the Father and of the Son indivisibly; the Holy Spirit certainly not being excluded from it, of whom it is expressly said, "She was found with child by the Holy Ghost." For perhaps our meaning will be more plainly unfolded, if we ask in what manner God sent his Son. He commanded that he should come, and he, complying with the commandment, came. Did he then request, or did he only suggest? But whichever of these it was, certainly it was done by a word, and the Word of God is the Son of God himself. Therefore, since the Father sent him by a word, his being sent was the work of both the Father and his Word; therefore the same Son was sent by the Father and the Son, because the Son himself is the Word of the Father. For who would embrace so impious an opinion as to think the Father to have uttered a word in time, in order that the eternal Son might thereby be sent and might appear in the flesh in the fulness of time? But assuredly it was in that Word of God itself which was in the beginning with God and was God, namely, in the wisdom itself of God, apart from time, at what time that wisdom must needs appear in the flesh. Therefore, since without any commencement of time, the Word was in the beginning, and the Word was with God, and the Word was God, it was in the Word itself without any time, at what time the Word was to be made flesh and dwell among us.[30] And when this fulness of time had come, "God sent his Son, made of a woman,"[31] that is, made in time, that the incarnate Word might appear to men; while it was in that Word himself, apart from time, at what time this was to be done; for the order of times is in the eternal wisdom of God without time. Since, then, that the Son should appear in the

[28] Rom. 8: 32.
[29] Gal. 2: 20.
[30] John 1: 1, 2, 14.
[31] Gal. 4: 4.

flesh was brought about by both the Father and the Son, it
is fitly said that he who appeared in that flesh was sent, and
that he who did not appear in it, sent him; because those things
which are transacted outwardly before the bodily eyes have
their existence from the inward machinery of the spiritual nature, and on that account are fitly said to be sent. Further,
that form of man which he took is the person of the Son,
not also of the Father; on which account the invisible Father,
together with the Son, who with the Father is invisible, is said
to have sent the same Son by making him visible. But if he
became visible in such way as to cease to be invisible with
the Father, that is, if the substance of the invisible Word were
turned by a change and transition into a visible creature, then
the Son would be so understood to be sent by the Father, that
he would be found to be only sent; not also, with the Father,
sending. But since he so took the form of a servant, as that
the unchangeable form of God remained, it is clear that that
which became apparent in the Son was done by the Father
and the Son not being apparent; that is, that by the invisible
Father, with the invisible Son, the same Son himself was sent
so as to be visible. Why, therefore, does he say, "Neither came
I of myself"? This, we may now say, is said according to the
form of a servant, in the same way as it is said, "I judge no
man."[32]

10. If, therefore, he is said to be sent, in so far as he appeared outwardly in the bodily creature, who inwardly in his
spiritual nature is always hidden from the eyes of mortals, it
is now easy to understand also of the Holy Spirit why he too
is said to be sent. For in due time a certain outward appearance of the creature was wrought, wherein the Holy Spirit
might be visibly shown; whether when he descended upon the
Lord himself in a bodily shape as a dove,[33] or when, ten days
having passed since his ascension, on the day of Pentecost a
sound came suddenly from heaven as of a rushing mighty
wind, and cloven tongues like as of fire were seen upon them,
and it sat upon each of them.[34] This operation, visibly exhib-

[32] John 8: 42, 15.
[33] Matt. 3: 16.
[34] Acts 2: 2–4.

ited, and presented to mortal eyes, is called the sending of the Holy Spirit; not that his very substance appeared, in which he himself also is invisible and unchangeable, like the Father and the Son, but that the hearts of men, touched by things seen outwardly, might be turned from the manifestation in time of him as coming to his hidden eternity as ever present.

CHAP. 6—*The creature is not so taken by the Holy Spirit as flesh is by the Word.*

11. It is, then, for this reason nowhere written, that the Father is greater than the Holy Spirit, or that the Holy Spirit is less than God the Father, because the creature in which the Holy Spirit was to appear was not taken in the same way as the Son of man was taken, as the form in which the person of the Word of God himself should be set forth; not that he might possess the word of God, as other holy and wise men have possessed it, but "above his fellows;"[35] not certainly that he possessed the word more than they, so as to be of more surpassing wisdom than the rest were, but that he was the very Word himself. For the word in the flesh is one thing, and the Word made flesh is another; i.e. the word in man is one thing, the Word that is man is another. For flesh is put for man, where it is said, "The Word was made flesh;"[36] and again, "And all flesh shall see the salvation of God."[37] For it does not mean flesh without soul and without mind; but "all flesh," is the same as if it were said, every man. The creature, then, in which the Holy Spirit should appear, was not so taken, as that flesh and human form were taken, of the Virgin Mary. For the Spirit did not beatify the dove, or the wind, or the fire, and join them for ever to himself and to his person in unity and "fashion." Nor, again, is the nature of the Holy Spirit mutable and changeable; so that these things were not made of the creature, but he himself was turned and changed first into one and then into another, as water is changed into ice. But these things appeared at the seasons at which they ought to have appeared, the creature serving the creator, and being changed and converted at the command of him who re-

[35] Heb. 1: 9.
[36] John 1: 14.
[37] Luke 3: 6.

mains immutably in himself, in order to signify and manifest
him in such way as it was fit he should be signified and manifested to mortal men. Accordingly, although that dove is called
the Spirit;[38] and in speaking of that fire, "There appeared to
them," he says, "cloven tongues, like as of fire, and it sat upon
each of them; and they began to speak with other tongues,
as the Spirit gave them utterance;"[39] in order to show that
the Spirit was manifested by that fire, as by the dove; yet we
cannot call the Holy Spirit both God and a dove, or both God
and fire, in the same way as we call the Son both God and
man; nor as we call the Son the lamb of God; which not only
John the Baptist says, "Behold the lamb of God,"[40] but also
John the Evangelist sees the lamb slain in the Apocalypse.[41]
For that prophetic vision was not shown to bodily eyes through
bodily forms, but in the spirit through spiritual images of bodily things. But whoever saw that dove and that fire, saw them
with their eyes. Although it may perhaps be disputed concerning the fire, whether it was seen by the eyes or in the spirit,
on account of the form of the sentence. For the text does not
say, They saw cloven tongues like fire, but, "There appeared
to them." But we do not usually say with the same meaning,
It appeared to me; as we say, I saw. And in those spiritual
visions of corporeal images the usual expressions are, both,
It appeared to me; and, I saw; but in those things which are
shown to the eyes through express corporeal forms, the common expression is not, It appeared to me; but, I saw. There
may, therefore, be a question raised respecting that fire, how
it was seen; whether within in the spirit as it were outwardly,
or really outwardly before the eyes of the flesh. But of that
dove, which is said to have descended in a bodily form, no
one ever doubted that it was seen by the eyes. Nor, again,
as we call the Son a rock (for it is written, "And that rock
was Christ"[42]), can we so call the Spirit a dove or fire. For
that rock was a thing already created, and after the mode of
its action was called by the name of Christ, whom it signified;

[38] Matt. 3: 16.
[39] Acts 2: 3 f.
[40] John 1: 29.
[41] Apoc. 5: 6.
[42] 1 Cor. 10: 4.

like the stone placed under Jacob's head, and also anointed, which he took in order to signify the Lord;[43] or as Isaac was Christ, when he carried the wood for the sacrifice of himself.[44] A particular significative action was added to those already existing things; they did not, as that dove and fire, suddenly come into being in order simply so to signify. The dove and the fire, indeed, seem to me more like that flame which appeared to Moses in the bush,[45] or that pillar which the people followed in the wilderness,[46] or the thunders and lightnings which came when the law was given in the mount.[47] For the corporeal form of these things came into being for the very purpose, that it might signify something, and then pass away.

CHAP. 7—*A doubt raised about divine appearances.*

12. The Holy Spirit, then, is also said to be sent, on account of these corporeal forms which came into existence in time, in order to signify and manifest him, as he must needs be manifested, to human senses; yet he is not said to be less than the Father, as the Son, because he was in the form of a servant, is said to be; because that form of a servant inhered in the unity of the person of the Son, but those corporeal forms appeared for a time, in order to show what was necessary to be shown, and then ceased to be. Why, then, is not the Father also said to be sent, through those corporeal forms, the fire of the bush, and the pillar of cloud or of fire, and the lightnings in the mount, and whatever other things of the kind appeared at that time, when (as we have learned from scripture testimony) he spoke face to face with the fathers, if he himself was manifested by those modes and forms of the creature, as exhibited and presented corporeally to human sight? But if the Son was manifested by them, why is he said to be sent so long after, when he was made of a woman, as the apostle says, "But when the fulness of time was come, God sent forth his Son, made of a woman,"[48] seeing that he was sent also before,

[43] Gen. 28: 18.
[44] Gen. 22: 6.
[45] Ex. 3: 2.
[46] Ex. 13: 21 f.
[47] Ex. 19: 16.
[48] Gal. 4: 4.

when he appeared to the fathers by those changeable forms of the creature? Or if he cannot rightly be said to be sent, unless when the Word was made flesh, why is the Holy Spirit said to be sent, of whom no such incarnation was ever wrought? But if by those visible things, which are put before us in the law and in the prophets, neither the Father nor the Son but the Holy Spirit was manifested, why also is he said to be sent now, when he was sent also before after these modes?

13. In the perplexity of this inquiry, the Lord helping us, we must ask, first, whether the Father, or the Son, or the Holy Spirit; or whether, sometimes the Father, sometimes the Son, sometimes the Holy Spirit; or whether it was without any distinction of persons, in such way as the one and only God is spoken of, that is, that the Trinity itself appeared to the fathers by those forms of the creature. Next, whichever of these alternatives shall have been found or thought true, whether for this purpose only the creature was fashioned, wherein God, as he judged it suitable at that time, should be shown to human sight; or whether angels, who already existed, were so sent, as to speak in the person of God, taking a corporeal form from the corporeal creature, for the purpose of their ministry, as each had need; or else, according to the power the creator has given them, changing and converting their own body itself, to which they are not subject, but govern it as subject to themselves, into whatever appearances they wished that were suited and apt to their several actions. Lastly, we shall discern that which it was our purpose to ask, viz. whether the Son and the Holy Spirit were also sent before; and, if they were so sent, what difference there is between that sending, and the one which we read of in the Gospel; or whether in truth neither of them were sent, except when either the Son was made of the Virgin Mary, or the Holy Spirit appeared in a visible form, whether in the dove or in tongues of fire.

CHAP. 8—*The entire Trinity invisible.*

14. Let us therefore say nothing of those who, with an over carnal mind, have thought the nature of the Word of God, and the wisdom, which, "remaining in herself, makes

all things new,"[49] whom we call the only Son of God, not only to be changeable, but also to be visible. For these, with more audacity than religion, bring a very dull heart to the inquiry into divine things. For whereas the soul is a spiritual substance, and whereas itself also was made, yet could not be made by any other than by him by whom all things were made, and without whom nothing is made,[50] it, although changeable, is yet not visible; and this they have believed to be the case with the Word himself and with the wisdom of God itself, by which the soul was made; whereas this wisdom is not only invisible, as the soul also is, but likewise unchangeable, which the soul is not. It is in truth the same unchangeableness in it, which is referred to when it was said, "Remaining in herself she makes all things new." Yet these people, endeavouring, as it were, to prop up their error in its fall by testimonies of the divine Scriptures, adduce the words of the apostle Paul; and take that, which is said of the one only God, in whom the Trinity itself is understood, to be said only of the Father, and neither of the Son nor of the Holy Spirit: "Now unto the king eternal, immortal, invisible, the only wise God, be honour and glory for ever and ever;"[51] and that other passage, "The blessed and only potentate, the king of kings, and Lord of lords; who only hath immortality, dwelling in the light which no man can approach to; whom no man has seen, nor can see."[52] How these passages are to be understood, I think we have already discoursed sufficiently.

CHAP. 9—*Against those who believed the Father only to be immortal and invisible. The truth to be sought by peaceful study.*

15. But they who will have these texts understood only of the Father, and not of the Son or the Holy Spirit, declare the Son to be visible, not by having taken flesh of the virgin, but beforehand also in himself. For he himself, they say, appeared to the eyes of the fathers. And if you say to them, In whatever manner, then, the Son is visible in himself, in that manner also he is mortal in himself; so that it plainly

[49] Wis. 7: 27.
[50] John 1: 3.
[51] 1 Tim. 1: 17.
[52] 1 Tim. 6: 15 f.

follows that you would have this saying also understood only of the Father, viz. "Who only hath immortality;" for if the Son is mortal from having taken upon him our flesh, then allow that it is on account of this flesh that he is also visible: they reply, that it is not on account of this flesh that they say that the Son is mortal; but that, just as he was also before visible, so he was also before mortal. For if they say the Son is mortal from having taken our flesh, then it is not the Father alone without the Son who has immortality; because his Word also has immortality, by which all things were made. For he did not therefore lose his immortality, because he took mortal flesh; seeing that it could not happen even to the human soul, that it should die with the body, when the Lord himself says, "Fear not them which kill the body, but are not able to kill the soul."[53] Or, perhaps, the Holy Spirit also took flesh: concerning whom certainly they will, without doubt, be troubled to say—if the Son is mortal on account of taking our flesh—in what manner they understand that the Father only has immortality without the Son and the Holy Spirit, since, indeed, the Holy Spirit did not take our flesh; and if he has not immortality, then the Son is not mortal on account of taking our flesh; but if the Holy Spirit has immortality, then it is not said only of the Father, "Who only has immortality." And therefore they think they are able to prove that the Son in himself was mortal also before the incarnation, because changeableness itself is not unfitly called mortality, according to which the soul also is said to die; not because it is changed and turned into body, or into some substance other than itself, but because, whatever in its own self-same substance is now after another mode than it once was, is discovered to be mortal, in so far as it has ceased to be what it was. Because then, they say, before the Son of God was born of the Virgin Mary, he himself appeared to our fathers, not in one and the same form only, but in many forms; first in one form, then in another; he is both visible in himself, because his substance was visible to mortal eyes, when he had not yet taken our flesh, and mortal, inasmuch as he is changeable. And so also the Holy Spirit, who appeared at one time as a dove, and

[53] Matt. 10: 28.

another time as fire. Therefore, they say, these texts do not belong to the Trinity, but singularly and properly to the Father only: "Now unto the king eternal, immortal, and invisible, the only wise God;" and, "Who only has immortality, dwelling in the light which no man can approach to; whom no man has seen, nor can see."

16. Passing by, then, these reasoners, who are unable to know the substance even of the soul, which is invisible, and therefore are very far indeed from knowing that the substance of the one and only God, that is, the Father and the Son and the Holy Spirit, remains ever not only invisible, but also unchangeable, and that hence it possesses true and real immortality; let us, who deny that God, whether the Father, or the Son, or the Holy Spirit, ever appeared to bodily eyes, unless through the corporeal creature made subject to his own power; let us, I say—ready to be corrected, if we are reproved in a fraternal and upright spirit, ready to be so, even if carped at by an enemy, so that he speak the truth—in catholic peace and with peaceful study inquire, whether God indiscriminately appeared to our fathers before Christ came in the flesh, or whether it was any one person of the Trinity, or whether severally, as it were by turns.

CHAP. 10—*Whether God the Trinity indiscriminately appeared to the Fathers, or any one person of the Trinity. The appearing of God to Adam. Of the same appearance. The vision to Abraham.*

17. And first, in that which is written in Genesis, viz. that God spoke with man whom he had formed out of the dust; if we set apart the figurative meaning, and treat it so as to place faith in the narrative even in the letter, it should appear that God then spoke with man in the appearance of a man. This is not indeed expressly laid down in the book, but the general tenor of its reading sounds in this sense, especially in that which is written, that Adam heard the voice of the Lord God, walking in the garden in the cool of the evening, and hid himself among the trees of the garden; and when God said, "Adam, where are you?"[54] replied, "I heard your voice, and I was afraid because I was naked, and I hid myself from your face." For I do not see how such a walking and conversation

[54] Gen. 3: 8–10.

of God can be understood literally, except he appeared as a man. For it can neither be said that a voice only of God was framed, when God is said to have walked, or that he who was walking in a place was not visible; while Adam, too, says that he hid himself from the face of God. Who then was he? Whether the Father, or the Son, or the Holy Spirit? Whether altogether indiscriminately did God the Trinity himself speak to man in the form of man? The context, indeed, itself of the scripture nowhere, it should seem, indicates a change from person to person; but he seems still to speak to the first man, who said, "Let there be light," and, "Let there be a firmament," and so on through each of those days; whom we usually take to be God the Father, making by a word whatever he willed to make. For he made all things by his word, which Word we know, by the right rule of faith, to be his only Son. If, therefore, God the Father spoke to the first man, and himself was walking in the garden in the cool of the evening, and if it was from his face that the sinner hid himself among the trees of the garden, why are we not to go on to understand that it was he also who appeared to Abraham and to Moses, and to whom he would, and how he would, through the changeable and visible creature, subjected to himself, while he himself remains in himself and in his own substance, in which he is unchangeable and invisible? But, possibly, it might be that the scripture passed over in a hidden way from person to person, and while it had related that the Father said "Let there be light," and the rest which it mentioned him to have done by the Word, went on to indicate the Son as speaking to the first man; not unfolding this openly, but intimating it to be understood by those who could understand it.

18. Let him, then, who has the strength whereby he can penetrate this secret with his mind's eye, so that to him it appears clearly, either that the Father also is able, or that only the Son and Holy Spirit are able, to appear to human eyes through a visible creature; let him, I say, proceed to examine these things if he can, or even to express and handle them in words; but the thing itself, so far as concerns this testimony of scripture, where God spoke with man, is, in my judgment, not discoverable, because it does not evidently appear even if Adam usually saw God with the eyes of his body; especially

as it is a great question what manner of eyes it was that
were opened when they tasted the forbidden fruit;[55] for before they had tasted, these eyes were closed. Yet I would not
rashly assert, even if that scripture implies Paradise to have
been a material place, that God could not have walked there
in any way except in some bodily form. For it might be said,
that only words were framed for the man to hear, without
seeing any form. Neither, because it is written, "Adam hid
himself from the face of God," does it follow forthwith that
he usually saw his face. For what if he himself indeed could
not see, but feared to be himself seen by him whose voice he
had heard, and had felt his presence as he walked? For Cain,
too, said to God, "From your face I will hide myself;"[56] yet
we are not therefore compelled to admit that he was accustomed to behold the face of God with his bodily eyes in any
visible form, although he had heard the voice of God questioning and speaking with him of his sin. But what manner of
speech it was that God then uttered to the outward ears of
men, especially in speaking to the first man, it is both difficult
to discover, and we have not undertaken to say in this discourse. But if words alone and sounds were made, by which
to bring about some sensible presence of God to those first
men, I do not know why I should not there understand the
person of God the Father, seeing that his person is manifested
also in that voice, when Jesus appeared in glory on the mount
before the three disciples;[57] and in that when the dove descended upon him at his baptism;[58] and in that where he cried
to the Father concerning his own glorification, and it was
answered him, "I have both glorified, and will glorify again."[59]
Not that the voice could be made without the work of the Son
and of the Holy Spirit (since the Trinity works indivisibly),
but that such a voice was made as to manifest the person of
the Father only; just as the Trinity made that human form
from the Virgin Mary, yet it is the person of the Son alone; for
the invisible Trinity made the visible person of the Son alone.

[55] Gen. 3: 7.
[56] Gen. 4: 14.
[57] Matt. 17: 5.
[58] Matt. 3: 17.
[59] John 12: 28.

Neither does anything forbid us, not only to understand those words spoken to Adam as spoken by the Trinity, but also to take them as manifesting the person of that Trinity. For we are compelled to understand of the Father only, that which is said, "This is my beloved Son."[60] For Jesus can neither be believed nor understood to be the Son of the Holy Spirit, or even his own Son. And where the voice uttered, "I have both glorified, and will glorify again," we confess it was only the person of the Father; since it is the answer to that word of the Lord, in which he had said, "Father, glorify thy Son," which he could not say except to God the Father only, and not also to the Holy Spirit, whose Son he was not. But here, where it is written, "And the Lord God said to Adam," no reason can be given why the Trinity itself should not be understood.

19. Likewise, also, in that which is written, "Now the Lord had said to Abraham, Get you out of your country, and from your kindred, and your father's house," it is not clear whether a voice alone came to the ears of Abraham, or whether anything also appeared to his eyes. But a little while after, it is somewhat more clearly said, "And the Lord appeared to Abraham, and said, To your seed will I give this land."[61] But neither there is it expressly said in what form God appeared to him, or whether the Father, or the Son, or the Holy Spirit appeared to him. Unless, perhaps, they think that it was the Son who appeared to Abraham, because it is not written, God appeared to him, but "the Lord appeared to him." For the Son seems to be called the Lord as though the name was appropriated to him; as e.g. the apostle says, "For though there be beings that are called gods, whether in heaven or in earth, (as there are many gods and many lords,) but to us there is but one God, the Father, of whom are all things, and we in him; and one Lord Jesus Christ, by whom are all things, and we by him."[62] But since it is found that God the Father also is called Lord in many places,—for instance, "The Lord has said to me, You are my Son; this day have I begotten you;"[63] and again, "The Lord said to my Lord, Sit

[60] Matt. 3: 17.
[61] Gen. 12: 1, 7.
[62] 1 Cor. 8: 5 f.
[63] Ps. 2: 7.

you at my right hand;"[64] since also the Holy Spirit is found
to be called Lord, as where the apostle says, "Now the Lord
is that Spirit;" and then, lest any one should think the Son to
be signified, and to be called the Spirit on account of his incorporeal substance, has gone on to say, "And where the Spirit of
the Lord is, there is liberty;"[65] and no one ever doubted the
Spirit of the Lord to be the Holy Spirit: therefore, neither here
does it appear plainly whether it was any person of the Trinity
that appeared to Abraham, or God himself the Trinity, of
which one God it is said, "You shall fear the Lord your God,
and him only shall you serve."[66] But under the oak at Mamre
he saw three men, whom he invited, and hospitably received,
and ministered to them as they feasted. Yet scripture at the
beginning of that narrative does not say, three men appeared
to him, but, "The Lord appeared to him." And then, setting
forth in due order after what manner the Lord appeared to
him, it has added the account of the three men, whom Abraham invites to his hospitality in the plural number, and afterwards speaks to them in the singular number as one; and
as one he promises him a son by Sarah, viz. the one whom the
scripture calls Lord, as in the beginning of the same narrative,
"The Lord," it says, "appeared to Abraham." He invites
them then, and washes their feet, and leads them forth at their
departure, as though they were men; but he speaks as with
the Lord God, whether when a son is promised to him, or
when the destruction is shown to him that was impending over
Sodom.[67]

CHAP. 11—*Of the same appearance.*

20. That place of scripture demands neither a slight nor a
passing consideration. For if one man had appeared, what
else would those at once cry out, who say that the Son was
visible also in his own substance before he was born of the
virgin, but that it was himself? since it is said, they say, of
the Father, "To the only invisible God."[68] And yet, I could

[64] Ps. 110: 1.
[65] 2 Cor. 3: 17.
[66] Deut. 6: 13.
[67] Gen. 18.
[68] 1 Tim. 1: 17.

still go on to demand, in what manner "he was found in fashion as a man," before he had taken our flesh, seeing that his feet were washed, and that he fed upon earthly food? How could that be, when he was still "in the form of God, and thought it not robbery to be equal with God"?[69] For, had he already "emptied himself, taking upon him the form of a servant, and made in the likeness of men, and found in fashion as a man"? when we know when it was that he did this through his birth of the virgin. How, then, before he had done this, did he appear as one man to Abraham? or, was not that form a reality? I could put these questions, if it had been one man that appeared to Abraham, and if that one were believed to be the Son of God. But since three men appeared, and no one of them is said to be greater than the rest either in form, or age, or power, why should we not here understand, as visibly intimated by the visible creature, the equality of the Trinity, and one and the same substance in three persons?

21. For, lest any one should think that one among the three is in this way intimated to have been the greater, and that this one is to be understood to have been the Lord, the Son of God, while the other two were his angels; because, whereas three appeared, Abraham there speaks to one as the Lord: Holy Scripture has not forgotten to anticipate, by a contradiction, such future cogitations and opinions, when a little while after it says that two angels came to Lot, among whom that just man also, who deserved to be freed from the burning of Sodom, speaks to one as to the Lord. For so scripture goes on to say, "And the Lord went his way, as soon as he left communing with Abraham; and Abraham returned to his place."[70]

CHAP. 12—*The appearance to Lot is examined.*

"But there came two angels to Sodom in the evening." Here, what I have begun to set forth must be considered more attentively. Certainly Abraham was speaking with three, and called that one, in the singular number, the Lord. Perhaps, some one may say, he recognised one of the three to be the

[69] Phil. 2: 6 f.
[70] Gen. 18: 33.

Lord, but the other two his angels. What, then, does that
mean which scripture goes on to say, "And the Lord went his
way, as soon as he had left communing with Abraham; and
Abraham returned to his place: and there came two angels
to Sodom in the evening"? Are we to suppose that the one
who, among the three, was recognised as the Lord, had departed, and had sent the two angels that were with him to
destroy Sodom? Let us see, then, what follows. "There came,"
it is said, "two angels to Sodom in the evening; and Lot sat
in the gate of Sodom: and Lot seeing them, rose up to meet
them; and he bowed himself with his face toward the ground;
and he said, Behold now, my lords, turn in, I beg you, into
your servant's house." Here it is clear, both that there were
two angels, and that in the plural number they were invited
to partake of hospitality, and that they were honourably designated lords, when they perchance were thought to be men.

22. Yet, again, it is objected that except they were known
to be angels of God, Lot would not have bowed himself with
his face to the ground. Why, then, is both hospitality and food
offered to them, as though they wanted such human succour?
But whatever may here lie hid, let us now pursue that which
we have undertaken. Two appear; both are called angels; they
are invited plurally; he speaks as with two plurally, until the
departure from Sodom. And then scripture goes on to say,
"And it came to pass, when they had brought them forth
abroad, that they said, Escape for your life; look not behind
you, and do not stay in all the plain; escape to the mountain,
and there you shall be saved, lest you be consumed. And Lot
said to them, Oh! not so, my lord: behold now, your servant
has found grace in your sight,"[71] etc. What is meant by his
saying to them, "Oh! not so, my lord," if he who was the Lord
had already departed, and had sent the angels? Why is it said,
"Oh! not so, my lord," and not, "Oh! not so, my lords"? Or if
he wished to speak to one of them, why does scripture say,
"But Lot said to them, Oh! not so, my lord: behold now, your
servant has found grace in your sight," etc.? Are we here,
too, to understand two persons in the plural number, but
when the two are addressed as one, there the one Lord God

[71] Gen. 19: 1–19.

of one substance? But which two persons do we here understand?—of the Father and of the Son, or of the Father and
of the Holy Spirit, or of the Son and of the Holy Spirit? The
last, perhaps, is the more suitable; for they said of themselves
that they were sent, which is that which we say of the Son
and of the Holy Spirit. For we find nowhere in the Scriptures
that the Father was sent.

CHAP. 13—*The appearance in the bush.*

23. But when Moses was sent to lead the children of Israel
out of Egypt, it is written that the Lord appeared to him thus:
"Now Moses kept the flock of Jethro his father-in-law, the
priest of Midian: and he led the flock to the back side of the
desert, and came to the mountain of God, even to Horeb.
And the angel of the Lord appeared to him in a flame of
fire, out of the midst of a bush; and he looked, and, behold,
the bush burned with fire, and the bush was not consumed.
And Moses said, I will now turn aside, and see this great
sight, why the bush is not burned. And when the Lord saw that
he turned aside to see, God called to him out of the midst of
the bush, and said, I am the God of your father, the God of
Abraham, the God of Isaac, and the God of Jacob."[72] He is
here also first called the angel of the Lord, and then God.
Was an angel, then, the God of Abraham, and the God of
Isaac, and the God of Jacob? Therefore he may be rightly
understood to be the Saviour himself, of whom the apostle
says, "Whose are the fathers, and of whom as concerning the
flesh Christ came, who is over all, God blessed for ever."[73]
He, therefore, "who is over all, God blessed for ever," is not
unreasonably here understood also to be himself the God of
Abraham, the God of Isaac, and the God of Jacob. But why is
he previously called the angel of the Lord, when he appeared
in a flame of fire out of the bush? Was it because it was one of
many angels, who by an economy bare the person of his Lord?
or was something of the creature assumed by him in order to
bring about a visible appearance for the business in hand,
and that words might thence be audibly uttered, whereby the

[72] Ex. 3: 1–6.
[73] Rom. 9: 5.

presence of the Lord might be shown, in such way as was
fitting, to the corporeal senses of man, by means of the creature made subject? For if he was one of the angels, who
could easily affirm whether it was the person of the Son which
was imposed upon him to announce, or that of the Holy
Spirit, or that of God the Father, or altogether of the Trinity
itself, who is the one and only God, in order that he might
say, "I am the God of Abraham, and the God of Isaac, and
the God of Jacob"? For we cannot say that the Son of God
is the God of Abraham, and the God of Isaac, and the God
of Jacob, and that the Father is not; nor will any one dare to
deny that either the Holy Spirit, or the Trinity itself, whom
we believe and understand to be the one God, is the God of
Abraham, and the God of Isaac, and the God of Jacob. For
he who is not God, is not the God of those fathers. Furthermore, if not only the Father is God, as all, even heretics,
admit; but also the Son, which, whether they will or not, they
are compelled to acknowledge, since the apostle says, "Who
is over all, God blessed for ever;" and the Holy Spirit, since
the same apostle says, "Therefore glorify God in your body;"
when he had said above, "Know you not that your body is
the temple of the Holy Ghost, which is in you, which you
have of God?"[74] and these three are one God, as catholic
soundness believes: it is not sufficiently apparent which person of the Trinity that angel bore, if he was one of the rest of
the angels, and whether any person, and not rather that of
the Trinity itself. But if the creature was assumed for the
purpose of the business in hand, whereby both to appear to
human eyes, and to sound in human ears, and to be called
the angel of the Lord, and the Lord, and God; then God
cannot here be understood to be the Father, but either the
Son or the Holy Spirit. Although I cannot call to mind that
the Holy Spirit is anywhere else called an angel, which yet
may be understood from his work; for it is said of him, "And
he will show you things to come;"[75] and "angel" in Greek
is certainly equivalent to "messenger" in Latin: but we read
most evidently of the Lord Jesus Christ in the prophet, that

[74] 1 Cor. 6: 20, 19.
[75] John 16: 13.

he is called "the angel of great counsel,"[76] while both the Holy Spirit and the Son of God is God and Lord of the angels.

CHAP. 14—*Of the appearance in the pillar of cloud and of fire.*

24. Also in the going forth of the children of Israel from Egypt it is written, "And the Lord went before them, by day in a pillar of cloud to lead them the way, and by night in a pillar of fire. He took not away the pillar of the cloud by day, nor the pillar of fire by night, from before the people."[77] Who here, too, would doubt that God appeared to the eyes of mortal men by the creature made subject to him, and that corporeal, not by his own substance? But it is not similarly apparent whether the Father, or the Son, or the Holy Spirit, or the Trinity itself, the one God. Nor is this made clear there either, in my judgment, where it is written, "The glory of the Lord appeared in the cloud, and the Lord spoke unto Moses, saying, I have heard the murmurings of the children of Israel,"[78] etc.

CHAP. 15—*Of the appearance on Sinai. Whether the Trinity spoke in that appearance or some one person specially.*

25. But now of the clouds, and voices, and lightnings, and the trumpet, and the smoke on Mount Sinai, when it was said, "And Mount Sinai was altogether on a smoke, because the Lord descended upon it in fire, and its smoke ascended as the smoke of a furnace; and all the people that were in the camp trembled; and when the voice of the trumpet sounded long and waxed louder and louder, Moses spoke, and God answered him by a voice."[79] And a little after, when the law had been given in the ten commandments, it follows in the text, "And all the people saw the thunderings, and the lightnings, and the noise of the trumpet, and the mountain smoking." And a little after, "And when the people saw it, they removed and stood afar off, and Moses drew near to the thick darkness where God was, and the Lord said to Moses,"[80]

[76] Is. 9: 6.
[77] Ex. 3: 21 f.
[78] Ex. 16: 10–12.
[79] Ex. 19: 18 f.
[80] Ex. 20: 18, 21.

etc. What shall I say about this, except that no one can be so insane as to believe the smoke, and the fire, and the cloud, and the darkness, and whatever there was of the kind, to be the substance of the word and wisdom of God which is Christ, or of the Holy Spirit? For not even the Arians ever dared to say that they were the substance of God the Father. All these things, then, were done through the creature serving the creator, and were presented in a suitable economy to human senses; unless, perhaps, because it is said, "And Moses drew near to the cloud where God was," carnal thoughts must suppose that the cloud was indeed seen by the people, but that within the cloud Moses with the eyes of the flesh saw the Son of God, whom doting heretics insist is seen in his own substance. Moses may have seen him with the eyes of the flesh, if not only the wisdom of God which is Christ, but even that of any man you please and however wise, can be seen with the eyes of the flesh; or if, because it is written of the elders of Israel, that "they saw the place where the God of Israel had stood," and that "there was under his feet as it were a paved work of a sapphire stone, and as it were the body of heaven in his clearness,"[81] therefore we are to believe that the word and wisdom of God in his own substance stood within the space of an earthly place, who indeed "reaches firmly from end to end, and sweetly orders all things;"[82] and that the Word of God, by whom all things were made,[83] is in such wise changeable, as now to contract, now to expand himself; (may the Lord cleanse the hearts of his faithful ones from such thoughts!). But indeed all these visible and sensible things are, as we have often said, exhibited through the creature made subject in order to signify the invisible and intelligible God, not only the Father, but also the Son and the Holy Spirit, "of whom are all things, and through whom are all things, and in whom are all things;"[84] although "the invisible things of God, from the creation of the world,

[81] Ex. 24: 10.
[82] Wis. 8: 1.
[83] John 1: 3.
[84] Rom. 11: 36.

are clearly seen, being understood by the things that are made, even his eternal power and Godhead."[85]

26. But as far as concerns our present undertaking, neither on Mount Sinai do I see how it appears, by all those things which were fearfully displayed to the senses of mortal men, whether God the Trinity spoke, or the Father, or the Son, or the Holy Spirit severally. But if it is allowable, without rash assertion, to venture upon a modest and hesitating conjecture from this passage, if it is possible to understand it of one person of the Trinity, why do we not rather understand the Holy Spirit to be spoken of, since the law itself also, which was given there, is said to have been written upon tables of stone with the finger of God,[86] by which name we know the Holy Spirit to be signified in the Gospel.[87] And fifty days are numbered from the slaying of the lamb and the celebration of the Passover until the day in which these things began to be done in Mount Sinai; just as after the passion of our Lord fifty days are numbered from his resurrection, and then came the Holy Spirit which the Son of God had promised. And in that very coming of his, which we read of in the Acts of the Apostles, there appeared cloven tongues like as of fire, and it sat upon each of them:[88] which agrees with Exodus, where it is written, "And Mount Sinai was altogether on smoke, because the Lord descended upon it in fire;" and a little after, "And the sight of the glory of the Lord," he says, "was like devouring fire on the top of the mount in the eyes of the children of Israel."[89] Or if these things were therefore done because neither the Father nor the Son could be there presented in that mode without the Holy Spirit, by whom the law itself must be written; then we know doubtless that God appeared there, not by his own substance, which remains invisible and unchangeable, but by the appearance above mentioned of the creature; but that some special person of the Trinity appeared, distinguished by a proper mark, as far as my capacity of understanding reaches, we do not see.

[85] Rom. 1: 20.
[86] Ex. 31: 18.
[87] Luke 11: 20.
[88] Acts 2: 1–4.
[89] Ex. 24: 17.

CHAP. 16—*In what manner Moses saw God.*

26. There is yet another difficulty which troubles most people, viz. that it is written, "And the Lord spoke unto Moses face to face, as a man speaks to his friend;" whereas a little after, the same Moses says, "Now therefore, I pray you, if I have found grace in your sight, show me now yourself plainly, that I may see you, that I may find grace in your sight, and that I may consider that this nation is your people;" and a little after Moses again said to the Lord, "Show me your glory." What means this then, that in everything which was done, as above said, God was thought to have appeared by his own substance; whence the Son of God has been believed by these miserable people to be visible not by the creature, but by himself; and that Moses, entering into the cloud, appeared to have had this very object in entering, that a cloudy darkness indeed might be shown to the eyes of the people, but that Moses within might hear the words of God, as though he beheld his face; and, as it is said, "And the Lord spoke unto Moses face to face, as a man speaks to his friend;" and yet, behold, the same Moses says, "If I have found grace in your sight, show me yourself plainly"? Assuredly he knew that he saw corporeally, and he sought the true sight of God spiritually. And that mode of speech accordingly which was made in words, was so modified, as if it were of a friend speaking to a friend. Yet who sees God the Father with the eyes of the body? And that Word, which was in the beginning, the Word which was with God, the Word which was God, by which all things were made,[90]—who sees him with the eyes of the body? And the Spirit of wisdom, again, who sees with the eyes of the body? Yet what is "Show me now yourself plainly, that I may see you," except Show me your substance? But if Moses had not said this, we would have to bear with those foolish people as we could, who think that the substance of God was made visible to his eyes through those things which, as above mentioned, were said or done. But when it is here demonstrated most evidently that this was not granted to him, even though he desired it; who will dare to say, that by the like forms which had ap-

[90] John 1: 1, 3.

peared visibly to him also, not the creature serving God, but that itself which is God, appeared to the eyes of a mortal man?

28. Add, too, that which the Lord afterwards said to Moses, "You cannot see my face: for there shall no man see my face, and live. And the Lord said, Behold, there is a place by me, and you shall stand upon a rock: and it shall come to pass, while my glory passes by, that I will put you into a watch-tower of the rock, and will cover you with my hand while I pass by: and I will take away my hand, and you shall see my back; but my face shall not be seen."[91]

CHAP. 17—*How the back of God was seen. The faith of the resurrection of Christ. The Catholic Church only is the place from whence the back of God is seen. The back of God was seen by the Israelites. It is a rash opinion to think that God the Father only was never seen by the fathers.*

Not unfitly is it commonly understood to be prefigured from the person of our Lord Jesus Christ, that his "back" is to be taken to be his flesh, in which he was born of the virgin, and died, and rose again; whether it is called back on account of the posteriority of mortality, or because it was almost in the end of the world, that is, at a late period, that he deigned to take it: but that his face was that form of God, in which he "thought it not robbery to be equal with God,"[92] which no one certainly can see and live; whether because after this life, in which we are absent from the Lord,[93] and where the corruptible body presses down the soul,[94] we shall see "face to face,"[95] as the apostle says—(for it is said in the Psalms of this life, "Truly every man living is altogether vanity;"[96] and again, "For in your sight shall no man living be justified;"[97] and in this life also, according to John, "It does not yet appear what we shall be, but we know," he says, "that when he shall appear, we shall be like him, for we shall

[91] Ex. 33: 11–23.
[92] Phil. 2: 6.
[93] 2 Cor. 5: 6.
[94] Wis. 9: 15.
[95] 1 Cor. 13: 12.
[96] Ps. 39: 5.
[97] Ps. 143: 2.

see him as he is,"[98] which he certainly intended to be understood as after this life, when we shall have paid the debt of
death, and shall have received the promise of the resurrection);—or whether that even now, in whatever degree we
spiritually understand the wisdom of God, by which all
things were made, in that same degree we die to carnal affections, so that, considering this world dead to us, we also
ourselves die to this world, and say what the apostle says,
"The world is crucified to me, and I to the world."[99] For it
was of this death that he also says, "Therefore, if you be
dead with Christ, why as though living in the world are you
subject to ordinances?"[100] Not therefore without cause will
no one be able to see the face, that is, the manifestation itself
of the wisdom of God, and live. For it is this very appearance,
for the contemplation of which every one sighs who strives
to love God with all his heart, and with all his soul, and
with all his mind; to the contemplation of which, he who
loves his neighbour, too, as himself builds up his neighbour
also as far as he may; on which two commandments hang all
the law and the prophets.[101] And this is signified also in
Moses himself. For when he had said, on account of the love
of God with which he was specially inflamed, "If I have
found grace in your sight, show me now yourself plainly,
that I may find grace in your sight;" he immediately subjoined, on account of the love also of his neighbour, "And
that I may know that this nation is your people." It is therefore that appearance which hurries away every rational soul
with the desire of itself, and the more ardently the more pure
that soul is; and it is the more pure the more it rises to spiritual things; and it rises the more to spiritual things the more
it dies to carnal things. But while we are absent from the
Lord, and walk by faith, not by sight,[102] we ought to see
the back of Christ, that is his flesh, by that very faith, that
is, standing on the solid foundation of faith, which the rock
signifies, and beholding it from such a safe watch-tower,

[98] 1 John 3: 2.
[99] Gal. 6: 14.
[100] Col. 2: 20.
[101] Matt. 22: 37–40.
[102] 2 Cor. 5: 6 f.

namely in the Catholic Church, of which it is said, "And upon this rock I will build my church."[103] For so much the more certainly we love that face of Christ, which we earnestly desire to see, as we recognise in his back how much first Christ loved us.

29. But in that flesh itself the faith of his resurrection saves and justifies us. For, "If you shall believe," he says, "in your heart, that God has raised him from the dead, you shall be saved;"[104] and again, "Who was delivered," he says, "for our offences, and was raised again for our justification."[105] So that the reward of our faith is the resurrection of the body of our Lord. For even his enemies believe that that flesh died on the cross of his passion, but they do not believe it to have risen again. Which we believing most firmly, gaze upon it as from the solidity of a rock: whence we wait with certain hope for the adoption, to wit, the redemption of our body;[106] because we hope for that in the members of Christ, that is, in ourselves, which by a sound faith we acknowledge to be perfect in him as in our head. Therefore it is that he would not have his back seen, unless as he passed by, that his resurrection may be believed. For that which is Pascha in Hebrew, is translated Passover.[107] Therefore John the Evangelist also says, "Before the feast of the Passover, when Jesus knew that his hour was come, that he should pass out of this world to the Father."[108]

30. But they who believe this, but believe it not in the Catholic Church, but in some schism or in heresy, do not see the back of the Lord from "the place that is by him." For what does that mean which the Lord says, "Behold, there is a place by me, and you shall stand upon a rock"? What earthly place is "by" the Lord, unless that is "by him" which touches him spiritually? For what place is not "by" the Lord, who "reaches from one end to another mightily, and sweetly

103 Matt. 16: 18.
104 Rom. 10: 9.
105 Rom. 4: 25.
106 Rom. 8: 23.
107 *Transitus* = passing by.
108 John 13: 1.

orders all things;"[109] and of whom it is said, "Heaven is his
throne, and earth is his footstool;" and who said, "Where
is the house that you build to me, and where is the place of
my rest? For has not my hand made all those things?"[110]
But manifestly the Catholic Church itself is understood to be
"the place by him," wherein one stands upon a rock, where
he healthfully sees the "Pascha Domini," that is, the "passing
by" of the Lord, and his back, that is, his body, who believes
in his resurrection. "And you shall stand," he says, "upon a
rock while my glory passes by." For in reality, immediately
after the majesty of the Lord had passed by in the glorification of the Lord, in which he rose again and ascended to
the Father, we stood firm upon the rock. And Peter himself
then stood firm, so that he preached him with confidence,
whom, before he stood firm, he had thrice from fear
denied;[111] although, indeed, already before placed in predestination upon the watch-tower of the rock, but with the
hand of the Lord still held over him that he might not see.
For he was to see his back, and the Lord had not yet "passed
by," namely, from death to life; he had not yet been glorified
by the resurrection.

31. For as to that, too, which follows in Exodus, "I will
cover you with my hand while I pass by, and I will take away
my hand and you shall see my back;" many Israelites, of
whom Moses was then a figure, believed in the Lord after his
resurrection, as if his hand had been taken off from their eyes,
and they now saw his back. And hence the evangelist also mentions that prophecy of Isaiah, "Make the heart of this people
fat, and make their ears heavy, and shut their eyes."[112] Lastly,
in the Psalm, that is not unreasonably understood to be said
in their person, "For day and night your hand was heavy upon
me." "By day," perhaps, when he performed manifest miracles, yet was not acknowledged by them; but "by night,"
when he died in suffering, when they thought still more certainly that, like any one among men, he was cut off and
brought to an end. But since, when he had already passed by,

109 Wis. 8: 1.
110 Is. 66: 1 f.
111 Matt. 26: 70–74.
112 Is. 6: 10; Matt. 13: 15.

so that his back was seen, upon the preaching to them by the
apostle Peter that it behoved Christ to suffer and rise again,
they were pricked in their hearts with the grief of repentance,[113] that that might come to pass among the baptized
which is said in the beginning of that Psalm, "Blessed are they
whose transgressions are forgiven, and whose sins are covered;" therefore, after it had been said, "Your hand is heavy
upon me," the Lord, as it were, passing by, so that now he
removed his hand, and his back was seen, there follows the
voice of one who grieves and confesses and receives remission
of sins by faith in the resurrection of the Lord: "My mois-
ture," he says, "is turned into the drought of summer. I acknowledged my sin to you, and my iniquity I have not hid.
I said, I will confess my transgressions to the Lord, and you
forgave the iniquity of my sin."[114] For we ought not to be
so wrapped up in the darkness of the flesh, as to think the
face indeed of God to be invisible, but his back visible, since
both appeared visibly in the form of a servant; but far be it
from us to think anything of the kind in the form of God;
far be it from us to think that the Word of God and the wisdom of God has a face on one side, and on the other a back,
as a human body has, or is at all changed either in place or
time by any appearance or motion.

32. Therefore, if in those words which were found in
Exodus, or in all those corporeal appearances, the Lord Jesus
Christ was manifested; or if in some cases Christ was manifested, as the consideration of this passage persuades us, in
others the Holy Spirit, as that which we have said above admonishes us; at any rate no such result follows, as that God
the Father never appeared in any such form to the fathers.
For many such appearances happened in those times, without
either the Father, or the Son, or the Holy Spirit being expressly named and designated in them; but yet with some intimations given through certain very probable interpretations,
so that it would be too rash to say that God the Father never
appeared by any visible forms to the fathers or the prophets.
For they gave birth to this opinion who were not able to un-

[113] Acts 2: 37, 41.
[114] Ps. 32: 4 f.

derstand in the unity of the Trinity such texts as, "Now unto
the king eternal, immortal, invisible, the only wise God;"[115]
and, "Whom no man has seen, nor can see."[116] Which texts
are understood by a sound faith of that substance itself, the
highest, and in the highest degree divine and unchangeable,
wherein both the Father and the Son and the Holy Spirit is
the one and only God. But those visions were effected through
the changeable creature, made subject to the unchangeable
God, and did not manifest God properly as he is, but by intimations such as suited the causes and times of the several
circumstances.

CHAP. 18—*The vision of Daniel.*

33. Although I do not know in what manner these men understand that the ancient of days appeared to Daniel, from
whom the Son of man, which he deigned to be for our sakes,
is understood to have received the kingdom; namely, from him
who says to him in the Psalms, "You are my Son; this day
have I begotten you; ask of me, and I shall give you the
heathen for your inheritance;"[117] and who has "put all things
under his feet."[118] If, therefore, both the Father giving the
kingdom, and the Son receiving it, appeared to Daniel in bodily form, how can those men say that the Father never appeared to the prophets, and, therefore, that he only ought to
be understood to be invisible whom no man has seen, nor can
see? For Daniel has told us thus: "I beheld," he says, "till
the thrones were set, and the ancient of days did sit, whose
garment was white as snow, and the hair of his head like the
pure wool: his throne was like the fiery flame, and his wheels
as burning fire; a fiery stream issued and came forth from before him: thousand thousands ministered unto him, and ten
thousand times ten thousand stood before him: the judgment
was set, and the books were opened," etc. And a little after,
"I saw," he says, "in the night visions, and behold, one like
the Son of man came with the clouds of heaven, and came
to the ancient of days, and they brought him near before him.

115 1 Tim. 1: 17.
116 1 Tim. 6: 16.
117 Ps. 2: 7 f.
118 Ps. 8: 8.

And there was given him dominion, and glory, and a kingdom, that all peoples, nations, and languages should serve him: his dominion is an everlasting dominion, which shall not pass away, and his kingdom that which shall not be destroyed."[119] Behold the Father giving, and the Son receiving, an eternal kingdom; and both are in the sight of him who prophesies, in a visible form. It is not, therefore, unsuitably believed that God the Father also was wont to appear in that manner to mortals.

34. Unless, perhaps, some one shall say, that the Father is therefore not visible, because he appeared within the sight of one who was dreaming; but that therefore the Son and the Holy Spirit are visible, because Moses saw all those things being awake; as if Moses saw the Word and the wisdom of God with fleshly eyes, or that even the human spirit which gives life to that flesh can be seen, or even that corporeal thing which is called wind;—how much less can that Spirit of God be seen, who transcends the minds of all men, and of angels, by the ineffable excellence of the divine substance? Or can any one fall headlong into such an error as to dare to say, that the Son and the Holy Spirit are visible also to men who are awake, but that the Father is not visible except to those who dream? How, then, do they understand that of the Father alone, "Whom no man has seen, nor can see"? When men sleep, are they then not men? Or cannot he, who can fashion the likeness of a body to signify himself through the visions of dreamers, also fashion that same bodily creature to signify himself to the eyes of those who are awake? Whereas his own very substance, whereby he himself is that which he is, cannot be shown by any bodily likeness to one who sleeps, or by any bodily appearance to one who is awake; but this not of the Father only, but also of the Son and of the Holy Spirit. And certainly, as to those who are moved by the visions of waking men to believe that not the Father, but only the Son, or the Holy Spirit, appeared to the corporeal sight of men,—to omit the great extent of the sacred pages, and their manifold interpretation, such that no one of sound reason ought to affirm that the person of the Father was nowhere shown to the eyes

[119] Dan. 7: 9–14.

of waking men by any corporeal appearance;—but, as I said, to omit this, what do they say of our father Abraham, who was certainly awake and ministering, when, after scripture had premised, "The Lord appeared to Abraham," not one, or two, but three men appeared to him; no one of whom is said to have stood prominently above the others, no one more than the others to have shone with greater glory, or to have acted more authoritatively?[120]

35. Therefore, since in our threefold division we determined to inquire, first, whether the Father, or the Son, or the Holy Spirit; or whether sometimes the Father, sometimes the Son, sometimes the Holy Spirit; or whether, without any distinction of persons, as it is said, the one and only God, that is, the Trinity itself, appeared to the fathers through those forms of the creature: now that we have examined, so far as appeared to be sufficient, what places of the Holy Scriptures we could, a modest and cautious consideration of divine mysteries leads, as far as I can judge, to no other conclusion, except that we may not rashly affirm which person of the Trinity appeared to this or that of the fathers or the prophets in some body or likeness of body, unless when the context attaches to the narrative some probable intimations on the subject. For the nature itself, or substance, or essence, or by whatever other name that very thing, which is God, whatever it be, is to be called, cannot be seen corporeally: but we must believe that by means of the creature made subject to him, not only the Son, or the Holy Spirit, but also the Father, may have given intimations of himself to mortal senses by a corporeal form or likeness. And since the case stands thus, that this second book may not extend to an immoderate length, let us consider what remains in those which follow.

[120] Gen. 18: 1.

BOOK 8

PREFACE

The conclusion of what has been said above. The rule to be observed in the more difficult questions of the faith.

We have said elsewhere, that those things are predicated specially in the Trinity as belonging severally to each person, which are predicated relatively the one to the other, as Father and Son, and the gift of both, the Holy Spirit; for the Father is not the Trinity, nor the Son the Trinity, nor the gift the Trinity: but that whenever each is singly spoken of in respect to themselves, then they are not spoken of as three in the plural number, but one, the Trinity itself, as the Father God, the Son God, and the Holy Spirit God; the Father good, the Son good, and the Holy Spirit good; and the Father omnipotent, the Son omnipotent, and the Holy Spirit omnipotent: yet neither three Gods, nor three goods, nor three omnipotents, but one God, good, omnipotent, the Trinity itself; and whatever else is said of them not relatively in respect to each other, but severally in respect to themselves. For they are thus spoken of according to essence, since in them to be is the same as to be great, as to be good, as to be wise, and whatever else is said of each person severally therein, or of the Trinity itself, in respect to themselves. And that therefore they are called three persons, or three substances, not in order that any difference of essence may be understood, but that we may be able to answer by some one word, should any one say what three, or what three things? And that there is so great an equality in that Trinity, that not only the Father is not greater than the Son, as regards divinity, but neither are the Father and Son together greater than the Holy Spirit; nor is each several person, whichever it be of the three, less than the Trinity itself. This is what we have said; and if it is handled and repeated frequently, it becomes, no doubt, more familiarly known: yet some limit, too, must be put to the discussion, and we must supplicate God with most devout piety, that he will open our understanding, and take away the inclination of disputing, in order that our minds may discern the essence of the truth, that has neither bulk nor moveableness. Now, therefore, so far as the creator himself aids us in his marvellous mercy, let us consider these subjects, into which we will enter more deeply than we entered into those which preceded, although they are in truth the same; preserving the while this rule, that what has not yet been made clear to our intellect, be nevertheless not loosened from the firmness of our faith.

CHAP. 1—*It is shown by reason that in God three are not anything greater than one person.*

2. For we say that in this Trinity two or three persons are not anything greater than one of them; which carnal associations do not receive, for no other reason except because they perceive as they can the true things which are created, but cannot discern the truth itself by which they are created; for if they could, then the very corporeal light would in no way be more clear than this which we have said. For in the substance of truth, since it alone truly is, nothing is greater, unless because it more truly is. But in whatsoever is intelligible and unchangeable, nothing is more truly than another, since all alike are unchangeably eternal; and that which therein is called great, is not great from any other source than from that by which it truly is. Therefore, where greatness itself is truth, whatever has more of greatness must needs have more of truth; whatever therefore has not more of truth, has not also more of greatness. Further, whatever has more of truth is certainly more true, just as that is greater which has more of greatness; therefore in the substance of truth that is more great which is more true. But the Father and the Son together are not more truly than the Father singly, or the Son singly. Both together, therefore, are not anything greater than each of them singly. And since also the Holy Spirit equally is truly, the Father and Son together are not anything greater than he, since neither are they more truly. The Father also and the Holy Spirit together, since they do not surpass the Son in truth (for they are not more truly), do not surpass him either in greatness. And so the Son and the Holy Spirit together are just as great as the Father alone, since they are as truly. So also the Trinity

itself is as great as each several person therein. For there, where truth itself is greatness, that is not more great which is not more true: since in the essence of truth to be true is the same as to be, and to be is the same as to be great; therefore to be great is the same as to be true. And in it, therefore, what is equally true must needs also be equally great.

CHAP. 2—*Every corporeal conception must be rejected, in order that God may be understood, as God is truth.*

3. But in bodies it may be the case that this gold and that may be equally true, but this may be greater than that, since greatness is not the same thing there as truth; and it is one thing for it to be gold, another to be great. So also in the nature of the soul; a soul is not called great in the same relation in which it is called true. For he, too, has a true soul who has not a great soul; since the essence of body and soul is not the essence of the truth itself; as is the Trinity, one God, alone, great, true, truthful, the truth. Of whom if we endeavour to think, so far as he himself permits and grants, let us not think of any touch or embrace in local space, as if of three bodies, or of any compactness of conjunction, as fables tell of three-bodied Geryon; but let whatever may occur to the mind, that is of such sort as to be greater in three than in each singly, and less in one than in two, be rejected without any doubt; for so everything corporeal is rejected. But also in spiritual things let nothing changeable that may have occurred to the mind be thought of God. For when we aspire from this depth to that height, it is a step towards no small knowledge, if, before we can know what God is, we can already know what he is not. For certainly he is neither earth nor heaven; nor, as it were, earth and heaven; nor any such thing as we see in the heaven; nor any such thing as we do not see, but which perhaps is in heaven. Neither if you were to magnify in the imagination of your thought the light of the sun as much as you are able, either that it may be greater, or that it may be brighter, a thousand times as much, or times without number; neither is this God. Neither if we think of the pure angels as spirits animating celestial bodies, and changing and dealing with them after the will by which they serve

God; not even if all, and there are "thousands of thousands,"[1] were brought together into one, and became one; neither is any such thing God. Neither if you were to think of the same spirits as without bodies—a thing indeed most difficult for carnal thought to do. Behold and see, if you can, O soul pressed down by the corruptible body, and weighed down by earthly thoughts, many and various; behold and see, if you can, God is truth.[2] For it is written that "God is light;"[3] not in such way that these eyes see, but in such way as the heart sees, when it is said, he is truth. Do not ask what is truth; for immediately the darkness of corporeal images and the clouds of phantasms will put themselves in the way, and will disturb that calm which at the first twinkling shone forth to you, when I said truth. See that you remain, if you can, in that first twinkling with which you are dazzled, as it were, by a flash, when it is said to you, truth. But you cannot; you will glide back into those usual and earthly things. And what weight is it that will cause you so to glide back, unless it be the bird-lime of the stains of appetite you have contracted, and the errors of your wandering from the right path?

CHAP. 3—*How God may be known to be the chief good. The mind does not become good unless by turning to God.*

4. Behold again, and see if you can. You certainly do not love anything except what is good, since good is the earth, with the loftiness of its mountains, and the due measure of its hills, and the level surface of its plains; and good is an estate that is pleasant and fertile; and good is a house that is arranged in due proportions, and is spacious and bright; and good are animal and animate bodies; and good is air that is temperate and salubrious; and good is food that is agreeable and fit for health; and good is health, without pains or lassitude; and good is the countenance of man that is disposed in fit proportions, and is cheerful in look, and bright in colour; and good is the mind of a friend, with the sweetness of agreement, and with the confidence of love; and good is a righteous man; and good are riches, since they are readily useful; and

[1] Apoc. 5: 11.
[2] Wis. 9: 15.
[3] 1 John 1: 5.

good is the heaven, with its sun, and moon, and stars; and good are the angels, by their holy obedience; and good is discourse that sweetly teaches and suitably admonishes the hearer; and good is a poem that is harmonious in its numbers and weighty in its sense. And why add yet more and more? This thing is good and that good, but take away this and that, and regard good itself if you can; so you will see God, not good by a good that is other than himself, but the good of all good. For in all these good things, whether those which I have mentioned, or any else that are to be discerned or thought, we could not say that one was better than another, when we judge truly, unless a conception of the good itself had been impressed upon us, such that according to it we might both approve some things as good, and prefer one good to another. So God is to be loved, not this and that good, but the good itself. For the good that must be sought for the soul is not one above which it is to fly by judging, but to which it is to cleave by loving; and what can this be except God? Not a good mind, or a good angel, or the good heaven, but the good good. For perhaps what I wish to say may be more easily perceived in this way. For when, for instance, a mind is called good, as there are two words, so from these words I understand two things—one whereby it is mind, and another whereby it is good. And itself had no share in making itself a mind, for there was nothing as yet to make itself to be anything; but to make itself to be a good mind, I see, must be brought about by the will: not because that by which it is mind is not itself anything good;—for how else is it already called, and most truly called, better than the body?—but it is not yet called a good mind, for this reason, that the action of the will still is wanted, by which it is to become more excellent; and if it has neglected this, then it is justly blamed, and is rightly called not a good mind. For it then differs from the mind which does perform this; and since the latter is praiseworthy, the former doubtless, which does not perform it, is blameable. But when it does this of set purpose, and becomes a good mind, it yet cannot attain to being so, unless it turn itself to something which itself is not. And to what can it turn itself that it may become a good mind, except to the good which it loves, and seeks, and obtains? And if it turns itself back again from this, and becomes not good, then by the very act of turning away from the good, unless that good remain in it from which it turns away, it cannot again turn itself back thither if it should wish to amend.

5. Therefore there would be no changeable goods, unless there were the unchangeable good. Whenever then you are told of this good thing and that good thing, which things can also in other respects be called not good, if you cannot put aside those things which are good by the participation of the good, and discern that good itself by the participation of which they are good (for when this or that good thing is spoken of, you understand together with them the good itself also): if, then, I say you can remove these things, and can discern the good in itself, then you will have discerned God. And if you shall cleave to him with love, you shall be forthwith blessed. But whereas other things are not loved, except because they are good, be ashamed, in cleaving to them, not to love the good itself whence they are good. That also, which is a mind, only because it is a mind, while it is not yet also good by the turning itself to the unchangeable good, but, as I said, is only a mind; whenever it so pleases us, as that we prefer it even, if we understand aright, to all corporeal light, does not please us in itself, but in that skill by which it was made. For it is thence approved as made, wherein it is seen to have been to be made. This is truth, and simple good: for it is nothing else than the good itself, and for this reason also the chief good. For no good can be diminished or increased, except that which is good from some other good. Therefore the mind turns itself, in order to be good, to that by which it comes to be a mind. Therefore the will is then in harmony with nature, so that the mind may be perfected in good, when that good is loved by the turning of the will to it, whence that other good also comes which is not lost by the turning away of the will from it. For by turning itself from the chief good, the mind loses being a good mind; but it does not lose being a mind. And this, too, is a good already, and one better than the body. The will, therefore, loses that which the will obtains. For the mind already was, that could wish to be turned to that from which it was: but that as yet was not, that could wish to be before it was. And herein is our good, when we see whether a thing

ought to be or to have been, of which we comprehend that
it ought to be or to have been, and when we see that a thing
could not have been unless it ought to have been, of which
we also do not comprehend in what manner it ought to have
been. This good then is not far from every one of us: for
in it we live, and move, and have our being.[4]

CHAP. 4—*God must first be known by an unerring faith, that he
may be loved.*

6. But it is by love that we must stand firm to this and cleave
to this, in order that we may enjoy the presence of that by
which we are, and in the absence of which we could not be
at all. For as "we walk as yet by faith, and not by sight,"[5]
we certainly do not yet see God, as the same [apostle] says,
"face to face:"[6] whom however we shall never see, unless now
already we love. But who loves what he does not know? For
it is possible something may be known and not loved: but I
ask whether it is possible that what is not known can be loved;
since if it cannot, then no one loves God before he knows
him. And what is it to know God except to behold him and
steadfastly perceive him with the mind? For he is not a body
to be searched out by carnal eyes. But before that also we
have power to behold and to perceive God, as he can be beheld
and perceived, which is permitted to the pure in heart; for
"blessed are the pure in heart, for they shall see God;"[7] except he is loved by faith, it will not be possible for the heart
to be cleansed, in order that it may be apt and suitable to
see him. For where are there those three, to build up which
in the mind the whole apparatus of the divine Scriptures has
been raised up, namely Faith, Hope, and Charity,[8] except in
a mind believing what it does not yet see, and hoping and
loving what it believes? Even he therefore who is not known,
but yet is believed, can be loved. But indisputably we must
take care, lest the mind believing that which it does not see,
feign to itself something which is not, and hope for and love

[4] Acts 17: 27 f.
[5] 2 Cor. 5: 7.
[6] 1 Cor. 13: 12.
[7] Matt. 5: 8.
[8] 1 Cor. 13: 13.

that which is false. For in that case, it will not be charity out
of a pure heart, and of a good conscience, and of faith unfeigned, which is the end of the commandment, as the same
apostle says.[9]

7. But it must needs be, that, when by reading or hearing
of them we believe in any corporeal things which we have not
seen, the mind frames for itself something in bodily features
and forms, just as it may occur to our thoughts; which either
is not true, or even if it is true, which can most rarely happen, yet this is of no benefit to us to believe in by faith, but
it is useful for some other purpose, which is intimated by
means of it. For who is there that reads or hears what the
apostle Paul has written, or what has been written of him,
that does not imagine to himself the countenance both of the
apostle himself, and of all those whose names are there mentioned? And whereas, among such a multitude of men to whom
these books are known, each imagines in a different way those
bodily features and forms, it is assuredly uncertain which it
is that imagines them more nearly and more like the reality.
Nor, indeed, is our faith busied therein with the bodily countenance of those men; but only that by the grace of God they
so lived and so acted as that scripture witnesses: this it is
which it is both useful to believe, and which must not be despaired of, and must be sought. For even the countenance of
our Lord himself in the flesh is variously fancied by the diversity of countless imaginations, which yet was one, whatever
it was. Nor in our faith which we have of our Lord Jesus
Christ, is that wholesome which the mind imagines for itself,
perhaps far other than the reality, but that which we think
of man according to his kind: for we have a notion of human
nature implanted in us, as it were by rule, according to which
we know forthwith, that whatever such thing we see is a man
or the form of a man.

CHAP. 5—*How the Trinity may be loved though unknown.*

Our conception is framed according to this notion, when
we believe that God was made man for us, as an example
of humility, and to show the love of God towards us. For this

[9] 1 Tim. 1: 5.

it is which it is good for us to believe, and to retain firmly
and unshakenly in our heart, that the humility by which God
was born of a woman, and was led to death through contume-
lies so great by mortal men, is the chiefest remedy by which
the swelling of our pride may be cured, and the profound
mystery by which the bond of sin may be loosed. So also, because we know what omnipotence is, we believe concerning
the omnipotent God in the power of his miracles and of his
resurrection, and we frame conceptions respecting actions of
this kind, according to the species and genera of things that
are either ingrafted in us by nature, or gathered by experience,
that our faith may not be feigned. For neither do we know
the countenance of the Virgin Mary; from whom, untouched
by a husband, nor tainted in the birth itself, he was wonderfully born. Neither have we seen what were the lineaments
of the body of Lazarus; nor yet Bethany; nor the sepulchre,
and that stone which he commanded to be removed when he
raised him from the dead; nor the new tomb cut out in the
rock, whence he himself arose; nor the Mount of Olives, from
whence he ascended into heaven. And, in short, whoever of
us have not seen these things, know not whether they are as
we conceive them to be, indeed judge them more probably not
to be so. For when the aspect either of a place, or a man,
or of any other body, which we happened to imagine before
we saw it, turns out to be the same when it occurs to our
sight as it was when it occurred to our mind, we are moved
with no little wonder. So scarcely and hardly ever does it happen. And yet we believe those things most steadfastly, because
we imagine them according to a special and general notion,
of which we are certain. For we believe our Lord Jesus Christ
to be born of a virgin who was called Mary. But what a virgin
is, or what it is to be born, and what is a proper name, we
do not believe, but certainly know. And whether that was the
countenance of Mary which occurred to the mind in speaking
of those things or recollecting them, we neither know at all,
nor believe. It is allowable, then, in this case to say without
violation of the faith, perhaps she had such or such a countenance, perhaps she had not: but no one could say without
violation of the Christian faith, that perhaps Christ was born
of a virgin.

8. Therefore, since we desire to understand the eternity, and equality, and unity of the Trinity, as much as is permitted us, but ought to believe before we understand; and since we must watch carefully, that our faith be not feigned; since we must have the fruition of the same Trinity, that we may live blessedly; but if we have believed anything false of it, our hope would be worthless, and our charity not pure: how then can we love, by believing, that Trinity which we do not know? Is it according to the special or general notion, according to which we love the apostle Paul? In whose case, even if he was not of that countenance which occurs to us when we think of him (and this we do not know at all), yet we know what a man is. For not to go far away, this we are; and it is manifest he, too, was this, and that his soul joined to his body lived after the manner of mortals. Therefore we believe this of him, which we find in ourselves, according to the species or genus under which all human nature alike is comprised. What then do we know, whether specially or generally, of that most excellent Trinity, as if there were many such trinities, some of which we had learned by experience, so that we may believe that Trinity, too, to have been such as they, through the rule of similitude, impressed upon us, whether a special or a general notion; and thus love also that thing which we believe and do not yet know, from the likeness of the thing which we do know? But this certainly is not so. Or is it that, as we love in our Lord Jesus Christ, that he rose from the dead, although we never saw any one rise from thence, so we can believe in and love the Trinity which we do not see, and the like of which we never have seen? But we certainly know what it is to die, and what it is to live; because we both live, and from time to time have seen and experienced both dead and dying persons. And what else is it to rise again, except to live again, that is, to return to life from death? When, therefore, we say and believe that there is a Trinity, we know what a Trinity is, because we know what three are; but this is not what we love. For we can easily have this whenever we will, to pass over other things, by just holding up three fingers. Or do we indeed love, not every trinity, but the Trinity, that is God? We love then in the Trinity, that it is God: but we never saw or knew any other God, because God is one; he alone whom

we have not yet seen, and whom we love by believing. But the question is, from what likeness or comparison of known things can we believe, in order that we may love God, whom we do not yet know?

CHAP. 6—*How the man not yet righteous can know the righteous man whom he loves.*

9. Return then with me, and let us consider why we love the apostle. Is it at all on account of his human kind, which we know right well, in that we believe him to have been a man? Assuredly not; for if it were so, he now is not, that we may love him, since he is no longer that man, for his soul is separated from his body. But we believe that which we love in him to be still living now, for we love his righteous mind. From what general or special measure then, except that we know both what a mind is, and what it is to be righteous? And we say indeed, not unfitly, that we therefore know what a mind is, because we too have a mind. For neither did we ever see it with our eyes, and gather a special or general notion from the resemblance of more minds than one, which we had seen; but rather, as I have said before, because we too have it. For what is known so intimately, and so perceives itself to be itself, as that by which also all other things are perceived, that is, the mind itself? For we recognise the movements of bodies also, by which we perceive that others live besides ourselves, from the resemblance of ourselves; since we also so move our body in living as we observe those bodies to be moved. For even when a living body is moved, there is no way opened to our eyes to see the mind, a thing which cannot be seen by the eyes; but we perceive something to be contained in that bulk, such as is contained in ourselves, so as to move in like manner our own bulk, which is the life and the soul. Neither is this, as it were, the property of human foresight and reason, since brute animals also perceive that not only they themselves live, but also other brute animals interchangeably, and the one the other, and that we ourselves do so. Neither do they see our souls, save from the movements of the body, and that immediately and most easily by some natural agreement. Therefore we both know the mind of any one from our own, and believe also from our own of him whom

we do not know. For not only do we perceive that there is
a mind, but we can also know what a mind is, by reflecting
upon our own: for we have a mind. But whence do we know
what a righteous man is? For we said above that we love
the apostle for no other reason except that he is a righteous
mind. We know, then, what a righteous man also is, just as
we know what a mind is. But what a mind is, as has been
said, we know from ourselves, for there is a mind in us. But
whence do we know what a righteous man is, if we are not
righteous? But if no one but he who is righteous knows what
is a righteous man, no one but a righteous man loves a righteous man; for one cannot love him whom one believes to be
righteous, for this very reason that one does believe him to
be righteous, if one does not know what it is to be righteous;
according to that which we have shown above, that no one
loves what he believes and does not see, except by some rule
of a general or special notion. And if for this reason no one
but a righteous man loves a righteous man, how will any one
wish to be a righteous man who is not yet so? For no one
wishes to be that which he does not love. But he certainly
must wish to be righteous, who, not yet being righteous, means
to be so; and in order that he may wish to be so, he loves
the righteous man. Therefore, even he who is not yet righteous
loves the righteous man. But he cannot love the righteous man,
who is ignorant what a righteous man is. Accordingly, even
he who is not yet righteous, knows what a righteous man is.
Whence then does he know this? Does he see it with his eyes?
Is any corporeal thing righteous, as it is white, or black, or
square, or round? Who could say this? Yet with one's eyes
one has seen nothing except corporeal things. But there is
nothing righteous in a man except the mind; and when a man
is called a righteous man, he is called so from the mind, not
from the body. For righteousness is in some sort the beauty
of the mind, by which men are beautiful, very many too, who
are misshapen and deformed in body. And as the mind is not
seen with the eyes, so neither is its beauty. From whence then
does he who is not yet righteous know what a righteous man
is, and love the righteous man that he may become righteous?
Do certain signs shine forth by the motion of the body, by
which this or that man is manifested to be righteous? But

whence does any one know that these are the signs of a righteous mind, when he is wholly ignorant what it is to be righteous? Therefore he does know. But whence do we know what
it is to be righteous, even when we are not yet righteous? If
we know from without ourselves, we know it by some bodily
thing. But this is not a thing of the body. Therefore we know
in ourselves what it is to be righteous. For I find this nowhere
else when I seek to utter it, except within myself; and if I
ask another what it is to be righteous, he seeks within himself
what to answer; and whoever hence can answer truly, he has
found within himself what to answer. And when indeed I wish
to speak of Carthage, I seek within myself what to speak, and
I find within myself a notion or image of Carthage; but I have
received this through the body, that is, through the perception
of the body, since I have been present in that city in the body,
and I saw and perceived it, and retained it in my memory,
that I might find within myself a word concerning it, whenever
I might wish to speak of it. For its word is the image itself
of it in my memory, not that sound of two syllables when
Carthage is named, or even when that name itself is thought
of silently from time to time, but that which I discern in my
mind, when I utter that dissyllable with my voice, or even before I utter it. So also, when I wish to speak of Alexandria,
which I never saw, an image of it is present with me. For
whereas I had heard from many and had believed that city
to be great, in such way as it could be told me, I formed an
image of it in my mind as I was able; and this is with me
its word when I wish to speak of it, before I utter with my
voice the five syllables which make the name that almost every
one knows. And yet if I could bring forth that image from
my mind to the eyes of men who know Alexandria, certainly
all either would say, It is not it; or if they said, It is, I should
greatly wonder; and as I gazed at it in my mind, that is, at
the image which was as it were its picture, I should yet not
know it to be it, but should believe those who retained an
image they had seen. But I do not so ask what it is to be
righteous, nor do I so find it, nor do I so gaze upon it, when
I utter it; neither am I so approved when I am heard, nor
do I so approve when I hear; as though I have seen such a
thing with my eyes, or learned it by some perception of the

body, or heard it from those who had so learned it. For when I say, and say knowingly, that mind is righteous which knowingly and of purpose assigns to every one his due in life and behaviour, I do not think of anything absent, as Carthage, or imagine it as I am able, as Alexandria, whether it be so or not; but I discern something present, and I discern it within myself, though I myself am not that which I discern: and many if they hear will approve it. And whoever hears me and knowingly approves, he too discerns this same thing within himself, even though he himself be not what he discerns. But when a righteous man says this, he discerns and says that which he himself is. And whence also does he discern it, except within himself? But this is not to be wondered at; for whence should he discern himself except within himself? The wonderful thing is, that the mind should see within itself that which it has seen nowhere else, and should see truly, and should see the very true righteous mind, and should itself be a mind, and yet not a righteous mind, which nevertheless it sees within itself. Is there another mind that is righteous in a mind that is not yet righteous? Or if there is not, what does it there see when it sees and says what is a righteous mind, nor sees it anywhere else but in itself, when itself is not a righteous mind? Is that which it sees an inner truth present to the mind which has power to behold it? Yet all have not that power; and they who have power to behold it, are not all also that which they behold, that is, they are not also righteous minds themselves, just as they are able to see and to say what is a righteous mind. And whence will they be able to be so, except by cleaving to that very same form itself which they behold, so that from thence they may be formed and may be righteous minds; not only discerning and saying that the mind is righteous which knowingly and of purpose assigns to every one that which is his due in life and behaviour, but so likewise that they themselves may live righteously and be righteous in character, by assigning to every one that which is his due, so as to owe no man anything, but to love one another.[10] And whence can any one cleave to that form but by loving it? Why then do we love another whom we believe to be righteous, and do not

[10] Rom. 13: 8.

love that form itself wherein we see what is a righteous mind, that we also may be able to be righteous? Is it that unless we loved that also, we should not love him at all, whom through it we love; but while we are not righteous, we love that form too little to allow of our being able to be righteous? The man therefore who is believed to be righteous, is loved through that form and truth which he who loves discerns and understands within himself; but that very form and truth itself cannot be loved from any other source than itself. For we do not find any other such thing besides itself, so that by believing we might love it when it is unknown, in that we here already know another such thing. For whatever of such a kind one may have seen, is itself; and there is not any other such thing, since itself alone is such as itself is. He therefore who loves men, ought to love them either because they are righteous, or that they may become righteous. For so also he ought to love himself, either because he is righteous, or that he may be righteous; for in this way he loves his neighbour as himself without any risk. For he who loves himself otherwise, loves himself wrongfully, since he loves himself to this end that he may be unrighteous; therefore to this end that he may be wicked; and hence it follows next that he does not love himself; for, "He who loves iniquity, hates his own soul."[11]

CHAP. 7—*Of true love, by which we arrive at the knowledge of the Trinity. God is to be sought, not outwardly, by seeking to do wonderful things with the angels, but inwardly, by imitating the piety of good angels.*

10. No other thing, then, is chiefly to be regarded in this inquiry, which we make concerning the Trinity and concerning knowing God, except what is true love, indeed, rather what is love. For that is to be called love which is true, otherwise it is desire; and so those who desire are said improperly to love, just as they who love are said improperly to desire. But this is true love, that cleaving to the truth we may live righteously, and so may despise all mortal things in comparison with the love of men, whereby we wish them to live righteously. For so we should be prepared also to die profitably for our brethren, as our Lord Jesus Christ taught us by

[11] Ps. 11: 6.

his example. For as there are two commandments on which hang all the law and the prophets, love of God and love of our neighbour;[12] not without cause the scripture mostly puts one for both: whether it be of God only, as is that text, "For we know that all things work together for good to them that love God;"[13] and again, "But if any man love God, the same is known of him;"[14] and that, "Because the love of God is shed abroad in our hearts by the Holy Ghost who is given to us;"[15] and many other passages; because he who loves God must both do what God has commanded, and loves him just in such proportion as he does so; therefore he must also love his neighbour, because God has commanded it: or whether it be that scripture only mentions the love of our neighbour, as in that text, "Bear ye one another's burdens, and so fulfil the law of Christ;"[16] and again, "For all the law is fulfilled in one word, even in this, You shall love your neighbour as yourself;"[17] and in the Gospel, "All things whatever you would that men should do to you, do you even so to them; for this is the law and the prophets."[18] And many other passages occur in the sacred writings, in which only the love of our neighbour seems to be commanded for perfection, while the love of God is passed over in silence; whereas the law and the prophets hang on both precepts. But this, too, is because he who loves his neighbour must also love above all else love itself. But "God is love; and he that dwells in love, dwells in God."[19] Therefore he must above all else love God.

11. Therefore they who seek God through those powers which rule over the world, or parts of the world, are removed and cast away far from him; not by intervals of space, but by difference of affections: for they endeavour to find a path outwardly, and forsake their own inward things, within which

[12] Matt. 22: 37–40.
[13] Rom. 8: 28.
[14] 1 Cor. 8: 3.
[15] Rom. 5: 5.
[16] Gal. 6: 2.
[17] Gal. 5: 14.
[18] Matt. 7: 12.
[19] 1 John 4: 6.

is God. Therefore, even although they may either have heard some holy heavenly power, or in some way or another may have thought of it, yet they rather covet its deeds at which human weakness marvels, but do not imitate the piety by which divine rest is acquired. For they prefer, through pride, to be able to do that which an angel does, more than, through devotion, to be that which an angel is. For no holy being rejoices in his own power, but in his from whom he has the power which he fitly can have; and he knows it to be more a mark of power to be united to the omnipotent by a pious will, than to be able, by his own power and will, to do what they may tremble at who are not able to do such things. Therefore the Lord Jesus Christ himself, in doing such things, in order that he might teach better things to those who marvelled at them, and might turn those who were intent and in doubt about unusual temporal things to eternal and inner things: "Come," he says, "to me, all you that labour and are heavy laden, and I will give you rest. Take my yoke upon you." And he does not say, Learn of me, because I raise those who have been dead four days; but he says, "Learn of me; for I am meek and lowly in heart." For humility, which is most solid, is more powerful and safer than pride, that is most inflated. And so he goes on to say, "And you shall find rest to your souls,"[20] for "Love is not puffed up;"[21] and "God is love;"[22] and "such as are faithful in love shall rest in him,"[23] called back from the din which is without to silent joys. Behold, "God is love:" why do we go forth and run to the heights of the heavens and the lowest parts of the earth, seeking him who is within us, if we wish to be with him?

CHAP. 8—*That he who loves his brother, loves God; because he loves love itself, which is of God, and is God.*

12. Let no one say, I do not know what I love. Let him love his brother, and he will love the same love. For he knows the love with which he loves, more than the brother whom he loves. So now he can know God more than he

[20] Matt. 11: 28 f.
[21] 1 Cor. 13: 4.
[22] 1 John 4: 8.
[23] Wis. 3: 9.

knows his brother: clearly known more, because more present; known more, because more within him; known more, because more certain. Embrace the love of God, and by love embrace God. That is love itself, which associates together all good angels and all the servants of God by the bond of sanctity, and joins together us and them mutually with ourselves, and joins us subordinately to himself. In proportion, therefore, as we are healed from the swelling of pride, in such proportion are we more filled with love; and with what is he full, who is full of love, except with God? Well, but you will say, I see love, and, as far as I am able, I gaze upon it with my mind, and I believe the scripture, saying, that "God is love; and he that dwells in love, dwells in God;"[24] but when I see love, I do not see in it the Trinity. But you do see the Trinity if you see love. But if I can I will put you in mind, that you may see that you see it; only let itself be present, that we may be moved by love to something good. Since, when we love love, we love one who loves something, and that on account of this very thing, that he does love something; therefore what does love love, that love itself also may be loved? For that is not love which loves nothing. But if it loves itself it must love something, that it may love itself as love. For as a word indicates something, and indicates also itself, but does not indicate itself to be a word, unless it indicates that it does indicate something; so love also loves indeed itself, but except it love itself as loving something, it loves itself not as love. What therefore does love love, except that which we love with love? But this, to begin from that which is nearest to us, is our brother. And listen how greatly the apostle John commends brotherly love: "He that loves his brother abides in the light, and there is no occasion of stumbling in him."[25] It is manifest that he placed the perfection of righteousness in the love of our brother; for he certainly is perfect in whom "there is no occasion of stumbling." And yet he seems to have passed by the love of God in silence; which he never would have done, unless he intends God to be understood in brotherly love itself. For in this same epistle, a little further

[24] 1 John 4: 16.
[25] 1 John 2: 10.

on, he says most plainly thus: "Beloved, let us love one another: for love is of God; and every one that loves is born of
God, and knows God. He that does not love, does not know
God; for God is love." And this passage declares sufficiently
and plainly, that this same brotherly love itself (for that is
brotherly love by which we love each other) is set forth by so
great authority, not only to be from God, but also to be God.
When, therefore, we love our brother from love, we love our
brother from God; neither can it be that we do not love above
all else that same love by which we love our brother: whence
it may be gathered that these two commandments cannot exist
unless interchangeably. For since "God is love," he who
loves love certainly loves God; but he must needs love love,
who loves his brother. And so a little after he says, "For he
that loves not his brother whom he has seen, how can he love
God whom he has not seen?"[26] because the reason that he
does not see God is, that he does not love his brother. For
he who does not love his brother, abides not in love; and he
who abides not in love, abides not in God, because God is
love. Further, he who abides not in God, abides not in light;
for "God is light, and in him is no darkness at all."[27] He
therefore who abides not in light, what wonder is it if he
does not see light, that is, does not see God, because he is in
darkness? But he sees his brother with human sight, with
which God cannot be seen. But if he loved with spiritual
love him whom he sees with human sight, he would see God,
who is love itself, with the inner sight by which he can be
seen. Therefore he who does not love his brother whom he
sees, how can he love God, whom on that account he does
not see, because God is love, which he has not who does not
love his brother? Neither let that further question disturb us,
how much of love we ought to spend upon our brother, and
how much upon God: incomparably more upon God than
upon ourselves, but upon our brother as much as upon ourselves; and we love ourselves so much the more, the more we
love God. Therefore we love God and our neighbour from

[26] 1 John 4: 7, 8, 20.
[27] 1 John 1: 5.

one and the same love; but we love God for the sake of God, and ourselves and our neighbours for the sake of God.

CHAP. 9—*Our love of the righteous is kindled from love itself of the unchangeable form of righteousness.*

13. For why is it that we burn when we hear and read, "Behold, now is the accepted time; behold, now is the day of salvation: giving no offence in anything, that the ministry be not blamed: but in all things approving ourselves as the ministers of God, in much patience, in afflictions, in necessities, in distresses, in stripes, in imprisonments, in tumults, in labours, in watchings, in fastings; by pureness, by knowledge, by long-suffering, by kindness, by the Holy Ghost, by love unfeigned, by the word of truth, by the power of God, by the armour of righteousness on the right hand and on the left, by honour and dishonour, by evil report and good report: as deceivers, and yet true; as unknown, and yet well known; as dying, and, behold, we live; as chastened, and not killed; as sorrowful, yet always rejoicing; as poor, yet making many rich; as having nothing, and yet possessing all things?"[28] Why is it that we are inflamed with love of the apostle Paul, when we read these things, unless that we believe him so to have lived? But we do not believe that the ministers of God ought so to live because we have heard it from any one, but because we behold it inwardly within ourselves, or rather above ourselves, in the truth itself. Him, therefore, whom we believe to have so lived, we love for that which we see. And except we loved above all else that form which we discern as always steadfast and unchangeable, we should not for that reason love him, because we hold fast in our belief that his life, when he was living in the flesh, was adapted to, and in harmony with, this form. But somehow we are stirred up the more to the love of this form itself, through the belief by which we believe some one to have so lived; and to the hope by which we do not any longer despair, that we, too, are able so to live—we who are men, from this fact itself, that some men have so lived, so that we both desire this more ardently, and pray for it more confidently. So both the love of that

[28] 2 Cor. 6: 2–10.

form, according to which they are believed to have lived, makes the life of these men themselves to be loved by us; and their life thus believed stirs up a more burning love towards that same form; so that the more ardently we love God, the more certainly and the more calmly do we see him, because we behold in God the unchangeable form of righteousness, according to which we judge that man ought to live. Therefore faith avails to the knowledge and to the love of God, not as though of one altogether unknown, or altogether not loved; but so that thereby he may be known more clearly, and loved more steadfastly.

CHAP. 10—*There are three things in love, as it were a trace of the Trinity.*

14. But what is love or charity, which divine scripture so greatly praises and proclaims, except the love of good? But love is of some one that loves, and with love something is loved. Behold, then, there are three things: he that loves, and that which is loved, and love. What, then, is love, except a certain life which couples or seeks to couple together some two things, namely, him that loves, and that which is loved? And this is so even in outward and carnal loves. But that we may drink in something more pure and clear, let us tread down the flesh and ascend to the mind. What does the mind love in a friend except the mind? There, then, also are three things: he that loves, and that which is loved, and love. It remains to ascend also from hence, and to seek those things which are above, as far as is given to man. But here for a little while let our purpose rest, not that it may think itself to have found already what it seeks; but just as usually the place has first to be found where anything is to be sought, while that thing itself is not yet found, but we have only found already where to look for it; so let it suffice to have said this much, that we may have, as it were, the hinge of some starting-point, whence to weave the rest of our discourse.

The *City of God* (twenty-two books) deals, as Augustine
says, with two cities, or rather societies, that of the good
angels and good men (the city of God, which, being the
better, gives the title to the work) and that of the fallen
angels and bad men (the city of the Earth or Devil). It is
therefore not about politics, but salvation. The first five books
(written between summer 413 and the end of 415) refute
the proposition that temporal prosperity results from polytheism. Augustine's center of reference is the Roman state.
The next five books (written between the end of 415 and
early 417) refute the proposition that eternal happiness results from polytheism: here his center of reference is Greek,
especially Neoplatonic, philosophy. The final twelve books
are positive and give the scriptural account of the origin of
man (Books 11–14, written from early 417 to early 418),
his secular history to date (Books 15–18, of 418–425) and
his final destiny—heaven or hell (Books 19–22, of 425–427).
Although the sack of Rome by Alaric in August 410 and
the charge that the Christians in prohibiting Roman polytheism had removed the very *foundation* of Rome's prosperity may have in part occasioned the work, the *City of God*
is really an interpretation of man's destiny arising from the
author's reflection on his own experience and adumbrated
in a number of works before 410. The work is a formal rec-
ognition of the Roman, Greek and Hebrew elements that
make the Christian era. Here are given the summary book
(5) on the Roman, or "political," section and the final book
of the Christian section (22)—recently described as contain-

ng some of the work's "most vivid pages" (D. Knowles, *Augustine, City of God*, Pelican, 1972, p. xxx). (The matter of the very significant and representative book [10] is already sufficiently found in *Confessions* 7.) The best edition is that of the BA, vols. 33–37 (Paris, 1959–60), which gives the text of Dombart and Kalb and introduction and notes by G. Bardy. The translation used here is that of J. J. Smith for Book 5 and M. Dods for Book 22, 2 vols. (Edinburgh, 1872). There are translations available also in the Everyman, Loeb and Pelican series, and a selection in translation in Image Books.

RECOMMENDED READING

T. O'Meara, *Charter of Christendom*, New York, 1961 (available from the Institute of Augustinian Studies, Villanova University, Villanova, Pa.).

S. Burleigh, *The City of God: A Study of St. Augustine's Philosophy*, London, 1949.

J. Ricaby, *St. Augustine's City of God*, London, 1925.

SPECIAL TOPICS

1. *Political theory* (Book 5)

One might get the impression from the title *City of God*, from its reputation in the Middle Ages as prescribing the relations of church and state and from the bibliography on the book in English that there is much political theory in the work. But: "There is an entire absence of any doctrine of church-state relationship in the *City of God*" (D. Knowles, op. cit., p. xx). It should be unnecessary to repeat that the work is overwhelmingly theological. What there is of political theory is to be found mainly by implication and mainly in the first and especially the fifth book—but there is also occasional political reference elsewhere. The basic point of reference is that any state that does not *formally* give cult to the Christian God lacks the quality of *true* justice vis-à-vis God and therefore is not a *true* state; it is for this reason that Augustine, rather too logically, declares that since no state, including the Roman state, prescribes this cult, no state is just (2.21) and states are but big brigandages (4.3). He accepts, of course, that a relative justice—what we, in fact, normally call justice —does exist in states. Secular states, such as the Roman, are

ordained by Providence and can serve not only to shame
Christians by the natural virtues (which, since they are not
directed to the Christian God, are logically but splendid vices)
of their citizens, but also serve to facilitate the spread of
Christianity throughout their dominions. Augustine also, in
Book 5.24, gives his version of the *speculum principis,* the
mirror of the Christian prince. It is sometimes imagined that
in the *City of God* Augustine gives a philosophy of history:
there is no foundation for this notion—but one might say that
he gives a theology of history, or, rather, a theological view of
history. See J. O'Meara, op. cit., pp. 54–61, 88–113; H. A.
Deane, *The Political and Social Ideas of St. Augustine* (New
York, 1963); R. A. Markus, *Saeculum: History and Society in
the Theology of St. Augustine* (Cambridge, 1970). The approaches of J. N. Figgis, *The Political Aspects of St. Augustine's "City of God"* (London, 1921); N. H. Baynes, "The
Political Ideas of St. Augustine's 'De civitate Dei,'" *Historical
Association Pamphlet* (London, 1936): and (especially)
E. Barker's introduction to the Everyman's Library edition of
the *City of God* create the impression that the *City of God* is
more concerned with political theory than it in fact is. See also
H.-X. Arquillière, *L'Augustinisme politique* (Paris, 1955);
J. Ratzinger, *Volk und Haus Gottes in Augustins Lehre von
der Kirche* (Munich, 1954); and T. E. Mommsen, "St. Augustine and the Christian Idea of Progress," *Journal of the History of Ideas,* 12 (1951), 346–74.

2. *Fate, astrology, foreknowledge, predestination and free will*
(Books 5.1–11, 22.24)
Augustine had learned, from the Stoics especially, of Fate (in
effect, a secular form of predestination) and its association
with the movements of the sun, moon and planets (an idea,
as we have seen [cf. *Confessions* 7.6.8] of importance to the
Manichaeans also). For all his fascination with astrology
(and especially the case of twins!), he dismissed it, without,
however, escaping from the problem of reconciling God's
foreknowledge with man's free will. Here and in the *De libero
arbitrio* (Book 3) he uses philosophical arguments against the
Stoic position as presented by Cicero. Later, in the Pelagian
controversy—and here in Book 22.24—he invokes Christian
theology. For Augustine, predestination applied not only to
the good (the general sense since the Middle Ages) but
equally to the wicked: "what will he give to those whom he
has predestined to life who has given such things even to those

whom he has predestined to death" (22.24). There is a difference, however, in God's will between the two cases. He *positively* wills for the good and only *permits* the evil (*Enchiridion* 24.95). God's positive will in favor of the good is
gratuitous and unmerited—but still respects free will. The doing
of evil arises from a particular exercise of that free will. See
O. Rottmanner, *Der Augustinismus* (Munich, 1892); H.
Rondet, *La liberté et la grace* (Paris, 1954); Portalié,
pp. 213–23. Other texts on predestination in Augustine: *Enchiridion* 25.95, 98; *De diversis quaestionibus ad Simplicianum*
1.11; *Contra Julianum* 4.8.45–46; *Contra duas epistulas
Pelagianorum* 11.13; *Epistulae* 186.12.15 f., 194.4.5.23. See
pp. 443 ff.

3. *Miracles* (Book 22)

Augustine grew up and lived his life in a period when ordinary men had a lively belief in the intervention of angels and
demons. *A fortiori*, they took it for granted that the Omnipotent could intervene to change the nature he had created.
Augustine's attitude to miracles within the Christian Church
was one of relative disinterest, it would appear, just before
his conversion. This changed, however, to one of enthusiastic
use in the apostolate by the end of his life—as is evidenced
by the last book of the *City of God*. The long series of miracles recounted here are necessary and (some might say) di-
verting reminders of how uncritical, in our sense, Augustine
was: if we are to know him and assess his work, we must expose ourselves to the evidence of this. His practical notion of
miracle was extensive enough to regard the "incredible" fact
of the spread of Christianity from a nucleus of a few poor
uneducated fishermen in a remote part of the empire to "the
whole world," high and low, as a "miracle" and sufficient
reason for believing. This idea had much to do with some of
his impatience with the obduracy, as he thought, of the
Donatists or Neoplatonists or even Pelagians. See F. van der
Meer, *Augustine the Bishop* (London and New York, 1961),
pp. 527–57 and P. Brown, *Religion and Society in the Age of
Saint Augustine* (London, 1972), pp. 325 ff. Other Augustine
texts on miracles: *De vera religione* 25.47; *De utilitate credendi* 16.34; 19.50; *Sermo* 88.2.2; 3.3. Augustine had also an
unusually highly developed sense of Providence (not uncon-
nected in his mind with miracles) arising not only from Roman Stoicism and Neoplatonist doctrine but also from reflec-

tion upon his own early unpredictable experiences: cf. *Contra Julianum* 4.3.16 f.

4. *Eschatology* (Book 22)

One of the most important and dangerous challenges to Christianity in the fourth century came from Porphyry (A.D. 232–305), who insisted that a soul could have no association whatever with any body in the after life: *omne corpus fugiendum* (22.26). This was one of the reasons given by Porphyry himself for his not being a Christian. Other Christian apologists, among them the Africans Arnobius and Lactantius, and Augustine were the more concerned with this objection because it came from that Neoplatonist source which appeared to commend so much of Christian doctrine. It therefore seemed vital to convince the Neoplatonists especially on this one point: for if this was achieved, then *all* argument would commend Christianity to all. Another aspect of the same problem was God's taking flesh of the virgin in the Incarnation—quite unthinkable to an immaterialistic Neoplatonist. This one point dominates, therefore, and is central to the whole argument of the *City of God*. This was in accordance with St. Paul's estimate of the importance of the resurrection. In the case made here (22.28), it is to be noted that Augustine ultimately appeals to the testimony of the Platonists themselves (Plato, Varro and Porphyry) to support his case and displays a fine eclectic Roman insouciance as to its real relevance or value. See J. O'Meara, *Charter of Christendom*, pp. 62–87, and *Porphyry's Philosophy from Oracles in Augustine* (Paris, 1959). Other Augustine texts on bodily resurrection: *De fide et symbolo* 6.13; *Enchiridion* 23.84–92; *De civitate Dei* 13.17 f. On eternal felicity, see *Epistulae* 92.2 f., 147.15, 148.17 f.

CITY OF GOD

BOOK 5

PREFACE

Since, then, it is established that the complete attainment of all we desire is that which constitutes felicity, which is no goddess, but a gift of God, and that therefore men can worship no god save him who is able to make them happy,— and if Felicity herself were a goddess, she would with reason be the only object of worship,—since, I say, this is established, let us now go on to consider why God, who is able to give with all other things those good gifts which can be possessed by men who are not good, and consequently not happy, has seen fit to grant such extended and long-continued dominion to the Roman empire; for that this was not effected by that multitude of false gods which they worshipped, we have both already adduced, and shall, as occasion offers, yet adduce considerable proof.

1. *That the cause of the Roman empire, and of all kingdoms, is neither fortuitous nor consists in the position of the stars.*

The cause, then, of the greatness of the Roman empire is neither fortuitous nor "fatal," according to the judgment or opinion of those who call those things *fortuitous* which either have no causes, or such causes as do not proceed from some intelligible order, and those things *fatal* which happen independently of the will of God and man, by the necessity of a certain *order*. In a word, human kingdoms are established by divine providence. And if any one attributes their existence to fate, because he calls the will or the power of God itself by the name of fate, let him keep his opinion, but correct his language. For why does he not say at first what he will say afterwards, when some one shall put the question to him, what he means by *fate*? For when men hear that word, according to the ordinary use of the language, they simply understand by it the virtue of that particular position of the stars which may exist at the time when any one is born or conceived, which some separate altogether from the will of God, while others affirm that this also is dependent on that will. But those who are of opinion that, apart from the will of God, the stars determine what we shall do, or what good things we shall possess, or what evils we shall suffer, must be refused a hearing by all, not only by those who hold the true religion, but by those who wish to be the worshippers of any gods whatsoever, even false gods. For what does this opinion really amount to but this, that no god whatever is to be worshipped or prayed to? Against these, however, our present disputation is not intended to be directed, but against those who, in defence of those whom they think to be gods, oppose the Christian religion. They, however, who make the position of the stars depend on the divine will, and in a manner decree what character each man shall have, and what good or evil shall happen to him, if they think that these same stars have that power conferred upon them by the supreme power of God, in order that they may determine these things according to their will, do a great injury to the celestial sphere, in whose most brilliant senate, and most splendid senate-house, as it were, they suppose that wicked deeds are decreed to be done, —such deeds as that if any terrestrial state should decree them, it would be condemned to overthrow by the decree of the whole human race. What judgment, then, is left to God concerning the deeds of men, who is Lord both of the stars and of men, when to these deeds a celestial necessity is attributed? Or, if they do not say that the stars, though they have indeed received a certain power from God, who is supreme, determine those things according to their own discretion, but simply that his commands are fulfilled by them instrumentally in the application and enforcing of such necessities, are we thus to think concerning God even what it seemed unworthy that we should think concerning the will of the stars? But, if the stars are said rather to signify these things than to effect them, so that that *position of the stars* is, as it were, a kind of speech predicting, not causing future things,—for this has been the opinion of men of no ordinary learning,—certainly the mathematicians[1] are not wont so to speak, saying, for example, Mars in such or such a position *signifies* a homicide, but *makes* a homicide. But, nevertheless, though we grant that they do not speak as they ought, and that we ought to accept as the proper form of speech that employed by the philosophers in predicting those things which they think they discover in the position of the stars, how comes it that they have never been able to assign any cause why, in the life of twins, in their actions, in the events which befall them, in their professions, arts, honours, and other things pertaining to human life, also in their very death, there is often so great a difference, that, as far as these things are concerned, many entire strangers are more like them than they are like each other, though separated at birth by the smallest interval of time, but at conception generated by the same act of copulation, and at the same moment?

2. *On the difference in the health of twins.*

Cicero says that the famous physician Hippocrates has left in writing that he had suspected that a certain pair of brothers were twins, from the fact that they both took ill at once, and their disease advanced to its crisis and subsided in the same time in each of them. Posidonius the Stoic, who was much given to astrology, used to explain the fact by supposing that they had been born and conceived under the same constellation. In this question the conjecture of the physician is by far more worthy to be accepted, and approaches much nearer to credibility, since, according as the parents were affected in body at the time of copulation, so might the first elements of the fœtuses have been affected, so that all that was necessary for their growth and development up till birth having been supplied from the body of the same mother, they might be born with like constitutions. After that, nourished in the same house, on the same kinds of food, where they would have

[1] I.e., astrologers.

also the same kinds of air, the same locality, the same quality of water,—which, according to the testimony of medical science, have a very great influence, good or bad, on the condition of bodily health,—and where they would also be accustomed to the same kinds of exercise, they would have bodily constitutions so similar that they would be similarly affected with sickness at the same time and by the same causes. But, to wish to adduce that particular position of the stars which existed at the time when they were born or conceived as the cause of their being simultaneously affected with sickness, manifests the greatest arrogance, when so many beings of most diverse kinds, in the most diverse conditions, and subject to the most diverse events, may have been conceived and born at the same time, and in the same district, lying under the same sky. But we know that twins do not only act differently, and travel to very different places, but that they also suffer from different kinds of sickness; for which Hippocrates would give what is in my opinion the simplest reason, namely, that, through diversity of food and exercise, which arises not from the constitution of the body, but from the inclination of the mind, they may have come to be different from each other in respect of health. Moreover, Posidonius, or any other asserter of the fatal influence of the stars, will have enough to do to find anything to say to this, if he is unwilling to impose upon the minds of the uninstructed in things of which they are ignorant. But, as to what they attempt to make out from that very small interval of time elapsing between the births of twins, on account of that point in the heavens where the mark of the natal hour is placed, and which they call the "horoscope," it is either disproportionately small to the diversity which is found in the dispositions, actions, habits, and fortunes of twins, or it is disproportionately great when compared with the status of twins, whether low or high, which is the same for both of them, the cause for whose greatest difference they place, in every case, in the hour in which one is born; and, for this reason, if the one is born so immediately after the other that there is no change in the horoscope, I demand an entire similarity in all that respects them both, which can never be found in the case of any twins. But if the slowness of the birth of the second give time for a change in the horoscope, I demand different parents, which twins can never have.

3. *Concerning the arguments which Nigidius the mathematician drew from the potter's wheel, in the question about the birth of twins.*

It is to no purpose, therefore, that that famous fiction about the potter's wheel is brought forward, which tells of the answer which Nigidius is said to have given when he was perplexed with this question, and on account of which he was called *Figulus*.[2] For, having whirled round the potter's wheel with all his strength, he marked it with ink, striking it twice with the utmost rapidity, so that the strokes seemed to fall on the very same part of it. Then, when the rotation had ceased, the marks which he had made were found upon the rim of the wheel at no small distance apart. Thus, said he, considering the great rapidity with which the celestial sphere revolves, even though twins were born with as short an interval between their births as there was between the strokes which I gave this wheel, that brief interval of time is equivalent to a very great distance in the celestial sphere. Hence, said he, come whatever dissimilitudes may be remarked in the habits and fortunes of twins. This argument is more fragile than the vessels which are fashioned by the rotation of that wheel. For if there is so much significance in the heavens which cannot be comprehended by observation of the constellations, that, in the case of twins, an inheritance may fall to the one and not to the other, why, in the case of others who are not twins, do they dare, having examined their constellations, to declare such things as pertain to that secret which no one can comprehend, and to attribute them to the precise moment of the birth of each individual? Now, if such predictions in connection with the natal hours of others who are not twins are to be vindicated on the ground that they are founded on the observation of more extended spaces in the heavens, while those very small moments of time which separated the births of twins, and correspond to minute portions of celestial space, are to be connected with trifling things about which the mathematicians are not wont to be consulted,—for

[2] I.e., the potter.

who would consult them as to when he is to sit, when to walk abroad, when and on what he is to dine?—how can we be justified in so speaking, when we can point out such manifold diversity both in the habits, doings, and destinies of twins?

4. *Concerning the twins Esau and Jacob, who were very unlike each other both in their character and actions.*

In the time of the ancient fathers, to speak concerning illustrious persons, there were born two twin brothers, the one so immediately after the other, that the first took hold of the heel of the second. So great a difference existed in their lives and manners, so great a dissimilarity in their actions, so great a difference in their parents' love for them respectively, that the very contrast between them produced even a mutual hostile antipathy. Do we mean, when we say that they were so unlike each other, that when the one was walking the other was sitting, when the one was sleeping the other was waking, —which differences are such as are attributed to those minute portions of space which cannot be appreciated by those who note down the position of the stars which exists at the moment of one's birth, in order that the mathematicians may be consulted concerning it? One of these twins was for a long time a hired servant; the other never served. One of them was beloved by his mother; the other was not so. One of them lost that honour which was so much valued among their people; the other obtained it. And what shall we say of their wives, their children, and their possessions? How different they were in respect to all these! If, therefore, such things as these are connected with those minute intervals of time which elapse between the births of twins, and are not to be attributed to the constellations, why are they predicted in the case of others from the examination of their constellations? And if, on the other hand, these things are said to be predicted, because they are connected, not with minute and inappreciable moments, but with intervals of time which can be observed and noted down, what purpose is that potter's wheel to serve in this matter, except it be to whirl round men who have hearts of clay, in order that they may be prevented from detecting the emptiness of the talk of the mathematicians?

5. *How the mathematicians are convicted of professing a vain science.*

Do not those very persons whom the medical sagacity of Hippocrates led him to suspect to be twins, because their disease was observed by him to develop to its crisis and to subside again in the same time in each of them,—do not these, I say, serve as a sufficient refutation of those who wish to attribute to the influence of the stars that which was owing to a similarity of bodily constitution? For why were they both sick of the same disease, and at the same time, and not the one after the other in the order of their birth? (for certainly they could not both be born at the same time.) Or, if the fact of their having been born at different times by no means necessarily implies that they must be sick at different times, why do they contend that the difference in the time of their births was the cause of their difference in other things? Why could they travel in foreign parts at different times, marry at different times, beget children at different times, and do many other things at different times, by reason of their having been born at different times, and yet could not, for the same reason, also be sick at different times? For if a difference in the moment of birth changed the horoscope, and occasioned dissimilarity in all other things, why has that simultaneousness which belonged to their conception remained in their attacks of sickness? Or, if the destinies of health are involved in the time of conception, but those of other things are said to be attached to the time of birth, they ought not to predict anything concerning health from examination of the constellations of birth, when the hour of conception is not also given, that its constellations may be inspected. But if they say that they predict attacks of sickness without examining the horoscope of conception, because these are indicated by the moments of birth, how could they inform either of these twins when he would be sick, from the horoscope of his birth, when the other also, who had not the same horoscope of birth, must of necessity fall sick at the same time? Again, I ask, if the distance of time between the births of twins is so great as to occasion a difference of their constellations on account of the difference of their horoscopes, and therefore of all the cardinal points to which so much influence is attributed, that even from such change there comes a difference of destiny, how is it possible that this should be so, since they cannot have been conceived at different times? Or, if two conceived at the same moment of time could have different destinies with respect to their births, why may not also two born at the same moment of time have different destinies for life and for death? For if the one moment in which both were conceived did not hinder that the one should be born before the other, why, if two are born at the same moment, should anything hinder them from dying at the same moment? If a simultaneous conception allows of twins being differently affected in the *womb*, why should not simultaneousness of birth allow of any two individuals having different fortunes in the *world?* and thus would all the fictions of this art, or rather delusion, be swept away. What strange circumstance is this, that two children conceived at the same time, indeed, at the same moment, under the same position of the stars, have different fates which bring them to different hours of birth, while two children, born of two different mothers, at the same moment of time, under one and the same position of the stars, cannot have different fates which shall conduct them by necessity to diverse manners of life and of death? Are they at conception as yet without destinies, because they can only have them if they are born? What, therefore, do they mean when they say that, if the hour of the conception is found, many things can be predicted by these astrologers? from which also arose that story which is reiterated by some, that a certain sage chose an hour in which to lie with his wife, in order to secure his begetting an illustrious son. From this opinion also came that answer of Posidonius, the great astrologer and also philosopher, concerning those twins who were attacked with sickness at the same time, namely, "that this had happened to them because they were conceived at the same time, and born at the same time." For certainly he added "conception," lest it should be said to him that they could not both be *born* at the same time, knowing that at any rate they must both have been conceived at the same time; wishing thus to show that he did not attribute the fact of their being similarly and simultaneously affected with sickness to the similarity of their bodily constitutions as its proximate cause, but that he held that even in respect of the similarity of their health, they were bound together by a sidereal connection. If, therefore, the time of conception has so much to do with the similarity of destinies, these same destinies ought not to be changed by the circumstances of birth; or, if the destinies of twins are said to be changed because they are born at different times, why should we not rather understand that they had been already changed in order that they might be born at different times? Does not, then, the will of men living in the world change the destinies of birth, when the order of birth can change the destinies they had at conception?

6. *Concerning twins of different sexes.*

But even in the very conception of twins, which certainly occurs at the same moment in the case of both, it often happens that the one is conceived a male, and the other a female. I know two of different sexes who are twins. Both of them are alive, and in the flower of their age; and though they resemble each other in body, as far as difference of sex will permit, still they are very different in the whole scope and purpose of their lives (consideration being had of those differences which necessarily exist between the lives of males and females),—the one holding the office of a count, and being almost constantly away from home with the army in foreign service, the other never leaving her country's soil, or her native district. Still more,—and this is more incredible, if the destinies of the stars are to be believed in, though it is not wonderful if we consider the wills of men, and the free gifts of God,—he is married; she is a sacred virgin: he has begotten a numerous offspring; she has never even married. But is not the virtue of the horoscope very great? I think I have said enough to show the absurdity of that. But, say those astrologers, whatever be the virtue of the horoscope in other respects, it is certainly of significance with respect to birth. But why not also with respect to conception, which takes place undoubtedly with one act of copulation? And, indeed, so great is the force of nature, that after a woman has once conceived, she ceases to be liable to conception. Or were they, perhaps, changed at birth, either he into a male, or she into a female, because of the difference in their horoscopes? But, while it is not altogether absurd to say that certain sidereal influences have some power to cause differences in bodies alone,—as, for instance, we see that the seasons of the year come round by the approaching and receding of the sun, and that certain kinds of things are increased in size or diminished by the waxings and wanings of the moon, such as sea-urchins, oysters, and the wonderful tides of the ocean, —it does not follow that the *wills of men* are to be made subject to the position of the stars. The astrologers, however, when they wish to bind our actions also to the constellations, only set us on investigating whether, even in these bodies, the changes may not be attributable to some other than a sidereal cause. For what is there which more intimately concerns a body than its sex? And yet, under the same position of the stars, twins of different sexes may be conceived. Therefore, what greater absurdity can be affirmed or believed than that the position of the stars, which was the same for both of them at the time of conception, could not cause that the one child should not have been of a different sex from her brother, with whom she had a common constellation, while the position of the stars which existed at the hour of their birth could cause that she should be separated from him by the great distance between marriage and holy virginity?

7. *Concerning the choosing of a day for marriage, or for planting, or sowing.*

Now, will any one bring forward this, that in choosing certain particular days for particular actions, men bring about certain new destinies for their actions? That man, for instance, according to this doctrine, was not born to have an illustrious son, but rather a contemptible one, and therefore, being a man of learning, he chose an hour in which to lie with his wife. He made, therefore, a destiny which he did not have before, and from that destiny of his own making something began to be "fatal" which was not contained in the destiny of his natal hour. Oh, singular stupidity! A day is chosen on which to marry; and for this reason, I believe, that unless a day be chosen, the marriage may fall on an unlucky day, and turn out an unhappy one. What then becomes of what the stars have already decreed at the hour of birth? Can a man be said to change by an act of choice that which has already been determined for him, while that which he himself has determined in the choosing of a day cannot be changed by another power? Thus, if men alone, and not all things under heaven, are subject to the influence of the stars, why do they choose some days as suitable for planting vines or trees, or for sowing grain, other days as suitable for taming beasts, or for putting the males to the females, that the cows and mares may be impregnated, and for such-like things? If it is said that certain chosen days have an influence on these things, because the constellations rule over all terrestrial bodies, animate and inanimate, according to differences in moments of time, let it be considered what innumerable multitudes of beings are born or arise, or take their origin at the very same instant of time, which come to ends so different, that they may persuade any little boy that these observations about days are ridiculous. For who is so mad as to dare affirm that all trees, all herbs, all beasts, serpents, birds, fishes, worms, have each separately their own moments of birth or commencement? Nevertheless, men are wont, in order to try the skill of the mathematicians, to bring before them the constellations of dumb animals, the constellations of whose birth they diligently observe at home with a view to this discovery; and they prefer those mathematicians to all others, who say from the inspection of the constellations that they indicate the birth of a beast and not of a man. They also dare tell what kind of beast it is, whether it is a wool-bearing beast, or a beast suited for carrying burdens, or one fit for the plough, or for watching a house; for the astrologers are also tried with respect to the fates of dogs, and their answers concerning these are followed by shouts of admiration on the part of those who consult them. They so deceive men as to make them think that during the birth of a man the births of all other beings are suspended, so that not even a fly comes to life at the same time that he is being born, under the same region of the heavens. And if this is admitted with respect to the fly, the reasoning cannot stop there, but must ascend

from flies till it lead them up to camels and elephants. Nor
are they willing to attend to this, that when a day has been
chosen on which to sow a field, so many grains fall into the
ground simultaneously, germinate simultaneously, spring up,
come to perfection, and ripen simultaneously; and yet, of all
the ears which are coeval, and, so to speak, *congerminal,* some
are destroyed by mildew, some are devoured by the birds, and
some are pulled by men. How can they say that all these
had their different constellations, which they see coming to so
different ends? Will they confess that it is folly to choose
days for such things, and to affirm that they do not come
within the sphere of the celestial decree, while they subject
men alone to the stars, on whom alone in the world God has
bestowed free wills? All these things being considered, we
have good reason to believe that, when the astrologers give
very many wonderful answers, it is to be attributed to the
occult inspiration of spirits not of the best kind, whose care
it is to insinuate into the minds of men, and to confirm in
them, those false and noxious opinions concerning the fatal
influence of the stars, and not to their marking and inspecting
of horoscopes, according to some kind of art which in reality
has no existence.

8. *Concerning those who call by the name of fate, not the position
   of the stars, but the connection of causes which depends on the
   will of God.*

But, as to those who call by the name of fate, not the disposition of the stars as it may exist when any creature is
conceived, or born, or commences its existence, but the whole
connection and train of causes which makes everything become what it does become, there is no need that I should labour and strive with them in a merely verbal controversy,
since they attribute the so-called order and connection of
causes to the will and power of God most high, who is most
rightly and most truly believed to know all things before they
come to pass, and to leave nothing unordained; from whom
are all powers, although the wills of all are not from him.
Now, that it is chiefly the will of God most high, whose power
extends itself irresistibly through all things which they call

fate, is proved by the following verses, of which, if I mistake not, Annæus Seneca is the author:—

Father supreme, Thou ruler of the lofty heavens,
Lead me where'er it is Thy pleasure; I will give
A prompt obedience, making no delay,
Lo! here I am. Promptly I come to do Thy sovereign will;
If Thy command shall thwart my inclination, I will still
Follow Thee groaning, and the work assigned,
With all the suffering of a mind repugnant,
Will perform, being evil; which, had I been good,
I should have undertaken and performed, though hard,
With virtuous cheerfulness.
The Fates do lead the man that follows willing;
But the man that is unwilling, him they drag.[3]

Most evidently, in this last verse, he calls that "fate" which he had before called "the will of the Father supreme," whom, he says, he is ready to obey that he may be led, being willing, not dragged, being unwilling, since "The Fates do lead the man that follows willing; But the man that is unwilling, him they drag."

The following Homeric lines, which Cicero translates into Latin, also favour this opinion:—

Such are the minds of men, as is the light
Which Father Jove himself doth pour
Illustrious o'er the fruitful earth.[4]

Not that Cicero wishes that a poetical sentiment should have any weight in a question like this; for when he says that the Stoics, when asserting the power of fate, were in the habit of using these verses from Homer, he is not treating concerning the opinion of that poet, but concerning that of those philosophers, since by these verses, which they quote in connection with the controversy which they hold about fate, is most distinctly manifested what it is which they reckon fate, since they call by the name of Jupiter him whom they

[3] Letter 107.11. Cleanthes frg. 527.
[4] *Odyssey*, 18. 136 ff.

reckon the supreme god, from whom, they say, hangs the whole chain of fates.

9. Concerning the foreknowledge of God and the free will of man, in opposition to the definition of Cicero.

The manner in which Cicero addresses himself to the task of refuting the Stoics, shows that he did not think he could effect anything against them in argument unless he had first demolished divination. And this he attempts to accomplish by denying that there is any knowledge of future things, and maintains with all his might that there is no such knowledge either in God or man, and that there is no prediction of events. Thus he both denies the foreknowledge of God, and attempts by vain arguments, and by opposing to himself certain oracles very easy to be refuted, to overthrow all prophecy, even such as is clearer than the light (though even these oracles are not refuted by him).

But, in refuting these conjectures of the mathematicians, his argument is triumphant, because truly these are such as destroy and refute themselves. Nevertheless, they are far more tolerable who assert the fatal influence of the stars than they who deny the foreknowledge of future events. For, to confess that God exists, and at the same time to deny that he has foreknowledge of future things, is the most manifest folly. This Cicero himself saw, and therefore attempted to assert the doctrine embodied in the words of scripture, "The fool has said in his heart, there is no God."[5] That, however, he did not do in his own person, for he saw how odious and offensive such an opinion would be; and, therefore in his book on the nature of the gods,[6] he makes Cotta dispute concerning this against the Stoics, and preferred to give his own opinion in favour of Lucilius Balbus, to whom he assigned the defence of the Stoical position, rather than in favour of Cotta, who maintained that no divinity exists. However, in his book on divination, he in his own person most openly opposes the doctrine of the prescience of future things. But all this he seems to do in order that he may not grant the doctrine of fate, and by so doing destroy free will. For he thinks that, the knowl-

[5] Ps. 14: 1.
[6] Book 3.

edge of future things being once conceded, fate follows as so necessary a consequence that it cannot be denied.

But, let these perplexing debatings and disputations of the philosophers go on as they may, we, in order that we may confess the most high and true God himself, do confess his will, supreme power, and prescience. Neither let us be afraid lest, after all, we do not do by will that which we do by will, because he, whose foreknowledge is infallible, foreknew that we would do it. It was this which Cicero was afraid of, and therefore opposed foreknowledge. The Stoics also maintained that all things do not come to pass by necessity, although they contended that all things happen according to destiny. What is it, then, that Cicero feared in the prescience of future things? Doubtless it was this,—that if all future things have been foreknown, they will happen in the order in which they have been foreknown; and if they come to pass in this order, there is a certain order of things foreknown by God; and if a certain order of things, then a certain order of causes, for nothing can happen which is not preceded by some efficient cause. But if there is a certain order of causes according to which everything happens which does happen, then by fate, says he, all things happen which do happen. But if this is so, then there is nothing in our own power, and there is no such thing as freedom of will; and if we grant that, says he, the whole economy of human life is subverted. In vain are laws enacted. In vain are reproaches, praises, chidings, exhortations had recourse to; and there is no justice whatever in the appointment of rewards for the good, and punishments for the wicked. And so that consequences so disgraceful, and absurd, and pernicious to humanity may not follow, Cicero chooses to reject the foreknowledge of future things, and shuts up the religious mind to this alternative, to make choice between two things, either that something is in our own power, or that there is foreknowledge,—both of which cannot be true; but if the one is affirmed, the other is thereby denied. He therefore, like a truly great and wise man, and one who consulted very much and very skilfully for the good of humanity, of those two chose the freedom of the will, to confirm which he denied the foreknowledge of future things; and thus, wishing to make men free, he makes them sacrilegious. But the religious mind chooses both, confesses both, and maintains both by the faith of piety. But how so? says Cicero; for the knowledge of future things being granted, there follows a chain of consequences which ends in this, that there can be nothing depending on our own free wills. And further, if there is anything depending on our wills, we must go backwards by the same steps of reasoning till we arrive at the conclusion that there is no foreknowledge of future things. For we go backwards through all the steps in the following order:—If there is free will, all things do not happen according to fate; if all things do not happen according to fate, there is not a certain order of causes; and if there is not a certain order of causes, neither is there a certain order of things foreknown by God,—for things cannot come to pass except they are preceded by efficient causes,—but, if there is no fixed and certain order of causes foreknown by God, all things cannot be said to happen according as he foreknew that they would happen. And further, if it is not true that all things happen just as they have been foreknown by him, there is not, says he, in God any foreknowledge of future events.

Now, against the sacrilegious and impious darings of reason, we assert both that God knows all things before they come to pass, and that we do by our free will whatsoever we know and feel to be done by us only because we will it. But that all things come to pass by fate, we do not say; indeed we affirm that nothing comes to pass by fate; for we demonstrate that the name of fate, as it is wont to be used by those who speak of fate, meaning thereby the position of the stars at the time of each one's conception or birth, is an unmeaning word, for astrology itself is a delusion. But an order of causes in which the highest efficiency is attributed to the will of God, we neither deny nor do we designate it by the name of fate, unless, perhaps, we may understand fate to mean that which is spoken, deriving it from *fari*, to speak; for we cannot deny that it is written in the sacred Scriptures, "God has spoken once; these two things have I heard, that power belongs to God. Also to you, O God, belongs mercy: for you will render to every man according to his works."[7] Now the expression,

[7] Ps. 62: 11 f.

"Once has he spoken," is to be understood as meaning *"immovably,"* that is, unchangeably has he spoken, inasmuch as he knows unchangeably all things which shall be, and all things which he will do. We might, then, use the word fate in the sense it bears when derived from *fari,* to speak, if it had not already come to be understood in another sense, into which I am unwilling that the hearts of men should unconsciously slide. But it does not follow that, though there is for God a certain order of all causes, there must therefore be nothing depending on the free exercise of our own wills; for our wills themselves are included in that order of causes which is certain to God, and is embraced by his foreknowledge; for human wills are also causes of human actions; and he who foreknew all the causes of things would certainly among those causes not have been ignorant of our wills. For even that very concession which Cicero himself makes is enough to refute him in this argument. For what does it help him to say that nothing takes place without a cause, but that every cause is not fatal, there being a fortuitous cause, a natural cause, and a voluntary cause? It is sufficient that he confesses that whatever happens must be preceded by a cause. For we say that those causes which are called fortuitous are not a mere name for the absence of causes, but are only latent, and we attribute them either to the will of the true God, or to that of spirits of some kind or other. And as to natural causes, we by no means separate them from the will of him who is the author and framer of all nature. But now as to voluntary causes. They are referable either to God, or to angels, or to men, or to animals of whatever description, if indeed those instinctive movements of animals devoid of reason, by which, in accordance with their own nature, they seek or shun various things, are to be called wills. And when I speak of the wills of angels, I mean either the wills of good angels, whom we call the angels of God, or of the wicked angels, whom we call the angels of the devil, or demons. Also by the wills of men I mean the wills either of the good or of the wicked. And from this we conclude that there are no efficient causes of all things which come to pass unless voluntary causes, that is, such as belong to that nature which is the spirit of life. For the air or wind is called spirit, but, inasmuch as it is a body, it is not the spirit of life. The spirit of life, therefore, which quickens all things, and is the creator of every body, and of every created spirit, is God himself, the uncreated spirit. In his supreme will resides the power which acts on the wills of all created spirits, helping the good, judging the evil, controlling all, granting power to some, not granting it to others. For, as he is the creator of all natures, so also is he the bestower of all powers, not of all wills; for wicked wills are not from him, being contrary to nature, which is from him. As to bodies, they are more subject to wills: some to our wills, by which I mean the wills of all living mortal creatures, but more to the wills of men than of beasts. But all of them are most of all subject to the will of God, to whom all wills also are subject, since they have no power except what he has bestowed upon them. The cause of things, therefore, which makes but is not made, is God; but all other causes both make and are made. Such are all created spirits, and especially the rational. Material causes, therefore, which may rather be said to be made than to make, are not to be reckoned among efficient causes, because they can only do what the wills of spirits do by them. How, then, does an order of causes which is certain to the foreknowledge of God necessitate that there should be nothing which is dependent on our wills, when our wills themselves have a very important place in the order of causes? Cicero, then, contends with those who call this order of causes "fatal," or rather designate this order itself by the name of fate; to which we have an abhorrence, especially on account of the word, which men have become accustomed to understand as meaning what is not true. But, whereas he denies that the order of all causes is most certain, and perfectly clear to the prescience of God, we detest his opinion more than the Stoics do. For he either denies that God exists,— which, indeed, in an assumed personage, he has laboured to do, in his book *On the Nature of the Gods,*—or if he confesses that he exists, but denies that he is prescient of future things, what is that but just "the fool saying in his heart there is no God?" For one who is not prescient of all future things is not God. Therefore our wills also have just so much power as God willed and foreknew that they should have; and therefore whatever power they have, they have it within most certain limits; and whatever they are to do, they are most assuredly to do, for he whose foreknowledge is infallible foreknew that they would have the power to do it, and would do it. Therefore, if I should choose to apply the name of fate to anything at all, I should rather say that fate belongs to the weaker of two parties, will to the stronger, who has the other in his power, than that the freedom of our will is excluded by that order of causes, which, by an unusual application of the word peculiar to themselves, the Stoics call *Fate*.

10. *Whether our wills are ruled by necessity.*

Therefore, neither is that necessity to be feared, for dread of which the Stoics laboured to make such distinctions among the causes of things as should enable them to rescue certain things from the dominion of necessity, and to subject others to it. Among those things which they wished not to be subject to necessity they placed our wills, knowing that they would not be free if subjected to necessity. For if that is to be called *our necessity* which is not in our power, but even though we be unwilling effects what it can effect,—as, for instance, the necessity of death,—it is manifest that our wills by which we live uprightly or wickedly are not under such a necessity; for we do many things which, if we were not willing, we should certainly not do. This is primarily true of the act of willing itself,—for if we will, it *is;* if we will not, it *is* not,—for we should not will if we were unwilling. But if we define necessity to be that according to which we say that it is necessary that anything be of such or such a nature, or be done in such and such a manner, I do not know why we should have any dread of that necessity taking away the freedom of our will. For we do not put the life of God or the foreknowledge of God under necessity if we should say that it is necessary that God should live for ever, and foreknow all things; as neither is his power diminished when we say that he cannot die or fall into error,—for this is in such a way impossible to him, that if it were possible for him, he would be of less power. But assuredly he is rightly called omnipotent, though he can neither die nor fall into error. For he is called omnipotent on account of his doing what he wills, not on account of his suffering what he wills not; for if that should befall him, he would by no means be omnipotent. Therefore, he cannot do some things for the very reason that he is omnipotent. So also, when we say that it is necessary that, when we will, we will by free choice, in so saying we both affirm what is true beyond doubt, and do not still subject our wills thereby to a necessity which destroys liberty. Our wills, therefore, *exist* as *wills*, and do themselves whatever we do by willing, and which would not be done if we were unwilling. But when any one suffers anything, being unwilling, by the will of another, even in that case will retains its essential validity,—we do not mean the will of the party who inflicts the suffering, for we resolve it into the power of God. For if a will should simply exist, but not be able to do what it wills, it would be overborne by a more powerful will. Nor would this be the case unless there had existed will, and that not the will of the other party, but the will of him who willed, but was not able to accomplish what he willed. Therefore, whatsoever a man suffers contrary to his own will, he ought not to attribute to the will of men, or of angels, or of any created spirit, but rather to his will who gives power to wills. It is not the case, therefore, that because God foreknew what would be in the power of our wills, there is for that reason nothing in the power of our wills. For he who foreknew this did not foreknow nothing. Moreover, if he who foreknew what would be in the power of our wills did not foreknow nothing, but something, assuredly, even though he did foreknow, there is something in the power of our wills. Therefore we are by no means compelled, either, retaining the prescience of God, to take away the freedom of the will, or, retaining the freedom of the will, to deny that he is prescient of future things, which is impious. But we embrace both. We faithfully and sincerely confess both. The former, that we may believe well; the latter, that we may live well. For he lives ill who does not believe well concerning God. Therefore, let it be far from us, in order to maintain our freedom, to deny the prescience of him by whose help we are or shall be free. Consequently, it is not in vain that laws are enacted, and that reproaches, exhortations, praises, and vituperations are had recourse to; for these also he foreknew, and they are of great avail, even as great as he foreknew that they would be. Prayers, also, are of avail to procure those things which he foreknew that he would grant to those who offered them; and with justice have rewards been appointed for good deeds, and punishments for sins. For a man does not therefore sin because God foreknew that he would sin. Nay, it cannot be doubted but that it is the man himself who sins when he does sin, because he, whose foreknowledge is infallible, foreknew not that fate, or fortune, or something else would sin, but that the man himself would sin, who, if he wills not, sins not. But if he shall not will to sin, even this did God foreknow.

11. *Concerning the universal providence of God in the laws of which all things are comprehended.*

Therefore God supreme and true, with his Word and Holy Spirit (which three are one), one God omnipotent, creator and maker of every soul and of every body; by whose gift all are happy who are happy through truth and not through vanity; who made man a rational animal consisting of soul and body, who, when he sinned, neither permitted him to go unpunished, nor left him without mercy; who has given to the good and to the evil, being in common with stones, vegetable life in common with trees, sensuous life in common with brutes, intellectual life in common with angels alone; from whom is every mode, every species, every order; from whom are measure, number, weight; from whom is everything which has an existence in nature, of whatever kind it be, and of whatever value; from whom are the seeds of forms and the forms of seeds, and the motion of seeds and of forms; who gave also to flesh its origin, beauty, health, reproductive fecundity, disposition of members, and the salutary concord of its parts; who also to the irrational soul has given memory, sense, appetite, but to the rational soul, in addition to these, has given intelligence and will; who has not left, not to speak of heaven and earth, angels and men, but not even the entrails of the smallest and most contemptible animal, or the feather of a bird, or the little flower of a plant, or the leaf of a tree, without a harmony, and, as it were, a mutual peace among all its parts; —that God can never be believed to have left the kingdoms of men, their dominations and servitudes, outside of the laws of his providence.

12. *By what virtues the ancient Romans merited that the true God, although they did not worship him, should enlarge their empire.*

Therefore let us go on to consider what virtues of the Romans they were which the true God, in whose power are also the kingdoms of the earth, condescended to help in order to raise the empire, and also for what reason he did so. And, in order to discuss this question on clearer ground, we have written the former books, to show that the power of those gods, who, they thought, were to be worshipped with such trifling and silly rites, had nothing to do in this matter; and also what we have already accomplished of the present volume, to refute the doctrine of fate, lest any one who might have been already persuaded that the Roman empire was not extended and preserved by the worship of these gods, might still be attributing its extension and preservation to some kind of fate, rather than to the most powerful will of God most high. The ancient and primitive Romans, therefore, though their history shows us that, like all the other nations, with the sole exception of the Hebrews, they worshipped false gods, and sacrificed victims, not to God, but to demons, have nevertheless this commendation bestowed on them by their historian, that they were "greedy of praise, prodigal of wealth, desirous of great glory, and content with a moderate fortune."[8] Glory they most ardently loved: for it they wished to live, for it they did not hesitate to die. Every other desire was repressed by the strength of their passion for that one thing. At length their country itself, because it seemed inglorious to serve, but glorious to rule and to command, they first earnestly desired to be free, and then to be mistress. Hence it was that, not enduring the domination of kings, they put the government into the hands of two chiefs, holding office for a year, who were called consuls, not kings or lords. But royal pomp seemed inconsistent with the administration of a ruler (*regentis*), or the benevolence of one who consults (that is, for the public good) (*consulentis*), but rather with the haughtiness of a lord (*dominantis*). King Tarquin, therefore, having been banished, and the consular government having been instituted, it followed, as the same author already alluded to says in his praises of

[8] Sallust, in *Cat.* 7.6.

the Romans, that "the state grew with amazing rapidity after it had obtained liberty, so great a desire of glory had taken possession of it." That eagerness for praise and desire of glory, then, was that which accomplished those many wonderful things, laudable, doubtless, and glorious according to human judgment. The same Sallust praises the great men of his own time, Marcus Cato, and Caius Cæsar, saying that for a long time the republic had no one great in virtue, but that within his memory there had been these two men of eminent virtue, and very different pursuits. Now, among the praises which he pronounces on Cæsar he put this, that he wished for a great empire, an army, and a new war, that he might have a sphere where his genius and virtue might shine forth. Thus it was ever the prayer of men of heroic character that Bellona would excite miserable nations to war, and lash them into agitation with her bloody scourge, so that there might be occasion for the display of their valour. This, indeed, is what that desire of praise and thirst for glory did. Therefore, by the love of liberty in the first place, afterwards also by that of domination and through the desire of praise and glory, they achieved many great things; and their most eminent poet testifies to their having been prompted by all these motives:

> Porsenna there, with pride elate,
> Bids Rome to Tarquin ope her gate;
> With arms he hems the city in,
> Æneas' sons stand firm to win.[9]

At that time it was their greatest ambition either to die bravely or to live free; but when liberty was obtained, so great a desire of glory took possession of them, that liberty alone was not enough unless domination also should be sought, their great ambition being that which the same poet puts into the mouth of Jupiter:

> Nay, Juno's self, whose wild alarms
> Set ocean, earth, and heaven in arms,
> Shall change for smiles her moody frown,
> And vie with me in zeal to crown

[9] *Aen.* 8. 646 ff.

> Rome's sons, the nation of the gown.
> So stands my will. There comes a day,
> While Rome's great ages hold their way,
> When old Assaracus's sons
> Shall quit them on the myrmidons,
> O'er Phthia and Mycenæ reign,
> And humble Argos to them chain.[10]

Which things, indeed, Vergil makes Jupiter predict as future, while, in reality, he was only himself passing in review in his own mind things which were already done, and which were beheld by him as present realities. But I have mentioned them with the intention of showing that, next to liberty, the Romans so highly esteemed domination, that it received a place among those things on which they bestowed the greatest praise. Hence also it is that that poet, preferring to the arts of other nations those arts which peculiarly belong to the Romans, namely, the arts of ruling and commanding, and of subjugating and vanquishing nations, says,

> Others, belike, with happier grace,
> From bronze or stone shall call the face,
> Plead doubtful causes, map the skies,
> And tell when planets set or rise;
> But Roman thou, do thou control
>   The nations far and wide;
> Be this thy genius, to impose
> The rule of peace on vanquished foes,
> Show pity to the humbled soul,
>   And crush the sons of pride.[11]

These arts they exercised with the more skill the less they gave themselves up to pleasures, and to enervation of body and mind in coveting and amassing riches, and through these corrupting morals, by extorting them from the miserable citizens and lavishing them on base stage-players. Hence these men of base character, who abounded when Sallust wrote and Vergil sang these things, did not seek after honours and glory by these arts, but by treachery and deceit. Therefore the same

[10] *Aen.* 1. 279 ff.
[11] Ibid. 6. 847 ff.

says, "But at first it was rather ambition than avarice that stirred the minds of men, which vice, however, is nearer to virtue. For glory, honour, and power are desired alike by the good man and by the ignoble; but the former," he says, "strives onward to them by the true way, while the other, knowing nothing of the good arts, seeks them by fraud and deceit."[12] And what is meant by seeking the attainment of glory, honour, and power by good arts, is to seek them by virtue, and not by deceitful intrigue; for the good and the ignoble man alike desire these things, but the good man strives to overtake them by the true way. The way is virtue, along which he presses as to the goal of possession—namely, to glory, honour, and power. Now that this was a sentiment engrained in the Roman mind, is indicated even by the temples of their gods; for they built in very close proximity the temples of Virtue and Honour, worshipping as gods the gifts of God. Hence we can understand what they who were good thought to be the end of virtue, and to what they ultimately referred it, namely, to honour; for, as to the bad, they had no virtue though they desired honour, and strove to possess it by fraud and deceit. Praise of a higher kind is bestowed upon Cato, for he says of him, "The less he sought glory, the more it followed him."[13] We say praise of a higher kind; for the glory with the desire of which the Romans burned is the judgment of men thinking well of men. And therefore virtue is better, which is content with no human judgment save that of one's own conscience. Whence the apostle says, "For this is our glory, the testimony of our conscience."[14] And in another place he says, "But let every one prove his own work, and then he shall have glory in himself, and not in another."[15] That glory, honour, and power, therefore, which they desired for themselves, and to which the good sought to attain by good arts, should not be sought after by virtue, but virtue by them. For there is no true virtue except that which is directed towards that end in which is the highest and ultimate good of

[12] Sallust, in *Cat.* 11.1 f.
[13] Sallust, in *Cat.* 54.6.
[14] 2 Cor. 1: 12.
[15] Gal. 6: 4.

man. Therefore even the honours which Cato sought he ought
not to have sought, but the state ought to have conferred them
on him unsolicited, on account of his virtues.

But, of the two great Romans of that time, Cato was he
whose virtue was by far the nearest to the true idea of virtue.
Therefore, let us refer to the opinion of Cato himself, to discover what was the judgment he had formed concerning the
condition of the state both then and in former times. "I do
not think," he says, "that it was by arms that our ancestors
made the republic great from being small. Had that been the
case, the republic of our day would have been by far more
flourishing than that of their times, for the number of our al-
lies and citizens is far greater; and, besides, we possess a far
greater abundance of armour and of horses than they did. But
it was other things than these that made them great, and we
have none of them: industry at home, just government abroad,
a mind free in deliberation, addicted neither to crime nor to
lust. Instead of these, we have luxury and avarice, poverty in
the state, opulence among citizens; we laud riches, we follow
laziness; there is no difference made between the good and
the bad; all the rewards of virtue are got possession of by intrigue. And no wonder, when every individual consults only
for his own good, when you are the slaves of pleasure at home,
and, in public affairs, of money and favour, no wonder that
an onslaught is made upon the unprotected republic."[16]

He who hears these words of Cato or of Sallust probably
thinks that such praise bestowed on the ancient Romans was
applicable to all of them, or, at least, to very many of them.
It is not so; otherwise the things which Cato himself writes,
and which I have quoted in the second book of this work,
would not be true. In that passage he says that, even from
the very beginning of the state, wrongs were committed by
the more powerful, which led to the separation of the people
from the Fathers, besides which there were other internal dissensions; and the only time at which there existed a just and
moderate administration was after the banishment of the kings,
and that no longer than while they had cause to be afraid of

16 Sallust, in *Cat.* 52.19–24.

Tarquin, and were carrying on the grievous war which had been undertaken on his account against Etruria; but afterwards the Fathers oppressed the people as slaves, flogged them as the kings had done, drove them from their land, and, to the exclusion of all others, held the government in their own hands alone. And to these discords, while the Fathers were wishing to rule, and the people were unwilling to serve, the second Punic war put an end; for again great fear began to press upon their disquieted minds, holding them back from those distractions by another and greater anxiety, and bringing them back to civil concord. But the great things which were then achieved were accomplished through the administration of a few men, who were good in their own way. And by the wisdom and forethought of these few good men, which first enabled the republic to endure these evils and mitigated them, it waxed greater and greater. And this the same historian affirms, when he says that, reading and hearing of the many illustrious achievements of the Roman people in peace and in war, by land and by sea, he wished to understand what it was by which these great things were specially sustained. For he knew that very often the Romans had with a small company contended with great legions of the enemy; and he knew also that with small resources they had carried on wars with opulent kings. And he says that, after having given the matter much consideration, it seemed evident to him that the pre-eminent virtue of a few citizens had achieved the whole, and that that explained how poverty overcame wealth, and small numbers great multitudes. But, he adds, after the state had been corrupted by luxury and indolence, again the republic, by its own greatness, was able to bear the vices of its magistrates and generals. Therefore even the praises of Cato are only applicable to a few; for only a few were possessed of that virtue which leads men to pursue glory, honour, and power by the true way,—that is, by virtue itself. This industry at home, of which Cato speaks, was the consequence of a desire to enrich the public treasury, even though the result should be poverty at home; and therefore, when he speaks of the evil arising out of the corruption of morals, he reverses the expression, and says, "Poverty in the state, riches at home."

13. Concerning the love of praise, which, though it is a vice, is reckoned a virtue, because by it greater vice is restrained.

Therefore, when the kingdoms of the East had been illustrious for a long time, it pleased God that there should also arise a Western empire, which, though later in time, should be more illustrious in extent and greatness. And, in order that it might overcome the grievous evils which existed among others nations, he purposely granted it to such men as, for the sake of honour, and praise, and glory, consulted well for their country, in whose glory they sought their own, and whose safety they did not hesitate to prefer to their own, suppressing the desire of wealth and many other vices for this one vice, namely, the love of praise. For he has the soundest perception who recognises that even the love of praise is a vice; nor has this escaped the perception of the poet Horace, who says,

> You're bloated by ambition? take advice:
> Yon book will ease you if you read it thrice.[17]

And the same poet, in a lyric song, has thus spoken with the desire of repressing the passion for domination:

> Rule an ambitious spirit, and thou hast
> A wider kingdom than if thou shouldst join
> To distant Gades Lybia, and thus
> Shouldst hold in service either Carthaginian.[18]

Nevertheless, they who restrain baser lusts, not by the power of the Holy Spirit obtained by the faith of piety, or by the love of intelligible beauty, but by desire of human praise, or, at all events, restrain them better by the love of such praise, are not indeed yet holy, but only less base. Even Cicero was not able to conceal this fact; for, in the books which he wrote, *De Republica,* when speaking concerning the education of a chief of the state, who ought, he says, to be nourished on glory, goes on to say that their ancestors did many wonderful and illustrious things through desire of glory. So far, therefore, from resisting this vice, they even thought that it ought

---

[17] Horace, *Epist.* 1.1.36 f.
[18] Horace, *Carm.* 2.2.

to be excited and kindled up, supposing that that would be beneficial to the republic. But not even in his books on philosophy does Cicero dissimulate this poisonous opinion, for he there avows it more clearly than day. For when he is speaking of those studies which are to be pursued with a view to the *true good,* and not with the vainglorious desire of human praise, he introduces the following universal and general statement:

Honour nourishes the arts, and all are stimulated to the prosecution of studies by glory; and those pursuits are always neglected which are generally discredited.[19]

14. *Concerning the eradication of the love of human praise, because all the glory of the righteous is in God.*

It is, therefore, doubtless far better to resist this desire than to yield to it, for the purer one is from this defilement, the more like one is to God; and, though this vice is not thoroughly eradicated from his heart,—for it does not cease to tempt even the minds of those who are making good progress in virtue,—at any rate, let the desire of glory be surpassed by the love of righteousness, so that, if there is seen anywhere "lying neglected things which are generally discredited," if they are good, if they are right, even the love of human praise may blush and yield to the love of truth. For so hostile is this vice to pious faith, if the love of glory be greater in the heart than the fear or love of God, that the Lord said, "How can you believe, who look for glory from one another, and do not seek the glory which is from God alone?"[20] Also, concerning some who had believed in him, but were afraid to confess him openly, the evangelist says, "They loved the praise of men more than the praise of God;"[21] which the holy apostles did not, who, when they proclaimed the name of Christ in those places where it was not only discredited, and therefore neglected,—according as Cicero says, "Those things always lie neglected which are generally discredited,"—but was even held in the utmost detestation, held to what they had heard from

[19] *Tusc. Disp.* 1.2.
[20] John 5: 44.
[21] John 12: 43.

the Good Master, who was also the physician of minds, "If any one shall deny me before men, him will I also deny before my Father who is in heaven and before the angels of God."[22] Amidst maledictions and reproaches, and most grievous persecutions and cruel punishments, they were not deterred from the preaching of human salvation by the noise of human indignation. And when, as they did and spoke divine things, and lived divine lives, conquering, as it were, hard hearts, and introducing into them the peace of righteousness, great glory followed them in the church of Christ, they did not rest in that as in the end of their virtue, but, referring that glory itself to the glory of God, by whose grace they were what they were, they sought to kindle, also by that same flame, the minds of those for whose good they consulted, to the love of him, by whom they could be made to be what they themselves were. For their Master had taught them not to seek to be good for the sake of human glory, saying, "Take heed that you do not your righteousness before men to be seen by them, or otherwise you shall not have a reward from your Father who is in heaven."[23] But again, lest, understanding this wrongly, they should, through fear of pleasing men, be less useful through concealing their goodness, showing for what end they ought to make it known, he says, "Let your works shine before men, that they may see your good deeds, and glorify your Father who is in heaven."[24] Not, observe, "that you may be seen by them, that is, in order that their eyes may be directed upon you,"—for of yourselves you are nothing,—but "that they may glorify your Father who is in heaven," by fixing their regards on whom they may become such as you are. These the martyrs followed, who surpassed the Scævolas, and the Curtiuses, and the Deciuses, both in true virtue, because in true piety, and also in the greatness of their number. But since those Romans were in an earthly city, and had before them, as the end of all the offices undertaken in its behalf, its safety, and a kingdom, not in heaven, but in earth,—not in the sphere of eternal life, but in the sphere of demise and succession, where the dead are succeeded by the dying,—what else but glory should

22 Matt. 10: 33.
23 Matt. 6: 1.
24 Matt. 5: 16.

they love, by which they wished even after death to live in the mouths of their admirers?

15. Concerning the temporal reward which God granted to the virtues of the Romans.

Now, therefore, with regard to those to whom God did not purpose to give eternal life with his holy angels in his own celestial city (to the society of which that true piety which does not render the service of religion, which the Greeks call *latreia*, to any save the true God conducts), if he had also withheld from them the terrestrial glory of that most excellent empire, a reward would not have been rendered to their good arts,—that is, their virtues,—by which they sought to attain so great glory. For as to those who seem to do some good that they may receive glory from men, the Lord also says, "Truly I say unto you, they have received their reward."[25] So also these despised their own private affairs for the sake of the republic, and for its treasury resisted avarice, consulted for the good of their country with a spirit of freedom, addicted neither to what their laws pronounced to be crime nor to lust. By all these acts, as by the true way, they pressed forward to honours, power, and glory; they were honoured among almost all nations; they imposed the laws of their empire upon many nations; and at this day, both in literature and history, they are glorious among almost all nations. There is no reason why they should complain against the justice of the supreme and true God,—"they have received their reward."

16. Concerning the reward of the holy citizens of the celestial city, to whom the example of the virtues of the Roman are useful.

But the reward of the saints is far different, who even here endured reproaches for that city of God which is hateful to the lovers of this world. That city is eternal. There none are born, for none die. There is true and full felicity,—not a goddess, but a gift of God. From there we receive the pledge of faith, while on our pilgrimage we sigh for its beauty. There rises not the sun on the good and the evil, but the sun of righteousness protects the good alone. There no great industry shall be expended to enrich the public treasury by suffering priva-

[25] Matt. 6: 2.

tions at home, for there is the common treasury of truth. And, therefore, it was not only for the sake of recompensing the citizens of Rome that her empire and glory had been so signally extended, but also that the citizens of that eternal city, during their pilgrimage here, might diligently and soberly contemplate these examples, and see what a love they owe to the supernal country on account of life eternal, if the terrestrial country was so much beloved by its citizens on account of human glory.

17. *To what profit the Romans carried on wars, and how much they contributed to the well-being of those whom they conquered.*

For, as far as this life of mortals is concerned, which is spent and ended in a few days, what does it matter under whose government a dying man lives, if they who govern do not force him to impiety and iniquity? Did the Romans at all harm those nations, on whom, when subjugated, they imposed their laws, except in as far as that was accomplished with great slaughter in war? Now, had it been done with consent of the nations, it would have been done with greater success, but there would have been no glory of conquest, for neither did the Romans themselves live exempt from those laws which they imposed on others. Had this been done without Mars and Bellona, so that there should have been no place for victory, no one conquering where no one had fought, would not the condition of the Romans and of the other nations have been one and the same—especially if that had been done at once which afterwards was done most humanely and most acceptably, namely, the admission of all to the rights of Roman citizens who belonged to the Roman empire, and if that had been made the privilege of all which was formerly the privilege of a few: with this one condition, that the humbler class who had no lands of their own should live at the public expense— an alimentary impost, which would have been paid with a much better grace by them into the hands of good administrators of the republic, of which they were members, by their own hearty consent, than it would have been had it to be extorted from them as conquered men? For I do not see what it makes for the safety, good morals, and certainly not for the dignity, of men, that some have conquered and others have been conquered, except that it yields them that most insane pomp of human glory, in which "they have received their reward," who burned with excessive desire of it, and carried on most eager wars. For do not their lands pay tribute? Have they any privilege of learning what the others are not privileged to learn? Are there not many senators in the other countries who do not even know Rome by sight? Take away outward show, and what are all men after all but men? But even though the perversity of the age should permit that all the better men should be more highly honoured than others, neither thus should human honour be held at a great price, for it is smoke which has no weight. But let us avail ourselves even in these things of the kindness of God. Let us consider how great things they despised, how great things they endured, what lusts they subdued for the sake of human glory, who merited that glory, as it were, in reward for such virtues; and let this be useful to us even in suppressing pride, so that, as that city in which it has been promised us to reign as far surpasses this one as heaven is distant from the earth, as eternal life surpasses temporal joy, solid glory empty praise, or the society of angels the society of mortals, or the glory of him who made the sun and moon the light of the sun and moon, the citizens of so great a country may not seem to themselves to have done anything very great, if, in order to obtain it, they have done some good works or endured some evils, when those men for this terrestrial country already obtained, did such great things, suffered such great things. And especially are all these things to be considered, because the remission of sins which collects citizens to the celestial country has something in it to which a shadowy resemblance is found in that asylum of Romulus, where the desire to escape from the punishment of all manner of crimes brought together that multitude with which the state was to be founded.

18. *How far Christians ought to be from boasting, if they have done anything for the love of the eternal country, when the Romans did such great things for human glory and a terrestrial city.*

What great thing, therefore, is it for that eternal and celestial city to despise all the charms of this world, however pleasant,

if for the sake of this terrestrial city Brutus could even put
to death his son,—a sacrifice which the heavenly city compels
no one to make? But certainly it is more difficult to put to
death one's sons, than to do what is required to be done for
the heavenly country, even to distribute to the poor those
things which were looked upon as things to be amassed and
laid up for one's children, or to let them go, if there arise
any temptation which compels us to do so, for the sake of
faith and righteousness. For it is not earthly riches which
make us or our sons happy; for they must either be lost by us
in our lifetime, or be possessed when we are dead, by whom
we know not, or perhaps by whom we would not. But it is God
who makes us happy, who is the true riches of minds. But
of Brutus, even the poet who celebrates his praises testifies that
it was the occasion of unhappiness to him that he slew his
son, for he says,

> And call his own rebellious seed
> For menaced liberty to bleed.
> Unhappy father! howsoe'er
> The deed be judged by after days.[26]

But in the following verse he consoles him in his unhappiness, saying,

> His country's love shall all o'erbear.

There are those two things, namely, liberty and the desire of
human praise, which compelled the Romans to admirable
deeds. If, therefore, for the liberty of dying men, and for the
desire of human praise which is sought after by mortals, sons
could be put to death by a father, what great thing is it, if,
for the true liberty which has made us free from the dominion
of sin, and death, and the devil,—not through the desire of
human praise, but through the earnest desire of freeing men,
not from King Tarquin, but from demons and the prince of
the demons,—we should, I do not say put to death our sons,
but reckon among our sons Christ's poor ones? If, also,
another Roman chief, surnamed Torquatus, slew his son, not

[26] *Aen.* 6.820 ff.

because he fought against his country, but because, being
challenged by an enemy, he through youthful impetuosity
fought, though for his country, yet contrary to orders which
his father had given as general; and this he did, notwithstanding that his son was victorious, lest there should be more
evil in the example of authority despised, than good in the
glory of slaying an enemy;—if, I say, Torquatus acted thus,
why should they boast themselves, who, for the laws of a
celestial country, despise all earthly good things, which are
loved far less than sons? If Furius Camillus, who was condemned by those who envied him, notwithstanding that he
had thrown off from the necks of his countrymen the yoke of
their most bitter enemies, the Veientes, again delivered his
ungrateful country from the Gauls, because he had no other
in which he could have better opportunities for living a life of
glory;—if Camillus did thus, why should he be extolled as
having done some great thing, who, having, it may be, suffered in the church at the hands of carnal enemies most
grievous and dishonouring injury, has not betaken himself
to heretical enemies, or himself raised some heresy against
her, but has rather defended her, as far as he was able, from
the most pernicious perversity of heretics, since there is not
another church, I say not in which one can live a life of
glory, but in which eternal life can be obtained? If Mucius,
in order that peace might be made with King Porsenna, who
was pressing the Romans with a most grievous war, when he
did not succeed in slaying Porsenna, but slew another by
mistake for him, reached forth his right hand and laid it on
a red-hot altar, saying that many such as he had conspired
for his destruction, so that Porsenna, terrified at his daring,
and at the thought of a conspiracy of such as he, without
any delay recalled all his warlike purposes, and made peace;
—if, I say, Mucius did this, who shall speak of his meritorious
claims to the kingdom of heaven, if for it he may have given
to the flames not one hand, but even his whole body, and that
not by his own spontaneous act, but because he was persecuted by another? If Curtius, spurring on his steed, threw
himself all armed into a precipitous gulf, obeying the oracles
of their gods, which had commanded that the Romans should
throw into that gulf the best thing which they possessed, and

they could only understand thereby that, since they excelled
in men and arms, the gods had commanded that an armed
man should be cast headlong into that destruction;—if he did
this, shall we say that that man has done a great thing for the
eternal city who may have died by a like death, not, however,
precipitating himself spontaneously into a gulf, but having suffered this death at the hands of some enemy of his faith, more
especially when he has received from his Lord, who is also
King of his country, a more certain oracle, "Fear not them
who kill the body, but cannot kill the soul?"[27] If the Decii
dedicated themselves to death, consecrating themselves in a
form of words, as it were, that falling, and pacifying by their
blood the wrath of the gods, they might be the means of
delivering the Roman army;—if they did this, let not the holy
martyrs carry themselves proudly, as though they had done
some meritorious thing for a share in that country where are
eternal life and felicity, if even to the shedding of their blood,
loving not only the brethren for whom it was shed, but, according as had been commanded them, even their enemies by
whom it was being shed, they have vied with one another in
faith of love and love of faith. If Marcus Pulvillus, when
engaged in dedicating a temple to Jupiter, Juno, and Minerva,
received with such indifference the false intelligence which
was brought to him of the death of his son, with the intention
of so agitating him that he should go away, and thus the
glory of dedicating the temple should fall to his colleague;—if
he received that intelligence with such indifference that he
even ordered that his son should be cast out unburied, the
love of glory having overcome in his heart the grief of bereavement, how shall any one affirm that he has done a great
thing for the preaching of the gospel, by which the citizens
of the heavenly city are delivered from divers errors, and
gathered together from divers wanderings, to whom his Lord
has said, when anxious about the burial of his father, "Follow me, and let the dead bury their dead?"[28] Regulus, in
order not to break his oath, even with his most cruel enemies,
returned to them from Rome itself, because (as he is said to

[27] Matt. 10: 28.
[28] Matt. 8: 22.

have replied to the Romans when they wished to retain him)
he could not have the dignity of an honourable citizen at
Rome after having been a slave to the Africans, and the
Carthaginians put him to death with the utmost tortures, because he had spoken against them in the senate. If Regulus
acted thus, what tortures are not to be despised for the sake
of good faith toward that country to whose beatitude faith
itself leads? Or what will a man have rendered to the Lord
for all he has bestowed upon him, if, for the faithfulness he
owes to him, he shall have suffered such things as Regulus
suffered at the hands of his most ruthless enemies for the
good faith which he owed to them? And how shall a Christian dare vaunt himself of his voluntary poverty, which he
has chosen in order that during the pilgrimage of this life he
may walk the more disencumbered on the way which leads
to the country where the true riches are, even God himself;
—how, I say, shall he vaunt himself for this, when he hears or
reads that Lucius Valerius, who died when he was holding the
office of consul, was so poor that his funeral expenses were
paid with money collected by the people?—or when he hears
that Quintius Cincinnatus, who, possessing only four acres of
land, and cultivating them with his own hands, was taken from
the plough to be made dictator,—an office more honourable
even than that of consul,—and that, after having won great
glory by conquering the enemy, he preferred notwithstanding
to continue in his poverty? Or how shall he boast of having
done a great thing, who has not been prevailed upon by the
offer of any reward of this world to renounce his connection
with that heavenly and eternal country, when he hears that
Fabricius could not be prevailed on to forsake the Roman
city by the great gifts offered to him by Pyrrhus king of the
Epirots, who promised him the fourth part of his kingdom,
but preferred to abide there in his poverty as a private individual? For if, when their republic,—that is, the interest of the
people, the interest of the country, the common interest,—
was most prosperous and wealthy, they themselves were so
poor in their own houses, that one of them, who had already
been twice a consul, was expelled from that senate of poor
men by the censor, because he was discovered to possess ten
pounds weight of silver-plate,—since, I say, those very men by

whose triumphs the public treasury was enriched were so poor, ought not all Christians, who make common property of their riches with a far nobler purpose, even that (according to what is written in the Acts of the Apostles) they may distribute to each one according to his need, and that no one may say that anything is his own, but that all things may be their common possession,[29]—ought they not to understand that they should not vaunt themselves, because they do that to obtain the society of angels, when those men did well-nigh the same thing to preserve the glory of the Romans?

How could these, and whatever like things are found in the Roman history, have become so widely known, and have been proclaimed by so great a fame, had not the Roman empire, extending far and wide, been raised to its greatness by magnificent successes? Therefore, through that empire, so extensive and of so long continuance, so illustrious and glorious also through the virtues of such great men, the reward which they sought was rendered to their earnest aspirations, and also examples are set before us, containing necessary admonition, in order that we may be stung with shame if we shall see that we have not held fast to those virtues for the sake of the most glorious city of God, which are, in whatever way, resembled by those virtues which they held fast for the sake of the glory of a terrestrial city, and that, too, if we shall feel conscious that we have held them fast, we may not be lifted up with pride, because, as the apostle says, "The sufferings of the present time are not worthy to be compared to the glory which shall be revealed in us."[30] But so far as regards human and temporal glory, the lives of these ancient Romans were reckoned sufficiently worthy. Therefore, also, we see, in the light of that truth which, veiled in the Old Testament, is revealed in the New, namely, that it is not in view of terrestrial and temporal benefits, which divine providence grants promiscuously to good and evil, that God is to be worshipped, but in view of eternal life, everlasting gifts, and of the society of the heavenly city itself;—in the light of this truth we see that the Jews were most righteously given as a

[29] Acts 2: 45.
[30] Rom. 8: 18.

trophy to the glory of the Romans; for we see that these Romans, who sought earthly glory, and sought to obtain it by virtues, such as they were, conquered those who, in their great depravity, slew and rejected the giver of true glory, and of the eternal city.

19. Concerning the difference between true glory and the desire of domination.

There is assuredly a difference between the desire of human glory and the desire of domination; for, though he who has an overweening delight in human glory will be also very prone to aspire earnestly after domination, nevertheless they who desire the true glory even of human praise strive not to displease those who judge well of them. For there are many good moral qualities, of which many are competent judges, although they are not possessed by many; and by those good moral qualities those men press on to glory, honour, and domination, of whom Sallust says, "But they press on by the true way."[31]

But whosoever, without possessing that desire of glory which makes one fear to displease those who judge his conduct, desires domination and power, very often seeks to obtain what he loves by most open crimes. Therefore he who desires glory presses on to obtain it either by the true way, or certainly by deceit and artifice, wishing to appear good when he is not. Therefore to him who possesses virtues it is a great virtue to despise glory; for contempt of it is seen by God, but is not manifest to human judgment. For whatever any one does before the eyes of men in order to show himself to be a despiser of glory, if they suspect that he is doing it in order to get greater praise,—that is, greater glory,—he has no means of demonstrating to the perceptions of those who suspect him that the case is really otherwise than they suspect it to be. But he who despises the judgment of praisers, despises also the rashness of suspectors. Their salvation, indeed, he does not despise, if he is truly good; for so great is the righteousness of that man who receives his virtues from the Spirit of God, that he loves his very enemies, and so loves them that

[31] *Cat.* 11.2.

he desires that his haters and detractors may be turned to
righteousness, and become his associates, and that not in an
earthly but in a heavenly country. But with respect to his
praisers, though he sets little value on their praise, he does
not set little value on their love; neither does he elude their
praise, lest he should forfeit their love. And, therefore, he
strives earnestly to have their praises directed to him from
whom every one receives whatever in him is truly praiseworthy. But he who is a despiser of glory, but is greedy of
domination, exceeds the beasts in the vices of cruelty and
luxuriousness. Such, indeed, were certain of the Romans, who,
wanting the love of esteem, wanted not the thirst for domination; and that there were many such, history testifies. But it
was Nero Cæsar who was the first to reach the summit,
and, as it were, the citadel, of this vice; for so great was his
luxuriousness, that one would have thought there was nothing
manly to be dreaded in him, and such his cruelty, that, had
not the contrary been known, no one would have thought
there was anything effeminate in his character. Nevertheless
power and domination are not given even to such men save
by the providence of the most high God, when he judges
that the state of human affairs is worthy of such lords. The
divine utterance is clear on this matter; for the wisdom of
God thus speaks: "By me kings reign, and tyrants possess the
land."[32] But, that it may not be thought that by "tyrants" is
meant, not wicked and impious kings, but brave men, in accordance with the ancient use of the word, as when Vergil
says,

> For know that treaty may not stand
> Where king greets king and joins not hand,[33]

in another place it is most unambiguously said of God, that
he "makes the man who is a hypocrite to reign on account
of the perversity of the people."[34] Therefore, though I have,
according to my ability, shown for what reason God, who
alone is true and just, helped forward the Romans, who were

[32] Prov. 8: 15.
[33] *Aen.* 7.266.
[34] Job 34: 30.

good according to a certain standard of an earthly state, to the acquirement of the glory of so great an empire, there may be, nevertheless, a more hidden cause, known better to God than to us, depending on the diversity of the merits of the human race. Among all who are truly pious, it is at all events agreed that no one without true piety—that is, true worship of the true God—can have true virtue; and that that is not true virtue which is the slave of human praise. Though, nevertheless, they who are not citizens of the eternal city, which is called the city of God in the sacred Scriptures, are more useful to the earthly city when they possess even that virtue than if they had not even that. But there could be nothing more fortunate for human affairs than that, by the mercy of God, they who are endowed with true piety of life, if they have the skill for ruling people, should also have the power. But such men, however great virtues they may possess in this life, attribute them solely to the grace of God since he has helped them—willing, believing, seeking. And, at the same time, they understand how far they are short of that perfection of righteousness which exists in the society of those holy angels for which they are striving to fit themselves. But however much that virtue may be praised and cried up, which without true piety is the slave of human glory, it is not at all to be compared even to the feeble beginnings of the virtue of the saints, whose hope is placed in the grace and mercy of the true God.

20. *That it is as shameful for the virtues to serve human glory as bodily pleasure.*

Philosophers,—who place the end of human good in virtue itself, in order to put to shame certain other philosophers, who indeed approve of the virtues, but measure them all with reference to the end of bodily pleasure, and think that this pleasure is to be sought for its own sake, but the virtues on account of pleasure,—are wont to paint a kind of word-picture, in which Pleasure sits like a luxurious queen on a royal seat, and all the virtues are subjected to her as slaves, watching her nod, that they may do whatever she shall command. She commands Prudence to be ever on the watch to discover how Pleasure may rule, and be safe. Justice she orders to grant what benefits she can, in order to secure those friendships which are necessary for bodily pleasure; to do wrong to no one, lest, on account of the breaking of the laws, Pleasure be not able to live in security. Fortitude she orders to keep her mistress, that is, Pleasure, bravely in her mind, if any affliction befall her body which does not occasion death, in order that by remembrance of former delights she may mitigate the stings of present pain. Temperance she commands to take only a certain quantity even of the most favourite food, lest, through immoderate use, anything should prove hurtful by disturbing the health of the body, and thus Pleasure, which the Epicureans make to consist chiefly in the health of the body, be grievously offended. Thus the virtues, with the whole dignity of their glory, will be the slaves of Pleasure, as of some imperious and disreputable woman.

There is nothing, say our philosophers, more disgraceful and monstrous than this picture, and which the eyes of good men can less endure. And they say the truth. But I do not think that the picture would be sufficiently becoming, even if it were made so that the virtues should be represented as the slaves of human glory; for, though that glory be not a luxurious woman, it is nevertheless puffed up, and has much vanity in it. Therefore it is unworthy of the solidity and firmness of the virtues to represent them as serving this glory, so that Prudence shall provide nothing, Justice distribute nothing, Temperance moderate nothing, except to the end that men may be pleased and vainglory served. Nor will they be able to defend themselves from the charge of such baseness, while they, by way of being despisers of glory, disregard the judgment of other men, seem to themselves wise, and please themselves. For their virtue,—if, indeed, it is virtue at all,—is only in another way subjected to human praise; for he who seeks to please himself seeks still to please man. But he who, with true piety towards God, whom he loves, believes, and hopes in, fixes his attention more on those things in which he displeases himself, than on those things, if there are any such, which please himself, or rather, not himself, but the truth, does not attribute that by which he can now please the truth to anything but to the mercy of him whom he has feared to displease, giving thanks for what in him is healed, and pouring out prayers for the healing of that which is yet unhealed.

21. *That the Roman dominion was granted by him from whom is all power, and by whose providence all things are ruled.*

These things being so, we do not attribute the power of giving kingdoms and empires to any save to the true God, who gives happiness in the kingdom of heaven to the pious alone, but gives kingly power on earth both to the pious and the impious, as it may please him, whose good pleasure is always just. For though we have said something about the principles which guide his administration, in so far as it has seemed good to him to explain it, nevertheless it is too much for us, and far surpasses our strength, to discuss the hidden things of men's hearts, and by a clear examination to determine the merits of various kingdoms. He, therefore, who is the one true God, who never leaves the human race without just judgment and help, gave a kingdom to the Romans when he would, and as great as he would, as he did also to the Assyrians, and even the Persians, by whom, as their own books testify, only two gods are worshipped, the one good and the other evil,—to say nothing concerning the Hebrew people, of whom I have already spoken as much as seemed necessary, who, as long as they were a kingdom, worshipped none save the true God. The same, therefore, who gave to the Persians harvests, though they did not worship the goddess Segetia, who gave the other blessings of the earth, though they did not worship the many gods which the Romans supposed to preside, each one over some particular thing, or even many of them over each several thing,—he, I say, gave the Persians dominion, though they worshipped none of those gods to whom the Romans believed themselves indebted for the empire. And the same is true in respect of men as well as nations. He who gave power to Marius gave it also to Caius Cæsar; he who gave it to Augustus gave it also to Nero; he also who gave it to the most benign emperors, the Vespasians, father and son, gave it also to the cruel Domitian; and, finally, to avoid the necessity of going over them all, he who gave it to the Christian Constantine gave it also to the apostate Julian, whose gifted mind was deceived by a sacrilegious and detestable curiosity, stimulated by the love of power. And it was because he was addicted through curiosity to vain oracles, that, confident of victory, he burned the ships which were laden with the provisions necessary for his army, and therefore, engaging with hot zeal in rashly audacious enterprises, he was soon slain, as the just consequence of his recklessness, and left his army unprovisioned in an enemy's country, and in such a predicament that it never could have escaped, save by altering the boundaries of the Roman empire, in violation of that omen of the god Terminus of which I spoke in the preceding book; for the god Terminus yielded to necessity, though he had not yielded to Jupiter. Manifestly these things are ruled and governed by the one God according as he pleases; and if his motives are hidden, are they therefore unjust?

22. *The durations and issues of war depend on the will of God.*

Thus also the durations of wars are determined by him as he may see meet, according to his righteous will, and pleasure, and mercy, to afflict or to console the human race, so that they are sometimes of longer, sometimes of shorter duration. The war of the Pirates and the third Punic war were terminated with incredible celerity. Also the war of the fugitive gladiators, though in it many Roman generals and the consuls were defeated, and Italy was terribly wasted and ravaged, was nevertheless ended in the third year, having itself been, during its continuance, the end of much. The Picentes, the Marsi, and the Peligni, not distant but Italian nations, after a long and most loyal servitude under the Roman yoke, attempted to raise their heads into liberty, though many nations had now been subjected to the Roman power, and Carthage had been overthrown. In this Italian war the Romans were very often defeated, and two consuls perished, besides other noble senators; nevertheless this calamity was not protracted over a long space of time, for the fifth year put an end to it. But the second Punic war, lasting for the space of eighteen years, and occasioning the greatest disasters and calamities to the republic, wore out and almost consumed the strength of the Romans; for in two battles about seventy thousand Romans fell. The first Punic war was terminated after having been waged for twenty-three years. The Mithridatic war was waged for forty years. And that no one may think that in the early and much praised times of the Romans they were far braver and more able to bring wars to a speedy termination, the Samnite war was protracted for nearly fifty years; and in this war the Romans were so beaten that they were even put under the yoke. But because they did not love glory for the sake of justice, but seemed rather to have loved justice for the sake of glory, they broke the peace and the treaty which had been concluded. These things I mention, because many, ignorant of past things, and some also dissimulating what they know, if in Christian times they see any war protracted a little longer than they expected, straightway make a fierce and insolent attack on our religion, exclaiming that, but for it, the deities would have been supplicated, according to ancient rites; and then, by that bravery of the Romans, which, with the help of Mars and Bellona, speedily brought to an end such great wars, this war also would be speedily terminated. Let them, therefore, who have read history recollect what long-continued wars, having various issues and involving woeful slaughter, were waged by the ancient Romans, in accordance with the general truth that the earth, like the tempestuous deep, is subject to agitations from tempests—tempests of such evils, in various degrees,—and let them sometimes confess what they do not like to admit, and not, by madly speaking against God, destroy themselves and deceive the ignorant.

23. *Concerning the war in which Radagaisus, king of the Goths, a worshipper of demons, was conquered in one day, with all his mighty forces.*

Nevertheless they do not mention with thanksgiving what God has very recently, and within our own memory, wonderfully and mercifully done, but as far as in them lies they attempt, if possible, to bury it in universal oblivion. But if we were to be silent about these things, we should be in like manner ungrateful. When Radagaisus, king of the Goths, having taken up his position very near to the city, with a vast and savage army, was already close upon the Romans, he was in one day so speedily and so thoroughly beaten, that, while not even one Roman was wounded, much less slain, far more than a hundred thousand of his army were prostrated, and he

himself and his sons, having been captured, were forthwith
put to death, suffering the punishment they deserved. For had
so impious a man, with so great and so impious a host, entered the city, whom would he have spared? what tombs of
the martyrs would he have respected? in his treatment of what
person would he have manifested the fear of God? whose
blood would he have refrained from shedding? whose chastity
would he have wished to preserve inviolate? But how loud
would they not have been in the praises of their gods! How
insultingly they would have boasted, saying that Radagaisus
had conquered, that he had been able to achieve such great
things, because he propitiated and won over the gods by daily
sacrifices,—a thing which the Christian religion did not allow
the Romans to do! For when he was approaching to those
places where he was overwhelmed at the nod of the Supreme
Majesty, as his fame was everywhere increasing, it was being
told us at Carthage that the pagans were believing, publishing, and boasting, that he, on account of the help and protection of the gods friendly to him, because of the sacrifices
which he was said to be daily offering to them, would certainly not be conquered by those who were not performing
such sacrifices to the Roman gods, and did not even permit
that they should be offered by any one. And now these
wretched men do not give thanks to God for his great mercy,
who, having determined to chastise the corruption of men,
which was worthy of far heavier chastisement than the corruption of the barbarians, tempered his indignation with such
mildness as, in the first instance, to cause that the king of the
Goths should be conquered in a wonderful manner, lest glory
should accrue to demons, whom he was known to be sup-
plicating, and thus the minds of the weak should be overthrown; and then, afterwards, to cause that, when Rome was
to be taken, it should be taken by those barbarians who,
contrary to any custom of all former wars, protected, through
reverence for the Christian religion, those who fled for refuge
to the sacred places, and who so opposed the demons themselves, and the rites of impious sacrifices, that they seemed to
be carrying on a far more terrible war with them than with
men. Thus did the true Lord and Governor of things both
scourge the Romans mercifully, and, by the marvellous de-

feat of the worshippers of demons, show that those sacrifices were not necessary even for the safety of present things; so that, true religion may not be deserted on account of the urgencies of the present time by those who do not obstinately hold out, but prudently consider the matter, but may be more clung to in most confident expectation of eternal life.

24. *What was the happiness of the Christian emperors, and how far it was true happiness.*

For neither do we say that certain Christian emperors were therefore happy because they ruled a long time, or, dying a peaceful death, left their sons to succeed them in the empire, or subdued the enemies of the republic, or were able both to guard against and to suppress the attempt of hostile citizens rising against them. These and other gifts or comforts of this sorrowful life even certain worshippers of demons have merited to receive, who do not belong to the kingdom of God to which these belong; and this is to be traced to the mercy of God, who would not have those who believe in him desire such things as the highest good. But we say that they are happy if they rule justly; if they are not lifted up amid the praises of those who pay them sublime honours, and the obsequiousness of those who salute them with an excessive humility, but remember that they are men; if they make their power the handmaid of his majesty by using it for the greatest possible extension of his worship; if they fear, love, worship God; if more than their own they love that kingdom in which they are not afraid to have partners; if they are slow to punish, ready to pardon; if they apply that punishment as necessary to government and defence of the republic, and not in order to gratify their own enmity; if they grant pardon, not that iniquity may go unpunished, but with the hope that the transgressor may mend his ways; if they compensate with the lenity of mercy and the liberality of benevolence for whatever severity they may be compelled to decree; if their luxury is as much restrained as it might have been unrestrained; if they prefer to govern depraved desires rather than any nation whatever; and if they do all these things, not through ardent desire of empty glory, but through love of eternal felicity, not neglecting to offer to the true God, who is their God, the sacrifices of humility, contrition, and prayer for their sins. Such Christian emperors, we say, are happy in the present time by hope, and are destined to be so in the enjoyment of the reality itself, when that which we wait for shall have arrived.

25. Concerning the prosperity which God granted to the Christian emperor Constantine.

For the good God, lest men, who believe that he is to be worshipped with a view to eternal life, should think that no one could attain to all this high estate, and to this terrestrial dominion, unless he should be a worshipper of the demons,— supposing that these spirits have great power with respect to such things,—for this reason he gave to the Emperor Constantine, who was not a worshipper of demons, but of the true God himself, such fulness of earthly gifts as no one would even dare wish for. To him also he granted the honour of founding a city, a companion to the Roman empire, the daughter, as it were, of Rome itself, but without any temple or image of the demons. He reigned for a long period as sole emperor, and unaided held and defended the whole Roman world. In conducting and carrying on wars he was most victorious; in overthrowing tyrants he was most successful. He died at a great age, of sickness and old age, and left his sons to succeed him in the empire. But again, lest any emperor should become a Christian in order to merit the happiness of Constantine, when every one should be a Christian for the sake of eternal life, God took away Jovian far sooner than Julian, and permitted that Gratian should be slain by the sword of a tyrant. But in his case there was far more mitigation of the calamity than in the case of the great Pompey, for he could not be avenged by Cato, whom he had left, as it were, heir to the civil war. But Gratian, though pious minds require not such consolations, was avenged by Theodosius, whom he had associated with himself in the empire, though he had a little brother of his own, being more desirous of a faithful alliance than of extensive power.

26. On the faith and piety of Theodosius Augustus.

And on this account, Theodosius not only preserved during the lifetime of Gratian that fidelity which was due to him, but also, after his death, he, like a true Christian, took his little brother Valentinian under his protection, as joint emperor, after he had been expelled by Maximus, the murderer of his father. He guarded him with paternal affection, though he might without any difficulty have got rid of him, who was entirely destitute of all resources, had he been animated with the desire of extensive empire, and not with the ambition of being a benefactor. It was therefore a far greater pleasure to him, when he had adopted the boy, and preserved to him his imperial dignity, to console him by his very humanity and kindness. Afterwards, when that success was rendering Maximus terrible, Theodosius, in the midst of his perplexing anxieties, was not drawn away to follow the suggestions of a sacrilegious and unlawful curiosity, but sent to John, whose abode was in the desert of Egypt,—for he had learned that this servant of God (whose fame was spreading abroad) was endowed with the gift of prophecy,—and from him he received assurance of victory. Immediately the slayer of the tyrant Maximus, with the deepest feelings of compassion and respect, restored the boy Valentinianus to his share in the empire from which he had been driven. Valentinianus being soon after slain by secret assassination, or by some other plot or accident, Theodosius, having again received a response from the prophet, and placing entire confidence in it, marched against the tyrant Eugenius, who had been unlawfully elected to succeed that emperor, and defeated his very powerful army, more by prayer than by the sword. Some soldiers who were at the battle reported to me that all the missiles they were throwing were snatched from their hands by a vehement wind, which blew from the direction of Theodosius' army upon the enemy; nor did it only drive with greater velocity the darts which were hurled against them, but also turned back upon their own bodies the darts which they themselves were throwing. And therefore the poet Claudian, although an alien from the name of Christ, nevertheless says in his praises of him, "O prince, too much beloved by God, for you Æolus pours armed tempests from their caves; for you the air fights, and the winds with one accord obey your bugles."[35]

[35] *De tert. consul. Honorii Aug. Panegyris* 96 ff.

But the victor, as he had believed and predicted, overthrew the statues of Jupiter, which had been, as it were, consecrated by I know not what kind of rites against him, and set up in the Alps. And the thunderbolts of these statues, which were made of gold, he mirthfully and graciously presented to his couriers, who (as the joy of the occasion permitted) were jocularly saying that they would be most happy to be struck by such thunderbolts. The sons of his own enemies, whose fathers had been slain not so much by his orders as by the vehemence of war, having fled for refuge to a church, though they were not yet Christians, he was anxious, taking advantage of the occasion, to bring over to Christianity, and treated them with Christian love. Nor did he deprive them of their property, but, besides allowing them to retain it, bestowed on them additional honours. He did not permit private animosities to affect the treatment of any man after the war. He was not like Cinna, and Marius, and Sylla, and other such men, who wished not to finish civil wars even when they were finished, but rather grieved that they had arisen at all, than wished that when they were finished they should harm any one. Amid all these events, from the very commencement of his reign, he did not cease to help the troubled church which the heretical Valens, favouring the Arians, had vehemently afflicted against the impious by most just and merciful laws. Indeed, he rejoiced more to be a member of this church than he did to be a king upon the earth. The idols of the Gentiles he everywhere ordered to be overthrown, understanding well that not even terrestrial gifts are placed in the power of demons, but in that of the true God. And what could be more admirable than his religious humility, when, compelled by the urgency of certain of his intimates, he avenged the grievous crime of the Thessalonians, which at the prayer of the bishops he had promised to pardon, and, being laid hold of by the discipline of the church, did penance in such a way that the sight of his imperial loftiness prostrated made the people who were interceding for him weep more than the consciousness of offence had made them fear it when enraged? These and other similar good works, which it would be long to tell, he carried with him from this world of time, where the greatest human nobility and loftiness are but vapour. Of these works the reward is eternal happiness, of which God is the giver, though only to those who are sincerely pious. But all other blessings and privileges of this life, as the world itself, light, air, earth, water, fruits, and the soul of man himself, his body, senses, mind, life, he lavishes on good and bad alike. And among these blessings is also to be reckoned the possession of an empire, whose extent he regulates according to the requirements of his providential government at various times. Therefore, I see, we must now answer those who, being confuted and convicted by the most manifest proofs, by which it is shown that for obtaining these terrestrial things, which are all the foolish desire to have, that multitude of false gods is of no use, attempt to assert that the gods are to be worshipped with a view to the interest, not of the present life, but of that which is to come after death. For as to those who, for the sake of the friendship of this world, are willing to worship vanities, and do not grieve that they are left to their puerile understandings, I think they have been sufficiently answered in these five books; of which books, when I had published the first three, and they had begun to come into the hands of many, I heard that certain persons were preparing against them an answer of some kind or other in writing. Then it was told me that they had already written their answer, but were waiting a time when they could publish it without danger. Such persons I would advise not to desire what cannot be of any advantage to them; for it is very easy for a man to seem to himself to have answered arguments, when he has only been unwilling to be silent. For what is more loquacious than vanity? And though it be able, if it like, to shout more loudly than the truth, it is not, for all that, more powerful than the truth. But let men consider diligently all the things that we have said, and if, maybe, judging without party spirit, they shall clearly perceive that they are such things as may rather be shaken than torn up by their most impudent garrulity, and, as it were, satirical and mimic levity, let them restrain their absurdities, and let them choose rather to be corrected by the wise than to be praised by the foolish. For if they are waiting an opportunity, not for liberty to speak the truth, but for licence to revile, may not that befall them which Cicero says concerning some one, "Oh, wretched man! who was at liberty to sin?"[36] Therefore, whoever he is who deems himself happy because of licence to revile, he would be far happier if that were not allowed him at all; for he might all the while, laying aside empty boast, question those to whose views he is opposed in free discussion with them, and hear honourably, gravely, candidly all that can be said by those whom he consults in friendly disputation.

BOOK 22

1. *Of the creation of angels and men.*

As we promised in the immediately preceding book, this, the last of the whole work, shall contain a discussion of the eternal blessedness of the city of God. This blessedness is named eternal, not because it shall endure for many ages, though at last it shall come to an end, but because, according to the words of the gospel, "of his kingdom there shall be no end."[1] Neither shall it enjoy the mere appearance of perpetuity which is maintained by the rise of fresh generations to occupy the place of those that have died out, as in an evergreen the same freshness seems to continue permanently, and the same appearance of dense foliage is preserved by the growth of fresh leaves in place of those that have withered and fallen; but in that city all the citizens shall be immortal, men now for the first time enjoying what the holy angels have never lost. And this shall be accomplished by God, the most almighty founder of the city. For he has promised it, and cannot lie, and has already performed many of his promises, and has done many unpromised kindnesses to those whom he now asks to believe that he will do this also.

For it is he who in the beginning created the world full of all visible and intelligible beings, among which he created nothing better than those spirits whom he endowed with intelligence, and made capable of contemplating and enjoying him, and united in our society, which we call the holy and heavenly

[36] Cf. *Tusc. Disp.* 5.19.
[1] Luke 1: 33.

city, and in which the material of their sustenance and blessedness is God himself, as it were their common food and nourishment. It is he who gave to this intellectual nature free-will of such a kind, that if it wished to forsake God its blessedness, misery should forthwith result. It is he who, when he foreknew that certain angels would in their pride desire to suffice for their own blessedness, and would forsake their great good, did not deprive them of this power, deeming it to be more befitting his power and goodness to bring good out of evil than to prevent the evil from coming into existence. And indeed evil would never have been, if the mutable nature —mutable, though good, and created by the most high God and immutable Good, who created all things good—had not brought evil upon itself by sin. And this its sin is itself proof that its nature was originally good. For if it had not been very good, though not equal to its creator, the desertion of God as its light could not have been an evil to it. For as blindness is a vice of the eye, and this very fact indicates that the eye was created to see the light, and as, consequently, vice itself proves that the eye is more excellent than the other members, because it is capable of light (for on no other supposition would it be a vice of the eye to want light), so the nature, which once enjoyed God, teaches, even by its very vice, that it was created the best of all, since it is now miserable because it does not enjoy God. It is he who with very just punishment doomed the angels who voluntarily fell to everlasting misery, and rewarded those who continued in their attachment to the supreme good with the assurance of endless stability as the reward of their fidelity. It is he who made also man himself upright, with the same freedom of will,—an earthly animal, indeed, but fit for heaven if he remained faithful to his creator, but destined to the misery appropriate to such a nature if he forsook him. It is he who, when he foreknew that man would in his turn sin by abandoning God and breaking his law, did not deprive him of the power of free-will, because he at the same time foresaw what good he himself would bring out of the evil, and how from this mortal race, deservedly and justly condemned, he would by his grace collect, as now he does, a people so numerous, that he thus

fills up and repairs the blank made by the fallen angels, and
that thus that beloved and heavenly city is not defrauded of
the full number of its citizens, but perhaps may even rejoice
in a still more overflowing population.

2. *Of the eternal and unchangeable will of God.*

It is true that wicked men do many things contrary to God's
will; but so great is his wisdom and power, that all things
which seem adverse to his purpose do still tend towards those
just and good ends and issues which he himself has foreknown. And consequently, when God is said to change his
will, as when, e.g., he becomes angry with those to whom he
was gentle, it is rather they than he who are changed, and
they find him changed in so far as their experience of suffering
at his hand is new, as the sun is changed to injured eyes, and
becomes as it were fierce from being mild, and hurtful from
being delightful, though in itself it remains the same as it
was. That also is called the will of God which he does in
the hearts of those who obey his commandments; and of this
the apostle says, "For it is God that works in you even to
will."[2] As God's "righteousness" is used not only of the
righteousness wherewith he himself is righteous, but also of
that which he produces in the man whom he justifies, so also
that is called his law, which, though given by God, is rather
the law of men. For certainly they were men to whom Jesus
said, "It is written in your law,"[3] though in another place
we read, "The law of his God is in his heart."[4] According
to this will which God works in men, he is said also to will
what he himself does not will, but causes his people to will;
as he is said to know what he has caused those to know who
were ignorant of it. For when the apostle says, "But now,
after you have known God, or rather are known of God,"[5]
we cannot suppose that God there for the first time knew
those who were foreknown by him before the foundation of
the world; but he is said to have known them then, because
then he caused them to know. But I remember that I dis-

[2] Phil. 2: 13.
[3] John 8: 17.
[4] Ps. 37: 31.
[5] Gal. 4: 9.

cussed these modes of expression in the preceding books. According to this will, then, by which we say that God wills what he causes to be willed by others, from whom the future is hidden, he wills many things which he does not perform.

Thus his saints, inspired by his holy will, desire many things which never happen. They pray, e.g., for certain individuals —they pray in a pious and holy manner—but what they request he does not perform, though he himself by his own Holy Spirit has made in them this will to pray. And consequently, when the saints, in conformity with God's mind, will and pray that all men be saved, we can use this mode of expression: God wills and does not perform,—meaning that he who causes them to will these things himself wills them. But if we speak of that will of his which is eternal as his foreknowledge, certainly he has already done all things in heaven and on earth that he has willed,—not only past and present things, but even things still future. But before the arrival of that time in which he has willed the occurrence of what he foreknew and arranged before all time, we say, it will happen when God wills. But if we are ignorant not only of the time in which it is to be, but even whether it shall be at all, we say, it will happen if God wills,—not because God will then have a new will which he had not before, but because that event, which from eternity has been prepared in his unchangeable will, shall then come to pass.

3. Of the promise of eternal blessedness to the saints, and everlasting punishment to the wicked.

Therefore, not to mention many other instances besides, as we now see in Christ the fulfilment of that which God promised to Abraham when he said, "In your seed shall all nations be blessed,"[6] so this also shall be fulfilled which he promised to the same race, when he said by the prophet, "They that are in their sepulchres shall rise again;"[7] and also, "There shall be a new heaven and a new earth: and they shall not remember former things, and nothing shall come into their mind; but they shall find joy and rejoicing: for I will make Jerusalem a rejoicing, and my people a joy. And I will rejoice

[6] Gen. 22: 18.
[7] Is. 26: 19.

in Jerusalem, and joy in my people, and the voice of weeping shall be no more heard in her."[8] And by another prophet he uttered the same prediction: "At that time your people shall be delivered, every one that shall be found written in the book. And many of them that sleep in the dust" (or, as some interpret it, "in the mound") "of the earth shall awake, some to everlasting life, and some to shame and everlasting contempt."[9] And in another place by the same prophet: "The saints of the Most High shall take the kingdom, and shall possess the kingdom for ever, even for ever and ever."[10] And a little after he says, "His kingdom is an everlasting kingdom."[11] Other prophecies referring to the same subject I have advanced in the twentieth book, and others still which I have not advanced are found written in the same Scriptures; and these predictions shall be fulfilled, as those also have been which unbelieving men supposed would be unfulfilled. For it is the same God who promised both, and predicted that both would come to pass,—the God whom the pagan deities tremble before, as even Porphyry, the noblest of pagan philosophers, testifies.

4. *Against the wise men of the world, who fancy that the earthly bodies of men cannot be transferred to a heavenly habitation.*

But men who use their learning and intellectual ability to resist the force of that great authority which, in fulfilment of what was so long before predicted, has converted all races of men to faith and hope in its promises, seem to themselves to argue acutely against the resurrection of the body while they cite what Cicero mentions in the third book of the *De Republica*. For when he was asserting the apotheosis of Hercules and Romulus, he says: "Whose bodies were not taken up into heaven; for nature would not permit a body of earth to exist anywhere except upon earth." This, indeed, is the profound reasoning of the wise men, whose thoughts God knows are vain. For if we were only souls, that is, spirits without any body, and if we dwelt in heaven and had no knowledge

8 Is. 65: 17–19.
9 Dan. 12: 1 f.
10 Dan. 7: 18.
11 Dan. 7: 27.

of earthly animals, and were told that we should be bound
to earthly bodies by some wonderful bond of union, and
should animate them, should we not much more vigorously
refuse to believe this, and maintain that nature would not
permit an incorporeal substance to be held by a corporeal
bond? And yet the earth is full of living spirits, to which
terrestrial bodies are bound, and with which they are in a
wonderful way implicated. If, then, the same God who has
created such beings wills this also, what is to hinder the
earthly body from being raised to a heavenly body, since a
spirit, which is more excellent than all bodies, and consequently than even a heavenly body, has been tied to an
earthly body? If so small an earthly particle has been able to
hold in union with itself something better than a heavenly
body, so as to receive sensation and life, will heaven disdain
to receive, or at least to retain, this sentient and living particle,
which derives its life and sensation from a substance more
excellent than any heavenly body? If this does not happen
now, it is because the time is not yet come which has been
determined by him who has already done a much more marvellous thing than that which these men refuse to believe.
For why do we not more intensely wonder that incorporeal
souls, which are of higher rank than heavenly bodies, are
bound to earthly bodies, rather than that bodies, although
earthly, are exalted to an abode which, though heavenly, is
yet corporeal, except because we have been accustomed to see
this, and indeed are this, while we are not as yet that other
marvel, nor have as yet ever seen it? Certainly, if we consult sober reason, the more wonderful of the two divine works
is found to be to attach somehow corporeal things to incorporeal, and not to connect earthly things with heavenly,
which, though diverse, are yet both of them corporeal.

5. *Of the resurrection of the flesh, which some refuse to believe,
though the world at large believes it.*

But granting that this was once incredible, behold, now, the
world has come to the belief that the earthly body of Christ
was received up into heaven. Already both the learned and
unlearned have believed in the resurrection of the flesh and
its ascension to the heavenly places, while only a very few

either of the educated or uneducated are still staggered by it. If this is a credible thing which is believed, then let those who do not believe see how stubborn they are; and if it is incredible, then this also is an incredible thing, that what is incredible should have received such credit. Here then we have two incredibles,—to wit, the resurrection of our body to eternity, and that the world should believe so incredible a thing; and both these incredibles the same God predicted should come to pass before either had as yet occurred. We see that already one of the two has come to pass, for the world has believed what was incredible; why should we despair that the remaining one shall also come to pass, and that this which the world believed, though it was incredible, shall itself occur? For already that which was equally incredible has come to pass, in the world's believing an incredible thing. Both were incredible: the one we see accomplished, the other we believe shall be; for both were predicted in those same Scriptures by means of which the world believed. And the very manner in which the world's faith was won is found to be even more incredible, if we consider it. Men uninstructed in any branch of a liberal education, without any of the refinement of heathen learning, unskilled in grammar, not armed with dialectic, not adorned with rhetoric, but plain fishermen, and very few in number,—these were the men whom Christ sent with the nets of faith to the sea of this world, and thus took out of every race so many fishes, and even the philosophers themselves, wonderful as they are rare. Let us add, if you please, or because you ought to be pleased, this third incredible thing to the two former. And now we have three incredibles, all of which have nevertheless come to pass. It is incredible that Jesus Christ should have risen in the flesh and ascended with flesh into heaven; it is incredible that the world should have believed so incredible a thing; it is incredible that a very few men, of mean birth and the lowest rank, and no education, should have been able so effectually to persuade the world, and even its learned men, of so incredible a thing. Of these three incredibles, the parties with whom we are debating refuse to believe the first; they cannot refuse to see the second, which they are unable to account for if they do not believe the third. It is indubitable that the resurrection of Christ, and his ascension into heaven with the flesh in which he rose, is already preached and believed in the whole world. If it is not credible, how is it that it has already received credence in the whole world? If a number of noble, exalted, and learned men had said that they had witnessed it, and had been at pains to publish what they had witnessed, it would not be wonderful that the world should have believed it, but it would be very stubborn to refuse credence; but if, as is true, the world has believed a few obscure, inconsiderable, uneducated persons, who state and write that they witnessed it, is it not unreasonable that a handful of wrong-headed men should oppose themselves to the creed of the whole world, and refuse their belief? And if the world has put faith in a small number of men, of mean birth and the lowest rank, and no education, it is because the divinity of the thing itself appeared all the more manifestly in such contemptible witnesses. The eloquence, indeed, which lent persuasion to their message, consisted of wonderful works, not words. For they who had not seen Christ risen in the flesh, nor ascending into heaven with his risen body, believed those who related how they had seen these things, and who testified not only with words but wonderful signs. For they marvelled to hear men whom they knew to be acquainted with only one, or at most two languages, speaking in the tongues of all nations. They saw a man, lame from his mother's womb, after forty years stand up healed by their word in the name of Christ; that handkerchiefs taken from their bodies had virtue to heal the sick; that countless persons, sick of various diseases, were laid in a row in the road where they were to pass, that their shadow might fall on them as they walked, and that they straightway received health; that many other stupendous miracles were done by them in the name of Christ; and, finally, that they even raised the dead. If it be admitted that these things occurred as they are related, then we have a multitude of incredible things to add to those three incredibles. That the one incredibility of the resurrection and ascension of Jesus Christ may be believed, we accumulate the testimonies of countless incredible miracles, but even so we do not bend the frightful obstinacy of these sceptics. But if they do not believe that these miracles were done by Christ's

apostles to gain credence for their preaching of his resurrection and ascension, this one grand miracle suffices for
us, that the whole world has believed without any miracles.

6. *That Rome made its founder Romulus a god because it loved
him; but the church loved Christ because it believed him to
be God.*

Let us here recite the passage in which Cicero expresses his
astonishment that the apotheosis of Romulus should have been
credited. I shall insert his words as they stand: "It is most
worthy of remark in Romulus, that other men who are said to
have become gods lived in less educated ages, when there was
a greater propensity to the fabulous, and when the uninstructed were easily persuaded to believe anything. But the
age of Romulus was barely six hundred years ago, and already
literature and science had dispelled the errors that attach to
an uncultured age." And a little later he says of the same
Romulus words to this effect: "From this we may perceive
that Homer had flourished long before Romulus, and that
there was now so much learning in individuals, and so generally diffused an enlightenment, that scarcely any room was
left for fable. For antiquity admitted fables, and sometimes
even very clumsy ones; but this age [of Romulus] was sufficiently enlightened to reject whatever had not the air of
truth."[12] Thus one of the most learned men, and certainly
the most eloquent, M. Tullius Cicero, says that it is surprising
that the divinity of Romulus was believed in, because the
times were already so enlightened that they would not accept
a fabulous fiction. But who believed that Romulus was a god
except Rome, which was itself small and in its infancy? Then
afterwards it was necessary that succeeding generations should
preserve the tradition of their ancestors; that, drinking in this
superstition with their mother's milk, the state might grow
and come to such power that it might dictate this belief, as
from a point of vantage, to all the nations over whom its
sway extended. And these nations, though they might not
believe that Romulus was a god, at least said so, that they
might not give offence to their sovereign state by refusing
to give its founder that title which was given him by Rome,

[12] *De Rep.* 2.18 f.

which had adopted this belief, not by a love of error, but an error of love. But though Christ is the founder of the heavenly and eternal city, yet it did not believe him to be God because it was founded by him, but rather it is founded by him, in virtue of its belief. Rome, after it had been built and dedicated, worshipped its founder in a temple as a god; but this Jerusalem laid Christ, its God, as its foundation, that the building and dedication might proceed. The former city loved its founder, and therefore believed him to be a god; the latter believed Christ to be God, and therefore loved him. There was an antecedent cause for the love of the former city, and for its believing that even a false dignity attached to the object of its love; so there was an antecedent cause for the belief of the latter, and for its loving the true dignity which a proper faith, not a rash surmise, ascribed to its object. For, not to mention the multitude of very striking miracles which proved that Christ is God, there were also divine prophecies heralding him, prophecies most worthy of belief, which being already accomplished, we have not, like our fathers, to wait for their verification. Of Romulus, on the other hand, and of his building Rome and reigning in it, we read or hear the narrative of what did take place, not prediction which beforehand said that such things should be. And so far as his reception among the gods is concerned, history only records that this was believed, and does not state it as a fact; for no miraculous signs testified to the truth of this. For as to that wolf which is said to have nursed the twin-brothers, and which is considered a great marvel, how does this prove him to have been divine? For even supposing that this nurse was a real wolf and not a mere courtezan, yet she nursed both brothers, and Remus is not reckoned a god. Besides, what was there to hinder any one from asserting that Romulus or Hercules, or any such man, was a god? Or who would rather choose to die than profess belief in his divinity? And did a single nation worship Romulus among its gods, unless it were forced through fear of the Roman name? But who can number the multitudes who have chosen death in the most cruel shapes rather than deny the divinity of Christ? And thus the dread of some slight indignation, which it was supposed, perhaps groundlessly, might exist in the minds of the Romans,

constrained some states who were subject to Rome to worship
Romulus as a god; whereas the dread, not of a slight mental
shock, but of severe and various punishments, and of death
itself, the most formidable of all, could not prevent an immense multitude of martyrs throughout the world from not
merely worshipping but also confessing Christ as God. The
city of Christ, which, although as yet a stranger upon earth,
had countless hosts of citizens, did not make war upon its
godless persecutors for the sake of temporal security, but
preferred to win eternal salvation by abstaining from war.
Its citizens were bound, imprisoned, beaten, tortured, burned,
torn in pieces, massacred, and yet they multiplied. It was not
given to them to fight for their eternal salvation except by
despising their temporal salvation for their Saviour's sake.

I am aware that Cicero, in the third book of his *De Republica,* if I mistake not, argues that a first-rate power will not
engage in war except either for honour or for safety. What
he has to say about the question of safety, and what he means
by safety, he explains in another place, saying, "Private persons frequently evade, by a speedy death, destitution, exile,
bonds, the scourge, and the other pains which even the most
insensible feel. But to states, death, which seems to emanci-
pate individuals from all punishments, is itself a punishment;
for a state should be so constituted as to be eternal. And
thus death is not natural to a republic as to a man, to whom
death is not only necessary, but often even desirable. But
when a state is destroyed, obliterated, annihilated, it is as if
(to compare great things with small) this whole world perished and collapsed."[13] Cicero said this because he, with the
Platonists, believed that the world would not perish. It is
therefore agreed that, according to Cicero, a state should
engage in war for the safety which preserves the state permanently in existence, though its citizens change; as the foliage of an olive or laurel, or any tree of this kind, is perennial,
the old leaves being replaced by fresh ones. For death, as he
says, is no punishment to individuals, but rather delivers them
from all other punishments, but it is a punishment to the state.
And therefore it is reasonably asked whether the Saguntines

[13] *De Rep.* 3. frg. 34.

did right when they chose that their whole state should perish rather than that they should break faith with the Roman republic; for this deed of theirs is applauded by the citizens of the earthly republic. But I do not see how they could follow the advice of Cicero, who tells us that no war is to be undertaken save for safety or for honour; neither does he say which of these two is to be preferred, if a case should occur in which the one could not be preserved without the loss of the other. For manifestly, if the Saguntines chose safety, they must break faith; if they kept faith, they must reject safety; as also it fell out. But the safety of the city of God is such that it can be retained, or rather acquired, by faith and with faith; but if faith be abandoned, no one can attain it. It is this thought of a most constant and patient spirit that has made so many noble martyrs, while Romulus has not had, and could not have, so much as one to die for his divinity.

7. *That the world's belief in Christ is the result of divine power, not of human persuasion.*

But it is thoroughly ridiculous to make mention of the false divinity of Romulus as any way comparable to that of Christ. Nevertheless, if Romulus lived about six hundred years before Cicero, in an age which already was so enlightened that it rejected all impossibilities, how much more, in an age which certainly was more enlightened, being six hundred years later, the age of Cicero himself, and of the emperors Augustus and Tiberius, would the human mind have refused to listen to or believe in the resurrection of Christ's body and its ascension into heaven, and have scouted it as an impossibility, if the divinity of the truth itself, or the truth of the divinity, and corroborating miraculous signs, had not proved that it could happen and had happened? Through virtue of these testimonies, and notwithstanding the opposition and terror of so many cruel persecutions, the resurrection and immortality of the flesh, first in Christ, and subsequently in all in the new generation, was believed, was intrepidly proclaimed, and was sown over the whole world, to be fertilized richly with the blood of the martyrs. For the predictions of the prophets that had preceded the events were read, they were corroborated by powerful signs, and the truth was seen to be not

contradictory to reason, but only different from customary
ideas, so that at length the world embraced the faith it had
furiously persecuted.

8. *Of miracles which were done that the world might believe in
Christ, and which have not ceased since the world believed.*

Why, they say, are those miracles, which you affirm were
done formerly, done no longer? I might, indeed, reply that
miracles were necessary before the world believed, in order
that it might believe. And whoever now-a-days demands to
see prodigies that he may believe, is himself a great prodigy,
because he does not believe, though the whole world does.
But they make these objections for the sole purpose of in-
sinuating that even those former miracles were never done.
How, then, is it that everywhere Christ is celebrated with
such firm belief in his resurrection and ascension? How is it
that in enlightened times, in which every impossibility is rejected, the world has, without any miracles, believed things
marvellously incredible? Or will they say that these things
were credible, and therefore were credited? Why then do
they themselves not believe? Our argument, therefore, is a
summary one—either incredible things which were not witnessed have caused the world to believe other incredible things
which both occurred and were witnessed, or this matter was
so credible that it needed no miracles in proof of it, and therefore convicts these unbelievers of unpardonable scepticism.
This I might say for the sake of refuting these most frivolous
objectors. But we cannot deny that many miracles were done
to confirm that one grand and health-giving miracle of
Christ's ascension to heaven with the flesh in which he rose.
For these most trustworthy books of ours contain in one
narrative both the miracles that were done and the creed
which they were done to confirm. The miracles were published that they might produce faith, and the faith which they
produced brought them into greater prominence. For they
are read in congregations that they may be believed, and
yet they would not be so read unless they were believed.
For even now miracles are done in the name of Christ,
whether by his sacraments or by the prayers or relics of his
saints; but they are not so brilliant and conspicuous as to

cause them to be published with such glory as accompanied the former miracles. For the canon of the sacred writings which had to be fixed, causes those to be everywhere recited, and to sink into the memory of all the congregations; but these modern miracles are scarcely known even to the whole population in the midst of which they are done, and at the best are confined to one spot. For frequently they are known only to a very few persons, while all the rest are ignorant of them, especially if the state is a large one; and when they are reported to other persons in other localities, there is no sufficient authority to give them prompt and unwavering credence, although they are reported to the faithful by the faithful.

The miracle which was done at Milan when I was there, and by which a blind man was restored to sight, could come to the knowledge of many; for not only is the city a large one, but also the emperor was there at the time, and the occurrence was witnessed by an immense concourse of people that had gathered to the bodies of the martyrs Protasius and Gervasius, which had long lain concealed and unknown, but were now made known to the bishop Ambrose in a dream, and discovered by him. By virtue of these relics the darkness of that blind man was scattered, and he saw the light of day.

But who but a very small number are aware of the cure which was done upon Innocentius, ex-advocate of the deputy prefecture, a cure done at Carthage, in my presence, and under my own eyes? For when I and my colleague Alypius, who were not yet clergymen, though already servants of God, came from abroad, this man received us, and made us live with him, for he and all his household were devotedly pious. He was being treated by medical men for fistulæ, of which he had a large number intricately seated in the rectum. He had already undergone an operation, and the surgeons were using every means at their command for his relief. In that operation he had suffered long-continued and acute pain; yet, among the many folds of the gut, one had escaped the operators so entirely, that, though they ought to have laid it open with the knife, they never touched it. And thus, though all those that had been opened were cured, this one remained as it was, and frustrated all their labour. The patient, having his suspicions awakened by the delay thus occasioned, and fearing greatly a second operation, which another medical man—one of his own domestics—had told him he must undergo, though this man had not even been allowed to witness the first operation, and had been banished from the house, and with difficulty allowed to come back to his enraged master's presence,—the patient, I say, broke out to the surgeons, saying, "Are you going to cut me again? Are you, after all, to fulfil the prediction of that man whom you would not allow even to be present?" The surgeons laughed at the unskilful doctor, and soothed their patient's fears with fair words and promises. So several days passed, and yet nothing they tried did him good. Still they persisted in promising that they would cure that fistula by drugs, without the knife. They called in also another old practitioner of great repute in that department, Ammonius (for he was still alive at that time); and he, after examining the part, promised the same result as themselves from their care and skill. On this great authority, the patient became confident, and, as if already well, vented his good spirits in facetious remarks at the expense of his domestic physician, who had predicted a second operation. To make a long story short, after a number of days had thus uselessly elapsed, the surgeons, wearied and confused, had at last to confess that he could only be cured by the knife. Agitated with excessive fear, he was terrified, and grew pale with dread; and when he collected himself and was able to speak, he ordered them to go away and never to return. Worn out with weeping, and driven by necessity, it occurred to him to call in an Alexandrian, who was at that time esteemed a wonderfully skilful operator, that he might perform the operation his rage would not suffer them to do. But when he had come, and examined with a professional eye the traces of their careful work, he acted the part of a good man, and persuaded his patient to allow those same hands the satisfaction of finishing his cure which had begun it with a skill that excited his admiration, adding that there was no doubt his only hope of a cure was by an operation, but that it was thoroughly inconsistent with his nature to win the credit of the cure by doing the little that remained to be done, and rob of their reward men whose consummate skill,

care, and diligence he could not but admire when he saw
the traces of their work. They were therefore again received
to favour; and it was agreed that, in the presence of the
Alexandrian, they should operate on the fistula, which, by the
consent of all, could now only be cured by the knife. The
operation was deferred till the following day. But when they
had left, there arose in the house such a wailing, in sympathy
with the excessive despondency of the master, that it seemed
to us like the mourning at a funeral, and we could scarcely
repress it. Holy men were in the habit of visiting him daily;
Saturninus of blessed memory, at that time bishop of Uzali,
and the priest Gelosus, and the deacons of the church of
Carthage; and among these was the bishop Aurelius, who
alone of them all survives,—a man to be named by us with due
reverence,—and with him I have often spoken of this affair,
as we conversed together about the wonderful works of God,
and I have found that he distinctly remembers what I am
now relating. When these persons visited him that evening
according to their custom, he besought them, with pitiable
tears, that they would do him the honour of being present next
day at what he judged his funeral rather than his suffering.
For such was the terror his former pains had produced, that
he made no doubt he would die in the hands of the surgeons.
They comforted him, and exhorted him to put his trust in
God, and nerve his will like a man. Then we went to prayer;
but while we, in the usual way, were kneeling and bending
to the ground, he cast himself down, as if some one were
hurling him violently to the earth, and began to pray; but in
what a manner, with what earnestness and emotion, with what
a flood of tears, with what groans and sobs, that shook his
whole body, and almost prevented him speaking, who can
describe! Whether the others prayed, and had not their attention wholly diverted by this conduct, I do not know. For
myself, I could not pray at all. This only I briefly said in my
heart: "O Lord, what prayers of your people do you hear
if you hear not these?" For it seemed to me that nothing
could be added to this prayer, unless he expired in praying.
We rose from our knees, and, receiving the blessing of the
bishop, departed, the patient beseeching his visitors to be present next morning, they exhorting him to keep up his heart.

The dreaded day dawned. The servants of God were present, as they had promised to be; the surgeons arrived; all that the circumstances required was ready; the frightful instruments are produced; all look on in wonder and suspense. While those who have most influence with the patient are cheering his fainting spirit, his limbs are arranged on the couch so as to suit the hand of the operator; the knots of the bandages are untied; the part is bared; the surgeon examines it, and, with knife in hand, eagerly looks for the abscess that is to be cut. He searches for it with his eyes; he feels for it with his finger; he applies every kind of scrutiny: he finds a perfectly firm cicatrix! No words of mine can describe the joy, and praise, and thanksgiving to the merciful and almighty God which was poured from the lips of all, with tears of gladness. Let the scene be imagined rather than described!

In the same city of Carthage lived Innocentia, a very devout woman of the highest rank in the state. She had cancer in one of her breasts, a disease which, as physicians say, is incurable. Ordinarily, therefore, they either amputate, and so separate from the body the member on which the disease has seized, or, that the patient's life may be prolonged a little, though death is inevitable even if somewhat delayed, they abandon all remedies, following, as they say, the advice of Hippocrates. This the lady we speak of had been advised to by a skilful physician, who was intimate with her family; and she betook herself to God alone by prayer. On the approach of Easter, she was instructed in a dream to wait for the first woman that came out from the baptistery after being baptized, and to ask her to make the sign of Christ upon her sore. She did so, and was immediately cured. The physician who had advised her to apply no remedy if she wished to live a little longer, when he had examined her after this, and found that she who, on his former examination, was afflicted with that disease was now perfectly cured, eagerly asked her what remedy she had used, anxious, as we may well believe, to discover the drug which should defeat the decision of Hippocrates. But when she told him what had happened, he is said to have replied, with religious politeness, though with a contemptuous tone, and an expression which made her fear he would utter some blasphemy against Christ, "I thought you would make some great discovery to me." She, shuddering at his indifference, quickly replied, "What great thing was it for Christ to heal a cancer, who raised one who had been four days dead?" When, therefore, I had heard this, I was extremely indignant that so great a miracle, done in that well-known city, and on a person who was certainly not obscure, should not be divulged, and I considered that she should be spoken to, if not reprimanded on this score. And when she replied to me that she had not kept silence on the subject, I asked the women with whom she was best acquainted whether they had ever heard of this before. They told me they knew nothing of it. "See," I said, "what your not keeping silence amounts to, since not even those who are so familiar with you know of it." And as I had only briefly heard the story, I made her tell how the whole thing happened, from beginning to end, while the other women listened in great astonishment, and glorified God.

A gouty doctor of the same city, when he had given in his name for baptism, and had been prohibited the day before his baptism from being baptized that year, by black woolly-haired boys who appeared to him in his dreams, and whom he understood to be devils, and when, though they trod on his feet, and inflicted the acutest pain he had ever yet experienced, he refused to obey them, but overcame them, and would not defer being washed in the font of regeneration, was relieved in the very act of baptism, not only of the extraordinary pain he was tortured with, but also of the disease itself, so that, though he lived a long time afterwards, he never suffered from gout; and yet who knows of this miracle? We, however, do know it, and so, too, do the small number of brethren who were in the neighbourhood, and to whose ears it might come.

An old comedian of Curubis was cured at baptism not only of paralysis, but also of hernia, and, being delivered from both afflictions, came up out of the font of regeneration as if he had had nothing wrong with his body. Who outside of Curubis knows of this, or who but a very few who might hear it elsewhere? But we, when we heard of it, made the man come to Carthage, by order of the holy bishop Aurelius,

although we had already ascertained the fact on the information of persons whose word we could not doubt.

Hesperius, of a tribunician family, and a neighbour of our
own, has a farm called Zubedi in the Fussalian district; and,
finding that his family, his cattle, and his servants were suffering from the malice of evil spirits, he asked our priests,
during my absence, that one of them would go with him
and banish the spirits by his prayers. One went, offered there
the sacrifice of the body of Christ, praying with all his might
that that vexation might cease. It did cease straightway,
through God's mercy. Now he had received from a friend
of his own some holy earth brought from Jerusalem, where
Christ, having been buried, rose again the third day. This
earth he had hung up in his bedroom to preserve himself
from harm. But when his house was purged of that demoni-
acal invasion, he began to consider what should be done
with the earth; for his reverence for it made him unwilling
to have it any longer in his bedroom. It so happened that
I and Maximinus bishop of Synita, and then my colleague,
were in the neighbourhood. Hesperius asked us to visit him,
and we did so. When he had related all the circumstances,
he begged that the earth might be buried somewhere, and
that the spot should be made a place of prayer where Christians might assemble for the worship of God. We made no
objection: it was done as he desired. There was in that neighbourhood a young countryman who was paralytic, who, when
he heard of this, begged his parents to take him without delay
to that holy place. When he had been brought there, he
prayed, and immediately went away on his own feet perfectly
cured.

There is a country-seat called Victoriana, less than thirty
miles from Hippo Regius. At it there is a monument to the
Milanese martyrs, Protasius and Gervasius. There a young
man was carried, who, when he was watering his horse one
summer day at noon in a pool of a river, had been taken
possession of by a devil. As he lay at the monument, near
death, or even quite like a dead person, the lady of the manor,
with her maids and religious attendants, entered the place
for evening prayer and praise, as her custom was, and they
began to sing hymns. At this sound the young man, as if

electrified, was thoroughly aroused, and with frightful scream-
ing seized the altar, and held it as if he did not dare or were
not able to let it go, and as if he were fixed or tied to it; and
the devil in him, with loud lamentation, besought that he
might be spared, and confessed where and when and how
he took possession of the youth. At last, declaring that he
would go out of him, he named one by one the parts of his
body which he threatened to mutilate as he went out; and
with these words he departed from the man. But his eye,
falling out on his cheek, hung by a slender vein as by a root,
and the whole of the pupil which had been black became
white. When this was witnessed by those present (others too
had now gathered to his cries, and had all joined in prayer
for him), although they were delighted that he had recovered
his sanity of mind, yet, on the other hand, they were grieved
about his eye, and said he should seek medical advice. But
his sister's husband, who had brought him there, said, "God,
who has banished the devil, is able to restore his eye at the
prayers of his saints." Then he replaced the eye that was
fallen out and hanging, and bound it in its place with his
handkerchief as well as he could, and advised him not to
loose the bandage for seven days. When he did so, he found
it quite healthy. Others also were cured there, but of them it
would be tedious to speak.

I know that a young woman of Hippo was immediately
dispossessed of a devil, on anointing herself with oil mixed
with the tears of the priest who had been praying for her.
I know also that a bishop once prayed for a demoniac young
man whom he never saw, and that he was cured on the spot.

There was a fellow-townsman of ours at Hippo, Florentius,
an old man, religious and poor, who supported himself as a
tailor. Having lost his coat, and not having means to buy
another, he prayed to the Twenty Martyrs, who have a very
celebrated memorial shrine in our town, begging in a distinct
voice that he might be clothed. Some scoffing young men,
who happened to be present, heard him, and followed him
with their sarcasm as he went away, as if he had asked the
martyrs for fifty pence to buy a coat. But he, walking on in
silence, saw on the shore a great fish, gasping as if just cast
up, and having secured it with the good-natured assistance of

the youths, he sold it for curing to a cook of the name of
Catosus, a good Christian man, telling him how he had come
by it, and receiving for it three hundred pence, which he laid
out in wool, that his wife might exercise her skill upon, and
make into a coat for him. But, on cutting up the fish, the
cook found a gold ring in its belly; and forthwith, moved
with compassion, and influenced, too, by religious fear, gave
it up to the man, saying, "See how the Twenty Martyrs have
clothed you."

When the bishop Projectus was bringing the relics of the
most glorious martyr Stephen to the waters of Tibilis, a great
concourse of people came to meet him at the shrine. There
a blind woman entreated that she might be led to the bishop
who was carrying the relics. She gave him the flowers she
was carrying. She took them back, applied them to her eyes,
and straightway saw. Those who were present were astounded,
while she, with every expression of joy, preceded them, pursuing her way without further need of a guide.

Lucillus bishop of Sinita, in the neighbourhood of the
colonial town of Hippo, was carrying in procession some relics
of the same martyr, which had been deposited in the castle
of Sinita. A fistula under which he had long laboured, and
which his private physician was watching an opportunity to
cut, was suddenly cured by the mere carrying of that sacred
burden,—at least, afterwards there was no trace of it in his
body.

Eucharius, a Spanish priest, residing at Calama, was for a
long time a sufferer from stone. By the relics of the same martyr, which the bishop Possidius brought him, he was cured.
Afterwards the same priest, sinking under another disease, was
lying dead, and already they were binding his hands. By the
help of the same martyr he was raised to life, the priest's cloak
having been brought from the oratory and laid upon the
corpse.

There was there an old nobleman named Martial, who had
a great aversion to the Christian religion, but whose daughter
was a Christian, while her husband had been baptized that
same year. When he was ill, they besought him with tears and
prayers to become a Christian, but he positively refused, and
dismissed them from his presence in a storm of indignation.

It occurred to the son-in-law to go to the oratory of St. Stephen, and there pray for him with all earnestness that God might give him a right mind, so that he should not delay believing in Christ. This he did with great groaning and tears, and the burning fervour of sincere piety; then, as he left the place, he took some of the flowers that were lying there, and, as it was already night, laid them by his father's head, and then slept. And lo! before dawn, the old man cries out for some one to run for the bishop; but he happened at that time to be with me at Hippo. So when he had heard that he was absent, he asked the priests to come. They came. To the joy and amazement of all, he declared that he believed, and he was baptized. As long as he remained in life, these words were ever on his lips: "Christ, receive my spirit," though he was not aware that these were the last words of the most blessed Stephen when he was stoned by the Jews. They were his last words also, for not long after he himself also gave up the ghost.

There, too, by the same martyr, two men, one a citizen, the other a stranger, were cured of gout; but while the citizen was absolutely cured, the stranger was only informed what he should apply when the pain returned; and when he followed this advice, the pain was at once relieved.

Audurus is the name of an estate, where there is a church that contains a memorial shrine of the martyr Stephen. It happened that, as a little boy was playing in the court, the oxen drawing a waggon went out of the track and crushed him with the wheel, so that immediately he seemed at his last gasp. His mother snatched him up, and laid him at the shrine, and not only did he revive, but also appeared uninjured.

A religious woman, who lived at Caspalium, a neighbouring estate, when she was so ill as to be despaired of, had her dress brought to this shrine, but before it was brought back she was gone. However, her parents wrapped her corpse in the dress, and, her breath returning, she became quite well.

At Hippo a Syrian called Bassus was praying at the relics of the same martyr for his daughter, who was dangerously ill. He too had brought her dress with him to the shrine. But as he prayed, behold, his servants ran from the house to tell him she was dead. His friends, however, intercepted them, and

forbade them to tell him, lest he should bewail her in public.
And when he had returned to his house, which was already
ringing with the lamentations of his family, and had thrown
on his daughter's body the dress he was carrying, she was restored to life.

There, too, the son of a man, Irenæus, one of our tax-
gatherers, took ill and died. And while his body was lying lifeless, and the last rites were being prepared, amidst the weeping and mourning of all, one of the friends who were consoling
the father suggested that the body should be anointed with the
oil[14] of the same martyr. It was done, and he revived.

Likewise Eleusinus, a man of tribunician rank among us,
laid his infant son, who had died, on the shrine of the martyr,
which is in the suburb where he lived, and, after prayer, which
he poured out there with many tears, he took up his child
alive.

What am I to do? I am so pressed by the promise of finishing this work, that I cannot record all the miracles I know;
and doubtless several of our adherents, when they read what
I have narrated, will regret that I have omitted so many which
they, as well as I, certainly know. Even now I beg these persons to excuse me, and to consider how long it would take
me to relate all those miracles, which the necessity of finishing
the work I have undertaken forces me to omit. For were I
to be silent of all others, and to record exclusively the miracles
of healing which were wrought in the district of Calama and
of Hippo by means of this martyr—I mean the most glorious
Stephen—they would fill many volumes; and yet all even of
these could not be collected, but only those of which narratives
have been written for public recital. For when I saw, in our
own times, frequent signs of the presence of divine powers
similar to those which had been given of old, I desired that
narratives might be written, judging that the multitude should
not remain ignorant of these things. It is not yet two years
since these relics were first brought to Hippo Regius, and
though many of the miracles which have been done by them
have not, as I have the most certain means of knowing, been
recorded, those which have been published amount to almost

[14] I.e., of the lamp before his shrine.

seventy at the hour at which I write. But at Calama, where
these relics have been for a longer time, and where more of
the miracles were narrated for public information, there are
incomparably more.

At Uzali, too, a colony near Utica, many signal miracles
were, to my knowledge, done by the same martyr, whose relics
had found a place there by direction of the bishop Evodius,
long before we had them at Hippo. But there the custom of
publishing narratives does not obtain, or, I should say, did not
obtain, for possibly it may now have been begun. For, when
I was there recently, a woman of rank, Petronia, had been
miraculously cured of a serious illness of long standing, in
which all medical appliances had failed, and, with the consent
of the above-named bishop of the place, I exhorted her to
publish an account of it that might be read to the people. She
most promptly obeyed, and inserted in her narrative a circumstance which I cannot omit to mention, though I am compelled
to hasten on to the subjects which this work requires me to
treat. She said that she had been persuaded by a Jew to wear
next her skin, under all her clothes, a hair girdle, and on this
girdle a ring, which, instead of a gem, had a stone which had
been found in the kidneys of an ox. Girt with this charm, she
was making her way to the threshold of the holy martyr. But,
after leaving Carthage, and when she had been lodging in her
own demesne on the river Bagrada, and was now rising to
continue her journey, she saw her ring lying before her feet.
In great surprise she examined the hair girdle, and when she
found it bound, as it had been, quite firmly with knots, she
conjectured that the ring had been worn through and dropped
off; but when she found that the ring was itself also perfectly
whole, she presumed that by this great miracle she had received somehow a pledge of her cure, whereupon she untied
the girdle, and cast it into the river, and the ring along with
it. This is not credited by those who do not believe either that
the Lord Jesus Christ came forth from his mother's womb
without destroying her virginity, and entered among his disciples when the doors were shut; but let them make strict inquiry into this miracle, and if they find it true, let them believe
those others. The lady is of distinction, nobly born, married
to a nobleman. She resides at Carthage. The city is distin-

guished, the person is distinguished, so that they who make inquiries cannot fail to find satisfaction. Certainly the martyr himself, by whose prayers she was healed, believed in the Son of her who remained a virgin; in him who came in among the disciples when the doors were shut; finally,—and to this tends all that we have been retailing,—in him who ascended into heaven with the flesh in which he had risen; and it is because he laid down his life for this faith that such miracles were done by his means.

Even now, therefore, many miracles are done, the same God who did those we read of still performing them, by whom he wills and as he wills; but they are not as well known, nor are they beaten into the memory, like gravel, by frequent reading, so that they cannot fall out of mind. For even where, as is now done among ourselves, care is taken that the accounts of those who receive benefit be read publicly, yet those who are present hear the narrative but once, and many are absent; and so it comes to pass that even those who are present forget in a few days what they heard, and scarcely one of them can be found who will tell what he heard to one who he knows was not present.

One miracle was done among ourselves, which, though no greater than those I have mentioned, was yet so signal and conspicuous, that I suppose there is no inhabitant of Hippo who did not either see or hear of it, none who could possibly forget it. There were seven brothers and three sisters of a noble family of the Cappadocian Cæsarea, who were cursed by their mother, a recent widow, on account of some wrong they had done her, and which she bitterly resented, and who were visited with so severe a punishment from heaven, that all of them were seized with a hideous shaking in all their limbs. Unable, while presenting this loathsome appearance, to endure the eyes of their fellow-citizens, they wandered over almost the whole Roman world, each following his own direction. Two of them came to Hippo, a brother and a sister, Paulus and Palladia, already known in many other places by the fame of their wretched lot. Now it was about fifteen days before Easter when they came, and they came daily to church, and specially to the relics of the most glorious Stephen, praying that God might now be appeased, and restore their former health. There, and wherever they went, they attracted the attention of every one. Some who had seen them elsewhere, and knew the cause of their trembling, told others as occasion offered. Easter arrived, and on the Lord's day, in the morning, when there was now a large crowd present, and the young man was holding the bars of the holy place where the relics were, and praying, suddenly he fell down, and lay precisely as if asleep, but not trembling as he was wont to do even in sleep. All present were astonished. Some were alarmed, some were moved with pity; and while some were for lifting him up, others prevented them, and said they should rather wait and see what would result. And behold! he rose up, and trembled no more, for he was healed, and stood quite well, looking at those who were looking at him. Who then refrained himself from praising God? The whole church was filled with the voices of those who were shouting and congratulating him. Then they came running to me, where I was sitting ready to come into the church. One after another they throng in, the last comer telling me as news what the first had told me already; and while I rejoiced and inwardly gave God thanks, the young man himself also enters, with a number of others, falls at my knees, is raised up to receive my kiss. We go in to the congregation: the church was full, and ringing with the shouts of joy, "Thanks to God! Praised be God!" every one joining and shouting on all sides, I saluted the people who started with still louder voice shouting again. Silence being at last obtained, the customary lessons of the divine Scriptures were read. And when I came to my sermon, I made a few remarks suitable to the occasion and the happy and joyful feeling, not desiring them to listen to me, but rather to consider the eloquence of God in this divine work. The man dined with us, and gave us a careful account of his own, his mother's, and his family's calamity. Accordingly, on the following day, after delivering my sermon, I promised that next day I would read his narrative to the people. And when I did so, the third day after Easter Sunday, I made the brother and sister both stand on the steps of the raised place from which I used to speak; and while they stood there their story was read. The whole congregation, men and women alike, saw the one standing without any unnatural movement, the other trembling in

all her limbs, so that those who had not before seen the man
himself saw in his sister what the divine compassion had removed from him. In him they saw matter of congratulation,
in her subject for prayer. Meanwhile, their story being finished, I instructed them to withdraw from the gaze of the people; and I had begun to discuss the whole matter somewhat
more carefully, when lo! as I was proceeding, other voices are
heard from the tomb of the martyr, shouting new congratula-
tions. My audience turned round, and began to run to the
tomb. The young woman, when she had come down from the
steps where she had been standing, went to pray at the holy
relics, and no sooner had she touched the bars than she, in the
same way as her brother, collapsed, as if falling asleep, and
rose up cured. While, then, we were asking what had happened, and what occasioned this noise of joy, they came into
the basilica where we were, leading her from the martyr's tomb
in perfect health. Then, indeed, such a shout of wonder rose
from men and women together, that the exclamations and the
tears seemed like never to come to an end. She was led to
the place where she had a little before stood trembling. They
now rejoiced that she was like her brother, as before they had
mourned that she remained unlike him; and as they had not
yet uttered their prayers in her behalf, they perceived that their
intention of doing so had been speedily heard. They shouted
God's praises without words, but with such a noise that our
ears could scarcely bear it. What was there in the hearts of
these exultant people but the faith of Christ, for which Stephen
had shed his blood?

9. *That all the miracles which are done by means of the martyrs
in the name of Christ testify to that faith which the martyrs had
in Christ.*

To what do these miracles witness, but to this faith which
preaches Christ risen in the flesh, and ascended with the same
into heaven? For the martyrs themselves were martyrs, that
is to say, witnesses of this faith, drawing upon themselves by
their testimony the hatred of the world, and conquering the
world not by resisting it, but by dying. For this faith they died,
and can now ask these benefits from the Lord in whose name
they were slain. For this faith their marvellous constancy was

exercised, so that in these miracles great power was manifested as the result. For if the resurrection of the flesh to eternal life had not taken place in Christ, and were not to be accomplished in his people, as predicted by Christ, or by the prophets who foretold that Christ was to come, why do the martyrs who were slain for this faith which proclaims the resurrection possess such power? For whether God himself did these miracles by that wonderful manner of working by which, though himself eternal, he produces effects in time; or whether he did them by servants, and if so, whether he made use of the spirits of martyrs as he uses men who are still in the body, or effects all these marvels by means of angels, over whom he exerts an invisible, immutable, incorporeal sway, so that what is said to be done by the martyrs is done not by their operation, but only by their prayer and request; or whether, finally, some things are done in one way, others in another, and so that man cannot at all comprehend them,—nevertheless these miracles attest this faith which preaches the resurrection of the flesh to eternal life.

10. *That the martyrs who obtain many miracles in order that the true God may be worshipped, are worthy of much greater honour than the demons, who do some marvels that they themselves may be supposed to be God.*

Here perhaps our adversaries will say that their gods also have done some wonderful things, if now they begin to compare their gods to our dead men. Or will they also say that they have gods taken from among dead men, such as Hercules, Romulus, and many others whom they fancy to have been received into the number of the gods? But our martyrs are not our gods; for we know that the martyrs and we have both but one God, and that the same. Nor yet are the miracles which they maintain to have been done by means of their temples at all comparable to those which are done by the tombs of our martyrs. If they seem similar, their gods have been defeated by our martyrs as Pharaoh's magi were by Moses. In reality, the demons did these marvels with the same impure pride with which they aspired to be the gods of the nations; but the martyrs do these wonders, or rather God does them while they pray and assist, in order that an impulse may be given to the faith by which we believe that they are not our gods, but have, together with ourselves, one God. In fine, they built temples to these gods of theirs, and set up altars, and ordained priests, and appointed sacrifices; but to our martyrs we build, not temples as if they were gods, but monuments as to dead men whose spirits live with God. Neither do we erect altars at these monuments that we may sacrifice to the martyrs, but to the one God of the martyrs and of ourselves; and in this sacrifice they are named in their own place and rank as men of God who conquered the world by confessing him, but they are not invoked by the sacrificing priest. For it is to God, not to them, he sacrifices, though he sacrifices at their monument; for he is God's priest, not theirs. The sacrifice itself, too, is the body of Christ, which is not offered to them, because they themselves are this body. Which then can more readily be believed to work miracles? They who wish themselves to be reckoned gods by those on whom they work miracles, or those whose sole object in working any miracle is to induce faith in God, and in Christ also as God? They who wished to turn even their crimes into sacred rites, or those who are unwilling that even their own praises be consecrated, and seek that everything for which they are justly praised be ascribed to the glory of him in whom they are praised? For in the Lord their souls are praised. Let us therefore believe those who both speak the truth and work wonders. For by speaking the truth they suffered, and so won the power of working wonders. And the leading truth they professed is that Christ rose from the dead, and first showed in his own flesh the immortality of the resurrection which he promised should be ours, either in the beginning of the world to come, or in the end of this world.

11. *Against the Platonists, who argue from the physical weight of the elements that an earthly body cannot inhabit heaven.*

But against this great gift of God, these reasoners, "whose thoughts the Lord knows are vain,"[15] bring arguments from the weights of the elements; for they have been taught by their master Plato that the two greatest elements of the world, and the furthest removed from one another, are coupled and

15 Ps. 94: 11.

united by the two intermediate, air and water. And consequently they say, since the earth is the first of the elements, beginning from the base of the series, the second the water
above the earth, the third the air above the water, the fourth
the heaven above the air, it follows that a body of earth cannot live in the heaven; for each element is poised by its own
weight so as to preserve its own place and rank. Behold with
what arguments human infirmity, possessed with vanity, con-
tradicts the omnipotence of God! What, then, do so many
earthly bodies do in the air, since the air is the third element
from the earth? Unless perhaps he who has granted to the
earthly bodies of birds that they be carried through the air by
the lightness of feathers and wings, has not been able to confer upon the bodies of men made immortal the power to abide
in the highest heaven. The earthly animals, too, which cannot
fly, among which are men, ought on these terms to live under
the earth, as fishes, which are the animals of the water, live
under the water. Why, then, can an animal of earth not live in
the second element, that is, in water, while it can in the third?
Why, though it belongs to the earth, is it immediately suffo-
cated if it is forced to live in the second element next above
earth, while it lives in the third, and cannot live out of it? Is
there a mistake here in the order of the elements, or is not the
mistake rather in their reasonings, and not in the nature of
things? I will not repeat what I said in the thirteenth book,
that many earthly bodies, though heavy like lead, receive from
the workman's hand a form which enables them to swim in
water; and yet it is denied that the omnipotent worker can
confer on the human body a property which shall enable it
to pass into heaven and dwell there.

But against what I have formerly said they can find nothing to say, even though they introduce and make the most of
this order of the elements in which they confide. For if the
order be that the earth is first, the water second, the air third,
the heaven fourth, then the soul is above all. For Aristotle
said that the soul was a fifth body, while Plato denied that
it was a body at all. If it were a fifth body, then certainly
it would be above the rest; and if it is not a body at all, so
much the more does it rise above all. What, then, does it do
in an earthly body? What does this soul, which is finer than

all else, do in such a mass of matter as this? What does the lightest of substances do in this heaviness? this swiftest substance in such sluggishness? Will not the body be raised to heaven by virtue of so excellent a nature as this? and if now earthly bodies can retain the souls below, shall not the souls be one day able to raise the earthly bodies above?

If we pass now to their miracles which as done by their gods they oppose to our martyrs, shall not even these be found to support us, and help out our argument? For if any of the miracles of their gods are great, certainly that is a great one which Varro mentions of a vestal virgin, who, when she was endangered by a false accusation of unchastity, filled a sieve with water from the Tiber, and carried it to her judges without any part of it leaking. Who kept the weight of water in the sieve? Who prevented any drop from falling from it through so many open holes? They will answer, some god or some demon. If a god, is he greater than the God who made the world? If a demon, is he mightier than an angel who serves the God by whom the world was made? If, then, a lesser god, angel, or demon could so sustain the weight of this liquid element that the water might seem to have changed its nature, shall not Almighty God, who himself created all the elements, be able to eliminate from the earthly body its heaviness, so that the live body shall dwell in whatever element the enlivening spirit pleases?

Then, again, since they give the air a middle place between the fire above and the water beneath, how is it that we often find it between water and water, and between the water and the earth? For what do they make of those watery clouds, between which and the seas air is constantly found intervening? I should like to know by what weight and order of the elements it comes to pass that very violent and stormy torrents are suspended in the clouds above the earth before they rush along upon the earth under the air? Shortly, why is it that throughout the whole globe the air is between the highest heaven and the earth, if its place is between the sky and the water, as the place of the water is between the sky and the earth?

Finally, if the order of the elements is so disposed that, as Plato thinks, the two extremes, fire and earth, are united by the two means, air and water, and that fire occupies the highest

part of the sky, and earth the lowest part, or as it were the foundation of the world, and that therefore earth cannot be in the heavens, how is fire in the earth? For, according to this reasoning, these two elements, earth and fire, ought to be so restricted to their own places, the highest and the lowest, that neither the lowest can rise to the place of the highest, nor the highest sink to that of the lowest. Thus, as they think that no particle of earth is or shall ever be in the sky, so we ought to see no particle of fire on the earth. But the fact is that it exists to such an extent, not only on but even under the earth, that the tops of mountains vomit it forth; besides, we see it to exist on earth for human uses, and even to be produced from the earth, since it is kindled from wood and stones, which are without doubt earthly bodies. But that [upper] fire, they say, is tranquil, pure, harmless, eternal; but this [earthly] fire is turbid, smoky, corruptible, and corrupting. But it does not corrupt the mountains and caverns of the earth in which it rages continually. But grant that the earthly fire is so unlike the other as to suit its earthly position, why then do they object to our believing that the nature of earthly bodies shall some day be made incorruptible and fit for the sky, even as now fire is corruptible and suited to the earth? They therefore adduce from their weights and order of the elements nothing from which they can prove that it is impossible for Almighty God to make our bodies such that they can dwell in the skies.

12. *Against the calumnies with which unbelievers throw ridicule upon the Christian faith in the resurrection of the flesh.*

But their way is to feign a scrupulous anxiety in investigating this question, and to cast ridicule on our faith in the resurrection of the body, by asking, whether abortions shall rise? And as the Lord says, "Truly I say unto you, not a hair of your head shall perish,"[16] shall all bodies have an equal stature and strength, or shall there be differences in size? For if there is to be equality, where shall those abortions, supposing that they rise again, get that bulk which they had not here? Or if they shall not rise because they were not born but cast out, they raise the same question about children who have died

[16] Luke 21: 18.

in childhood, asking us whence they get the stature which we see they had not here; for we will not say that those who have been not only born, but born again, shall not rise again. Then, further, they ask of what size these equal bodies shall be. For if all shall be as tall and large as were the tallest and largest in this world, they ask us how it is that not only children but many full-grown persons shall receive what they here did not possess, if each one is to receive what he had here. And if the saying of the apostle, that we are all to come to the "measure of the age of the fulness of Christ,"[17] or that other saying, "Whom he predestinated to be conformed to the image of his Son,"[18] is to be understood to mean that the stature and size of Christ's body shall be the measure of the bodies of all those who shall be in his kingdom, then, say they, the size and height of many must be diminished; and if so much of the bodily frame itself be lost, what becomes of the saying, "Not a hair of your head shall perish?" Besides, it might be asked regarding the hair itself, whether all that the barber has cut off shall be restored? And if it is to be restored, who would not shrink from such deformity? For as the same restoration will be made of what has been pared off the nails, much will be replaced on the body which a regard for its appearance had cut off. And where, then, will be its beauty, which assuredly ought to be much greater in that immortal condition than it could be in this corruptible state? On the other hand, if such things are not restored to the body, they must perish; how, then, they say, shall not a hair of the head perish? In like manner they reason about fatness and leanness; for if all are to be equal, then certainly there shall not be some fat, others lean. Some, therefore, shall gain, others lose something. Consequently there will not be a simple restoration of what formerly existed, but, on the one hand, an addition of what had no existence, and, on the other, a loss of what did before exist.

The difficulties, too, about the corruption and dissolution of dead bodies,—that one is turned into dust, while another evaporates into the air; that some are devoured by beasts, some by fire, while some perish by shipwreck or by drowning in

[17] Eph. 4: 13.
[18] Rom. 8: 29.

one shape or other, so that their bodies decay into liquid,—these difficulties give them immoderate alarm, and they believe that all those dissolved elements cannot be gathered again and reconstructed into a body. They also make eager use of all the deformities and blemishes which either accident or birth has produced, and accordingly, with horror and derision, cite monstrous births, and ask if every deformity will be preserved in the resurrection. For if we say that no such thing shall be reproduced in the body of a man, they suppose that they confute us by citing the marks of the wounds which we assert were found in the risen body of the Lord Christ. But of all these, the most difficult question is, into whose body that flesh shall return which has been eaten and assimilated by another man constrained by hunger to use it so; for it has been converted into the flesh of the man who used it as his nutriment, and it filled up those losses of flesh which famine had produced. For the sake, then, of ridiculing the resurrection, they ask, shall this return to the man whose flesh it first was, or to him whose flesh it afterwards became? And thus, too, they seek to give promise to the human soul of alternations of true misery and false happiness, in accordance with Plato's theory; or, in accordance with Porphyry's, that, after many transmigrations into different bodies, it ends its miseries, and never more returns to them, not, however, by obtaining an immortal body, but by escaping from every kind of body.

13. *Whether abortions, if they are numbered among the dead, shall not also have a part in the resurrection.*

To these objections, then, of our adversaries which I have thus detailed, I will now reply, trusting that God will mercifully assist my endeavours. That abortions, which, even supposing they were alive in the womb, did also die there, shall rise again, I make bold neither to affirm nor to deny, although I fail to see why, if they are not excluded from the number of the dead, they should not attain to the resurrection of the dead. For either all the dead shall not rise, and there will be to all eternity some souls without bodies, though they once had them,—only in their mother's womb, indeed; or, if all human souls shall receive again the bodies which they had wherever they lived, and which they left when they died, then I do not see how I can say that even those who died in their mother's womb shall have no resurrection. But whichever of these opinions any one may adopt concerning them, we must at least apply to them, if they rise again, all that we have to say of infants who have been born.

14. *Whether infants shall rise in that body which they would have had had they grown up.*

What, then, are we to say of infants, if not that they will not rise in that diminutive body in which they died, but shall receive by the marvellous and rapid operation of God that body which time by a slower process would have given them? For in the Lord's words, where he says, "Not a hair of your head shall perish,"[19] it is asserted that nothing which was possessed shall be wanting; but it is not said that nothing which was not possessed shall be given. To the dead infant there was wanting the perfect stature of its body; for even the perfect infant lacks the perfection of bodily size, being capable of further growth. This perfect stature is, in a sense, so possessed by all that they are conceived and born with it,—that is, they have it potentially, though not yet in actual bulk; just as all the members of the body are potentially in the seed, though, even after the child is born, some of them, the teeth for example, may be wanting. In this seminal principle of every substance, there seems to be, as it were, the beginning of everything which does not yet exist, or rather does not appear, but which in process of time will come into being, or rather into sight. In this, therefore, the child who is to be tall or short is already tall or short. And in the resurrection of the body, we need, for the same reason, fear no bodily loss; for though all should be of equal size, and reach gigantic proportions, lest the men who were largest here should lose anything of their bulk and it should perish, in contradiction to the words of Christ, who said that not a hair of their head should perish, yet why should there lack the means by which that wonderful worker should make such additions, seeing that he is the creator, who himself created all things out of nothing?

[19] Luke 21: 18.

15. *Whether the bodies of all the dead shall rise the same size as the Lord's body.*

It is certain that Christ rose in the same bodily stature in which he died, and that it is wrong to say that, when the general resurrection shall have arrived, his body shall, for the sake of equalling the tallest, assume proportions which it had not when he appeared to the disciples in the figure with which they were familiar. But if we say that even the bodies of taller men are to be reduced to the size of the Lord's body, there will be a great loss in many bodies, though he promised that not a hair of their head should perish. It remains, therefore, that we conclude that every man shall receive his own size which he had in youth, though he died an old man, or which he would have had, supposing he died before his prime. As for what the apostle said of the measure of the age of the fulness of Christ, we must either understand him to refer to something else, namely to the fact that the measure of Christ will be completed when all the members among the Christian communities are added to the head; or if we are to refer it to the resurrection of the body, the meaning is that all shall rise neither beyond nor under youth, but in that vigour and age to which we know that Christ had arrived. For even the world's wisest men have fixed the bloom of youth at about the age of thirty; and when this period has been passed, the man begins to decline towards the defective and duller period of old age. And therefore the apostle did not speak of the measure of the body, nor of the measure of the stature, but of "the measure of the age of the fulness of Christ."

16. *What is meant by the conforming of the saints to the image of the Son of God.*

Then, again, these words, "Predestinate to be conformed to the image of the Son of God,"[20] may be understood of the inner man. So in another place he says to us, "Be not conformed to this world, but be transformed in the renewing of your mind."[21] In so far, then, as we are transformed so as not to be conformed to the world, we are conformed to the

[20] Rom. 8: 29.
[21] Rom. 12: 2.

Son of God. It may also be understood thus, that as he was conformed to us by assuming mortality, we shall be conformed to him by immortality; and this indeed is connected with the resurrection of the body. But if we are also taught in these words what form our bodies shall rise in, as the measure we spoke of before, so also this conformity is to be understood not of size, but of age. Accordingly all shall rise in the stature they either had attained or would have attained had they lived to their prime, although it will be no great disadvantage even if the form of the body be that of an infant or aged, while no infirmity shall remain in the mind nor in the body itself. So that even if any one contends that every person will rise again in the same bodily form in which he died, we need not spend much labour in disputing with him.

17. *Whether the bodies of women shall retain their own sex in the resurrection.*

From the words, "Till we all come to a perfect man, to the measure of the age of the fulness of Christ,"[22] and from the words, "Conformed to the image of the Son of God,"[23] some conclude that women shall not rise women, but that all shall be men, because God made man only of earth, and woman of the man. For my part, they seem to be wiser who make no doubt that both sexes shall rise. For there shall be no lust, which is now the cause of confusion. For before they sinned, the man and the woman were naked, and were not ashamed. From those bodies, then, vice shall be withdrawn, while nature shall be preserved. And the sex of woman is not a vice, but nature. It shall then indeed be free from carnal intercourse and child-bearing; nevertheless the female members shall remain adapted not to the old uses, but to a new beauty, which, so far from provoking lust, now extinct, shall excite praise to the wisdom and clemency of God, who both made what was not and delivered from corruption what he made. For at the beginning of the human race the woman was made of a rib taken from the side of the man while he slept; for it seemed fit that even then Christ and his church should

22 Eph. 4: 13.
23 Rom. 8: 29.

be foreshadowed in this event. For that sleep of the man was the death of Christ, whose side, as he hung lifeless upon the cross, was pierced with a spear, and there flowed from it blood and water, and these we know to be the sacraments by which the church is "built up." For scripture used this very word, not saying "he formed" or "framed," but "built her up into a woman;"[24] whence also the apostle speaks of the *edification* of the body of Christ,[25] which is the church. The woman, therefore, is a creature of God even as the man; but by her creation from man unity is commended; and the manner of her creation prefigured, as has been said, Christ and the church. He, then, who created both sexes will restore both. Jesus himself also, when asked by the Sadducees, who denied the resurrection, which of the seven brothers should have to wife the woman whom all in succession had taken to raise up seed to their brother, as the law enjoined, says, "You do err, not knowing the Scriptures nor the power of God."[26] And though it was a fit opportunity for his saying, she about whom you make inquiries shall herself be a man, and not a woman, he said nothing of the kind; but "In the resurrection they neither marry nor are given in marriage, but are as the angels of God in heaven."[27] They shall be equal to the angels in immortality and happiness, not in flesh, nor in resurrection, which the angels did not need, because they could not die. The Lord then denied that there would be in the resurrection, not women, but marriages; and he uttered this denial in circumstances in which the question mooted would have been more easily and speedily solved by denying that the female sex would exist, if this had in truth been foreknown by him. But, indeed, he even affirmed that the sex should exist by saying, "They shall not be given in marriage," which can only apply to females; "Neither shall they marry," which applies to males. There shall therefore be those who are in this world accustomed to marry and be given in marriage, only they shall there make no such marriages.

24 Gen. 2: 22.
25 Eph. 4: 12.
26 Matt. 22: 29.
27 Matt. 22: 30.

18. *Of the perfect man, that is, Christ; and of his body, that is, the church, which is his fulness.*

To understand what the apostle means when he says that we shall all come to a perfect man, we must consider the connection of the whole passage, which runs thus: "He that descended is the same also that ascended up far above all heavens, that he might fill all things. And he gave some, apostles; and some, prophets; and some, evangelists; and some, pastors and teachers; for the perfecting of the saints, for the work of the ministry, for the edifying of the body of Christ: till we all come to the unity of the faith and knowledge of the Son of God, to a perfect man, to the measure of the age of the fulness of Christ: that we henceforth be no more children, tossed and carried about with every wind of doctrine, by the sleight of men, and cunning craftiness, by which they lie in wait to deceive; but, speaking the truth in love, may grow up in him in all things, who is the head, even Christ: from whom the whole body fitly joined together and compacted by that which every joint supplies, according to the effectual working in the measure of every part, makes increase of the body, to the edifying of itself in love."[28] Behold what the perfect man is—the head and the body, which is made up of all the members, which in their own time shall be perfected. But new additions are daily being made to this body while the church is being built up, to which it is said, "You are the body of Christ and his members;"[29] and again, "For his body's sake," he says, "which is the church;"[30] and again, "We being many are one bread and one body."[31] It is of the edification of this body that it is here, too, said, "For the perfecting of the saints, for the work of the ministry, for the edification of the body of Christ;" and then that passage of which we are now speaking is added, "Till we all come to the unity of the faith and knowledge of the Son of God, to a perfect man, to the measure of the age of the fulness of Christ," and so on. And he shows of what body we are to

[28] Eph. 4: 10–16.
[29] 1 Cor. 12: 27.
[30] Col. 1: 24.
[31] 1 Cor. 10:17.

understand this to be the measure, when he says, "That we may grow up into him in all things, which is the head, even Christ: from whom the whole body fitly joined together and compacted by that which every joint supplies, according to the effectual working in the measure of every part." As, therefore, there is a measure of every part, so there is a measure of the fulness of the whole body which is made up of all its parts, and it is of this measure it is said, "To the measure of the age of the fulness of Christ." This fulness he spoke of also in the place where he says of Christ, "And gave him to be the head over all things to the church, which is his body, the fulness of him that fills all in all."[32] But even if this should be referred to the form in which each one shall rise, what should hinder us from applying to the woman what is expressly said of the man, understanding both sexes to be included under the general term "man?" For certainly in the saying, "Blessed is he who feareth the Lord,"[33] women also who fear the Lord are included.

19. *That all bodily blemishes which mar human beauty in this life shall be removed in the resurrection, the natural substance of the body remaining, but the quality and quantity of it being altered so as to produce beauty.*

What am I to say now about the hair and nails? Once it is understood that no part of the body shall so perish as to produce deformity in the body, it is at the same time understood that such things as would have produced a deformity by their excessive proportions shall be added to the total bulk of the body, not to parts in which the beauty of the proportion would thus be marred. Just as if, after making a vessel of clay, one wished to make it over again of the same clay, it would not be necessary that the same portion of the clay which had formed the handle should again form the new handle, or that what had formed the bottom should again do so, but only that the whole clay should go to make up the whole new vessel, and that no part of it should be left unused. Therefore, if the hair that has been cropped and the nails that have been cut would cause a deformity if they were to be restored to their

[32] Eph. 1: 22 f.
[33] Ps. 112: 1.

places, they shall not be restored; and yet no one will lose
these parts at the resurrection, for they shall be changed into
the same flesh, their substance being so altered as to preserve
the proportion of the various parts of the body. However, what
our Lord said, "Not a hair of your head shall perish," might
more suitably be interpreted of the number, and not of the
length of the hairs, as he elsewhere says, "The hairs of your
head are all numbered."[34] Nor would I say this because I
suppose that any part naturally belonging to the body can perish, but that whatever deformity was in it, and served to exhibit
the penal condition in which we mortals are, should be restored in such a way that, while the substance is entirely preserved, the deformity shall perish. For if even a human workman, who has, for some reason, made a deformed statue, can
recast it and make it very beautiful, and this without suffering
any part of the substance, but only the deformity to be lost,—
if he can, for example, remove some unbecoming or dispropor-
tionate part, not by cutting off and separating this part from
the whole, but by so breaking down and mixing up the whole
as to get rid of the blemish without diminishing the quantity
of his material,—shall we not think as highly of the almighty
worker? Shall he not be able to remove and abolish all deformities of the human body, whether common ones or rare and
monstrous, which, though in keeping with this miserable life,
are yet not to be thought of in connection with that future
blessedness; and shall he not be able so to remove them that,
while the natural but unseemly blemishes are put an end to,
the natural substance shall suffer no diminution?

And consequently overgrown and emaciated persons need
not fear that they shall be of such a figure in heaven as they
would not be even in this world if they could help it. For
all bodily beauty consists in the proportion of the parts, together with a certain agreeableness of colour. Where there
is no proportion, the eye is offended, either because there is
something wanting, or too small, or too large. And thus there
shall be no deformity resulting from want of proportion in that
state in which all that is wrong is corrected, and all that is

[34] Luke 12: 7.

defective supplied from resources the creator knows of, and
all that is excessive removed without destroying the integrity
of the substance. And as for the pleasant colour, how conspicuous shall it be where "the just shall shine forth as the
sun in the kingdom of their Father!"[35] This brightness we
must rather believe to have been concealed from the eyes of
the disciples when Christ rose, than to have been wanting.
For weak human eyesight could not bear it, and it was necessary that they should so look upon him as to be able to recognise him. For this purpose also he allowed them to touch
the marks of his wounds, and also ate and drank,—not because he needed nourishment, but because he could take it
if he wished. Now, when an object, though present, is invisible to persons who see other things which are present, as
we say that that brightness was present but invisible by those
who saw other things, this is called in Greek *aorasia;* and our
Latin translators, for want of a better word, have rendered
this *cæcitas* (blindness) in the book of Genesis. This blindness the men of Sodom suffered when they sought the just
Lot's gate and could not find it. But if it had been blindness,
that is to say, if they could see nothing, then they would not
have asked for the gate by which they might enter the house,
but for guides who might lead them away.

But the love we bear to the blessed martyrs causes us, I
know not how, to desire to see in the heavenly kingdom the
marks of the wounds which they received for the name of
Christ, and possibly we shall see them. For this will not be a
deformity, but a mark of honour, and will add lustre to their
appearance, and a spiritual, if not a bodily beauty. And yet
we need not believe that they to whom it has been said, "Not
a hair of your head shall perish," shall, in the resurrection,
want such of their members as they have been deprived of in
their martyrdom. But if it will be seemly in that new kingdom
to have some marks of these wounds still visible in that immortal flesh, the places where they have been wounded or
mutilated shall retain the scars without any of the members
being lost. While, therefore, it is quite true that no blemishes
which the body has sustained shall appear in the resurrection,

35 Matt. 13: 43.

yet we are not to reckon or name these marks of virtue blemishes.

20. *That, in the resurrection, the substance of our bodies, however disintegrated, shall be entirely reunited.*

Far be it from us to fear that the omnipotence of the creator cannot, for the resuscitation and reanimation of our bodies, recall all the portions which have been consumed by beasts or fire, or have been dissolved into dust or ashes, or have decomposed into water, or evaporated into the air. Far from us be the thought, that anything which escapes our observation in any most hidden recess of nature either evades the knowledge or transcends the power of the creator of all things. Cicero, the great authority of our adversaries, wishing to define God as accurately as possible, says, "God is a mind free and independent, without materiality, perceiving and moving all things, and itself endowed with eternal movement."[36] This he found in the systems of the greatest philosophers. Let me ask, then, in their own language, how anything can either lie hidden from him who perceives all things, or irrevocably escape him who moves all things?

This leads me to reply to that question which seems the most difficult of all,—to whom, in the resurrection, will belong the flesh of a dead man which has become the flesh of a living man? For if some one, famishing for want and pressed with hunger, use human flesh as food,—an extremity not unknown, as both ancient history and the unhappy experience of our own days have taught us,—can it be contended, with any show of reason, that all the flesh eaten has been evacuated, and that none of it has been assimilated to the substance of the eater, though the very emaciation which existed before, and has now disappeared, sufficiently indicates what large deficiencies have been filled up with this food? But I have already made some remarks which will suffice for the solution of this difficulty also. For all the flesh which hunger has consumed finds its way into the air by evaporation, whence, as we have said, God Almighty can recall it. That flesh, therefore, shall be restored to the man in whom it first became

[36] Cic. *Tusc. Disp.* 1.27.

human flesh. For it must be looked upon as borrowed by the other person, and, like a pecuniary loan, must be returned to the lender. His own flesh, however, which he lost by famine, shall be restored to him by him who can recover even what has evaporated. And though it had been absolutely annihilated, so that no part of its substance remained in any secret spot of nature, the Almighty could restore it by such means as he saw fit. For this sentence, uttered by the truth, "Not a hair of your head shall perish," forbids us to suppose that, though no hair of a man's head can perish, yet the large portions of his flesh eaten and consumed by the famishing can perish.

From all that we have thus considered, and discussed with such poor ability as we can command, we gather this conclusion, that in the resurrection of the flesh the body shall be of that size which it either had attained or should have attained in the flower of its youth, and shall enjoy the beauty that arises from preserving symmetry and proportion in all its members. And it is reasonable to suppose that, for the preservation of this beauty, any part of the body's substance, which, if placed in one spot, would produce a deformity, shall be distributed through the whole of it, so that neither any part, nor the symmetry of the whole, may be lost, but only the general stature of the body somewhat increased by the distribution in all the parts of that which, in one place, would have been unsightly. Or if it is contended that each will rise with the same stature as that of the body he died in, we shall not obstinately dispute this, provided only there be no deformity, no infirmity, no slowness, no corruption,—nothing of any kind which would ill become that kingdom in which the children of the resurrection and of the promise shall be equal to the angels of God, if not in body and age, at least in happiness.

21. *Of the new spiritual body into which the flesh of the saints shall be transformed.*

Whatever, therefore, has been taken from the body, either during life or after death, shall be restored to it, and, in conjunction with what has remained in the grave, shall rise again, transformed from the oldness of the animal body into the newness of the spiritual body, and clothed in incorruption and immortality. But even though the body has been all quite ground to powder by some severe accident, or by the ruthlessness of enemies, and though it has been so diligently scattered to the winds, or into the water, that there is no trace of it left, yet it shall not be beyond the omnipotence of the creator,—no, not a hair of its head shall perish. The flesh shall then be spiritual, and subject to the spirit, but still flesh, not spirit, as the spirit itself, when subject to the flesh, was fleshly, but still spirit and not flesh. And of this we have experimental proof in the deformity of our penal condition. For those persons were carnal, not in a fleshly, but in a spiritual way, to whom the apostle said, "I could not speak to you as unto spiritual, but as unto carnal."[37] And a man is in this life spiritual in such a way, that he is yet carnal with respect to his body, and sees another law in his members warring against the law of his mind; but even in his body he will be spiritual when the same flesh shall have had that resurrection of which these words speak, "It is sown an animal body, it shall rise a spiritual body."[38] But what this spiritual body shall be, and how great its grace, I fear it would be but rash to pronounce, seeing that we have as yet no experience of it. Nevertheless, since it is fit that the joyfulness of our hope should utter itself, and so show forth God's praise, and since it was from the profoundest sentiment of ardent and holy love that the Psalmist cried, "O Lord, I have loved the beauty of your house,"[39] we may, with God's help, speak of the gifts he lavishes on men, good and bad alike, in this most wretched life, and may do our best to conjecture the great glory of that state which we cannot worthily speak of, because we have not yet experienced it. For I say nothing of the time when God made man upright; I say nothing of the happy life of "the man and his wife" in the fruitful garden, since it was so short that none of their children experienced it: I speak only of this life which we know, and in which we now are, from the temptations of which we cannot escape so long as we are in it, no matter what progress we make, for it is

[37] 1 Cor. 3: 1.
[38] 1 Cor. 15: 42.
[39] Ps. 26: 8.

all temptation, and I ask, who can describe the tokens of God's goodness that are extended to the human race even in this life?

22. *Of the miseries and ills to which the human race is justly exposed through the first sin, and from which none can be delivered save by Christ's grace.*

That the whole human race has been condemned in its first origin, this life itself, if life it is to be called, bears witness by the host of cruel ills with which it is filled. Is this not proved by the profound and dreadful ignorance which produces all the errors that enfold the children of Adam, and from which no man can be delivered without toil, pain, and fear? Is it not proved by his love of so many vain and hurtful things, which produces gnawing cares, disquiet, griefs, fears, wild joys, quarrels, law-suits, wars, treasons, angers, hatreds, deceit, flattery, fraud, theft, robbery, perfidy, pride, ambition, envy, murders, parricides, cruelty, ferocity, wickedness, luxury, insolence, impudence, shamelessness, fornications, adulteries, incests, and the numberless uncleannesses and unnatural acts of both sexes, which it is shameful so much as to mention; sacrileges, heresies, blasphemies, perjuries, oppression of the innocent, calumnies, plots, falsehoods, false witnessings, unrighteous judgments, violent deeds, plunderings, and whatever similar wickedness has found its way into the lives of men, though it cannot find its way into the conception of pure minds? These are indeed the crimes of wicked men, yet they spring from that root of error and misplaced love which is born with every son of Adam. For who is there that has not observed with what profound ignorance, manifesting itself even in infancy, and with what superfluity of foolish desires, beginning to appear in boyhood, man comes into this life, so that, if he were left to live as he pleased, and to do whatever he pleased, he would plunge into all, or certainly into many of those crimes and iniquities which I mentioned, and could not mention?

But because God does not wholly desert those whom he condemns, nor shuts up in his anger his tender mercies, the human race is restrained by law and instruction, which keep guard against the ignorance that besets us, and oppose the assaults of vice, but are themselves full of labour and sorrow. For what mean those multifarious threats which are used to restrain the folly of children? What mean pedagogues, masters, the birch, the strap, the cane, the schooling which scripture says must be given a child, "beating him on the sides lest he wax stubborn,"[40] even if it is hardly possible or not possible at all to subdue him? Why all these punishments, except to overcome ignorance and control evil desires—these evils with which we come into the world? For why is it that we remember with difficulty, and without difficulty forget? learn with difficulty, and without difficulty remain ignorant? are diligent with difficulty, and without difficulty are indolent? Does not this show what vitiated nature inclines and tends to by its own weight, and what help it needs if it is to be delivered? Inactivity, sloth, laziness, negligence, are vices which shun labour, since labour, though useful, is itself a punishment.

But, besides the punishments of childhood, without which there would be no learning of what the parents wish,—and the parents rarely wish anything useful to be taught,—who can describe, who can conceive the number and severity of the punishments which afflict the human race,—pains which are not only the accompaniment of the wickedness of godless men, but are a part of the human condition and the common misery,—what fear and what grief are caused by bereavement and mourning, by losses and condemnations, by fraud and falsehood, by false suspicions, and all the crimes and wicked deeds of other men? For at their hands we suffer robbery, captivity, chains, imprisonment, exile, torture, mutilation, loss of sight, the violation of chastity to satisfy the lust of the oppressor, and many other dreadful evils. What numberless casualties threaten our bodies from without,—extremes of heat and cold, storms, floods, inundations, lightning, thunder, hail, earthquakes, houses falling; or from the stumbling, or shying, or vice of horses; from countless poisons in fruits, water, air, animals; from the painful or even deadly bites of wild animals; from the madness which a mad dog communicates, so that even the animal which of all others is most gentle and friendly to its own master, becomes an object of intenser fear than a

[40] Sir. 30: 12.

lion or dragon, and the man whom it has by chance infected with this pestilential contagion becomes so rabid, that his parents, wife, children, dread him more than any wild beast! What disasters are suffered by those who travel by land or sea! What man can go out of his own house without being exposed on all hands to unforeseen accidents? Returning home sound in limb, he slips on his own door-step, breaks his leg, and never recovers. What can seem safer than a man sitting in his chair? Eli the priest fell from his, and broke his neck. How many accidents do farmers, or rather all men, fear that the crops may suffer from the weather, or the soil, or the ravages of destructive animals? Commonly they feel safe when the crops are gathered and housed. Yet, to my certain knowledge, sudden floods have driven the labourers away, and swept the barns clean of the finest harvest. Is innocence a sufficient protection against the various assaults of demons? That no man might think so, even baptized infants, who are certainly unsurpassed in innocence, are sometimes so tormented, that God, who permits it, teaches us hereby to bewail the calamities of this life, and to desire the felicity of the life to come. As to bodily diseases, they are so numerous that they cannot all be contained even in medical books. And in very many, or almost all of them, the cures and remedies are themselves tortures, so that men are delivered from a pain that destroys by a cure that pains. Has not the madness of thirst driven men to drink human urine, and even their own? Has not hunger driven men to eat human flesh, and that the flesh not of bodies found dead, but of bodies slain for the purpose? Have not the fierce pangs of famine driven mothers to eat their own children, incredibly savage as it seems? Finally, sleep itself, which is justly called repose, how little of repose there sometimes is in it when disturbed with dreams and visions; and with what terror is the wretched mind overwhelmed by the appearances of things which are so presented, and which, as it were, so stand out before the senses, that we cannot distinguish them from realities! How wretchedly do false appearances distract men in certain diseases! With what astonishing variety of appearances are even healthy men sometimes deceived by evil spirits, who produce these delusions for the sake of perplexing the senses of their victims, if they cannot succeed in seducing them to their side!

From this hell upon earth there is no escape, save through the grace of the Saviour Christ, our God and Lord. The very name Jesus shows this, for it means saviour; and he saves us especially from passing out of this life into a more wretched and eternal state, which is rather a death than a life. For in this life, though holy men and holy pursuits give us great consolations, yet the blessings which men crave are not invariably bestowed upon them, lest religion should be cultivated for the sake of these temporal advantages, while it ought rather to be cultivated for the sake of that other life from which all evil is excluded. Therefore, also, does grace aid good men in the midst of present calamities, so that they are enabled to endure them with a constancy proportioned to their faith. The world's sages affirm that philosophy contributes something to this,—that philosophy which, according to Cicero, the gods have bestowed in its purity only on a few men. They have never given, he says, nor can ever give, a greater gift to men. So that even those against whom we are disputing have been compelled to acknowledge, in some fashion, that the grace of God is necessary for the acquisition, not, indeed, of any philosophy, but of the true philosophy. And if the true philosophy—this sole support against the miseries of this life—has been given by heaven only to a few, it sufficiently appears from this that the human race has been condemned to pay this penalty of wretchedness. And as, according to their acknowledgment, no greater gift has been bestowed by God, so it must be believed that it could be given only by that God whom they themselves recognise as greater than all the gods they worship.

23. *Of the miseries of this life which attach peculiarly to the toil of good men, irrespective of those which are common to the good and bad.*

But, irrespective of the miseries which in this life are common to the good and bad, the righteous undergo labours peculiar to themselves, in so far as they make war upon their vices, and are involved in the temptations and perils of such a contest. For though sometimes more violent and at other times slacker, yet without intermission does the flesh lust against the spirit and the spirit against the flesh, so that we cannot do the things we would,[41] and extirpate all lust, but can only refuse consent to it, as God gives us ability, and so keep it under, vigilantly keeping watch lest a semblance of truth deceive us, lest a subtle discourse blind us, lest error involve us in darkness, lest we should take good for evil or evil for good, lest fear should hinder us from doing what we ought, or desire precipitate us into doing what we ought not, lest the sun go down upon our wrath, lest hatred provoke us to render evil for evil, lest unseemly or immoderate grief consume us, lest an ungrateful disposition make us slow to recognise benefits received, lest calumnies fret our conscience, lest rash suspicion on our part deceive us regarding a friend, or false suspicion of us on the part of others give us too much uneasiness, lest sin reign in our mortal body to obey its desires, lest our members be used as the instruments of unrighteousness, lest the eye follow lust, lest thirst for revenge carry us away, lest sight or thought dwell too long on some evil thing which gives us pleasure, lest wicked or indecent language be willingly listened to, lest we do what is pleasant but unlawful, and lest in this warfare, filled so abundantly with toil and peril, we either hope to secure victory by our own strength, or attribute it when secured to our own strength, and not to his grace of whom the apostle says, "Thanks be to God, who gives us the victory through our Lord Jesus Christ;"[42] and in another place he says, "In all these things we are more than conquerors through him that loved us."[43] But yet we are to know this, that however valorously we resist our vices, and however successful we are in overcoming them, yet as long as we are in this body we have always reason to say to God, "Forgive us our debts."[44] But in that kingdom where we shall dwell for ever, clothed in immortal bodies, we shall no longer have either conflicts or debts,—as indeed we should not have had at any time or in any condition, if our nature had continued upright as it was created. Consequently even this conflict of ours, in

[41] Gal. 5: 17.
[42] 1 Cor. 15: 57.
[43] Rom. 8: 37.
[44] Matt. 6: 12.

which we are exposed to peril, and from which we hope to be delivered by a final victory, belongs to the ills of this life, which is proved by the witness of so many grave evils to be a life under condemnation.

24. *Of the blessings with which the creator has filled this life, subject though it be to the curse.*

But we must now contemplate the rich and countless blessings with which the goodness of God, who cares for all he has created, has filled this very misery of the human race, which reflects his retributive justice. That first blessing which he pronounced before the fall, when he said, "Increase, and multiply, and replenish the earth,"[45] he did not hold back after man had sinned, but the fecundity originally bestowed remained in the condemned stock; and the vice of sin, which has involved us in the necessity of dying, has yet not deprived us of that wonderful power of seed, or rather of that still more marvellous power by which seed is produced, and which seems to be as it were inwrought and inwoven in the human body. But in this river, as I may call it, or torrent of the human race, both elements are carried along together,—both the evil which is derived from him who begets, and the good which is bestowed by him who creates us. In the original evil there are two things, sin and punishment; in the original good, there are two other things, propagation and conformation. But of the evils, of which the one, sin, arose from our audacity, and the other, punishment, from God's judgment, we have already said as much as suits our present purpose. I mean now to speak of the blessings which God has conferred or still confers upon our nature, vitiated and condemned as it is. For in condemning it he did not withdraw all that he had given it, otherwise it would have been annihilated; neither did he, in penally subjecting it to the devil, remove it beyond his own power; for not even the devil himself is outside of God's government, since the devil's nature subsists only by the supreme creator, who gives being to all that in any form exists.

Of these two blessings, then, which we have said flow from God's goodness, as from a fountain, towards our nature, viti-

[45] Gen. 1: 28.

ated by sin and condemned to punishment, the one, propoga-
tion, was conferred by God's benediction when he made those
first works, from which he rested on the seventh day. But the
other, conformation, is conferred in that work of his wherein
"he works until now."[46] For were he to withdraw his effi-
cacious power from things, they should neither be able to go
on and complete the periods assigned to their measured movements, nor should they even continue in possession of that nature they were created in. God, then, so created man that he
gave him what we may call fertility, whereby he might propagate other men, giving them a congenital capacity to propagate
their kind, but not imposing on them any necessity to do so.
This capacity God withdraws at pleasure from individuals,
making them barren; but from the whole race he has not withdrawn the blessing of propagation once conferred. But though
not withdrawn on account of sin, this power of propagation
is not what it would have been had there been no sin. For
since "man placed in honour fell, he has become like the
beasts,"[47] and generates as they do, though the little spark
of reason, which was the image of God in him, has not been
quite quenched. But if conformation were not added to propagation, there would be no reproduction of one's kind. For even
though there were no such thing as copulation, and God
wished to fill the earth with human inhabitants, he might create
all these as he created one without the help of human generation. And, indeed, even as it is, those who copulate can
generate nothing except by the creative energy of God. As,
therefore, in respect of that spiritual growth whereby a man
is formed to piety and righteousness, the apostle says, "Neither
is he that plants anything, neither he that waters, but God that
gives the increase,"[48] so also it must be said that it is not
he that generates that is anything, but God that gives the essential form; that it is not the mother who carries and nurses
the fruit of her womb that is anything, but God that gives
the increase. For he alone, by that energy by which "he works
until now," causes the seed to develop, and to evolve from

46 John 5: 17.
47 Ps. 49: 12.
48 1 Cor. 3: 7.

certain secret and invisible folds into the visible forms of
beauty which we see. He alone, coupling and connecting in
some wonderful fashion the spiritual and corporeal natures,
the one to command, the other to obey, makes a living being.
And this work of his is so great and wonderful, that not only
man, who is a rational animal, and consequently more excellent than all other animals of the earth, but even the most
diminutive insect, cannot be considered attentively without astonishment and without praising the creator.

It is he, then, who has given to the human soul a mind,
in which reason and understanding lie as it were asleep during
infancy, and as if they were not, destined, however, to be
awakened and exercised as years increase, so as to become
capable of knowledge and of receiving instruction, fit to understand what is true and to love what is good. It is by this capacity the soul drinks in wisdom, and becomes endowed with
those virtues by which, in prudence, fortitude, temperance, and
justice, it makes war upon error and the other inborn vices,
and conquers them by fixing its desires upon no other object
than the supreme and unchangeable Good. And even though
this be not uniformly the result, yet who can competently utter
or even conceive the grandeur of this work of the almighty,
and the unspeakable good he has conferred upon our rational
nature, by giving us even the capacity of such attainment? For
over and above those arts which are called virtues, and which
teach us how we may spend our life well, and attain to endless
happiness,—arts which are given to the children of the promise
and the kingdom by the sole grace of God which is in Christ,—
has not the genius of man invented and applied countless
astonishing arts, partly the result of necessity, partly the result
of exuberant invention, so that this vigour of mind, which is
so active in the discovery not merely of superfluous but even
of dangerous and destructive things, betokens an inexhaustible
wealth in the nature which can invent, learn, or employ such
arts? What wonderful—one might say stupefying—advances has
human industry made in the arts of weaving and building, of
agriculture and navigation! With what endless variety are de-
signs in pottery, painting, and sculpture produced, and with
what skill executed! What wonderful spectacles are exhibited
in the theatres, which those who have not seen them cannot

credit! How skilful the contrivances for catching, killing, or taming wild beasts! And for the injury of men, also, how many kinds of poisons, weapons, engines of destruction, have been invented, while for the preservation or restoration of health the appliances and remedies are infinite! To provoke appetite and please the palate, what a variety of seasonings have been concocted! To express and gain entrance for thoughts, what a multitude and variety of signs there are, among which speaking and writing hold the first place! what ornaments has eloquence at command to delight the mind! what wealth of song is there to captivate the ear! how many musical instruments and strains of harmony have been devised! What skill has been attained in measures and numbers! with what sagacity have the movements and connections of the stars been discovered! Who could tell the thought that has been spent upon nature, even though, despairing of recounting it in detail, he endeavoured only to give a general view of it? In short, even the defence of errors and misapprehensions, which has illustrated the genius of heretics and philosophers, cannot be sufficiently appreciated. For at present it is the nature of the human mind which adorns this mortal life which we are extolling, and not the faith and the way of truth which lead to immortality. And since this great nature has certainly been created by the true and supreme God, who administers all things he has made with absolute power and justice, it could never have fallen into these miseries, nor have gone out of them to miseries eternal,—except only those who are redeemed,—had not an exceeding great sin been found in the first man from whom the rest have sprung.

Moreover, even in the body, though it dies like that of the beasts, and is in many ways weaker than theirs, what goodness of God, what providence of the great creator, is apparent! The organs of sense and the rest of the members, are they not so placed, the appearance, and form, and stature of the body as a whole, is it not so fashioned, as to indicate that it was made for the service of a reasonable soul? Man has not been created stooping towards the earth, like the irrational animals; but his bodily form, erect and looking heavenwards, admonishes him to mind the things that are above. Then the marvellous nimbleness which has been given to the tongue and the hands, fitting them to speak, and write, and execute so many duties, and practise so many arts, does it not prove the excellence of the soul for which such an assistant was provided? And even apart from its adaptation to the work required of it, there is such a symmetry in its various parts, and so beautiful a proportion maintained, that one is at a loss to decide whether, in creating the body, greater regard was paid to utility or to beauty. Assuredly no part of the body has been created for the sake of utility which does not also contribute something to its beauty. And this would be all the more apparent, if we knew more precisely how all its parts are connected and adapted to one another, and were not limited in our observations to what appears on the surface; for as to what is covered up and hidden from our view, the intricate web of veins and nerves, the vital parts of all that lies under the skin, no one can discover it. For although, with a cruel zeal for science, some medical men, who are called anatomists, have dissected the bodies of the dead, and sometimes even of sick persons who died under their knives, and have inhumanly pried into the secrets of the human body to learn the nature of the disease and its exact seat, and how it might be cured, yet those relations of which I speak, and which form the concord, or, as the Greeks call it, "harmony," of the whole body outside and in, as of some instrument, no one has been able to discover, because no one has been audacious enough to seek for them. But if these could be known, then even the inward parts, which seem to have no beauty, would so delight us with their exquisite fitness, as to afford a profounder satisfaction to the mind—and the eyes are but its ministers—than the obvious beauty which gratifies the eye. There are some things, too, which have such a place in the body, that they obviously serve no useful purpose, but are solely for beauty, as e.g. the nipples on a man's breast, or the beard on his face; for that this is for ornament, and not for protection, is proved by the bare faces of women, who ought rather, as the weaker sex, to enjoy such a defence. If, therefore, of all those members which are exposed to our view, there is certainly not one in which beauty is sacrificed to utility, while there are some which serve no purpose but only beauty, I think it can readily be concluded that in the creation of the human body comeliness was more regarded than necessity. In truth, necessity is a transitory thing; and the time is coming when we shall enjoy one another's beauty without any lust,—a condition which will specially redound to the praise of the creator, who, as it is said in the psalm, has "put on praise and comeliness."[49]

How can I tell of the rest of creation, with all its beauty and utility, which the divine goodness has given to man to please his eye and serve his purposes, condemned though he is, and hurled into these labours and miseries? Shall I speak of the manifold and various loveliness of sky, and earth, and sea; of the plentiful supply and wonderful qualities of the light; of sun, moon, and stars; of the shade of trees; of the colours and perfume of flowers; of the multitude of birds, all differing in plumage and in song; of the variety of animals, of which the smallest in size are often the most wonderful,—the works of ants and bees astonishing us more than the huge bodies of whales? Shall I speak of the sea, which itself is so grand a spectacle, when it arrays itself as it were in vestures of various colours, now running through every shade of green, and again becoming purple or blue? Is it not delightful to look at it in storm, and experience the soothing complacency which it inspires, by suggesting that we ourselves are not tossed and shipwrecked?[50] What shall I say of the numberless kinds of food to alleviate hunger, and the variety of seasonings to stimulate appetite which are scattered everywhere by nature, and for which we are not indebted to the art of cookery? How many natural appliances are there for preserving and restoring health! How grateful is the alternation of day and night! how pleasant the breezes that cool the air! how abundant the supply of clothing furnished us by trees and animals! Who can enumerate all the blessings we enjoy? If I were to attempt to detail and unfold only these few which I have indicated in the mass, such an enumeration would fill a volume. And all these are but the solace of the wretched and condemned, not the rewards of the blessed. What then shall these rewards be, if such be the blessings of a condemned state? What will he give to those whom he has predestined to life, who has given

49 Ps. 104: 1.
50 Cf. Lucretius 2.1 ff.

such things even to those whom he has predestined to death? What blessings will he shower in the blessed life upon those for whom, even in this state of misery, he has been willing that his only-begotten son should endure such sufferings even to death? Thus the apostle reasons concerning those who are predestined to that kingdom: "He that spared not his own son, but delivered him up for us all, how shall he not with him also give us all things?"[51] When this promise is fulfilled, what shall we be? What blessings shall we receive in that kingdom, since already we have received as the pledge of them Christ's dying? In what condition shall the spirit of man be, when it has no longer any vice at all; when it neither yields to any, nor is in bondage to any, nor has to make war against any, but is perfected, and enjoys undisturbed peace with itself? Shall it not then know all things with certainty, and without any labour or error, when unhindered and joyfully it drinks the wisdom of God at the fountainhead? What shall the body be, when it is in every respect subject to the spirit, from which it shall draw a life so sufficient, as to stand in need of no other nutriment? For it shall no longer be animal, but spiritual, having indeed the substance of flesh, but without any fleshly corruption.

25. *Of the obstinacy of those individuals who impugn the resurrection of the body, though, as was predicted, the whole world believes it.*

The foremost of the philosophers agree with us about the spiritual felicity enjoyed by the blessed in the life to come; it is only the resurrection of the flesh they call in question, and deny with all their might. But the mass of men, learned and unlearned, the world's wise men and its fools, have believed, and have left in meagre isolation the unbelievers, and have turned to Christ, who in his own resurrection demonstrated the reality of that which seems to our adversaries absurd. For the world has believed this which God predicted, as it was also predicted that the world would believe,—a prediction not due to the sorceries of Peter, since it was uttered so long before. He who has predicted these things, as I have already said, and am not ashamed to repeat, is the God before

[51] Rom. 8: 32.

whom all other divinities tremble, as Porphyry himself admits and seeks to prove, by testimonies from the oracles of these gods, and goes so far as to call him God the Father and King. Far be it from us to interpret these predictions as they do who have not believed, along with the whole world, in that which it was predicted the world would believe in. For why should we not rather understand them as the world does, whose belief was predicted, and leave that handful of unbelievers to their idle talk and obstinate and solitary infidelity? For if they maintain that they interpret them differently only to avoid charging scripture with folly, and so doing an injury to that God to whom they bear so notable a testimony, is it not a much greater injury they do him when they say that his predictions must be understood otherwise than the world believed them, though he himself praised, promised, accomplished this belief on the world's part? And why can he not cause the body to rise again, and live for ever? or is it not to be believed that he will do this, because it is an undesirable thing, and unworthy of God? Of his omnipotence, which effects so many great miracles, we have already said enough. If they wish to know what the Almighty cannot do, I shall tell them he cannot lie. Let us therefore believe what he can do, by refusing to believe what he cannot do. Refusing to believe that he can lie, let them believe that he will do what he has promised to do; and let them believe it as the world has believed it, whose faith he predicted, whose faith he praised, whose faith he promised, whose faith he now points to. But how do they prove that the resurrection is an undesirable thing? There shall then be no corruption, which is the only evil thing about the body. I have already said enough about the order of the elements, and the other fanciful objections men raise; and in the thirteenth book I have, in my own judgment, sufficiently illustrated the facility of movement which the incorruptible body shall enjoy, judging from the ease and vigour we experience even now, when the body is in good health. Those who have either not read the former books, or wish to refresh their memory, may read them for themselves.

26. *That the opinion of Porphyry, that the soul, in order to be blessed, must be separated from every kind of body, is demol-*

ished by Plato, who says that the supreme God promised the gods[52] *that they should never be expelled from their bodies.*

But, say they, Porphyry tells us that the soul, in order to be blessed, must escape connection with every kind of body. It does not avail, therefore, to say that the future body shall be incorruptible, if the soul cannot be blessed till delivered from every kind of body. But in the book above mentioned I have already sufficiently discussed this. This one thing only will I repeat,—let Plato, their master, correct his writings, and say that their gods, in order to be blessed, must quit their bodies, or, in other words, die; for he said that they were shut up in celestial bodies, and that, nevertheless, the God who made them promised them immortality,—that is to say, an eternal tenure of these same bodies, such as was not provided for them naturally, but only by the further intervention of his will, that thus they might be assured of felicity. In this he obviously overturns their assertion that the resurrection of the body cannot be believed because it is impossible; for, according to him, when the uncreated God promised immortality to the created gods, he expressly said that he would do what was impossible. For Plato tells us that he said, "As you have had a beginning, so you cannot be immortal and incorruptible; yet you shall not decay, nor shall any fate destroy you or prove stronger than my will, which more effectually binds you to immortality than the bond of your nature keeps you from it."[53] If they who hear these words have, we do not say understanding, but ears, they cannot doubt that Plato believed that God promised to the gods he had made that he would effect an impossibility. For he who says, "You cannot be immortal, but by my will you shall be immortal," what else does he say than this, "I shall make you what you cannot be?" The body, therefore, shall be raised incorruptible, immortal, spiritual, by him who, according to Plato, has promised to do that which is impossible. Why then do they still exclaim that this which God has promised, which the world has believed on God's promise as was predicted, is an impossibility? For what we say is, that the God who, even according to Plato, does impos-

[52] I.e., lesser, "created" gods; cf. *Timaeus* 40 b, d.
[53] Ibid.

sible things, will do this. It is not, then, necessary to the blessedness of the soul that it be detached from a body of any kind whatever, but that it receive an incorruptible body. And in what incorruptible body will they more suitably rejoice than in that in which they groaned when it was corruptible? For thus they shall not feel that dire craving which Vergil, in imitation of Plato, has ascribed to them when he says that they wish to return again to their bodies.[54] They shall not, I say, feel this desire to return to their bodies, since they shall have those bodies to which a return was desired, and shall, indeed, be in such thorough possession of them, that they shall never lose them even for the briefest moment, nor ever lay them down in death.

27. *Of the apparently conflicting opinions of Plato and Porphyry, which would have conducted them both to the truth if they could have yielded to one another.*

Statements were made by Plato and Porphyry singly, which if they could have seen their way to hold in common, they might possibly have become Christians. Plato said that souls could not exist eternally without bodies; for it was on this account, he said, that the souls even of wise men must some time or other return to their bodies. Porphyry, again, said that the purified soul, when it has returned to the father, shall never return to the ills of this world. Consequently, if Plato had communicated to Porphyry that which he saw to be true, that souls, though perfectly purified, and belonging to the wise and righteous, must return to human bodies; and if Porphyry, again, had imparted to Plato the truth which he saw, that holy souls shall never return to the miseries of a corruptible body, so that they should not have each held only his own opinion but should both have held both truths, I think they would have seen that it follows that the souls return to their bodies, and also that these bodies shall be such as to afford them a blessed and immortal life. For, according to Plato, even holy souls shall return to the body; according to Porphyry, holy souls shall not return to the ills of this world. Let Porphyry then say with Plato, they shall return to the body; let Plato say with Porphyry, they shall not return to their old misery: and

[54] *Aen.* 6.751.

they will agree that they return to bodies in which they shall suffer no more. And this is nothing else than what God has promised,—that he will give eternal felicity to souls joined to their own bodies. For this, I presume, both of them would readily concede, that if the souls of the saints are to be re-united to bodies, it shall be to their own bodies, in which they have endured the miseries of this life, and in which, to escape these miseries, they served God with piety and fidelity.

28. *What Plato or Labeo, or even Varro, might have contributed to the true faith of the resurrection, if they had adopted one another's opinions in one scheme.*

Some Christians, who have a liking for Plato on account of his magnificent style and the truths which he now and then uttered, say that he even held an opinion similar to our own regarding the resurrection of the dead. Cicero, however, alluding to this in his *De Republica,* asserts that Plato meant it rather as a playful fancy than as a reality; for he introduces a man[55] who had come to life again, and gave a narrative of his experience in corroboration of the doctrines of Plato. Labeo, too, says that two men died on one day, and met at a cross-roads, and that, being afterwards ordered to return to their bodies, they agreed to be friends for life, and were so till they died again. But the resurrection which these writers instance resembles that of those persons whom we have ourselves known to rise again, and who came back indeed to this life, but not so as never to die again. Marcus Varro, however, in his work *On the Origin of the Roman People,* records something more remarkable; I think his own words should be given. "Certain astrologers," he says, "have written that men are destined to a new birth, which the Greeks call *palingenesis.* This will take place after four hundred and forty years have elapsed; and then the same soul and the same body, which were formerly united in the person, shall again be reunited." This Varro, indeed, or those nameless astrologers,—for he does not give us the names of the men whose statement he cites, —have affirmed what is indeed not altogether true; for once the souls have returned to the bodies they wore, they shall never afterwards leave them. Yet what they say upsets and

[55] *Republic* 10. 614 b.

demolishes much of that idle talk of our adversaries about the impossibility of the resurrection. For those who have been or are of this opinion, have not thought it possible that bodies which have dissolved into air, or dust, or ashes, or water, or into the bodies of the beasts or even of the men that fed on them, should be restored again to that which they formerly were. And therefore, if Plato and Porphyry, or rather, if their disciples now living, agree with us that holy souls shall return to the body, as Plato says, and that, nevertheless, they shall not return to misery, as Porphyry maintains,—if they accept the consequence of these two propositions which is taught by the Christian faith, that they shall receive bodies in which they may live eternally without suffering any misery,—let them also adopt from Varro the opinion that they shall return to the same bodies as they were formerly in, and thus the whole question of the eternal resurrection of the body shall be resolved out of their own mouths.

29. *Of the beatific vision.*

And now let us consider, with such ability as God may grant us, how the saints shall be employed when they are clothed in immortal and spiritual bodies, and when the flesh shall live no longer in a fleshly but a spiritual fashion. And indeed, to tell the truth, I am at a loss to understand the nature of that employment, or, shall I rather say, repose and ease, for it has never come within the range of my bodily senses. And if I should speak of my mind or understanding, what is our understanding in comparison of its excellence? For then shall be that "peace of God which," as the apostle says, "passes all understanding,"[56]—that is to say, all human, and perhaps all angelic understanding, but certainly not the divine. That it passes ours there is no doubt; but if it passes that of the angels,—and he who says *"all"* understanding" seems to make no exception in their favour,—then we must understand him to mean that neither we nor the angels can understand, as God understands, the peace which God himself enjoys. Doubtless this passes all understanding but his own. But as we shall one day be made to participate, according to our

[56] Phil. 4: 7.

slender capacity, in his peace, both in ourselves, and with our neighbour, and with God our chief good, in this respect the angels understand the peace of God in their own measure, and men too, though now far behind them, whatever spiritual advance they have made. For we must remember how great a man he was who said, "We know in part, and we prophesy in part, until that which is perfect is come;"[57] and "Now we see through a glass, darkly; but then face to face."[58] Such also is now the vision of the holy angels, who are also called our angels, because we, being rescued out of the power of darkness, and receiving the guarantee of the Spirit, are translated into the kingdom of Christ, and already begin to belong to those angels with whom we shall enjoy that holy and most delightful city of God of which we have now written so much. Thus, then, the angels of God are our angels, as Christ is God's and also ours. They are God's, because they have not abandoned him; they are ours, because we are their fellow-citizens. The Lord Jesus also said, "See that you despise not one of these little ones: for I say to you, that in heaven their angels do always see the face of my Father who is in heaven."[59] As, then, they see, so shall we also see; but we do not thus see yet. Therefore the apostle uses the words cited a little while ago, "Now we see through a glass, darkly; but then face to face." This vision is reserved as the reward of our faith; and of it the apostle John also says, "When he shall appear, we shall be like him, for we shall see him as he is."[60] By "the face" of God we are to understand his manifestation, and not a part of the body similar to that which in our bodies we call by that name.

And so, when I am asked how the saints shall be employed in that spiritual body, I do not say what I see, but I say what I believe, according to that which I read in the psalm, "I believed, therefore have I spoken."[61] I say, then, they shall in the body see God; but whether they shall see him by means of the body, as we now see the sun, moon, stars, sea, earth,

[57] 1 Cor. 13: 9 f.
[58] 1 Cor. 13: 12.
[59] Matt. 18: 10.
[60] 1 John 3: 2.
[61] Ps. 116: 10.

and all that is in it, that is a difficult question. For it is hard to say that the saints shall then have such bodies that they shall not be able to shut and open their eyes as they please; while it is harder still to say that every one who shuts his eyes shall lose the vision of God. For if the prophet Elisha, though at a distance, saw his servant Gehazi, who thought that his wickedness would escape his master's observation and accepted gifts from Naaman the Syrian, whom the prophet had cleansed from his foul leprosy, how much more shall the saints in the spiritual body see all things, not only though their eyes are shut, but though they themselves are at a great distance? For then shall be "that which is perfect," of which the apostle says, "We know in part, and we prophesy in part; but when that which is perfect is come, then that which is in part shall be done away." Then, that he may illustrate as well as possible, by a simile, how superior the future life is to the life now lived, not only by ordinary men, but even by the foremost of the saints, he says, "When I was a child, I understood as a child, I spoke as a child, I thought as a child; but when I became a man, I put away childish things. Now we see through a glass, darkly; but then face to face: now I know in part; but then shall I know even as also I am known."[62] If, then, even in this life, in which the prophetic power of remarkable men is no more worthy to be compared to the vision of the future life than childhood is to manhood, Elisha, though distant from his servant, saw him accepting gifts, shall we say that when that which is perfect is come, and the corruptible body no longer oppresses the soul, but is incorruptible and offers no impediment to it, the saints shall need bodily eyes to see, though Elisha had no need of them to see his servant? For, following the Septuagint version, these are the prophet's words: "Did not my heart go with you, when the man came out of his chariot to meet you, and you took his gifts?"[63] Or, as the priest Jerome rendered it from the Hebrew, "Was not my heart present when the man turned from his chariot to meet you?" The prophet said that he saw this with his heart, miraculously aided by God, as no one can

[62] 1 Cor. 13: 11 f.
[63] 2 Kings 5: 26.

doubt. But how much more abundantly shall the saints enjoy this gift when God shall be all in all? Nevertheless the bodily eyes also shall have their office and their place, and shall be used by the spirit through the spiritual body. For the prophet did not forego the use of his eyes for seeing what was before them, though he did not need them to see his absent servant, and though he could have seen these present objects in spirit, and with his eyes shut, as he saw things far distant in a place where he himself was not. Far be it, then, from us to say that in the life to come the saints shall not see God when their eyes are shut, since they shall always see him with the spirit.

But the question arises, whether, when their eyes are open, they shall see him with the bodily eye? If the eyes of the spiritual body have no more power than the eyes which we now possess, manifestly God cannot be seen with them. They must be of a very different power if they can look upon that incorporeal nature which is not contained in any place, but is all in every place. For though we say that God is in heaven and on earth, as he himself says by the prophet, "I fill heaven and earth,"[64] we do not mean that there is one part of God in heaven and another part on earth; but he is all in heaven and all on earth, not at alternate intervals of time, but both at once, as no bodily nature can be. The eye, then, shall have a vastly superior power,—the power not of keen sight, such as is ascribed to serpents or eagles, for however keenly these animals see, they can discern nothing but bodily substances, —but the power of seeing things incorporeal. Possibly it was this great power of vision which was temporarily communicated to the eyes of the holy Job while yet in this mortal body, when he says to God, "I have heard of you by the hearing of the ear; but now my eye sees you: therefore I abhor myself, and melt away, and count myself dust and ashes;"[65] although there is no reason why we should not understand this of the eye of the heart, of which the apostle says, "having the eyes of your heart illuminated."[66] But that God shall be seen with these eyes no Christian doubts who believingly accepts what

[64] Jer. 23: 24.
[65] Job 43: 5 f.
[66] Eph. 1: 18.

our God and master says, "Blessed are the pure in heart: for
they shall see God."[67] But whether in the future life God
shall also be seen with the bodily eye, this is now our question.

The expression of scripture, "And all flesh shall see the salvation of God,"[68] may without difficulty be understood as if
it were said, "And every man shall see the Christ of God."
And he certainly was seen in the body, and shall be seen in
the body when he judges the living and the dead. And that
Christ is the salvation of God, many other passages of scripture witness, but especially the words of the venerable Simeon,
who, when he had received into his hands the infant Christ,
said, "Now you let your servant depart in peace, according
to your word: for my eyes have seen your salvation."[69] As for
the words of the above-mentioned Job, as they are found in
the Hebrew manuscripts, "And in my flesh I shall see God,"[70]
no doubt they were a prophecy of the resurrection of the
flesh; yet he does not say *by* the flesh." And indeed, if he
had said this, it would still be possible that Christ was meant
by "God;" for Christ shall be seen by the flesh in the flesh.
But even understanding it of God, it is only equivalent to saying, I shall be in the flesh when I see God. Then the apostle's
expression, "face to face,"[71] does not oblige us to believe that
we shall see God by the bodily face in which are the eyes
of the body, for we shall see him without intermission in spirit.
And if the apostle had not referred to the face of the inner
man, he would not have said, "But we, with unveiled face beholding as in a glass the glory of the Lord, are transformed
into the same image, from glory to glory, as by the Spirit of
the Lord."[72] In the same sense we understand what the Psalmist sings, "Draw near to him, and be enlightened; and your
faces shall not be ashamed."[73] For it is by faith we draw near
to God, and faith is an act of the spirit, not of the body. But
as we do not know what degree of perfection the spiritual body

[67] Matt. 5: 8.
[68] Luke 3: 6.
[69] Luke 2: 29 f.
[70] Job 19: 26.
[71] 1 Cor. 13: 12.
[72] 2 Cor. 3: 18.
[73] Ps. 34: 5.

shall attain,—for here we speak of a matter of which we have no experience, and upon which the authority of scripture does not definitely pronounce,—it is necessary that the words of the Book of Wisdom be illustrated in us: "The thoughts of mortal men are timid, and our forecastings uncertain."[74]

For if that reasoning of the philosophers, by which they attempt to make out that intelligible or mental objects are so seen by the mind, and sensible or bodily objects so seen by the body, that the former cannot be discerned by the mind through the body, nor the latter by the mind itself without the body,—if this reasoning were trustworthy, then it would certainly follow that God could not be seen by the eye even of a spiritual body. But this reasoning is exploded both by true reason and by prophetic authority. For who is so little acquainted with the truth as to say that God has no cognisance of sensible objects? Has he therefore a body, the eyes of which give him this knowledge? Moreover, what we have just been relating of the prophet Elisha, does this not sufficiently show that bodily things can be discerned by the spirit without the help of the body? For when that servant received the gifts, certainly this was a bodily or material transaction, yet the prophet saw it not by the body, but by the spirit. As, therefore, it is agreed that bodies are seen by the spirit, what if the power of the spiritual body shall be so great that spirit also is seen by the body? For God is a spirit. Besides, each man recognises his own life—that life by which he now lives in the body, and which vivifies these earthly members and causes them to grow—by an interior sense, and not by his bodily eye; but the life of other men, though it is invisible, he sees with the bodily eye. For how do we distinguish between living and dead bodies, except by seeing at once both the body and the life which we cannot see save by the eye? But a life without a body we cannot see thus.

Therefore it may very well be, and it is thoroughly credible, that we shall in the future world see the material forms of the new heavens and the new earth in such a way that we shall most distinctly recognise God everywhere present and governing all things, material as well as spiritual, and shall

[74] Wis. 9: 14.

see him, not as now we understand the invisible things of God, by the things which are made,[75] and see him darkly, as in a mirror, and in part, and rather by faith than by bodily vision of material appearances, but by means of the bodies we shall wear and which we shall see wherever we turn our eyes. As we do not believe, but see that the living men around us who are exercising vital functions are alive, though we cannot see their life without their bodies, but see it most distinctly by means of their bodies, so, wherever we shall look with those spiritual eyes of our future bodies, we shall then, too, by means of bodily substances behold God, though a spirit, ruling all things. Either, therefore, the eyes shall possess some quality similar to that of the mind, by which they may be able to discern spiritual things, and among these God,—a supposition for which it is difficult or even impossible to find any support in scripture,—or, which is more easy to comprehend, God will be so known by us, and shall be so much before us, that we shall see him by the spirit in ourselves, in one another, in himself, in the new heavens and the new earth, in every created thing which shall then exist; and also by the body we shall see him in every body which the keen vision of the eye of the spiritual body shall reach. Our thoughts also shall be visible to all, for then shall be fulfilled the words of the apostle, "Judge nothing before the time, until the Lord come, who both will bring to light the hidden things of darkness, and will make manifest the thoughts of the heart, and then shall every one have praise of God."[76]

30. *Of the eternal felicity of the city of God, and of the perpetual Sabbath.*

How great shall be that felicity, which shall be tainted with no evil, which shall lack no good, and which shall afford leisure for the praises of God, who shall be all in all! For I do not know what other employment there can be where no lassitude shall slacken activity, nor any want stimulate to labour. I am admonished also by the sacred song, in which I read or hear the words, "Blessed are they that dwell in your house,

[75] Rom. 1: 20.
[76] 1 Cor. 4: 5.

O Lord; they will be still praising you."[77] All the members and organs of the incorruptible body, which now we see to be suited to various necessary uses, shall contribute to the praises of God; for in that life necessity shall have no place, but full, certain, secure, everlasting felicity. For all those parts of the bodily harmony, which are distributed through the whole body, within and without, and of which I have just been saying that they at present elude our observation, shall then be discerned; and, along with the other great and marvellous discoveries which shall then kindle rational minds in praise of the great artificer, there shall be the enjoyment of a beauty which appeals to the reason. What power of movement such bodies shall possess, I have not the audacity rashly to define, as I have not the ability to conceive. Nevertheless I will say that in any case, both in motion and at rest, they shall be, as in their appearance, worthy; for into that state nothing which is unworthy shall be admitted. One thing is certain, the body shall straightway be wherever the spirit wills, and the spirit shall will nothing which is unbecoming either to the spirit or to the body. True honour shall be there, for it shall be denied to none who is worthy, nor yielded to anyone unworthy; neither shall any unworthy person so much as seek it, for none but the worthy shall be there. True peace shall be there, where no one shall suffer opposition either from himself or any other. God himself, who is the author of virtue, shall there be its reward; for, as there is nothing greater or better, he has promised himself. What else was meant by his word through the prophet, "I will be your God, and you shall be my people,"[78] than, I shall be their satisfaction, I shall be all that men honourably desire,—life, and health, and nourishment, and plenty, and glory, and honour, and peace, and all good things? This, too, is the right interpretation of the saying of the apostle, "That God may be all in all."[79] He shall be the end of our desires who shall be seen without end, loved without surfeit, praised without weariness. This outgoing of affection, this employment, shall certainly be, like eternal life itself, common to all.

[77] Ps. 84: 4.
[78] Lev. 26: 12.
[79] 1 Cor. 15: 12.

But who can conceive, not to say describe, what degrees of honour and glory shall be awarded to the various degrees of merit? Yet it cannot be doubted that there shall be degrees. And in that blessed city there shall be this great blessing, that no inferior shall envy any superior, as now the archangels are not envied by the angels, because no one will wish to be what he has not received, though bound in strictest concord with him who has received; as in the body the finger does not seek to be the eye, though both members are harmoniously included in the complete structure of the body. And thus, along with his gift, greater or less, each shall receive this further gift of contentment—to desire no more than he has.

Neither are we to suppose that because sin shall have no power to delight them, free will must be withdrawn. It will, on the contrary, be all the more truly free, because set free from delight in sinning to take unfailing delight in not sinning. For the first freedom of will which man received when he was created upright consisted in an ability not to sin, but also in an ability to sin; whereas this last freedom of will shall be superior, inasmuch as it shall not be able to sin. This, indeed, shall not be a natural ability, but the gift of God. For it is one thing to be God, another thing to be a partaker of God. God by nature cannot sin, but the partaker of God receives this inability from God. And in this divine gift there was to be observed this gradation, that man should first receive a free will by which he was able not to sin, and at last a free will by which he was not able to sin,—the former being adapted to the acquiring of merit, the latter to the enjoying of the reward. But the nature thus constituted, having sinned when it had the ability to do so, it is by a more abundant grace that it is delivered so as to reach that freedom in which it cannot sin. For as the first immortality which Adam lost by sinning consisted in his being able not to die, while the last shall consist in his not being able to die; so the first free will consisted in his being able not to sin, the last in his not being able to sin. And thus piety and justice shall be as secure as happiness. For certainly by sinning we lost both piety and happiness; but when we lost happiness, we did not lose the love of it. Are we to say that God himself is not free because he cannot sin? In that city, then, there shall be free will, one in all the citizens, and indivisible in each, delivered from all ill, filled with all good, enjoying securely the delights of eternal joys, oblivious of sins, oblivious of sufferings, and yet not so oblivious of its deliverance as to be ungrateful to its deliverer.

The soul, then, shall have an intellectual remembrance of its past ills; but, so far as regards sensible experience, they shall be quite forgotten. For a skilful physician knows, indeed, professionally almost all diseases; but experimentally he is ignorant of a great number which he himself has never suffered from. As, therefore, there are two ways of knowing evil things,—one by mental insight, the other by sensible experience, for it is one thing to understand all vices by the wisdom of a cultivated mind, another to understand them by the foolishness of an abandoned life,—so also there are two ways of forgetting evils. For a well-instructed and learned man forgets them one way, and he who has experimentally suffered from them forgets them another,—the former by neglecting what he has learned, the latter by escaping what he has suffered. And in this latter way the saints shall forget their past ills, for they shall have so thoroughly escaped them all, that they shall be quite blotted out of their experience. But their intellectual knowledge, which shall be great, shall keep them acquainted not only with their own past woes, but with the eternal sufferings of the lost. For if they were not to know that they had been miserable, how could they, as the Psalmist says, for ever sing the mercies of God? Certainly that city shall have no greater joy than the celebration of the grace of Christ, who redeemed us by his blood. There shall be accomplished the words of the psalm, "Be still, and know that I am God."[80] There shall be the great Sabbath which has no evening, which God celebrated among his first works, as it is written, "And God rested on the seventh day from all his works which he had made. And God blessed the seventh day, and sanctified it; because in it he had rested from all his work which God began to make."[81] For we shall ourselves be the seventh day, when we shall be filled and replenished with God's blessing and sanctification. There shall we be still, and know that he

[80] Ps. 46: 10.
[81] Gen. 2: 2 f.

is God; that he is that which we ourselves aspired to be when we fell away from him, and listened to the voice of the seducer, "You shall be as gods,"[82] and so abandoned God, who would have made us as gods, not by deserting him, but by participating in him. For without him what have we accomplished, save to perish in his anger? But when we are restored by him, and perfected with greater grace, we shall have eternal leisure to see that he is God, for we shall be full of him when he shall be all in all. For even our good works, when they are understood to be rather his than ours, are imputed to us that we may enjoy this Sabbath rest. For if we attribute them to ourselves, they shall be servile; for it is said of the Sabbath, "You shall do no servile work in it."[83] Therefore also it is said by Ezekiel the prophet, "And I gave them my Sabbaths to be a sign between me and them, that they might know that I am the Lord who sanctify them."[84] This knowledge shall be perfected when we shall be perfectly at rest, and shall perfectly know that he is God.

This Sabbath shall appear still more clearly if we count the ages as days, in accordance with the periods of time defined in scripture, for that period will be found to be the seventh. The first age, as the first day, extends from Adam to the deluge; the second from the deluge to Abraham, equalling the first, not in length of time, but in the number of generations, there being ten in each. From Abraham to the advent of Christ there are, as the evangelist Matthew calculates, three periods, in each of which are fourteen generations,—one period from Abraham to David, a second from David to the captivity, a third from the captivity to the birth of Christ in the flesh. There are thus five ages in all. The sixth is now passing, and cannot be measured by any number of generations, as it has been said, "It is not for you to know the times, which the father hath put in his own power."[85] After this period God shall rest as on the seventh day, when he shall give us (who shall be the seventh day) rest in himself. But there is not now space to treat of these ages; suffice it to say that the seventh

82 Gen. 3: 5.
83 Deut. 5: 14.
84 Ezek. 20: 12.
85 Acts 1: 7.

shall be our Sabbath, which shall be brought to a close, not by an evening, but by the Lord's day, as an eighth and eternal day, consecrated by the resurrection of Christ, and prefiguring the eternal repose not only of the spirit, but also of the body. There we shall rest and see, see and love, love and praise. This is what shall be in the end without end. For what other end do we propose to ourselves than to attain to the kingdom of which there is no end?

I think I have now, by God's help, discharged my obligation in writing this large work. Let those who think I have said too little, or those who think I have said too much, forgive me; and let those who think I have said just enough join me in giving thanks to God. Amen.

The Grace of Christ and Original Sin
(A.D. 418)
Book 2

The monk Pelagius, commonly taken to have come from the British Isles, was in Rome by 410 where he converted a lawyer, Cœlestius. This latter and Julian, bishop of Eclanum, near Capua, made a trio of brilliant supporters of the cause of the virtue of human nature independent of grace. They were not alone, however; for they had many and influential followers in Rome and elsewhere. Pelagius and Cœlestius were in Africa about 411, but did not meet Augustine. Subsequently Cœlestius was accused of false doctrine before an African council (presided over by Augustine) in 412 and condemned—he then went on to Ephesus. Meanwhile Pelagius had gone to Palestine where he was also accused at a council at Diospolis in 415 for holding views similar to those for which Cœlestius had been condemned. Pelagius, explaining that Cœlestius was indiscreet, escaped censure. The matter came up for decision by Pope Innocent, who died, and then Pope Zosimus who eventually (but only under pressure from Africa) condemned both Pelagius and Cœlestius. A score of Italian bishops, of whom Julian was one, sided with Pelagius, now in Constantinople. We know nothing of Pelagius or Cœlestius subsequently. Their ideas survived in a modified form known as Semi-Pelagianism. The Council of Orange (539) upheld Augustine's views—apart, however, from his more extreme formulations on predestination. The essential problem in the Pelagian controversy is the relating of human free will with God's action. Pelagius spoke in the tradition of the civic virtues of Rome ("splendid vices" to Augustine; see p. 316). He also spoke in the tradition of the

Stoic philosophy which, while admitting that the Stoic Wise Man had never perhaps existed, insisted that he *could* exist. Likewise man unaided might not save himself—but the possibility of this must be held. In particular, Adam's progeny was not flawed by original sin—and therefore did not automatically require Christ's grace—at birth. This is the point at which Book 2 becomes relevant: there the central problems of original sin itself, sexuality and marriage (in which original sin is transmitted), free will and Christ's grace are treated at a mature stage and in a lively controversial context. The translation here is by Peter Holmes (Edinburgh, 1885).

RECOMMENDED READING

Portalié, pp. 177–229.

Battenhouse, pp. 203–34.

J. Ferguson, *Pelagius*, Cambridge, 1956.

R. F. Evans, *Pelagius: Inquiries and Reappraisals*, London, 1968.

G. Bonner, "Rufinus of Syria and African Pelagianism," *Augustinian Studies*, 1970, pp. 31–48.

P. Brown, *Religion and Society in the Age of Saint Augustine* (London, 1972), pp. 183–226; *Augustine of Hippo* (London, 1967), pp. 340–52.

Other Augustine texts on Pelagianism: *De peccatorum meritis et remissione; De spiritu et littera; De gratia Novi Testamenti; De natura et gratia; De perfectione iustitiae hominis; De gestis Pelagii; De nuptiis et concupiscentia; De anima et eius origine; Contra duas epistulas Pelagianorum; Contra Julianum; De gratia et libero arbitrio; De correptione et gratia; De praedestinatione sanctorum; De dono perseverantiae; Opus imperfectum contra secundam Juliani responsionem.*

SPECIAL TOPICS

1. *Grace and free will* (Book 2.28 ff.; see also pp. 316 f.)

Up to A.D. 395 or so Augustine held the view that God does not give grace unless an act of man's free will precedes (*De diversis quaestionibus*, 83.68.3–5; *Epistulae ad Romanos quarumdam propositionum expositio* 55–62). By 397, however, according to himself (*De dono perseverantiae* 21.55) Augustine had changed his opinion and had in fact formulated what was to be his final view on grace and free will—before any pressure from the Pelagians. This doctrine can be seen in the *De diversis quaestionibus ad Simplicianum* (A.D. 396). In any consideration of Augustine's treatment of free will it has to be remembered that he distinguished between "the exercise of the will itself and the exercise of its power. Not everyone that has the will has the power also . . . we sometimes will what we cannot do, and sometimes can do what we do not will" (*De spiritu et littera* 53). For Augustine the real exercise of free will lies in the power to execute—the exercise of the will itself is the area for the influence of grace. Augustine accepts that God prepares our will—while leaving it free: "not because it is not in the choice of man's free will to believe or not to believe, but because in the elect the will is prepared by God" (*De praedestinatione sanctorum* 5.10). In the afterlife man's free will will consist in his not being able to sin, whereas in Adam it consisted in his being able not to sin (*City of God* 22.30). A nerve center of the Pelagian position is exposed at considerable length and with perhaps tedious (for us) historical details in the book given here: infants, according to the Pelagians, are born now as Adam was—that is without supernatural elevation and without inherited ("original") sin. This position negatives the propositions that man fell from a higher state to the mortal one known to us; that death and concupiscence resulted from that fall; and that the sin of Adam injured his descendants. In brief: man does not have to be liberated by another from any original sin; he is wholly responsible for himself. Pelagius employed a formula not unlike that of Augustine himself before 395: "if something precedes [the act of will], the will is destroyed" (*Opus imperfectum* 5.41). The Council of Carthage in 418, on the contrary, held that Adam had been immortal before the fall; his sin is transmitted to his descendants; infants must be baptized to be released from this sin; grace is absolutely necessary to avoid sin. Augustine developed further the idea of the gratuitousness of grace. Portalié sums up the Augustinian position as follows: "First, God, through his grace, is the absolute master of all the determinations of the will. Second, man remains just as free under the influence of grace as he is in its absence. Third, the reconciliation of these two truths depends upon the method of the divine government" (p. 192). The third is the crucial point. Here Augustine's extraordinary conviction on Providence makes it possible for him to accept that God's grace and man's good will do in fact coincide. See pp. 316 f.

2. Original sin and concupiscence (Book 2.38 ff.)

While previous theologians concerned themselves with *punishment* or loss of privileges caused by original sin, Augustine stressed the additional *guilt* aspect arising from man's moral union with Adam. Readers should note Augustine's use in this book (36) of the phrase *massa perdita* ("ruined mass") of all children born of Adam. Some commentators believe that Augustine simply identified original sin with concupiscence. It seems more likely, however, that in Augustine's view the culpability that arises from our moral union with Adam is the sin. Concupiscence on the other hand is its effect, is independent of our free will, but is not in itself a sin. Nevertheless, as the present book only too clearly illustrates, Augustine used such exaggerated terms of concupiscence that his views on marriage were greatly affected. See Portalié, pp. 204–29; H. Rondet, *Original Sin* (New York, 1972), pp. 113–32.

3. Concupiscence, sexuality and marriage (Book 2.38 ff.)

In effect, Augustine appears to say that original sin is transmitted through concupiscence—in sexual pleasure. This is at best a rather jaundiced view of sex in itself. Marriage, however, is unambiguously commended for its three goods: children, guarantee of chastity, pledge of union (2.39). It is clear, however, that according to Augustine sexual pleasure must be "reduced to the good purposes of the moderate procreation of children" (2.38) and that good Christians should not—as others do—expose themselves to morbid concupiscence. Continence, even in marriage, is better than the normal use of marriage: contraception, he pronounces, even by the rhythm method, and abortion are wrong. The literary prejudices of the ancient world, Neoplatonism and Manichaeism—as well as the pressures of the Pelagian controversy centering on sexual pleasure in conception—and many other factors had an undue influence on Augustine's view of sexuality. See J. O'Meara, "Augustine's Attitude to Love," *Arethusa*, vol. 2 (1969), 1, pp. 46–60; L. Janssens, "Morale Congugale et Progestogènes," *Ephemerides Theologicae Lovanienses* 39.4, pp. 787–826; B. Pereira, *La doctrine du mariage selon s. Augustin* (Paris, 1930); A. Reuter, *S. Augustini doctrina de bonis matrimonii* (Rome, 1942). Other Augustine texts on marriage: *De bono conjugali; De nuptiis et concupiscentia; De conjugiis adulterinis.*

THE GRACE OF CHRIST AND ORIGINAL SIN

BOOK 2

ON ORIGINAL SIN.

CHAP. 1.

Next I beg of you, Albina, Pinianus, and Melania,[1] to observe carefully with what caution you ought, on the question of the baptism of infants, to lend an ear to men of this character, who have not the courage to refuse openly the font of regeneration and the forgiveness of sins to this early age, for fear that Christians would not bear to listen to them; and who yet persist in holding and urging their opinion, that the children of our first parent were not born in sin, although they apparently allow infants to be baptized for the remission of sins. You have, indeed, yourselves informed me in your letter, that you heard Pelagius say in your presence, reading out of that book of his which he declared that he had actually sent to Rome, that his party maintain that "infants ought to be baptized with the same formula of sacramental words as adults." Who, after that statement, would suppose that they ought to raise any question at all on this subject? Or if he did suppose so, to whom would he not seem to indulge a very calumnious disposition—previous, at all events, to the perusal of their plain assertions, in which they deny that infants inherit original sin, and contend that all persons are by birth free from all sinful taint?

---

[1] These were friends—a mother, her son and his wife respectively —somewhat under the influence of Pelagius.

CHAP. 2.—*Cœlestius, on his trial at Carthage, refuses to condemn this error; the written statement which he gave to Zosimus, bishop of Rome.*

Cœlestius, indeed, maintained this erroneous doctrine with less restraint. To such an extent did he push his freedom as actually to refuse, when on trial before the bishops at Carthage, to condemn those who say, "That Adam's sin injured only Adam himself, and not the human race, and that infants at their birth are in the same state that Adam was in before his transgression and fall."[2] In the written statement, too, which he presented to the most blessed Pope Zosimus at Rome, he declared with especial plainness, "that original sin binds not a single infant." Concerning the proceedings at Carthage we copy the following account from his words.

CHAP. 3.—*Part of the acts of the Council of Carthage against Cœlestius.*

"The bishop Aurelius said: Let what follows be recited. It was accordingly recited, that the sin of Adam injured only himself, and not the human race. Then, after the recital, Cœlestius said: I said that I was in doubt about the transmission of sin,[3] but so as to yield assent to any man whom God has gifted with the grace of knowledge; for the fact is, that I have heard different opinions from men who have even been appointed priests in the Catholic Church. The deacon Paulinus[4] said: Tell us their names. Cœlestius answered: The holy priest Rufinus, who lived at Rome with the holy Pammachius. I heard him declare that there is no transmitted sin. The deacon Paulinus then asked: Is there any one else? Cœlestius replied: I heard others say the same. The deacon Paulinus rejoined: Tell us their names. Cœlestius said: Is not one priest enough for you?" Then afterwards in another passage we read: "The bishop Aurelius said: Let the rest of the

[2] Pelagius condemned this position of Cœlestius.

[3] *De traduce peccati*, the technical phrase to express the conveyance by birth of original sin.

[4] This Paulinus, was the deacon of Ambrose, bishop of Milan, and the author of his biography, which he wrote at the instance of Augustine. He lived in Africa when John was pretorian prefect, i.e. either in the year 412, or 413, or 422. The trial mentioned in the text took place about the commencement of the year 413.

book be read." It then went on to recite how infants at their birth are in the same state as Adam was before his transgression; and they read to the very end of the little book which had been previously put in. "The bishop Aurelius inquired: Have you, Cœlestius, taught at any time, as the deacon Paulinus has stated, that infants are at their birth in the same state as Adam was previous to his transgression? Cœlestius answered: Let him explain what he meant when he said, *'previous to his transgression.'* The deacon Paulinus then said: Do you on your side deny that you ever taught this doctrine? It must be one of two things: he must either say that he never so taught, or else he must now condemn the opinion. Cœlestius rejoined: I have already said, Let him explain the words he mentioned, *'previous to the transgression.'* The deacon Paulinus then said: You must deny ever having taught this. The bishop Aurelius said: I ask, What conclusion I have on my part to draw from this man's obstinacy; my affirmation is, that although Adam, as created in Paradise, is said to have been made incapable of dissolution at first, he afterwards became corruptible through transgressing the commandment. Do you say so, brother Paulinus? I do, my lord, answered the deacon Paulinus. Then the bishop Aurelius said: As regards the condition of infants before baptism at the present day, the deacon Paulinus wishes to be informed whether it is such as Adam's was before his transgression; and whether at least it derives the guilt of transgression from the original sin wherein it is born? The deacon Paulinus asked: Whether he actually taught this, or could not deny the allegation? Cœlestius answered: With regard to the transmission of original sin, I have already asserted, that I have heard many persons of acknowledged position in the Catholic Church deny it altogether; and on the other hand, many affirm it: it may be fairly deemed a matter for inquiry, but not a heresy. I have always maintained that infants require baptism, and ought to be baptized. What else does he want?"

CHAP. 4.

You, of course, see that Cœlestius here conceded baptism for infants only in such a manner as to be unwilling to confess that the sin of the first man, which is washed away in the font of regeneration, is transferred to them, although at the same time he did not venture to deny the transmission; but by reason of his uncertainty and doubt he refused to condemn those who maintain "that Adam's sin injured only himself, and not the human race; and that infants at their birth are in the self-same condition wherein Adam was before he fell."

CHAP. 5.—*Cœlestius' book which was produced in the proceedings at Rome.*

But in the book which he published at Rome, and produced in the proceedings before the church there, he speaks on this question in such a way as to show that he really believed that about which he had professed to be in doubt. For these are his words: "That infants, however, ought to be baptized for the remission of sins, according to the rule of the church universal, and according to the meaning of the Gospel, we readily admit. For the Lord has determined that the kingdom of heaven should be conferred only on baptized persons;[5] and since the resources of nature do not possess it, it must necessarily be conferred by God's free grace." Now if he had not said anything elsewhere on this subject, who would not have supposed that he acknowledged the remission of original sin in infants at their baptism, by saying that they ought to be baptized for the remission of sins? Hence the point of what you have stated in your letter, that Pelagius' answer to you was on this line, "that infants are baptized with the same words of sacramental formula as adults," and that you rejoiced to hear the very thing which you were desirous of hearing, and yet that we preferred holding a consultation concerning his words.

CHAP. 6.—*Cœlestius the disciple is in this work bolder than his master.*

Observe carefully, then, what Cœlestius has advanced so very openly, and you will discover what amount of concealment Pelagius has practised upon you. Cœlestius goes on to say as follows: "That infants, however, must be baptized for the remission of sins, was not admitted by us with the view of our seeming to affirm the doctrine of original sin, which

[5] John 3: 5.

is very alien from the sentiment of Catholics. Because sin is not born with a man; it is subsequently committed by the man: for it is shown to be a fault, not of nature, but of the human will. It is fitting, indeed, to confess this, lest we should seem to make different kinds of baptism; it is, moreover, necessary to lay down this preliminary safeguard, lest by the occasion of this mystery evil should, to the disparagement of the creator, be said to be conveyed to man by nature, previous to man's having committed it at all." Now Pelagius was either afraid or ashamed to avow this to be his own opinion before you; although his disciple experienced neither a qualm nor a blush in openly professing it to be his, without any obscure subterfuges, in presence of the Apostolic See.

CHAP. 7.—Pope Zosimus kindly excuses him.

The bishop, however, who presides over this See, upon seeing him hurrying headlong in so great presumption, like a madman, chose in his great compassion, with a view to the man's repentance, if it might be, rather to bind him tightly by eliciting from him answers to questions proposed by himself, than by the stroke of a severe condemnation to drive him over the precipice, down which he seemed to be even now ready to fall. I say advisedly, "down which he seemed to be ready to fall," rather than "over which he had actually fallen," because he had already in this same book of his forecast the subject with an intended reference to questions of this sort in the following words: "If it should so happen that any error of ignorance has stolen over us, who are but human beings, let it be corrected by your decisive sentence."

CHAP. 8.—Cælestius condemned by Zosimus.

The venerable Pope Zosimus, keeping in view this deprecatory preamble, dealt with the man, puffed up as he was with the blasts of false doctrine, in such a way as to condemn all the objectionable points which had been alleged against him by the deacon Paulinus, while yielding his assent to the rescript of the Apostolic See which had been issued by his predecessor of sacred memory. The accused man, however, refused to condemn the objections raised by the deacon, yet he did not venture to hold out against the letter of the blessed

Pope Innocent; indeed, he went so far as to promise "that he would condemn all the points which the Apostolic See condemned." Thus the man was treated with gentle remedies, as a delirious patient who required rest; but, at the same time, he was not regarded as being yet ready to be released from the restraints of excommunication. The interval of two months was granted him, until communications could be received from Africa, with the further concession of a provision for penance, under the mild restorative of the sentence which had been pronounced. For the truth is, if he would have laid aside his vain obstinacy, and be now willing to carry out what he had undertaken, and would carefully read the very letter to which he had replied by promising submission, he would yet come to a better mind. But after the rescripts were duly issued from the council of the African bishops, there were very good reasons why the sentence should be carried out against him, in strictest accordance with equity. What these reasons were you may read for yourselves, for we have sent you all the particulars.

CHAP. 9.—*Pelagius deceived the council in Palestine, but was unable to deceive the church at Rome. The faith of the Romans deserved to be spoken of. Pelagius lived at Rome for some time.*

From these you will find that even Pelagius, if he will only reflect candidly on his own position and writings, has no reason for saying that he ought not to have been banned with such a sentence. For although he deceived the council in Palestine, seemingly clearing himself before it, he entirely failed in imposing on the church at Rome (where, as you well know, he is by no means a stranger), although he went so far as to make the attempt to succeed by one means or another. But, as I have just said, he entirely failed. For the most blessed Pope Zosimus recollected what his predecessor, who had set him so worthy an example, had thought of these very proceedings. Nor did he omit to observe what opinion was entertained about this man by the trusty Romans, whose faith deserved to be spoken of in the Lord,[6] and whose consistent zeal in defence of catholic truth against this heresy he saw prevailing among them with warmth, and at the same time

6 Rom. 1: 8.

most perfect harmony. Pelagius had lived among them for a long while, and his opinions could not escape their notice; moreover, they had so completely found out his disciple Cœlestius, as to be able at once to adduce the most trustworthy and irrefragable evidence on this subject. Now what was the solemn judgment which the holy Pope Innocent formed respecting the proceedings in the Synod of Palestine, by which Pelagius boasts of having been acquitted, you may indeed read in the letter which he addressed to me. It is duly mentioned also in the answer which was forwarded by the African Synod to the venerable Pope Zosimus, and which, along with the other instructions, we have despatched to your charity.[7] But it seems to me, at the same time, that I ought not to omit producing the particulars in the present work.

CHAP. 10.—*The judgment of Innocent respecting the proceedings in Palestine.*

Five bishops, then, of whom I was one, wrote him a letter,[8] wherein we mentioned the proceedings in Palestine, of which the report had already reached us. We informed him that in the East, where this man lived, there had taken place certain ecclesiastical proceedings, in which he is thought to have been acquitted on all the charges. To this communication from us Innocent replied in a letter which contains the following among other words: "There are," he says, "sundry positions, as stated in these very acts, which, when they were objected against him, he partly suppressed by avoiding them altogether, and partly confused in absolute obscurity, by wresting many words from their relative meaning; while there are other allegations which he cleared off,—not, indeed, in the honest way which he seemed at the time to resort to, but rather by methods of sophistry, meeting some of the objections with a flat denial, and tampering with others by a fallacious interpretation. Would to God, however, that he would even now adopt what is the far more desirable course of turning from his own error back to the true ways of catholic faith; that he would also, duly considering God's daily grace, and acknowledging its help, be willing and desirous to appear, amidst the approbation

---

[7] I.e., Albina, Pinianus and Melania.
[8] *Letter* 177.

of all men, to be truly corrected by the method of open conviction,—not, indeed, by judicial process, but by a hearty conversion to the catholic faith. We are therefore unable either
to approve of or to blame their proceedings at that trial; for
we cannot tell whether the proceedings were true, or even,
if true, whether they do not really show that the man escaped
by subterfuge, rather than that he cleared himself by entire
truth."[9] You see clearly from these words, how the most
blessed Pope Innocent without doubt speaks of this man as
of one who was by no means unknown to him. You see what
opinion he entertained about his acquittal. You see, moreover,
what his successor the holy Pope Zosimus was bound to recollect,—as in truth he did,—even to confirm without doubt or
wavering the judgment in this case of his predecessor.

CHAP. 11.—*How Pelagius deceived the Synod of Palestine.*

Now I pray you to observe carefully by what evidence
Pelagius is shown to have deceived his judges in Palestine on
this very question of the baptism of infants, not to mention
other points; and I make this request of you, lest we should
seem to any one to have used calumny and suspicion, rather
than to have ascertained the certain fact, when we alleged
that Pelagius concealed the opinion which Cœlestius expressed with greater frankness, while at the same time he
actually entertained the same views. Now, from what has
been stated above, it has been clearly seen that, when
Cœlestius refused to condemn the assertion that "Adam's
sin injured only himself, and not the human race, and that
infants at their birth are in the same state that Adam was
before his transgression," he did so because he saw that, by
condemning these propositions, he would in fact affirm that
there was in infants a transmission to them of Adam's sin.
When, however, it was objected to Pelagius that he was of
one mind with Cœlestius on this point, he condemned the
words without hesitation or recall. I am quite aware that you
have read all this before. Since, however, we are not writing
this account simply for yourselves, we proceed to transcribe
the very words of the synodal acts, lest the reader should be

[9] *Letter* 183.3.4.

unwilling either to turn to the record for himself, or if he does not possess it, take any trouble to procure a copy. Here, then, are the words:—

Chap. 12.—*A portion of the acts of the Synod of Palestine in the cause of Pelagius.*

"The Synod said: now, since Pelagius has pronounced his anathema on this shifting utterance of folly, rightly replying that a man can with God's help and grace live *anamartētos,* that is to say, without sin, let him give us his answer on some other articles also. Another particular in the teaching of Cœlestius, disciple of Pelagius, selected from the heads which were mentioned and heard before the holy Aurelius bishop of Carthage, and other bishops, was to this effect: 'That Adam was made mortal, and that he must have died, whether he sinned or not; that Adam's sin injured himself alone, and not the human race; that the law no less than the gospel leads us to the kingdom of heaven; that before the coming of Christ there were persons who lived without sin; that new-born infants are in the same condition as Adam was before his transgression; that, on the one hand, the entire human race does not die owing to Adam's death and transgression, nor, on the other hand, does the whole human race rise again through the resurrection of Christ; that the holy bishop Augustine wrote a book in answer to his followers in Sicily, on articles which were subjoined; and in this book, which was addressed to Hilary, are contained the following statements: that a man can be without sin if he wishes; that infants, even if they die unbaptized, have eternal life; that rich men, even if they are baptized, unless they renounce and give up all, have, whatever good they may seem to have done, nothing of it put to their credit, nor can they possess the kingdom of heaven.' Pelagius then said: As regards man's power to live without sin, my opinion has been already given. With respect, however, to the allegation that there were even before the Lord's coming persons who lived without sin, we also on our part say that before the coming of Christ there certainly were persons who passed their lives in holiness and righteousness, according to the accounts which have been handed down to us in the Holy Scriptures. As for the other points, indeed, even on their own showing, they are not of a character which obliges me to be answerable for them; but yet, for the satisfaction of the sacred Synod, I anathematize those who either now hold or have ever held these opinions."

CHAP. 13.—*Cœlestius the bolder heretic; Pelagius the more subtle.*

You see, indeed, not to mention other points, how Pelagius pronounced his anathema against those who hold that "Adam's sin injured only himself, and not the human race; and that infants are at their birth in the same condition in which Adam was before he transgressed." Now what else could the bishops who sat in judgment on him have possibly understood him to mean by this, but that the sin of Adam is transmitted to infants? It was to avoid making such an admission that Cœlestius refused to condemn this statement, which *he* on the contrary anathematized. If, therefore, I shall show that he did not really entertain any other opinion concerning infants than that they are born without any contagion of a single sin, what difference will there remain on this question between him and Cœlestius, except this, that the one is more open, the other more reserved; the one more pertinacious, the other more mendacious; or, at any rate, that the one is more candid, the other more astute? The one even in the presence of the church of Carthage refused to condemn what he afterwards in the church at Rome publicly confessed to be a tenet of his own; at the same time professing himself "ready to submit to correction if an error had stolen over him, considering that he was but human;" whereas the other both condemned this dogma likewise as being contrary to the truth (lest he should himself be condemned by his Catholic judges), and yet kept it in reserve for subsequent defence, so that either his condemnation was a lie, or his interpretation a trick.

CHAP. 14.—*He shows that, even after the Synod of Palestine, Pelagius held the same opinions as Cœlestius on the subject of original sin.*

I see, however, the very great justice of the demand made on me, that I would not defer my promised demonstration, that he actually entertains the same views as Cœlestius. In

the first book of his more recent work, written in defence of
the freedom of the will (which work he mentions in the letter he despatched to Rome), he says: "Nothing good, and
nothing evil, on account of which we are deemed either
laudable or blameworthy, is born with us, but is done by us:
for we are born not fully developed, but with a capacity for
either conduct; we are formed naturally without either virtue
or vice; and previous to the action of our own proper will,
the only thing in man is what God has formed in him." Now
you perceive in these words of Pelagius, that therein is contained the dogma of both these men, that infants are born
without the contagion of any sin from Adam. It is therefore
not astonishing that Cœlestius refused to condemn such as
say that Adam's sin injured only himself, and not the human
race; and that infants are at their birth in the same state in
which Adam was before he fell. But it is very much to be
wondered at, that Pelagius had the effrontery to anathematize
these opinions. For if, as he alleges, "evil is not born with
us, and we are begotten without fault or sin, and the only
thing in man previous to the action of his own will is that
which God created in him," then of course the sin of Adam
did only injure himself, inasmuch as it did not pass on to his
offspring. For there is no sin which is not an evil; otherwise
sin is not a flaw or fault; or else sin was created by God.
But *he* says: "Nothing evil is born with us, and we are procreated without vice; and the only thing in men at their birth
is what God created in them." Now, since by this language he
supposes it to be most true, that, according to the well-known
sentence of his: "Adam's sin was injurious to himself alone,
and not to the human race," why did Pelagius condemn this,
if it were not for the purpose of deceiving his Catholic
judges? By equal reasoning, it may also be argued: "If evil is
not born with us, and if we are procreated without vice, and
if the only thing found in man at the time of his birth is what
God created in him," it follows beyond a doubt that "infants
at their birth are in the same condition that Adam was before
he fell," to whom no evil or vice was incidental, and in whom
no quality existed which was not made by God. And yet
Pelagius pronounced anathema on all those persons "who
hold now, or have at any time held, that new-born babes are

placed by their birth in the same state that Adam was in previous to his fall,"—in other words, are without any sin or any vice, simply possessing whatever quality God had created in them. Now, why again did Pelagius condemn this tenet also, if it were not for the purpose of deceiving the Catholic Synod, and saving himself from condemnation as an heretical innovator?

CHAP. 15.—*Pelagius by his mendacity and deception stole his acquittal from the Synod in Palestine.*

For my own part, however, I, as you are quite aware, and as I also stated in the book which I addressed to our venerable old bishop Aurelius on the proceedings in Palestine, really felt glad that Pelagius in that answer of his had exhausted the whole of this question. To me, indeed, he seemed most plainly to have acknowledged that there is original sin in infants, by the anathema which he pronounced against those persons who supposed that by the sin of Adam only himself, and not the human race, was injured, and who entertained the opinion that infants are in the same state in which the first man was before his transgression. When, however, I had read his four books (from the first of which I copied the words which I have just now quoted), and discovered that he was still cherishing thoughts which were opposed to the Catholic faith touching infants, I felt all the greater surprise at a mendacity which he so unblushingly maintained in a synod of the church, and on so great a question. For if he had already written these books, how did he profess to anathematize those who ever entertained the opinions alluded to? If he purposed, however, afterwards to publish such a work, how could he anathematize those who at the same time were holding the opinions? Unless, to be sure, by some ridiculous subterfuge he meant to say that the objects of his anathema were such persons as had in some previous time held, or were then holding, these opinions; but that in respect of the future—that is, as regards those persons who were about to take up such views—he felt that it would be impossible for him to prejudge either himself or other people, and that therefore he was guilty of no lie or deception when he was afterwards detected in the maintenance of similar errors. This plea, however, he does not advance, not only because it is a ridiculous one, but because it cannot possibly be true; because in these very books of his he both argues against the transmission of sin from Adam to infants, and glories in the proceedings of the Synod in Palestine, where he was supposed to have sincerely anathematized such as hold the opinions in dispute, and where he, in fact, pilfered his acquittal by practising deceit.

CHAP. 16.—*Pelagius' fraudulent and crafty excuses.*

For what have his answers to his followers to do with the matter on which we are at present treating, when he tells them that "the reason why he condemned the points which were objected against him, was because he himself maintains that the primal sin was injurious not only to the first man, but to the whole human race; not because it was transmitted by birth, but because it was an example;" in other words, not on the ground of his offspring having derived any fault from him, but because all who afterwards sinned imitated him who committed the first sin? Or when he says that "the reason why infants are not in the same state in which Adam was before his transgression, is because they are not yet able to understand the commandment, whereas he was able; and because they do not yet possess that choice of a rational will which he indeed possessed, for otherwise no commandment would have been given to him"? How does such an exposition as this of the points alleged against him justify him in thinking that he rightly condemned the propositions, "Adam's sin injured only himself, and not the whole race of man;" and "infants at their birth are in the self-same state as Adam was before he sinned;" and that by the said condemnation he is not guilty of deceit in holding such opinions as are found in his subsequent writings, namely, that "infants are born without any fault or sin, and that there is nothing in them but what God created,"—no wound, in short, inflicted by an enemy?

CHAP. 17.

Now, by making such statements as these, meeting objections which are urged in one sense with explanations which are meant in another, is it his aim to prove to us that he did not deceive those who sat in judgment on him? Then he utterly fails in his purpose. In proportion to the craftiness of his explanations, was the stealthiness with which he deceived them. For, Catholic bishops as they were, when they heard the man pouring out anathemas upon those who maintained that "Adam's sin was injurious to none but himself, and not to the human race," they understood him to assert nothing but what the Catholic Church has been accustomed to declare, on the strength of which it truly baptizes infants for the remission of sins—not, indeed, sins which they have committed by imitation of the example of the first sinner, but sins which they have contracted by their very birth, owing to the taint and flaw of their nature. When, again, they heard him anathematizing those who assert that "infants at their birth are in the same state as Adam previous to his fall," they supposed him simply to refer to those persons who think that infants have derived no sin from Adam, and that they are accordingly in the same state that *he* was in previous to his sin. For, of course, no other objection would be brought against him than that on which the question turned. When, therefore, he so explains the objection as to say that infants are not in the same state that Adam was before he sinned, simply because they have not yet arrived at the same firmness of mind or body, not because sin has passed on to them by birth, he must be answered thus: when the objections were laid against you for condemnation, the Catholic bishops did not understand them in this sense; therefore, when you condemned them, they believed that you were a Catholic. That, accordingly, which they supposed you to maintain, deserved to be released from censure; but that which you really maintained was worthy of condemnation. It was not you, then, that were acquitted, who held tenets which ought to be condemned; but that opinion was freed from censure which you ought to have held and maintained. You could only be supposed to be acquitted by having been believed to entertain opinions worthy to be praised; for your judges could not suppose that you were concealing opinions which merited condemnation. Rightly have you been adjudged an accomplice of Cœlestius, in whose opinions you prove yourself to be a sharer. Though you kept your books shut during your trial, you published them to the world after it was over.

CHAP. 18.—*The condemnation of Pelagius; after Pelagius and Cælestius were excommunicated, many of their followers were converted.*

This being the case, you[10] of course feel that episcopal councils, and the Apostolic See, and the whole church of Rome, and the Roman Empire itself, which by God's gracious favour has become Christian, has been most righteously moved against the authors of this wicked error, until they repent and escape from the snares of the devil. For who can tell whether God may not give them repentance to discover, and acknowledge, and even declare his truth, and to condemn their own truly damnable error? But whatever may be the bent of their own will, we cannot doubt that the merciful kindness of the Lord has sought the good of many persons who followed them, for no other reason than because they saw them joining in communion with the Catholic Church.

CHAP. 19.—*Pelagius' attempt to deceive the Apostolic See; he inverts the bearings of the controversy.*

But I would like you to observe carefully the way in which Pelagius endeavoured by stealth to overreach even the judgment of the bishop of the Apostolic See on this very question of the baptism of infants. He sent a letter to Rome to Pope Innocent of blessed memory; and when it did not find him alive, it was handed to the holy Pope Zosimus, and by him directed to us. In this letter he complains of being "defamed by certain persons for refusing the sacrament of baptism to infants, and promising the kingdom of heaven irrespective of Christ's redemption." The objections, however, are not urged against them in the manner he has stated. For they neither deny the sacrament of baptism to infants, nor do they promise the kingdom of heaven to any irrespective of the redemption of Christ. As regards, therefore, his complaint of being defamed by sundry persons, he has set it forth in such terms as to be able to give a ready answer to the alleged charge against him, without injury to his own dogma. The

10 I.e., Albina, Pinianus and Melania.

real objection against them is, that they refuse to confess that
unbaptized infants are liable to damnation because of the first
Adam, and that original sin has been transmitted to them,
and requires to be purged by regeneration; their contention
being that infants must be baptized solely for the purpose of
being admitted to the kingdom of heaven, as if they could
only have eternal death without the kingdom of heaven, who
cannot have eternal life without partaking of the Lord's body
and blood. This, you must know, is the real objection to
them respecting the baptism of infants; and not as he has
represented it, for the purpose of enabling himself to save his
own dogmas while answering what is actually a proposition
of his own, under colour of meeting the objection of his accusers.

CHAP. 20.—*Pelagius provides a refuge for his falsehood in ambiguous subterfuges.*

And then observe how he makes his answer, how he provides in the obscure mazes of his double sense retreats for
his false doctrine, quenching the truth in his dark mist of
error; and he succeeded so well, that even we, on our first
perusal of his words, rejoiced almost at their propriety and
correctness. But the fuller discussions in his books, in which
he is generally forced, in spite of all his efforts at concealment, to explain his meaning, have made even his better
statements suspicious to us, lest on a closer inspection of them
we should detect them to be ambiguous. For, after saying that
"he had never heard even an impious heretic say this"
(namely, what he set forth as the objection) "about infants,"
he goes on to ask: "Who indeed is so unacquainted with
Gospel lessons, as not only to attempt to make such a statement, but even be able to sketch it slightly, or only let it
enter his thought? And then who is so impious as to wish
to exclude infants from the kingdom of heaven, by forbidding them to be baptized and to be born again in Christ?"

CHAP. 21.

Now it is to no purpose that he says all this. He does not
clear himself thereby; for even they have never denied the
impossibility of infants entering the kingdom of heaven

without baptism. But this is not the question; what we are now discussing concerns the obliteration of original sin in infants. Let him clear himself on this point, since he refuses to acknowledge that there is anything in infants which the font of regeneration has to cleanse. On this account we ought carefully to consider what he has afterwards to say. After adducing, then, the passage of the Gospel which declares that "whoever is not born again of water and the Spirit cannot enter into the kingdom of heaven"[11] (on which matter, as we have said, they raise no question), he goes on at once to ask: "Who indeed is so impious as to have the heart to refuse the common redemption of the human race to an infant of any age whatever?" But this is ambiguous language; for what *redemption* does he mean? Is it from evil to good? or from good to better? Now even Cœlestius, in his book at Carthage, allowed a redemption for infants; although, at the same time, he would not admit the transmission of sin to them from Adam.

CHAP. 22.

Then, again, observe what he adds to the last remark: "Can any one," says he, "deny his second birth to an eternal and certain life, who has been born to this present uncertain life?" In other words: who is so impious as to forbid his being born again to the life which is sure and eternal, who has been born to this life of uncertainty? When we first read these words, we supposed that by the phrase "uncertain life" he meant to designate this present temporal life; although it appeared to us that he ought rather to have called it "mortal" than "uncertain," on the ground that it is brought to a close by certain death. But for all this, we thought that he had only shown a preference for calling this mortal life an *uncertain* one, because of the general view which men take that there is undoubtedly not a moment in our lives when we are free from this uncertainty. And so it happened that our anxiety about him was allayed to some extent by the following consideration, which rose almost to a proof, notwithstanding the fact of his unwillingness openly to confess that

[11] John 3: 5.

infants incur eternal death who depart from this life without the sacrament of baptism. We argued: If, as he seems to admit, eternal life can only accrue to them who have been baptized, it follows of course that they who die unbaptized incur everlasting death. This destiny, however, cannot by any means justly befall those who never in this life committed any sins of their own, who therefore only possessed original sin.

CHAP. 23.—*The opinion of Pelagius concerning infants who die unbaptized; how he shelters himself under his ambiguous phrases.*

Certain brethren, however, afterwards did not fail to remind us that Pelagius possibly expressed himself in this way, because on this question he is represented as having his answer ready for all inquirers, to this effect: "As for infants who die unbaptized, I know indeed where they do not go; yet where they go, I do not know;" as much as to say, I know they do not go into the kingdom of heaven. But as to where they actually go, he was (and for the matter of that, *still is*) in the habit of saying that he did not know, for no other reason than because he had not the courage to say that those persons went to eternal death, who he was persuaded had never committed sin in this life, and whom he would not admit to have contracted original sin. Consequently those very words of his which were forwarded to Rome to secure his absolute acquittal, are so steeped in ambiguity that they afford a shelter for their doctrine, out of which may sally forth an heretical sense to entrap the unwary straggler; for when no one is at hand who can give the answer, any man may find himself weak in his solitary condition.

CHAP. 24.—*Pelagius' long residence at Rome.*

The truth indeed is, that in the document of his faith which he sent to Rome with this very letter which we have been discussing, to the already mentioned Pope Innocent, to whom he had also written the letter, he only set himself in a clearer light by his efforts at concealment. He says: "We hold one baptism, which we insist ought to be administered in the same formula of sacramental words in the case of infants as in the case of adults." He did not, however, say, "in the same sacrament" (although if he had said so, there would still have been ambiguity), but "in the same formula of sacramental words,"—as if remission of sins in infants were only a matter of verbal sound, instead of a fact effectually achieved. For the time, indeed, he seemed to say what was agreeable with the catholic faith; but he did not have it in his power permanently to deceive the Holy See. Subsequent to the rescript of the Council of Carthage, into which province this pestilent doctrine had stealthily made its way—without, however, spreading widely or sinking deeply—other opinions also of this man were discovered by the industry of some faithful brethren and brought to light at Rome, where he had lived for a very long while, and had already engaged in sundry discourses and controversies. In order to procure the condemnation of these opinions, Pope Zosimus, as you may read, annexed them to his letter, which he wrote for publication throughout the Catholic world. Among these statements, Pelagius, pretending to expound the apostle Paul's Epistle to the Romans, argues in these words: "As even Adam's sin did not injure sinners, so Christ's righteousness also does not profit those who believe." He says other things, too, in the same sense; but they have all been refuted and answered by me with the Lord's help in the books which I wrote, *On the Baptism of Infants*. But he had not the courage to make those objectionable statements in his own person in the forementioned so-called exposition. This particular one, however, having been enunciated in a place where he was so well known, his words and their meaning could not be disguised. In those books, from the first of which I have already quoted above, he treats this point without any suppression of his views. With all the energy of which he is capable, he most plainly asserts that human nature in infants cannot in any wise be supposed to be tainted by birth; and by claiming salvation for them as their due, he does discredit to the Saviour.

CHAP. 25.—*The condemnation of Pelagius and Cœlestius.*

These things, then, being as I have stated, it is now evident that there has arisen a deadly heresy which, with the Lord's help, the church by this time guards against more directly—now that those two men, Pelagius and Cœlestius, have been either offered repentance, or on their refusal been wholly condemned. They are reported, or perhaps are actually proved, to be the authors of this perversion; at all events, if not the authors (having learned it from others), they are yet boastfully set forth as its abettors and teachers, through whose agency the heresy has advanced and grown to a wider extent. This boast, too, is made even in their own statements and writings, and in unmistakeable signs of reality, as well as in the fame which arises and grows out of all these circumstances. What, therefore, remains to be done? Must not every Catholic, with all the energies wherewith the Lord endows him, confute this pestilential doctrine, and oppose it with all vigilance; so that whenever we contend for the truth, compelled to answer, but not fond of the contest, the untaught may be instructed, and that thus the church may be benefited by that which the enemy devised for her destruction; in accordance with that word of the apostle's, "There must be heresies, that they who are approved may be made manifest among you"?[12]

CHAP. 26.—*The Pelagians maintain that raising questions about original sin does not endanger the faith.*

Therefore, after the full discussion with which we have been able to rebut in writing this error of theirs, which is so inimical to the grace of God given to small and great through our Lord Jesus Christ, it is now our duty to examine and explode that assertion of theirs, which in their desire to avoid the odious imputation of heresy they astutely advance, to the effect that "calling this subject into question produces no danger to the faith,"—in order that they may appear, while under the conviction of having departed from the usual track, to have erred only by a sort of offence against courtesy, and not to have incurred any charge of hostility to the faith. This, accordingly, is the language which Cœlestius used in the ecclesiastical process at Carthage: "With regard to the transmission of original sin," he said, "I have already asserted that I have heard many persons of acknowledged position in

[12] 1 Cor. 11: 19.

the Catholic Church deny it altogether, and on the other hand many affirm it; it may fairly, indeed, be deemed a matter for inquiry, but not a heresy. I have always maintained that infants require baptism, and ought to be baptized. What else does he want?" He said this, as if he wanted to intimate that only then could he be deemed chargeable with heresy, if he were to assert that they ought not to be baptized. As the case stood, however, since he acknowledged that they ought to be baptized, he thought that he was not in error, and therefore ought not to be adjudged a heretic, even though he maintained the reason of their baptism to be other than the truth holds, or the faith claims as its own. On the same principle, in the book which he sent to Rome, he first explained his belief, so far as it suited his pleasure, on all the articles of the creed, from the Trinity of the One Godhead down to the Resurrection of the Dead, as it is to be; on all which points, however, no one had ever questioned him, or been questioned by him. And when his discourse reached the question which was under consideration, he said: "If, indeed, any questions have arisen beyond the compass of the creed, on which there might be perhaps dissension on the part of a great many persons, in no case have I pretended to pronounce a decision on any dogma, as if I possessed a definitive authority in the matter myself; but whatever I have derived from the fountain of the prophets and the apostles, I have presented for determination to the sentence of your apostolic office; so that if any error has crept in among us, human as we are, through our ignorance, it may be corrected by your decision and sentence." You of course clearly see that in this action of his he used all this deprecatory preamble in order that, if he had been discovered to have erred at all, he might seem to have erred not on a matter of faith, but on questionable points outside the creed; where, however necessary it may be to correct the error, it is not corrected as a heresy; where also the person who undergoes the correction is declared indeed to be in error, but for all that is not adjudged a heretic.

CHAP. 27.—*On questions outside the creed—what they are, and instances of the same.*

But he is greatly mistaken in this opinion. The questions

which he supposes to be outside the creed are of a very
different character from those in which, without any detri-
ment to the faith whereby we are Christians, there exists
either an ignorance of the real fact, and a consequent suspension of any fixed opinion, or else a conjectural view of
the case, which, owing to the infirmity of human thought,
issues in conceptions at variance with truth: as when a question arises about the description and locality of that paradise
where God placed man whom he formed out of the earth,
without any disturbance, however, of the Christian belief
that there undoubtedly is such a paradise; or as when it is
asked where Elijah is at the present moment, and where
Enoch—whether in this paradise or in some other place,
although we do not doubt that they exist still in the same
bodies in which they were born; or as when one inquires
whether it was in the body or out of the body that the apostle
was caught up to the third heaven,—an inquiry, however,
which betokens great immodesty on the part of those who
want to know what he who is the subject of the mystery itself
expressly declares his ignorance of,[13] without impairing his
own belief of the fact; or as when the question is started,
how many are those heavens, to the "third" of which he tells
us that he was caught up; or whether the elements of this
visible world are four or more; what it is which causes those
eclipses of the sun or the moon which astronomers are in the
habit of foretelling for certain appointed seasons; why, again,
men of ancient times lived to the age which Holy Scripture
assigns to them; and whether the period of their puberty,
when they begat their first son, was postponed to an older
age, proportioned to their longer life; or where Methuselah
could possibly have lived, since he was not in the ark, inasmuch as (according to the chronological notes of most
copies of the scripture, both Greek and Latin) he is found
to have survived the deluge; or whether we must rather follow the order of the fewer copies—and they happen to be
extremely few—which so arrange the years as to show that he
died before the deluge. Now who does not feel, amidst the
various and innumerable questions of this sort, which relate

[13] 2 Cor. 12: 2.

either to God's most hidden operations or to most obscure passages of the Scriptures, and which it is difficult to embrace and define in any certain way, that ignorance may on many points be compatible with sound Christian faith, and that occasionally erroneous opinion may be entertained without any room for the imputation of heretical doctrine?

CHAP. 28.—*The heresy of Pelagius and Cœlestius aims at the very foundations of our faith. The Christian belief is principally concerned about the two men who are at the head of the old and the new creation. Without faith in Christ, no man could possibly be either justified or saved. Faith in Christ an entirely gratuitous gift.*

There is, however, subject-matter of quite a different kind in the case of the two representative men, who have affected our race so diversely, that by one of them we are sold under sin, by the other redeemed from our sins—by the one have been precipitated into death, by the other are liberated unto life: the former of whom has ruined us in himself, by doing his own will instead of his who created him; whereas the other has saved us in himself, by not doing his own will, but the will of him who sent him.[14] Now it is in what concerns these two men that the Christian faith properly consists. For "there is one God, and one mediator between God and men, the man Christ Jesus;"[15] since "there is no other name under heaven given to men, by which we must be saved;"[16] and "in him God defined unto all men their faith, in that he raised him from the dead."[17] Now without this faith, that is to say, without a belief in the one mediator between God and men, the man Christ Jesus; without faith, I say, in his resurrection, by which God has given assurance to all men, and which no man could of course truly believe, were it not for his incarnation and death; without faith, therefore, in the incarnation and death and resurrection of Christ, the Christian verity unhesitatingly declares that the ancient saints could not possibly have been cleansed from sin, so as to have become holy, and justified by the grace of God. And this is true

14 John 4: 34 and 5: 30.
15 1 Tim. 2: 5.
16 Acts 4: 12.
17 Acts 17: 31.

both of the saints who are mentioned in Holy Scripture, and
of those also who are not indeed commemorated therein, but
must yet be supposed to have existed,—either before the deluge, or in the interval between that event and the giving
of the law, or in the period of the law itself,—not merely
among the children of Israel, as the prophets, but even outside that nation, as for instance Job. It was no doubt by the
self-same faith in the one mediator that the hearts of even
these were cleansed, in which also was "shed abroad the
love of God by the Holy Ghost,"[18] "who blows where he
wills,"[19] never following men's merits, but ever producing
them himself; since the grace of God will in no way exist
unless it be wholly free.

CHAP. 29.—*The righteous men who lived in the time of the law were
nevertheless not under the law, but under grace. The grace of
the New Testament hidden under the Old. The veil of the temple.
Gideon's fleece.*

Death indeed reigned from Adam until Moses,[20] because
it was not possible even for the law given through Moses to
overcome death: it was not given, in fact, with a view to its
being able to give life;[21] but its proper function was to show
that all were dead,—not only as being prostrated under the
dominion of original sin, but as being also convicted of the
additional guilt of breaking the law itself,—and that grace
was needed to give them life: so that no man might perish
who in the mercy of God understood this even in that early
age; but that, destined though he were to punishment, owing
to the dominion of sin, and conscious, too, of guilt through his
own violation of the law, he might seek God's help; so that
where sin abounded, grace might much more abound,[22] even
the grace which alone delivers from the body of this death.[23]
Yet, notwithstanding this, although the very law which Moses
gave was unable to liberate any man from the dominion of
death, there were even then, at the time of the law, men of

[18] Rom. 5: 5.
[19] John 3: 8.
[20] Rom. 5: 14.
[21] Gal. 3: 21.
[22] Rom. 5: 20.
[23] Rom. 7: 24 f.

God who were not living under the terrors and conviction and punishment of the law, but under the delights and healing and liberating influence of grace. There were some who said, "I was shapen in iniquity, and in sin did my mother conceive me;"[24] and, "There is no rest in my bones, by reason of my sins;"[25] and, "Create in me a clean heart, O God; and renew a right spirit in my inward parts;"[26] and, "Uphold me with a willing spirit;"[27] and, "Take not your Holy Spirit from me."[28] There were some, again, who said: "I believed, therefore have I spoken."[29] For they too were cleansed with the self-same faith with which we ourselves are. Whence the apostle also says: "We having the same spirit of faith, according as it is written, I believe, and therefore have I spoken; we also believe, and therefore speak."[30] In faith was it said, "Behold, a virgin shall conceive and bear a son, and they shall call his name Emmanuel,"[31] "which is, being interpreted, God with us."[32] In faith too it was said concerning him: "As a bridegroom he comes out of his chamber; as a giant did he exult to run his course. His going forth is from the extremity of heaven, and his circuit runs to the other end of heaven; and no one is hidden from his heat."[33] In faith, again, was it said to him: "Your throne, O God, is for ever and ever; a sceptre of righteousness is the sceptre of your kingdom. You have loved righteousness, and hated iniquity; therefore God, your God, has anointed you with the oil of gladness above your fellows."[34] By the self-same spirit of faith were all these things foreseen by them as about to happen, by which they are believed by us as having happened. They, indeed, who were able in faithful love to foretell these things to us were not

[24] Ps. 51: 5.
[25] Ps. 38: 3.
[26] Ps. 51: 10.
[27] Ps. 51: 12.
[28] Ps. 51: 11.
[29] Ps. 116: 10.
[30] 2 Cor. 4: 13.
[31] Isa. 7: 14.
[32] Matt. 1: 23.
[33] Ps. 19: 5, 6.
[34] Ps. 45: 6 f.

themselves partakers of them. The apostle Peter says, "Why
do you tempt God to put a yoke upon the neck of the disciples, which neither our fathers nor we were able to bear?
But we believe that through the grace of the Lord Jesus
Christ we shall be saved, even as they."[35] Now on what
principle does he make this statement, if it is not because
even those ancient saints were saved through the grace of the
Lord Jesus Christ, and not the law of Moses, from which
comes not the cure, but only the knowledge of sin?[36] "Now,
however, the righteousness of God apart from the law is
manifested, being witnessed by the law and the prophets."[37]
If, therefore, it is now manifested, it even then existed, but
it was hidden. This concealment was symbolized by the veil
of the temple. When Christ was dying, this veil was rent
asunder,[38] to signify the full revelation of him. Even of old,
therefore, there existed among the people of God this grace
of the one mediator between God and men, the man Christ
Jesus. As, however, in the fleece the rain which God sets
apart for his inheritance,[39] not of debt, but of his own will,
was but latently inherent, it is now patently visible among
all nations as its "floor," the fleece being dry; in other words,
the Jewish people having become reprobate.[40]

CHAP. 30.—*Pelagius and Cœlestius deny that the ancient saints
were saved by Christ.*

We must not therefore divide the periods, as Pelagius and
his disciples do, who say: "Men first lived righteously by
nature, then under the law, thirdly under grace." By their
period "by nature," they mean all the long time before the
giving of the law. "For then," say they, "the creator was
known by the guidance of nature; and the rule of living
rightly was carried in the hearts of men, written not in the
law of the letter, but of nature. But men's manners became
corrupt; and then," they say, "when nature now tarnished

[35] Acts 15: 10 f.
[36] Rom. 3: 20.
[37] Rom. 3: 21.
[38] Matt. 27: 51.
[39] Ps. 68: 9.
[40] Judg. 6: 36–40.

began to be insufficient, the law was added to it, by which as by a moon the original lustre was restored to nature after its blush was impaired. But after the habit of sin had become excessive by over-indulgence among men, and the law was unequal to the task of curing it, Christ came; and the physician himself, through his own self, and not through his disciples, brought relief to the malady at its most desperate development."

CHAP. 31.—*Christ's incarnation was of avail to the fathers, even though it had not yet happened.*

By disputation of this sort, they attempt to shut off the ancient saints from the grace of the mediator, as if the man Christ Jesus were not the mediator between God and *them;* on the ground that, not having yet taken flesh of the virgin's womb, he was not man yet at the time when those righteous men lived. If this, however, were true, in vain would the apostle say: "By man came death, by man came also the resurrection of the dead; for as in Adam all die, even so in Christ shall all be made alive."[41] For as those ancient saints, according to the vain conceits of these men, found their nature self-sufficient, and did not require the man Christ to be their mediator to reconcile them to God, so neither shall they be made alive in him, to whose body they are shown not to belong as members, according to the statement that it was on man's account that he became man. Since, however, as the truth says through his apostles, all shall be made alive in Christ, even as all die in Adam, because resurrection from death comes through the one, even as death comes through the other, what Christian man can be bold enough to doubt, that even those righteous men who pleased God in the fresher periods of the human race are destined to attain to the resurrection of eternal life, and not eternal death, because they shall be made alive in Christ; that they are made alive in Christ, because they belong to the body of Christ; that they belong to the body of Christ, because Christ is the head even to them;[42] and that Christ is the head even to them, because there is but one mediator between God and

41 1 Cor. 15: 21 f.
42 1 Cor. 11: 3.

men, the man Christ Jesus? But this he could not have been
to them, unless through his grace they had believed in his
resurrection. And how could they have done this, if they had
not known that he was to come in the flesh, and if they had
not turned this faith to good and pious account in their lives?
Now, if the incarnation of Christ could be of no concern to
them, on the ground that it had not yet come about, it must
follow that Christ's judgment can be of no concern to us,
because it has not yet taken place. But if we shall stand at
the right hand of Christ through our faith in his judgment,
which has not yet transpired, but is to come to pass, it follows
that those ancient saints are members of Christ through their
faith in his resurrection, which had not in their day happened, but which was one day to come to pass.

CHAP. 32.—*He shows by the example of Abraham that the ancient
saints believed in the incarnation of Christ; why Abraham
wished his servant to swear with his hand under his thigh.*

For it must not be supposed that those saints of old only
profited by Christ's divinity, which was ever existent, and not
also by the revelation of his humanity, which had not yet
come to pass. What the Lord Jesus says, "Abraham desired
to see my day, and he saw it, and was glad,"[43] meaning by
the phrase *his day* to understand *his time* or dispensation,
affords of course a clear testimony that Abraham was fully
impressed with the belief of his incarnation; for it is only in
respect of *this* that he possesses any temporal attribute at all.
His divinity, indeed, transcends all time, for it was by it that
time and all its dispensations were created. If, however, any
one supposes that the phrase in question must be understood
of that eternal "day" which is limited by no morrow, and
preceded by no yesterday,—in a word, of the very eternity in
which he is co-eternal with the Father,—how would Abraham
really desire this, without being aware that there was to be
a mortality belonging to him for whose eternity he wished?
Or, perhaps, some one would confine the meaning of the
phrase so far as to say, that nothing else is meant in the
Lord's saying, "He desired to see my day," than "He desired
to see me," who am the never-ending day, or the unfailing

[43] John 8: 56.

light, as when we mention the life of the Son, concerning which it is said in the gospel: "So he has given to the Son to have life in himself."[44] Here the life is nothing less than himself. So we understand the Son himself to be the life, when he said, "I am the way, the truth, and the life;"[45] of whom also it was said, "He is the true God, and eternal life."[46] Supposing, then, that Abraham desired to see this equal divinity of the Son's with the Father, without any precognition of his coming in the flesh—as certain philosophers sought him, who knew nothing of his flesh—can that other act of Abraham, when he orders his servant to place his hand under his thigh, and to swear by the God of heaven,[47] be rightly understood by any one otherwise than as showing that Abraham well knew that the flesh in which the God of heaven was to come was the offspring of that very thigh?

CHAP. 33.—How Christ is our mediator.

Of this flesh and blood Melchizedek also, when he blessed Abram himself,[48] gave the testimony which is very well known to Christian believers, so that long afterwards it was said to Christ in the Psalms: "You are a priest for ever, after the order of Melchizedek."[49] This was not then an accomplished fact, but was still future; yet that faith of the fathers, which is the self-same faith as our own, used to chant the prophecy as a certain truth. Now, to all who meet with death in Adam, Christ is of this avail, that he is the mediator for obtaining life. He is, however, not a mediator, as being equal with the Father; for in this respect he is himself as far distant from us as the Father; and how can there be any mediatorial function in a case where there is an absolute identity of distance in the parties? Therefore the apostle does not say, "There is one mediator between God and men, even Jesus Christ;" but his words are, "The man Christ Jesus."[50] He is the medi-

44 John 5: 26.
45 John 14: 6.
46 1 John 5: 20.
47 Gen. 24: 2 f.
48 Gen. 14: 18–20.
49 Ps. 110: 4.
50 1 Tim. 2: 5.

ator, then, in that he is man. He is inferior to the Father, in being nearer to ourselves; and superior to us, in being nearer to the Father. A doctrine which is more openly expressed thus: "He is inferior to the Father, because in the form of a servant;"[51] superior to us, because without spot of sin.

CHAP. 34.

Now, whoever maintains that human nature at any period did not require the second Adam for its physician, as not having been diseased in the first Adam, is convicted as an enemy to the grace of God; not in a question where doubt or error might be compatible with soundness of belief, but in that very rule of faith which makes us Christians. How does it happen, then, that the human nature, which first existed, is praised by these men as being so far less tainted with evil manners? How is it that they overlook the fact that men were even then sunk in so many intolerable sins, that, with the exception of one man of God and his wife, and three sons and their wives, the whole world was in God's just judgment destroyed by the flood, even as the little land of Sodom was afterwards with fire?[52] From the moment, then, when "by one man sin entered into the world, and death by sin, and so death passed upon all men, because all men sinned,"[53] the entire mass of our nature was ruined beyond doubt, and fell into the possession of its destroyer. And from him no one—no, not one—has been delivered, or is being delivered, or ever will be delivered, except by the grace of the redeemer.

CHAP. 35.—*Why the circumcision of infants was enjoined under pain of so great a punishment; what is meant in the Scriptures by "being cut off from one's people."*

The scripture does not inform us whether before Abraham's time righteous men and their children were marked by any bodily or visible sign. Abraham himself, indeed, received the sign of circumcision, a seal of the righteousness of faith.[54] And he received it with this accompanying injunction: all the

51 Phil. 2: 7.
52 See Gen. 7 and 19.
53 Rom. 5: 12.
54 Rom. 4: 11.

male infants of his household were from that very time to be circumcised, while fresh from their mother's womb, on the eighth day from their birth;[55] so that even they who were not yet able with the heart to believe to righteousness, should nevertheless receive the seal of the righteousness of faith. And this command was imposed with so fearful a sanction, that God said: "That soul shall be cut off from his people, the flesh of whose foreskin is not circumcised on the eighth day."[56] If inquiry be made into the justice of so terrible a penalty, will not the entire argument of these men about the free will, and laudable soundness and purity of our nature, however cleverly maintained, fall to pieces, struck down and fractured to atoms? For, tell me, what evil has an infant committed of his own will, that, for the negligence of another in not circumcising him, he must be actually condemned, and with so severe a condemnation, that that soul must be cut off from his people? It was not of any temporal death that this fear was injected, since of righteous persons, when they died, it used rather to be said, "And he was gathered unto his people;"[57] or, "He was gathered to his fathers:"[58] for no attempt to separate a man from his people is long fearful to him, when his own people is itself the people of God.

CHAP. 36.—*The Platonists' opinion about the existence of the soul previous to the body rejected; circumcision; prophecy of Christ's grace.*

What, then, is the purport of so severe a condemnation, when no wilful sin has been committed? For the opinion of certain Platonists has no relevance here, that every such infant is thus paid back in his soul for what it did of its own wilfulness previous to the present life, as having possessed previous to its present bodily state a free choice to live either well or ill; since the apostle Paul says most plainly, that before they were born they did neither good nor evil.[59] On what account, therefore, is an infant rightly punished with such ruin, if it

---

[55] Gen. 17: 10.
[56] Gen. 17: 14.
[57] Gen. 25: 17.
[58] 1 Macc. 2: 69.
[59] Rom. 9: 11.

is not because he belongs to the ruined mass, and is properly regarded as born of Adam, condemned under the bond of the ancient debt of original sin, unless he has been released from the bond—not indeed by any merit of his own, but by grace? And what grace but God's, through our Lord Jesus Christ? Now there was a forecast of his coming undoubtedly contained not only in other sacred institutions of the ancient Jews, but also in their circumcision of the foreskin. For the eighth day, when it was administered, in the recurrence of weeks, became the Lord's day, on which the Lord arose from the dead; and Christ was the rock[60] whence was formed the stony blade for the circumcision;[61] and the flesh of the foreskin was the body of sin.

CHAP. 37.—*In what sense Christ is called "sin."*

There was a change of the sacramental ordinances made after the coming of him whose advent they prefigured; but there was no change in the mediator's help, who, even previous to his coming in the flesh, all along delivered the ancient members of his body by their faith in his incarnation; and in respect of ourselves too, though we were dead in sins and in the uncircumcision of our flesh, we are made alive together in Christ, in whom we are circumcised with the circumcision not made with the hand,[62] such as was prefigured by the old manual circumcision, that the body of sin might be done away with,[63] which was born with us from Adam. The propagation of a condemned original nature condemns ourselves, if we are not cleansed in the likeness of sinful flesh, in which he was sent without sin, who nevertheless concerning sin condemned sin, having been made sin for us.[64] Accordingly the apostle says: "We beseech you in Christ's stead, be reconciled to God. For he has made him to be sin for us, who knew no sin; that we might be made the righteousness of God in him."[65] God, therefore, to whom we are reconciled, has made

[60] 1 Cor. 10: 4.
[61] Ex. 4: 25.
[62] Col. 2: 11, 13.
[63] Rom. 6: 6.
[64] Rom. 8: 3 and Gal. 3: 13.
[65] 2 Cor. 5: 20, 21.

him to be sin for us,—that is to say, a sacrifice by which our sins may be remitted; for sins are designated as the sacrifices for sins. And indeed he was sacrificed for our sins, the only one among men who had no sins, even as in those early times a faultless animal was sought for among the flocks, to prefigure the faultless one who was to come to heal our offences. On whatever day, therefore, an infant may be baptized after his birth, he is as if circumcised on the eighth day; inasmuch as he is circumcised in him who rose again the third day indeed after he was crucified, but the eighth according to the weeks. He is circumcised for the putting off of the body of sin; in other words, that the grace of spiritual regeneration may do away with the debt which the contagion of carnal generation contracted. "For no one is pure from uncleanness" (what uncleanness, tell me, but that of sin?), "not even the infant, whose life is but that of a single day upon the earth."[66]

CHAP. 38.—*Original sin does not render marriage evil. Conjugal chastity the blessing of the nuptial state.*

But they captiously argue, saying: "Is not, then, marriage an evil, and surely the human being which is produced by marriage is not God's work?" As if the good of the married life were that morbid concupiscence with which they, who know not God, love their wives—a course which the apostle forbids;[67] and not rather that conjugal chastity, by which carnal lust is reduced to the good purposes of the moderate procreation of children. Or as if a man could possibly be anything but God's work, not only when born in wedlock, but even if he is produced in fornication or adultery. In the present inquiry, however, when the question is not for what purpose the creator is wanted, but the saviour, we have not to consider what good there is in natural procreation, but what evil there is in sin, whereby our nature has been certainly vitiated. No doubt the two are generated simultaneously—both nature and nature's flaw; one, however, of these is good, the other evil. The one comes to us from the bounty of the creator, the other is contracted from the original condemnation; the one has its cause in the goodwill of the supreme, the other in the depraved

66 Job 14: 4, 5 (Septuagint).
67 1 Thess. 4: 5.

will of the first man; the one exhibits God as the maker of
the creature, the other as the punisher of disobedience. In
short, the very same Christ was *man's maker* for the creation
of the one, and *man-made* for the healing of the other.

CHAP. 39.—*Three things good and laudable in matrimony. Lust.
Good out of evil. Whence arises modesty in the members of
our body.*

Marriage, therefore, is a good in all the things which are
the properties of the nuptial state. And these are three: it is
the ordained means of procreation, it is the guarantee of chastity, it is the pledge and security of sexual union. In respect
of its ordinance for generation the scripture says, "I will therefore that the younger women marry, bear children, guide the
house;"[68] as regards its guaranteeing chastity, it is said of it,
"The wife has not power of her own body, but the husband;
and likewise also the husband has not power of his own body,
but the wife;"[69] and considered as the sacramental pledge and
security of sexual union, the scripture gives it this sanction,
"What God has joined together, let not man put asunder."[70]
As regards these points, we do not forget that we have treated
at sufficient length, with whatever ability the Lord has given
us, in other works of ours, which are not unknown to you.[71]
In relation to all these properties the scripture has this general
praise: "Marriage is honourable in all, and the bed unde-
filed."[72] For, to the extent that the wedded state is good, to
that extent it produces a very large amount of good in respect
of the evil of concupiscence; for it is not lust, but reason,
which makes a good use of concupiscence. Now lust lies in
that law of the "disobedient" members which the apostle notes
as "warring against the law of the mind;"[73] whereas reason
lies in that law of the wedded state which makes good use
of concupiscence. If, however, it were not possible for any
good to arise out of evil, not even God could create man out

[68] 1 Tim. 5: 14.
[69] 1 Cor. 7: 4.
[70] Matt. 19: 6.
[71] Cf. *De bono Conjugali*, 3 ff.
[72] Heb. 13: 4.
[73] Rom. 7: 23.

of the embraces of adultery. As, therefore, the damnable evil
of adultery, whenever man is born in it, is not chargeable on
God, who certainly amid man's evil work actually produces
a good work; so, likewise, all which causes shame in that re-
bellion of the members which brought the accusing blush on
those who after their sin covered the said members with the
fig-tree leaves,[74] is not laid to the charge of marriage, by virtue of which the conjugal embrace is not only allowable, but
is even useful and honourable; but it is imputable to the sin
of that disobedience which was followed by the penalty of
man's finding his own members emulating against himself that
very disobedience which he had practised against God. Then,
abashed at their action, since they moved no more at the bidding of his rational will, but at their own arbitrary choice as
it were, instigated by lust, he devised the covering which
should conceal such of them as he judged to be worthy of
shame. For man, as the handiwork of God, deserved not confusion of face; nor were the members which it seemed fit to
the creator to form and appoint by any means designed to
bring the blush to the creature. Accordingly, that naked simplicity of Eden was displeasing neither to God nor to man:
there was nothing to be ashamed of, because nothing at first
accrued which deserved punishment.

CHAP. 40.—*Marriage existed before sin was committed. How God's
blessing operated in our first parents.*

There must, however, undoubtedly have been marriage,
even when sin had no prior existence; and for no other reason
was it that woman, and not a second man, was created as a
help suitable for the man. Moreover, those grand words of
God, "Be fruitful and multiply,"[75] are not prophetic of sins
to be condemned, but a benediction upon the fertility of marriage. For by these ineffable words of his, I mean by the divine
methods which are inherent in the truth of that wisdom by
which all things were made, God endowed the primeval pair
with their seminal power. Suppose, however, that nature had
not been tarnished by sin, God forbid that we should think
that marriages in paradise must have been such, that in them

[74] Gen. 3: 7.
[75] Gen. 1: 28.

the procreative members would be excited by the mere ardour of lust, and not at the bidding of the will,—as the foot is for walking, the hand for labour, and the tongue for speech. Nor, as now happens, would the purity of the virgin state be excited to the conception of the womb by the force of a turbid heat, but it would rather be submissive to the power of the gentlest love; and thus there would be no pain, no blood-effusion of the companion virgin, as there would also be no groan of the parturient mother. This, however, men refuse to believe, because it has not been verified in the actual condition of our mortal state. Nature, having been vitiated by sin, has never experienced an instance of that primeval purity. But we address ourselves to faithful men, who have learned to believe the inspired Scriptures, even though no examples are adduced of actual reality. For how could I now possibly *prove* that a man was made of the dust, without any parents, and a wife formed for him out of his own side?[76] And yet faith takes on trust what the eye no longer discovers.

CHAP. 41.—*Lust and travail come from sin. Whence our members became a cause of shame.*

Granted, therefore, that we have no means of showing that the nuptial acts of even that primeval marriage were quietly discharged, undisturbed by lustful passion, and that the motion of the organs of generation, like that of any other members of the body, was not instigated by the ardour of lust, but directed by the deliberate choice of the will (in which tranquillity marriage would have continued, had not the disgrace of sin intervened); still, from all that is stated in the sacred Scriptures on divine authority, we have reasonable grounds for believing that such was the original condition of wedded life. Although, it is true, I am not told that the nuptial embrace was unattended with prurient desire; as also I do not find it on record that parturition was unaccompanied with groans and pain, or that actual birth did not lead to future death; yet, at the same time, if I follow the truth of the Holy Scriptures, I must conclude that the travail of the mother and the death of the human offspring would never have supervened if sin

[76] Gen. 2: 7, 22.

had not preceded. Nor would that have happened which abashed the man and woman when they covered their loins; because in the same sacred records it is expressly written that the sin was first committed, and then immediately followed this hiding of their shame.[77] For unless some indelicacy of motion had shown to their eyes—which were of course not closed, though not open to this point in the sense of earnest perception—that those particular members required chastisement, they would not have perceived anything on their own persons, which God had entirely made worthy of all praise, that called for either shame or concealment. If, indeed, the sin had not first occurred which they had dared to commit in their disobedience, there would not have followed the disgrace which their shame wished to conceal.

CHAP. 42.—*The evil of lust ought not to be ascribed to marriage. The three good results of the nuptial ordinance: offspring, chastity, and the sacramental union. Original sin the result of carnal concupiscence.*

It is then manifest that that must not be laid to the account of marriage, in spite of which, even if it had not come into being, marriage would have existed. The good of marriage is not taken away by the evil, although the evil is by marriage turned to a good use. Such, however, is the present condition of mortal men, that the connubial intercourse and lust are simultaneous in action; and on this account it happens, that as the lust is blamed, so also the nuptial commerce, however lawful and honourable, is thought to be reprehensible by those persons who either are unwilling or unable to draw the distinction between them. They are, moreover, inattentive to that good of the nuptial state which is the glory of matrimony; I mean offspring, chastity, and the sacramental union. The evil, however, at which even marriage blushes for shame is not the fault of marriage, but of the lust of the flesh. Yet because without this evil it is impossible to effect the good purpose of marriage, even the procreation of children, whenever this process is approached, secrecy is sought, witnesses are removed, and even the presence of the very children who happen to be born of the process is avoided as soon as they reach the age of

[77] Gen. 3: 7.

observation. Thus it comes to pass that marriage is permitted
to effect all that is lawful in its state, only it must not forget
to conceal all that is improper. Hence it follows that infants,
although incapable of sinning, are yet not born without the
contagion of sin,—not, indeed, because of what is lawful in
matrimony, but of its improper element: for from the lawful
a natural creature is born; from the improper, sin. Of the natural creature so born, God is the maker, who created man, and
who united male and female under the law of the nuptial
union; but the origin of the sin lies in the subtlety of the devil
who deceives, and in the will of the man who yields to the
deception.

CHAP. 43.—*Human offspring, even previous to birth, under condemnation at the very root. Uses of matrimony undertaken for mere
pleasure not without venial fault.*

Where God has done nothing else than by a just sentence
to condemn the man who wilfully sins, root and all; there also,
and as a matter of course, everything pertaining to human offspring is in its sinful root under condemnation. In this radical
ruin carnal generation involves every man; and from it nothing but spiritual regeneration liberates him. In the case, therefore, of regenerate parents, if they continue in the same state
of grace, there will undoubtedly ensue no injurious consequence of their radical ruin, by reason of the remission of
sins which has been bestowed upon them. It is only when they
make a perverse use of this grace that the ruin operates, not
only in improper and corrupt practices of all kinds, but also
in the marriage state itself, whenever husband and wife toil
at procreation, not from the desire of natural propagation of
their species, but are mere slaves to the gratification of their
lust out of mere wantonness. As for the permission which the
apostle gives to husbands and wives, "not to defraud one another, except with consent for a time, that they may have leisure for prayer,"[78] he concedes it by way of indulgent allowance, and not as a command; but this very form of the
concession evidently implies some degree of fault. The connubial embrace, however, which marriage-contracts point to as
intended for the procreation of children, considered in itself

[78] 1 Cor. 7: 5.

simply, and without any reference to fornication, is good and right; because, although it is on account of this body of death (which is unrenewed as yet by the resurrection) impracticable without a certain amount of bestial motion, which puts human nature to the blush, yet the embrace is not after all a sin in itself, when reason applies the concupiscence to a good end, and is not overmastered to evil.

CHAP. 44.—*A full renewal through the resurrection, the effect of baptism.*

This concupiscence of the flesh would be prejudicial to good, even so far only as it is inherent in us, if the remission of sins did not prove so beneficial, that while it is inherent in men, both in the natural and the regenerate, it may in the former be prejudicial as well as inherent, but in the latter inherent simply, but never prejudicial. In the unregenerate it is prejudical to such an extent indeed, that, unless they are born again, it can contribute no advantage to them, even if they are born of regenerate parents. The fault of our nature remains in our offspring so deeply impressed as to make it guilty, even when the guilt of the self-same fault has been washed away in the parent by the remission of sins—until every defect which ends in sin by the consent of the human will is consumed and done away with in the last regeneration. This will be identical with that renovation of the very flesh itself which is promised in its future resurrection, when we shall not only commit no sins, but be even free from those vitiated desires which lead us to sin by yielding consent to them. To this blessed consummation advances are even now made by us, through the grace of that holy font which we have put within our reach. The same regeneration which now renews our spirit, so that all our past sins are remitted, will by and by also operate, as might be expected, to the renewal to eternal life of that very flesh, by the resurrection of which to an incorruptible state the incentives of all sins will be purged out of our nature. But this salvation is as yet only accomplished in hope: it is not absolutely realized in fact; it is not in present possession, but it is looked forward to with patience. And thus there is a whole and perfect cleansing, in the self-same baptismal font, not only of all the sins remitted now in our baptism, which make us guilty owing to the consent we yield to wrong desires, and to the sinful acts in which they issue; but of these said wrong desires also, which, if not consented to by us, would contract no guilt of sin, and which, though not removed in this present life, will yet have no existence in the life beyond.

CHAP. 45.—*Man's deliverance suited to the character of his very captivity. Exorcism, exsufflation, and renunciation of Satan, among the ceremonies of baptism.*

The guilt, therefore, of that fault of our nature of which we are speaking will remain in the carnal offspring of the regenerate, until in them also it will be washed in the font of regeneration. A regenerate man does not regenerate, but generates, sons according to the flesh; and thus he hands on to his posterity, not the condition of the regenerate, but only of natural birth. Therefore, if a man is guilty of unbelief, or is a perfect believer, he does not in either case beget faithful children, but sinners; in the same way that the seeds, not only of a wild olive, but also of a cultivated one, produce not cultivated olives, but wild ones. So, likewise, his first birth holds a man in that bondage from which only his second birth delivers him. The devil holds him, Christ liberates him; Eve's deceiver holds him, Mary's Son frees him: he holds him, who approached the man through the woman; he frees him, who was born of a woman that never approached a man: he holds him, who injected into the woman the cause of lust; he liberates him, who without any lust was conceived in the woman. The former was wholly able to hold all men in his grasp through one; nor does any deliver them out of his power but one, whom he was unable to grasp. The very sacraments indeed of the church, which she administers with due ceremony, according to the authority of very ancient tradition (and these opponents of the truth, notwithstanding their opinion that the sacraments are only feignedly and not really used in the case of infants, still do not venture to reject them with open disapproval),—the very sacraments, I say, of the holy church show plainly enough that infants, even when fresh from the womb, are delivered from the bondage of the devil through the grace of Christ. For, to say nothing of the fact that they are baptized for the remission of sins by no fallacious pretence, but in a true and faithful mystery, there is effected in them previously the exorcism and the exsufflation of the hostile power, which they profess to renounce by the mouth of those who bring them to baptism. Now, by all these consecrated and evident signs of hidden realities, they are shown to pass from their worst oppressor to their most excellent redeemer, who, by taking on himself our infirmity in our behalf, has bound the strong man, that he may spoil his goods;[79] seeing that the weakness of God is stronger, not only than men, but also than angels. While, therefore, God delivers small as well as great, he shows in both instances that the apostle spoke under the direction of him who is the truth. For it is not merely adults, but little babes too, whom he rescues from the power of darkness, in order to transfer them to the kingdom of God's dear Son.[80]

CHAP. 46.—*Difficulty of believing original sin. Man's vice is a beast's nature.*

No one should feel surprise, and ask: "Why does God's goodness create anything for the devil's malignity to take possession of?" The truth is, God's gift of creation is bestowed on the seminal elements of his creature with the same bounty by which "He makes his sun to rise on the evil and on the good, and sends rain on the just and on the unjust."[81] It is with so large a bounty that God has blessed the very seeds, as it were, of our nature, and by blessing has constituted and built it up. Nor has this blessing been eliminated out of our excellent nature by a fault which puts us under condemnation. Owing, indeed, to God's justice, who punishes, this fatal flaw has so far prevailed, that men are born with the fault of original sin; but yet its influence has not extended so far as to stop the birth of men. Just so does it happen in persons of adult age: whatever sins they commit, these defects of character do not eliminate his manhood from man; nay, God's good workmanship continues still, however evil are the deeds of the impious. For although "man being in honour abides not; and being without understanding, is compared with the beasts, and

[79] Matt. 12: 29.
[80] Col. 1: 13.
[81] Matt. 5: 45.

is like them,"[82] yet the resemblance is not so absolute that he becomes a beast. There is a comparison, no doubt, between the two; but it is not by reason of nature, but through vice—not vice in the beast, but fault in nature. For so excellent is a man in comparison with a beast, that man's vice is a beast's nature; still man's nature is never on this account changed into the nature of a beast. God, therefore, condemns man because of the fault by which his nature is disgraced, and not because of his nature, which is not removed out of existence in consequence of its fault. Heaven forbid that we should think beasts are subject to the sentence of condemnation which lies on ourselves! It is only proper that they should be free from our misery, since they cannot partake of our blessedness. What, then, is there surprising or unjust in man's being subjected to an impure spirit—not owing to his nature, but on account of that impurity of his which he has contracted in the stain of his birth, and which proceeds from the will of man,—the impure spirit itself being a good thing considered as spirit, but an evil in that it is impure? For the substance is of God, and is his work, while the bad quality emanates from man's own will. The stronger nature, therefore, that is, the angelic one, keeps the lower, or human, nature in subjection, by reason of the association of vice with the latter. Accordingly the mediator, who was stronger than the angels, became weak for man's sake.[83] So that the pride of the destroyer is destroyed by the humility of the redeemer; and he who makes his boast over the sons of men of his angelic strength, is vanquished by the Son of God in the human weakness which he assumed.

CHAP. 47.—*Sentences from Ambrose in favour of original sin. Every male which opens the womb.*

And now that we are about to bring this book to a conclusion, we think it proper to do on this subject of *Original Sin* what we did before in our treatise *On Grace,*—adduce in evidence against the injurious talk of these persons that servant of God, the Archbishop Ambrose, whose orthodoxy is claimed by Pelagius as being the most perfect among the writers of the Latin church; and there is a consistency in this testimony,

[82] Ps. 49: 12.
[83] 2 Cor. 8: 9.

for *grace* is more especially honoured in doing away with *original sin*. In the work which the saintly Ambrose wrote, *Concerning the Resurrection,* he says: "I fell in Adam, in Adam was I expelled from Paradise, in Adam I died; and he only recalls me to a state of salvation because he has found me in Adam—subject, indeed, to the guilt of sin in him, and subject to death, but also justified in Christ." Then, again, writing against the Novatians, he says: "We men are all of us born in sin; our very origin is wrapped in sin; as you may read when David says, 'Behold, I was shapen in iniquity, and in sin did my mother conceive me.'[84] Hence it is that Paul's flesh is 'a body of death;'[85] even as he says himself, 'Who shall deliver me from the body of this death?' Christ's flesh, however, has condemned sin, which he experienced not by being born, and which by dying he crucified, that in our flesh there might be justification through grace, where previously there was impurity through sin."[86] The same holy man also, in his *Exposition of Isaiah,* speaking of Christ, says: "Therefore as man he was tried in all things, and in the likeness of men he endured all things; but as born of the spirit of God, he was free from sin. For every man is a liar, and no one but God alone is without sin. It is therefore an observed and settled fact, that no man born of a man and a woman, that is, by means of their bodily commerce, is clearly free from sin. Whosoever, indeed, is free from sin, is free also from a conception and birth of this kind."[87] Moreover, when expounding the Gospel according to Luke, he says: "It was no cohabitation with a husband which opened the secret energies of the virgin's womb; rather was it the Holy Ghost which infused immaculate seed into her unviolated womb. For the Lord Jesus alone of those who are born of woman is holy, inasmuch as he experienced not the contact of earthly corruption, by reason of the novelty of his immaculate birth; indeed, he repelled it by his heavenly majesty."[88]

[84] Ps. 51: 5.
[85] Rom. 7: 24.
[86] *De Pœnitentia,* 1. 2 f.
[87] Quoted from a work by St. Ambrose, *On Isaiah,* not now extant.
[88] *Commentary on St. Luke,* 2.56.

CHAP. 48.

These words, however, of the man of God are contradicted by Pelagius, notwithstanding all his commendation of his author, when he himself declares that "we are born, as without virtue, so without vice."[89] What remains, then, but that Pelagius should condemn and renounce this error of his; or else be sorry that he has quoted Ambrose in the way he has? Since, however, the blessed Ambrose, Catholic bishop as he is, has expressed himself in the above-quoted passages in accordance with the Catholic faith, it follows that Pelagius, along with his disciple Cœlestius, was justly condemned by the authority of the Catholic Church for having turned aside from the true way of faith, since he repented not for having bestowed commendation on Ambrose, and for having at the same time entertained opinions in opposition to him. I know full well with what insatiable avidity you read whatever is written for edification and in confirmation of the faith; but yet, notwithstanding its utility as contributing to such an end, I must at last bring this treatise to a conclusion.

[89] See above, ch. 14.

Christian Instruction
(A.D. 396–426)

Book 4

The first three books of *Christian Instruction*, written about
396, discuss how to discover (especially through the use of
allegory) the *meaning* of the Bible. The fourth book, written
in 426, describes how to *communicate* that meaning to one's
audience. While the work is, therefore, concerned for the
most part with exegesis and homiletics, it reveals many of
Augustine's attitudes on education for Christians. Although at
the outset of his life as a Christian Augustine professed his
active interest in secular knowledge (particularly in Cicero,
Varro and the Platonists old and new), in this fourth book
of *Christian Instruction* he reveals his final attitude of detachment from the traditional culture as exemplified in Cicero's
great oratorical works. Brown speaks of the work as "one of
the most original that Augustine ever wrote. For it dealt, explicitly, with the ties that had bound educated Christians to
the culture of their age . . . it cut forever, in Augustine's
mind at least, the Gordian knot that had bound him to his
past education" (*Augustine of Hippo,* London, 1967, p. 264).
Not that Augustine was hostile to or did not want to use
that education; but he wanted to *develop the possibilities* on
the Christian side. The great themes of Augustine on education center on the distinction between instruction and learning, between general fact and Christian fact and between use
and enjoyment. Augustine strongly approves of book learning,
language (and logic), history, geography, mathematics, practical arts (but he has little enthusiasm for painting), rhetoric
and philosophy—but nothing to excess! The translation here
is by J. F. Shaw (Edinburgh, 1883).

RECOMMENDED READING

T. Sullivan, *De doctrina Christiana: A Commentary*, Washington, D.C., 1930.

H. I. Marrou, *S. Augustin et la fin de la culture antique*, Paris, 1949.

E. Kevane, *Augustine the Educator*, Westminster, Md., 1964; "Augustine's *de doctrina Christiana*," *Recherches Augustiniennes*, 4 (1966), pp. 97–133.

G. Howie, *Educational Theory and Practice in St. Augustine*, London, 1969.

Battenhouse, pp. 127–47.

Other Augustine texts on the topic: *De musica; De magistro; De catechizandis rudibus; Enchiridion.*

CHRISTIAN INSTRUCTION

BOOK 4

CHAP. 1—*This work not intended as a treatise on rhetoric.*

1. This work of mine, which is entitled *On Christian Doctrine,* was at the commencement divided into two parts. For, after a preface, in which I answered by anticipation those who were likely to take exception to the work, I said, "There are two things on which all interpretation of scripture depends: the mode of ascertaining the proper meaning, and the mode of making known the meaning when it is ascertained. I shall treat first of the mode of ascertaining, next of the mode of making known the meaning."[1] As, then, I have already said a great deal about the mode of ascertaining the meaning, and have given three books to this one part of the subject, I shall only say a few things about the mode of making known the meaning, in order if possible to bring them all within the compass of one book, and so finish the whole work in four books.

2. In the first place, then, I wish by this preamble to put a stop to the expectations of readers who may think that I am about to lay down rules of rhetoric such as I have learned, and taught too, in the secular schools, and to warn them that they need not look for any such from me. Not that I think such rules of no use, but that whatever use they have is to be learned elsewhere; and if any good man should happen to have leisure for learning them, he is not to ask me to teach them either in this work or any other.

[1] Book 1 chap. 1.

CHAP. 2—*It is lawful for a Christian teacher to use the art of rhetoric.*

3. Now, the art of rhetoric being available for the enforcing either of truth or falsehood, who will dare to say that truth in the person of its defenders is to take its stand unarmed against falsehood? For example, that those who are trying to persuade men of what is false are to know how to introduce their subject, so as to put the hearer into a friendly, or attentive, or teachable frame of mind, while the defenders of the truth shall be ignorant of that art? That the former are to tell their falsehoods briefly, clearly, and plausibly, while the latter shall tell the truth in such a way that it is tedious to listen to, hard to understand, and in short, not easy to believe it? That the former are to oppose the truth and defend falsehood with sophistical arguments, while the latter shall be unable either to defend what is true, or to refute what is false? That the former, while imbuing the minds of their hearers with erroneous opinions, are by their power of speech to awe, to melt, to enliven, and to rouse them, while the latter shall in defence of the truth be sluggish, and frigid, and somnolent? Who is such a fool as to think this wisdom? Since, then, the faculty of eloquence is available for both sides, and is of very great service in the enforcing either of wrong or right, why do not good men study to engage it on the side of truth, when bad men use it to obtain the triumph of wicked and worthless causes, and to further injustice and error?

CHAP. 3—*The proper age and the proper means for acquiring rhetorical skill.*

4. But the theories and rules on this subject (to which, when you add a tongue thoroughly skilled by exercise and habit in the use of many words and many ornaments of speech, you have what is called *eloquence* or *oratory*) may be learned apart from these writings of mine, if a suitable space of time be set aside for the purpose at a fit and proper age. But only by those who can learn them quickly; for the masters of Roman eloquence themselves did not shrink from saying that any one who cannot learn this art quickly can never thoroughly learn it at all.[2] Whether this is true or not, why need we in-

[2] Cicero, *de Oratore*, 3.31; Quintilian, *Inst. Orat.* 1.1.2.

quire? For even if this art can occasionally be in the end mastered by men of slower intellect, I do not think it of so much importance as to wish men who have arrived at mature age to spend time in learning it. It is enough that boys should give attention to it; and even of these, not all who are to be fitted for usefulness in the church, but only those who are not yet engaged in any occupation of more urgent necessity, or which ought evidently to take precedence of it. For men of quick intellect and glowing temperament find it easier to become eloquent by reading and listening to eloquent speakers than by following rules for eloquence. And even outside the canon, which to our great advantage is fixed in a place of secure authority, there is no want of ecclesiastical writings, in reading which a man of ability will acquire a tinge of the eloquence with which they are written, even though he does not aim at this, but is solely intent on the matters treated of; especially, of course, if in addition he practise himself in writing, or dictating, and at last also in speaking, the opinions he has formed on grounds of piety and faith. If, however, such ability be wanting, the rules of rhetoric are either not understood, or if, after great labour has been spent in enforcing them, they come to be in some small measure understood, they prove of no service. For even those who have learned them, and who speak with fluency and elegance, cannot always think of them when they are speaking so as to speak in accordance with them, unless they are discussing the rules themselves. Indeed, I think there are scarcely any who can do both things—that is, speak well, and, in order to do this, think of the rules of speaking while they are speaking. For we must be careful that what we have got to say does not escape us while we are thinking about saying it according to the rules of art. Nevertheless, in the speeches of eloquent men, we find rules of eloquence carried out which the speakers did not think of as aids to eloquence at the time when they were speaking, whether they had ever learned them, or whether they had never even met with them. For it is because they are eloquent that they exemplify these rules; it is not that they use them in order to be eloquent.

5. And, therefore, as infants cannot learn to speak except by learning words and phrases from those who do speak, why should not men become eloquent without being taught any art

of speech, simply by reading and learning the speeches of eloquent men, and by imitating them as far as they can? And
what do we find from the examples themselves to be the case
in this respect? We know numbers who, without acquaintance
with rhetorical rules, are more eloquent than many who have
learned these; but we know no one who is eloquent without
having read and listened to the speeches and debates of eloquent men. For even the art of grammar, which teaches correctness of speech, need not be learned by boys, if they have
the advantage of growing up and living among men who speak
correctly. For without knowing the names of any of the faults,
they will, from being accustomed to correct speech, lay hold
upon whatever is faulty in the speech of any one they listen
to, and avoid it; just as city-bred men, even when illiterate,
seize upon the faults of rustics.

CHAP. 4—*The duty of the Christian teacher.*

6. It is the duty, then, of the interpreter and teacher of Holy
Scripture, the defender of the true faith and the opponent of
error, both to teach what is right and to refute what is wrong,
and in the performance of this task to conciliate the hostile,
to rouse the careless, and to tell the ignorant both what is oc-
curring at present and what is probable in the future. But once
his hearers are friendly, attentive, and ready to learn, whether
he has found them so, or has himself made them so, the remaining objects are to be carried out in whatever way the case
requires. If the hearers need teaching, the matter treated of
must be made fully known by means of narrative. On the other
hand, to clear up points that are doubtful requires reasoning
and the exhibition of proofs. If, however, the hearers require
to be roused rather than instructed, in order that they may
be diligent to do what they already know, and to bring their
feelings into harmony with the truths they admit, greater vigour of speech is needed. Here entreaties and reproaches, exhortations and upbraidings, and all the other means of rousing
the emotions, are necessary.

7. And all the methods I have mentioned are constantly
used by nearly every one in cases where speech is the agency
employed.

CHAP. 5—*Wisdom of more importance than eloquence to the Christian teacher.*

But as some men employ these coarsely, inelegantly, and frigidly, while others use them with acuteness, elegance, and spirit, the work that I am speaking of ought to be undertaken by one who can argue and speak with wisdom, if not with eloquence, and with profit to his hearers, even though he profit them less than he would if he could speak with eloquence too. But we must beware of the man who abounds in eloquent nonsense, and so much the more if the hearer is pleased with what is not worth listening to, and thinks that because the speaker is eloquent what he says must be true. And this opinion is held even by those who think that the art of rhetoric should be taught: for they confess that "though wisdom without eloquence is of little service to states, yet eloquence without wisdom is frequently a positive injury, and is of service never."[3] If, then, the men who teach the principles of eloquence have been forced by truth to confess this in the very books which treat of eloquence, though they were ignorant of the true, that is, the heavenly wisdom which comes down from the father of lights, how much more ought we to feel it who are the sons and the ministers of this higher wisdom! Now a man speaks with more or less wisdom just as he has made more or less progress in the knowledge of scripture; I do not mean by reading them much and committing them to memory, but by understanding them aright and carefully searching into their meaning. For there are some who read and yet neglect them; they read to remember the words, but are careless about knowing the meaning. It is plain we must set far above these the men who are not so retentive of the words, but see with the eyes of the heart into the heart of scripture. Better than either of these, however, is the man who, when he wishes, can repeat the words, and at the same time correctly apprehends their meaning.

8. Now it is especially necessary for the man who is bound to speak wisely, even though he cannot speak eloquently, to retain in memory the words of scripture. For the more he discerns the poverty of his own speech, the more he ought to

[3] Cicero, *de Inventione Rhetorica*, 1.1.

draw on the riches of scripture, so that what he says in his own words he may prove by the words of scripture; and he himself, though small and weak in his own words, may gain strength and power from the confirming testimony of great men. For his proof gives pleasure when he cannot please by his mode of speech. But if a man desire to speak not only with wisdom, but with eloquence also (and assuredly he will prove of greater service if he can do both), I would rather send him to read, and listen to, and exercise himself in imitating, eloquent men, than advise him to spend time with the teachers of rhetoric; especially if the men he reads and listens to are justly praised as having spoken, or as being accustomed to speak, not only with eloquence, but with wisdom also. For eloquent speakers are heard with pleasure; wise speakers with profit. And, therefore, scripture does not say that the multitude of the eloquent, but "the multitude of the wise is the welfare of the world."[4] And as we must often swallow wholesome bitters, so we must always avoid unwholesome sweets. But what is better than wholesome sweetness or sweet wholesomeness? For the sweeter we try to make such things, the easier it is to make their wholesomeness serviceable. And so there are writers of the church who have expounded the Holy Scriptures, not only with wisdom, but with eloquence as well; and there is not more time for the reading of these than is sufficient for those who are studious and at leisure to exhaust them.

CHAP. 6—*The sacred writers unite eloquence with wisdom.*

9. Here, perhaps, some one inquires whether the authors whose divinely-inspired writings constitute the canon, which carries with it a most wholesome authority, are to be considered wise only, or eloquent as well. A question which to me, and to those who think with me, is very easily settled. For where I understand these writers, it seems to me not only that nothing can be wiser, but also that nothing can be more eloquent. And I venture to affirm that all who truly understand what these writers say, perceive at the same time that it could not have been properly said in any other way. For as there is a kind of eloquence that is more becoming in youth, and

[4] Wis. 6: 24.

a kind that is more becoming in old age, and nothing can be called eloquence if it be not suitable to the person of the speaker, so there is a kind of eloquence that is becoming in men who justly claim the highest authority, and who are evidently inspired of God. With this eloquence they spoke; no other would have been suitable for them; and this itself would be unsuitable in any other, for it is in keeping with their character, while it mounts as far above that of others (not from empty inflation, but from solid merit) as it seems to fall below them. Where, however, I do not understand these writers, though their eloquence is then less apparent, I have no doubt but that it is of the same kind as that I do understand. The very obscurity, too, of these divine and wholesome words was a necessary element in eloquence of a kind that was designed to profit our understandings, not only by the discovery of truth, but also by the exercise of their powers.

10. I could, however, if I had time, show those men who cry up their own form of language as superior to that of our authors (not because of its majesty, but because of its inflation), that all those powers and beauties of eloquence which they make their boast, are to be found in the sacred writings which God in his goodness has provided to mould our characters, and to guide us from this world of wickedness to the blessed world above. But it is not the qualities which these writers have in common with the heathen orators and poets that give me such unspeakable delight in their eloquence; I am more struck with admiration at the way in which, by an eloquence peculiarly their own, they so use this eloquence of ours that it is not conspicuous either by its presence or its absence: for it did not become them either to condemn it or to make an ostentatious display of it; and if they had shunned it, they would have done the former; if they had made it prominent, they might have appeared to be doing the latter. And in those passages where the learned do note its presence, the matters spoken of are such, that the words in which they are put seem not so much to be sought out by the speaker as spontaneously to suggest themselves; as if wisdom were walking out of its house,—that is, the breast of the wise man, and eloquence, like an inseparable attendant, followed it without being called for.

CHAP. 7—*Examples of true eloquence drawn from the Epistles of Paul and the Prophecies of Amos.*

11. For who would not see what the apostle meant to say, and how wisely he has said it, in the following passage: "We glory in tribulations also: knowing that tribulation works patience; and patience, experience; and experience, hope: and hope makes not ashamed; because the love of God is shed abroad in our hearts by the Holy Ghost who is given to us"?[5] Now if any man were unlearnedly learned (if I may use the expression) to contend that the apostle had here followed the rules of rhetoric, would not every Christian, learned or unlearned, laugh at him? And yet here we find the figure which is called in Greek *climax*, and by some in Latin *gradatio*, for they do not care to call it *scala* (a ladder), when the words and ideas have a connection of dependency the one upon the other, as we see here that patience arises out of tribulation, experience out of patience, and hope out of experience. Another ornament, too, is found here; for after certain statements finished in a single tone of voice, which we call clauses and sections (*membra et cæsa*), but the Greeks *kōla* and *kommata*, there follows a rounded sentence (*ambitus sive circuitus*) which the Greeks call *periodos*, the clauses of which are suspended on the voice of the speaker till the whole is completed by the last clause. For of the statements which precede the period, this is the first clause, "knowing that tribulation works patience;" the second, "and patience, experience;" the third, "and experience, hope." Then the period which is subjoined is completed in three clauses, of which the first is, "and hope makes not ashamed;" the second, "because the love of God is shed abroad in our hearts;" the third, "by the Holy Ghost who is given to us." But these and other matters of the same kind are taught in the art of elocution. As then I do not affirm that the apostle was guided by the rules of eloquence, so I do not deny that his wisdom naturally produced, and was accompanied by, eloquence.

12. In the Second Epistle to the Corinthians, again, he refutes certain false apostles who had gone out from the Jews, and had been trying to injure his character; and being com-

[5] Rom. 5: 3 ff.

pelled to speak of himself, though he ascribes this as folly to himself, how wisely and how eloquently he speaks! But wisdom is his guide, eloquence his attendant; he follows the first, the second follows him, and yet he does not spurn it when it comes after him. "I say again," he says, "let no man think me a fool: if otherwise, yet as a fool receive me, that I may boast, myself, a little. That which I speak, I speak it not after the Lord, but as it were foolishly, in this confidence of boasting. Seeing that many glory after the flesh, I will glory also. For you suffer fools gladly, seeing you yourselves are wise. For you suffer, if a man bring you into bondage, if a man devour you, if a man take of you, if a man exalt himself, if a man smite you on the face. I speak as concerning reproach, as though we had been weak. However, in whatever anyone is bold (I speak foolishly), I am bold also. Are they Hebrews? so am I. Are they Israelites? so am I. Are they the seed of Abraham? so am I. Are they ministers of Christ? (I speak as a fool), I am more: in labours more abundant, in stripes above measure, in prisons more frequent, in deaths oft. Of the Jews five times I received forty stripes save one, three times was I beaten with rods, once was I stoned, three times I suffered shipwreck, a night and a day I have been in the deep; in journeyings often, in perils of waters, in perils of robbers, in perils by my own countrymen, in perils by the heathen, in perils in the city, in perils in the wilderness, in perils in the sea, in perils among false brethren; in weariness and painfulness, in watchings often, in hunger and thirst, in fastings often, in cold and nakedness. Besides those things which are without, that which comes upon me daily, the care of all the churches. Who is weak, and I am not weak? who is offended, and I do not burn? If I must needs glory, I will glory of the things which concern my infirmities."[6] The thoughtful and attentive perceive how much wisdom there is in these words. And even a man sound asleep must notice what a stream of eloquence flows through them.

13. Further still, the educated man observes that those sections which the Greeks call *kommata*, and the clauses and periods of which I spoke a short time ago, being intermingled

[6] 2 Cor. 11: 16–30.

in the most beautiful variety, make up the whole form and features (so to speak) of that diction by which even the unlearned are delighted and affected. For, from the place where I commenced to quote, the passage consists of periods: the first the smallest possible, consisting of two members; for a period cannot have less than two members, though it may have more: "I say again, let no man think me a fool." The next has three members: "if otherwise, yet as a fool receive me, that I may boast, myself, a little." The third has four members: "That which I speak, I speak it not after the Lord, but as it were foolishly, in this confidence of boasting." The fourth has two: "Seeing that many glory after the flesh, I will glory also." And the fifth has two: "For you suffer fools gladly, seeing you yourselves are wise." The sixth again has two members: "for you suffer, if a man bring you into bondage." Then follow three sections (*cæsa*): "if a man devour you, if a man take of you, if a man exalt himself." Next three clauses (*membra*): "if a man smite you on the face. I speak as concerning reproach, as though we had been weak." Then is subjoined a period of three members: "However, in whatever is bold (I speak foolishly), I am bold also." After this, certain separate sections being put in the interrogatory form, separate sections are also given as answers, three to three: "Are they Hebrews? so am I. Are they Israelites? so am I. Are they the seed of Abraham? so am I." But a fourth section being put likewise in the interrogatory form, the answer is given not in another section (*cæsum*) but in a clause (*membrum*): "Are they the ministers of Christ? (I speak as a fool.) I am more." Then the next four sections are given continuously, the interrogatory form being most elegantly suppressed: "in labours more abundant, in stripes above measure, in prisons more frequent, in deaths often." Next is interposed a short period; for, by a suspension of the voice, "of the Jews five times" is to be marked off as constituting one member, to which is joined the second, "I received forty stripes save one." Then he returns to sections, and three are set down: "Three times was I beaten with rods, once was I stoned, three times I suffered shipwreck." Next comes a clause: "a night and a day I have been in the deep." Next fourteen sections burst forth with a vehemence which is most appropriate: "In journeyings often, in perils of waters, in perils of robbers, in perils by my own coun-trymen, in perils by the heathen, in perils in the city, in perils in the wilderness, in perils in the sea, in perils among false brethren, in weariness and painfulness, in watchings often, in hunger and thirst, in fastings often, in cold and nakedness." After this comes in a period of three members: "Besides those things which are without, that which comes upon me daily, the care of all the churches." And to this he adds two clauses in a tone of inquiry: "Who is weak, and I am not weak? who is offended, and I do not burn?" In short, this whole passage, as if panting for breath, winds up with a period of two mem-bers: "If I must needs glory, I will glory of the things which concern my infirmities." And I cannot sufficiently express how beautiful and delightful it is when after this outburst he rests himself, and gives the hearer rest, by interposing a slight narrative. For he goes on to say: "The God and Father of our Lord Jesus Christ, who is blessed for evermore, knows that I do not lie." And then he tells very briefly the danger he had been in, and the way he escaped it.

14. It would be tedious to pursue the matter further, or to point out the same facts in regard to other passages of Holy Scripture. Suppose I had taken the further trouble, at least in regard to the passages I have quoted from the apostle's writ-ings, to point out figures of speech which are taught in the art of rhetoric? Is it not more likely that serious men would think I had gone too far, than that any of the studious would think I had done enough? All these things when taught by masters are reckoned of great value; great prices are paid for them, and the vendors puff them magniloquently. And I fear lest I too should smack of that puffery while thus descanting on matters of this kind. It was necessary, however, to reply to the ill-taught men who think our authors contemptible; not because they do not possess, but because they do not display, the eloquence which these men value so highly.

15. But perhaps some one is thinking that I have selected the apostle Paul because he is our great orator. For when he says, "Though I am rude in speech, yet not in knowledge,"[7] he seems to speak as if granting so much to his detractors,

---

[7] 2 Cor. 11: 6.

not as confessing that he recognised its truth. If he had said, "I am indeed rude in speech, but not in knowledge," we could not in any way have put another meaning upon it. He did not hesitate plainly to assert his knowledge, because without it he could not have been the teacher of the gentiles. And certainly if we bring forward anything of his as a model of eloquence, we take it from those epistles which even his very detractors, who thought his bodily presence weak and his speech contemptible, confessed to be weighty and powerful.[8]

I see, then, that I must say something about the eloquence of the prophets also, where many things are concealed under a metaphorical style, which the more completely they seem buried under figures of speech, give the greater pleasure when brought to light. In this place, however, it is my duty to select a passage of such a kind that I shall not be compelled to explain the matter, but only to commend the style. And I shall do so, quoting principally from the book of that prophet who says that he was a shepherd or herdsman, and was called by God from that occupation, and sent to prophesy to the people of God.[9] I shall not, however, follow the Septuagint translators, who, being themselves under the guidance of the Holy Spirit in their translation, seem to have altered some passages with the view of directing the reader's attention more particularly to the investigation of the spiritual sense (and hence some passages are more obscure, because more figurative, in their translation); but I shall follow the translation made from the Hebrew into Latin by the priest Jerome, a man thoroughly acquainted with both tongues.

16. When, then, this rustic, or *quondam* rustic prophet, was denouncing the godless, the proud, the luxurious, and therefore the most neglectful of brotherly love, he called aloud, saying: "Woe to you who are at ease in Zion, and trust in the mountain of Samaria, who are heads and chiefs of the people, entering with pomp into the house of Israel! Pass to Calneh, and see; and from there go to Hamath the great; then go down to Gath of the Philistines, and to all the best kingdoms of these: is their border greater than your border? You that are set apart

[8] 2 Cor. 10: 10.
[9] Amos 1: 1.

for the day of evil, and that come near to the seat of oppression; that lie upon beds of ivory, and stretch yourselves upon couches; that eat the lamb of the flock, and the calves out of the midst of the herd; that chant to the sound of the viol. They thought that they had instruments of music like David; drinking wine in bowls, and anointing themselves with the costliest ointment: and they were not grieved for the affliction of Joseph."[10] Suppose those men who, assuming to be themselves learned and eloquent, despise our prophets as untaught and unskilful of speech, had been obliged to deliver a message like this, and to men such as these, would they have chosen to express themselves in any respect differently—those of them, at least, who would have shrunk from raving like madmen?

17. For what is there that sober ears could wish changed in this speech? In the first place, the invective itself; with what vehemence it throws itself upon the drowsy senses to startle them into wakefulness: "Woe to you who are at ease in Zion, and trust in the mountains of Samaria, who are heads and chiefs of the people, entering with pomp into the house of Israel!" Next, that he may use the favours of God, who has bestowed upon them ample territory, to show their ingratitude in trusting to the mountain of Samaria, where idols were worshipped: "Pass to Calneh," he says, "and see; and from there go to Hamath the great; then go down to Gath of the Philistines, and to all the best kingdoms of these: is their border greater than your border?" At the same time also that these things are spoken of, the style is adorned with names of places as with lamps, such as "Zion," "Samaria," "Calneh," "Hamath the great," and "Gath of the Philistines." Then the words joined to these places are most appropriately varied: "you are at ease," "you trust," "pass on," "go," "descend."

18. And then the future captivity under an oppressive king is announced as approaching, when it is added: "You that are set apart for the day of evil, and come near to the seat of oppression." Then are subjoined the evils of luxury: "you that lie upon beds of ivory, and stretch yourselves upon couches; that eat the lamb from the flock, and the calves out of the

---

[10] Amos 6: 1–6. The version given is a literal translation of Jerome's Latin, as quoted by Augustine.

midst of the herd." These six clauses form three periods of two members each. For he does not say: You who are set apart for the day of evil, who come near to the seat of oppression, who sleep upon beds of ivory, who stretch yourselves upon couches, who eat the lamb from the flock, and calves out of the herd." If he had so expressed it, this would have had its beauty: six separate clauses running on, the same pronoun being repeated each time, and each clause finished by a single effort of the speaker's voice. But it is more beautiful as it is, the clauses being joined in pairs under the same pronoun, and forming three sentences, one referring to the prophecy of the captivity: "You that are set apart for the day of evil, and come near the seat of oppression;" the second to lasciviousness: "you that lie upon beds of ivory, and stretch yourselves upon couches;" the third to gluttony: "who eat the lamb from the flock, and the calves out of the midst of the herd." So that it is at the discretion of the speaker whether he finish each clause separately and make six altogether, or whether he suspend his voice at the first, the third, and the fifth, and by joining the second to the first, the fourth to the third, and the sixth to the fifth, make three most elegant periods of two members each: one describing the imminent catastrophe; another, the lascivious couch; and the third, the luxurious table.

19. Next he reproaches them with their luxury in seeking pleasure for the sense of hearing. And here, when he had said, "You who chant to the sound of the viol," seeing that wise men may practise music wisely, he, with wonderful skill of speech, checks the flow of his invective, and not now speaking to, but of, these men, and to show us that we must distinguish the music of the wise from the music of the voluptuary, he does not say, "You who chant to the sound of the viol, and think that you have instruments of music like David;" but he first addresses to themselves what it is right the voluptuaries should hear, "You who chant to the sound of the viol;" and then, turning to others, he intimates that these men have not even skill in their art: "they thought that they had instruments of music like David; drinking wine in bowls, and anointing themselves with the costliest ointment." These three clauses are best pronounced when the voice is suspended on the first two members of the period, and comes to a pause on the third.

20. But now as to the sentence which follows all these: "and they were not grieved for the affliction of Joseph." Whether this be pronounced continuously as one clause, or whether with more elegance we hold the words, "and they were not grieved," suspended on the voice, and then add, "for the affliction of Joseph," so as to make a period of two members; in any case, it is a touch of marvellous beauty not to say, "and they were not grieved for the affliction of their brother;" but to put Joseph for brother, so as to indicate brothers in general by the proper name of him who stands out illustrious from among his brethren, both in regard to the injuries he suffered and the good return he made. And, indeed, I do not know whether this figure of speech, by which Joseph is put for brothers in general, is one of those laid down in that art which I learned and used to teach. But how beautiful it is, and how it comes home to the intelligent reader, it is useless to tell any one who does not himself feel it.

21. And a number of other points bearing on the laws of eloquence could be found in this passage which I have chosen as an example. But an intelligent reader will not be so much instructed by carefully analysing it as kindled by reciting it with spirit. Nor was it composed by man's art and care, but it flowed forth in wisdom and eloquence from the divine mind; wisdom not aiming at eloquence, yet eloquence not shrinking from wisdom. For if, as certain very eloquent and acute men have perceived and said, the rules which are laid down in the art of oratory could not have been observed, and noted, and reduced to system, if they had not first had their birth in the genius of orators, is it wonderful that they should be found in the messengers of him who is the author of all genius? Therefore let us acknowledge that the canonical writers are not only wise but eloquent also, with an eloquence suited to a character and position like theirs.

CHAP. 8—*The obscurity of the sacred writers, though compatible with eloquence, not to be imitated by Christian teachers.*

22. But although I take some examples of eloquence from those writings of theirs which there is no difficulty in understanding, we are not by any means to suppose that it is our duty to imitate them in those passages where, with a view to

exercise and train the minds of their readers, and to break in upon the satiety and stimulate the zeal of those who are willing to learn, and with a view also to throw a veil over the minds of the godless either that they may be converted to piety or shut out from a knowledge of the mysteries, from one or other of these reasons they have expressed themselves with a useful and wholesome obscurity. They have indeed expressed themselves in such a way that those who in after ages understood and explained them aright have in the church of God obtained an esteem, not indeed equal to that with which they are themselves regarded, but coming next to it. The expositors of these writers, then, ought not to express themselves in the same way, as if putting forward their expositions as of the same authority; but they ought in all their deliverances to make it their first and chief aim to be understood, using as far as possible such clearness of speech that either he will be very dull who does not understand them, or that if what they say should not be very easily or quickly understood, the reason will lie not in their manner of expression, but in the difficulty and subtlety of the matter they are trying to explain.

CHAP. 9—*How, and with whom, difficult passages are to be discussed.*

23. For there are some passages which are not understood in their proper force, or are understood with great difficulty, at whatever length, however clearly, or with whatever eloquence the speaker may expound them; and these should never be brought before the people at all, or only on rare occasions when there is some urgent reason. In books, however, which are written in such a style that, if understood, they, so to speak, draw their own readers, and if not understood, give no trouble to those who do not care to read them, and in private conversations, we must not shrink from the duty of bringing the truth which we ourselves have reached within the comprehension of others, however difficult it may be to understand it, and whatever labour in the way of argument it may cost us. Only two conditions are to be insisted upon, that our hearer or companion should have an earnest desire to learn the truth, and should have capacity of mind to receive it in whatever form

it may be communicated, the teacher not being so anxious about the eloquence as about the clearness of his teaching.

CHAP. 10—*The necessity for perspicuity of style.*

24. Now a strong desire for clearness sometimes leads to neglect of the more polished forms of speech, and indifference about what sounds well, compared with what clearly expresses and conveys the meaning intended. Therefore a certain author, when dealing with speech of this kind, says that there is in it "a kind of careful negligence."[11] Yet while taking away ornament, it does not bring in vulgarity of speech; though good teachers have, or ought to have, so great an anxiety about teaching that they will employ a word (which cannot be made pure Latin without becoming obscure or ambiguous, but which when used according to the vulgar idiom is neither ambiguous nor obscure) not in the way the learned, but rather in the way the unlearned employ it. For if our translators did not shrink from saying, *non congregabo conventicula eorum de sanguinibus*,[12] because they felt that it was important for the sense to put a word here in the plural which in Latin is used only in the singular; why should a teacher of godliness who is addressing an unlearned audience shrink from using *ossum* instead of *os*, if he fear that the latter might be taken not as the singular of *ossa*, but as the singular of *ora*, seeing that African ears have no quick perception of the shortness or length of vowels? And what advantage is there in purity of speech which does not lead to understanding in the hearer, seeing that there is no use at all in speaking, if they do not understand us for whose sake we speak? He, therefore, who teaches will avoid all words that do not teach; and if instead of them he can find words which are at once pure and intelligible, he will take these by preference; if, however, he cannot, either because there are no such words, or because they do not at the time occur to him, he will use words that are not quite pure, if only the substance of his thought be conveyed and apprehended in its integrity.

25. And this must be insisted on as necessary to our being

---

[11] Cicero, *Orator.* 23.
[12] "I shall not assemble their assemblies of blood," Ps. 16: 4 (Vulgate).

understood, not only in conversations, whether with one person or with several, but much more in the case of a speech delivered in public: for in conversation any one has the power of asking a question; but when all are silent that one may be heard, and all faces are turned attentively upon him, it is neither customary nor decorous for a person to ask a question about what he does not understand; and on this account the speaker ought to be especially careful to give assistance to those who cannot ask it. Now a crowd anxious for instruction generally shows by its movements if it understands what is said; and until some indication of this sort be given, the subject discussed ought to be turned over and over, and put in every shape and form and variety of expression, a thing which cannot be done by men who are repeating words prepared beforehand and committed to memory. As soon, however, as the speaker has ascertained that what he says is understood, he ought either to bring his address to a close, or pass on to another point. For if a man gives pleasure when he throws light upon points on which people wish for instruction, he becomes wearisome when he dwells at length upon things that are already well known, especially when men's expectation was fixed on having the difficulties of the passage removed. For even things that are very well known are told for the sake of the pleasure they give, if the attention be directed not to the things themselves, but to the way in which they are told. Indeed, even when the style itself is already well known, if it is pleasing to the hearers, it is almost a matter of indifference whether he who speaks is a speaker or a reader. For things that are gracefully written are often not only read with delight by those who are making their first acquaintance with them, but reread with delight by those who have already made acquaintance with them, and have not yet forgotten them; both these classes will derive pleasure even from hearing another man repeat them. And if a man has forgotten anything, when he is reminded of it he is taught. But I am not now treating of the mode of giving pleasure. I am speaking of the mode in which men who desire to learn ought to be taught. And the best mode is that which secures that he who hears shall hear the truth, and that what he hears he shall understand. And when this point has been reached, no further labour need be spent on the truth itself, as if it required further explanation; but perhaps some trouble may be taken to enforce it so as to bring it home to the heart. If it appear right to do this, it ought to be done so moderately as not to lead to weariness and impatience.

CHAP. 11—*The Christian teacher must speak clearly, but not inelegantly.*

26. For teaching, of course, true eloquence consists, not in making people like what they disliked, nor in making them do what they shrank from, but in making clear what was obscure; yet if this is done without grace of style, the benefit does not extend beyond the few eager students who are anxious to know whatever is to be learned, however rude and unpolished the form in which it is put; and who, when they have succeeded in their object, find the plain truth pleasant food enough. And it is one of the distinctive features of good intellects not to love words, but the truth in words. For of what service is a golden key, if it cannot open what we want it to open? Or what objection is there to a wooden one if it can, seeing that to open what is shut is all we want? But as there is a certain analogy between learning and eating, the very food without which it is impossible to live must be flavoured to meet the tastes of the majority.

CHAP. 12—*The aim of the orator, according to Cicero, is to teach, to delight, and to move. Of these, teaching is the most essential.*

27. Accordingly a great orator has truly said that "an eloquent man must speak so as to teach, to delight, and to persuade."[13] Then he adds: "To teach is a necessity, to delight is a beauty, to persuade is a triumph." Now of these three, the one first mentioned, the teaching, which is a matter of necessity, depends on what we say; the other two on the way we say it. He, then, who speaks with the purpose of teaching should not suppose that he has said what he has to say as long as he is not understood; for although what he has said be intelligible to himself, it is not said at all to the man who does not understand it. If, however, he is understood, he has said his say, whatever may have been his manner of saying

[13] Cicero, *Orator*. 21.

it. But if he wishes to delight or persuade his hearer as well, he will not accomplish that end by putting his thought in any shape no matter what, but for that purpose the style of speaking is a matter of importance. And as the hearer must be pleased in order to secure his attention, so he must be persuaded in order to move him to action. And as he is pleased if you speak with sweetness and elegance, so he is persuaded if he be drawn by your promises, and awed by your threats; if he reject what you condemn, and embrace what you commend; if he grieve when you heap up objects for grief, and rejoice when you point out an object for joy; if he pity those whom you present to him as objects of pity, and shrink from those whom you set before him as men to be feared and shunned. I need not go over all the other things that can be done by powerful eloquence to move the minds of the hearers, not telling them what they ought to do, but urging them to do what they already know ought to be done.

28. If, however, they do not yet know this, they must of course be instructed before they can be moved. And perhaps the mere knowledge of their duty will have such an effect that there will be no need to move them with greater strength of eloquence. Yet when this is needful, it ought to be done. And it is needful when people, knowing what they ought to do, do it not. Therefore, to teach is a necessity. For what men know, it is in their own hands either to do or not to do. But who would say that it is their duty to do what they do not know? On the same principle, to persuade is not a necessity: for it is not always called for; as, for example, when the hearer yields his assent to one who simply teaches or gives pleasure. For this reason also to persuade is a triumph, because it is possible that a man may be taught and delighted, and yet not give his consent. And what will be the use of gaining the first two ends if we fail in the third? Neither is it a necessity to give pleasure; for when, in the course of an address, the truth is clearly pointed out (and this is the true function of teaching), it is not the fact, nor is it the intention, that the style of speech should make the truth pleasing, or that the style should of itself give pleasure; but the truth itself, when exhibited in its naked simplicity, gives pleasure, because it is the truth. And hence even falsities are frequently a source of

pleasure when they are brought to light and exposed. It is not, of course, their falsity that gives pleasure; but as it is true that they are false, the speech which shows this to be true gives pleasure.

CHAP. 13—*The hearer must be moved as well as instructed.*

29. But for the sake of those who are so fastidious that they do not care for truth unless it is put in the form of a pleasing discourse, no small place has been assigned in eloquence to the art of pleasing. And yet even this is not enough for those stubborn-minded men who both understand and are pleased with the teacher's discourse, without deriving any profit from it. For what does it profit a man that he both confesses the truth and praises the eloquence, if he does not yield his consent, when it is only for the sake of securing his consent that the speaker in urging the truth gives careful attention to what he says? If the truths taught are such that to believe or to know them is enough, to give one's assent implies nothing more than to confess that they are true. When, however, the truth taught is one that must be carried into practice, and that is taught for the very purpose of being practised, it is useless to be persuaded of the truth of what is said, it is useless to be pleased with the manner in which it is said, if it is not so learned as to be practised. The eloquent divine, then, when he is urging a practical truth, must not only teach so as to give instruction, and please so as to keep up the attention, but he must also sway the mind so as to subdue the will. For if a man is not moved by the force of truth, though it is demonstrated to his own confession, and clothed in beauty of style, nothing remains but to subdue him by the power of eloquence.

CHAP. 14—*Beauty of diction to be in keeping with the matter.*

30. And so much labour has been spent by men on the beauty of expression here spoken of, that not only is it not our duty to do, but it is our duty to shun and abhor, many and heinous deeds of wickedness and baseness which wicked and base men have with great eloquence recommended, not with a view to gaining assent, but merely for the sake of being read with pleasure. But may God avert from his church what the prophet Jeremiah says of the synagogue of the Jews:

"A wonderful and horrible thing is committed in the land: the prophets prophesy falsely, and the priests applaud them with their hands; and my people love to have it so: and what will you do in the end?"[14] O eloquence, which is the more terrible from its purity, and the more crushing from its solidity! Assuredly it is "a hammer that breaks the rock in pieces." For to this God himself has by the same prophet compared his own word spoken through his holy prophets.[15] God forbid, then, God forbid that with us the priest should applaud the false prophet, and that God's people should love to have it so. God forbid, I say, that with us there should be such terrible madness! For what shall we do in the end? And assuredly it is preferable, even though what is said should be less intelligible, less pleasing, and less persuasive, that truth be spoken, and that what is just, not what is iniquitous, be listened to with pleasure. But this, of course, cannot be, unless what is true and just be expressed with elegance.

31. In a serious assembly, moreover, such as is spoken of when it is said, "I will praise you among much people,"[16] no pleasure is derived from that species of eloquence which indeed says nothing that is false, but which buries small and unimportant truths under a frothy mass of ornamental words, such as would not be graceful or dignified even if used to adorn great and fundamental truths. And something of this sort occurs in a letter of the blessed Cyprian, which, I think, came there by accident, or else was inserted designedly with this view, that posterity might see how the wholesome discipline of Christian teaching had cured him of that redundancy of language, and confined him to a more dignified and modest form of eloquence, such as we find in his subsequent letters, a style which is admired without effort, is sought after with eagerness, but is not attained without great difficulty. He says, then, in one place, "Let us seek this abode: the neighbouring solitudes afford a retreat where, while the spreading shoots of the vine trees, pendulous and intertwined, creep among the supporting reeds, the leafy covering has made a portico

14 Jer. 5: 30 f.
15 Jer. 23: 29.
16 Ps. 35: 18.

of vine."[17] There is wonderful fluency and exuberance of language here; but it is too florid to be pleasing to serious minds. But people who are fond of this style are apt to think that men who do not use it, but employ a more chastened style, do so because they cannot attain the former, not because their judgment teaches them to avoid it. Therefore this holy man shows both that he can speak in that style, for he has done so once, and that he does not choose, for he never uses it again.

CHAP. 15—*The Christian teacher should pray before preaching.*

32. And so our Christian orator, while he says what is just, and holy, and good (and he ought never to say anything else), does all he can to be heard with intelligence, with pleasure, and with obedience; and he need not doubt that if he succeed in this object, and so far as he succeeds, he will succeed more by piety in prayer than by gifts of oratory; and so he ought to pray for himself, and for those he is about to address, before he attempts to speak. And when the hour is come that he must speak, he ought, before he opens his mouth, to lift up his thirsty soul to God, to drink in what he is about to pour forth, and to be himself filled with what he is about to distribute. For, as in regard to every matter of faith and love there are many things that may be said, and many ways of saying them, who knows what it is expedient at a given moment for us to say, or to be heard saying, except God who knows the hearts of all? And who can make us say what we ought, and in the way we ought, except him in whose hand both we and our speeches are? Accordingly, he who is anxious both to know and to teach should learn all that is to be taught, and acquire such a faculty of speech as is suitable for a divine. But when the hour for speech arrives, let him reflect upon that saying of our Lord's, as better suited to the wants of a pious mind: "Take no thought how or what you shall speak; for it shall be given you in that same hour what you shall speak. For it is not you that speak, but the Spirit of your Father which speaks in you."[18] The Holy Spirit, then, speaks thus in those who for Christ's sake are delivered to the persecutors; why

[17] Cyprian, *ad Donat. Ep.* 1.
[18] Matt. 10: 19 f.

not also in those who deliver Christ's message to those who
are willing to learn?

CHAP. 16—*Human directions not to be despised, though God makes
the true teacher.*

33. Now if any one says that we need not direct men how
or what they should teach, since the Holy Spirit makes them
teachers, he may as well say that we need not pray, since our
Lord says, "Your Father knows what things you have need
of before you ask him;[19] or that the apostle Paul should not
have given directions to Timothy and Titus as to how or what
they should teach others. And these three apostolic epistles
ought to be constantly before the eyes of every one who has
obtained the position of a teacher in the church. In the First
Epistle to Timothy do we not read: "These things command
and teach"?[20] What these things are, has been told previously.
Do we not read there: "Rebuke not an elder, but exhort him
as a father"?[21] Is it not said in the Second Epistle: "Hold
fast the form of sound words, which you have heard from
me"?[22] And is he not there told: "Study to show yourself
approved to God, a workman that needs not to be ashamed,
rightly handling the word of truth"?[23] And in the same place:
"Preach the word; be instant in season, out of season; reprove,
rebuke, exhort, with all long-suffering and doctrine."[24] And
so in the Epistle to Titus, does he not say that a bishop ought
to "hold fast the faithful word as he has been taught, that
he may be able by sound doctrine both to exhort and to convince those who contradict"?[25] There, too, he says: "But
speak the things which become sound doctrine: that the aged
men be sober," and so on.[26] And there, too: "These things
speak, and exhort, and rebuke with all authority. Let no man
despise you. Put them in mind to be subject to principalities

[19] Matt. 6: 8.
[20] 1 Tim. 4: 11.
[21] 1 Tim. 5: 1.
[22] 2 Tim. 1: 13.
[23] 2 Tim. 2: 15.
[24] 2 Tim. 4: 2.
[25] Tit. 1: 9.
[26] Tit. 2: 1 f.

and powers,"[27] and so on. What then are we to think? Does the apostle in any way contradict himself, when, though he says that men are made teachers by the operation of the Holy Spirit, he yet himself gives them directions how and what they should teach? Or are we to understand, that though the duty of men to teach even the teachers does not cease when the Holy Spirit is given, yet that neither he who plants is anything, nor he who waters, but God who gives the increase?[28] Therefore though holy men are our helpers, or even holy angels assist us, no one learns rightly the things that pertain to life with God, until God makes him ready to learn from himself, that God who is thus addressed in the psalm: "Teach me to do your will; for you are my God."[29] And so the same apostle says to Timothy himself, speaking, of course, as teacher to disciple: "But continue in the things which you have learned, and been assured of, knowing from whom you have learned them."[30] For as the medicines which men apply to the bodies of their fellowmen are of no avail except God gives them virtue (who can heal without their aid, though they cannot without his), and yet they are applied; and if it is done from a sense of duty, it is esteemed a work of mercy or benevolence; so the aids of teaching, applied through the instrumentality of man, are of advantage to the soul only when God works to make them of advantage, who could give the gospel to man even without the help or agency of men.

CHAP. 17—*Threefold division of the various styles of speech.*

34. He then who, in speaking, aims at enforcing what is good, should not despise any of those three objects, either to teach, or to give pleasure, or to move, and should pray and strive, as we have said above, to be heard with intelligence, with pleasure, and with ready compliance. And when he does this with elegance and propriety, he may justly be called eloquent, even though he do not carry with him the assent of his hearer. For it is these three ends, viz. teaching, giving pleasure, and moving, that the great master of Roman eloquence

[27] Tit. 2: 15; 3: 1.
[28] 1 Cor. 3: 7.
[29] Ps. 143: 10.
[30] 2 Tim. 3: 14.

himself seems to have intended that the following three directions should subserve: "He, then, shall be eloquent, who can say little things in a subdued style, moderate things in a temperate style, and great things in a majestic style:"[31] as if he had taken in also the three ends mentioned above, and had embraced the whole in one sentence thus: "He, then, shall be eloquent, who can say little things in a subdued style, in order to give instruction, moderate things in a temperate style, in order to give pleasure, and great things in a majestic style, in order to sway the mind."

CHAP. 18—*The Christian orator is constantly dealing with great matters.*

35. Now the author I have quoted could have exemplified these three directions, as laid down by himself, in regard to legal questions: he could not, however, have done so in regard to ecclesiastical questions,—the only ones that an address such as I wish to give shape to is concerned with. For of legal questions those are called small which have reference to pecuniary transactions; those great where a matter relating to man's life or liberty comes up. Cases, again, which have to do with neither of these, and where the intention is not to get the hearer to do, or to pronounce judgment upon anything, but only to give him pleasure, occupy as it were a middle place between the former two, and are on that account called middling, or moderate. For moderate things get their name from *modus* (a measure); and it is an abuse, not a proper use of the word *moderate*, to put it for *little*. In questions like ours, however, where all things, and especially those addressed to the people from the place of authority, ought to have reference to men's salvation, and that not their temporal but their eternal salvation, and where also the thing to be guarded against is eternal ruin, everything that we say is important; so much so, that even what the preacher says about pecuniary matters, whether it have reference to loss or gain, whether the amount be great or small, should not seem unimportant. For justice is never unimportant, and justice ought assuredly to be observed, even in small affairs of money, as our Lord says: "He that is faith-

[31] Cicero, *Orator.* 29.

ful in that which is least, is faithful also in much."[32] That which is least, then, is very little; but to be faithful in that which is least is great. For as the nature of the circle, viz. that all lines drawn from the centre to the circumference are equal, is the same in a great disk as it is in the smallest coin; so the greatness of justice is in no degree lessened, though the matters to which justice is applied are small.

36. And when the apostle spoke about trials in regard to secular affairs (and what were these but matters of money?), he says: "Dare any of you, having a matter against another, go to law before the unjust, and not before the saints? Do you not know that the saints shall judge the world? and if the world shall be judged by you, are you unworthy to judge the smallest matters? Do you not know that we shall judge angels? how much more things that pertain to this life? If, then, you have judgments of things pertaining to this life, set them to judge who are least esteemed in the church. I speak to your shame. Is it so, that there is not a wise man among you? no, not one that shall be able to judge between his brethren? But brother goes to law with brother, and that before the unbelievers. Now therefore there is clearly a fault among you, because you go to law one with another: why do you not rather suffer wrong? why do you not rather suffer yourselves to be defrauded? You do wrong, and defraud, and that your brethren. Do you not know that the unrighteous shall not inherit the kingdom of God?"[33] Why is it that the apostle is so indignant, and that he thus accuses, and upbraids, and chides, and threatens? Why is it that the changes in his tone, so frequent and so abrupt, testify to the depth of his emotion? Why is it, in short, that he speaks in a tone so exalted about matters so very trifling? Did secular matters deserve so much at his hands? God forbid. No; but all this is done for the sake of justice, charity, and piety, which in the judgment of every sober mind are great, even when applied to matters the very least.

37. Of course, if we were giving men advice as to how they ought to conduct secular cases, either for themselves or for

[32] Luke 16: 10.
[33] 1 Cor. 6: 1–9.

their connections, before the church courts, we would rightly advise them to conduct them quietly as matters of little moment. But we are treating of the manner of speech of the man who is to be a teacher of the truths which deliver us from eternal misery and bring us to eternal happiness; and wherever these truths are spoken of, whether in public or private, whether to one or many, whether to friends or enemies, whether in a continuous discourse or in conversation, whether in tracts, or in books, or in letters long or short, they are of great importance. Unless indeed we are prepared to say that, because a cup of cold water is a very trifling and common thing, the saying of our Lord that he who gives a cup of cold water to one of his disciples shall in no wise lose his reward,[34] is very trivial and unimportant. Or that when a preacher takes this saying as his text, he should think his subject very unimportant, and therefore speak without either eloquence or power, but in a subdued and humble style. Is it not the case that when we happen to speak on this subject to the people, and the presence of God is with us, so that what we say is not altogether unworthy of the subject, a tongue of fire springs up out of that cold water which inflames even the cold hearts of men with a zeal for doing works of mercy in hope of an eternal reward?

CHAP. 19—*The Christian teacher must use different styles on different occasions.*

38. And yet, while our teacher ought to speak of great matters, he ought not always to be speaking of them in a majestic tone, but in a subdued tone when he is teaching, temperately when he is giving praise or blame. When, however, something is to be done, and we are speaking to those who ought, but are not willing, to do it, then great matters must be spoken of with power, and in a manner calculated to sway the mind. And sometimes the same important matter is treated in all these ways at different times, quietly when it is being taught, temperately when its importance is being urged, and powerfully when we are forcing a mind that is averse to the truth to turn and embrace it. For is there anything greater than God

[34] Matt. 10: 42.

himself? Is nothing, then, to be learned about him? Or ought he who is teaching the Trinity in unity to speak of it otherwise than in the method of calm discussion, so that in regard to a subject which it is not easy to comprehend, we may understand as much as it is given us to understand? Are we in this case to seek out ornaments instead of proofs? Or is the hearer to be moved to do something instead of being instructed so that he may learn something? But when we come to praise God, either in himself, or in his works, what a field for beauty and splendour of language opens up before man, who can task his powers to the utmost in praising him whom no one can adequately praise, though there is no one who does not praise him in some measure! But if he be not worshipped, or if idols, whether they are demons or any created being whatever, are worshipped with him or in preference to him, then we ought to speak out with power and impressiveness, show how great a wickedness this is, and urge men to flee from it.

CHAP. 20—*Examples of the various styles drawn from scripture.*

39. But now to come to something more definite. We have an example of the calm, subdued style in the apostle Paul, where he says: "Tell me, you that desire to be under the law, do you not hear the law? For it is written, that Abraham had two sons; the one by a bond maid, the other by a free woman. But he who was born of the bond woman was born after the flesh; but he of the free woman was by promise. Which things are an allegory: for these are the two covenants; the one from the Mount Sinai, which gives birth to bondage, which is Hagar. For this Hagar is Mount Sinai in Arabia, and answers to Jerusalem which now is, and is in bondage with her children. But the Jerusalem that is above is free, which is the mother of us all;"[35] and so on. And in the same way where he reasons thus: "Brethren, I speak after the manner of men: Though it is but a man's covenant, yet if it is confirmed, no man annuls or adds to it. Now to Abraham and his seed were the promises made. He does not say, and to seeds, as of many; but as of one, and to your seed, which is Christ. And this I say, that the covenant, that was confirmed before by God in

[35] Gal. 4: 21–26.

Christ, the law, which was four hundred and thirty years after, cannot annul, that it should make the promise of no effect. For if the inheritance is of the law, it is no more of promise: but God gave it to Abraham by promise."[36] And because it might possibly occur to the hearer to ask, if there is no inheritance by the law, why then was the law given? he himself anticipates this objection and asks, "What use, then, is the law?" And the answer is given: "It was added because of transgressions, till the seed should come to whom the promise was made; and it was ordained by angels in the hand of a mediator. Now a mediator is not a mediator of one; but God is one." And here an objection occurs which he himself has stated: "Is the law then against the promises of God?" He answers: "God forbid." And he also states the reason in these words: "For if there had been a law given which could have given life, truly righteousness should have been by the law. But the scripture concluded all under sin, that the promise by faith of Jesus Christ might be given to them that believe."[37] It is part, then, of the duty of the teacher not only to interpret what is obscure, and to unravel the difficulties of questions, but also, while doing this, to meet other questions which may chance to suggest themselves, lest these should cast doubt or discredit on what we say. If, however, the solution of these questions suggests itself as soon as the questions themselves arise, it is useless to disturb what we cannot remove. And besides, when out of one question other questions arise, and out of these again still others; if these be all discussed and solved, the reasoning is extended to such a length, that unless the memory is exceedingly powerful and active, the reasoner finds it impossible to return to the original question from which he set out. It is, however, very desirable that whatever occurs to the mind as an objection that might be urged should be stated and refuted, lest it turn up at a time when no one will be present to answer it, or lest, if it should occur to a man who is present but says nothing about it, it might never be thoroughly removed.

40. In the following words of the apostle we have the tem-

36 Gal. 3: 15–18.
37 Gal. 3: 19–22.

perate style: "Do not rebuke an elder, but exhort him as a
father; and the younger men as brethren; the elder women as
mothers, the younger as sisters."[38] And also in these: "I beseech you, therefore, brethren, by the mercies of God, that
you present your bodies a living sacrifice, holy, acceptable to
God, which is your reasonable service."[39] And almost the
whole of this hortatory passage is in the temperate style of
eloquence; and those parts of it are the most beautiful in
which, as if paying what was due, things that belong to each
other are gracefully brought together. For example: "Having
then gifts, differing according to the grace that is given to us,
whether prophecy, let us prophesy according to the proportion
of faith; or ministry, let us minister; or he that teaches, in
teaching; or he that exhorts, in exhortation: he that gives, let
him do it with simplicity; he that rules, with diligence; he that
shows mercy, with cheerfulness. Let love be without dissimulation. Abhor that which is evil, cleave to that which is good.
Be kindly disposed one to another with brotherly love; in honour preferring one another; not slothful in business; fervent
in spirit; serving the Lord; rejoicing in hope; patient in tribulation; continuing instant in prayer; distributing to the needs of
saints; given to hospitality. Bless them that persecute you:
bless, and curse not. Rejoice with them that rejoice, and weep
with them that weep. Be of the same mind one toward another."[40] And how gracefully all this is brought to a close
in a period of two members: "Mind not high things, but condescend to men of low estate!" And a little afterwards: "Render therefore to all their dues: tribute to whom tribute is due;
custom to whom custom; fear to whom fear; honour to whom
honour."[41] And these also, though expressed in single clauses,
are terminated by a period of two members: "Owe no man
anything, but to love one another." And a little farther on:
"The night is far spent, the day is at hand: let us therefore
cast off the works of darkness, and let us put on the armour
of light. Let us walk honestly, as in the day; not in rioting
and drunkenness, not in chambering and wantonness, not in

[38] 1 Tim. 5: 1 f.
[39] Rom. 12: 1.
[40] Rom. 12: 6–16.
[41] Rom. 13: 7.

strife and envying: but put on the Lord Jesus Christ, and make
not provision for the flesh, to fulfil the lusts thereof."[42] Now
if the passage were rendered thus, "et carnis providentiam ne
in concupiscentiis feceritis,"[43] the ear would no doubt be
gratified with a more harmonious ending; but our translator,
with more strictness, preferred to retain even the order of the
words. And how this sounds in the Greek language, in which
the apostle spoke, those who are better skilled in that tongue
may determine. My opinion, however, is, that what has been
translated to us in the same order of words does not run very
harmoniously even in the original tongue.

41. And, indeed, I must confess that our authors are very
defective in that grace of speech which consists in harmonious
endings. Whether this be the fault of the translators, or
whether, as I am more inclined to believe, the authors designedly avoided such ornaments, I dare not affirm; for I confess I do not know. This I know, however, that if any one who
is skilled in this species of harmony would take the closing sentences of these writers and arrange them according to the law
of harmony (which he could very easily do by changing some
words for words of equivalent meaning, or by retaining the
words he finds and altering their arrangement), he will learn
that these divinely-inspired men are not defective in any of
those points which he has been taught in the schools of the
grammarians and rhetoricians to consider of importance; and
he will find in them many kinds of speech of great beauty,—
beautiful even in our language, but especially beautiful in the
original,—none of which can be found in those writings of
which they boast so much. But care must be taken that, while
adding harmony, we take away none of the weight from these
divine and authoritative utterances. Now our prophets were
so far from being deficient in the musical training from which
this harmony we speak of is most fully learned, that Jerome,
a very learned man, describes even the metres employed by
some of them,[44] in the Hebrew language at least; though, in
order to give an accurate rendering of the words, he has not

---

[42] Rom. 13: 12–14.

[43] Instead of *"ne feceritis in concupiscentiis,"* which is the translation as quoted by Augustine.

[44] In his preface to Job.

preserved these in his translation. I, however (to speak of my own feeling, which is better known to me than it is to others, and than that of others is to me), while I do not in my own speech, however modestly I think it done, neglect these harmonious endings, am just as well pleased to find them in the sacred authors very rarely.

42. The majestic style of speech differs from the temperate style just spoken of, chiefly in that it is not so much decked out with verbal ornaments as exalted into vehemence by mental emotion. It uses, indeed, nearly all the ornaments that the other does; but if they do not happen to be at hand, it does not seek for them. For it is borne on by its own vehemence; and the force of the thought, not the desire for ornament, makes it seize upon any beauty of expression that comes in its way. It is enough for its object that warmth of feeling should suggest the fitting words; they need not be selected by careful elaboration of speech. If a brave man be armed with weapons adorned with gold and jewels, he works feats of valour with those arms in the heat of battle, not because they are costly, but because they are arms; and yet the same man does great execution, even when anger furnishes him with a weapon that he digs out of the ground.[45] The apostle in the following passage is urging that, for the sake of the ministry of the gospel, and sustained by the consolations of God's grace, we should bear with patience all the evils of this life. It is a great subject, and is treated with power, and the ornaments of speech are not wanting: "Behold," he says, "now is the accepted time; behold, now is the day of salvation. Giving no offence in anything, that the ministry be not blamed: but in all things approving ourselves as the ministers of God, in much patience, in afflictions, in necessities, in distresses, in strifes, in imprisonments, in tumults, in labours, in watchings, in fastings; by pureness, by knowledge, by long-suffering, by kindness, by the Holy Ghost, by love unfeigned, by the word of truth, by the power of God, by the armour of righteousness on the right hand and on the left, by honour and dishonour, by evil report and good report: as deceivers, and yet true; as unknown, and yet well known; as dying, and, behold, we live;

[45] An allusion to Vergil, *Aen.* 7.508.

as chastened, and not killed; as sorrowful, yet always rejoicing; as poor, yet making many rich; as having nothing, and yet possessing all things."[46] See him still burning: "O you Corinthians, our mouth is opened to you, our heart is enlarged," and so on; it would be tedious to go through it all.

43. And in the same way, writing to the Romans, he urges that the persecutions of this world should be overcome by charity, in assured reliance on the help of God. And he treats this subject with both power and beauty: "We know," he says, "that all things work together for good to them that love God, to them who are the called according to his purpose. For whom he did foreknow, he also did predestinate to be conformed to the image of his Son, that he might be the firstborn among many brethren. Moreover, whom he did predestinate, them he also called; and whom he called, them he also justified; and whom he justified, them he also glorified. What shall we then say to these things? If God is for us, who can be against us? He that spared not his own Son, but delivered him up for us all, how shall he not with him also freely give us all things? Who shall lay anything to the charge of God's elect? It is God that justifies; who is he that condemns? It is Christ that died, or rather, that is risen again, who is even at the right hand of God, who also makes intercession for us. Who shall separate us from the love of Christ? shall tribulation, or distress, or persecution, or famine, or nakedness, or peril, or sword? (As it is written, for your sake we are killed all the day long; we are accounted as sheep for the slaughter.) In all these things we are more than conquerors, through him that loved us. For I am persuaded, that neither death, nor life, nor angels, nor principalities, nor powers, nor things present, nor things to come, nor height, nor depth, nor any other creature, shall be able to separate us from the love of God, which is in Christ Jesus our Lord."[47]

44. Again, in writing to the Galatians, although the whole epistle is written in the subdued style, except at the end, where it rises into a temperate eloquence, yet he interposes one passage of so much feeling that, notwithstanding the absence of

[46] 2 Cor. 6: 2–10.
[47] Rom. 8: 28–39.

any ornaments such as appear in the passages just quoted, it cannot be called anything but powerful: "You observe days, and months, and times, and years. I am afraid of you, lest I have bestowed upon you labour in vain. Brethren, I beseech you, be as I am; for I am as you are: you have not injured me at all. You know how, through infirmity of the flesh, I preached the gospel to you at the first. And my temptation which was in my flesh you despised not, nor rejected; but received me as an angel of God, even as Christ Jesus. Where is then the blessedness you spoke of? for I bear you witness, that, if it had been possible, you would have plucked out your own eyes, and have given them to me. Am I therefore become your enemy, because I tell you the truth? They zealously affect you, but not well; they would exclude you, that you might affect them. But it is good to be zealously affected always in a good thing, and not only when I am present with you. My little children, of whom I travail in birth again until Christ be formed in you, I desire to be present with you now, and to change my voice; for I stand in doubt of you."[48] Is there anything here of contrasted words arranged antithetically, or of words rising gradually to a climax, or of sonorous clauses, and sections, and periods? Yet, notwithstanding, there is a glow of strong emotion that makes us feel the fervour of eloquence.

CHAP. 21—*Examples of the various styles, drawn from the teachers of the church, especially Ambrose and Cyprian.*

45. But these writings of the apostles, though clear, are yet profound, and are so written that one who is not content with a superficial acquaintance, but desires to know them thoroughly, must not only read and hear them, but must have an expositor. Let us, then, study these various modes of speech as they are exemplified in the writings of men who, by reading the Scriptures, have attained to the knowledge of divine and saving truth, and have ministered it to the church. Cyprian of blessed memory writes in the subdued style in his treatise on the sacrament of the cup. In this book he resolves the question, whether the cup of the Lord ought to contain water only,

48 Gal. 4: 10–20.

or water mingled with wine. But we must quote a passage by way of illustration. After the customary introduction, he proceeds to the discussion of the point in question. "Observe," he says, "that we are instructed, in presenting the cup, to maintain the custom handed down to us from the Lord, and to do nothing that our Lord has not first done for us: so that the cup which is offered in remembrance of him should be mixed with wine. For, as Christ says, 'I am the true vine,'[49] it follows that the blood of Christ is wine, not water; and the cup cannot appear to contain his blood by which we are redeemed and quickened, if the wine be absent; for by the wine is the blood of Christ typified, that blood which is foreshadowed and proclaimed in all the types and declarations of scripture. For we find that in the book of Genesis this very circumstance in regard to the sacrament is foreshadowed, and our Lord's sufferings typically set forth, in the case of Noah, when he drank wine, and was drunken, and was uncovered within his tent, and his nakedness was exposed by his second son, and was carefully hidden by his elder and his younger sons.[50] It is not necessary to mention the other circumstances in detail, as it is only necessary to observe this point, that Noah, foreshadowing the future reality, drank, not water, but wine, and thus showed forth our Lord's passion. In the same way we see the sacrament of the Lord's supper prefigured in the case of Melchizedek the priest, according to the testimony of the Holy Scriptures, where it says: 'And Melchizedek king of Salem brought forth bread and wine: and he was the priest of the most high God. And he blessed Abraham.'[51] Now, that Melchizedek was a type of Christ, the Holy Spirit declares in the Psalms, where the Father addressing the Son says, 'You are a priest for ever after the order of Melchizedek.'[52]"[53] In this passage, and in all of the letter that follows, the subdued style is maintained, as the reader may easily satisfy himself.

46. St. Ambrose also, though dealing with a question of very great importance, the equality of the Holy Spirit with the

[49] John 15: 1.
[50] Gen. 9: 20–24.
[51] Gen. 14: 18 f.
[52] Ps. 110: 4.
[53] *Ad Cæcilium*, Ep. 63. 1 f.

Father and the Son, employs the subdued style, because the object he has in view demands, not beauty of diction, nor the swaying of the mind by the stir of emotion, but facts and proofs. Accordingly, in the introduction to his work, we find the following passage among others: "When Gideon was startled by the message he had heard from God, that, though thousands of the people failed, yet through one man God would deliver his people from their enemies, he brought forth a kid of the goats, and by direction of the angel laid it with unleavened cakes upon a rock, and poured the broth over it; and as soon as the angel of God touched it with the end of the staff that was in his hand, there rose up fire out of the rock and consumed the offering.[54] Now this sign seems to indicate that the rock was a type of the body of Christ, for it is written, 'They drank of that spiritual rock that followed them, and that rock was Christ;'[55] this, of course, referring not to Christ's divine nature, but to his flesh, whose everflowing fountain of blood has ever satisfied the hearts of his thirsting people. And so it was at that time declared in a mystery that the Lord Jesus, when crucified, should abolish in his flesh the sins of the whole world, and not their guilty acts merely, but the evil lusts of their hearts. For the kid's flesh refers to the guilt of the outward act, the broth to the allurement of lust within, as it is written, 'And the mixed multitude that was among them fell a lusting; and the children of Israel also wept again and said, who shall give us flesh to eat?'[56] When the angel, then, stretched out his staff and touched the rock, and fire rose out of it, this was a sign that our Lord's flesh, filled with the Spirit of God, should burn up all the sins of the human race. Therefore also the Lord says, 'I am come to send fire on the earth.' "[57] And in the same style he pursues the subject, devoting himself chiefly to proving and enforcing his point.[58]

47. An example of the temperate style is the celebrated encomium on virginity from Cyprian: "Now our discourse ad-

[54] Judg. 6: 14–21.
[55] 1 Cor. 10: 4.
[56] Num. 11: 4.
[57] Luke 12: 49.
[58] *De Spiritu Sancto*, 1. Prologue.

dresses itself to the virgins, who, as they are the objects of higher honour, are also the objects of greater care. These are the flower on the tree of the church, the glory and ornament of spiritual grace, the joy of honour and praise, a work unbroken and unblemished, the image of God answering to the holiness of the Lord, the brighter portion of the flock of Christ. The glorious fruitfulness of their mother the church rejoices in them, and in them flourishes more abundantly; and in proportion as bright virginity adds to her numbers, in the same proportion does the mother's joy increase.'[59] And at another place in the end of the epistle, 'As we have borne,' he says, 'the image of the earthly, we shall also bear the image of the heavenly.'[60] Virginity bears this image, integrity bears it, holiness and truth bear it; they bear it who are mindful of the chastening of the Lord, who observe justice and piety, who are strong in faith, humble in fear, steadfast in the endurance of suffering, meek in the endurance of injury, ready to pity, of one mind and of one heart in brotherly peace. And every one of these things ought you, holy virgins, to observe, to cherish, and fulfil, who having hearts at leisure for God and for Christ, and having chosen the greater and better part, lead and point the way to the Lord, to whom you have pledged your vows. You who are advanced in age, exercise control over the younger. You who are younger, wait upon the elders, and encourage your equals; stir up one another by mutual exhortations; provoke one another to glory by emulous examples of virtue; endure bravely, advance in spirituality, finish your course with joy; only be mindful of us when your virginity shall begin to reap its reward of honour."[61]

48. Ambrose also uses the temperate and ornamented style when he is holding up before virgins who have made their profession a model for their imitation, and says: "She was a virgin not in body only, but also in mind; not mingling the purity of her affection with any dross of hypocrisy; serious in speech; prudent in disposition; sparing of words; delighting in study; not placing her confidence in uncertain riches, but

[59] *De habitu Virginum*, 7.
[60] 1 Cor. 15: 49.
[61] *De habitu Virginum*, 18.

in the prayer of the poor; diligent in labour; reverent in word; accustomed to look to God, not man, as the guide of her conscience; injuring no one, wishing well to all; dutiful to her elders, not envious of her equals; avoiding boastfulness, following reason, loving virtue. When did she wound her parents even by a look? When did she quarrel with her neighbours? When did she spurn the humble, laugh at the weak, or shun the indigent? She is accustomed to visit only those haunts of men that pity would not blush for, nor modesty pass by. There is nothing haughty in her eyes, nothing bold in her words, nothing wanton in her gestures: her bearing is not voluptuous, nor her gait too free, nor her voice petulant; so that her outward appearance is an image of her mind, and a picture of purity. For a good house ought to be known for such at the very threshold, and show at the very entrance that there is no dark recess within, as the light of a lamp set inside sheds its radiance on the outside. Why need I detail her sparingness in food, her superabundance in duty,—the one falling beneath the demands of nature, the other rising above its powers? The latter has no intervals of intermission, the former doubles the days by fasting; and when the desire for refreshment does arise, it is satisfied with food such as will support life, but not minister to appetite."[62] Now I have cited these latter passages as examples of the temperate style, because their purpose is not to induce those who have not yet devoted themselves to take the vows of virginity, but to show of what character those who have taken vows ought to be. To prevail on any one to take a step of such a nature and of so great importance, requires that the mind should be excited and set on fire by the majestic style. Cyprian the martyr, however, did not write about the duty of taking up the profession of virginity, but about the dress and deportment of virgins. Yet that great bishop urges them to their duty even in these respects by the power of a majestic eloquence.

49. But I shall select examples of the majestic style from their treatment of a subject which both of them have touched. Both have denounced the women who colour, or rather discolour, their faces with paint. And the first, in dealing with

---

[62] *De Virginibus*, 2.1.

this topic, says: "Suppose a painter should depict in colours that rival nature's the features and form and complexion of some man, and that, when the portrait had been finished with consummate art, another painter should put his hand over it, as if to improve by his superior skill the painting already completed; surely the first artist would feel deeply insulted, and his indignation would be justly roused. Do you, then, think that you will carry off with impunity so audacious an act of wickedness, such an insult to God the great artificer? For, granting that you are not immodest in your behaviour towards men, and that you are not polluted in mind by these meretricious deceits, yet, in corrupting and violating what is God's, you prove yourself worse than an adulteress. The fact that you consider yourself adorned and beautified by such arts is an impeachment of God's handiwork, and a violation of truth. Listen to the warning voice of the apostle: 'Purge out the old leaven, that you may be a new lump, as you are unleavened. For even Christ our passover is sacrificed for us: therefore let us keep the feast, not with old leaven, neither with the leaven of malice and wickedness; but with the unleavened bread of sincerity and truth.'[63] Now can sincerity and truth continue to exist when what is sincere is polluted, and what is true is changed by meretricious colouring and the deceptions of quackery into a lie? Your Lord says, 'You cannot make one hair white or black;'[64] and do you wish to have greater power so as to bring to nought the words of your Lord? With rash and sacrilegious hand you would like to change the colour of your hair: I wish you would, with a prophetic look to the future, dye it the colour of flame."[65] It would be too long to quote all that follows.

50. Ambrose again, inveighing against such practices, says: "Hence arise these incentives to vice, that women, in their fear that they may not prove attractive to men, paint their faces with carefully-chosen colours, and then from stains on their features go on to stains on their chastity. What folly it is to change the features of nature into those of a painting, and from fear of incurring their husband's disapproval, to proclaim

[63] 1 Cor. 5: 7 f.
[64] Matt. 5: 36.
[65] Cyprian, *de habitu Virginum*, 12.

openly that they have incurred their own! For the woman who desires to alter her natural appearance pronounces condemnation on herself; and her eager endeavours to please another prove that she has first been displeasing to herself. And what testimony to your ugliness can we find, O woman, that is more unquestionable than your own, when you are afraid to show yourself? If you are comely, why do you hide your comeliness? If you are plain, why do you lyingly pretend to be beautiful, when you cannot enjoy the pleasure of the lie either in your own consciousness or in that of another? For he loves another woman, you want to please another man; and you are angry if he love another, though he is taught adultery in you. You are the evil promptress of your own injury. For even the woman who has been the victim of a pander shrinks from acting the pander's part, and though she is vile, it is herself she sins against and not another. The crime of adultery is almost more tolerable than yours; for adultery tampers with modesty, but you with nature."[66] It is sufficiently clear, I think, that this eloquence calls passionately upon women to avoid tampering with their appearance by deceitful arts, and to cultivate modesty and fear. Accordingly, we notice that the style is neither subdued nor temperate, but majestic throughout. Now in these two authors whom I have selected as specimens of the rest, and in other ecclesiastical writers who both speak the truth and speak it well,—speak it, that is, judiciously, pointedly, and with beauty and power of expression,—many examples may be found of the three styles of speech, scattered through their various writings and discourses; and the diligent student may by assiduous reading, intermingled with practice on his own part, become thoroughly imbued with them all.

CHAP. 22—*The necessity of variety in style.*

51. But we are not to suppose that it is against rule to mingle these various styles: on the contrary, every variety of style should be introduced so far as is consistent with good taste. For when we keep monotonously to one style, we fail to retain the hearer's attention; but when we pass from one style to another, the discourse goes off more gracefully, even though

---

[66] Ambrose, *de Virginibus,* 1.6.28.

it extends to greater length. Each separate style, again, has varieties of its own which prevent the hearer's attention from cooling or becoming languid. We can bear the subdued style, however, longer without variety than the majestic style. For the mental emotion which it is necessary to stir up in order to carry the hearer's feelings with us, when once it has been sufficiently excited, the higher the pitch to which it is raised, can be maintained the shorter time. And therefore we must be on our guard, lest, in striving to carry to a higher point the emotion we have excited, we rather lose what we have already gained. But after the interposition of matter that we have to treat in a quieter style, we can return with good effect to that which must be treated forcibly, thus making the tide of eloquence to ebb and flow like the sea. It follows from this, that the majestic style, if it is to be long continued, ought not to be unvaried, but should alternate at intervals with the other styles; the speech or writing as a whole, however, being referred to that style which is the prevailing one.

CHAP. 23—*How the various styles should be mingled.*

52. Now it is a matter of importance to determine what style should be alternated with what other, and the places where it is necessary that any particular style should be used. In the majestic style, for instance, it is always, or almost always, desirable that the introduction should be temperate. And the speaker has it in his discretion to use the subdued style even where the majestic would be allowable, in order that the majestic when it is used may be the more majestic by comparison, and may as it were shine out with greater brilliance from the dark background. Again, whatever may be the style of the speech or writing, when knotty questions turn up for solution, accuracy of distinction is required, and this naturally demands the subdued style. And accordingly this style must be used in alternation with the other two styles whenever questions of that sort turn up; just as we must use the temperate style, no matter what may be the general tone of the discourse, whenever praise or blame is to be given without any ulterior reference to the condemnation or acquittal of any one, or to obtaining the concurrence of any one in a course of action. In the majestic style, then, and in the quiet likewise, both the

other two styles occasionally find place. The temperate style, on the other hand, not indeed always, but occasionally, needs the quiet style; for example, when, as I have said, a knotty question comes up to be settled, or when some points that are susceptible of ornament are left unadorned and expressed in the quiet style, in order to give greater effect to certain exuberances (as they may be called) of ornament. But the temperate style never needs the aid of the majestic; for its object is to gratify, never to excite, the mind.

CHAP. 24—*The effects produced by the majestic style.*

53. If frequent and vehement applause follows a speaker, we are not to suppose on that account that he is speaking in the majestic style; for this effect is often produced both by the accurate distinctions of the quiet style, and by the beauties of the temperate. The majestic style, on the other hand, frequently silences the audience by its impressiveness, and even calls forth their tears. For example, when at Cæsarea in Mauritania I was dissuading the people from that civil, or worse than civil, war which they called *Caterva* ('band'—for it was not fellow-citizens merely, but neighbours, brothers, fathers and sons even, who, divided into two factions and armed with stones, fought annually at a certain season of the year for several days continuously, every one killing whomsoever he could), I strove with all the vehemence of speech that I could command to root out and drive from their hearts and lives an evil so cruel and inveterate; it was not, however, when I heard their applause, but when I saw their tears, that I thought I had produced an effect. For the applause showed that they were instructed and delighted, but the tears that they were subdued. And when I saw their tears I was confident, even before the event proved it, that this horrible and barbarous custom (which had been handed down to them from their fathers and their ancestors of generations long gone by, and which like an enemy was besieging their hearts, or rather had complete possession of them) was overthrown; and immediately after my sermon was finished I called upon them with heart and voice to give praise and thanks to God. With the blessing of Christ, it is now eight years or more since anything of the sort was attempted there. In many other cases besides

I have observed that men show the effect made on them by the powerful eloquence of a wise man, not by clamorous applause so much as by groans, sometimes even by tears, finally by change of life.

54. The quiet style, too, has made a change in many; but it was to teach them what they were ignorant of, or to persuade them of what they thought incredible, not to make them do what they knew they ought to do but were unwilling to do. To break down hardness of this sort, speech needs to be vehement. Praise and censure, too, when they are eloquently expressed, even in the temperate style, produce such an effect on some, that they are not only pleased with the eloquence of the encomiums and censures, but are led to live so as themselves to deserve praise, and to avoid living so as to incur blame. But no one would say that all who are thus delighted change their habits in consequence, whereas all who are moved by the majestic style act accordingly, and all who are taught by the quiet style know or believe a truth which they were previously ignorant of.

CHAP. 25—*How the temperate style is to be used.*

55. From all this we may conclude, that the end arrived at by the two styles last mentioned is the one which it is most essential for those who aspire to speak with wisdom and eloquence to secure. On the other hand, what the temperate style properly aims at, viz. to please by beauty of expression, is not in itself an adequate end; but when what we have to say is good and useful, and when the hearers are both acquainted with it and favourably disposed towards it, so that it is not necessary either to instruct or persuade them, beauty of style may have its influence in securing their prompter compliance, or in making them adhere to it more tenaciously. For as the function of all eloquence, whichever of these three forms it may assume, is to speak persuasively, and its object is to persuade, an eloquent man will speak persuasively, whatever style he may adopt; but unless he succeeds in persuading, his eloquence has not secured its object. Now in the subdued style, he persuades his hearers that what he says is true; in the majestic style, he persuades them to do what they are aware they ought to do, but do not; in the temperate style, he persuades

them that his speech is elegant and ornate. But what use is there in attaining such an object as this last? They may desire it who are vain of their eloquence and make a boast of panegyrics, and such-like performances, where the object is not to instruct the hearer, or to persuade him to any course of action, but merely to give him pleasure. We, however, ought to make that end subordinate to another, viz. the effecting by this style of eloquence what we aim at effecting when we use the majestic style. For we may by the use of this style persuade men to cultivate good habits and give up evil ones, if they are not so hardened as to need the vehement style; or if they have already begun a good course, we may induce them to pursue it more zealously, and to persevere in it with constancy. Accordingly, even in the temperate style we must use beauty of expression not for ostentation, but for wise ends; not contenting ourselves merely with pleasing the hearer, but rather seeking to aid him in the pursuit of the good end which we hold out before him.

CHAP. 26—*In every style the orator should aim at perspicuity, beauty, and persuasiveness.*

56. Now in regard to the three conditions I laid down a little while ago[67] as necessary to be fulfilled by any one who wishes to speak with wisdom and eloquence, viz. perspicuity, beauty of style, and persuasive power, we are not to understand that these three qualities attach themselves respectively to the three several styles of speech, one to each, so that perspicuity is a merit peculiar to the subdued style, beauty to the temperate, and persuasive power to the majestic. On the contrary, all speech, whatever its style, ought constantly to aim at, and as far as possible to display, all these three merits. For we do not like even what we say in the subdued style to pall upon the hearer; and therefore we want to be listened to, not with intelligence merely, but with pleasure as well. Again, why do we enforce what we teach by divine testimony, except that we wish to carry the hearer with us, that is, to compel his assent by calling in the assistance of him of whom it is said, "Your testimonies are very sure"?[68] And when any

---

[67] Chaps. 15 and 17.
[68] Ps. 93: 5.

one narrates a story, even in the subdued style, what does he
wish but to be believed? But who will listen to him if he does
not arrest attention by some beauty of style? And if he is not
intelligible, is it not plain that he can neither give pleasure
nor enforce conviction? The subdued style, again, in its own
naked simplicity, when it unravels questions of very great difficulty, and throws an unexpected light upon them; when it
worms out and brings to light some very acute observations
from a quarter whence nothing was expected; when it seizes
upon and exposes the falsity of an opposing opinion, which
seemed at its first statement to be unassailable; especially when
all this is accompanied by a natural, unsought grace of expression, and by a rhythm and balance of style which is not ostentatiously obtruded, but seems rather to be called forth by the
nature of the subject: this style, so used, frequently calls forth
applause so great that one can hardly believe it to be the subdued style. For the fact that it comes forth without either ornament or defence, and offers battle in its own naked simplicity,
does not hinder it from crushing its adversary by weight of
nerve and muscle, and overwhelming and destroying the falsehood that opposes it by the mere strength of its own right arm.
How explain the frequent and vehement applause that waits
upon men who speak thus, except by the pleasure that truth
so irresistibly established, and so victoriously defended, naturally affords? Therefore the Christian teacher and speaker
ought, when he uses the subdued style, to endeavour not only
to be clear and intelligible, but to give pleasure and to bring
home conviction to the hearer.

57. Eloquence of the temperate style, also, must, in the
case of the Christian orator, be neither altogether without
ornament, nor unsuitably adorned nor is it to make the giving
of pleasure its sole aim, which is all it professes to accomplish
in the hands of others; but in its encomiums and censures it
should aim at inducing the hearer to strive after or hold more
firmly by what it praises, and to avoid or renounce what it
condemns. On the other hand, without perspicuity this style
cannot give pleasure. And so the three qualities, perspicuity,
beauty, and persuasiveness, are to be sought in this style also;
beauty, of course, being its primary object.

58. Again, when it becomes necessary to stir and sway the

hearer's mind by the majestic style (and this is always necessary when he admits that what you say is both true and agreeable, and yet is unwilling to act accordingly), you must, of
course, speak in the majestic style. But who can be moved
if he does not understand what is said? and who will stay to
listen if he receives no pleasure? Therefore, in this style, too,
when an obdurate heart is to be persuaded to obedience, you
must speak so as to be both intelligible and pleasing, if you
want to be heard with a submissive mind.

CHAP. 27—*The man whose life is in harmony with his teaching
will teach with greater effect.*

59. But whatever may be the majesty of the style, the life
of the speaker will count for more in securing the hearer's
compliance. The man who speaks wisely and eloquently, but
lives wickedly, may, it is true, instruct many who are anxious
to learn; though, as it is written, he "is unprofitable to himself."[69] Therefore, also, the apostle says: "Whether in pretence or in truth Christ is preached."[70] Now Christ is the
truth; yet we see that the truth can be preached, though not
in truth,—that is, what is right and true in itself may be
preached by a man of perverse and deceitful mind. And thus
it is that Jesus Christ is preached by those that seek their own,
and not the things that are Jesus Christ's. But since true believers obey the voice, not of any man, but of the Lord himself,
who says, "All therefore whatsoever they bid you observe, that
observe and do: but do not imitate their works; for they say
and do not;"[71] therefore it is that men who themselves lead
unprofitable lives are heard with profit by others. For though
they seek their own objects, they do not dare to teach their
own doctrines, sitting as they do in the high places of ecclesiastical authority, which is established on sound doctrine.
Therefore our Lord himself, before saying what I have just
quoted about men of this stamp, made this observation: "The
scribes and the Pharisees sit in Moses' seat."[72] The seat they
occupied, then, which was not theirs but Moses', compelled

[69] Sir. 37: 19.
[70] Phil. 1: 18.
[71] Matt. 23: 3.
[72] Matt. 23: 2.

them to say what was good, though they did what was evil.
And so they followed their own course in their lives, but were
prevented by the seat they occupied which belonged to another, from preaching their own doctrines.

60. Now these men do good to many by preaching what
they themselves do not perform; but they would do good to
very many more if they lived as they preach. For there are
numbers who seek an excuse for their own evil lives in comparing the teaching with the conduct of their instructors, and
who say in their hearts, or even go a little further, and say
with their lips: why do you not do yourself what you bid
me do? And thus they cease to listen with submission to a
man who does not listen to himself, and in despising the
preacher they learn to despise the word that is preached.
Therefore the apostle, writing to Timothy, after telling him,
"Let no man despise your youth," adds immediately the course
by which he would avoid contempt: "but be an example to
the believers, in word, in conversation, in charity, in spirit,
in faith, in purity."[73]

CHAP. 28—*Truth is more important than expression. What is meant
by strife about words.*

61. Such a teacher as is here described may, to secure compliance, speak not only quietly and temperately, but even vehemently, without any breach of modesty, because his life protects him against contempt. For while he pursues an upright
life, he takes care to maintain a good reputation as well, pro-
viding things honest in the sight of God and men,[74] fearing
God, and caring for men. In his very speech even he prefers
to please by matter rather than by words; thinks that a thing
is well said in proportion as it is true in fact, and that a teacher
should govern his words, not let the words govern him. This
is what the apostle says: "Not with wisdom of words, lest the
cross of Christ should be made of no effect."[75] To the same
effect also is what he says to Timothy: "Charging them before
the Lord that they do not strive about words to no profit, but

[73] 1 Tim. 4: 12.
[74] 2 Cor. 8: 21.
[75] 1 Cor. 2: 17.

to the subverting of the hearers."[76] Now this does not mean that, when adversaries oppose the truth, we are to say nothing in defence of the truth. For where, then, would be what he says when he is describing the sort of man a bishop ought to be: "that he may be able by sound doctrine both to exhort and convince those who contradict"?[77] To strive about words is not to be careful about the way to overcome error by truth, but to be anxious that your mode of expression should be preferred to that of another. The man who does not strive about words, whether he speak quietly, temperately, or vehemently, uses words with no other purpose than to make the truth plain, pleasing, and effective; for not even love itself, which is the end of the commandment and the fulfilling of the law,[78] can be rightly exercised unless the objects of love are true and not false. For as a man with a comely body but an ill-conditioned mind is a more painful object than if his body too were deformed, so men who teach lies are the more pitiable if they happen to be eloquent in speech. To speak eloquently, then, and wisely as well, is just to express truths which it is expedient to teach in fit and proper words,—words which in the subdued style are adequate, in the temperate, elegant, and in the majestic, forcible. But the man who cannot speak both eloquently and wisely should speak wisely without eloquence, rather than eloquently without wisdom.

CHAP. 29—*It is permissible for a preacher to deliver to the people what has been written by a more eloquent man than himself.*

If, however, he cannot do even this, let his life be such as shall not only secure a reward for himself, but afford an example to others; and let his manner of living be an eloquent sermon in itself.

63. There are, indeed, some men who have a good delivery, but cannot compose anything to deliver. Now, if such men take what has been written with wisdom and eloquence by others, and commit it to memory, and deliver it to the people, they cannot be blamed, supposing them to do it without deception. For in this way many become preachers of the truth

[76] 2 Tim. 2: 14.
[77] Tit. 1: 9.
[78] 1 Tim. 1: 5 and Rom. 13: 10.

(which is certainly desirable), and yet not many teachers; for all deliver the discourse which one real teacher has composed, and there are no divisions among them. Nor are such men to be alarmed by the words of Jeremiah the prophet, through whom God denounces those who steal his words every one from his neighbour.[79] For those who steal take what does not belong to them, but the word of God belongs to all who obey it; and it is the man who speaks well, but lives badly, who really takes the words that belong to another. For the good things he says seem to be the result of his own thought, and yet they have nothing in common with his manner of life. And so God has said that they steal his words who would appear good by speaking God's words, but are in fact bad, as they follow their own ways. And if you look closely into the matter, it is not really themselves who say the good things they say. For how can they say in words what they deny in deeds? It is not for nothing that the apostle says of such men: "They profess that they know God, but in works they deny him."[80] In one sense, then, they do say the things, and in another sense they do not say them; for both these statements must be true, both being made by him who is the truth. Speaking of such men, in one place he says, "Whatsoever they bid you observe, that observe and do; but do not imitate their works;"—that is to say, what you hear from their lips, that do; what you see in their lives, that do you not;—"for they say and do not."[81] And so, though they do not, yet they say. But in another place, upbraiding such men, he says, "O generation of vipers, how can you, being evil, speak good things?"[82] And from this it would appear that even what they say, when they say what is good, it is not themselves who say, for in will and in deed they deny what they say. Hence it happens that a wicked man who is eloquent may compose a discourse in which the truth is set forth to be delivered by a good man who is not eloquent; and when this takes place, the former draws from himself what does not belong to him, and the latter receives from another what really belongs to himself. But when

[79] Jer. 23: 30.
[80] Tit. 1: 16.
[81] Matt. 23: 3.
[82] Matt. 12: 34.

true believers render this service to true believers, both parties speak what is their own, for God is theirs, to whom belongs all that they say; and even those who could not compose what they say make it their own by composing their lives in harmony with it.

CHAP. 30—*The preacher should commence his discourse with prayer to God.*

63. But whether a man is going to address the people or to dictate what others will deliver or read to the people, he ought to pray God to put into his mouth a suitable discourse. For if Queen Esther prayed, when she was about to speak to the king touching the temporal welfare of her race, that God would put fit words into her mouth,[83] how much more ought he to pray for the same blessing who labours in word and doctrine for the eternal welfare of men? Those, again, who are to deliver what others compose for them ought, before they receive their discourse, to pray for those who are preparing it; and when they have received it, they ought to pray both that they themselves may deliver it well, and that those to whom they address it may give ear; and when the discourse has a happy issue, they ought to render thanks to him from whom they know such blessings come, so that all the praise may be his "in whose hand are both we and our words."[84]

CHAP. 31—*Apology for the length of the work.*

64. This book has extended to a greater length than I expected or desired. But the reader or hearer who finds pleasure in it will not think it long. He who thinks it long, but is anxious to know its contents, may read it in parts. He who does not care to be acquainted with it need not complain of its length. I, however, give thanks to God that with what little ability I possess I have in these four books striven to depict, not the sort of man I am myself (for my defects are very many), but the sort of man he ought to be who desires to labour in sound, that is, in Christian doctrine, not for his own instruction only, but for that of others also.

[83] Esther 4: 16.
[84] Wis. 7: 16.

BIBLIOGRAPHICAL GUIDE

Specialized bibliographies are given under the Special Topics in the Sectional Introductions. The references there to Augustine's works give the Latin titles which can easily be used in connection with the table of the principal works of Augustine given on pp. 546 ff.

1. *Bibliography*
To 1928: E. Nebreda, *Bibliographia Augustiniana,* Rome, 1928.
To 1962: C. Andresen, *Bibliographia Augustiniana,* Darmstadt, 1962.
1950–60: T. van Bavel, *Répertoire bibliographique de saint Augustin,* The Hague, 1963.
From 1949: *Bulletin augustinien* of the *Revue des Études Augustiniennes,* Paris = REA

2. Editions of all Augustine's works in Latin: J. P. Migne, *Patrologia Latina,* Paris, vols. 32–46 = PL
   A large number of his works in Latin: *Corpus Scriptorum Ecclesiasticorum Latinorum,* Vienna = CSEL

3. Edition of many of Augustine's works with good texts and up-to-date introductions, commentaries and indexes: *Bibliothèque Augustinienne,* Paris = BA

4. English translations of works of Augustine (while there are individual translations, some of them well known, of single works, especially of the *Confessions* and the *City of God,* reference at this point will be only to translations in series)
The Works of Aurelius Augustinus, Edinburgh, 1871–76 = E;
A Select Library of Nicene and Post-Nicene Fathers, New

York, 1887–1902 = NPN; *The Fathers of the Church,* Washington, 1947– = FC; *Ancient Christian Writers,* Westminster, Md., 1946– = ACW; *Catholic University of America,* Patristic Studies, Washington, 1922– = CUA; and the *Library of Christian Classics,* Philadelphia = CC.

The translations used in this *Reader* are, except for the extracts from the *Soliloquies* and *Sermons,* those of the Edinburgh versions: these are sometimes used by preference even still (see REA XVI, 1970, p. 235, n. 5). They have been adapted considerably here.

5. Table of the principal works of Augustine of which English translations are available in series.

Date of composition A.D.	Title	PL	CSEL	English translations
386	Academicos (contra) *Against the Academics*	32	63	FC 5; ACW 12
396	Agone christiano (de) *The Christian Combat*	40	41	FC 2
419	Anima et eius origine (de) *The Soul and Its Origin*	44	60	E 12; NPN 5
401	Baptismo (de) *Baptism*	43	51	E 3; NPN 4
386	Beata vita (de) *The Happy Life*	32	63	FC 5; CUA 72
401	Bono coniugali (de) *The Good of Marriage*	40	41	NPN 3; FC 27
414	Bono viduitatis (de) *The Excellence of Widowhood*	40	41	NPN 3; FC 16
399	Catechizandis rudibus (de) *The Catechizing of the Uninstructed*	40		E 9; NPN 3; ACW 2; CUA 8
	Catechumenos de symbolo (ad) *To the Catechumens on the Creed*	40		NPN 3; FC 27

Date of composition A.D.	Title	PL	CSEL	English translations
13–27	Civitate Dei (de) *City of God*	41	40	E 12; NPN 2; FC 8, 14, 24
97	Confessiones *Confessions*	32	33	E 14; NPN 1; FC 21; CC 7
19	Coniugiis adulterinis (de) *Adulterous Marriages*	40	41	FC 27
00	Consensu evangelistarum (de) *The Harmony of the Evangelists*	34	43	E 8; NPN 6
fter 412	Continentia (de) *Continence*	40	41	NPN 3; FC 16
17	Correctione Donatistarum (de) = Ep. 185 *The Correction of the Donatists*	33	57	E 3; NPN 4
26	Correptione et gratia (de) *Rebuke and Grace*	44		E 15; NPN 5; FC 2
21	Cura pro mortuis gerenda (de) *The Care to be Taken for the Dead*	40	41	NPN 3; FC 27
92	Disputatio contra Fortunatum *Debate with Fortunatus*	42	25,1	NPN 4
06	Divinatione daemonum (de) *The Divination of Demons*	40	41	FC 27
96, 426	Doctrina christiana (de) *Christian Instruction*	34		E 9; NPN 2; FC 2; CUA 23
29	Dono perseverantiae (de) *The Gift of Perseverance*	45		E 15; NPN 5; CUA 91

Date of composition A.D.	Title	PL	CSEL	English translations
392	Duabus animabus (de) *The Two Souls*	42	25, 1	NPN 4
394?–418	Enarrationes in Psalmos *Expositions on the Book of the Psalms*	36, 37		NPN 8; ACW 29 30
421–22	Enchiridion ad Laurentium *Faith, Hope and Charity*	40		E 9; NPN 3; FC 2 ACW 3; CC 7
396	Epistulam quam vocant Fundamenti (contra) *Against the Epistle of Manichaeus Entitled Fundamental*	42	25, 1	E 5; NPN 4
Winter 419–20	Epistulas Pelagianorum (contra duas) *Against Two Letters of the Pelagians*	44	60	E 15; NPN 5
386–429	Epistulae *Letters*	33	34, 44, 57, 58	E 6, 13; NPN 1 FC 12, 18, 20 30, 32
397–98	Faustum Manichaeum (contra) *Reply to Faustus the Manichaean*	42	25, 1	E 5; NPN 4
393	Fide et symbolo (de) *Faith and the Creed*	40	41	E 9; NPN 3; FC 27 CC 6
412–13	Fide et operibus (de) *Faith and Works*	40	41	FC 27; CUA 47
400	Fide rerum quae non videntur (de) *Faith in Things Unseen*	40		NPN 3; FC 4; CUA 84

Date of mposition A.D.	Title	PL	CSEL	English translations
7?	Firmum (epistola ad)* *Letter to Firmus*			FC 8
7	Gestis Pelagii (de) *The Proceedings of Pelagius*	44	42	E 4; NPN 5
8	Gratia Christi et peccato originali (de) *The Grace of Christ and Original Sin*	44	42	E 12; NPN 5
5	Gratia et libero arbitrio (de) *Grace and Free Will*	44		E 15; NPN 5; FC 59
8–29	Haeresibus ad Quodvultdeum (de) *To Quodvultdeus, on Heresies*	42		CUA 90
7	Immortalitate animae (de) *The Immortality of the Soul*	32		FC 4; CUA 90
9/430?	Iudaeos (adversus) *In Answer to the Jews*	42		FC 27
1	Iulianum libri VI (contra) *Against Julian*	44		FC 35
8, 394–95	Libero arbitrio (de) *The Free Choice of the Will*	32	74	ACW 22; FC 59
1, 402, 405	Litteras Petiliani (contra) *Answer to Letters of Petilian*	43	52	E 3; NPN 4
9	Magistro (de) *The Teacher*	32		FC 59; ACW 9; CC 6

* Cf. C. Lambot, "Lettre inédite de S. Augustin relative au *De vitate Dei*," *Revue Bénédictine*, 51 (1939), pp. 109–21.

Date of composition A.D.	Title	PL	CSEL	English translations
394–95	Mendacio (de) *Lying*	40	41	NPN 3; FC 16
419	Mendacium (contra) *Against Lying*	40	41	NPN 3; FC 16
388, 389–90	Moribus ecclesiae Catholicae et de moribus Manichaeorum (de) *The Catholic and Manichaean Ways of Life*	32		E 5; NPN 4; FC
389	Musica (de) *On Music*	32		FC 4
399	Natura boni contra Manichaeos (de) *The Nature of the Good*	42	25, 2	NPN 4; CUA 8 CC 6
415	Natura et gratia (de) *Nature and Grace*	44	60	E 4; NPN 5
418–19, 419–20	Nuptiis et concupiscentia (de) *Marriage and Concupiscence*	44	42	E 12
401	Opere monachorum (de) *The Work of Monks*	40	41	NPN 3; FC 16
End of 386	Ordine (de) *Divine Providence and the Problem of Evil*	32	63	FC 5
Before 418?	Patientia (de) *Patience*	40	41	NPN 3; FC 16
411, 412	Peccatorum meritis et remissione (de) *Forgiveness of Sin and Baptism*	44	60	E 4; NPN 5
415?	Perfectione iustitiae hominis (de) *Man's Perfection in Righteousness*	44	42	E 4; NPN 5

Date of composition A.D.	Title	PL	CSEL	English translations
429	Praedestinatione sanctorum (de)	44		
	The Predestination of the Saints			E 15; NPN 5
396	Quaestionibus ad Simplicianum (de diversis)	40		
	On Various Questions to Simplicianus			CC 6
422	Quaestionibus Dulcitii (de, VIII)	40		
	The Eight Questions of Dulcitius			FC 16
388	Quantitate animae (de)	32		
	The Greatness of the Soul			FC 4; ACW 9
426–27	Retractationes	32	36	
	Retractations			FC 60
401	Sancta virginitate (de)	40	41	
	Holy Virginity			NPN 3; FC 27
394	Sermone Domini in monte (de)	34		
	The Lord's Sermon on the Mount			E 8; NPN 6; FC 11; ACW 5
	Sermones	38–39		
	Sermons			NPN 6; FC 38; ACW 15
Winter 386–87	Soliloquia	32		
	Soliloquies			NPN 7; FC 5; CC 6
412	Spiritu et littera (de)	44	60	
	The Spirit and the Letter			E 4; NPN 5; CC 8
415	Tractatus in Epistulam Joannis ad Parthos	35		
	Homilies on St. John's Epistle to the Parthi			NPN 7; CC 8

Date of composition A.D.	Title	PL	CSEL	English translations
414–16/17	Tractatus in Joannis Evangelium	35		
	Homilies on St. John's Gospel			E 10, 11; NPN 7
399–419	Trinitate (de)	42		
	The Trinity			E 7; NPN 3; FC 45; CC 8
End of 410?	Urbis excidio (de)	40		
	The Destruction of the City			CUA 89
391	Utilitate credendi (de)	42	25,1	
	The Advantage of Believing			NPN 3; FC 4; CC 6
?	Utilitate jejunii (de)	40		
	The Usefulness of Fasting			FC 16; CUA 85
390	Vera religione (de)	34		
	True Religion			CC 6

6. *General Short Bibliography*

Reference is kept throughout as far as possible to books in English. Sometimes, however, it was found necessary or desirable to refer to items in a foreign language. Frequently a work is published in both Britain and America although one place of publication only is given here.

A. Over-all Surveys

B. Altaner, *Patrology*, 5th ed., London, 1960 = Altaner

R. W. Battenhouse, *A Companion to the Study of St. Augustine*, New York, 1955 = Battenhouse

F. Copleston, *A History of Philosophy*, Garden City, N.Y., 1962, Image Books (Vol. 2, Pt. 1), pp. 55–105.

E. Gilson, *The Christian Philosophy of Saint Augustine*, London, 1961 = Gilson

H. I. Marrou, *St. Augustine and his Influence through the Ages* (Men of Wisdom Book), New York, 1957.

E. Portalié, *A Guide to the Thought of Saint Augustine*, London, 1960 = Portalié

E. Te Selle, *Augustine the Theologian*, New York, 1970.

Reference might also be made to the *New Catholic Encyclopedia*, New York, 1967.

B. General Biographies

G. Bonner, *St. Augustine of Hippo: Life and Controversies*, London, 1963.

V. J. Bourke, *Augustine's Quest of Wisdom*, Milwaukee, 1945.

P. Brown, *Augustine of Hippo*, London, 1967.

A. Mandouze, *Saint Augustin*, Paris, 1968.

J. O'Meara, *The Young Augustine*, New York, 1965.

F. van der Meer, *Augustine the Bishop*, trans. by B. Battershaw and G. R. Lamb, London and New York, 1961.

C. Chronology

A.-M. La Bonnardière, *Recherches de chronologie augustinienne*, Paris, 1965.

S. Zarb, *Chronologia operum s. Augustini*, Rome, 1934.

D. General Background

C. N. Cochrane, *Christianity and Classical Culture*, New York, 1957, pp. 376–516.

H. I. Marrou, *Saint Augustin et la fin de la culture antique*, 2nd ed. (with *Retractatio*), Paris, 1949.

INDEX OF TOPICS

Ascent of the Soul, 18, 34, 129 f., 175–77
Astrology, 128, 316, 319–30

Baptism, 204–34
Bibliography, 545–53

Christian Education (Instruction), 235, 491–543
Christology, 17, 21, 27, 35 ff., 253, 255–92
Church, 19, 20, 21, 205, 227 f.
City of God, 17, 18 ff., 23, 26, 29, 31, 33, 314–442
Concupiscence, 446, 455. *See* Sexuality
Confessions, 17 ff., 22, 31, 33, 35, 127, 202 f., 252, 254
Conversion, 16, 28, 33, 127 ff., 154 f., 180
Correspondence, 16 ff., 28, 65–126
Creation, 18, 20, 127, 129, 180–87

Donatism, 17, 28, 204–15, 231

Eschatology, 318, 370–442
Exegesis, 33, 252, 491

Faith, 20, 21, 24, 35 f.
Fate, 316, 330 ff.
Foreknowledge, 316, 332–37
Free Will, 21, 316, 337–39, 444 f., 446

Grace, 21, 24, 26–28, 30, 34, 443–90

Illumination, 20, 21, 34, 36

Justice, 35

Letters, 65–126
Life of Augustine, 12, 25 ff., 127 ff.

Manichaeism, 13 ff., 17, 26, 28, 30, 33, 127 ff., 171, 446
Miracles, 317, 382–98
Marriage, 444, 446, 479–85
Mysticism, 15, 18, 23, 25, 27, 31, 130

Neoplatonism, 15, 17, 20, 21, 22, 26 ff., 33, 35 f., 127, 129, 317 f.,
    446

Original Sin, 21, 24, 30, 443, 446, 447–90

Pelagianism, 17 ff., 24, 28, 30, 443, 446
Political Theory, 19, 23, 33, 314–16
Predestination, 21, 23 ff., 33, 316
Problem of Evil, 14, 26, 34, 136, 446
Providence, 27 ff., 127, 316, 317

Reason, 20, 34 ff.

Sacraments, 21, 205, 229
Sermons, 235–51
Sexuality, 21, 29 f., 444, 446. *See* Concupiscence
Soliloquies, 18, 34–64
Speculum principis, 316

Time, 127, 129, 186–200
Trinity, 17 ff., 20, 27, 33, 252–313
Trinity and Psychological Analogies, 253, 293–313

OTHER IMAGE BOOKS

THE IMITATION OF CHRIST – Thomas à Kempis. Edited with an Introduction by Harold C. Gardiner, S.J. (D17) – $1.75

SAINT THOMAS AQUINAS – G. K. Chesterton (D36) – $1.45

ST. FRANCIS OF ASSISI – G. K. Chesterton (D50) – $1.45

VIPER'S TANGLE – François Mauriac. A novel of evil and redemption (D51) – 95¢

THE CITY OF GOD – St. Augustine. Edited by Vernon J. Bourke. Introduction by Étienne Gilson. Specially abridged (D59) – $2.95

RELIGION AND THE RISE OF WESTERN CULTURE – Christopher Dawson (D64) – $1.95

THE LITTLE FLOWERS OF ST. FRANCIS – Translated by Raphael Brown (D69) – $1.95

DARK NIGHT OF THE SOUL – St. John of the Cross. Edited and translated by E. Allison Peers (D78) – $1.45

THE CONFESSIONS OF ST. AUGUSTINE – Translated with an Introduction by John K. Ryan (D101) – $1.75

A HISTORY OF PHILOSOPHY: VOLUME 1 – GREECE AND ROME (2 Parts) – Frederick Copleston, S.J. (D134a, D134b) – $1.75 ea.

A HISTORY OF PHILOSOPHY: VOLUME 2 – MEDIAEVAL PHILOSOPHY (2 Parts) – Frederick Copleston, S.J. Part I – Augustine to Bonaventure. Part II – Albert the Great to Duns Scotus (D135a, D135b) – Pt. I, $1.95; Pt. II, $1.75

A HISTORY OF PHILOSOPHY: VOLUME 3 – LATE MEDIAEVAL AND RENAISSANCE PHILOSOPHY (2 Parts) – Frederick Copleston, S.J. Part I – Ockham to the Speculative Mystics. Part II – The Revival of Platonism to Suárez (D136a, D136b) – Pt. I, $1.75; Pt. II, $1.45

A HISTORY OF PHILOSOPHY: VOLUME 4 – MODERN PHILOSOPHY: Descartes to Leibniz – Frederick Copleston, S.J. (D137) – $1.75

A HISTORY OF PHILOSOPHY: VOLUME 5 – MODERN PHILOSOPHY: The British Philosophers, Hobbes to Hume (2 Parts) – Frederick Copleston, S.J. Part I – Hobbes to Paley (D138a) – $1.45. Part II – Berkeley to Hume (D138b) – $1.75

A HISTORY OF PHILOSOPHY: VOLUME 6 – MODERN PHILOSOPHY (2 Parts) – Frederick Copleston, S.J. Part I – The French Enlightenment to Kant (D139a, D139b) – $1.45 ea.

A HISTORY OF PHILOSOPHY: VOLUME 7 – MODERN PHILOSOPHY (2 Parts) – Frederick Copleston, S.J. Part I – Fichte to Hegel. Part II – Schopenhauer to Nietzsche (D140a, D140b) – $1.75 ea.

These prices subject to change without notice

OTHER IMAGE BOOKS

A HISTORY OF PHILOSOPHY: VOLUME 8 – MODERN PHILOSOPHY: Bentham to Russell (2 Parts) – Frederick Copleston, S.J. Part I – British Empiricism and the Idealist Movement in Great Britain. Part II – Idealism in America, the Pragmatist Movement, the Revolt against Idealism (D141a, D141b) – $1.75 ea.

THE SPIRITUAL EXERCISES OF ST. IGNATIUS – Translated by Anthony Mottola, Ph.D. Introduction by Robert W. Gleason, S.J. (D170) – $1.45

LIFE AND HOLINESS – Thomas Merton (D183) – $1.25

WITH GOD IN RUSSIA – Walter J. Ciszek, S.J., with Daniel L. Flaherty, S.J. (D200) – $1.95

A HOPKINS READER – Ed. by John Pick (D203) – $2.45

THE TWO-EDGED SWORD – John L. McKenzie, S.J. (D215) – $1.45

NO MAN IS AN ISLAND – Thomas Merton (D231) – $1.45

CONJECTURES OF A GUILTY BYSTANDER – Thomas Merton (D234) – $1.45

THE NOONDAY DEVIL: Spiritual Support in Middle Age – Bernard Basset, S.J. (D237) – $1.25

HEALTH OF MIND AND SOUL – Ignace Lepp (D239) – 95¢

RELIGION AND PERSONALITY – Adrian van Kaam, C.S.Sp. (D240) – $1.45

RELIGIONS OF THE WORLD (2 Volumes) – John A. Hardon, S.J. (D241a) – $1.95; (D241b) – $1.45

CHRISTIAN SACRAMENTS AND CHRISTIAN PERSONALITY – Bernard J. Cooke, S.J. (D246) – $1.25

THOUGHTS IN SOLITUDE – Thomas Merton (D247) – $1.25

NEW TESTAMENT ESSAYS – Raymond E. Brown, S.S. (D251) – $1.45

TEILHARD DE CHARDIN AND THE MYSTERY OF CHRIST – Christopher Mooney, S.J. (D252) – $1.45

THE NEW TESTAMENT OF THE JERUSALEM BIBLE: Reader's Edition – Alexander Jones, General Editor (D253) – $1.65

THE FOUR GOSPELS: AN INTRODUCTION (2 Volumes) – Bruce Vawter, C.M. (D255a, D255b) – $1.25 ea.

THE PROTESTANT CHURCHES OF AMERICA – Revised Edition – John A. Hardon (D259) – $2.45

EXISTENTIAL FOUNDATIONS OF PSYCHOLOGY – Adrian van Kaam (D260) – $1.75

MORALITY FOR OUR TIME – Marc Oraison (D266) – $1.25

These prices subject to change without notice

OTHER IMAGE BOOKS

SUMMA THEOLOGIAE – Thomas Aquinas – Thomas Gilby, O.P., General Editor
Volume 1: The Existence of God; Part One: Questions 1–13 (D270) – $1.45

THE GOSPELS AND THE JESUS OF HISTORY – Xavier Léon-Dufour, S.J. (D276) – $1.95

THE SEVEN STOREY MOUNTAIN – Thomas Merton (D281) – $1.95

THE PSALMS OF THE JERUSALEM BIBLE – Alexander Jones, General Editor (D283) – $1.45

CONTEMPLATIVE PRAYER – Thomas Merton (D285) – $1.45

THE CHALLENGES OF LIFE – Ignace Lepp (D286) – $1.25

THE ROMAN CATHOLIC CHURCH – John L. McKenzie (D287) – $1.95

BEING TOGETHER: OUR RELATIONSHIPS WITH OTHER PEOPLE – Marc Oraison (D289) – $1.25

THE ABORTION DECISION – Revised Edition – David Granfield (D294) – $1.45

CHRIST IS ALIVE! – Michel Quoist (D298) – $1.45

THE MAN IN THE SYCAMORE TREE: The Good Times and Hard Life of Thomas Merton – Edward Rice (D299) – $1.95

THE NEW TESTAMENT OF THE NEW AMERICAN BIBLE (D300) – $1.75

TOWARD A NEW CATHOLIC MORALITY – John Giles Milhaven (D302) – $1.45

THE POWER AND THE WISDOM – John L. McKenzie (D303) – $1.95

INFALLIBLE? AN INQUIRY – Hans Küng (D304) – $1.45

THE DECLINE AND FALL OF RADICAL CATHOLICISM – James Hitchcock (D305) – $1.25

IN THE SPIRIT, IN THE FLESH – Eugene C. Kennedy (D306) – $1.45

THE GOD OF SPACE AND TIME – Bernard J. Cooke (D308) – $1.45

AN AQUINAS READER (Image Original) – Edited with an Intro. by Mary T. Clark (D309) – $2.45

CHRISTIANITY IN THE TWENTIETH CENTURY – John A. Hardon (D310) – $2.45

THE OLD TESTAMENT OF THE JERUSALEM BIBLE – Reader's Edition – Alexander Jones, General Editor
Volume 1: Genesis – Ruth (D311) – $1.95
Volume 2: 1 Samuel – 2 Maccabees (D312) – $1.95
Volume 3: Job – Ecclesiasticus (D313) – $1.95
Volume 4: The Prophets – Malachi (D314) – $1.95

These prices subject to change without notice

OTHER IMAGE BOOKS

CHRISTIAN COMMUNITY: Response to Reality – Bernard J. Cooke (D315) – $1.45

THE JESUS MYTH – Andrew M. Greeley (D316) – $1.45

THE SURVIVAL OF DOGMA – Avery Dulles, S.J. (D317) – $1.75

CONTEMPLATION IN A WORLD OF ACTION – Thomas Merton (D321) – $2.45

AN AUGUSTINE READER (An Image Original) – Edited with an Intro. by John J. O'Meara (D322) – $2.45

HOPE IS THE REMEDY – Bernard Häring, C.Ss.R. (D323) – $1.25

SEX: THOUGHTS FOR CONTEMPORARY CHRISTIANS – Edited by Michael J. Taylor, S.J. (D324) – $1.45

WE ARE FUTURE – Ladislaus Boros, S.J. (D326) – $1.45

THE NEW SEXUALITY: Myths, Fables and Hang-ups – Eugene C. Kennedy (D328) – $1.45

CATHOLIC AMERICA – John Cogley (D332) – $1.75

PROTESTANTISM – Martin E. Marty (D334) – $2.45

OUR PRAYER – Louis Evely (D338) – $1.45

A RELIGION FOR OUR TIME – Louis Evely (D339) – $1.45

A THOMAS MERTON READER – Revised Edition – Ed. by Thomas P. McDonnell (D341) – $2.95

THE MYSTERY OF SUFFERING AND DEATH – Edited by Michael J. Taylor, S.J. (D342) – $1.75

THOMAS MERTON ON PRAYER – John J. Higgins (D345) – $1.75

IN THE CHRISTIAN SPIRIT – Louis Evely (D348) – $1.45

THE SINAI MYTH – Andrew M. Greeley (D350) – $1.75

These prices subject to change without notice